RILEY ON BUSINESS INTERRUPTION INSURANCE

AUSTRALIA

The Law Book Company
Sydney

CANADA

The Carswell Company
Toronto, Ontario

INDIA

N.M. Tripathi (Private) Ltd
Bombay

Eastern Law House (Private) Ltd
Calcutta

M.P.P. House
Bangalore

Universal Book Traders
Delhi

ISRAEL

Steimatzky's Agency Ltd
Tel Aviv

PAKISTAN

Pakistan Law House
Karachi

RILEY ON BUSINESS INTERRUPTION INSURANCE

SEVENTH EDITION

by

DAVID CLOUGHTON B.A., (Hons.)
*Fellow of the Chartered
Insurance Institute*

LONDON
SWEET & MAXWELL
1991

First Edition	(1956)
Second Edition	(1959)
Reprint	(1961)
Third Edition	(1967)
Fourth Edition	(1977)
Fifth Edition	(1981)
Sixth Edition	(1985)
Seventh Edition	(1991)

Published in 1991 by
Sweet & Maxwell Limited of
South Quay Plaza, 183 Marsh Wall, London E14 9FT.
Computerset by Promenade Graphics Limited, Cheltenham
and printed in Great Britain by
Richard Clay Limited,
Bungay, Suffolk.

**A catalogue record for this book is available
from the British Library.**

ISBN 0 421–40720 4

All rights reserved.
No part of this publication may be
reproduced or transmitted in any form
or by any means, electronic, mechanical, photocopying,
recording or otherwise, or stored in any retrieval
system of any nature without the written permission
of the copyright holder and the publisher, application
for which shall be made to the publisher.

©
Sweet & Maxwell Limited
1991

Editor's Preface to Seventh Edition

This Seventh Edition marks my second attempt to maintain "Riley" as a contemporary work of comment and reference.

The world is a smaller place—even since 1985—and a work of the standing of "Riley" needs to encompass as much of what is being done in the various insurance markets of the world as is practicable. There is therefore more comment on activities, philosophies, etc., in Asia, Africa, the Americas, Australasia, etc., than in the previous Edition.

In the United States, new wordings were introduced in 1986 with the object of making business interruption insurance more acceptable and more readily intelligible to the buying public. Time will tell if the endeavours of the Insurance Services Office have been successful.

Domestically, in the United States, the gross earnings forms which were endorsements to property damage policies have thus given way to the new Business Income Coverage forms which can stand alone if need be. Nevertheless, because the gross earnings forms are still used outside the United States, I have retained much of Denis Riley's original comment on them. Perhaps in some later Edition (or amendment) these comments will fall away naturally as the new wordings find acceptance wherever the U.S. basis is followed.

Of course, any new wordings (particularly those formulated in a foreign country) are difficult to assimilate readily and I trust therefore that readers will share with me my attempts first of all to compare the new wordings with the old and then to contrast them with the U.K. wordings.

In the United Kingdom, new wordings have been developed by the Association of British Insurers. These are more refinements of previous wordings than fundamentally new concepts as in the United States but again the idea is to make this class of insurance more coherent to potential (and actual) insured. At the same time, following the demise of the U.K. Tariff system in 1985, these new wordings are simply *recommended* to members of A.B.I. who can choose to what extent they individually accept or amend them.

We are presented each day with new words and expressions and the A.B.I. have created definitions for the new word "Incident" (to replace our old friend "damage") and for our equally old friend "consequential loss" (to clarify its contextual meaning). Nevertheless I have continued to use the generally understood words "damage" and "fire" where there is no direct reference to current U.K. wordings.

Wages or payroll covers are now rarely written separately from gross profit in the United Kingdom but because they continue to be written outside the United Kingdom and because it is of interest to see the background to the current United Kingdom situation, I have retained some information and comment on the subject.

The title "Consequential Loss" has now all but disappeared from official usage and "Business Interruption" can be regarded as the generic title for this form of cover wherever it is met throughout the world. It is strange that as the United Kingdom has accepted the inevitable and once again adopted a phrase used by the Americans (*cf.* deductibles) so our colleagues in the United States have moved on to Business Income Coverage—although "business interruption" remains the generic title.

On a minor (but often irksome) point, we appear to be witnessing the return (on both sides of the Atlantic) of the capital initial, particularly where the word, or group of words, is defined elsewhere in the policy. Where litigation is on the increase it is natural to ensure that words and phrases are clearly identified as being used in their *particular* sense (as defined) rather than their (more debatable) *general* sense.

There are fewer "tariffs" in the world now than in the 1970s and 1980s. Whether the relaxation of market discipline is a good or a bad thing it has happened in nearly all markets and individual insurers can now act with a greater degree of independence than ever before. The discipline gap in the U.K. market is to an extent being filled by "philosophical" guidance from the A.B.I. and by the central collation and promulgation (among A.B.I. members) of "market" statistics which can (depending on their accuracy) provide underwriters with a basic "burning cost" indication for each type of business insured.

International affairs move on rapidly and it is the task of the Editor of "Riley" to try to keep up with them—as far as "business interruption" insurance is concerned. At the same time it is right to remind ourselves of Denis Riley's original intention for his book. The opening paragraphs of his last Preface—to the Fifth Edition in 1981—were as follows:

"There are relatively few businesses which in the event of damage being caused by fire or other perils at their premises or possibly those of their suppliers or customers would not suffer financially either through a loss of trade or the additional expenditure involved during the period following the occurrence. Protection against such financial loss by means of consequential loss insurance—alternatively termed business interruption insurance—has developed progressively during the present century until it may now be said that in the United Kingdom it is taken out by practically all prudent business undertakings as an essential complement of their material damage insurances.

As a result there is a constant demand for information and guidance on the part of those concerned with affecting, maintaining or claiming under such insurances. Towards meeting this situation information beyond that in a students' textbook is required, exemplified by the statement from a leading insurance company that in 1978 over 40 per cent. of consequential loss claims had to be settled for less than the full amount of the loss. The need is for a book of ready reference on the subject for business people requiring immediate and practical answers to practical problems.

The present book is an attempt to meet that need and to deal fully yet as far as possible in a readable form with the principles, conditions and available scope of modern consequential loss policies—including the pitfalls—as related to the practical task confronting those who have to arrange, advise upon or supply information in connection with such contracts or the settlement of claims under them. It is hoped that accountants whether in private practice or in the employ of industrial concerns, company secretaries and directors, insurance brokers, underwriters, insurance company officials (particularly non-specialist fieldmen) and loss adjusters will find it of practical value as a book of quick and easy reference."

Finally, may I acknowledge my indebtedness to former colleagues at the "Royal" for much of my "overseas" information, and to the Association of British Insurers and the Insurance Services Office for their co-operation in providing recommended wordings.

June 1991   DAVID CLOUGHTON

Contents

Editor's Preface to Seventh Edition   v

	PARA.
1. Measurement of loss of future earnings—the basis of business interruption insurance	1
2. The framework of the cover—policy forms used in the United Kingdom	12
3. The framework of the cover—policy forms used in the United States	24
4. Operation of the cover—United Kingdom basis	35
5. Operation of the cover—United States basis	61
6. Worldwide practices and procedures	72
7. Gross profit, gross earnings or business income: specifications and definitions—United Kingdom	81
8. Gross profit, gross earnings or busines income: specifications and definitions (continued)—United States	97
9. Standing charges and variable expenses—United Kingdom and United States	104
10. Insurance of payroll cost—United Kingdom and United States	189
11. Calculating the amount to be insured—United Kingdom and United States	218
12. Risk management—analysis, treatment and financing (insurance)	241
13. Special forms of insurance—separate items or policies	261
14. Perils (United Kingdom) or causes of loss (United States)	280
15. Engineering business interruption insurance—United Kingdom	311
16. Boiler and machinery coverage—United States	328

CONTENTS

17. Dependence on other businesses and premises—United Kingdom and United States ... 340
18. Miscellaneous clauses and covers ... 378
19. Book debts (United Kingdom): accounts receivable (United States) ... 393
20. Claim settlements ... 411

Appendices

PARA.

A. Standard United Kingdom Fire Policy Form (Business Interruption) ... 447
B. Standard United Kingdom "All Risks" Policy Form (Business Interruption) ... 448
C. United Kingdom Business Interruption ("Difference" Basis) Specification—Gross Profit Wording—Sum Insured Basis ... 449
D. United Kingdom Business Interruption ("Difference" Basis) Specification—Gross Profit Wording—Declaration-Linked Basis ... 450
E. United Kingdom Business Interruption ("Additions" Basis) Specification—Gross Profit Wording—Sum Insured Basis ... 451
F. United Kingdom Business Interruption Specification—Gross Revenue Wording—Sum Insured Basis ... 452
G. United Kingdom Business Interruption Specification—to Insure Trading Profit (Example) ... 453
H. United Kingdom Business Interruption Specification—Item Insuring Wages under the Dual Basis Scheme ... 454
I. United Kingdom Business Interruption Specification—Item Insuring Notice Wages on the "Pro Rata" Basis ... 455
J. United Kingdom Business Interruption Specification—for Advance Profits (Example) ... 456
K. United Kingdom Business Interruption Specification—for the Insurance of Loss of Book Debts (Example) ... 457
L. United Kingdom Business Interruption Specification—for the Insurance of Research Expenditure ... 458
M. United Kingdom Engineering Business Interruption Policy (Example) ... 459
N. United Kingdom Engineering Business Interruption Specification ... 460

CONTENTS

O. United Kingdom Business Interruption Extension Wording for Notifiable Disease, etc. — 461
P. United Kingdom Business Interruption Specification—to Insure Loss of Interest (Example) — 462
Q. United States Business Interruption Insurance of Gross Earnings for Mercantile and Non-Manufacturing Businesses — 463
R. United States Business Interruption Insurance of Gross Earnings for Manufacturing and Mining Businesses — 464
S. United States Business Income Coverage Forms (including Causes of Loss—Basic Form—and Commercial Property Conditions) — 465
T. United Kingdom Overseas ("Home Foreign") Standard Consequential Loss Policy Form — 466
U. Specimen Settlement of a Simple Loss Claim under a United Kingdom Business Interruption Policy Claim — 467
V. Reduction in Turnover—Effect on Accounts (United Kingdom) — 468
W. Illustration of Settlement of a Claim under a United Kingdom Business Interruption Policy with Wages Insured on the Dual Basis — 469
X. Specimen Settlement of a More Complicated Loss Claim under a United Kingdom Business Interruption Policy — 470
Y. Illustration of a Claim Settlement under a United Kingdom Business Interruption Specification including a Departmental Clause — 471
Z. Simplified Specimen Claim Settlement under a United States Business Income (and Extra Expense) Coverage — 472

Index — 571

CHAPTER 1

MEASUREMENT OF LOSS OF FUTURE EARNINGS—THE BASIS OF BUSINESS INTERRUPTION INSURANCE

1. Earnings at risk

All kinds of businesses are carried on in all areas of the world either as part of a developed capitalist system or as part of a socialist, centrally-controlled, state monopoly. The difference, apart from any question of efficiency, would appear to be the presence or the absence of a profit motive. In either case the individual business enterprise stands to be affected as the result of damage caused by fire or a kindred peril, its cashflow interrupted and part of its future earnings lost. Insurance is therefore necessary to afford protection against that loss of future earnings: and in the event of a claim a method of measuring that loss of future earnings must be applied.

2. Loss of turnover—the United Kingdom approach

When buildings or their contents are damaged by fire or kindred perils, the condition and value of the property before the damage and the cost of its restoration or replacement are tangible factors on which assessment of the amount to be paid under the insurance covering them can be based. What method of general application is there to ascertain for the purposes of protection by insurance the intangible, often hypothetical, loss which commences when the fire engines have driven away—the loss of future earnings?

Experience shows that the proportionate effects of a fire upon the earning capacity of a business can be readily and accurately measured, in most cases, by comparing the turnover in the months following the damage with that in the corresponding period in the 12 months preceding it, subject to appropriate adjustments for special circumstances or trends of business. For example, if a fire causes interruption of business throughout October, November and December the loss of turnover during those months can be found by means of a comparison with the turnover for October, November and December in the preceding year. In general, the loss of turnover during any other period of whatever length, can be used as a yardstick for measuring the interruption of trading provided that provision is made for any necessary adjustments.

As turnover figures can usually be ascertained satisfactorily for each day or week, or at the outside each month, this method provides a sensitive index for measuring the proportionate effects of a fire without waiting until the end of a financial year. It also shows the loss sustained when the end of an insured's financial year falls within the period of interference, a loss which could not be ascertained by a comparison of the profit earned in each of the two years. For instance, if damage takes place three months before the end of a firm's financial year and the business is affected from that date until three months into the next financial year, there might be little or no difference between the profit earned in those two years although altogether something approaching six months profit may have been lost. In circumstances of that kind a comparison of the profit and loss accounts cannot show the amount of loss sustained, but the shortage of turnover throughout the period of interruption is ascertainable and would provide an accurate basis for measuring the insured's loss.

Moreover, the use of turnover as an index provides for businesses of a seasonal nature in which sales are not constant throughout the months of the year and it is also suitable for businesses in which turnover is either increasing or decreasing because trends can be assessed for calculating the loss of sales consequent upon a fire.

3. How turnover can be used as a yardstick

But loss of turnover is not synonymous with loss of profit. How can the yardstick of turnover be used to assess the net effect of a fire upon the earnings of a business? In this way, each £ of turnover may be assumed to bear an equal share of:

(a) prime costs, conventionally entered in the first section of a trading account, such as purchases, whether for resale or for use in manufacture, productive wages, consumable stores, fuel for trade purposes, power, and other process charges. These may be described as variable or working expenses, that is, they vary proportionately with the rise or fall of turnover;

(b) overhead expenses such as administrative, selling and distributive costs which generally appear in the second section of a trading account and in the profit and loss account. Because they are not controllable as are prime costs they are for insurance purposes referred to as standing charges, a term which aptly describes their nature;

(c) the residual net profit.

Should turnover fall in consequence of damage by fire the prime costs will, by and large, be reduced proportionately and no loss will be sustained by the business under (a) above. Standing charges, however, as they do not vary directly with turnover will not fall proportionately; therefore in the event of a reduction in turnover (b) above will bear an increased incidence beyond its normal ratio. This relative increase in the amount of the standing charges will have a corresponding inverse effect by reducing the residue (c) above, that is, the net profit. At the same time there will be a concurrent loss of net profit taking place due to there being a smaller volume of turnover on which it can be earned.

However, if compensation is provided by insurance during a period of interruption caused by fire, for the amount of (b) and (c) normally borne by each £ of turnover, on every £ of turnover lost, the revenue of a business will be restored to the extent necessary to cover the normal amount of standing charges and net profit.

4. Basis of business interruption insurance in the United Kingdom

(a) *Principle*

The simple principle that reduction in turnover after a fire is a reliable guide to and a suitable index for measuring the proportionate effect of the fire upon the earnings of a business, and that the actual loss can be ascertained by applying to this reduction the ratio which standing charges and net profit together normally bear to turnover, is the basis of most of the business interruption insurance transacted in the United Kingdom.

As the ratio of variable charges to turnover is generally constant the balance of charges and net profit combined must also be constant even though the relative proportions of the latter two may vary. Recognition of this factor is given for insurance purposes by dealing with "gross profit", that is, net profit and standing charges combined instead of treating them separately. The effect is the same whether gross profit is defined in the policy in that way or as being the amount of turnover less variable expenses as explained in paragraph 6.

A U.K. policy undertakes to provide an indemnity for the loss during a period of interruption after fire. So far as the loss due to reduction in turnover is concerned the policy agrees to pay, on the amount of turnover lost, the percentage which the gross profit insured bore to the turnover in the last financial year before the fire. This percentage is called the rate of gross profit but it is necessary to explain at the outset that the definition of gross profit given in the policy attaches to it a meaning which generally differs in several respects from the gross profit shown in the accounts of a business. A more detailed explanation as to how and why it differs is given in later chapters. It may, however, be stated at this point that some portion of the direct costs in the trading account, such as wages or power, might for various reasons require to be included in the insurance on gross profit. On the other hand it may be unnecessary to insure some items shown in the profit and loss accounts, such as discounts allowed and agents commission, which will vary proportionately with a fall in turnover.

(b) *Operation*

At this point a very simple illustration may be useful to show how under a U.K. business interruption policy the basic principle of measuring the loss resulting from damage by fire—application of the rate of gross profit to the reduction in turnover—restores an insured's financial result at the end of a period of interruption, *i.e.* the net trading profit, to what it would have been but for the fire. (*The illustration is as follows.*)

Accounts for last financial year preceding a fire

	£		£
Purchases	360,000	Sales	1,000,000
Productive wages etc	400,000		
Overheads	160,000 } rate of gross		
Net profit	80,000 } profit 24%		
	1,000,000		1,000,000

Accounts for 12 months during which a 50 per cent. reduction in sales has resulted from the fire

	£		£
Purchases	180,000	Sales	500,000
Productive wages etc	200,000	Business interruption insurance claim: rate of gross profit (24%) applied to the reduction in turnover (500,000)	120,000
Overheads	160,000		
Net profit	80,000		
	620,000		620,000

5. Alternatives to turnover specification

The specification using reduction in turnover as the index by which to measure the loss of gross profit has now been in general use for so many years by all insurance companies that there is ample experience whereby it can be judged. There is no doubt that it has stood the test of time and that the consensus of opinion is in favour of its use for the majority of industrial and commercial businesses excepting those for which the use of specifications insuring gross income, fees, revenue, commission, rent, etc., are recommended elsewhere in this book. On the other hand, manufacturing on any sizeable scale today involves so many complex factors that alternative methods of insuring which superficially may appear simple can prove, on analysis, to have drawbacks which render them less satisfactory than the turnover specification.

With this as in most things, however, there are exceptions and when necessary insurers will consider the use of some alternative index of loss which may be thought more appropriate to meet the special features of a particular business. It must be borne in mind in this connection that it is a major loss which is to be chiefly considered and not the relatively small damage which results in an interruption of the business for a short period of hours or days. It is not disputed that in the latter event the actual loss of gross profit may not be readily ascertainable by the turnover formula or that the work involved in doing so may be out of proportion to the amount of loss sustained. This does not invalidate the contention that turnover is the best index of loss for trading concerns since it is the possibility of substantial loss which is the real reason why an insurance is effected.

Indeed, it may be said that in practice in the case of a very limited interruption of a business insurers are quite agreeable to measure the loss by whatever yardstick is most convenient and convert the result into turnover figures for producing an equitable settlement with a minimum of labour. The guiding principle in such cases is that the object of the insurance is to provide, within its terms, an indemnity. At the same time it must be appreciated that the settlement of a small claim in this manner cannot be taken as establishing a binding precedent for any subsequent claim.

For reasons given above the use of various alternative forms of specification which have had at best limited appeal over past years has declined to the point of now being of little more than historic interest. To recall them indicates the evolution over some 90 years to the present standard use of the turnover basis. Output basis; Sale Value of Output; Alternative Output/Turnover; Input; Throughput; Productive Wages; Spindles specification; Looms specification. These have all been explained in previous editions of this book but as requests for any of them are today so rare in the U.K. they have for economy been left out of the present edition.

6. Old and new definitions of gross profit

From the inception of this form of insurance the accepted method of determining and defining insurable gross profit was by the addition of the amount of the standing charges to the net profit. But in the late 1950's a simpler method was introduced in which the total of the variable expenses is deducted from the turnover. This innovation necessitated a new definition of insurable gross profit which is in a sense a reversal of the traditional one. The latter started at the end of the accounts with net profit and added back the amount of the insurable standing charges. The new one starts at the head of the accounts with turnover—the money receivable for goods sold and services rendered—and then deducts the total of the variable charges, the difference between the two amounts being the insurable gross profit. Hence the newer specification wording in which the "turnover less variables" definition of gross profit is used is called the "difference" basis and because it is a more logical method and generally a simpler one it has become standard practice for insurers to recommend it.

But as the "net profit plus standing charges" form is still sometimes used in the U.K. and more so abroad and in the Canadian "Profits" form (refer paragraph 73(a)) it is necessary to keep in mind that whilst the two methods work on the same basic principles and produce the same end-results in claims, they treat gross profit from opposite directions. The variable charges which in a "difference" definition of gross profit are termed the uninsured working expenses are the reverse of standing charges. An alternative name for them which is often used is specified working expenses but, since all expenses in the manufacturing section of accounts which may normally be thought of as working expenses are not necessarily variable charges for the purposes of a business interruption insurance (for instance, see paragraph 133 on power and paragraph 174 on fuel), the term uninsured working expenses seems preferable in order to avoid misunderstandings.

Whether the old or the new definition of gross profit is used in a specification it is necessary to understand why the various charges incurred in the running of a business are or are not, as the case may be, to be included in the insurances of different businesses. They will be dealt with accordingly in subsequent chapters so as to give guidance for application under either definition.

7. Increased ratio of standing charges

Mention was made in paragraph 3 that a reduction in turnover will affect net profit in two ways. The more obvious is that with a smaller volume of business on which net profit can be earned there will be a corresponding reduction in the amount of net profit. But the more serious aspect may be the increased ratio of standing charges caused by the reduction in turnover because that will automatically reduce any net profit earned by the turnover maintained and may not only cancel it out but be sufficient to create a net trading loss.

It will be appreciated that in this way a heavy loss due to the increased incidence of standing charges for even a limited period of two or three months could offset the whole of a year's net profit or possibly result in a trading deficit. The following simplified illustration of the effects of a fire shows how this might arise.

On an annual turnover of £2 million the variable charges are £1.4 million (70 per cent.), the standing charges are £500,000 (25 per cent.) and the net profit is £100,000 (5 per cent.). Fire causes an interruption of business during six months of the year resulting in a loss of turnover amounting to

£720,000. The actual loss due to this is, therefore, 30 per cent. (non-variable charges 25 per cent. and net profit 5 per cent.) on the shortage in turnover (720,000), namely £216,000, more than twice the normal annual net profit.

For a more detailed illustration of such effects of a fire, see the claim illustrations set out in Appendix V, paragraph 468 which shows how a 50 per cent. reduction in turnover in 12 months can wipe out the net profit which it would take more than three years of normal trading to earn.

This potential loss due to an increased incidence of standing charges after a fire makes it essential to have the protection of a business interruption policy even during a time of adverse trading. Some businessmen are apt to think that such an insurance can be dispensed with when trading conditions are difficult and economies in overheads are necessary or that such a policy must be valueless when a business is running at a loss. Accountants in particular will understand the fallacy of such a line of thought and also that the effect of a small trading loss resulting from a fire, which would be relatively unimportant when good profits are being made and act as a cushion, can be most serious during a difficult trading period when no profit is being earned.

8. Compensation for additional expenditure

Interruption of trading which follows damage by fire or other perils generally involves additional expenditure of one kind or another with the object of minimising the loss of turnover and restoring normal conditions as quickly as possible. Any insurance which is intended to give an indemnity for loss consequent upon such damage must therefore provide compensation for additional expenditure undertaken to reduce the prospective loss of turnover during a period of interruption.

Without provision being made for the additional expenditure insurers would benefit through their insured's action whilst the latter would suffer the loss of the amount incurred. In practice such additional expenditure is generally of considerable amount and because of its effectiveness frequently exceeds the loss arising from reduction in turnover.

Consequently provision is made in the policy as explained in paragraph 45 for the payment of increase in cost of working. This rounds off the indemnity provided for loss of gross profit and the broad lines of the U.K. business interruption insurance may be summarised as giving compensation for:

(i) loss of net profit due to shortage in turnover;
(ii) loss due to the increased ratio of continuing charges to a reduced amount of turnover;
(iii) loss due to additional expenditure incurred with the object of minimising the effects of the damage on turnover.

The alternative way of stating this for an insurance, where the definition of gross profit is on the modern difference basis, would be compensation for:

(i) loss of net turnover *i.e.*, turnover less purchases and other variable charges;
(ii) loss due to additional expenditure incurred with the object of minimising the effects of the damage on turnover.

9. Loss of Business Income—the United States approach

Because of the enormous size of the United States the diversity of conditions (commercial as well as geographic) and the complications of State legislation, the development of business interruption insurance has in the past lacked the uniformity of U.K. practices which were primarily the outcome of the central authority and pooled experience of the U.K. tariff organisation (dissolved in 1985 and replaced by the Association of British Insurers which is an advisory body). However, over the years the hard work of various bureaux, associations and conferences aiming at improved policy terms and conditions culminated in the formation in the United States of the Insurance Services Office (I.S.O.) and the adoption by the majority of U.S. insurers of standard forms.

In 1986 new standard forms were introduced by the I.S.O. to replace the long-standing business interruption gross earnings forms. Called Business Income Coverage forms their purpose is basically the same as those they replaced but the language in which they are now written is new and (it is to be hoped) more readily understandable. For example "we" and "you" have placed "insurer" and "insured" and the point made by the new title is that it is the "income" of a business rather than its "interruption" that is the subject-matter of the insurance. Further, that income is no longer described as "gross earnings" because "gross earnings" is not a familiar expression in U.S. accounting practices. It is of interest to note that "Business Income" is defined as net profit plus continuing charges whereas "gross earnings" were defined as net sales less non-continuing charges.

Again the purposes of both the old and the new forms is the same as that of business interruption insurance in the United Kingdom and other countries namely to provide indemnity for loss of earnings and additional expenditure resulting from damage to or destruction of property by the operation of specified contingencies. Methods of achieving such indemnity differ in various respects between the United Kingdom and the United States forms but because the end results arrived at are in essence the same—reimbursement for loss of net profit and the maintenance of continuing charges which would have been earned but for the occurrence of the damage—many of the day-to-day problems which arise are comparable and solutions may often be found on similar lines.

10. "Actual loss of Business Income you sustain"

One fundamental and important difference exists in the two methods of providing an indemnity for loss resulting from a reduction in income. In the United Kingdom there is a formula set out in the specification in the policy which is based on a reduction in turnover. In the United States the indemnity for loss of earnings is described as the "actual loss of Business Income you sustain" (somewhat clearer than the previous "actual loss sustained") and although the Loss Determination condition which I.S.O. have introduced (see paragraph 61) sets out the basic ingredients in arriving at the Business Income loss no "formula" for loss calculation has yet been incorporated.

11. Expenses to Reduce Loss (or Extra Expense)

As far as increased costs are concerned a U.S. Business Income coverage form will also cover either Expenses to Reduce Loss, which is equivalent in its operation to the U.K. cover within the insurance of gross profit and is subject to the "economic limit" of the amount of loss that otherwise would have been payable under the form, or the broader Extra Expense which is not subject to such limitations and includes other items of "necessary" expenditure. (See further comment in paragraph 64.)

Chapter 2

The Framework of the Cover—Policy Forms Used in the United Kingdom

12. The standard policy

The framework of the cover, applicable to all United Kingdom business interruption insurances, is the legal document called the policy and within this is inserted the more detailed description of the cover provided for each individual case, which is termed the specification (Chapter 4—paragraph 35 *et seq.*).

The policy is a printed document in a standardised form of wording which is a recently "modernised" version of that which was adopted for use in Great Britain and Ireland by the tariff insurance companies in 1939 and which resulted from experience gained during the preceding 40 years and subsequently being adopted by non-tariff companies and by underwriters at Lloyd's. A specimen of the current (1990) standard policy which has been produced by the Association of British Insurers (A.B.I.) as part of their Recommended Practices for the Conduct of Material Damage and Business Interruption Insurance in Great Britain and Northern Ireland is given in Appendix A. It contains conditions common to most forms of insurance policy but the following features (paragraphs 13 to 19) call for special mention.

The overall title of this class of insurance in the United Kingdom is now accepted as "business interruption" insurance. However, the words "consequential loss" are still to be found. In the past confusion has arisen over the different interpretations of "consequential loss" the same words also being encountered in property damage and liability insurances. So as to help clarify the situation the A.B.I. have added the following definition to their recommended business interruption policy wordings—

> "The words 'CONSEQUENTIAL LOSS', in capital letters, shall mean loss resulting from interruption of or interference with the Business carried out by the Insured at the Premises in consequence of loss or destruction of or damage to property used by the Insured at the Premises for the purpose of the Business".

However, where the words "consequential loss" appear (in both property damage and business interruption policies) other than in capital letters they refer in the main to consequential damage.

13. Perils insured

(a) Named perils

The perils insured against are the same as those covered under the standard fire policy. These are shown on the face of the policy as being fire (but excluding loss, destruction or damage caused by explosion resulting from fire, or caused by earthquake, subterranean fire or spontaneous heating, etc.), lightning, explosion of boilers used for domestic purposes, and explosion of gas used for domestic purposes (excluding loss, destruction or damage caused by earthquake or subterranean fire). Riot, civil commotion, war, etc., which was once an exclusion on the face of the policy is now a General Exclusion (see paragraph 148, Appendix A). In addition, however, the risk of business interruption loss arising from the explosion of *any* boiler or economiser on the premises is included. This latter benefit is a valuable one in the case of industrial premises containing a steam boiler, for the explosion of such a boiler could have a very serious effect upon the productive capacity of a business.

No definition is given of the meaning of each of the insured perils. It is unnecessary to do so because the inclusion later in the preamble of the "material damage proviso" (paragraph 15(e) *et seq.*) provides for the business interruption policy to follow the material damage insurance in the interpretation of the meaning of any damage giving rise to a claim. In the case of a fire policy the meaning of fire, etc., is long established by common law and case law and includes resulting smoke damage and damage caused by water or other means in efforts to extinguish or limit the spread of a fire; so these are treated as damage by fire although this is not mentioned on the policy. Loss resulting from damage occasioned by or happening through explosion, whether the explosion be caused by fire or otherwise, is not covered except as stated on the face of the policy, that is, as mentioned above. It should be noted from this that fire resulting from explosion is an insured peril.

So far as the explosion of any boiler or economiser on the premises is concerned, the meaning would, because of the material damage proviso, be taken as being that defined in a boiler insurance policy. In such a policy a boiler means those parts of the permanent structure which are subject to steam or other fluid pressure up to and including fittings and direct attachments subject to such pressure which are connected to the permanent structure without intervening valve or cock. This automatically excludes flue gas explosion and explosion of steam pipes and vessels, regarding which see paragraphs 282 and 283.

The perils included on the face of the policy are usually referred to as the "standard perils" whilst the additional contingencies for which cover can be obtained described in Chapter 14 are for purposes of distinction spoken of as "special perils" or "extra perils". A specific standard fire and special perils policy has been formulated by the A.B.I. but individual special perils can still be added to the standard fire business interruption policy (Appendix A).

(b) *All risks*

The perils insured against are those covered under the equivalent material damage "all risks" policy (or section if the policy is a combined document).

The cover is in respect of "all risks" of accidental loss, destruction or damage, with named exclusions, some of which can be "bought back" (at additional premium) with the remainder (including mechanical or electrical breakdown) not being generally available to be "bought back".

The intention is to preserve the cover afforded by the full standard fire and special perils wording but at the same time to include "accidental damage" other than that denied to the insured by the excluded "perils".

In this way, explosion cover is provided, other than that caused by or consisting of:

> "the bursting of any vessel, machine or apparatus (not being a boiler or economiser on the premises or a boiler used for domestic purposes only) in which internal pressure is due to steam only and belonging to or under the control of the Insured, but this shall not exclude subsequent CONSEQUENTIAL LOSS which itself results from a cause not otherwise excluded".

Also included automatically in the all risks wording are perils not previously available in a standard fire and perils cover, *e.g.* impact by own vehicles, spontaneous heating and sprinkler leakage. Perils which it is possible to "buy back" include subsidence and theft.

An example of this wording is shown in Appendix B and it is worth making a comparison with the standard form in Appendix A, which to be strictly comparable should be extended to include the usual special perils of explosion, aircraft, earthquake, riot, etc., malicious damage, storm and tempest, flood, etc., and sprinkler leakage (refer Chapter 14). It will be noted that the cover is restricted at various places to "defined perils". A specific definition is included:

> "The words "Defined Peril" shall mean fire, lightning, explosion, aircraft or other aerial devices or articles dropped therefrom, riot, civil commotion, strikers, locked-out workers, persons taking part in labour disturbances, malicious persons, earthquake, storm, flood, escape of water from any tank apparatus or pipe or impact by any road vehicle or animal".

The purpose of this restriction is to avoid including loss caused by unknown contingencies.

14. General exclusions

(a) *Radioactivity from nuclear fuel, waste or assembly*

This exclusion is in respect of loss, destruction or damage arising from ionising radiations or contamination by radioactivity from any nuclear fuel or from any nuclear waste from the combustion of nuclear fuel.

It was introduced by all insurers when the Nuclear Installations (Licensing and Insurance) Act 1959 (now revoked and replaced by the Nuclear Installations Act 1965) came into force, which imposed liabilities upon operators of atomic installations for injury or damage suffered from an escape of radioactivity. Special insurance facilities were then provided for such operators by the British Insurance (Atomic Energy) Committee, which comprises the whole of the British insurance market, to meet claims for compensation and the Committee announced that it is neither necessary nor possible for the general public to insure against loss from radioactive contamination.

The above radioactive contamination clause was subsequently extended to exclude also the radioactive, toxic, explosive or other hazardous properties of any explosive nuclear assembly or nuclear component thereof. The full clause is shown in each of the A.B.I. standard policies in Appendices A and B.

(b) *Northern Ireland*

This was added to the standard policy in 1978 with the effect of excluding all loss resulting from damage in Northern Ireland caused by civil commotion or by persons acting on behalf of a proscribed organisation engaged in terrorism. An insured can now claim compensation for such loss from the Secretary of State for Northern Ireland under a government scheme if a legally enforceable interest in the damaged property can be established. For the full wording of the exclusion see the specimen policies in Appendices A and B (for fuller information refer to paragraph 290).

The standard all risks wording (refer paragraph 448, Appendix B) contains a wider version which also excludes loss resulting from damage caused by riot and (except in respect of damage by fire or explosion) strikers, locked-out workers or persons taking part in labour disturbances or malicious persons. Opportunity exists under the standard fire and the standard fire and special perils policies for insurers to decline to add these additional causes.

(c) *Pollution or contamination*

The occurrence of large losses in various parts of the world resulting in the pollution or contamination of property beyond the site of the loss has led to concern over the extent of property insurers' liability to pay for damage so caused. Such concern has been strengthened by the attitude taken in the United States with regard to pollution or contamination after insurers had found themselves liable in respect of clean-up costs to third party properties for which they had never intended giving cover.

Following due consideration the current A.B.I. recommended wordings for fire, material damage and business interruption policies specifically exclude loss resulting from pollution or contamination. The exclusion is however overridden by a qualification which states (for business interruption) that

> "this shall not exclude loss resulting from destruction of or damage to property used by the Insured at the Premises for the purpose of the Business, not otherwise excluded, caused by (a) pollution or contamination at the Premises which itself results from a peril hereby insured against, or (b) any peril hereby insured against which itself results from pollution or contamination".

15. Conditions for a valid claim

In order to provide valid grounds for a claim under the policy the following five conditions (a) to (e) must be met in accordance with the preamble on the face of the policy.

(a) The business interruption loss must be the result of loss, destruction or damage by one of the perils mentioned in paragraph 13 subsequently referred to and defined in the specification by the single word "Incident"—"Loss or destruction of or damage to property used by the Insured at the Premises for the purpose of the Business".

(b) The damage must occur at premises used by the insured for the purpose of the business the addresses of which are stated in the policy schedule or in the specification. It is possible for an insured's business to sustain loss of turnover as the result of an Incident (as defined) at premises not occupied by them, for instance those of suppliers of materials, components or finished products or of processors or customers or at public warehouses or other premises where the insured may have stock temporarily stored. Loss resulting from loss, destruction or damage at such premises not used by the insured for purposes of the business can be brought within the scope of the insurance only by their specific inclusion and the manner in which this is effected is fully described in Chapter 17.

Further, new premises and major extensions to existing premises for the purpose of the business are not until they are "used" by the insured within the terms of the policy. Loss, destruction or damage occurring during the period of construction and fitting out will almost inevitably delay commencement of production or sales in all or part of the new unit with a consequent loss of turnover. This is a contingency which should be insured under an Advance Profits policy, for details of which see paragraph 268(a).

Another aspect of extensions or alterations to an insured's premises is introduced by the Alteration Condition under which if any alteration be made whereby the risk of loss, destruction or damage is increased the policy shall be not voidable but voided, unless its continuance be admitted by the insurer. (See paragraph 17.)

(c) The loss, destruction or damage must cause interruption of or interference with the business carried on by the insured at the premises stated in the policy schedule or in the specification and the indemnity is confined to loss arising from such interruption or interference at those premises. An insured firm may have more than one premises and loss, destruction or damage at one may adversely affect turnover at another but unless the latter has been included in the description of the premises as well as that at which the loss, destruction or damage occurs the loss arising at the undamaged premises is not covered.

The importance of this condition has been increased with the intensification of business take-overs and combinations and general diversification of trading activities. It is obviously essential that insurers should know exactly which firms, premises and business operations come within the insurance cover and if owing to an oversight or mistake by a member of an insured firm they are not notified of an addition which should be made to the insurance they cannot be held liable for any loss arising from the omission.

(d) The interruption of or interference with the business must be in consequence of an Incident (as defined). This may rule out loss due to personal injuries or death of an insured or of directors, members or employees of a firm, even though this is caused by one of the insured perils if such injury cannot be construed as being damage to "property" (see paragraph 421). The meaning of "any building or other property" is not confined to fixed assets but includes plant, machinery and stock and such need not be actually owned by the insured; it can be rented buildings, hired plant or machinery, or stock held on credit—any property "used" by the insured for the purposes of the business.

Further, the loss covered is that sustained by "the business", that is, the business as described on the policy schedule. Therefore, if an insured is engaged in more than one business at the premises the insurance will apply only to such as may be mentioned in the schedule description (see paragraph 23(b)).

(e) There must be in existence a fire policy and/or a boiler policy covering the interest of the insured in the material damage sustained (and similar insurance appropriate to any special perils which may have been added, subject to certain exceptions, as detailed in paragraphs 280 to 309, Chapter 14), and the claim under such policy must be admitted by the insurer concerned. The clause in which this is stated is known as the "material damage proviso" (see following paragraphs 16(a) and (b)).

It should be noted that this clause cannot be applied to extensions of cover to the premises of suppliers, processors and customers, etc., because it refers to *the interest of the insured* in the property which is lost, destroyed or damaged. Further, whilst it stipulates that there must be material damage insurance in force in respect of the perils insured by the business interruption policy the latter need not cover all the risks insured by the material damage policy if for some reason insurance in respect of some of those perils is not required.

The foregoing five conditions (a) to (e) though wide in scope are specific in regard to matters covered by them. Yet no mention is made in them, nor in the Alteration condition of the policy dealt with in paragraph 17, about the introduction of factors such as new machines of more complicated design or greater vulnerability than those they replace, new materials in short or seasonal supply, computers on which the whole factory might be dependent, or new processes or production and selling techniques which do not change the purpose or nature of the business or use of the premises or the risk of inception or degree of loss, destruction or damage but may very considerably increase the incidence and length of the interruption risk. This may well be a grey area in which insurers could in certain circumstances feel justified in invoking the doctrine of *uberrima fides*, the policy being a contract of the utmost good faith. Whilst the duty of disclosure of material facts only applies to negotiations preceding the formation of the contract, at each renewal thereafter any fresh material facts neither known or presumed to be known by the insurers must be disclosed to them. It would therefore seem advisable when an insured introduces into a business a new factor of appreciable importance regarding the interruption risk to notify and consult the insurers and obtain their acknowledgment of its existence.

16. Material damage proviso

(a) *General application*

The primary object of this proviso (paragraph 15(e)) is to ensure that insured will be in a financial position to make good any damage to their own property—buildings or contents. Otherwise the reinstatement of a business might be delayed or be impossible and in that event part of the business interruption loss would not be proximately caused by the damage but by the insured's lack of financial means to rehabilitate the business. Payment of material damage claims monies does not always guarantee replacement of property destroyed. For instance, the basis of settlement may be indemnity only and what has been paid may also be called in by creditors. As a result, the insured may have no alternative but to attempt to borrow the required amount of money and to request the largest possible payment on account under the business interruption policy. However, the material damage proviso does not stipulate that the material damage cover is sufficient to restore the lost, destroyed or damaged property, nor that the money is used for restoration if the claim is not settled on a reinstatement basis. Nevertheless, the requirement that the insured must minimise the business interruption loss should ensure that the material damage claims monies are properly used (refer also paragraph 420(a)).

It must also be borne in mind that material damage policies usually contain a number of warranties and conditions compliance with which is a condition precedent to liability of the insurers for any loss. The necessity which would otherwise arise for the insurers of the business interruption loss to place similar warranties and conditions on their policies, thus making these more lengthy, is avoided by the use of this proviso. It also relieves them of the need to investigate the circumstances of the damage in order to ascertain whether all such stipulations have been complied with.

Further, the possibility of a fire being deliberately caused or of other dishonest circumstances attaching to it must not be overlooked. The insurers who are responsible for providing an indemnity for the material damage are in the better position to investigate any suspicious cases and so the insurers of the business interruption loss leave that aspect to them. If the claim under the fire insurance is not paid because it is fraudulent or because of a breach of warranty or for any other reason then there can be no valid claim under the business interruption insurance.

Circumstances sometimes arise of such a nature that liability for the material damage caused is not admitted by the insurers under a fire or other policy but nevertheless an *ex gratia* payment is made by them to the insured. In such cases the exact wording of the material damage proviso in the business interruption policy may be of considerable importance; it reads:

> "provided that at the time of the happening of the loss, destruction or damage there shall be in force an insurance covering the interest of the Insured in the property at the Premises against such loss, destruction or damage and that payment shall have been made or liability admitted therefor".

The legal position will presumably depend upon whether a denial of liability by insurers of the material damage means that although an *ex gratia* payment is made their insurance was not regarded as being "in force . . . against such damage" at the time it happened. In practice the business interruption insurers generally follow the action of the material damage insurers in making an *ex gratia* payment. But it is possible that if damage of a very small amount at say a key point in a productive process caused a very much greater business interruption loss, insurers of the latter might understandably look at the request for an *ex gratia* payment in a different light from the insurers of the material damage.

(b) *Exceptions*

The material damage proviso is inoperative if the insured have no financial interest in the property the loss or destruction of or damage to which gives rise to the business interruption loss as, for example, when they do not own the building or plant, or in the case of an extension of cover to the factory of a supplier or customer, etc., (as explained in Chapter 17). The proviso is concerned only with property in which the insured have a direct and insurable interest and which they can reasonably be expected to insure.

In a number of material damage policies in respect of fire or other perils the amount payable is made subject to an excess. This applies to insurances against malicious damage and to storm and flood policies; and also to "deductibles" (paragraph 24(b)). In general, a similar excess is not applied to the business interruption insurances for malicious damage (paragraph 291) and for storm and flood (paragraph 294).

But if the material damage sustained at any time is less in amount than the excess on the fire or other policy, no claim is payable under such policy and consequently the material damage proviso printed on the face of the business interruption policy would debar a claim for loss under the latter. Even though there might be on a business interruption policy, a deductible of the same amount as that on the fire policy circumstances could arise in which whilst the material damage is less than the deductible, the business interruption loss exceeds it.

In order that in such circumstances the material damage proviso on the business interruption policy does not act as a bar to a claim under that insurance, the following is now incorporated into the material damage proviso:

> "Payment would have been made or liability admitted therefor but for the operation of a proviso in such insurance excluding liability for losses below a specified amount.".

17. Alteration condition

This condition states that the insurance will be avoided if the business is wound up or carried on by a liquidator or receiver or permanently discontinued, or if the insured's interest ceases otherwise than by death, or if any alteration be made in the business or premises or property therein whereby the risk of loss, destruction or damage is increased, unless the insurer agrees to the change.

This condition applies to the state of affairs before damage takes place. Once the latter has occurred liability is established on the basis of conditions appertaining at that time and the position with regard to the claim is then governed by the claims condition—to which reference is made in paragraph 18.

The first part of the condition is of particular interest to accountants. The appointment of a liquidator generally signifies the winding up of a business as soon as possible and in such cases when the point of closing down the business is reached there would be no call for the continuation of a business interruption insurance designed to protect future earnings. But where it is intended to carry on the business for some time, for instance, to complete unfulfilled orders or contracts or to dispose of the business as a viable concern, the liquidator may desire to continue the insurance. In such circumstances the insurers will generally agree to do so, vesting in the liquidator an interest in the policy.

When a receiver is appointed it is in the interests of the parties for whom he is acting that the business interruption insurance should be continued until the business is sold or liabilities to creditors are discharged. The insurers must, however, be notified and a formal transfer of interest to the receiver be agreed to by them.

The further stipulation that if "the insured's interest cease other than by death" the policy shall be avoided unless the insurer agrees to its continuance makes sense because the moral hazard is of great importance in a business interruption insurance which covers the loss of something hypothetical and so is very dependent upon the business integrity of an insured.

It may be noted that the reference to alterations being made in the business or premises or property therein is limited to increase in the risk of *damage* and does not include increases in what is known as the "interruption risk". Consequently, if an insured effects alterations such as the installation of new machinery which would take much longer to replace after damage than that which it supersedes, or introduces automation in a factory which in the event of a fire would involve greater dislocation of production than previously would have been the case, there is no stipulation that the insurers be informed. It would therefore seem that although the potential liability of the latter may be greatly increased the policy remains valid provided that the physical hazard, that is, the risk of material damage taking place or extending, is not increased. See also remarks in final paragraph of paragraph 15.

The risk of a business interruption loss arising from damage to a computer which controls factory production is proving in practice to be a very serious matter and it may be that at some time in the future insurers will decide that the condition will have to provide for their being notified of an increase in the interruption risk. But the practical difficulties of this are very great because of the wide range in degrees of increase of interruption risk and the wide area for disagreement on this feature, unless the scope of the condition were confined, as on the French standard policy, to the presence of or the installation of computers and mini computers.

It is interesting to note the attitude of U.S. insurers in the above matter as evidenced by the condition on all business interruption policies which limits the period of indemnity in respect of loss resulting from damage to electronic data processing, etc., as given in paragraph 63(c).

18. Obligations of insured: the claims conditions

The claims condition dealing with "Action by the Insured" is to a large extent an embodiment of the implied obligations in the event of loss under the doctrine of *uberrima fides*—"utmost good faith"—which continues throughout the insurance. But it amplifies these, states specifically the action which an insured must take or permit to be taken when damage occurs which is likely to give rise to a claim under the insurance, and sets a time limit for furnishing details of the claim.

This matter is dealt with more fully in Chapter 20 on Claim Settlements but it is advisable at this point to note one implication which occasionally arises in practice. The condition states in effect that on the occurrence of loss, destruction or damage the insured must do and concur in doing and permit to be done all things reasonably practicable to minimise the resulting loss. It will be seen from this that the policy does not provide for, say, an elderly insured who might wish to take out an insurance with the intention, if serious interruption of the business should follow damage, of retiring and drawing the compensation provided by the policy. That would in any event be nonfulfilment of the obligations implied under the doctrine of good faith. On the other hand, if unforeseen circumstances are brought about by the damage which make it expedient for an insured to discontinue the business insurers are not precluded from reaching an agreement for a suitable settlement of the claim on the basis of a compromise if it appears reasonable to do so.

An elderly owner of a business with no member of his family or staff interested to continue the business on his retirement may express the opinion that as he would not wish to restore his business in the event of destruction of the premises by fire, and could not in those circumstances obtain compensation under a business interruption insurance, there is no necessity for such a policy. This overlooks the possibility of a fire or other insured peril causing only partial damage and interference with the business. In such circumstances the proprietor would probably not wish to retire immediately and insurance would be very valuable to ensure restoration of the business either for continued operation by the insured for his own benefit or for sale by him later as a going concern. The other claims conditions are dealt with in Chapter 20, paragraphs 439 to 442.

19. Implied conditions

The implied conditions of good faith, indemnity and insurable interest established in connection with fire insurance practice by common law and case law over the past 280 years, attach similarly to a business interruption insurance. Where necessary these are emphasised or implemented by the terms and conditions of the policy and specification, as explained in paragraphs 435 to 442 in the chapter on claim settlements.

20. An annual contract: days of grace for renewal

With regard to the more general terms of the policy it may be mentioned that the normal contract is an annual one and although the maximum indemnity period during which compensation is payable (described in paragraph 245(a)) may be for any length of time commencing with the date of loss, destruction or damage from a few months to a number of years according to the insured's choice, the policy itself is renewable yearly.

When the traditional 15 days of grace are allowed for the payment of the renewal premium each year, as with an annual fire material damage policy, this fact is shown on the renewal notice although it is not mentioned on the policy. It should be borne in mind, however, that this concession only applies if the insured intend to renew the policy and are not taking steps to transfer it to another insurance company. Should the latter position appertain at the time of a loss occurring the insured would have no legal claim to the benefit of the days of grace and if cover had not already been arranged with the new insurer, would be without insurance protection.

In U.S. insurances if a "grace period" applies this is usually for 31 days following the due date.

21. Long term agreements

In the majority of insurances the insurers are willing to enter into a long term agreement whereby the insured contract to renew the insurance for an agreed number of years on what is termed an "offer basis", for which a discount of 5 per cent. is allowed off the premium.

Under such an agreement the insured undertake to offer annually, for a stated period of either three or five years, to renew the insurance on the terms and conditions which would be applicable each renewal date. The contract states that the insurers are under no obligation to accept the offer of renewal. Should they agree to do so but only on increased terms then the insured have the right not to renew.

Apart from this option not to renew if the conditions proposed by the insurers are unacceptable, the insured cannot terminate an insurance before the expiry of a term agreement even though they may be willing to refund the amount of the discount already allowed during its current term. If insurers were to accede to such requests term agreements would be reduced to an absurdity.

In the event of a business being wound up or carried on by liquidator or receiver or permanently discontinued, or if an insured's interest ceases by sale or other cause, the agreement will automatically lose its validity but normally no claim will be made by the insurers for a refund of the discounts which may have been allowed during its current term.

The wording of a term agreement to be signed for a policy with a single insurer is as follows:

> "In consideration of the above-named Insurer agreeing to allow a discount of 5 per cent. off the net premiums on the above numbered policy, we hereby undertake from . . . to offer annually for . . . years the insurance under the said policy on the terms and conditions in force at the expiry of each period of insurance and to pay the premium thereon annually in advance.
> It is understood that:
>
> > (a) the Insurer shall be under no obligation to accept an offer made in accordance with this undertaking
> > (b) the sum insured may be reduced at any time to correspond with any reduction in the business.
>
> This undertaking shall apply to any policy or policies which may be issued by the Insurer within the said period of . . . years in substitution for the above-mentioned policy and the same discount of 5 per cent. shall be allowed off the net premium of any subsituted policy or policies issued by the Insurer aforesaid".

This wording is varied appropriately where a number of insurers share the insurance.

It will be noticed that the agreement permits a reduction in the sum insured, at any time during its currency, to correspond with any reduction in the insured's business. Further, insurance companies have put it on record that an alteration in the length of a maximum indemnity period is not a breach of an agreement. Consequently, the possibility of a period of adverse trading conditions should not deter an insured from entering into a term agreement.

In the United States and Canada long term agreements of the foregoing nature are not used and the expression "long term insurance" refers to a three-years policy contract.

22. "Collective" policies

A collective policy is the same in content as and practically identical in wording with the standard form already described, but is one in which a number of insurance companies share the risk in stated proportions, one policy being issued on behalf of all the insurers by the "leading office". Similarly, whenever an endorsement is necessary to give effect to an alteration to the insurance under such a policy one document is issued on behalf of all the insurers and at renewal date only one renewal notice and one receipt are issued. The convenience of this arrangement to an insured, in lieu of separate documents being issued by a number of insurers, is obvious and it is now the accepted practice to issue a collective policy for an insurance shared by more than one insurer.

Should an insured have good and sufficient reasons to support a request for the introduction of another insurance company for a share of the insurance during the currency of a long term agreement, this may be acceded to, provided that the interest of all existing insurers is maintained, each taking a proportionate reduction to accommodate the introduction of the new insurer.

In the United States the expression "lead company" corresponds to "leading office" or " lead insurers" in U.K. insurances.

23. Schedule details

(a) *The Insured*

Part of the printed standard policy form is a schedule (for a specimen of which see Appendix A) in which certain necessary details of the insurance are inserted and regarding these the following points may be noted.

It is essential that the full and correct title of the insured be stated because the policy is a legal contract covering the loss sustained solely by the party or parties named in it as the insured.

Where more than one legal entity is to be insured in the same policy as in the case of a parent firm and its subsidiaries, or associated companies, the name of all of them should be stated even though one or other may be only a trading name provided that it is a properly constituted company.

Difficulty sometimes arises when the insured wish to include subsidiary and associated concerns in their own policy without the names of these being stated, possibly because they do not wish the relationship to become common knowledge or because they wish to safeguard themselves against overlooking notification to the insurers of the subsequent acquisition of another subsidiary. They may suggest that the policy description should be on some such lines as "The X.Y.Z. Manufacturing Co. Ltd. and its Associated Companies", or "The X.Y.Z. Manufacturing Co. Ltd. and its Subsidiary and Associated Companies". But a description of this kind is not acceptable as a definition of the insured.

There is in U.K. law no definition of "associated company" and no reference to it appears in the various Companies Acts including the 1980 Act. The term is undoubtedly in common use but is so very frequently either misused or loosely used that there is no certainty as to its meaning. Its reference may be to companies with no closer association than interlocking directorates and with no legal title to be named jointly in a business interruption policy.

The meaning of "subsidiary company" is defined in the Companies Act 1948 (in Part IV, s.154) and is retained by the Companies Act 1980, Part IV, s.49. Even so, the use of the expression in the description of the insured without the names of the subsidiary company or companies being stated may give rise to misunderstanding or misconstruction as to the extent of the cover, particularly where there are subsidiaries of subsidiaries or if at some date after the insurance is arranged another company is acquired and no notification is given of intention to include it in the group insurance. Also, it might lead an accountant inadvertently to give a certified figure for purposes of the return of premium clause which does not include all the companies in the group especially if, as is sometimes the case, all the firms in the group do not employ the same auditors.

The fact that a business interruption insurance is subject to the "average proviso" (paragraph 52) makes it essential that the insurers should know the names of all the firms which are included in the cover. It is sometimes suggested that the description of the premises provides an adequate safeguard but this is not necessarily so because subsidiary companies are often trading concerns operating from the same premises as the parent company. It must further be borne in mind that a policy of insurance is a legal document and a valid discharge in respect of a claim under it should be signed by all parties included as the insured.

(b) *The Business*

It is even more important than in the case of a fire material damage insurance that the description of the insured's trade should be adequately and accurately stated on the policy. On a fire policy it is necessary to have an accurate description of the insured's business mainly because the risk of loss, destruction or damage is intimately related to the trade processes; but the property covered by the fire insurance is identifiable. A business interruption policy, however, is concerned with something intangible, the loss resulting from interruption of or interference with "the business carried on by the insured at the premises" and an insured may in some cases carry on more than one business at the same premises.

For example, a firm may have (a) a factory producing goods for sale to wholesalers (b) a separate merchanting business which occupies part of the premises as a warehouse for the sale of a different class of goods and (c) a section for the recovery and treatment of the by-products of the factory and their sale. Separate accounts may be kept for each branch or division of the business and all the earnings be brought together into one profit and loss account but the firm may not wish to include all three sections of their business in the business interruption policy. In these or similar circumstances it is obviously essential that the insurers should know the extent of their cover.

As the description of the insurance on the printed policy form limits it to loss in respect of the business carried on by the insured at the premises the cover will only apply to the business as described in the schedule.

A point of frequent relevance in this connection is that where the insured receive income from the letting of property in addition to their main trade and insure it under an item on rent receivable (see paragraph 263(a)) the words "and property owners" should be added to the description of the insured's business in order to conform with the policy wording.

There is a tendency for the larger insured to have a definition of Business on the following lines—"Any activity now or hereafter carried on by the Insured". It is essential for such a definition to be reinforced by full and accurate details to be lodged with the leading insurer.

(c) *The Premises*

The description inserted in this part of the schedule likewise needs to be a full and accurate list of the premises at which the insured carry on business and which are to be included in the insurance. As the printed policy wording restricts the cover to loss resulting from interruption of or interference with the business carried on by the insured at the premises the insurers will have no legal liability in respect of loss at any addresses not named in the schedule. "The premises" does, however, include property of the insured in the yards or open spaces forming part of those premises.

This wording also makes it essential to notify the insurers when any additional premises are taken for the purposes of the business in order that these can be included in the insurance by endorsement of the policy.

As with Business, so Premises are often defined on a deliberately comprehensive basis for large insured, *e.g.* "All premises in . . . (country) owned and/or occupied by the Insured for the purpose of the Business". Again full and accurate details should be lodged with the leading insurer.

A further important matter is the possibility of an insured's business being interrupted as a result of loss, destruction or damage at some other firm's premises, for example, a supplier of components for the insured's products. The potential loss from such loss, destruction or damage cannot be covered by inserting the address of the suppliers in the description of the premises because the insured's business is not carried on there. To provide for the insurance of this contingency a special memorandum has to be added to the specification as explained in paragraph 344.

On the other hand a "shop within a shop" meaning that a firm rents space within a department store for the sale of its own products, or services such as hairdressing salon, travel and theatre ticket agencies, is regarded as the insured's premises and the appropriate address can be added to the list of these.

When the insured have a town office in London or elsewhere away from the works it is advisable to include this in the list of the premises. At first thought it might be considered that in the case of a manufacturing concern no advantage is gained by doing so if such an office is unconnected with administration or production at the works, as loss, destruction or damage at the office would not affect the manufacturing capacity and therefore the turnover of the business. But the expense of maintaining such an office would not be incurred unless it was of some administrative or economic benefit to the business and in the event of its being closed because of loss, destruction or damage alternative office accommodation would have to be found as soon as possible. Even if the lack of office facilities and records would not cause a loss of sales it might involve additional expenditure within the cover provided for increase in cost of working (as subsequently explained in paragraph 45). If it does and the office address has been included in the schedule the extra expense will be met by the insurance. It may be said that in general there is unlikely to be any additional premium cost involved by including such premises. (Refer also paragraph 382.)

Somewhat similar considerations apply to hostel premises provided and maintained by firms in the textile and other industries to house workpeople from Italy and other Continental countries who do not intend to stay permanently in this country. Loss, destruction or damage at such a hostel would affect production if no alternative accommodation were provided locally for the workpeople living there and they left their employment. To provide suitable alternative premises and possibly transport for employees to and from the works would involve additional expenditure.

In the case of London or provincial town showrooms and depots the possibility of loss of turnover or additional expenditure resulting from loss, destruction or damage is probably obvious but the necessity of naming the addresses on the policy should not be overlooked.

Similar remarks apply to the garage where the insured's own vehicles are housed when this is not part of their main premises. Specific mention should be made of the garage address in the description of the premises to ensure that it is included in the cover. Loss, destruction or damage which puts out of use delivery or service vehicles might involve a loss of earnings or additional expenditure on hiring and the amount of this can be very substantial when the vehicles are of special design or the number involved is considerable. In businesses such as that of quarry owners the housing together at night of a large fleet of vehicles and the mechanics' shop for maintenance work might constitute a greater potentiality of loss than the quarry buildings and plant.

Finally, the description of The Premises in the policy schedule must be read in conjunction with the contractual undertaking which refers to loss, destruction or damage to "any building or other property or any part thereof *used by the Insured* at the premises for the purpose of the business". As mentioned in paragraph 15(b) the effect of this could be that where an insured builds a major extension to existing premises which might be regarded as a separate unit of production even though it is within the precincts of the existing premises, until such time as the new building can be said to be "used" by the insured for the purposes of the business a strict interpretation of the policy wording would exclude loss arising from loss, destruction or damage there. A business interruption loss could be sustained although the use of such buildings had not actually started because loss, destruction or damage by fire or other perils would delay the time when their contribution to the turnover of the business would otherwise have commenced. For protection against this possibility an Advance Profits insurance on the lines of that for a new factory, explained in paragraph 268(a), is the answer.

(d) *The Insurer's liability*

This is the heading to a further section of the policy schedule, and the description of the liability is generally shown as being:

"The Insurer's liability under this policy is limited to . . . per cent. of its amount otherwise payable under the provision of the Specification".

It will be noticed that although the schedule states the maximum sum recoverable under the policy it makes the specification the part of the policy which sets out in detail the method of arriving at the indemnity provided.

In a collective policy (paragraph 22) the heading "The Insurer's Liability" is further defined as:

"The liability of each of the insurers individually shall be limited to the proportion set against its name".

Chapter 3

THE FRAMEWORK OF THE COVER (CONTINUED)—POLICY FORMS USED IN THE UNITED STATES

24. The standard policy forms

Until 1986 the legal instrument setting out the terms of a business interruption insurance was not usually a separate policy (with specification attached) as in U.K. practice but was part and parcel of the actual property damage (fire) policy in respect of the insured's business and premises.

The most important standard business interruption forms were the Gross Earnings—Mercantile and Non-manufacturing form, the Gross Earnings—Manufacturing and Mining form, the Earnings—Short Form (with no coinsurance), the Extra Expenses forms, and the Combined Business Interruption and Extra Expense form. However, in 1986 the Insurance Services Office (I.S.O.), which provides a wide range of advisory and other services to United States underwriters, replaced these forms with the Business Income Coverage and Extra Expense forms which are designed to stand alone as separate policies. It must be stressed that the I.S.O. is an advisory organisation and that it may well be that some insurers are continuing to use the previous forms. It must also be said that the previous forms were often the basis of policy wordings used outside the United States and may still be so.

Because they may still be used and for comparison purposes with the new forms a specimen of a gross earnings form for non-manufacturing businesses is given in Appendix Q, paragraph 463, and in Appendix R, paragraph 464, the form for manufacturing businesses is given by showing only its terms and conditions where these differ from those for non-manufacturing.

The I.S.O. recommended form for Business Income Coverage (and Extra Expense) is set out in Appendix S, paragraph 465. The more restricted form—Business Income Coverage (without Extra Expense)—is largely the same with the removal of the Extra Expense additional coverage and its replacement by the more limited Expenses to Reduce Loss; for this reason there is no separate wording in the Appendices. The separate Extra Expense coverage form largely follows the Business Income Coverage form but with reference exclusively where necessary to Extra Expense rather than Business Income. It also includes a time limitation for the payment of loss (see paragraph 278(b)) which does not feature in the Extra Expense additional coverage within the Business Income Coverage form.

The basic Business Income Coverage form has been designed to replace the previous forms mentioned already (with the exception of Earnings) as well as the old Rental Value Insurance Coinsurance form. The optional coverages in the form can if required replace the old Earnings Insurance forms, Rental Value Insurance Monthly Limitation form, Loss of Business Income form, and the Agreed Amount Endorsement.

25. Causes insured

The causes giving rise to damage from which resulting loss of business income is insured are not mentioned on the Business Income Coverage or Extra Expense Coverage forms. Instead the appropriate Causes of Loss form is attached. These forms are the same for Property Damage as for Business Income Coverage.

The coverage forms refer to "direct physical loss of or damage to property at the premises . . . . caused by or resulting from any Covered Cause of Loss".

(a) *Causes of Loss—Basic Form*

This form lists the following causes—fire and lightning (without any qualification); and (with qualification as necessary in each case) explosion (but excluding the explosion of steam boilers—refer Boiler and Machinery Insurance, paragraphs 328 *et seq.*), windstorm or hail, smoke, aircraft or vehicles, riot or civil commotion, vandalism, sprinkler leakage, sinkhole collapse and volcanic action.

Exclusions which affect the Business Income Coverage or Extra Expense Coverage forms are:

(i) Any loss caused by or resulting from damage or destruction of "finished stock"; or the time required to reproduce "finished stock". (This exclusion does not apply to Extra Expense.)

(ii) Any loss caused by or resulting from direct physical loss or damage to radio or television antennas, including their lead-in wiring, masts or towers.

(iii) Any increase of loss caused by or resulting from:
  (a) Delay in rebuilding, repairing or replacing the property or resuming "operations", due to interference at the location of the rebuilding, repair or replacement by strikers or other persons; or
  (b) Suspension, lapse or cancellation of any license, lease or contract. But if the suspension, lapse or cancellation is directly caused by the suspension of "operations", cover will apply to such loss that affects the income of the Business during the "period of restoration".

(iv) Any Extra Expense caused by or resulting from suspension, lapse or cancellation of any license, lease or contract beyond the "period of restoration".

(v) Any other consequential loss.

(b) *Causes of Loss—Broad Form*

This form provides the same Causes as the Basic Form with the addition of—breakage of glass, falling objects, weight of snow, ice or sleet, and water damage (roughly equivalent to "burst pipes" in the United Kingdom). The Exclusions are the same as in the Basic Form.

(c) *Causes of Loss—Special Form*

This form is akin to the "All Risks" coverage in the United Kingdom and relates to "RISKS OF DIRECT PHYSICAL LOSS" unless the loss is "(specifically) excluded or limited".

The Exclusions are the same as those set out in the Basic or Broad Forms but extended to include those that are usually found in "All Risks" coverages *e.g.* wear and tear, rust, corrosion, deterioration, latent defect, mechanical breakdown, changes in temperature, dishonest acts on the part of the insured (or their employees), etc. The explosion of steam boilers is also excluded.

The Limitations relate to further exclusions which are then qualified, *e.g.*:

> "We will not pay for loss of or damage to:
> (i) Steam boilers, steam pipes, steam-engines or steam turbines caused by or resulting from any condition or event inside such equipment. But we will pay for loss of or damage to such equipment caused by or resulting from an explosion of gases or fuel within the furnace of any fired vessel or within the flues or passages through which the gases of combustion pass.
> (ii) Hot water boilers or other water heating equipment caused by or resulting from any condition or event inside such boilers or equipment, other than an explosion".

Additional coverage is provided for collapse of buildings subject to detailed qualifications; for property in transit subject to qualification; and for water damage, other liquids, powder or molten material damage again subject to qualifications.

26. Nuclear Hazard Exclusion

This states that loss by nuclear reaction or radiation or radioactive contamination is not insured even if caused by or aggravated by fire or other insured perils but that loss by fire resulting from nuclear reaction, etc., is insured by the policy.

Insurance of property and economic damages is arranged through two pools of major U.S. insurance companies, the American Nuclear Insurers and the Mutual Energy Reinsurance Pool. In 1973 competition was introduced by Nuclear Mutual Limited, a Bermuda company set up by 14 U.S. nuclear utilities with a capacity that later grew to $500 million.

Claims for hundreds of millions of dollars were filed in respect of the Three Mile Island nuclear plant disaster in Pennsylvania in 1979, revealing significant underinsurance in certain areas of expense. A Bermuda-based captive company called Nuclear Electric Insurance Limited was established in September 1980 by U.S. utilities. It provided cover for "replacement power" (subject to a 26 weeks' waiting period). In November 1982 an excess property policy was also introduced for $500 million in excess of the original $500 million.

27. Conditions for a valid claim—loss of Business Income

In order to sustain a valid claim under a Business Income Coverage policy the following conditions must be fulfilled.

(a) The loss must be the actual loss of Business Income sustained due to the necessary suspension of "operations" during the "period of restoration". The suspension must be caused by *direct* physical loss of or damage to property at the premises. "Operations" are defined as the insured's "business activities occurring at the described premises", and the "period of restoration" as:

> "The period of time that—
> (i) Begins with the date of direct physical loss or damage caused by or resulting from any Covered Cause of Loss at the described premises; and
> (ii) Ends on the date when the property at the described premises should be repaired, rebuilt or replaced with reasonable speed and similar quality".

The definition of "period of restoration" goes on to say that:

> "It does not include any increased period required due to the enforcement of any ordinance or law that:
> 1. Regulates the construction, use or repair, or requires the tearing down of any property; or
> 2. Requires any insured or others to test for, monitor, clean up, remove, contain, treat, detoxify or neutralize, or in any way respond to, or assess the effects of 'pollutants'".

"Pollutants" are defined as meaning "any solid, liquid, gaseous or thermal irritant or contaminant, including smoke, vapour, soot, fumes, acids, alkalis, chemicals and waste. Waste includes materials to be recycled, reconditioned or reclaimed".

The whole question of pollution and contamination has become so important in the United States that every opportunity is taken to exclude its effects in property damage and business interruption covers (refer paragraph 302).

(b) The above must take place on premises situated as described in the Declarations (the schedule of essential information attached to the policy). This makes it vital for an accurate description of both property and premises to be given because an insured might be dependent in small or large degree, perhaps totally, upon the uninterrupted functioning of another firm's business; interruption of the latter due to damage at its premises may adversely affect the earnings of the insured. This dependency may be upon suppliers of materials, components or finished products, or upon processors or customers, or upon other premises where the insured may temporarily have property deposited or services carried out. The new form does not specifically stipulate, as did the old form, that the premises must be "occupied" by the insured. Coverage is also provided for personal property (machinery, plant, etc.) in the open (or in a vehicle) within 100 feet of the described premises.

Loss of Business Income or Extra Expense incurred for the purpose of avoiding or minimising possible loss resulting from "other people's fires" is not insured under the terms of the standard Business Income Coverage policy but can be covered by the addition of a Business Income from Dependent Properties form—see Chapter 15.

(c) The damage must be caused during the term of the policy by a Covered Cause of Loss but this does not limit the payment of the indemnity to loss during a period ending with the expiry date of the policy if the period of interruption continues beyond that date. This fact is made clear by the words—"The expiration date of this policy will not cut short the 'period of restoration'".

An exclusion to the Covered Causes of Loss is any loss caused by or resulting from damage or destruction of "finished stock". "Finished stock" is now defined as "stock you have manufactured". A qualification to that definition states that " 'finished stock' does not include stock you have manufactured that is held for sale on the premises of any retail outlet insured under this Coverage Part". This brings back, where applicable, the cover previously provided under a separate Mercantile form.

28. Property damage cover

It is important that there be parallel, adequate, property damage cover so that sufficient resources are available to rebuild, repair, restore, etc., when the damage occurs.

(a) *Own premises*

As the Business Income Coverage form can stand alone with its own separate conditions, etc., there appears to be no requirement in the wording that there be an underlying property damage policy covering the same causes of loss and with a sum insured which is adequate to meet any property damage claim that might be made. Inadequacy of property damage cover might well cause some restriction on loss payment under the Business Income Coverage policy in that the "period of restoration" talks of *"should be repaired"*, etc., and of *"reasonable* speed". However, it is assumed that the situation is closely monitored so as to avoid such inadequacy of property damage cover.

(b) *Outside dependencies*

The Business Income from Dependent Properties forms refer to suspension being caused by direct physical loss of or damage to "contingent business property" at the premises described—contributing locations, recipient locations, manufacturing locations and leader locations (refer paragraphs 347 and 374. "Contingent business property" means "property operated by others whom you depend on", and the insured cannot therefore be responsible for or have any direct influence over the extent of the property damage cover arranged in respect of such property.

29. Obligations of insured when loss occurs

Under the Loss Conditions, Duties in the Event of Loss require that several steps must be taken by the insured. These range from notifying the police if a law may have been broken, providing insurers as soon as possible with a full description of the circumstances of the loss or damage and of the property involved, and protecting the covered property from further damage, to allowing insurers to inspect the property and question the insured (under oath) about any relevant matter, providing a sworn statement of loss (within 60 days of insurers requesting it), co-operating with insurers in the investigation or settlement of the claim and resuming all or part of the "operations" as quickly as possible.

30. Additional Coverages and Coverage Extension

These are dealt with in greater depth in Chapter 5.

The following are referred to as Additional Coverages—Extra Expense (or Expenses to Reduce Loss—depending on the form chosen), Civil Authority, Alterations and New Buildings and Extended Business Income. These additional coverages either extend or replace covers already available under the old forms.

The Coverage Extension relates to Newly Acquired Locations and provides an additional 10 per cent. of the Limit of Insurance for Business Income, subject to a limit of $100,000 at each location and to time restrictions on the period during which seperate cover is provided.

It is to be noted that although referred to as "Additional" the "Additional Coverages" are an integral part of the overall cover, whereas the "Coverage Extension" is an available extra cover with an additional premium chargeable.

31. Additional Condition—Coinsurance

This is set out at greater length than the previous coinsurance or contribution condition and translates a single sentence of a few lines to an elaborate mathematical progression (with examples) which is intended to add clarity to a condition which has always perhaps caused difficulty to the uninitiated. An important change in effect is that the basis for comparison with the sum insured is now the income for the 12 months of the policy year rather than the 12 months following the date of the loss, (refer paragraph 67(b) for further comment).

32. Conditions Forms

Whether the Business Income Coverage form is combined with a Commercial Fire Coverage Form (as part of a Commercial Property Policy or, more broadly, as part of a Commercial Package Policy which includes various Parts—Boiler and Machinery, Commercial Auto, Commercial Crime, Commercial General Liability, Commercial Inland Marine and Commercial Farm Coverages) two Conditions Forms must be included—the Common Policy Conditions Form and the Commercial Property Conditions Form.

The Common Policy Conditions relate to such matters as cancellation, changes in terms, examination of books and records, inspections and surveys, premium payments and transfer of rights and duties under the policy.

The Commercial Property Conditions (refer Appendix S, paragraph 465) are akin to the U.K. policy conditions and relate to such matters as concealment, misrepresentation or fraud, control of property, insurance under two or more coverages (within the overall coverage), legal action against insurers, liberalization (of cover), other insurance (contribution), transfer of rights of recovery against others to insurers (subrogation), and the restriction of loss or damage to the policy period and named territory (the United States, Puerto Rico and Canada).

33. Declarations

Besides the Common Policy Declarations Page there is a particular Declarations Page for the Commercial Property Coverage Part which sets out the essential details of the insured and the cover provided.

(a) Description of Premises—sets out the location, construction and occupancy.
(b) Coverages Provided—sets out the coverage, the limit of insurance, the covered causes of loss and the coinsurance percentage chosen.
(c) Optional Coverages—sets out a list of possible extra covers including, for Business Income, Monthly Limit of Indemnity (Fraction), Maximum Period of Indemnity (X) and Extended Period of Indemnity (Days). For further information on the Optional Coverages see Chapter 5, paragraphs 63(b), 68 and 71.

34. Policy construction—summary

The new U.S. "Simplified" policy forms can relate to a "package" of "lines" or to a single "line" only. A single "line" policy for Business Income Coverage must be made up of the following Pages and Forms—

(a) Common Policy Declarations
(b) Common Policy Conditions
(c) Commercial Property Conditions
(d) Commercial Property Declarations
(e) Business Income Coverage
(f) Causes of Loss

CHAPTER 4

OPERATION OF THE COVER—UNITED KINGDOM BASIS

35. Formula for claims is part of the policy—the specification

A description of the cover granted within the framework of the printed terms and conditions of the policy itself and a formula for ascertaining the amount to be paid under a claim are set out in the Specification. This is attached to and declared to be an integral part of the policy.

The provision of this formula is a peculiarity which distinguishes a U.K. business interruption policy from the policies issued for practically all other classes of insurance. It could, like a contract of fire insurance to which it is complementary, omit any reference to the method to be adopted for ascertaining an insured's loss. This would on the face of it be the ultimate in simplicity, a goal towards which insurers are constantly urged to direct their efforts. The position, however, is vastly different from that under a fire policy which deals with tangible, identifiable forms of property and the material loss sustained in respect of them at a fixed point of time. Moreover, with fire insurances a procedure for assessing a loss can be followed based on precedents of common law, court decisions and accepted practice stretching back for more than 280 years. But a business interruption policy is concerned with something both intangible and hypothetical—the effect of damage on trading results which might have materialised in the future had the damage not occurred. So far as precedents are concerned there are few decided law cases from which to obtain guidance.

Because of this it is in the interests of both insured and insurers that some method should be determined and set out in the contract by which to assess the amount of loss sustained by an insured through the happening of the contingency insured against.

36. "Turnover" specification recommended

The form of specification recommended by insurance companies for general use incorporates reduction in turnover as the yardstick by which to calculate a loss. To this basic wording variations or additions can be made to provide for the particular circumstances of different businesses.

The collective experience of insurance companies over many years has provided ample proof that turnover is the most satisfactory general standard by which to measure the effect of damage upon the anticipated earnings of a business. Where special circumstances in a particular business suggest that a different index of loss would be more appropriate and practicable this might be adopted in lieu of turnover. Some alternative indices of limited usefulness are mentioned in paragraph 5 and insurance of gross revenue, gross income, gross fees or similar standard is recommended for various types of business in paragraphs 275 and 276 but otherwise all general references to specifications are in respect of those using turnover as the basis.

At first reading the specification may seem to be a rather formidable document. Perhaps necessarily so, because it has to deal with future profit earnings and, although this is a hypothetical matter upon which it is unwise to prognosticate for even a single business in normal conditions, it has to lay down a formula of universal application for calculating the loss of them for almost any business during abnormal conditions following damage. In spite of this it is capable of being readily understood by any intelligent person with a mind accustomed to business practice.

It will be appreciated from subsequent pages that every sentence in the policy and in the specification is of importance. The wording of all the clauses and terms used and the definitions are the result of very careful drafting with the object of stating as explicitly as possible not only the scope of the cover but also its limitations. For there are various forms of loss which might be sustained following damage which it is not intended to cover and which do not come within the scope of the policy and it is a mistake to assume that a business interruption policy will compensate for all losses consequent upon damage. It is noteworthy that whereas there is no reported case of a dispute over the 1939 form for U.K. business interruption insurances going to Court, since its introduction there have been during the intervening years many cases heard in U.S. Courts on policies issued on the equivalent American insurance forms.

37. Two forms of recommended specifications

The form of specification which from its introduction in 1939 until the 1960s was regarded by U.K. insurance companies as the standard form, incorporating turnover as the index for measuring a loss with gross profit defined as net profit plus insured standing charges, and during that time termed the "recommended" wording, is reproduced in Appendix E. The specification now recommended is known as the "difference" or "sales less variables" wording, so-called because instead of defining gross profit as being the net profit plus standing charges, as in the 1939 form, it treats gross profit as being the difference between turnover and the total of the variable charges. This newer form, which also uses reduction in turnover as the index for measuring a loss, is reproduced in Appendix C.

It may perhaps seem almost superfluous in the 1990s to include details relevant to the older form of specification which in the United Kingdom is now seldom used. They are included for two reasons. First, when the "difference" wording is used it states the working expenses which are excluded from the cover on gross profit and thereby leaves in it all other charges in the accounts. These latter being unmentioned thus become in effect insured standing charges and a proper understanding of their nature and the reasons for insuring them, in whole or in part, is just as necessary as when they are named in the older form of specification. The fact that nearly two hundred charges are mentioned in this book indicates the scope for error or for saving premium in arranging the details of a business interruption insurance. The inclusion in the "difference" specification of an "Uninsured standing charges clause" (paragraph 49) is of some significance in this matter. Secondly, the "difference" wording now regarded as standard practice in the United Kingdom has not yet been adopted as such in many other countries in which net trading profit plus insured standing charges is currently used, as for instance the Canadian "Profits form" (refer paragraph 73(a)). Hence it seems appropriate and necessary in a book which may be used in such countries for reference on this class of insurance to include detailed descriptions of the insurable nature or otherwise of the charges in business accounts.

The only differences between the two forms of specification are in the definition of gross profit and in the textual matters which stem from this definition and as the two forms are in all other respects the same they are dealt with together in this chapter, only points of difference being mentioned specifically.

38. Description of the indemnity

At the head of the specification appear the words:
Item No. 1. On Gross Profit . . . . . . Sum insured £ . . . . . .

followed by a statement that the insurance under the item is limited to loss of gross profit due to (a) reduction in turnover and (b) increase in cost of working. The amount payable as indemnity under these two headings is then described and it should be noted that the declared object is to provide indemnity, that is, the insured must be fully compensated for loss to the extent to which insurance has been effected, within its terms and conditions, but not overcompensated.

Clause (a) gives effect to the basic principle referred to in Chapter 1 by stating that the amount payable is the sum produced by applying the rate of gross profit to the amount by which the turnover during the indemnity period shall, in consequence of the damage (or "Incident"—see below), fall short of the standard turnover.

Each of these terms is later defined under the general heading of Definitions, which since the end of 1989 has included a new word—"Incident" which is defined as "Loss or destruction of or damage to property used by the Insured at the Premises for the sake of the Business". This word has been introduced to replace the word "damage" and although it has basically the same meaning as "damage" its use is intended to avoid confusion with the definition of "DAMAGE" recently introduced into material damage policies meaning "Loss or destruction of or damage to the Property Insured".

39. Turnover

(a) *General*

The normal definition of turnover is "the money paid or payable to the insured for goods sold and delivered and for services rendered in course of the business at the premises".

By using the ordinary meaning of sales, together with receipts for services rendered, the definition of turnover caters for practically all types of business. It also provides for credit transactions in connection with the sale of goods or services by the use of the phrase "the money paid or payable". Further, it tallies with the normal accountancy practice for the figure credited in the trading account by referring to "goods sold and delivered", that is, when they are entered in the sales book, and does not include orders, or forward sales or contracts, until the goods are manufactured and invoiced or the services are actually performed.

In certain classes of business turnover may be predominantly or wholly in respect of services rendered; for instance, laundries, dry-cleaners, cinemas, theatres, dance halls, removal contractors, haulage contractors, transport operators, public warehouses and cold stores. Whilst the standard definition of turnover embraces the revenue in all such businesses, if it is more satisfactory to an insured to give prominence to or to define more specifically the services aspect the definition can be appropriately amended, *e.g.* "charges for laundering, dyeing, dry-cleaning and repairing services" or "admission charges for entertainment and revenue for advertisements and for refreshments provided" or "charges for transport, storage and other services". But such more specific definitions may sometimes leave room for the omission of some present or future source of revenue from sales and generally it may be better simply to transpose words in the standard definition of turnover so that it reads: "the money paid or payable to the insured for services rendered and for goods sold and delivered in course of the business at the premises." Where goods have been sold but have not been delivered, and there is a condition in the sale contract which provides that the contract can be cancelled in the event of fire, it is possible to insure on a "contract price" basis under a material damage policy. Such a cover is particularly attractive to wholesalers who are often likely not to carry business interruption insurance.

(b) *Turnover: sales on instalment or hire-purchase systems*

Mention might be made of the difficulty which is sometimes experienced about the meaning of turnover in the case of a business in which an appreciable part of the sales is of goods on an instalment credit or hire-purchase system financed by the vendors. Although different methods of accountancy are employed in such cases, the general practice appears to be not to take credit for the goods sold beyond the amount of cash received for them in the current financial year or possibly that amount plus a fixed percentage of it. Consequently each year's accounts include an amount for sales which were made in the previous year or years. Should damage interfere with trading, subsequent sales may be less than normal but revenue will continue to be received in respect of the outstanding payments on goods sold and delivered in preceding years.

It may be thought that this revenue will increase the figure of turnover during the indemnity period whilst if the business has been growing that of the standard turnover in the year before the damage, used for comparison, may be less than the actual sales because credit was not taken in that year's accounts for outstanding balances. Hence the claims formula might not provide full compensation for the insured's true loss. This is not so, because the figure used in each case must be in accordance with the definition of turnover, which is the money *paid or payable* in respect of goods *sold and delivered* during the respective periods.

Therefore in order to ascertain the reduction in turnover the figures used for both the pre-damage and the post-damage periods are those representing the sale price of the goods sold during the respective periods. The time when the insured actually realise the profit on the goods they sell, or credit all or part of it in their accounts, is beside the point. If the damage causes a reduction in normal sales the loss of gross profit will follow sooner or later; a business interruption policy is designed to make good that loss.

The outstanding instalments due on goods sold before the damage are in effect book debts with which the policy is not concerned as they are unconnected with turnover in the period after the damage has taken place. Loss may, indeed, be experienced in respect of such debts if the records in respect of them are destroyed by fire or other perils. Such loss, however, is in respect of goods sold and delivered before a fire and is not recoverable under a normal business interruption policy which is concerned with reduction of post-fire trading. Insurance against loss of outstanding balances can be arranged but this has to be done under a separate policy (see Chapter 19 regarding insurance against loss of book debts).

(c) *Turnover: payments in advance, stage or progress payments*

The difference here is that payments are being made prior to or during the manufacture of goods to be sold, or prior to or during the provision of a service. Circumstances can arise where a contract needs to be cancelled because of a prolonged interruption following damage and some, if not all, the money paid to date is to be returned. The exact nature of the contract must dictate the manner in which the situation is dealt with, but the loss of turnover is again based on the extent to which turnover has been *earned* whether actual money has changed hands or not.

40. Rate of Gross Profit

(a) *General*

The rate of Gross Profit is defined as being "the rate of gross profit earned on the turnover during the financial year immediately before the date of the damage (or "Incident"—see paragraph 38). It should be noted that this definition, without mentioning accounts, makes the results of the nearest pre-fire accounting year the basis for the calculation of the profit ratio, this being likely to give the most up-to-date information and therefore the best indication of what the rate of gross profit would have been in the post-fire period.

Whilst this is quite sound theoretically in practice many points arise for which it does not provide. For instance, the gross profit margin can be affected by changes, either before or after damage, in trading conditions, prices of materials, wage rates and so on. However, all such circumstances are taken care of very adequately by the incorporation of a clause under which appropriate adjustments of figures may be made (see paragraph 55(a)—Other Circumstances Clause).

Another factor which will influence the rate of gross profit of some businesses and cause fluctuations in it from year to year applies where dealings are made in "futures" on commodity exchanges. Gains or losses made in this way are the result of speculation and are not earnings from business activities which are dependent upon and bear a stable ratio to its turnover. The effect of such speculative dealings in accounts for the financial year before damage occurs is no indication or guarantee of similar gains or losses in the period of interruption following the damage. Hence the other circumstances clause which is bracketed against the definition of rate of gross profit may have to be used to ensure a proper indemnity by excluding any gains or losses of that nature which are independent of the productive activities of a business.

(b) *Rate of Gross Profit: sales on instalment or hire-purchase systems*

Difficulty about the meaning of the rate of gross profit, as with that of turnover, may be experienced in the case of a business selling goods on an instalment credit or hire-purchase system financed by the vendors, because the gross profit shown in the accounts will include revenue from previous years but will not take full credit in respect of goods sold in the current year. This problem can be resolved by reference to the operative word in the definition. It is the rate of gross profit *earned* on the turnover during the financial year immediately before the date of the damage (or Incident) with which the policy is concerned. The meaning of turnover in such businesses has already been explained (paragraph 39); if to this is applied the amount of gross profit earned on that turnover, including outstanding balances due on it but excluding revenue from instalments on sales made in previous years, the correct rate of gross profit can be ascertained.

41. Indemnity Period and Maximum Indemnity Period

The definition of Indemnity Period is self-explanatory, being "the period beginning with the occurrence of the Incident and ending not later than the maximum indemnity period thereafter during which the results of the business shall be affected in consequence thereof". To this is added a definition of the "maximum indemnity period" which simply states the number of months decided by the insured when the insurance was arranged. This matter is fully dealt with in Chapter 12 (see paragraphs 245 *et seq.*).

It is interesting to note the different approaches to indemnity period in the United Kingdom and the United States and the extent to which the United States is now moving towards the inclusion of the continuing effects on the business beyond the end of the "period of restoration".

42. Standard Turnover

The Standard Turnover, as its name implies, is the standard against which comparison is to be made in order to ascertain the shortage in turnover resulting from the Incident being, in brief, the turnover during the period in the 12 months immediately before the date of the Incident which corresponds with the indemnity period, that is, which corresponds with the period of interruption within the selected maximum limit.

For example, if the turnover were affected during the period from the middle of February to the end of August the standard turnover would be that for the same six-and-a-half months in the preceding year. If turnover were affected during the nine months September to the following May inclusive, the standard turnover would be that for the corresponding months of September to May 12 months previously. This method of comparison against the same calendar period in the 12 months preceding the Incident provides for the seasonal fluctuations which in greater or less degree affect a large proportion of businesses. It also uses the most up-to-date pre-Incident figures suitable for purposes of comparison and calculation of the loss of turnover.

The definition of standard turnover is, however, qualified by the "other circumstances clause" (paragraph 52), which provides for adjustments to be made for trends of business and for variations in or other circumstances affecting the business either before or after the Incident. The steps to take when the indemnity period is greater than 12 months are explained in paragraph 251.

43. "In consequence of the Incident"

It is important to bear in mind that the indemnity in respect of reduction in turnover is qualified by the words "in consequence of the Incident". Therefore if the reduction is attributable wholly or in part to causes not connected with the Incident which would have affected turnover irrespective of the Incident having occurred, an adjustment must be made to the figure of standard turnover in order to reflect as accurately as possible the loss solely due to the Incident. For this purpose the other circumstances clause referred to in the preceding paragraph is employed.

For example, if during the time when the turnover of a business is partially reduced as a result of an Incident turnover is further reduced because supplies of raw materials are held up owing to a strike in another industry, the loss due to the latter cause would not be the responsibility of the insurers. Such loss would have been experienced had there been no Incident. Similarly, if the insured's business was at a standstill because of an Incident and an extraneous circumstance such as a strike in their own industry took place which would in any event have meant a reduction in turnover, an appropriate adjustment must be made to the figures from which the shortage in turnover is calculated. Otherwise the insured would be compensated for loss outside the scope of the policy the expressed intention of which is an indemnity for loss due to reduction in turnover "in consequence of the Incident". (See also paragraph 420(a).)

On the other hand the opposite position can apply. For example, the strikes mentioned above might have happened in the comparative period in the year before the Incident; in such a case the figure of standard turnover would by means of the other circumstances clause be stepped up in order to provide a true indemnity by increasing the figure for the shortage in turnover.

44. Prolongation—delays in restoration of business (extraneous causes and proximate cause)

A distinction must be drawn, however, between circumstances which would have affected the trading results had there been no interference with the business caused by an Incident, as stated in the preceding paragraph 43, and those which prolong the period of interruption. For example, a strike in the building industry might delay the restoration of damaged premises.

As such a contingency could not have affected the insured's business had it not happened during a period of rehabilitation following the Incident insurers regard the Incident as the prime cause of an insured loss for which they have accepted premium. They therefore hold themselves liable for the lengthened period of interruption up to the maximum indemnity period limit.

It might be suggested that this may be contrary to the time-honoured maxim *causa proxima non remota spectatur*, that is, not the latest but the dominant cause of a loss must be regarded as the operative one. If this cause is within the risks covered the insurers are liable for the loss; if it is within the excepted perils the insurers are not liable; in cases which are indeterminate it depends upon the presumed intention of the parties to the policy. There are more than 70 reported cases on proximate cause decided one way or another in the Courts in the United Kingdom and in North America over the past two centuries, continuing until 1977, so it may be concluded that it is a rule not easy to apply in practice!

Basically, common law is applied common-sense and this would appear to be the final arbiter in determining what is the proximate cause of a loss. It is a common-sense view which insurers take in their acknowledgment that intervening factors between the date of the Incident and the end of the indemnity period of a nature which would not have affected the business had the Incident not occurred do not constitute a new cause to break the chain of causation. This is consistent with the fact that the possibility of intervening causes prolonging the period of interruption are a factor which insurers advise their policy holders to keep in mind when deciding about the maximum indemnity period for an insurance. It is also significant that not one case is on record of U.K. insurers being involved in litigation through disputing a claim on grounds of proximate cause. For further discussion of this matter see paragraphs 420 and 421.

45. Increase in cost of working

It is in an insured's interest to restore a business to normal trading conditions as quickly as possible after Incident and, moreover, there is a duty to do so imposed by the policy claims conditions (see paragraph 435). This however may involve considerable expense in undertaking special measures to reduce the loss of turnover during the indemnity period and to hasten the resumption of normal trading. But action on these lines is also of benefit to the insurers as its effect is to reduce the amount which would otherwise be payable for loss of gross profit. Therefore clause (b) under the heading Increase in Cost of Working compensates the insured for "the additional expenditure necessarily and reasonably incurred for the sole purpose of avoiding or diminishing the reduction in turnover" which would otherwise have taken place.

No sum insured is stated in respect of this benefit nor is anything to be added to the amount insured on gross profit to provide for it because it is an alternative to loss which would otherwise be payable under the latter heading. An exception to this arises, however, when it is anticipated that the amount which may have to be expended on increase in cost of working in the event of a claim will exceed the amount of the gross profit which will be conserved by such expenditure. Specific insurance in then required in respect of the excess amount as described in paragraph 50.

Payments under the provisions for increase in cost of working can be made for very varied expenditure. The payment of the additional part of overtime wages, either to an insured's employees to try to make good the loss of production or to builder's or other tradesmen's workers to speed up the restoration of the damaged property and plant, is a regular feature of claims. Other typical examples are the cost of having provisional repairs effected to buildings or plant, of temporary roofing or flooring, or of the installation of heating, lighting or power arrangements of a provisional nature, which subsequently have to be scrapped. It might be possible to promote some turnover by having work done on commission or by having components or finished products made by other firms, thus incurring an increase in productive costs which can be claimed under this clause. Changes in works shop-floor practice and other provisional production expedients can involve heavy extra expense. The occupation of temporary premises generally entails additional expenditure of various kinds which may continue for a prolonged period. Sometimes it is necessary to purchase premises, or buy out another business, purely as a temporary measure, with a subsequent loss on resale when the insured's permanent premises are again ready for occupation. Heavy advertising expenditure may be necessary for a considerable period after the restoration of the damaged property in order to regain lost custom.

The cost of demolition and of the removal of debris in connection with damaged buildings and their contents does not constitute increase in cost of working (it can be included in a fire policy), but additional expenditure involved to speed up such work in order to hasten rebuilding operations would be admitted.

46. Abnormal expenditure only is covered

Although the heading to clause (b) is "in respect of increase in cost of working" as an appropriate indication of the scope of the cover provided it is not always appreciated that this does not mean "increase in *ratio* of cost of working". That it does not is made clear by the operative words of the description which follows the heading stating that the indemnity provided is for "the *additional* expenditure . . . incurred". If after an Incident certain charges do not fall proportionately with a reduction in turnover their increased incidence will mean financial loss for the business concerned. The object of insuring "standing" charges along with the net profit is largely to protect the latter against the effect of the increased ratio to turnover which such standing charges bear when the turnover is reduced. Consequently when loss arises because the ratio to turnover of charges which have not been included in the insurance goes up it would be untenable to expect payment of such loss as increase in cost of working.

Clause (b) is therefore specifically restricted to the additional, or what might be called abnormal, expenditure incurred. Whether or not it includes the loss due to an increased ratio of productive charges to turnover was decided in the case of *Polikoff Ltd.* v. *North British & Mercantile Insurance Co. Ltd.* (1936) 55 LIL.R. 279, when Branson J. disallowed a claim for uninsured wages and expenses which after a fire bore a higher percentage to turnover than the same wages and expenses bore to turnover before the fire. He confirmed the view of the arbitrator that there was no additional expenditure involved. This decision illustrates, incidentally, the danger of assuming that productive charges are never standing charges and consequently omitting them from an insurance. Unless they are of such a nature that they will under all circumstances be reduced in amount proportionately with any fall in production the possibility of loss will exist and in some businesses this may be very serious. (See paragraph 175.)

47. "Economic limit" to additional expenditure

(a) *Theory*

The increase in cost of working section of the cover is invoked in most claims and involves insurers in very substantial payments which often exceed the amount paid concurrently in respect of loss of gross profit. Provided however that the expenditure is "necessarily and reasonably incurred for the sole purpose of avoiding or diminishing the reduction in turnover . . . " and the amount of it is less than the insurers would otherwise have had to pay under clause (a) for the loss of gross profit which that expenditure has avoided, the policy compensates for it and insurers welcome the steps taken. A provision that the insurance will not contribute in respect of increase in cost of working an amount greater than that saved by the expenditure on it, that is, will not pay more than £x to save £x, is a natural and equitable one. Effect is given to this so-called "economic limit" by the final sentence of clause (b) in the words "but not exceeding the sum produced by applying the rate of gross profit to the amount of the reduction (in turnover) thereby avoided".

(b) *Application*

Sufficient attention is not always given to this economic limit because it is not readily apparent, nor sometimes even foreseeable, how it may be necessary to incur additional expenditure in excess of the resultant saving.

There is also a widespread impression that it is not possible to apply the limitation, through inability to measure the reduction in turnover avoided by additional expenditure. But circumstances do sometimes arise after an Incident when for one reason or another the limit is exceeded and, as there is generally a means of measuring the amount of the excess expenditure, some loss devolves upon the insured.

For example, if temporary premises are rented and fitted up following an Incident the turnover resulting from such action, which represents the "reduction in turnover avoided", can be measured exactly. To this the rate of gross profit is applied to give the limit in respect of the policy contribution towards the additional expenditure incurred. Another instance would be the purchase of goods from a competitor, for resale, in order to fulfil contracts or to maintain the goodwill of customers, the price of the purchases being as much as or more than the insured's normal selling price. Apart from exceptional circumstances which may arise under a contract the sale of those goods will represent the saving in turnover. The application to this of the rate of gross profit will show the maximum amount the insurers can be called upon to pay in respect of the increased cost of carrying on the business in that way. The additional expenditure would be the difference between the purchase price of the goods and the insured's own normal productive costs for the same quantity of goods. If this difference exceeded the limit mentioned the insured would suffer loss in respect of the excess.

It is worth noting that the greater the proportion of the wage roll which is included in the item on gross profit the higher will be the limit on the amount recoverable for increase in cost of working. This is because the rate of gross profit used to calculate the limit can be considerably increased by the inclusion of wages, from perhaps 25 per cent. without any wages to possibly 50 per cent. or more with all wages insured. If all wages are insured under a separate item on the "dual basis" (paragraphs 205 to 211), the rate of gross profit will be correspondingly lower because it will not include any amount for wages. However, the dual basis wages item more than compensates for this by including a provision for payment of the amount of any increase in cost of working in excess of that recoverable under the item insuring gross profit. (See paragraph 209.)

In certain businesses it is recognised that continuous trading must be maintained at all costs whatever additional expenditure may be involved. This will probably mean that in the event of an Incident taking place it will be necessary to exceed the limitation on increase in cost of working. In such cases it is advisable to obtain cover for the possible excess expenditure by means of a separate item in the specification, on Additional Increase in Cost of Working, as explained in paragraph 50.

There can sometimes be a further difficulty in the strict interpretation of the phrase "reasonable and necessary". Immediately following an Incident additional expenditure might appear to all parties concerned to be "reasonable" but in the event not to have been "necessary" because it did not save the amount of turnover originally envisaged, if it saved any turnover at all. The expenditure might have been in respect of some form of action which if successful would have been of significant benefit to insured and insurers. In such a situation, if insurers have given their prior assent to the expenditure, being fully aware of the risk involved, then they are likely to pay the additional expenditure as increase in cost of working.

Similarly, where additional expenditure is "necessary" (*i.e.* unavoidable) but is not *deliberately* incurred, insurers may again agree to pay. An example is where goods which continue to be delivered despite severe damage to the insured's manufacturing facilities need to be stored at extra cost, and the abrupt cancellation of the contract (so as to stop the supply) might lead to an even greater loss.

48. Further limitation on additional expenditure

(a) *"For the sole purpose"*

The additional expenditure must be necessarily and reasonably incurred "for the sole purpose of avoiding or diminishing the reduction in turnover". Although this limitation must be applied as strictly as possible a degree of flexibility must enter into negotiations with loss adjusters where part of an item of expenditure is deemed to qualify for treatment as increase in cost of working.

(b) *"During the indemnity period"*

Another limitation in clause (b) is introduced by a proviso which restricts the payment by insurers to the additional expenditure incurred to minimise the reduction in turnover *during the indemnity period*. Therefore should it happen that the period of interruption following an Incident exceeds the maximum indemnity period the insurers will not be liable for that proportion of any additional expenditure incurred which will benefit the business after the end of that limit. This may be a difficult apportionment to determine in actual practice but it is a reasonable provision against an insured embarking on expenditure at the insurers' expense with a view to helping turnover after the period of their liability has ended.

Similarly, if additional expenditure is incurred during the period of interruption which benefits turnover after the end of that period but still within the maximum indemnity period the insured are entitled to only an equitable proportion of such expenditure. But in those circumstances an adjustment would be effected by crediting the amount of such benefit as an offset to the reduction in turnover claimed, that is, by extending the period of interruption to include the period of increased turnover, as explained in paragraph 247.

The point to note in this matter is that "indemnity period" does not necessarily mean the number of months stated in the definition of maximum indemnity period; that is only the maximum limit. The length of the indemnity period is the period during which the results of the business are affected by the Incident, within the limit of the stated number of months. (See paragraph 245(a).)

On the other hand "the results of the business" means more than just turnover. The latter might be restored to normal and maintained at that level only by means of additional expenditure under the provisions of clause (b). But the net profit of the business would be reduced by the amount of such continuing expenditure, extending correspondingly the period "during which the results of the business shall be affected in consequence" of the Incident and, therefore, the period during which the insurers would (within the limit of the maximum indemnity period insured) be liable for such additional expenditure.

Circumstances can also arise where the insured incurs additional expenditure which *contractually* continues beyond the end of the indemnity period, *e.g.* the insured is obliged to sign a lease for a number of years in order to obtain alternative accommodation. In the event insurers would probably pay for this additional expense (subject to the other limitations) because it benefited the turnover *during* the indemnity period. To be sure, however, the insured could add an item on Additional Increase in Cost of Working (refer preceding paragraph 47(b), and paragraph 50) not only for an additional amount but also for a maximum indemnity period in excess of that for the main gross profit item.

49. Apportionment under the "uninsured standing charges" clause

The form of specification in which gross profit is defined as being net profit plus insured standing charges incorporates a further condition relative to the payment of increase in cost of working, making it "subject to the provisions of the uninsured standing charges clause". This clause states:

> "If any standing charges of the Business be not insured by this policy then in computing the amount recoverable hereunder as increase in cost of working that proportion only of the additional expenditure shall be brought into account which the sum of the Net Profit and the Insured Standing Charges bears to the sum of the Net Profit and all the standing charges".

This provision is equitable because if additional expenditure is incurred to minimise the potential loss of turnover the turnover thus preserved will help to pay not only for those standing charges which have been included in the insurance on gross profit but also for those which have been omitted. So it is right that the insured should bear the relative part of the additional expenditure which is responsible for providing revenue towards the payment of those insured standing charges.

Although the clause does not state the accounting period from which the figures for this operation of apportionment are to be taken it is probably most reasonable and practicable to use the same figures as for the computation of the rate of gross profit, that is, to take them from the accounts for the last financial year before the Incident.

For a specification on the "difference" wording in which gross profit is defined as turnover less variables there would appear to be no necessity for such an apportionment of the increase in cost of working because all the standing charges are automatically included in the insurance by the definition of gross profit. However, it is possible that an insured may from choice, misunderstanding, or doubt if it is a debatable borderline or optional charge, include in the list of uninsured working expenses, that is, the variable charges excluded from the gross profit insurance, certain expenses or a portion of them which it might be considered could rank in some circumstances as being not wholly variable charges. To provide for this contingency an appropriately worded uninsured standing charges clause is included in the specification, reading:

> "If any standing charges of the Business be not insured by this policy (having been deducted in arriving at the Gross Profit as defined herein) then in computing the amount recoverable hereunder as Increase in Cost of Working, that proportion only of any additional expenditure shall be brought into account which the Gross Profit bears to the sum of the Gross Profit and the uninsured standing charges".

This clause can be omitted where the Uninsured Working Expenses are recognised variable charges *e.g.* purchases, carriage, etc.

50. Necessity for adequate insurance—additional increase in cost of working

Foregoing paragraphs on increase in cost of working may have created the impression that the provision of compensation under clause (b) is so hedged round with restrictions and limitations that its value is largely nugatory. It should be appreciated, however, that these only operate in cases where the insurance has not been arranged on an adequate basis; when it is adequate the additional expenditure will be recovered in full. The point to be emphasised is the necessity for a full insurance not only in amount and maximum indemnity period but also in the inclusion in the gross profit of all insurable charges and where special circumstances appertain for an extra item on additional expenditure if a complete indemnity is to be provided.

As explained in paragraphs 45 to 48 under an item insuring gross profit an insured is indemnified under clause (b) for additional expenditure necessarily and reasonably incurred in order to minimise or avoid altogether the potential loss of turnover. The amount provided for this is, however, limited to the sum which would otherwise have been payable for loss of gross profit had such additional expenditure not been incurred. In other words the insurer will not pay in respect of additional expenditure more than £ per £ of gross profit saved. This limit is calculated by applying the rate of gross profit to the amount of the turnover that has been achieved as a result of the additional expenditure.

Although this "economic limit" is normally sufficient to provide fully for an insured's loss there are businesses in which the circumstances are such that it may be inadequate. Some insured must try to continue their production or services without a break whatever the cost involved in doing so in order to keep competitors out of their connections or to retain the goodwill of their customers or to maintain what are tantamount to public utility services.

Publishers of newspapers and periodicals would make every effort to maintain circulation after an Incident irrespective of what might be extremely heavy extra cost because in such a highly competitive industry the future profitability of a business depends upon continuity of production. In the milk, bakery and laundry trades profit margins are low and any sizeable additional expenditure incurred to maintain normal services—even the cost of hiring transport for door-to-door deliveries if vehicles in the garage are damaged—might exceed the "economic limit", that is, the loss of gross profit avoided by the expenditure. Firms holding agencies for products such as agricultural machinery must try to maintain their services without interruption in order to avoid the loss of agencies. Insured in quite a number of other trades where they might be able to get their work done by competitors but only at heavy extra cost and perhaps considerable transport expenses because of the distance factor have this problem; printers, ice-cream manufacturers, dry-cleaners, milk processing, cheese and bacon factories and ice factories are typical examples. An Incident at a boarding school or college might result in heavy expenditure on accommodation of pupils and staff in hotels considerably in excess of the amount recoverable under the provisions of the increase in cost of working clauses of the insurance because of the substantially higher standard and, therefore, cost of accommodation, staffing and catering at hotels.

Provided that the maximum indemnity period for the item on gross profit is not less than 12 months an indemnity for additional expenditure beyond that recoverable under clauses (b) of the items on gross profit and on wages (if insured separately) can be obtained by a supplementary item under the heading On Additional Expenditure. The general wording for such an item is:

"The insurance under this item is limited to such further additional expenditure beyond that recoverable under clause (b) of item no. 1 on Gross Profit and clause (b) of item no. 2 on Wages/Payroll as the insured shall necessarily and reasonably incur during the Indemnity Period in consequence of the Incident for the purpose of avoiding or diminishing the reduction in Turnover".

Because the sum insured is of necessity an arbitrary amount it is not subject to average; the premium rating is generally the same as that for the gross profit item.

A somewhat similar item may be advisable for brickworks, iron and steel works and glassworks, potteries, etc., in respect of the heavy fuel cost which might be incurred in the cooling and reheating of kilns or furnaces.

Another variation of the "additional expenditure" cover is to make the item operative from the end of the maximum indemnity period of the gross profit insurance for a further indemnity period of one or more years. The usual reason for such cover is to provide against the possibility, for example, of alternative premises being taken after the Incident and then occupied permanently at considerable higher rent and rates than was paid at those destroyed and such heavy extra cost continuing subsequent to restoration of normal working, without any corresponding increase over the pre-Incident turnover to carry it, after the end of the maximum indemnity period. It may be necessary for some businesses, *e.g.* those providing public services like television and radio broadcasting companies (paragraph 272) to restore activities to normal by any available means as soon as ever possible after an Incident. Measures taken to do this might involve increase in cost of working of a period much longer that the maximum indemnity period of the item on gross profit.

51. The savings clause

(a) *Explanation*

Following the description of the cover provided under clauses (a) and (b) the next step in the formula for ascertaining the insured's loss is set out, and this termed the "savings clause". This provides for a deduction from the claim, as ascertained up to that point, of any sum saved during the indemnity period in respect of such of the charges included in the insurance on gross profit as may cease or be reduced in consequence of the Incident.

For example, if some of the buildings forming part of the premises are destroyed and no alternative accommodation can be found several expenses relating to the destroyed buildings will cease. In calculating under the specification formula the amount of the loss recoverable under clause (a), however, the insurers will automatically contribute towards the normal amount of any of these items which are included in the insurance on gross profit because they are similarly included as components of the rate of gross profit. Thus, on the one hand the insured will obtain from the insurers a proportionate part corresponding with the shortage in turnover, of the normal amount of these expenses, the balance being provided by any turnover maintained. But the insured will not have to disburse them. This would be more than an indemnity; it would in fact be making a profit out of the Incident. Hence the insertion of the savings clause to redress the position by stipulating that any sum saved in this way shall be deducted in the computation of the claim. It should not, however, be regarded as being a reduction of the insured's claim, which it is not. It is an adjustment foreseen in the method adopted for calculations under clause (a), which without the savings clause would provide for the payment of charges that the insured do not have to meet.

In the "difference" specification, as the definition of gross profit includes all charges in the accounts except the variables which are listed as the uninsured working expenses, the savings clause reads:

> "less any sum saved during the Indemnity Period in respect of such of the charges and expenses of the Business payable out of Gross Profit as may cease or be reduced in consequence of the Incident".

But in the older form of specification, as the insured gross profit is defined as the sum of the net profit and the insured standing charges, the savings clause has to make specific mention of the latter, being worded:

> "less any sum during the indemnity period in respect of such of the insured standing charges as may cease or be reduced in consequence of the Incident".

(b) *Limitations in application*

It is possible, however, that certain charges will be less during the period of interruption than they were in the comparable period of the preceding year due to causes quite unconnected with the Incident. For example, shortly before the Incident occurred an insured may have reduced the amount of a large overdraft at the bank, resulting in a lower interest charge in the period after the Incident than previously. As reductions in charges from causes of that kind would have taken place irrespective of the Incident it would be inequitable to deprive an insured of the benefit.

This point is of considerable importance in connection with those charges of a substantial amount, such as repairs and renewals, which with many businesses fluctuate widely from year to year. The appropriate "savings" during an indemnity period should be regarded as the amount of any reduction in the *normal* expenditure in respect of each charge which is included in the insurance on gross profit.

Moreover, insurers are not entitled to take credit for any reduction in the amount of any charges which are not included in the insurance on gross profit because they are not providing any indemnity in respect of such charges in the calculation of loss under clause (a). Therefore the savings clause is limited in application to those charges which (i) are insured and (ii) are reduced in consequence of the Incident.

Difficulties can arise where there are savings in respect of charges which are only partially insured. It is assumed that if savings are made "in respect of such of the charges and expenses of the business payable out of gross profit", then the benefit accrues *wholly* to the insurers.

52. The "average" proviso (underinsurance)

(a) *Principle*

To complete the formula for ascertaining the amount payable by the insurers there follows a very important proviso by which the principle of average is applied. This is introduced because the equitable fixing of premiums depends upon the assumption that insurances are always for the full amount at risk and any insured who carry less than a full insurance are regarded as being, in effect, their own insurer for the difference. The "average proviso" legislates for this by stipulating that if there is underinsurance the insured must bear a proportionate share of the claim as ascertained under the preceding part of the formula in the specification. This means that when there is underinsurance even though the amount of the claim is much less than the sum insured it cannot be recovered in full because the insurers are responsible only for their proportion of the loss, however large or small it may be.

By placing the average proviso at the end of the formula after the savings clause, insurers provided that in the event of underinsurance the insured will obtain the benefit of a relative proportion of any "savings" in the charges included in the gross profit insurance which has been deducted in the calculation of the claim, according to the degree to which average applies.

The average clause undoubtedly creates difficulties for insured because it requires them to estimate their sums insured at least 12 months in advance and to maintain them on this forward looking basis as explained in following paragraphs. But this is considered to be essential in order to provide insured with a true indemnity and also maintain sound principles of underwriting. Nevertheless, in 1982, companies who were members of the Consequential Loss Committee did in fact offer an alternative scheme which dispensed with the need for the average proviso. This is known as the Declaration-Linked specification wording (refer paragraph 53 and Appendix D, paragraph 450).

(b) *Operation*

It is very important that the manner in which the average proviso operates should be thoroughly understood. The figure used to determine whether the sum insured is adequate and, if it is not, to be used for calculating the relative proportions which are the respective liabilities of the insured and insurers, is not the gross profit computed from the accounts for the last financial year before the Incident.

The proviso states "that if the sum insured by this item be less than the sum produced by applying the Rate of Gross Profit to the Annual Turnover (or to a proportionately increased multiple thereof where the Maximum Indemnity Period exceeds 12 months) the amount payable shall be proportionately reduced". As annual turnover is defined in the specification as "the turnover during the 12 months immediately before the date of the Incident" the figure produced by this calculation can be very different from the amount of gross profit in the last financial year, which may have ended several months before the Incident occurred. This is another instance of the endeavour of insurers to provide that for the calculation of a claim figures as up to date as possible shall be used.

The same objective of using the latest available figures lies behind the method adopted for the application of average where the maximum indemnity period insured exceeds 12 months. It will be noticed that in the average proviso given above there is provision within the brackets for the use of a multiplier when the maximum indemnity period is longer that 12 months. For instance, it would be one-and-a-half-times for an 18 months and twice for a 24 months maximum indemnity period. Thus in the latter case the proviso applies the rate of gross profit to which the annual turnover, which by definition is the turnover during the 12 months immediately before the Incident; not, it should be noted, to the turnover in the 24 months preceding the Incident.

(c) *Effect (sum insured an estimate of future earnings)*

On completion of their accounts at the end of each financial year many firms revise the sum insured on gross profit by making it the same amount as that computed from the accounts. They consider that by this means they are keeping their policy up to date and ensuring a full insurance. Actually they may be running a serious risk of being underinsured at the time of a loss.

The explanation of this is that as the object of the insurance is to provide an indemnity for loss of earnings sustained *after* Incident the specification formula for calculating the loss takes cognisance of the most up-to-date trading results available. The rate of gross profit is taken from the accounts for the last completed financial year before the Incident because they give the most recent figure. This rate of gross profit is then applied to the shortage in turnover which also is calculated from the most up-to-date figures available, that is, by a comparison between the turnover in the months during the indemnity period and that in the corresponding period in the 12 months immediately preceding the Incident. Consequently the same basis must be used to calculate the figure for comparison purposes under the average proviso.

Therefore the formula in the latter provides for the rate of gross profit arrived at as above to be applied to the annual turnover, which is the turnover for the 12 months immediately preceding the Incident, and not to the turnover in the last financial year. From this there arises danger in fixing as the sum insured the amount of gross profit computed from the last completed accounts. It could be at least 12 months before the next revision is due and an Incident may happen at any time during the period—say, in the eleventh month. If there has been an upward trend of turnover in the interim the annual turnover, *i.e.* turnover during the 12 months immediately before the date of the Incident, will be larger than the figure in the accounts of the last financial year. The amount of gross profit will be calculated from the higher turnover figure and so will also be greater than that shown in the last accounts. But it is on this hypothetical amount that the policy undertakes to provide an indemnity and that the average proviso is applied. So unless the sum insured has been arranged sufficiently high to allow for the increasing business the insured will be penalised in the event of a claim because of the underinsurance. (See paragraph 431 in the chapter on Claim Settlements regarding ante-dating alterations in the sum insured.)

Not only trends in turnover but also forthcoming planned changes in the business such as an extension of manufacturing capacity, the opening of additional selling outlets, the introduction of new lines, a special advertising campaign, etc., the fruits of which might not be fully realised in the event of an Incident, must be taken into account when estimating the appropriate sum insured. But in addition to considering any such factors it is vitally important to allow for the overall effect of economic inflation on future turnover and gross profit in order to maintain sums insured at adequate amounts. For some points of guidance on calculating sums insured refer to paragraph 224 and for new businesses see paragraphs 229, 268(a) and 383.

This means that the figures in the last available accounts should be used only as a guide and that the sum insured must be based on an estimate of future earnings. With a maximum indemnity period of 12 months it is necessary to estimate what the gross profit might be during 12 months commencing from the time when the next revision of the sum insured will be made. If that is a year ahead it means that a forward projection or estimated gross profit will have to be made two years into the future. Estimates for the amount of cover must similarly be projected further ahead to correspond with longer maximum indemnity periods. Forward budgeted accounts can be very helpful in this. With a maximum indemnity period in excess of 12 months the projection will need to be longer than 24 months, although the average proviso operates only on a proportionately increased amount base on annual turnover.

It is impossible to estimate so far ahead with complete accuracy and so provision is made in the specification to allow for a margin of up to 100 per cent. overinsurance without forfeiting premium for the amount insured which actual future results show to have been not required. (See details of Return Premium Clause in paragraph 225(a).)

53. Declaration-Linked basis: no average proviso

As the title implies, the basis on which it is possible to dispense with the average proviso involves the insured adhering to certain *declaration* rules:

(i) The insured is required at the inception of the insurance and prior to each renewal to advise insurers of the Estimated Gross Profit for the period of insurance. This figure is shown in the policy but the liability of insurers can be up to a maximum of 133.33 per cent. of this amount.

(ii) The premium at the inception of any period of insurance will be charged on the Estimated Gross Profit and will be subject to adjustment by a return premium (maximum 50 per cent.) or additional premium (no prescribed maximum), according to the declaration of actual gross profit for the relative financial year. Such declaration must be confirmed by the insured's auditors and is mandatory not later than six months after the expiry of each period of insurance.

(iii) Adequate underwriting information, including details of current levels of earnings and future plans and projections must be supplied by the insured prior to each renewal and when significant changes are anticipated.

Failure to comply with any of these requirements will render a case ineligible for such treatment. Insurers also expect the insured to advise them of any alteration in risk during the period of insurance so that underwriting bases can be amended as necessary.

The Estimated Gross Profit figure is increased proportionately where the maximum indemnity period is longer than 12 months. A suppliers or customers extension percentage limit is a percentage of the limit of liability. (Refer also paragraph 348, and Appendix D, paragraph 450.)

54. Formula for settlement of loss

In the specification the meaning of the various terms used is set down in precise form under the heading Definitions. A careful study of these will make it possible to follow without difficulty the logical steps already dealt with and thereby construct the formula to be applied in the settlement of a claim.

A specimen of the settlement of a simple loss is given in Appendix U (paragraph 467) which illustrates the basic stages of the specification formula just described namely:

(1) ascertainment of the loss of turnover and the application to this of the rate of gross profit earned in the last financial year before the Incident;
(2) the addition of the amount expended on increase in cost of working;
(3) the deduction of savings in insured charges;
(4) application of the average proviso (if there is one).

55. "Other circumstances clause"

(a) *Explanation*

A most important provision for the adjustment of certain figures which is usually referred to as the "other circumstances clause" is bracketed jointly against the definitions of rate of gross profit, annual turnover and standard turnover and reads:

> "to which such adjustments shall be made as may be necessary to provide for the trend of the Business and for variations in or other circumstances affecting the Business either before or after the Incident which would have affected the Business had the Incident not occurred, so that the figures thus adjusted shall represent as nearly as may be reasonably practicable the results which but for the Incident would have been obtained during the relative period after the Incident".

This clause is also known as the "adjustments clause" and sometimes termed "the bracketed provisions". It is so wide in scope that it will permit adjustments to the rate of gross profit and the turnover figures used in calculating a claim to meet almost any actual or potential variation in their amount. Even so, its application is confined solely to figures and only to those for the three definitions against which it is bracketed. For example, it could be invoked in a claim settlement to increase the percentage figure of the rate of gross profit but not to do so by incorporating in it a charge which was not already included in the definition of gross profit. The latter would not constitute a "trend of business" or a "variation in or other circumstances affecting the business" but would be altering the definition of gross profit.

Without this clause the policy cannot be regarded as fulfilling the basic principle of an insurance, that is to indemnify, because the turnover, charges and profits which would have been realised during a period of interruption are hypothetical and never capable of absolute proof. By the use of this clause it is possible to make adjustments in a loss settlement to produce as near as is reasonably possible a true indemnity for an insured's loss.

An illustration of a claim settlement which includes adjustments to the rate of gross profit and turnover figures is given in Appendix X, paragraph 470.

(b) *Importance*

Because of the unstable and fluctuating national and international trading conditions of recent decades the provision for the adjustment of figures in a claim settlement has throughout that period played a vital role. Experience has proved it to be a most useful—perhaps the most useful—and essential part of the contract and it is of necessity invoked in most claims of any size. An indication of the importance placed on its application is the fact that until 1970 the clause referred to "special" circumstances and, significantly, that word was then changed to "other" which gives even wider scope in its application. This was timely because the acute economic inflation which started in the early 1970s is now accepted as a permanent threat which must be taken into account in all calculations of sums insured and in all claim settlements as being a normal, not a special, circumstance.

Quite apart from the effects of a period of general prosperity or of economic inflation there are many other factors due to the influence of which the turnover of a business during a period of interruption would, but for the Incident, have been relatively higher than that during the corresponding period before the Incident. Such an increase may be the result of one or more of a number of causes such as credit restrictions, a trade recession or an industrial dispute at some time during the 12 months preceding the Incident. Alternatively it may be that greater turnover would have come about in the period of interruption as the result of a special advertising campaign conducted in the previous year, the securing of some large new contract or customers, opening of additional shops, automation, new plant and processes or lay-out of a factory, the efforts of time and motion study engineers, or merely because of a general upward trend of trade.

An increase in selling prices will probably create an automatic increase in turnover; a reduction in prices by stimulating sales sometimes has the same result. Even changes in the pattern of social habits can have a very marked effect on the manufacture and sales of different commodities whilst for some business the vagaries of the weather can make the difference between a profit and a loss. For some firms the expiry of a patent or copyright held by them or by a competitor may have a big influence on their trading results. Changes in the fiscal policy or import and export restrictions and imposts or currency regulations of our own or other countries can also have either harmful or beneficial effects upon many businesses.

Because the turnover of most businesses is subject to variation due to external influences an adjustment of the standard turnover figure is very frequently necessary in the settlement of claims. The actual extent to which such an adjustment should be made is not always easy to determine and often some degree of compromise is required in order to reach an equitable settlement. For example, assume a situation in which Smith & Co., one of two firms in competition in identical lines of business has a serious fire and during the period of interruption its rival Jones & Co., also has a fire: such coincidences do occur especially in present times when arson seems to be a popular sport. In their business interruption claim Smith & Co. might claim that but for their own premises being out of action they would have obtained additional trade because of the interruption of the business of Jones & Co. by the fire at the latter's premises. How much extra turnover?—a neat problem for the loss adjuster!

Moreover, factors of the nature mentioned in the foregoing paragraphs sometimes result in the turnover during a period of interruption after an Incident even exceeding the standard turnover. Consequently a straight comparison reveals no shortage in turnover which is the index by which the loss is to be be measured. But it may be demonstrable that the Incident has adversely affected the turnover of the business. What is apparently a paradox is resolved by the use of the other circumstances clause to adjust the standard turnover figure according to the particular circumstances.

(c) *Effect*

If the other circumstances clause is invoked by an insured in a claim settlement in order to obtain the benefit of an upward trend by increasing the figure of the standard turnover the same percentage increase is, in the absence of other special circumstances which would condition it in some way, automatically applied to the annual turnover. The effect of this latter adjustment is to increase the figure to be used for comparison with the sum insured in applying the average proviso. Thus the benefit obtained from an adjustment of the standard turnover to give a larger figure for the shortage consequent upon the Incident will be to some extent lost if the sum insured is not sufficient to provide a full insurance when compared with the correspondingly adjusted figure under the average proviso. The degree to which the benefit is offset will depend upon relative figures and also upon the relationship of the amount claimed under clause (a) reduction in turnover, *vis-à-vis* that claimed under clause (b) increase in cost of working. The greater the proportion of the latter the heavier will be the incidence of the adjusted average proviso. Because of this, in cases in which increase in cost of working constitutes the whole, of, or a preponderant part of, the claim, an insured could recover less as a result of an upward adjustment of the standard turnover if the sum insured proved inadequate after a corresponding adjustment of the annual turnover.

Similar results are obtained if the other circumstances clause is brought into operation to increase the rate of gross profit. This might be done to provide for an anticipated higher ratio of gross profit resulting from new plant or processes, from lower costs of materials, or from higher selling prices, the benefit of which would have accrued in the months after the Incident had the Incident not occurred. Or if the net profit in the last financial year preceding the Incident was reduced by a non-recurring and non-insurable charge, such as a bad debt, the other circumstances clause would be operated to adjust the net profit figure to what it would have been but for the bad debt. (See paragraph 82(c) on non-recurring charges.) By adjusting the rate of gross profit upwards the figure produced under the average proviso for purposes of comparison with the sum insured is automatically increased.

It will be realised from the foregoing that, valuable as the other circumstances clause is, the full benefit of its use in a claim settlement will only be obtained if the sum insured is adequate to allow for the application of the average proviso on the basis of adjusted figures. This means that it is generally advisable to fix the sum insured with a generous margin of overinsurance; this matter will be explained more fully in paragraphs 239 and 240 in Chapter 11 which deals with the arrangement of the sum insured.

See also paragraph 432 regarding variations in the application of the other circumstances clause to figures for the average proviso in claims.

(d) *Reverse application*

It must also be understood that this clause can be invoked by the insurers in the calculation of a claim to reduce the amount of the standard turnover or the rate of gross profit when conditions warrant such action. For example, increased competition may force down selling prices during the period of interruption with a lowering effect on both the rate of gross profit and turnover. Similarly a general trade recession, unseasonable weather conditions, or a strike or lock-out either in the particular trade concerned or in transport or other industries are typical of circumstances which may cause a reduction in turnover concurrently with that due to the Incident. Such events would have had the effect of lowering the insured's gross profit in the months after the Incident even had the Incident not taken place. Unless allowance is made for such circumstances an insured would be over-indemnified and this point is specifically covered by the words which follow and qualify the reference in clause (a) to reduction in turnover, namely "in consequence of the Incident". (See paragraphs 43 and 44.)

56. Adjustments to calculations

As the stated purpose of the other circumstances clause is to produce figures for the loss settlement "as near as may be reasonably practicable" there must be on both sides a willingness to give and take in its operation.

This need for a reasonable and understanding attitude in the application of the clause is well illustrated by circumstances in which a double adjustment may be required. For example, some time prior to an Incident taking place the insured might have put into effect a reduction in the selling price of their products at the expense of their normal percentage of net profit with the idea of expanding sales in order to oust competitors in a particular commodity or territory. In the claim calculation the rate of gross profit would need reducing to correspond with the cut in net profit but the standard turnover would require two adjustments, one to allow for the fact that the same quantity of goods would produce a lower sales figure than previously because of the reduction in price and a second one to take into account the increase in volume of sales anticipated from the price reductions. Such an increase would be largely hypothetical because competitors might reduce their prices in retaliation and if the Incident took place so soon after the price reduction became effective that no conclusive evidence of its success could be gathered the matter would rest largely on the fact that the insured must have been fairly confident of successful results when they decided to embark on the scheme. But bearing in mind that boards of directors are human and can make wrong decisions how far can that be taken an evidence that the scheme would have succeeded? The task of loss adjusters can be an unenviable one!

57. Full formula for settlement of claims

As this chapter has introduced the several factors which may modify the four basic steps laid down in the specification for the calculation of a claim (see paragraph 54), the full formula is now set out, as follows:

LOSS OF GROSS PROFIT:
    clause (a)—application of the rate of gross profit (adjusted if necessary) to the reduction in turnover (after any necessary adjustment of the standard turnover figure) during the indemnity period

INCREASE IN COST OF WORKING:
    clause (b)—addition to the above of any additional expenditure necessarily and reasonably incurred, etc., after
        (i) apportionment of the amount if any insurable charges have not been included in the definition of gross profit
        (ii) application of the "economic limit" proviso that the amount, after that apportionment, shall not exceed the loss of gross profit avoided by the additional expenditure

SAVINGS: deduction from the foregoing of the amount of any savings in the charges included in the gross profit insurance, consequent upon the Incident.

AVERAGE: application of the average proviso after adjustment of the figures of the rate of gross profit and the annual turnover to correspond with any adjustment made in clause (a) above.

An illustration of a loss settlement is given in Appendix X (paragraph 470) which shows how the above formula works when (i) some standing charges are not included in an insurance (ii) the annual turnover is greater than the turnover in the financial year preceding the Incident (iii) there is underinsurance (iv) adjustments are made under the other circumstances clause to the figures of standard turnover and to the rate of gross profit.

58. Alternative trading clause—turnover elsewhere after damage

The formula and the definitions of the terms used in it do not quite complete the specification. A memorandum called the alternative trading clause is included, which reads:

> "If during the Indemnity Period goods shall be sold or services shall be rendered elsewhere than at the Premises for the benefit of the Business either by the Insured or by others on their behalf the money paid or payable in respect of such sales or services shall be brought into account in arriving at the Turnover during the Indemnity Period".

For example, after premises are damaged the insured may during the period of interruption take temporary premises from which to continue trading. Or they may during the period of interruption arrange with another firm in the same trade to manufacture, label and dispatch goods in the insured's name direct to the latter's customers. The additional cost of any such arrangement will be borne under clause (b) of the specification as increase in cost of working.

It seems obviously equitable and in accordance with the principle of indemnity that the money earned on sales or services promoted during a period of interruption, as a result of the Incident, should be credited to the turnover during the indemnity period and so the memorandum might be thought to be superfluous. It was found advisable, however, to introduce this memorandum so as to leave no room for doubt on the matter, because of the case of *City Tailors Ltd.* v. *Evans* (1921) 91 L.J.K.B. 379 (C.A.) when the point arose under a policy which did not contain a clause of this nature. See paragraph 232 for an interesting problem in which this clause is relevant.

59. Necessity for specification

As the contents of this chapter may have produced in the reader's mind the idea that the assessment of the loss which an insured might suffer in consequence of an Incident is a very complex matter a rider needs to be added. This is to the effect that most claims are simple, straightforward settlements and in any event insurers always try to introduce flexibility into them and are willing to compromise where there are reasonable grounds for doing so.

59 CHAPTER 4

But the fact remains that a great many claims *are* complicated, generally because of the complex nature of business activities, the play upon them of so many outside factors, and the unpredictable consequences of an Incident; often, too, because unfortunately the insurance is inadequate or has been incorrectly arranged.

One thing certain is that involved claim settlements would be much worse to settle without the specification formula and frequent recourse to arbitration or law over the many points on which disagreement might arise would be inevitable. The standard form of specification introduced in 1939 was drafted as an attempt to obviate such difficulties by providing for the purpose of settling claims a workable basis which can be approved by an insured before entering into the contract. Basically the same today, from its introduction to the time of writing the absence of any law case arising from it confirms that it is soundly constructed.

60. Valued bases

(a) *Percentage of fire loss*

Not unnaturally it is often suggested that the whole business of insuring business interruption could, and should, be greatly simplified. One method introduced in the early days of Profits insurance known as Percentage of Fire Loss Insurance undertook to pay a fixed percentage of the sums recoverable by an insured for material damage to the contents of the premises. Whilst there is no doubt as to the simplicity of calculating the amount payable in the event of a claim under a policy of this nature it can be most erratic in its results and may provide either more or less than an indemnity. Being inflexible it can take no account of the effect of an Incident upon the productive capacity of a business nor compensate for the large business interruption loss which may arise from a small amount of fire damage at a vulnerable point nor provide for the loss during a long period which may be required to rehabilitate premises and plant and regain lost customers.

For businesses such as those of wholesale warehousemen and merchants in raw materials and imported commodities, a percentage of fire loss insurance might provide an indemnity if new premises could be obtained practically straight away without any additional expenditure on rent, rate, fitting-up, etc. But otherwise, such an insurance would not compensate for the additional loss sustained, that is, the loss due to the lack of a warehouse preventing their turning stock over in the normal way in subsequent months.

Should an Incident occur when warehouse stocks are at a seasonal lowest point with a correspondingly small fire loss, shortage immediately thereafter of warehouse accommodation for the new season's goods could result in a loss of profit on the potential sale of a much greater quantity of stock than that destroyed. Further, and of considerable importance, no provision is made for increase in cost of working; experience under normal "turnover" policies shows that warehouse claims often involve substantial payments under that heading.

(b) *Pay as paid*

A similar form of insurance known as a "pay as paid" policy has been provided by some Underwriters at Lloyd's in respect of a firm's stock on its own premises. Under such a policy the amount payable following an Incident is the same percentage of the sum insured as the total paid for loss under the fire insurance on stock bears to the total sum insured on stock in the premises. As a safeguard against overinsurance a policy condition limits the sum insured to the amount of the gross profit in the preceding financial year. Previous remarks about the shortcomings of percentage of fire loss insurances apply equally to a "pay as paid" policy.

It must further be borne in mind that many merchants and wholesalers are open to serious loss if supplies of the goods or commodities in which they deal are curtailed as the result of a fire at the premises of a manufacturer or processor. Neither a percentage of fire loss policy nor a pay as paid policy makes provision for this risk, which may involve greater loss than a fire at an insured's own warehouse. To provide against loss arising from "other people's fires" it is essential to have a normal U.K. business interruption policy with an appropriate "suppliers extension", or a U.S. Business Income from Dependent Properties form", as explained in paragraphs 346 and 347 respectively.

CHAPTER 5

OPERATION OF THE COVER—UNITED STATES BASIS

61. Contract to indemnify—actual loss (of Business Income) sustained

A comparison of the specimen wordings for Gross Earnings and Business Income coverages given in Appendices Q, R and S with that in Appendix C for a U.K. business interruption specification will show that the U.S. and U.K. forms differ fundamentally. Whilst the U.K. form makes reduction in turnover the yardstick of primary measurement of a loss, agreed to by both insurer and insured, the U.S. Business Income Coverage policies state that "we will pay for the actual loss of Business Income you sustain" but do not say precisely how this "actual loss" is to be ascertained. Some progress has been made beyond the gross earnings forms in that under Loss Determination the new form sets out the factors upon which the loss of Business Income will be determined, *viz.*:

"(1) The Net Income of the business before the direct physical loss or damage occurred;
(2) The likely Net Income of the business if no loss or damage occurred;
(3) The operating expenses, including payroll expenses, necessary to resume 'operations' etc. with the same quality of service that existed before the direct physical loss or damage, etc.".

A feature of the description of coverage of the U.S. gross earnings is that it does not actually say that the indemnity is for loss of gross earnings but is for the actual loss sustained not exceeding the reduction in gross earnings. This latter together with the Special Exclusion of liability for any consequential or remote loss will exclude claims arising from, for example, breach of contract or spoilage of undamaged fruit, etc. The Canadian form (refer paragraph 73(a)) is perhaps more definitive in this matter by reversing the wording so that "the measure of recovery shall be the reduction in gross earnings . . . not exceeding the actual loss sustained". It also carries a Special Exclusion of loss due to fines or damages for breach of contract for late or non-completion of orders or for any penalties of whatever nature.

Apart from the above the provisions for indemnification of an insured embody the same principles in the U.S. as in the U.K. forms; any variations in their actual application will be discussed in subsequent paragraphs. One important point is that the gross earnings coverage for manufacturing risks excludes finished stock (as does the Business Income Coverage form) and the differences from the non-manufacturing form which stem from this are shown in Appendix R and examined in paragraph 97(b).

62. Savings in charges and expenses

The insurer's liability for the actual loss of Business Income sustained by an insured is qualified in the description of coverage by the stipulation that Business Income shall represent "Net Income (Net Profit or Loss before income taxes) that would have been earned or incurred; and continuing normal operating expenses incurred, including payroll". This means that any reduction in the wages of non-essential workers who are dismissed following the damage is a saving which benefits the insurer. This is in accordance with the principle that an insured must not be over-indemnified by being paid for charges which are reduced or cease because of the interruption of business. This is in line with the "savings clause" in a U.K. business interruption specification (see paragraphs 51 *et seq.*).

There is no attempt to mention individual "normal operating expenses" other than payroll. Presumably this means that a decision as to which charges and expenses and employees' wages shall continue to be paid during a period of interruption or are to be deducted as savings to the benefit of the insurer depends on the latter's opinion.

As the clause refers to "*normal* operating expenses" what would be the attitude of an insurer should an abnormal charge be involved, or is the payment of optional charges such as agents' commission and some forms of advertising to be regarded as a *de facto* normal operating system? The charge of most importance in this respect is that of payroll expenses: different businesses will have different requirements regarding the retention of employees during a period of interruption. Provision to meet this situation is possible by arranging the insurance on payroll for less than the standard 100 per cent. coverage—see paragraphs 217(a)–(c).

63. Period of indemnity

(a) *For the actual loss of Business Income sustained*

The period of the interruption of business during which indemnity will be paid is open-ended so far as time is concerned. It commences with the date of the damage but continues until "the date when the property at the described premises should be repaired, rebuilt or replaced with reasonable speed and similar quality". As the word "property" includes the contents of premises the time required after rebuilding to re-equip, refurnish, decorate and stock-up with new merchandise is covered. The words "should be" are important if through some cause, such as a landlord or the insured deciding not to rebuild, the premises are not restored.

Under this definition the Business Income coverage could prove more beneficial to an insured than it would have been under a U.K. business interruption cover if following an Incident the period required for restoration of the property turned out to be longer than the maximum indemnity period. On the other hand there seem to be more chances that a Business Income coverage would be inferior as in the following circumstances.

The indemnity for loss of Business Income ceases on the date when it is estimated that the damaged property could have been rebuilt, repaired or replaced. This makes no provision for loss of income or increased expenditure after that date. Such losses may continue for many months during which production or income of a business is still affected and below normal, continuing loss of this nature generally being the result of loss of customers during the period of interruption with consequent difficulty in regaining their custom after competitors have gained a foothold in connections. Most businesses dealing direct with the public are open to continuing loss of trade—shopkeepers, factory outlets, hoteliers, restaurants, etc. It may also arise because during a closure of part or the whole of a factory the labour force has been largely dispersed and when the works are rebuilt and re-equipped there is a shortage of technicians and skilled workers and it takes time to recruit and train new operatives. There is also the possibility of a period of teething troubles during the running in of new plant and machinery and the integration of departments and processes to secure a continuous flow of production. It may be that after the rehabilitation of the damaged premises and contents additional expenditure such as special advertising or overtime working is required to restore the level of pre-fire earnings.

Continuing loss of the foregoing nature is covered under a U.K. business interruption policy until the results of the business are restored to normal up to the limit of the maximum indemnity period insured (see paragraph 245(a)) but under a U.S. Business Income coverage form such loss is not insured and to do so requires extra coverage as explained below.

(b) *Additional and Optional Coverages*

As mentioned in paragraph 63(a) the indemnity under a Business Income coverage form ends on the date when the property has been or should have been restored to pre-damage condition and this limitation may leave an insured open to serious loss in subsequent weeks or months. It is very doubtful in a great many cases whether a business can function at its normal level of production or sales immediately after restoration of damaged property. Experience over the years of losses suffered by insured because of this shortcoming in coverage and consequent widespread criticism has resulted in insurers including Extended Business Income under Additional Coverages and offering an Extended Period of Indemnity under the Optional Coverages.

(i) Extended Business Income

This Additional Coverage provides for the payment of actual loss of Business Income during the period beginning with the end of the "period of restoration" when "operations" are resumed and ending either on "the date you could restore your business, with reasonable speed, to the condition that would have existed if no direct physical loss or damage occurred" or after "30 consecutive days" whichever is the earlier. What makes this Additional Coverage come closer in intention to the U.K. business interruption cover is the introduction of a reference to the restoration of "business" where the basic coverage refers only to the restoration of "property".

(ii) Extended Period of Indemnity

The effect of the insured taking up this Optional Coverage is to increase the cover provided by Extended Business Income, the "30 consecutive days" being replaced by a number of consecutive days chosen by the insured and shown in the Declarations for this Optional Coverage.

As with the Period of Indemnity Extension Endorsement which was attached to a gross earnings coverage the additional indemnity period purchased is in units of 30 days (up to 180 days and then 90 days units up to 360 days) and the rating is on a sliding scale with 60 days (*i.e.* 30 days beyond the basic guaranteed cover) having a factor of 1.10 to be applied to the Business Income rates otherwise applicable and 360 days (*i.e.* 330 days extra) having a factor of 1.50 to be so applied.

The insurance under this Optional Coverage is subject to all the terms and conditions of the basic coverage including the coinsurance percentage applicable. This latter fact necessitates an uplift in the amount insured to allow for the probable greater loss of earnings corresponding to the longer period of interruption now insured. In estimating the amount to be insured extra care has to be taken if the business is of a seasonal nature to provide for the position that if the period of return to normal does not end until partway through or just after the second season the whole of two season's earnings might be lost. See paragraph 252(a)–(c) regarding seasonal businesses.

There are two classes of business undertakings which are especially vulnerable to the possibilities of loss if the period of indemnity is limited to the time required for physical restoration of damaged premises plus 30 days. Although such businesses might insure against their continuing loss by the Optional Coverage there is possibly still available for each class of business a coverage which is specially designed to give them better protection than this.

The Seasonal Crops or Seasonal Foodstuffs endorsement used to be given without extra premium to operators of packing and processing plants for vegetable and fruit purchased under advance contracts with the growers. If, due to damage at their plant, an insured could not take delivery of the crops as harvested but restoration was completed before the end of the growing season, they might be put in the position that the growers had meanwhile contracted to sell their crops to other packers or processors rather than risk having no sale of them and seeing them rot. This would leave the insured with either a diminished quantity, or none at all, of fruit and vegetables to put through their plant in the period following expiry of the indemnity period of a standard gross earnings coverage, thus suffering a loss of what might be a substantial part of or even the whole of a season's work and earnings.

These special endorsements operate from the date of damage for a period not exceeding 12 months on an actual loss sustained basis to insure loss due to the shortage of seasonal crops or foodstuffs which would have been obtainable by the insured but for the damage to their premises or plant. The cover is probably provided by use of the Optional Coverage.

The other category of businesses is schools and colleges and for these a special Tuition and Fees endorsement is available. As with the foregoing a period of indemnity will end with the physical rehabilitation of the damaged premises; but loss of fees may continue beyond that time because students have of necessity to continue their studies and this may mean enrolling at other places of learning. This applies especially following serious damage when there is uncertainty as to the date of restoration or if this appears likely to be part-way through a term or semester.

The insurance covers actual loss of tuition and fees and extra expenses less any savings in charges which do not continue, for a period including the school term after restoration irrespective of the time required for the latter.

There are two forms of cover—"Limited" where Business Income is limited to "tuition and fees from students, including fees from room, board, laboratories and other similar sources", and "Broad" where "Business Income is revised to include tuition, fees and other income from educational services and related activities, including laboratory fees, bookstores, athletic events and research grants".

(c) *Limitation: Electronic Media and Records*

This limitation on an insurer's liability for loss resulting from damage by the Covered Causes of Loss to media for, or programming records pertaining to, electronic data processing or electrically controlled equipment, including data thereon has at present no counterpart on U.K. policies. It states that "the length of time for which the insurer shall be liable shall not exceed (a) 60 consecutive calendar days or (b) the length of time that would be required to rebuild, repair or replace with reasonable speed and similar quality such other property herein described as has been damaged or destroyed, whichever is the greater length of time".

As the time limit (b) is already incorporated in the general description of coverage it might at first sight appear redundant to repeat it and instead the clause might simply state "not exceeding 60 days" as the limit in respect of electronic media. However, the clause is not so restrictive and it would appear probable that the seeming ambiguity arises because the intention is to separate electronic media from the general meaning of "property" in view of the increased risk of business interruption attaching to it, and make the 60 days limit apply only if damage is confined to such media alone and no other property is damaged or the time for restoration of the latter is less than 60 days. If the period of indemnity for loss resulting from damage to "other property" exceeds 60 days loss due to damage to electronic media, etc., is covered up to the same period.

The period of 60 days in the clause can be extended to either 180 consecutive days or an unlimited period by endorsement if required.

64. Extra Expense/Expenses to Reduce Loss

There are two basic Business Income Coverage Forms: "(And Extra Expense)"—which is akin to the old Gross Earnings and Extra Expense Form and "Without Extra Expense"—which provides the restricted Gross Earnings Forms cover. The alternative "increased costs" Additional Coverages are described below. The separate Extra Expense Coverage Form is dealt with in paragraph 278(b).

(a) *Extra Expense*

This Additional Coverage covers the expenses *necessarily* incurred by the insured during the "period of restoration" that would not have been incurred if there had been no damage. Three categories of Extra Expense payable by insurers are listed—

1. Any Extra Expense to avoid or minimise the suspension of business and to continue "operations": at the described premises; or at replacement premises or at temporary locations, including relocation expenses and costs to equip and operate the replacement or temporary locations.
2. Any Extra Expense to minimise the suspension of business if the insured cannot continue "operations".
3. Any Extra Expense to repair or replace any property; or research, replace or restore the lost information on damaged valuable papers and records; but only to the extent that it reduces the amount of loss that otherwise would have been payable under the Coverage form.

Extra Expense incurred in respect of the reproduction of "finished stock" is payable by not being excluded under the Causes of Loss forms.

(b) *Expenses to Reduce Loss*

Under this heading those expenses other than fire extinguishing expenses which are necessarily incurred for the purpose of reducing loss, generally called "expediting expenses", are automatically included in the insurance, that is, are additional to the payment for loss of Business Income subject to the overall limit of the amount insured. This cover corresponds to the additional expenditure insured under the Increase in Cost of Working provision in a U.K. business interruption policy (see paragraph 45 *et seq.*) and similarly an "economic limit" as in paragraph 47(a) is included by insurers agreeing to pay for such expenses "to the extent that they do not exceed the amount of loss that otherwise would have been payable under this Coverage form". In other words the insurers will not pay more than X dollars to save X dollars. Some of the many directions in which this provision for expediting expenses might be utilised to shorten the period of interruption are mentioned in paragraph 45.

The Additional Condition—Coinsurance in the policy is exempted from application to both Extra Expense and Expenses to Reduce Loss and this gives an insured an added incentive to make every possible use of these Additional Coverages, to reduce the loss of earnings.

65. Prolongation

(a) *Interruption by civil authority (prevention of access)*

Under the Additional Coverage of Civil Authority insurers promise to pay for the actual loss of Business Income sustained and necessary Extra Expense (where this is covered)—

> "caused by action of civil authority that prohibits access to the described premises due to direct physical loss of or damage to property, other than that at the described premises, caused by or resulting from any Covered Cause of Loss. This coverage will apply for a period of up to two consecutive weeks from the date of that action".

Although this cover is wider than that previously given under a gross earnings form (in that it applies with respect to loss at any location "other than the described premises" and not just to loss at "adjacent premises") it is not as wide as the U.K. Prevention of Access extension as described in paragraph 373.

(b) *Exclusion—enforcement of law*

This special exclusion on a gross earnings policy of any increase of loss resulting from enforcement of any ordinance or law regulating the use, construction, repair or demolition of property is repeated in the new forms where:

> "any increased period required due to the enforcement of any ordinance or law that:
> (1) Regulates the construction, use or repair, or requires the tearing down of any property; or

(2) Requires any insured or others to test for, monitor, clean up, remove, contain, treat, detoxify or neutralize, or in any way respond to, or assess the effects of 'pollutants'."

is not deemed to be part of the "period of restoration". Under the latter if restoration of damaged property is delayed by the action of a planning authority the extended period of interruption would be treated as an extraneous cause to be dealt with in the light of the particular circumstances of the case. For further information on this type of contingency and the doctrine of proximate cause see paragraphs 44 and 420(a).

Although instances do arise in the United Kingdom of delays in rebuilding due to the special requirements of planning authorities as, for instance, for the provision of parking facilities in a new building, the problem is not as acute as in North America. The exclusion exists in U.S. forms because in most U.S. cities there are building and zoning regulations governing the construction and sites of new buildings. Many older premises were built before the passage of some of these laws but in the event of such buildings sustaining a certain extent of damage they must be demolished and new buildings erected in their place which conform with current regulations. Compliance with this can add very considerably to "the period of restoration" beyond the "date when the property at the described premises should be repaired, rebuilt or replaced with reasonable speed and similar quality". Insurance for this potential loss beyond the normal coverage can be obtained by a special endorsement to include the extra contingent liability which might arise from the operation of city or state laws governing restoration which prolong the "period of restoration".

(c) *Exclusion—interference by strikers, etc.*

Another disadvantage of the U.S. coverage compared with a U.K. insurance is that losses during a period of interruption which is extended by certain extraneous causes which would be claimable under the latter are not covered under a U.S. policy because of a special exclusion which states that the insurer will not pay for any increase in loss caused by or resulting from interference by strikers or other persons with rebuilding, repairing or replacing the property or with the resumption of "operations". This exclusion means that an insured is liable to suffer serious loss due to prolongation of the period of interruption of business—and it may be weeks or even months—through causes entirely outside his control, *e.g.* a strike by construction workers or damage by vandals.

This exclusion refers only to actions at the "location of the rebuilding", etc., and might give grounds for thinking that an extension of a period of interruption due to extraneous causes elsewhere is not covered. The word "directly" is included in paragraph 1 of the description of coverage in a gross earnings policy so that it "insures against loss resulting *directly* from necessary interruption of business caused by damage" and it could be construed to mean that increase of loss due to strikes elsewhere than at the insured's premises or any other extraneous contingencies which may arise to delay the rehabilitation of a business are not insured. The new wording does not include the word "directly" and by inference from the exclusion of increased loss due to strikers and other persons being confined specifically to action at the "location of the rebuilding", etc., increased loss due to external factors which would not have affected the Business Income had the damage not occurred should be met by insurers. Such a construction on the intention of the coverage would bring it into line on this particular issue with the attitude adopted by U.K. insurers as explained in paragraphs 44 and 420(a).

(d) *Exclusion—suspension, lapse or cancellation of any license, etc.*

This is another special exclusion which is not on a U.K. policy. It states that the insurer will no be liable for any increase of loss resulting from the suspension, lapse or cancellations of any license, lease or contract unless this results directly from the suspension of "operations" and then only for such loss as affects the insured's Business Income during, and limited to, "the period of restoration" covered under the policy. An insurance specially designed to cover loss of leasehold interest would pick up an insured's continuing loss which is not covered because of this exclusion. (See paragraph 266(b).)

66. Resumption of operations

Under the Loss Conditions the last of the insured's Duties in the Event of Loss is to resume all or part of their "operations" as quickly as possible. By saying this insurers are reintroducing the idea of "due diligence and dispatch" mentioned in the gross earnings policy and it allows them to avoid liability when the insured have obviously been slow in resuming operations through inefficiency or lack of interest, or have decided not to resume operations at all.

Later in the Loss Conditions, under the heading of Resumption of Operations, the insurers state that they will reduce the amount of the insured's Business Income loss, other than Extra Expense, to the extent they can resume their "operations", in whole or in part, by using damaged or undamaged property (including merchandise or stock) at the described premises or elsewhere. The amount of Extra Expense loss will also be reduced to the extent the insured can return "operations" to normal and discontinue such Extra Expense.

These conditions are on a par with the Alternative Trading Clause in a U.K. policy (see paragraph 58) but differ inasmuch as the latter refer only to goods actually sold or services actually rendered elsewhere whereas the U.S. form goes beyond this saying that payment will be reduced to the extent the insured can resume their "operations". This means that insurers are entitled to the benefit of any possible reduction in loss by the stated means even though an insured does not actually put them into effect.

The Loss Conditions also place on the insured the duty of protecting the property from further damage which might result in extension of the period of interruption and of providing written notification with details and proofs about the interruption of business and resulting claim. The Loss Conditions are lengthy and are given in full in the policy wording in Appendix S. (See also paragraph 435.)

67. Coinsurance

(a) *Gross earnings*

This very important clause on gross earnings policies gave rise to a considerable amount of misunderstanding as to how it operated. Its purpose was similar to that of the "average clause" incorporated in a U.K. specification (paragraph 52 *et seq*. namely to provide that in the event of there being underinsurance at the time when a loss occurs, based on figures adjusted for prospective earnings, the insured would bear an equitable share of the loss. The method by which this was achieved by a coinsurance clause differs from a U.K. average clause by providing what was in effect a "first loss" coverage so long as the amount insured was at least equal to the coinsurance percentage of what would have been a full insurance. Operation of the coinsurance clause was not as simple as it may at first sight have appeared and was not as easy to grasp as the straightforward application of average in a U.K. policy. The coinsurance clause (also called the contribution clause in which case the two words are transposed), reads:

> "The insurer shall not be liable for a greater proportion of any loss than the amount of insurance specified bears to the amount produced by multiplying the gross earnings that would have been earned (had no loss occurred) during the 12 months immediately following the date of damage to or destruction of the described property by the coinsurance percentage specified on this policy".

(b) *Business Income Coverage*

The Additional Condition—Coinsurance occupies three-quarters of a page in the new wording and is intended to explain at length and with mathematical clarity the operation of the condition.

It begins by stating that insurers will not pay the full amount of any loss if the Limit of Insurance for Business Income (shown in the Declarations) is less than the stated coinsurance percentage times the sum of the Net Income (Net Profit or Loss before income taxes), and *all* operating expenses, including payroll expenses. (What is not explained is the meaning of "operating expenses": without a definition it must be assumed that such expenses include the cost of materials, and in the event of a loss *savings* are expected to be made in the cost of materials and similar *variable* costs so as to justify the coinsurance percentage chosen and to allow for the deduction of further non-continuing expenses so as to avoid over-indemnification.)

There then follows a statement of how the maximum amount payable is calculated with two specimen calculations, one demonstrating an underinsurance situation, and the other a situation where there is adequacy of insurance. (Refer Appendix S, paragraph 465.)

(c) *The "coinsurance percentage"*

The size of the "coinsurance percentage" agreed for the insurance is reflected in the premium rating table, the higher the percentage the lower the relative rate charged, as shown in paragraph 256(b). The normal range of coinsurance percentages is from a minimum of 50 per cent. up to 80 per cent., which is the most usual, and in some parts of the States 100 per cent. The choice depends upon the practice of different insurers and type of business and for some heavy industrial risks a specified percentage may be obligatory. (See also paragraph 235.)

If at the time of damage occurring the amount insured under a U.S. coverage, which is, for instance, subject to a 50 per cent. coinsurance clause, is equal to at least 50 per cent. of the Business Income, which it is estimated would, after adjustments for trends of business, inflation and other circumstances, have been earned in the 12 months of the policy year, the loss is recoverable in full up to the amount insured. This would provide indemnity up to that amount for total loss over a period of six months (unless income was of a seasonal nature) or a partial loss of income over a longer period of interruption. In addition any expenditure incurred in order to reduce the potential loss of Business Income is insured in full because the Extra Expense and Expenses to Reduce Loss and Additional Coverages (paragraph 64) exempts such expenditure from application of the coinsurance condition.

The coinsurance condition is so worded that it allows an insured to arrange an insurance for an amount less than a full 12 months projected Business Income without incurring the penalty of bearing a proportionate share of a loss, as would arise under a U.K. policy with "average", provided that the amount of any loss does not exceed the figure produced by the formula in the coinsurance clause. This is because the clause limits the recovery for loss not to the coinsurance percentage either of the amount insured or of the loss but allows for recovery in full up to the amount produced by the formula:

$$\frac{\text{Limit of Insurance}}{\text{coinsurance percentage of Business Income for policy year}} \times \text{amount of loss.}$$

This figure together with the amount of extra expense or expenses incurred to reduce the loss is then subject to the overall limit of the amount insured.

Although directed towards ensuring adequate insurance coverage the condition allows flexibility for an insured to arrange this, with due allowances for the coinsurance percentage chosen, from knowledge of his own business and on his own estimate of possible maximum loss taking into account the period which might be necessary to rehabilitate the property damaged and the severity and proportionate effect on Business Income.

It is essential however to take into account the fact that the coinsurance condition applied (under the gross earnings forms) on the basis of the gross earnings which would have been realised (had no loss occurred) during the 12 months immediately following the date of the damage. This necessitated basing a calculation of the amount to be insured on an estimate of the gross earnings which might have been earned during a period of 12 months or longer beyond the expiry date of the policy as explained in connecting with the operation of the average clause on a U.K. policy in paragraph 52(c).

This potential difficulty is now avoided by making the basis the 12 months of the policy year, although the business income which would have been earned in the remainder of the policy year following the date of the loss (had the loss not occurred) must still be estimated.

68. Optional Coverage: Agreed Value

The foregoing paragraph 67 gives some indication of the difficulties confronting the insured in understanding just how the coinsurance condition operates and in maintaining insurance at an adequate figure to avoid being penalised by the condition in the event of a claim. The problem was met under the gross earnings form (where the coinsurance clause was more difficult to comply with because of the projected time base) by the incorporation of an Agreed Amount clause—which substituted for the percentage in the coinsurance condition a dollar amount.

Under the new wording the Agreed Value Optional Coverage achieves the same end. Under the terms of this coverage a Business Income Report/ Work Sheet must be made a part of the policy and must show *actual* financial data for the insured's "operations" during the 12 months prior to the date of the Work Sheet and *estimated* data for the 12 months immediately following the inception of the Optional Coverage. An Agreed Value must be shown, either in the Declarations or in the Work Sheet, which is at least equal to the stated coinsurance percentage times the amount of Net Income And Operating Expenses for the following 12 months reported in the Work Sheet.

This makes the cover very much like the U.K. Declaration-Linked basis (see paragraph 53), the similarity being reinforced by the further statement that the coinsurance condition is suspended until 12 months after this

Optional Coverage is effected or the policy expires, whichever is the sooner. If a new Work Sheet is not submitted together with a new Agreed Value, within 12 months of the effective date of the Optional Coverage or when a change in Business Income Limit of Insurance is requested, the coinsurance condition will be reinstated.

The "honesty clause" under the gross earnings form by which it was required that a form of pro rata average be applied if the earnings amount reported on the worksheet was found to be less than actual gross earnings, is not included in the new wording.

69. Business Income: manufacturing/non-manufacturing

The new simplified form describes Business Income as Net Income (Net Profit or Loss before income taxes) that would have been earned or incurred; and continuing normal operating expenses incurred, including payroll. What is missing is a definition of "normal operating expenses" (see also paragraph 67(b) and 101). Due to the net income approach it is not necessary to have a separate policy for non-manufacturing concerns, and the qualification in the definition of "Finished Stock" that the exclusion "does not include stock you have manufactured that is held for sale on the premises of any retail outlet insured under this Coverage Part" further does away with the need for separate cover (for further comment refer paragraph 97(c)).

70. Adjustment for probable experience

Following the definition of gross earnings in the older wording there is an innocuous looking clause of only three lines of print which is nevertheless of considerable importance and can have a great influence on the amount payable in claims. It states that "in determining gross earnings due consideration shall be given to the experience of the business before the date of damage and the probable experience thereafter had no loss occurred".

This states more succinctly what is said in the U.K. "Other Circumstances Clause" (paragraph 55(a)) although its brevity and commitment only to "due consideration" might on occasion place upon a loss adjuster an onerous burden in agreeing an adjustment of figures.

Its purpose is to fulfil the aim of the policy to provide a true indemnity by permitting trends and circumstances which may have influenced trading results one way or another either before or after the date of damage or would have influenced them had no damage occurred, to be considered in a claim settlement. Such a provision for adjustments to be made when necessary to actual figures of gross earnings is essential because there are so many factors which can influence businesses (see paragraphs 55(b) to (d).)

In the new wording it is stated that "the amount of Business Income loss will be determined based on the Net Income of the business before the direct physical loss or damage occurred" and "the likely Net Income of the business if no loss or damage occurred". Other factors such as "operating expenses, including payroll expenses" are mentioned but it is Net Income that is highlighted because it is the more fluctuating part of Business Income.

71. "Valued" bases

(a) *Earnings (short) form*

This simplified form of coverage was introduced in the 1950s to try to overcome the reluctance of small and medium sized businesses to insure on gross earnings forms because of the apparently complicated nature of these, particularly the coinsurance provisions, and the necessity for completion of worksheets. Originally confined to mercantile and non-manufacturing risks it grew over the years in popularity and demand and was later made available for manufacturing businesses.

The Monthly Limit of Indemnity Optional Coverage on the new form maintains the same form of cover, the main attraction of which is the fact that the Coinsurance condition does not apply.

In order to try to obtain an amount insured and premium commensurate with the risk underwritten by insurers the purpose of a coinsurance clause is taken over by a Monthly Limit of Liability. Under this, recovery for loss is restricted for any period of 30 consecutive calendar days to a selected fraction of the amount insured and this fraction limit is applied separately to each successive 30-day period. But the amount of cover for 30-day periods is not cumulative.

To illustrate how the monthly limit may operate an example is shown in the wording.

The reason why an insured may lose, as in the example, $10,000 when there is in three 30-day periods a total insurance of $90,000 against a total loss during that time of the same amount is because the Monthly Limit of Liability condition imposes a limit of $30,000 for each period of 30 days.

There is no stipulation that the fraction limit per 30-day period selected by an insured must equal the earnings for any month of the year nor that the amount insured represents the annual figure of Business Income: an insured's estimate is the deciding factor and as there is no coinsurance clause and no average clause it is in effect a first-loss coverage per 30 calendar day period. But even an amount insured, which may appear to be adequate on a careful advance assessment of any loss which might be visualised if based on the normal pattern of trading, may leave an insured open to serious loss if sufficient allowance is not made for economic inflation, trends of business and other factors and unforeseen special circumstances which might arise.

The above applies particularly to businesses in which Business Income is of a seasonal nature. For these the amount of insurance available per 30-day period, calculated on the fraction limit applicable, should be arranged at a figure adequate to meet the maximum possible loss in any month of a year or more ahead. For instance, with a one-quarter monthly limit of liability full indemnity would be obtained for a total loss during the busiest month of a year's trading only if the insurance had been arranged for an amount equal to four times the heaviest monthly loss which might be anticipated at the height of the season. There is a general tendency to look upon one-quarter as a satisfactory standard limitation for most businesses and insured are consequently generally recommended to carry insurance equal to four times their best month's earnings. This is the practice in Canada where the use of the Earnings short form is generally confined to small retail outlets and a 25 per cent. limit is the maximum normally permitted.

Because of the first-loss nature of the Earnings form or the Monthly Limit of Indemnity coverage it may appear insurers obtain less premium income than they would from insurances on a full Gross Earnings or Business Income basis. On the other hand, since "Earnings" are defined as the sum of total net profit, payroll expenses, taxes, interest, rents and all other operating expenses earned by the business, it may well be that under that form more insurance is carried than is actually necessary in many cases. The new Business Income Coverage form in which the Monthly Limit of Indemnity coverage is incorporated does not go into that kind of detail, referring only to "continuing normal operating expenses, including payroll".

(b) *"Per diem"*, etc.

Another simplified method, long popular in the United States, was known as Use and Occupancy insurance. This provides for the payment of the actual amount of loss sustained without stating how it should be ascertained, but limited to a proportionate amount of annual earnings for each day, week or month (as selected for the insurance) of total suspension and a proportionate amount for partial interruption of business. Although this was an improvement on the percentage of fire loss cover as the sum insured represented estimated annual profits, the method made insufficient allowance for seasonal or other fluctuations of trade and in the event of only partial interruption, which happens in the majority of cases, shortage in turnover had to be adopted in some form to measure the loss. It is doubtful whether this form of coverage is any longer used, except in very exceptional circumstances.

Chapter 6

World-Wide Practices and Procedures

72. Practice in overseas countries

Wherever business interruption covers are written it is common practice for the format of the policies to be very much like the U.K. policy and specification, which incorporates a loss calculation formula and a defined indemnity period dealing with the whole of the period during which the insured's business is affected by the damage. However there is a strong leaning towards U.S. types of cover in certain countries (*e.g.* South and Central America, parts of the Far East, and some countries in Northern Europe) where U.S. commercial interests are particularly influential.

In countries which have always looked to the U.K. for guidance (having been assisted in the past by the foreign arm of the U.K. Fire Offices Committee) there is an agreement among local "associations" to utilise the so-called U.P.C. (Uniform Policy Conditions) wording as the basis of local policies. This wording is the same as that used in the United Kingdom for the writing of overseas risks which is generally known as the "Home Foreign" policy (see paragraph 79 and Appendix T).

The foreign department of the A.B.I. continues this service and is reviewing the current wording which has stood the test of time for many decades but which is now in need of revision to bring it more in line with current practices in the United Kingdom.

73. North America (excluding the United States)

The area of North America is taken for this study to include not only the United States and Canada but also Mexico, Central America and the islands of the Caribbean. The main influence of course from the point of view of insurance is that of the United States but the U.K. philosophy is followed in some areas, notably Canada and the Caribbean, *i.e.* those territories formerly under direct British political and commercial control.

(a) *Canada*

Canadian business interruption forms are a mixture of the more traditional U.S. and U.K. forms—gross earnings (U.S.) and gross profit (U.K.) the latter being on the "additions" basis—net profit and insured standing charges (see Appendix E). Forms are authorised by the Insurance Advisory Organisation (I.A.O.). U.S. forms are used in the minority of cases (say 10 per cent.) mainly for non-manufacturing and U.S.-owned insured. More popular is the U.K.-style Profits Form but elements of U.S. influence are detectable even in this form with the inclusion of a version of the civil authority condition and the limiting of the indemnity period in respect of damage to or destruction of electronic media and records.

Gross profit is made up of net profit and all or named standing charges with the following in no event being deemed to be insurable standing charges—depreciation of stock, bad debts, and wages and salaries other than salaries to permanent staff and wages to foremen and important employees whose services would not be dispensed with should the business be interrupted or interfered with. Full payroll cover can, however, be arranged although cover is usually for only 90 or 180 days. No account is taken of legal requirements for retention of employees.

The usual maximum indemnity period is 12 months with the sum insured based on the 12 months following the expiry date of the policy. Policies are subject to average provisos or coinsurance clauses but non-average, first loss, policies are available, particularly where the sums insurable are very large and there are relatively small loss limitations.

Suppliers' and customers' covers are available (usually by separate policies) but not often sold. Advance profits is rarely sold and then usually only on non-manufacturing businesses with a "waiting period" of two weeks.

Deductibles are used—mostly on a monetary basis, but large processing risks often carry "waiting periods" (presumably with the *whole* of the cover available thereafter). Loss limitations are also sometimes applied to very large risks, usually in respect of combined property damage and business interruption coverage.

All risks covers are available as are special engineering covers for boiler and machinery risks. Computer insurances are usually written on an all risks basis in respect of extra expenses.

Losses are usually calculated by reputable chartered accountants employed by the insurers who work with the loss adjuster to reach an equitable settlement. The insured can, if they wish, employ their own accountants to assist in the negotiating process.

(b) *Central America*

There is little business interruption insurance except through the activities in the region of large foreign concerns who recognise the value of the cover and can control its application. The basis of coverage is either U.K. or U.S. forms.

(c) *Caribbean*

Little business interruption insurance is written in the Caribbean compared with property damage insurance. Where it is written the U.K. form is used with gross profit defined on the "difference" basis. U.S. forms are used only when it is advantageous so to do—for hotels, etc. There are unofficial market agreements and rating guides in certain islands, *e.g.* Jamaica and Trinidad.

All policies are subject to average (although there are signs that Declaration-Linked covers—see paragraph 53 and Appendix D—are becoming known) and there appears to be no restriction on the length of maximum indemnity periods. Payroll is often insured on the dual basis and sometimes (although rarely) fully included in the gross profit cover. Attention is paid to local employment legislation, including redundancy payments regulations.

Suppliers' and customers' extensions are generally available with top limits of 50 per cent. of the sum insured for specified and 10 per cent. for unspecified suppliers, and customers' extensions restricted to named customers only.

The use of deductibles and loss limitations is rare. Advance profits can be written for fire and allied perils or for contractors all risks perils, with a time exclusion for testing and commissioning, but it is not a familiar form of cover throughout the Carribbean.

Industrial all risks is available in Barbados but is not popular in other islands except where U.S. companies provide it. A wide range of special perils is available including windstorm. The provision of engineering covers is not uniform throughout the Carribbean although cover can usually be obtained on a U.K. or U.S. (or perhaps Swiss or German) basis. In a similar manner computer insurances are written by some and not written by others depending perhaps on whose advice (U.K. insurers, etc.) is being taken.

Losses are usually handled on the U.K. system of independent loss adjusters. For the larger, catastrophic, losses (the results of windstorm damage, etc.), loss adjusters come from the United Kingdom and elsewhere. Accountants will often be involved.

74. South America

South America ranks fourth in area among the continents but only fifth in size of population. There are 10 large independent republics—Argentina, Bolivia, Brazil, Chile, Colombia, Ecuador, Paraguay, Peru, Uruguay and Venezuela. Although originally ruled by either Spain or Portugal, these countries have, in varying degrees, adopted the U.K. or the U.S. forms of business interruption insurance (often both), depending on the extent of commercial influence from either of those nations. Little guidance could be provided by their former colonisers for reasons given in the commentaries on the Spanish and Portuguese markets (see paragraphs 78(l) and (m)).

Business interruption insurance is written mostly in Argentina, Brazil, Chile, Colombia, Peru, Uruguay and Venezuela.

(a) *Argentina*

Business interruption insurance mainly follows U.K. practices, but U.S. covers are available. Although there is a tariff for property insurance there is no such control over business interruption covers. Maximum indemnity periods can be from one to 36 months. Cover is usually in respect of net profit plus insured standing charges. Policies are subject to average. Payroll (wages) cover can be written on the dual basis reflecting to an extent obligations under labour laws.

Although the market is reasonably professional in its handling of business interruption risks, difficulties can occur because of such factors as high inflation, currency exchange problems and the integration of Argentinian insured into international programmes made complicated by the restrictions put on reinsurance by the national reinsurance institute (I.N.D.E.R.).

(b) *Brazil*

Business interruption insurance is written on the U.K. system (and very profitably in recent years with loss ratios of less than 20 per cent.). There is a tariff with rates and policy conditions set by the Brazilian Reinsurance Institute (I.R.B.). U.S. covers are not written but special covers may be written with the particular authority of the I.R.B.

Gross profit is defined as net profit plus insured standing charges, with payroll written as a standing charge or on the dual basis (wages only): due provision is normally made for statutory obligations. All policies are subject to average and there is no restriction on the length of maximum indemnity periods.

Suppliers' and customers' extensions are available on the U.K. basis, but advance profits insurance is not written. Deductibles are always imposed on petrochemical risks, there is a standard 48 hours deductible in the policy and there is an option of 1 per cent. of sum insured for risks other than petrochemicals for which a premium discount of 12.5 per cent. is granted.

All risks policies have not been introduced but the normal list of perils can include "full" explosion (including boiler explosion) and electrical breakdown. Mechanical breakdown cover is available as a separate policy but a specialist computer policy is not yet on the market.

Losses are handled by independent loss adjusters.

(c) *Chile*

Forms in Chile follow the U.K. wordings generally but also show Swiss influences. U.S. covers are rarely seen. There is no tariff except for earthquake and the market is a free one.

Gross profit is defined either as net profit and insured standing charges or as turnover less uninsured (variable) charges. Payroll is covered in accordance with employee protection legislation. Rarely are policies not subject to average.

There is a growing demand for suppliers' and customers' extensions, but none for advance profits. Deductibles are used where necessary and are either monetary or time, but loss limitations are rare. All risks covers are not written, but mechanical and electrical breakdown covers are issued. Boiler explosion is, it seems, only requested by multinational companies. Computer covers are available.

Losses are dealt with by independent loss adjusters appointed by insurers working with a team of experts—accountants, engineers, etc. The insured usually have their own advisors.

(d) *Colombia*

This is a very active market which has developed well and, on the whole, profitably in the field of business interruption insurance. Both U.S. and U.K. forms are used but the U.K. form is preferred. There is a universal tariff controlling both U.S. and U.K. insurances which is under the control of the Banking Superintendency.

Gross profit is insured on the "difference" basis, with maximum indemnity periods from one to 36 months. Payroll (wages) can be written on the U.K. dual basis or on the various U.S. payroll bases (90, 180, etc., days). It is still possible to cover wages on a "period" or a "tiered" basis which are, in the U.K., early forms of tailor-made wages covers. Provision is made in wages sums insured for severance pay, pension reserves, etc. There is an average proviso in every policy.

Suppliers' and customers' extensions are written within the tariff rules. Advance profits is written on a normal U.K. form suitably adjusted, but the premium cost often reduces the cover to standing charges only. Time deductibles are used for machinery breakdown and may be used for fire business interruption covers in due course if monetary deductibles are not preferred.

All risks covers are generally not written, but all standard fire and allied perils are written. A point of interest is that because Colombia is subject to earthquakes, net profit and net earnings cannot be insured against loss by this peril; only standing charges can be insured. Boiler explosion is an extension of the fire policy, but mechanical and electrical breakdown risks are the subject of separate policies. There is a special form of insurance covering computers and other electrical apparatus.

Losses are nearly always handled by professional adjusters who work closely with the insured's own accountants. Loss assessors are rarely appointed by insured.

(e) Peru

This is a market which is largely government-controlled. Both U.S. and U.K. forms are used—gross earnings and gross profit—in accordance with the tariff.

Under the U.K. form maximum indemnity periods allowed by the tariff range from three to 12 months with extensions up to 36 months by special approval. Under the U.S. form 50 per cent., 60 per cent. and 80 per cent. coinsurance bases are available. All policies are subject to a form of average proviso.

Payroll is generally insured fully within the gross profit or gross earnings cover reflecting the difficulty with which workers can be discharged in the event of damage. Covers in respect of suppliers or customers are available specially. Deductibles can be applied as percentages of the insured amount (with appropriate discounts off the premium).

All risks insurance is rarely written but there is a long list of perils available including earthquake which is potentially the most catastrophic peril in Peru. Machinery breakdown is written specially under the tariff.

Losses are usually settled by independent adjusters.

(f) Uruguay

Although the cover is known in Uruguay the number of cases written is still relatively small. There are no set tariff regulations for rating, etc., but the (fire) tariff committee agrees each case submitted by private insurers. The State Insurance Organisation does not submit cases for rating. U.S. covers are not written.

Gross profit is normally defined on the "difference" basis and payroll is insured in full because of employment legislation. Maximum indemnity periods of any reasonable length are allowed, and there is an average proviso in every policy.

Suppliers' extensions are available to named suppliers, but there is no experience of customers' extensions. Nor is there any knowledge of advance profits. The market would be prepared, however, to consider both customers' extensions and advance profits covers. Deductibles and loss limitations are not used in Uruguay.

All risks covers are not available from private insurers. The normal list of perils written is fire, explosion, windstorm, impact and riot (fire). Engineering risks are not known but could be considered. There is no special computer policy.

With a small portfolio insurers' experience of serious business interruption losses is limited and independent loss adjusters would be called in—from Argentina, if necessary.

(g) *Venezuela*

Business interruption is a developing class of insurance in Venezuela. Although there is strict control for property damage insurance there is no tariff for business interruption insurance. The majority of covers (say 70 per cent.) are on the U.S. basis mainly because of the importance of U.S. commercial influence in Venezuela.

Gross profit, where this is the basis of the cover, is defined as net profit plus insured standing charges. Payroll (wages) covers are written on a restricted basis because there are no strong labour laws and can be for 90 days (U.S. basis) or on a dual basis (U.K.). All policies are subject to average.

Suppliers' and customers' extensions are available. Advance profits is little known but can be written subject to extensive facultative reinsurance support. Time deductibles are applied where necessary.

All risks cover is not available but an extensive list of perils can be written. Clearly earthquake, flood and other water damage are the perils which particularly concern local insurers. On the engineering side mechanical and electrical breakdown covers are available as is cover for boiler explosion. There is no special cover for computer risks.

Small losses are dealt with by local loss adjusters but large losses are usually handled by international loss adjusters, often from the United Kingdom.

75. Australasia

Australasia is part of the area known as Oceania which comprises Australia, New Zealand, Papua New Guinea and the islands of the South Pacific. The two largest commercial and industrial territories are clearly Australia and New Zealand.

(a) *Australia*

The Australian market has always been closely aligned to the United Kingdom as far as business interruption insurance is concerned. However, the tariff ceased to regulate property damage and business interruption rating, wordings, etc., in 1973 since when the market has developed on pragmatic lines. It has now evolved an industrial special risks insurance policy which is used (perhaps with some variations introduced by brokers) as a standard wording for most insurers in Australia and contains both a "Material Loss or Damage" Section and a "Consequential Loss" Section.

Standard items under the "Consequential Loss" cover relate to loss of gross profit (defined on the "difference" basis), professional fees, etc., for preparation of claims (under both Sections of the policy), payroll (on the dual basis) and increase in cost of working (not otherwise recoverable under the policy). The cover provided is subject to an average proviso and there would appear to be no restriction in the length of maximum indemnity period.

Payroll is defined as "the remuneration (including but not limited to payroll tax, bonuses, holiday pay, workers' compensation premiums and/or accident compensation levies, superannuation and pension fund contributions and the like) of all employees". Covers other than dual basis are available and the extent of cover takes due account of Australian employment legislation.

The wording also includes the following memoranda—departmental clause, new business, accumulated stocks, salvage sale and the turnover/output alternative. These are indications of the inherent flexibility of the basic cover which are not always regarded as necessary to include in a U.K. wording.

U.S. covers are issued in Australia but these are predominantly for U.S. commercial or industrial concerns.

Suppliers' and customers' extensions are provided where required. Extensions provided within the standard policy are to public utilities ("on or immediately adjacent to the premises"), to computer installations utilised by the insured anywhere in Australia and to "premises in the vicinity (prevention of access)".

Advance profits is written with caution, usually for future rental risks. Deductibles are also used, in all their forms, depending on the risk. There is a small deductible on the policy in respect of any one event arising out of earthquake, subterranean fire or volcanic eruption.

The industrial special risks insurance policy is on an all risks basis. There is, however, a substantial list of both property and perils exclusions. As in the United Kingdom loss resulting from the explosion of boilers or economisers is excluded from the "Material Loss or Damage" Section but is not excluded from the "Consequential Loss" Section.

Separate mechanical breakdown covers can be provided but covers for electrical breakdown are rarely given. A form of boiler explosion cover is included in the special risks policy. Separate policies can be issued for computers or the cover can be incorporated in the special risks policy.

Claims are usually handled by independent loss adjusters.

(b) *New Zealand*

Historically the New Zealand market has closely followed U.K. principles. There are virtually no U.S. type covers written. Regulatory tariffs are forbidden by law. A basic Industrial Special Risks (I.S.R.) cover—similar in intent to that issued in Australia—is used by all insurers, with variations introduced by brokers where necessary.

Cover in respect of gross profit is usually defined on the "difference" basis. Payroll is covered in a variety of ways—fully (within gross profit), by dual basis or in lieu of notice basis—depending not so much on legal requirements as on the decision of the insured.

Insurers are willing to provide cover for outside dependencies. I.S.R. policies include automatic extensions to suppliers, customers, utilities, transit and storage situations, prevention of access, etc., in New Zealand, subject sometimes (for the larger risks) to a limit of say 10 per cent. of sums insured. Otherwise there are no ceilings for such extensions, in New Zealand or overseas, except for earthquake in respect of Japanese dependency risks.

Advance profits cover is available but few insurers will write it on contractors' all risks business. The use of deductibles and loss limitations generally is not wide but some insurers do actively seek to impose substantial monetary (or even time) deductibles where the risks call for them.

Not all policies are subject to average. Those which are not are often subject to an "upwards adjustment" clause so that an adequate premium can be collected.

The I.S.R. policy is a form of all risks cover the perils being accidental loss or damage with a modest (compared with the Australian policy) list of exclusions, boiler, etc., explosion, and earthquake (which includes earthquakes, fire or shock; volcanic eruption, hydrothermal activity, landslip, tsunami or tidal wave; and rainwater damage following earthquake). Although the New Zealand government provides indemnity against damage caused by earthquake (fire and shock), as well as other defined catastrophe perils (under the Earthquake and War Damage Act, 1944), only property damage claims are paid and then only for indemnity values. Cover in respect of the difference between indemnity and reinstatement, and business interruption insurance must be arranged with an insurance company.

Both mechanical and electrical breakdown covers are available. Special computer covers, on loss of revenue or increased costs, are issued in response to an awareness of risk, particularly in regard to loss of data.

Most policies for exporters include cover in respect of the loss of increased exports incentive or export performance incentive tax deductions. These are deductions provided for under the Income Tax Act in New Zealand to encourage exports and are related to the increase in export sales in a particular year by comparison with the average figure over a stipulated three years period. If as the result of an interruption of an insured's business through the operation of an insured peril export sales are curtailed there will be a resultant loss of incentive tax deduction which would otherwise have been earned. Similar tax relief schemes exist in other countries—for example in the Republic of Ireland (see paragraph 78(i)).

The adjustment of business interruption insurance losses is almost always carried out by independent loss adjusters, experienced in the subject, who are appointed by insurers. It is sometimes stated in the policy that such appointment will be made with the mutual agreement of the insured.

76. Africa

The continent of Africa which stretches from the Mediterranean down to South Africa contains many markets the more advanced, from the point of view of business interruption insurance, being those previously under the influence of the U.K. (and to an extent France—Cameroun, Gabon, Ivory Coast, Morocco, Senegal, Togo). In some markets (Libya, Mozambique, Tanzania, Zambia) there is full "nationalisation" of the insurance industry (by compulsory insurance with a national corporation) and guidance often comes from the major international professional reinsurance organisations.

The following comments relate to South Africa, Kenya and Zimbabwe which are relatively free markets.

(a) *South Africa*

This is a well-developed business interruption insurance market befitting a highly industrialised economy. Covers written are essentially on the U.K. basis and no U.S. covers are available. There is no tariff but there is an agreed market wording which is usually part of a property damage and business interruption combined policy.

The majority of covers written are for gross profit either on a net profit plus insured standing charges or on a "difference" basis. There are some special policies on revenue in respect of mining, farming, etc., risks. All policies are subject to average and there would appear to be no restriction on the length of maximum indemnity periods.

Payroll is either fully insured within gross profit or on the dual basis (wages). Pro rata wages cover (for a limited number of weeks) can also be given. Regard is paid to employment protection legislation.

Suppliers' and customers' extensions are available, usually restricted to a limit of a percentage of sum insured. Advance profits covers are written, but often subject to a substantial time deductible. Deductibles used elsewhere are usually monetary except for extensions to public utilities and engineering covers. Little use is made of loss limitations.

All risks covers are available, particularly for large insured. Otherwise the usual perils are fire, explosion, storm, etc., earthquake and malicious damage. There is an exclusion of loss following damage caused by a peril either insured by the South African Special Risks Insurance Association (S.A.S.R.I.A.—a special government insurance pool, established in 1979 and run by private insurers) or which could be insured by S.A.S.R.I.A., or which but for the situation of the property could be insured by S.A.S.R.I.A. A particular peril which has been insured by S.A.S.R.I.A. is that of "political" riot. However this cover is in respect of loss of or damage to property only; no cover is provided for consequential or indirect loss of any kind or description whatsoever other than loss of rent if specifically insured. Private insurers have not themselves provided this cover (it has only been sometimes available in the Lloyd's market) and political developments in South Africa make it difficult always to be up to date with attitudes towards its provision.

Engineering covers are available for mechanical and electrical breakdown and boiler explosion. An all risks cover is written for computer risks in response to the growing recognition among businessmen of the importance of such systems.

In most instances independent loss adjusters are employed by insurers to handle claims. It is unusual for insured to employ an independent loss assessor.

(b) *Kenya*

U.K. influence introduced business interruption insurance into Kenya where it is written on a steady if unexciting basis. There are no tariff regulations but in effect rates need to be approved by the Kenya Reinsurance Corporation to whom 20 per cent. of all business written in Kenya must be ceded. Only rarely is a U.S. type cover written.

Gross profit is defined on the "difference" basis and payroll is insured either fully as part of gross profit or on the dual basis, taking account of employment legislation. All policies are subject to average, and there would appear to be no limitation on the length of maximum indemnity periods.

Suppliers' and customers' extensions are written, as is advance profits, in carefully selected cases. Deductibles are rarely used except for engineering covers (time) and all risks (money). No use is made of loss limitations.

An all risks cover is available but policies are usually issued on a fire and special perils basis. Mechanical and electrical breakdown and boiler explosion covers are written. Computer risks are usually insured for mechanical or electrical breakdown on an increased costs basis.

Losses are handled by local independent loss adjusters.

(c) *Zimbabwe*

This market is still developing but its roots lie in U.K. influences. There is no tariff for business interruption insurance but some control over rating comes from the rule that 20 per cent. of all business must be ceded to the Zimbabwe Reinsurance Corporation.

Gross profit is defined either on a net profit and insured standing charges or a "difference" basis. Payroll is normally insured fully within gross profit. Average is applied on all policies. There is no limit on the length of maximum indemnity periods although six to 12 months is considered adequate by some insured who almost certainly underestimate the extent of their risks.

Advance profits insurance is written with caution as are extensions to other premises except for storage or transit. There is often an exclusion of liability for a prolongation (see also paragraph 44) of the interruption period due to delay in the replacement or repair of the property destroyed or damaged where such delay results from import and/or export restrictions, customs regulations, currency restrictions or any other regulations imposed by a Government or public or local authority.

Usual covers are on a fire and special perils basis. Some engineering policies are written but boiler explosion is available under the fire policy.

Losses are dealt with by independent loss adjusters and claims can only be settled under Zimbabwean jurisdiction.

77. Asia

Asia is the largest of the continents comprising one-third of the Earth's land mass and containing one-half of the world's population. Although there is widespread poverty certain areas are very dynamic and are developing commercially at an astonishing rate. Ethnic and religious attitudes have made it difficult for European or American insurance philosophies to gain footholds but industrial and commercial progress has brought with it the need for more sophisticated insurance protection including business interruption coverage.

The region which has developed fastest recently is the Far East with the highly commercialised and industrialised territories of Hong Kong, Japan, South Korea and Singapore in the forefront. Other territories such as Indonesia, Malaysia, the Philippines, Taiwan and Thailand have also developed well, their strength often being based on the exploitation of their rich natural resources (oil, gas, rubber, minerals, etc.) which require specialised forms of business interruption insurance protection.

India and Pakistan must also be mentioned among markets which are strictly outside the Far East region. Their insurance methods are derived from U.K. practices and business interruption insurance is freely written in both countries although perhaps not on as sophisticated a basis as in the United Kingdom.

Middle Eastern countries write business interruption insurance, particularly where the industry to be protected has an international sales base such as oil and petrochemical, chemical, aluminium, etc., production.

Particular comment follows on Hong Kong, Japan, South Korea and Singapore.

(a) *Hong Kong*

Despite the intense business activity in Hong Kong (involving the maximum utilisation of plant and machinery), demand for business interruption insurance protection is low. Larger organisations will seek full cover while others prefer the simplicity of increased costs only cover. Policies are usually U.K. type with very few U.S. wordings issued. There is no tariff system.

Gross profit is usually defined on the "difference" basis although the net profit plus insured standing charges basis is still sometimes used. Payroll is insured on whatever basis suits the insured best (100 per cent. payroll, dual basis wages, notice wages, etc.,) with local employment legislation being rudimentary and having little influence on the cover sought. All full covers (on gross profit, gross revenue, gross rentals, etc.,) are subject to average and there would appear to be no restriction on the length of maximum indemnity periods.

Suppliers' and customers' extensions are available, usually on a named but sometimes on an unspecified basis, after due consideration of the circumstances. Deductibles are rarely used except for extensions to public utilities where time deductibles of 24, 36 or 72 hours are applied. There is little evidence of loss limitations being employed. Advance profits is written where required—on loss of gross profit, gross rentals, etc.,—with restrictions for periods of testing and commissioning.

All risks covers are issued occasionally but usually the cover is for fire and special perils (aircraft, bush fire, earthquake, explosion, impact, sprinkler leakage, typhoon windstorm and flood, burst pipes, riot and strike, malicious damage, etc., and including sometimes subsidence, landslip and all water damage). Boiler explosion cover can be written as well as mechanical and electrical breakdown (particularly in respect of computer covers).

A pragmatic attitude is often taken to the settlement of claims. Usually loss adjusters are appointed by insurers but where the circumstances of the interruption are clearly understood insurers will often accept the position and settle directly with the insured on an agreed compromise basis.

(b) *Japan*

This market has written business interruption insurance since 1939 when, among other considerations, it took advice from the Fire Offices Committee in London and adopted a basically U.K. form of policy wording. The form was revised in 1959, still on the U.K. basis, and again in 1981 when some regard was taken of U.S. gross earnings forms. There is a strict tariff with ultimate control of all insurance resting in the hands of the Ministry of Finance.

Covers are available for normal commercial and industrial risks on a gross profit (net profit plus insured standing charges) basis; for service risks, *e.g.* newspapers, hospitals, banks, etc., on an extra expenses basis; for smaller retail stores, restaurants, etc., on a specialised basis; and for owners of apartment houses, etc., on a loss of rent basis. The first three covers are written on separate policies while the loss of rent is written by endorsement to a fire policy.

All policies are subject to average. The longest maximum indemnity period allowed is 12 months and it is possible to limit the indemnity period further by applying the U.S. idea of termination, *i.e.* at the time of completion of the restoration of the insured property.

Suppliers' and customers' extensions are available with a percentage limit overall (based on the highest dependency) of at least 50 per cent. Advance profits is not written. Deductibles are imposed for certain perils, *i.e.* for electrical damage, strikes, riot and civil commotion, and malicious damage—48 hours; and for wind, hail, snow and flood—72 hours.

No all risks covers are written. Standard perils are fire, lightning and explosion with special perils available being windstorm, hail, snow, flood, strikes riot and civil commotion, malicious damage, aircraft, impact, burst pipes, electrical damage and glass damage. There is of course restricted earthquake cover, the extent and cost of which depends on the situation in Japan of the insured risk. Mechanical and electrical breakdown cover is written as an endorsement to the material damage policy. Boiler explosion cover can also be written. Special computer covers are written with a combination of fire and machinery perils.

Loss assessment is usually based on an accountant's report.

(c) *South Korea*

Business interruption insurance has been written in the Republic of Korea only since the early 1970s but shows signs of development. U.S. forms are more commonly used because of early U.S. influence although U.K. wordings are used for engineering insurances. It is a controlled market with the national reinsurers regulating rating, etc.

Gross earnings forms are used (manufacturing and non-manufacturing), with payroll normally fully insured. A coinsurance or contribution clause is contained in every policy.

Suppliers' and customers' dependency risks are catered for by the use of U.S. contingent business interruption forms. These are particularly important for the Korean petrochemical industry where cover must be extended to the premises of the suppliers of oil and electrical power and to the ethylene producers as customers.

Advance profits is written usually within specialised erection or contractors all risks policies arranged by foreign insurers. Deductibles are used particularly for the heavy, continuous process industries where time deductibles of up to 60 days may be applied.

All risks covers are available but otherwise the range of perils is usually restricted to fire and special perils and mechanical and electrical breakdown. Boiler explosion can be covered. Engineering covers are normally written on a U.K. form, but computer covers are written on a German electronic equipment policy, usually for increased costs only.

Losses are usually handled by independent loss adjusters appointed by the insurers.

(d) *Singapore*

This is a developing market which has become very interested in business interruption insurance of recent years. U.K. type covers are written although some U.S. policies may be issued by U.S. insurers. There are no tariffs.

Gross profit is defined on the "difference" basis. Wages are usually insured on the dual basis with salaries as an insured standing charge, but the whole of payroll can be insured as a standing charge. Laws on employment protection, redundancy payments, etc., are influential. All policies are subject to average. There is no restriction on the length of maximum indemnity periods.

Suppliers' and customers' extensions are given reasonably freely with unspecified suppliers' cover restricted to a low percentage limit (*e.g.* 10 per cent. of sum insured). Advance profits is provided on a very cautious basis. Deductibles can be used, normally on a monetary basis, except for extensions to public utilities where time deductibles are used.

An all risks cover is available although the usual list of perils is fire, lightning, explosion, aircraft, impact, burst pipes, earthquake, windstorm, flood, extended flood, riot, strike, malicious damage and sprinkler leakage. Mechanical breakdown is written as well as boiler explosion, and computer insurances are normally provided for revenue, additional expenditure and the reconstitution of data.

Losses are usually handled by independent loss adjusters assisted by accountants where the loss is substantial and the accounting systems complex.

78. Western Europe

The countries of Western Europe, including the United Kingdom and the Republic of Ireland, have a long history of industrial and commercial development. Business interruption insurance however has developed to markedly different degrees in the various markets of the overall area. In each of the markets where it is written extensively it has its own identity and its own inbuilt procedures but throughout most of the region the turnover/gross profit basis is in common use in one way or another on very similar lines to traditional U.K. practice.

The following is a brief comment on practices and procedures in the countries of Western Europe.

(a) *Austria*

Business interruption insurance is available in Austria, although it is not widely written. There are general agreements on rating and insurance conditions which are regulated by the Bureau of Insurance Control at the Federal Ministry of Finance and are subject to the law of the land.

The normal method of insuring income is on the basis of net profit plus standing charges (including salaries and wages): the "difference" basis has not yet been adopted as it has in other European countries. Maximum indemnity periods are usually 12 months, or less, although longer periods are available. Many policies include time deductibles. All policies are subject to average.

Outside dependency extensions are not available; advance profits is not written; there are no industrial all risks covers; and U.S. business interruption insurance is not purchased in Austria.

Machinery breakdown covers are written, including business interruption with a maximum indemnity period of 12 months and time deductibles. There is also a separate computer cover on an increased cost of working basis with the maximum indemnity period measured in working days, subject to an agreed time deductible.

Loss adjustment in Austria is similar in procedure to that in Germany with the use of independent experts in accordance with the general policy conditions.

(b) *Belgium*

There is a market for business interruption insurance in Belgium but because it is heavily influenced by foreign insurers and reinsurers no truly standard Belgian approach to matters such as policy wordings, rating or risk assessment exists on the fire side. Greater stability exists on the machinery breakdown side as there are fewer insurers and greater control from reinsurers.

Net profit plus standing charges has been the traditional method of insuring gross profit but the "difference" basis is becoming more popular. Salaries are always insured as a standing charge. One week pro rata basis cover is usually sufficient for wages to deal with statutory requirements but dual basis wages is also frequently used. Maximum indemnity periods tend on the whole to be short and probably inadequate. Policies are usually subject to a form of average provision although first-loss, valued, *per diem* indemnity basis covers are often issued for shops, restaurants, etc.

Little interest is shown in extensions of cover to suppliers, customers, etc., nor is there any real demand for advance profits cover. Industrial all risks covers are issued for material damage and it is likely that the demand will spread to business interruption. U.S. business interruption policies are usually issued only to U.S. industrial and commercial insured and then as part of an international programme of insurance. Deductibles and loss limitations do not appear in Belgian fire business interruption policies.

Machinery breakdown covers follow the same format as far as fire but time deductibles are always imposed. Computer increased costs covers are also issued as an engineering cover.

Accountants are employed by insurance companies to calculate losses.

(c) Denmark

The majority of industrial and commercial organisations in Denmark enjoy business interruption insurance and have done so for many years. Insurance companies use mutually agreed standard policy conditions: until about 1980 there was a form of tariff but this was dissolved.

Although there are still a few policies which define gross profit on the net profit plus standing charges basis, there has been a general change since about 1975 to the "difference" basis. Direct wages are often insured by a separate item for a predetermined percentage of the annual wages expenditure. Policies are usually subject to an average provision.

Maximum indemnity periods vary from six to 24 months. If an actual indemnity period does not exceed 30 days an eight hour time deductible is imposed. Where the maximum indemnity period is at least 12 months, the insured has the right following damage to request a delay of up to six months from the date of the damage in the commencement of the indemnity period. This right must be exercised within 14 days of the damage and the insured must name the hour and day when the indemnity period should begin. This facility recognises the benefit to the insured of the use of accumulated stocks to maintain turnover (refer paragraph 246 for the U.K. approach).

U.S. business interruption insurance covers are not written in Denmark nor are industrial all risks covers except in a few special cases. Deductibles, other than the standard time excess, are arranged for individual covers on a percentage of loss basis but usually with fixed minimum and maximum monetary amounts. Loss limitations are rarely found but can be stated as a percentage of sum insured.

Advance profits covers are not written as such but due care is taken in projecting sums insured to deal with future business developments. Suppliers and customers extensions are given. Machinery breakdown policies are issued on a similar basis to the fire policies but with the premium calculated with reference to key machinery. Computer covers are in respect of increased costs and re-establishment of data.

Claims are usually assessed by the insurance companies' experts in co-operation with the insured and the insured's accountants.

(d) Finland

The insurance of business interruption is highly specialised in Finland and the amount written has grown considerably over the last decade or so. There is no tariff control but because of the nature of the market a single company, Otso, owned by a consortium of leading insurance companies, writes the vast majority of all business interruption insurances and applies its own rules, derived from its experience and developed expertise in this class.

Gross profit is now generally defined on the "difference" basis but it is possible to insure those variable charges that do not vary strictly in line with a variation in turnover as a separate item. Wages cover is purchased as a percentage of annual wages, the usual practice being to select a percentage in excess of the minimum demanded by legislation. The normal maximum indemnity period is 12 months. Most covers are subject to a form of average: policies on very large risks contain a sum insured adjustment provision—50 per cent. decrease, 20 per cent. increase—to allow insured a degree of flexibility. Some sums insured are on an agreed amount basis. The U.S. business interruption basis is not used in Finland.

Otso is prepared to provide extensions to both suppliers and customers, subject to separate maximum loss limits. An increasing number of these covers is being written. Advance profits has been developed by Otso on special conditions which include the restriction of the cover to standing charges (interest costs, etc.) only, *i.e.* no cover on anticipated net profit. These policies are also proving to be popular.

Industrial all risks covers are now written both generally and specifically for computer policies and certain engineering policies in respect of all plant and machinery used by the insured. Normally, mechanical breakdown covers are in respect of specified machines (*e.g.* turbines) and the gross profit derived from their use. Computer policies are usually on an additional expenditure basis (with a loss limit) but sometimes full gross profit is insured for the larger computer service centres.

There is always a deductible in every policy. Time deductibles have been used most frequently, but the percentage (of sum insured) variety is becoming more popular. For some industrial all risks covers, a monetary deductible has been introduced which is subject to an annual aggregate. Loss limitations are found in some very large covers and in industrial all risks policies.

There are no loss adjusters in Finland. Instead, Otso employ technical specialists who concentrate on the minimisation of the loss and the most efficient handling of the repair or replacement of damaged or destroyed plant, machinery, etc. Accountants who are experienced in this field are also employed to assist in the calculation of the loss and to be responsible for the settlement of the claim.

(e) *France*

The market has developed significantly since the early 1970s, before which a narrowly-based portfolio had suffered a number of very large losses. This growth has been assisted by deliberate advertising by the Assemblée Plenière des Sociétés d'Assurances (French Fire Offices' Committee) and through the efforts of brokers although even now, less than 20 per cent. of industrial and commercial concerns purchase the cover. In 1979, following the French government's Free Market Commission report, the rating of property damage and business interruption covers by tariff agreements became advisory only and not binding on any insurer in France.

There is a standard form for industrial risks (other more simplified forms are used for small businesses, etc.) which is used by all insurers. The U.S. business interruption form is not used, except in very exceptional circumstances. Until recently gross profit had been defined as net profit plus standing charges, but with the introduction in 1984 of a new standardised European accounting system the definition in the General Policy Conditions was changed to the difference between turnover and variable charges. The current trend is also towards the insurance of total payroll, although partial covers are still written, in particular by the "option" method which equates with the U.K. dual basis wages system. Suppliers' extensions are provided but requests for customers' extensions are usually resisted.

Advance profits insurance is usually only provided as a machinery breakdown cover or as part of contractors all risks covers.

Deductibles are often used on major risks. They are always expressed as a monetary figure (or as a percentage of declared gross profit) except for losses resulting from "electrical" damage where there is a time excess of a minimum of three days. Similarly, covers are often subject to an upper limit of indemnity in respect of any one loss, but where this is applied there is usually a discount in the rate.

The standard form contains an average condition. However, the sum insured on gross profit can be adjusted upwards by 20 per cent. in the event of loss. In effect a deposit premium is paid on 100/120ths of the policy liability and is adjusted at the end of the insurance year either by rebate of up to 50 per cent. or further payment of premium not exceeding 20 per cent. of that already paid. Average applies if 120 per cent. of the sum insured proves to be inadequate. It is possible, however, for a form to be issued with a waiver of average. In this case a deposit premium is paid which is adjusted without limitation on the actual gross profit declared for the year. The amount of cover is restricted to the sum insured, or where appropriate the policy limit of indemnity (refer paragraph 53 for comparison with the Declaration-Linked wording introduced in the United Kingdom in 1982).

Insurances on an industrial all risks basis have been virtually prohibited except for very specific situations—big distribution companies. Engineering business is handled similarly to fire, although the assessment of risk is based on a careful analysis of the importance of key machinery. Specific computer risks can be insured by a machinery breakdown policy with the cover extended to cover extra costs where the computer function is solely for administrative purposes; where computers are used for process-control full gross profit cover is arranged with the fire risks provided by the fire business interruption policy.

An interesting development occurred in July 1982 with the introduction in France of legislation relating to the insurance of natural catastrophes. A compulsory surcharge is levied on all property damage and business interuption policies and insurers are required to indemnify losses in the event of a catastrophe being declared by the government—the word "catastrophe" is not defined. Further legislation in 1983 required insurers to offer "criminal acts" (including riot, civil commotion, sabotage and terrorism).

Loss adjustment is usually by a system of "experts" appointed by both insurers and insured with a third "expert" appointed by the two parties if they are not in agreement. The three experts then work together to calculate the loss, with a majority decision operating if necessary.

There is an interesting variation in the standard French policy as regards the material damage proviso compared with that usually found in the United Kingdom (refer paragraph 16(a)). It stipulates that there be a "sufficiency" of material damage cover on the day of the loss and that, if there is not, then the business interruption loss payment will be reduced (on the ruling of "experts") on a pro rata basis measured against the degree of insufficiency of the material damage cover.

(f) *Germany*

Because of its advanced industrialisation the German Federal Republic writes almost as much business interruption insurance as the United Kingdom although perhaps there is not the same spread of risk. There is no strict tariff control, but guidelines are provided by the Association of Property Insurers and recommend certain bases of rating, etc., which most insurers would support so as to achieve a stable market and good underwriting results. All conditions used in business interruption forms must have the agreement of the German Insurance Supervisory Authority.

A form of "difference" wording is the basis of the definition of gross profit, with the cost of raw, etc., materials being excluded by a general condition of the policy along with such uninsured costs as sales tax, carriage outwards, insurance premiums dependent on turnover, royalties dependent on turnover, and others not connected with trading. Salaries and wages are covered as part of gross profit but can be insured as a separate item for a maximum indemnity period less than 12 months which is the obligatory minimum period for the insurance of gross profit. In general costs are indemnified only so far as continued expenditure is legally necessary or economically justifiable. Most policies are subject to average.

Outside dependency extensions are generally unavailable, except in special situations where an extension is allowed to named suppliers, subject to a maximum indemnity period (for the extension) of 12 months, a time deductible of 48 hours, a loss limit of no more than 10 per cent. per named supplier, and no premium rebate provision on declarations. Customers' extensions are not usually given.

Industrial all risks covers are not written at present; advance profits is not available (except possibly under erection covers); and U.S. business interruption insurance is rarely bought, mainly because the forms and conditions have not been officially approved.

The general conditions include a rule that the insurer is not liable for insignificant interruptions the consequences of which can be made good within the business without substantial expenditure. For insurances of a certain size (annual sums insured in excess of DM.750,000) a time franchise of 48 hours is agreed, without discount. Special time deductibles can be arranged for iron and steel works, at a discount, where there is a coverage on molten metal. Otherwise monetary deductibles can be agreed for discounts in accordance with a guide table, with the amount expressed as a percentage of the sum insured (or loss limitation).

Loss limitations are usually found only in covers on "large risks" (with an annual sum insured in excess of DM.50 million). There is a guide table of discounts for loss limitations up to a certain amount (DM.150 million) and surcharges if the limitation is higher.

Engineering breakdown policies are issued in accordance with relevant general conditions, and special covers on computers are also obtainable, again subject to relevant general conditions.

In the event of a claim, both insured and insurers can demand that the amount of the loss will be ascertained by "experts" working separately for each side with an "umpire" appointed to settle only differences of calculation.

The standard German policy also contains a proviso to the effect that insurers are not liable in so far as the business interruption loss is considerably increased (a) by extraordinary events taking place during the interruption, (b) by restrictions imposed by the authorities on the reconstruction or operation of the business, or (c) due to the insured's lack of sufficient capital, for timely restoration of property lost, destroyed or damaged. (See also paragraphs 16(a), 44 and 78(e).)

(g) *Greece*

This is a very underdeveloped market for business interruption insurance. Where cover has been arranged it has been largely by multinational companies with factories in Greece. There are consequently no tariff or market agreements as there are for property damage insurance.

Definition of gross profit is on the net profit plus standing charges basis, and wages cover is usually in respect of severance pay and/or the continued payment of key workers; legislation in Greece provides for the payment of one month's salary or wages following a catastrophe which results in the closure of the business. There is an average proviso in all policies.

Suppliers', customers', etc., extensions are given, but advance profits insurance is unknown. Deductibles are a feature of business interruption policies, usually as three to five day "waiting periods". No use is made of loss limitations.

Industrial all risks cover is prohibited because of the compulsory tariff for fire, earthquake, explosion, strike, riot and civil commotion property damage risks. Only computer insurances are on an all risks basis, less the tariff perils separately insured. There are no business interruption covers against engineering perils.

Loss adjustment is usually carried out by chartered accountants appointed by the insurers.

(h) *Holland*

There is a well-developed market in Holland for business interruption insurance. The market agreement between insurers which for many years had a stabilising influence on the market was abolished in line with the dissolution of the industrial fire tariff upon which it was based for rating purposes. Unofficial market agreements do, however, still exist.

Cover is usually in respect of net profit plus all standing charges which are incurred by the insured: a kind of reference list of common standing charges is often listed in the policy, with those (and others) insured which relate to the insured's trading. Where the insured interest is in terms of gross profit the definition is on the "difference" basis. Dutch industrial companies do not purchase U.S. business interruption covers. All policies are subject to average and there is no restriction on the lengths of maximum indemnity periods.

Payroll is fully insured as a standing charge, because insurers have accepted the situation that the obligation to pay wages during a period of interruption following insured damage is their responsibility and not that of the government. It would appear that the government has not attempted to argue against this view. Nevertheless dual basis wages cover is available for firms with large workforces.

Suppliers' and customers' extensions are available as is advance profits but there is no great enthusiasm for the latter. The use of deductibles is rare in Dutch business interruption contracts but where they appear they can be in terms of money, time, or percentage of sum insured. Loss limitations are only found in very large covers where there is a need to create additional market capacity.

Industrial all risks policies have not been introduced, reflecting the lack of interest generally in Europe, apart from a few markets. Boiler explosion is normally insured in the fire business interruption policy. Mechanical breakdown business interruption is written on the same lines as the fire business interruption policies. Separate covers are issued in respect of the loss arising from the breakdown of computers: these are usually on an additional expenses basis.

Losses are usually settled by an adjuster who possesses accountancy expertise. He will employ technical experts to fix reinstatement or replacement periods for buildings or machinery. It is also standard practice for the insured to appoint their own assessor who will negotiate with the adjuster on their behalf. Otherwise the system is similar to that followed in the United Kingdom.

(i) *Ireland, Republic of*

Practices and procedures in the Republic of Ireland tend to follow closely those of the U.K. market. In fact policies issued may contain virtually the same wordings. The only vital differences would appear to lie in the currency used, the jurisdiction applied and the terms of the arbitration condition where "all differences" may be referred and not merely the question of "amount".

A special cover has been established in respect of tax relief schemes. This is similar to the cover in New Zealand in respect of export tax relief (see paragraph 75(b)). A new low rate of tax on profits was introduced in 1981 for manufacturers, and because claims payments will attract the full rate, it has been regarded as essential that all business interruption covers issued in respect of manufacturing risks should also include an item on tax relief.

(j) *Italy*

There was never a great demand for business interruption insurance in Italy, but there has been some increase in the number of policies sold over the last decade or so as businessmen become less reluctant to disclose financial information to insurers. Perhaps 30 per cent. of industrial firms now purchase the cover in one form or another. U.S. business interruption insurance covers are quite popular with subsidiaries of U.S. commercial or industrial companies and are recommended by U.S. brokers to their Italian clients. There is no tariff but a Concordato (tariff organisation) committee exists for the provision of technical advice, wordings, etc.

The "difference" basis of turnover less uninsured variable charges is used most frequently, which incorporates the total insurance of salaries and wages within the gross profit cover. As in the United Kingdom, (see paragraph 205(a)), the dual basis wages method has become less popular as employee protection legislation has made it increasingly difficult to insure on a partial basis. All policies are subject to an average proviso, but a margin of extra cover is provided by a "leeway clause" which can add an agreed percentage to the sum insured; adjustment of premium at end of year is limited to 50 per cent. rebate or the chosen percentage additional.

Extensions to suppliers are normally provided but the market is not yet sufficiently sophisticated to show any significant interest in extensions to customers or in the insurance of advance profits. Deductibles are used extensively, in the form of either time or money. Limitations of loss are rarely introduced.

There has been some interest shown in industrial all risks covers and in the area of engineering business interruption insurances. Computer covers are usually limited to extra expenses.

Loss adjustment is carried out by certain independent firms of fire loss adjusters who have acquired a degree of specialist knowledge of business interruption claims. If necessary, assistance would be sought additionally from accountants and other experts.

(k) *Norway*

There is a very healthy business interruption insurance market in Norway. In fact, this form of cover is regarded as so important that many bank loans stipulate in their terms that not only should there be full material damage cover in force throughout the terms of the loan but also full business interruption protection. There is no longer a tariff in force (dissolved at the end of 1982) partly because the market is now dominated by three or four large insurance groups. However, the general terms and conditions of the old Norwegian tariff union are still largely followed.

Gross profit is calculated on the "difference" basis, which superseded the previous net profit plus insured standing charges in 1967. Variable charges excluded from the cover can include 80 per cent. of wages to all hourly, daily or weekly paid workers, leaving 20 per cent. insured as a standing charge. Alternatively, wages can be wholly excluded from gross profit and insured separately for a 14 days minimum period (in accordance with the labour laws). Maximum indemnity periods for industrial risks usually vary from 12 to 24 months. There is always an average provision. Very little use is made of U.S. business interruption wordings.

All covers carry a deductible of at least 24 or 48 hours: occasionally monetary deductibles are used. Loss limitations are not used. Extensions to outside suppliers and customers are available, to the extent possible. Advance profits covers are not written. In the early 1980s, a form of industrial all risks was introduced with extended perils in respect of fire, burglary, "water" and fire following electrical faults but excluding cover for elemental perils. Mechanical breakdown policies are issued for individual items of machinery and for complete installations and are usually subject to a seven day deductible. There is a special policy form for computer cover.

Independent loss adjusters are not used in Norway. Instead claims are settled by representatives from the insurance company and the insured. In the case of complicated losses insurers employ specialists as consultants; and in some other cases insurers and insured choose a consultant each and the two consultants then settle the amount of the claim.

(l) *Portugal*

Over recent years there has been an increase in the number of business interruption insurance policies issued but there is still no great demand for this form of cover. The U.K. form is followed, with the usual U.K. multipliers (refer paragraph 256(a)) being used for rating purposes. The basis rates are taken from the official fire tariff but there is no official tariff for business interruption. Maximum indemnity periods range from three to 24 months.

Gross profit is defined either on the "additions" basis (net profit plus insured standing charges) or on the "difference" basis (turnover less uninsured variable charges). Wages are covered generously, reflecting the extent of the employee protection legislation. In the event of a prolonged shutdown of a factory following damage, wages or redundancy payments receive preferential treatment under the law. There is always an average provision. Suppliers' and customers' extensions are possible, depending on the nature of the particular circumstances. U.S. gross earnings covers are available but they are normally issued only as part of an international programme of covers for a U.S. company.

Policies can be written with deductibles which are usually on a time basis. Engineering covers normally carry a deductible of 48 hours. Advance profits insurance is not known in the Portuguese market; nor is there an all risks cover available, but basic "fire" covers can be "extended" to include explosion, aircraft, water damage, windstorm, sprinkler leakage, riot and strike and civil commotion, vandalism and malicious mischief, flood and earthquake.

Use is made of independent loss adjusters (who have their own accountancy, etc., experts) for the settlement of claims.

(m) *Spain*

The development of business interruption insurance in Spain remains at a very low level, partly because not all insurance companies have the government's authority to write this form of cover, and partly because of the Spanish businessman's natural reluctance to disclose trading figures. There was an attempt in the mid-1970s to create a tariff and perhaps to expand therefrom but this came to naught. Consequently it is usually only the very big risks that are protected in this way, with consequent large exposures.

The usual definition of gross profit is net profit and insured standing charges. Cover for wages and salaries is fully included in accordance with social security, redundancy protection, etc., regulations. Standing charges are defined in the policy as "the expenses which do not vary in direct ratio to the activities of the business and which in consequence must be maintained despite a total or partial interruption in the operation caused by the damage". All policies are subject to an average proviso, but it is possible to incorporate an "adjustability" whereby losses are indemnifiable up to 125 per cent. of the sum insured.

It is possible to extend covers to suppliers' and customers' premises but such extensions are rare. Advance profits covers are not issued. Deductibles are used, sometimes in monetary terms but more often as time with a minimum period of three days. Loss limitations are not often found but can be introduced if necessary.

Machinery breakdown policies are issued with conditions in line with those for fire business interruption policies. There is no special policy form for the insurance of business interruption following damage to computers but it is possible for a cover to be issued in exceptional circumstances.

A form of industrial all risks cover has been introduced but its application is confined to certain large risks. In addition there exists in Spain a facility to provide cover for business interruption arising out of the operations of the so-called "Consorcio" perils written by a material damage policy. The "Consorcio de Compensacion de Seguros" is a government agency which administers a kind of national disaster fund. When an event is not deemed a national disaster the material damage insurers of the "Consorcio" perils may nevertheless declare the event a catastrophe loss payable by their policies. In these circumstances, the business interruption covers will also be regarded as liable, and it is even possible for the business interruption insurers to make payments in proportion to "Consorcio" payments when an event is, in fact, declared a national disaster. The "Consorcio" perils are "acts of a political or social nature, riot, disturbances or popular commotion, military force or measures in time of peace, flood, volcanic eruption, hurricane, seismic movement, landslide, other seismic or meteorological phenomena of an exceptional nature, and, in general, any cause of an unwonted nature not covered by an ordinary policy".

Another form of cover still exists in Spain called Paralizacion which is a form of percentage of fire loss cover and issued as an extension to a fire material damage policy. Payment under this policy is taken into account when settlement under a normal business interruption policy is calculated.

Loss adjusters exist in Spain, working closely in association with insurers.

(n) *Sweden*

Business interruption insurance is written extensively in Sweden and there is an acute awareness of the potential losses, both material damage and business interruption, that can arise from a major fire or explosion. There has not been a regulatory body in Sweden since the tariff union was dissolved in 1967, but the market is dominated by two large companies who thereby influence the manner in which business interruption insurance is dealt with.

Gross profit is defined on the "difference" basis and until recently there were particular variations of this definition in accordance with the type of business insured. Definition Classes A and B related to small businesses, with Class A being specifically for the one-man businesses with few variable charges deducted and the payment of wages and salaries treated as an insured charge, Class B treated wages as a variable charge and excluded them. Classes C and D were for larger industrial concerns, with Class C being based on the sales value of production and mostly used for processing industries, and Class D being based on the sale value of sold and delivered goods, and the definition most commonly used.

Worksheets (similar to those found in the U.S.) are used by insured to calculate gross profit for insurance, for end of year premium adjustment declaration and for claims formulation purposes. Deducted from insurable gross profit as an uninsured manufacturing cost are wages and attendant benefits. However wages are generally insured partly because of employee protection legislation and partly because of collective agreements between employers and employees. This is done by a separate cover for an arbitrary percentage of total wage costs, which reflects the insured's obligations, and which is never less than 20 per cent. The cover includes a proviso which states that the insured should make every effort to employ elsewhere in the business those employees whose services cannot otherwise be utilised because of the damage. In the event that the business suffers a consequent loss of "profitability", this loss is payable under the gross profit cover as an increase in cost of working. Average applies to the wages cover as it does to all business interruption covers in Sweden.

There have been developments towards full wages cover because of legislation and there is increasing use of the agreed value basis of insurance for gross profit with negotiated agreed values put on units of production. Extensions to suppliers and customers are freely available, as is advance profits in respect of buildings, etc., in course of erection. Industrial all risks covers have also been introduced and are popular. There are separate covers issued on machinery and on computers. Machinery business interruption is effected either on individual machines or on a total installation. Deductibles are negotiable but for individual machines there is usually a "waiting period" of seven days. Computer business interruption policies are either on a full gross profit basis or for increased costs only (depending on the importance of the equipment to the insured's business) subject to a deductible. No U.S. business interruption insurance is bought in Sweden.

Deductibles can be negotiated for the main business interruption covers. These are usually on the basis of an amount (the general system is for policies to carry a deductible amount which is 7 per cent. of a basic amount, indexed for annual inflation, so that in 1983 it was 7 per cent. of SK.19,000 and in 1984 7 per cent. of SK.20,300), a number of days (two, four or eight days "waiting period" before the indemnity period begins for certain high hazard industries) or a percentage of the sum insured. Loss limitations are not found in policies, insurers preferring to rely on active loss settlement procedures. Claims are in the main dealt with by the insurers themselves, although outside experts can be called in.

(o) *Switzerland*

Business interruption insurance is widely purchased in Switzerland. This was particularly true in the mid-1970s but there has been some retraction since then. There is strict control of wordings and rates. All general policy conditions and wordings must be approved by the Federal Office for Private Insurance Business and all rates must conform with the tariff of the Swiss Property Insurance Association.

Various methods are used to insure business interruption—Systems A, B, C and KT. Of these, System C relates to the insurance of manufacturing risks, and gross profit is defined on the "difference" basis. Cover is on a first loss basis with the insured freely choosing a sum insured between 10 per cent. and 80 per cent. of the gross profit amount. There is a declaration of gross profit every three years and this serves as the basis for an evaluation of adequacy of insurance: average will only be applied in the event of a loss if the gross profit achieved *at the time of the declaration* is higher than the amount declared, even if there has been an increase in gross profit between declaration date and the date of the loss.

Maximum indemnity periods can range from the usual 12 months up to 36 months, and groups of standing charges can be covered as separate items for different maximum indemnity periods; this latter rule also applies to salaries and wages cover.

Of the other three Systems, System A is primarily for seasonal businesses (hotels, etc.), is on a "full value" basis with gross profit defined as net profit plus insured standing charges, and is subject to annual adjustment of sum insured on declaration (thereby avoiding the strict application of average). Maximum indemnity periods can be of the order of one to three months. System B is a form of percentage of fire loss and usually found applied to warehouse risks. System KT is for small shops and traders, is in respect of gross profit defined on the "difference" basis, and has a sum insured chosen by the insured of between 5 per cent. and 60 per cent. of turnover, with the maximum indemnity period usually 12 months but possibly larger.

Deductibles are available, expressed as an amount and reflecting a certain percentage of the sum insured, but the authorities allow such low discounts that insured are normally not attracted. Suppliers' extensions are given for named suppliers but customers' extensions are not permitted. Advance profits covers are generally not available but insurers can provide them as long as they are extensions to existing contracts or in connection with a contractors all risks cover.

The U.S. gross earnings form is not available in Switzerland and industrial all risks covers are prohibited by the insurance authorities. There is a separate policy form for machinery breakdown business interruption with the indemnity based on an agreed amount per day during a period of interruption in output. There is also a special EDP form for business interruption following the electrical or mechanical breakdown of computer equipment.

Loss adjustment for large and/or complex claims is carried out by independent adjusters. Otherwise insurers settle claims directly with insured, but in case of non-agreement there is a facility for the appointment of experts who will assist in the resolution of the claim.

79. "Home Foreign" arrangements

Business interruption policies issued in the United Kingdom for business overseas, generally called either "standard overseas" or "home foreign" policies, follow very closely the principles applicable to insurances for business in the United Kingdom and incorporate specifications on similar lines to those dealt with later in this book. As compared with insurances in the United Kingdom (policy form in Appendix A) conditions are in general more stringent; the main differences in the policy terms and conditions are, briefly:

(a) the absence of cover for loss resulting from the explosion of boilers on the insured's premises;
(b) the immediate cessation of cover in respect of any part of the insured premises where there is increased risk due to a fall or displacement of a substantial part of the buildings caused by an insured peril;
(c) the exclusion of loss occasioned by or in consequence of the burning of property on the order of any public authority;
(d) the exclusion of loss occasioned by or in consequence of the burning, whether accidental or otherwise, of forests, bush, prairie, pampas or jungle and the clearing of lands by fire;
(e) the exclusion of loss resulting from damage by the insured perils occasioned by or in consequence of, directly or indirectly, volcanic eruption or other convulsion of nature, typhoon, hurricane, tornado, cyclone or other atmospheric disturbance, mutiny, martial law, etc.,;
(f) the exclusion of loss resulting from damage by the insured perils during abnormal conditions occasioned by earthquake, war, etc., or any of the occurrences in (e), except for damage which the insured shall prove happened independently of the existence of such abnormal conditions;
(g) notice must be given to the insurers of any increase in the fire insurance rate for the premises and additional premium paid;
(h) both insured and insurers have the option to terminate the policy at any time, with an appropriate refund of premium;
(i) the insurers will not be liable in respect of any claim after the expir-

ation of one year from the end of the indemnity period or, if later, three months from the date when liability is admitted by the insurers of the material damage, unless the claim is the subject of pending action or arbitration.

A specimen of the policy and conditions is given in Appendix T, paragraph 466.

As mentioned in paragraph 72 this form, which is also used as the basis for covers in certain countries outside the United Kingdom is subject to review at present and a revised version is awaited which is closer in concept to current United Kingdom practices.

80. World-wide cover arrangements

The growth of industrial concerns to embrace manufacturing and selling activities on a universal scale with subsidiary companies and factories operating in all parts of the world and the implications of regional areas of "common market" trading agreements have of recent years opened up the question of providing business interruption cover of almost limitless scope for holding companies. The advantages sought are simplicity, efficient arrangement and control at the centre and adequate but flexible overall cover. One suggested solution is a single business interruption policy for such a company to insure against loss arising from an interruption of trading activities at the premises of any member of the group organisation anywhere in the world or of any supplier or customer, including its effects on the earnings of other businesses within the group.

Such a policy would carry considerable benefits for both insured and insurers. But insurance on such lines entails obvious difficulties due to legislation in so many countries restricting the conduct of insurance business, financial dealings and transfers of currency, the variations in policy conditions, insurance practice and law in different parts of the world, and problems for insurers of premium rating commensurate with the risks involved as well as those of limits to the maximum liabilities they can carry. An initial step towards a global cover may well be a form of "European policy" to meet the circumstances and needs of members of the E.C. The practical political, legal and technical difficulties in this more limited sphere are less formidable than those which would have to be overcome for a world-wide cover and the Treaty of Rome allows freedom to offer services throughout the Community. The European directive on non-life insurance services adopted in 1988 should be law in all member states by 1992 and insurers should then be able to apply the "rules" of their own markets to risks in other E.C. states.

Although the provision in a single policy of the all-embracing cover desired by multinationals may not be easy at present, greater uniformity in the policy terms and insurance covers available throughout the E.C. would be a practical step forward. A "European business interruption policy" even in this limited sense would, as the countries of Europe come closer together in economic affairs, be advantageous to both insurers and insured and would certainly help multi-national groups in the arrangement of their insurance requirements.

Meanwhile in cases where an insured in the U.K. is not satisfied that policies for factories overseas are providing cover as adequate as those in this county would, insurers here issue a "Difference in Conditions" policy to make good shortcomings in each individual policy, usually a matter of dependency extensions (with a particular emphasis on the interdependency between group companies) and special perils.

Alternatively, a "master" policy can be issued centrally which would be the model for all local policies and which will provide the cover which local policies cannot (for whatever reason) provide themselves. Such a system involves central control, by the insured's holding or parent company over the arrangement of cover throughout the group world-wide and the co-operation of the local management of subsidiary companies in whatever country they are situated. (Refer also comments in paragraphs 382 and 446.)

Chapter 7

Gross Profit, Gross Earnings or Business Income: Specifications and Definitions—United Kingdom

81. Meaning of gross profit

Profit is a simple word of wide general usage but it is said that efforts to define this facile word have been the subject of more decisions in the courts than any other single financial issue, and as mentioned in the opening chapter of this book the meaning of gross profit as defined in a U.K. business interruption insurance specification may differ very materially from the gross profit brought down in an insured's trading accounts. This will become clear from Chapter 9 on Standing Charges and Variable Expenses in which it will be explained that the charges which are selected as components of gross profit for insurance purposes may exclude some items which are included in the gross profit of the accounts or, on the other hand, include some charges from the preceding manufacturing account or section of the trading account.

The definition in the current "difference" form of specification (see full specification in Appendix C, paragraph 449) reads:

"**Gross Profit**—the amount by which
  (1) the sum of the turnover and the amounts of the closing stock and work in progress shall exceed
  (2) the sum of the amounts of the opening stock and work in progress and the amount of the uninsured working expenses.
Note: The amounts of the opening and closing stocks and work in progress shall be arrived at in accordance with the Insured's normal accountancy methods, due provision being made for depreciation.

Uninsured Working Expenses—
  (1) Purchases (less discounts received);
  (2) Discounts allowed;
  (3)
  (4)   here are listed other
  (5)   }   variable charges appropriate
  (6)   to each particular
  (7)   case.
Note: The words and expressions used in this definition (other than wages) shall have the meaning usually attached to them in the books and accounts of the Insured."

In the older form of specification, introduced in 1939 as the recommended specification (see Appendix E, paragraph 451) and now superseded by the above, the definition reads:

"**Gross Profit**—The sum produced by adding to the net profit the amount of the insured standing charges or if there be no net profit the amount of the insured standing charge less such a proportion of any net trading loss as the amount of the insured standing charges bears to all the standing charges of the business."

82. Advantages of insuring composite gross profit

As explained in Chapter 4, clause (a) of the specification gives effect to the principle that the loss of gross profit consequent upon an Incident can be measured by applying to the shortage in turnover the anticipated rate of gross profit. The components of gross profit for this purpose, whichever of the foregoing definitions is used, are in effect the net profit earned by the business and the standing charges which it is decided to include in the insurance and the fact that they are combined without division in the sum insured and also in the rate of gross profit, carries certain important advantages.

(a) It avoids any confidential information such as the remuneration of directors or the amount of net profit having to be divulged to the insurers or shown in the policy where members of the insured's staff might see it.

(b) It allows for fluctuations in the amount either of individual standing charges or of the net profit from year to year without affecting the rate of gross profit, that is, their combined ratio to turnover, which will be brought into the calculation of a claim. Some variation from year to year in the relative amount of individual charges is a normal feature of most businesses, with a corresponding alteration in the balance left for net profit. But the ratio of the combined amount of charges and net profit to turnover is fairly constant over the years and as the combined rate is the one used for measuring a loss this method suitably provides for any annual fluctuations in the relative proportions of charges and net profit. This is not to suggest that because the rate of gross profit is reasonably static the amount of gross profit will not change from year to year. Even though the rate does not alter, annual changes in the total turnover will automatically produce a variation in the amount of gross profit.

(c) This method also provides for the appearance as a charge against revenue in one year's accounts of an item of a non-recurring nature such as exceptional expenditure on consultant's, architects' or legal fees. Although this will reduce the amount of net profit in that particular year the overall amount of net profit plus standing charges will be unaffected. Therefore in the following year with the same amount of gross profit the figure for net profit will return to normal. If an Incident were to occur in the interim the insured would quite rightly expect to be recouped at that normal rate of net profit as would have been forthcoming had the Incident not taken place. Because the loss is calculated by using a combined rate of gross profit taken from the accounts of the preceding year the insured would in fact be fully recompensed provided that the sum insured on gross profit was adequate. No deduction would be made under the savings clause, because that refers only to any reduction in the charges included in the insurance on gross profit "in consequence of the Incident" (see paragraph 51(b)); the reduction in respect of any non-recurring charge would have taken place had there been no Incident.

This self-balancing feature should be specially noted to avoid the mistake which is frequently made of omitting from the computation of the amount to be insured any item of a non-recurring nature such as those just mentioned, or of the excess beyond the usual amount of any charge which has been abnormally high during the year under consideration.

(d) The use of a composite figure takes care of the position when the production or sales of a business are expanding. Although the overall rate of gross profit may remain fairly constant, the ratio within it of standing charges may fall and that of net profit rise, perhaps very considerably. The insured is, however, adequately covered for the increase of net profit because the policy measures the loss after an Incident by using the rate of *gross* profit and is not concerned as to how this is apportioned as between charges and net profit.

83. "Difference" specification: uninsured working expenses

As explained in paragraph 6, the "difference" wording is virtually a reversal of the traditional net profit plus standing charges basis for defining and calculating the insurable gross profit. But even though standing charges are not mentioned in the newer form of specification and their key position is now occupied by their opposites, the uninsured working (or variable) expenses, the importance previously attached to them still remains.

Uninsured working expenses are the charges which it is considered will vary proportionately with rises or falls in turnover—the charges which are to be excluded from the gross profit insurance. They have to be specified in the definition of gross profit for each insurance. The list of them is almost invariably much shorter than the list of insured standing charges would be for the same business, a distinct advantage and one which greatly simplifies the future figure work in computing sums insured and in the production of accountants' certificates.

But the original compilation of the list involves going through all items in the accounts to decide which charges can, as variable expenses, be excluded from the insurance, in the same manner as would have had to be done to decide under the older form of specification which were to be included as standing charges.

It is probably most useful, therefore, to deal first with the definition of uninsured working expenses—or specified working expenses, or excluded variable expenses, which are alternative definitions used by many insurers—by briefly mentioning the charges which are most frequently included under it, leaving the detailed consideration of all other charges to Chapter 9 on Standing Charges and Variable Expenses.

84. List of uninsured working expenses

For most businesses the first item in the list of variable charges to be excluded from the insurance on gross profit will be *purchases* and this is intended to refer to purchases of direct materials and indirect, consumable, materials. It is not intended to relate to purchases of electricity and other utilities, and other services which should come under separate headings (refer also paragraph 234(a)—U.S. worksheets). Purchases are less discounts received, followed by discounts allowed, because these charges almost invariably rise or fall in strict ratio to turnover. This means that discounts received are, but discounts allowed are not, included in the gross profit—see paragraphs 85(b), 152 and 222 regarding discounts. The next item can be a proportion of the wage roll but in the U.K. such an item rarely appears since the virtually universal adoption of 100 per cent. payroll cover (refer paragraph 204). Carriage (other than own transport costs), freightage and packing materials are perhaps the charges which next appear most frequently in lists of uninsured working expenses but these should be mentioned only when they are strictly variable with turnover. (See paragraphs 154–156.)

There are several other charges such as those classified as "semi-variable costs" where flexible budgeting is employed as, for instance, repairs and renewals, power, fuel, and also commission, which may or may not be included according to the particular circumstances of a business. All these are dealt with individually in Chapter 9 but it may be noted here that cases do arise in large insurances in which it is impracticable to segregate some of the variables from the general factory overheads account. In such cases the insurers should be consulted in order that special provision may be made for an adequate cover to be arranged at an equitable premium cost.

The list of uninsured working expenses on a specification is concluded with a note to the effect that the words and expressions used in the definition (other than wages) shall have the meaning usually attached to them in the books and accounts of the insured.

85. "Difference" specification

(a) *Work in progress*

It may be noted that the definition of gross profit given in paragraph 81 carries a provision that the amounts of the opening and closing stocks shall be arrived at in accordance with the insured's normal accountancy methods, *due provision being made for depreciation*. This footnote is necessary to ensure that a true gross profit figure is brought into the insurance (see paragraph 147 on depreciation). Also the method of calculating the value of work in progress, whether by historical cost accounting or by current cost accounting, needs to be taken into account as per paragraph 219.

A further point in connection with the definition is that in many businesses there is always a considerable value in unfinished production on the shop floor and this is shown in the accounts as "work in progress" as a separate item from stock in hand. For instance, in the motor and aeroplane manufacturing, machine tool, engineering and allied industries, furniture making and television factories, etc., it is always a very substantial figure. Differences in the value of this work in progress at the beginning and end of any financial year can have a considerable effect on the amount shown as gross profit for that year as can differences in stock values each year end. If the definition of gross profit did not mention work in progress then in relevant cases an incorrect figure would be brought into the insurance; hence the reference to it in the definition of gross profit given in paragraph 81.

(b) *Discounts received, etc.*

A further point of considerable importance for many businesses when the "difference" specification is used is that provision must be made in it for the inclusion of discounts received. Since this form of revenue comes from purchases and not from sales the definition of turnover and therefore of gross profit does not include discounts received. The amount is frequently very substantial in relation to the net profit of a business and it is essential to be certain that it is included in the insured gross profit.

It may well be argued that in the definition of the gross profit "purchases" listed as an uninsured working expense is understood to mean the net cost of same and, therefore, discounts received are automatically included in the gross profit although not specifically mentioned. However, as they are generally shown as a separate item on the credit side of the accounts it is advisable to put the matter beyond a doubt and, also, to avoid their being overlooked in any computation of the amount of gross profit, by specifically mentioning discounts received.

This can be done by including them in the opening words of the definition so that this reads: "The amount by which the sum of the turnover, discounts received and the amount of the closing stock and work in progress shall exceed, etc." or alternatively by showing the first of the uninsured working expenses as: "Purchases less discounts received". Further discussion of discounts received is in paragraph 222.

Care must also be exercised where there is revenue which does not arise from the normal trading operations of an insured and is shown in the second section of the accounts but which nevertheless depends for its continuation upon the functioning of the business, for instance, payments by a subsidiary company for administrative services or office accommodation. If necessary the definition of gross profit should be amended to include such income and in any event its amount should be included in any computation of the sum insured.

(c) *Sale of scrap*

Saleable scrap from manufacturing processes is a very important source of income for many firms, particularly in the motor and other engineering industries, often representing as much as 10 per cent. of the overall gross profit.

Such income is included automatically in the older form of specification in which gross profit is defined as net profit plus standing charges. In the "difference" wording, it may be considered that it is brought in through the definition of turnover as being "goods sold". When it is shown in the accounts as a separate item from sales of the insured's products care must be exercised to ensure that the amount of it is included in the computation of gross profit and to avoid its being overlooked at that time or when an accountant is furnishing a certificate for return of premium it might be advisable to mention sale of scrap in the definition of gross profit.

(d) *Other variations*

In addition to the particular points already mentioned, there may be others calling for special consideration, for instance, where the accounts are drawn up not altogether in conformity with the conventional pattern. Modern methods of business management often involve unorthodox accounting or there may be certain items of credit arising from trading activities which should be included but do not fall within the standard definition of gross profit. Conversely, where there is a debit in the accounts, such as for work done by other firms on commission or by outworkers, which is a variable charge but is neither purchases nor a premises working expense, mention must be made of it in the list of uninsured working expenses.

(e) *No definition of net profit*

One important benefit of the method of arriving at the gross profit under the "difference" definition is that unlike the older wording no reference is necessary to net profit. A net trading profit or loss is automatically taken care of in the "difference" definition of gross profit. This obviates any need to adjust the figures when computing the amount of insurable gross profit to allow for non-trading revenue or expenses.

However, whilst it is clear from this definition that items of non-trading revenue are not embraced by it the question as to whether they, and also certain disbursements, should not be included in the insurance in some form or other remains to be settled by the individuals arranging the insurance.

Hence whilst the following paragraphs 86 to 96 are concerned with the meaning and implications of the definition of net profit in the older form of specification they can be of relevance also to the "difference" wording and to U.S. forms dealt with in Chapter 3.

86. Meaning of net profit

The older form of ("additions" basis—refer Appendix E, paragraph 451) specification in which the insurable gross profit is defined as net profit plus insured standing charges gives the following definition of net profit:

> "Net Profit—The net trading profit (exclusive of all capital receipts and accretions and all outlay properly chargeable to capital) resulting from the business of the Insured at the premises after due provision has been made for all standing and other charges including depreciation but before the deduction of any taxation chargeable on profits".

The first important point to be noticed is that the definition refers to the net *trading* profit after provision for all charges (which *inter alia* include directors' remuneration of all kinds) and depreciation (this being mentioned because it is not an expense paid out of revenue but is a provision for replacement). The inclusion of the word "trading" makes it clear that charges which appear in the profit and loss appropriation account, that is, dividends of all categories, including cumulative preference share dividends, amounts set aside for taxation and dividends or in a corporation tax equalisation account, or other special allocations of net profit, are automatically included in the insurance without specific mention as they come within the definition of net profit. For this reason, no reference is made to such charges in Chapter 9 on Standing Charges and Variable Expenses.

The intention of the word "trading" in relation to net profit is put beyond a doubt with regard to any capital receipts or accretions by the specific exclusion of such credits. Therefore the sale of or appreciation of capital assets, investment grants received from the government on U.K. capital expenditure on fixed assets (see paragraph 88), premium on the issue of share capital, or similar revenue attributable to capital, and interest or dividends on investments or loans, is not to be included in the net profit for purposes of insurance.

For similar reasons, in order to provide for a full indemnity the definition of net profit then excludes "all outlay properly chargeable to capital" from the calculation of the insurable figure of net profit. For example, a non-recurring item of capital outlay such as legal costs in connection with the purchase of premises or a capital reconstruction may be charged to revenue by debiting it to the profit and loss account. It is not, however, insurable as a standing charge, yet it will have reduced the net trading profit shown in the accounts for the year in question below the amount actually earned.

Consequently to bring out for purposes of the insurance, the true rate of gross profit earned it will be necessary to add back the amount of this item to the figure of net profit shown in the accounts. Special consideration is required for businesses which engage in large production contracts extending over periods of years on which the net profit is not receivable until completion of the contract (refer to paragraph 94).

87. Non-trading revenue

The words "net trading profit" are qualified as being those resulting from the business of the insured at the premises. This is in accordance with the limitation in the policy itself which confines the indemnity to loss due to interruption of the business of the insured arising from an Incident at the premises. Consequently any revenue such as rent from property, commissions, compensation, fees, or royalties, which is not derived from the trading activities at the premises (and would not be affected by an Incident there) is to be excluded from the computation of the insurable amount of gross profit even if not already regarded as being within the exclusion of "capital receipts and accretions".

Although there is no specific exclusion in the definition of net profit of amounts brought in from stock reserves or bad debts reserves, as these are "resulting from the business", albeit of previous years, the point is covered in the definition of the rate of gross profit, namely that "earned on the turnover during the financial year immediately before the Incident".

There are cases in which a credit is shown in the accounts for "dividends" which are not dividends on invested money but are a special trading discount, as in the case of Working Men's Clubs (of which there were 31,000 in the United Kingdom in 1980) formed into a federation which may secure privileged terms from a brewery company. In a case of this nature the payment is made to the "federation" by the brewers and then divided amongst member clubs in proportion to their purchases of beer from the brewery concerned. Consequently it is really an additional profit margin for the clubs and as it would be affected by a reduction in their turnover should be brought into the computation of gross profit in the same way as discounts received (see paragraph 222). A similar discount known as "barrelage" is sometimes paid by brewers direct to employees of individual Working Men's Clubs ostensibly for handing over to the club treasurer. In such cases if the payments appear in the club's accounts they should be included in the insurance.

88. Investment grants and regional development grants

These Government grants in respect of U.K. capital expenditure on fixed assets whether credited in full in the year in which the expenditure is incurred or spread over the estimated average life of the relative assets are non-trading revenue. In a specification on the net profit plus standing charges basis they are excluded under the definition of net profit (the net *trading* profit exclusive of all capital receipts and accretions). Therefore whether they appear in the accounts as an item of income or are shown as a deduction from current taxation or depreciation the amount must be deducted from the net profit shown in order to arrive at the correct amount of the gross profit insurance.

The amount of Government grants will be automatically excluded from the insured gross profit by the wording of a "difference" specification whether they are shown in the insured's accounts as a deduction from taxation or as depreciation debits or are credited as a separate item of income.

89. Insurance of extraneous revenue

Some adjustment will be necessary to arrive at the figure of net profit as defined in the specification if there are any extraneous items of revenue present in the accounts, as explained in paragraph 87. Where there is such income and it is liable to diminution through any of the insured perils it is advisable to arrange for it to be insured—possibly under a separate item of the specification. For example, many firms obtain revenue from the letting of part of their premises or of other property owned by them and an insurance against loss of rents receivable can be arranged as explained in paragraphs 294 *et seq.* Manufacturers often receive revenue from other firms in the form of royalties on production under patent rights by the latter, an interruption of whose business by fire would result in a reduction in the royalties payable. Another form of royalties arises in the widespread practice of franchising of business (see paragraph 162). An appropriate item of insurance on royalties receivable should be arranged to cover the potential loss of any such income as explained in paragraph 275(a).

It should be noted here that the standard definition of gross profit in a "difference" wording similarly does not include extraneous revenue of the foregoing nature and where necessary steps should be taken to arrange for it to be insured under a separate item.

90. Proprietor's earnings

In a business owned by a single individual the proprietor may draw a weekly or monthly sum as wages or salary. As this remuneration is an advance drawing on account of net profit dependent upon the latter being earned, it is included within the definition of net profit in the older form of specification and therefore should not be shown as a standing charge. It will be automatically included in a "difference" specification if it is not mentioned as an uninsured working expense.

91. Partnership drawings

In the case of a partnership the same position as with a sole proprietor applies to partners' drawings because of the provisions of the Partnership Act of 1890 unless there is an agreement to provide for the payment of a wage or salary either together with, or in lieu of, a share of the profits. In the event of there being such an agreement, designated partners' salaries (or wages) although in the nature of preferential shares of the divisible profit, might be allowed as an insurable standing charge.

In the United States the official handbook "Employers Guide to Unemployment Insurance" states that "amounts withdrawn from a business by the individual owner or partner are considered a withdrawal of profits and are *not* wages". Presumably this would be acceptable evidence as the position regarding payroll in a gross earnings or Business Income coverage if the question should arise in a claim.

92. Workers' share of profits

Of recent years there has been a steady growth in the number of firms operating profit-sharing schemes and in many of these the annual payments to employees run into six or seven figures.

In businesses where provision is made for the payment to workers of a share of the annual net profit, even though this may be called "workers' bonus", the position is different from the normal production bonus paid weekly on wages which is really a higher rate of wages. In the latter circumstances a corresponding amount of bonus should be included as an integral part of the wages to whatever extent they may be insured.

In a profit-sharing scheme, however, the share of profits is not a charge on the business paid weekly with wages according to the production above a certain target or norm but is an allocation of the net profit if and when any is earned and probably only when prior claims on it have been met. The insured net profit will therefore include the whole of the workers' share and not merely that of the "standing charge" workers and if there is a reduction in turnover following an Incident the insurance will make good the whole amount of the loss of net profit. This will include the share normally allocated to all the workers although a proportion of them may no longer be employed by the firm due to dismissal as a result of the Incident. The amount of the payment under the business interruption insurance will then be available, together with the net profit earned by whatever turnover is maintained, for payment of the appropriate amount under the profit-sharing scheme to those workers remaining on the payroll or otherwise as provided in the memorandum governing its distribution.

93. Employee share schemes

Payments under this head differ from those under a scheme such as the foregoing in paragraph 92 in which a share of net profit earned is allocated to employees but is only payable to them provided that sufficient net profit has been earned. The reference to "share" in an "employee share scheme" is to shares in the capital of the company which are given without charge to workers with a minimum service qualification under the 1980 Finance Act as a reward for their commitment to the successful operation of the company. Where there is such a scheme which provides for the expense of this to be carried each year as a standing charge debited against trading profit, payable to purchase shares for employees irrespective of the net profit earned, it will similarly require to be included in the list of insured standing charges where the definition of gross profit is on that basis.

94. Firms with construction contracts uncompleted

A rather perplexing position arises with firms whose output consists in the main of a small number of contracts each of considerable magnitude, who do not receive payment for or take credit for the net profit on any contract in a year's accounts unless the work is wholly delivered by the end of that year. For example, shipbuilders, aircraft manufacturers, constructors of steel-rolling mills, petrochemical complexes, electricity works, atomic power stations and similar large industrial units, and fabricators of large engineering products such as oil drilling platforms, gasholders or bridges.

It follows that the net profit of such firms in any financial year depends within wide limits upon the number of major contracts completed within that year. The profit on a contract taking three years to complete will not appear in the accounts until the final year and then it will swell the net profit for that year with the amount earned throughout three years' working.

For many firms this may result in wide variations in the net profit shown each financial year end, particularly if there are time gaps between contracts with but little work being done and an uneven spread of work as between one year and another. In such circumstances, as the net profit for each individual contract is really earned over the period of construction the computation of gross profit might be calculated by arrangement with the insurers to correspond with the amount of work actually carried out each year, from the firm's costing system.

In some businesses, in which the net profit position from year to year is fairly evenly balanced, the normal method of insuring gross profit at an amount based on each individual year's results might be satisfactory with recourse to the other circumstances clause in the event of a claim.

95. Where there is a net trading loss

Where there has been no net profit, but a net trading loss, the question arises as to the need for a business interruption policy. If a business is showing a loss on its manufacturing account or first section of the trading account, that is, a *gross* trading loss, and is likely to continue to do so there seems to be little object in insuring because the business is not meeting any of the standing charges. Where it is earning sufficient to pay for a portion of them the net loss would be increased and the financial position of the business worsened if turnover were adversely affected by an Incident. In these latter circumstances not only is a business interruption insurance advisable, there being no net profit earned which might cushion the effect of loss due to an increased ratio of standing charges following an Incident, but it may be for that reason even more essential than when a business is making a profit. Moreover as always with business interruption insurance it is future prospective profit which is being protected and this must be a dominant factor in reaching a decision.

Where insurance is effective for a business showing a net trading loss the question arises as to how the amount of gross profit should be computed. With the "difference" specification there is no problem because by subtracting the amount of the uninsured working expenses from the turnover, the resulting figure will be minus the amount of any net loss there might be but will include the net profit if and when any is earned. This is another advantage of the "difference" wording over the older definition of gross profit. When the latter form is used, however, reference to the second part of the definition of gross profit which is quoted in full in paragraph 81 will show that in such circumstances the amount of the net trading loss is to be deducted from the total of the insured standing charges. This is necessary to maintain the principle of indemnity as the effect of such a deduction is to limit the payment under the insurance to the portion of the insured standing charges which but for the Incident would have been earned by the business. The insured must not be placed in a better financial position following the Incident than they would have been in had it not occurred; so as the business was not earning all its charges before the Incident the indemnity provided by insurance must be limited to a similar extent. When the "difference" wording is used this limitation arises automatically from the method of calculating the gross profit.

Because the build-up of gross profit under the "difference" definition is confined to accounts items for turnover and working expenses complications of revenue from non-trading sources do not arise in considering the position where a business is trading at a loss: another advantage over the older form of wording. But in the latter wording the definition refers to the net *trading* loss. This means the net loss arising from the conduct of the business at the insured premises and not necesssarily the net loss disclosed in the profit and loss account. The latter may be less than the trading loss because of revenue from some extraneous source such as rents, royalties, interest on invested money or dividends on shares, being brought into the profit and loss account. For the reasons explained in paragraphs 86 and 87 any income in the nature of capital receipts or accretions or which would be unaffected by an interruption of the business by an Incident at the premises is not brought into the computation of the gross profit. Similarly, but in reverse, it must be added back to the net loss disclosed by the profit and loss account to give the net *trading* loss to be deducted from the amount of the insured standing charges. Also any charges included in the list of insured standing charges which are shown in the accounts after the net trading loss should be added back to arrive at the net trading loss for purposes of the insurance.

96. Trading loss

(a) *Some charges uninsured*

In the case of an insurance where for one reason or another all the standing charges are not included it would be unfair to the insured to deduct the whole of the net trading loss when calculating the amount of the insured gross profit. All the standing charges, both insured and uninsured, are responsible for that loss having arisen and it should therefore be allocated proportionately between them. Consequently the actual clause in the older form of definition of gross profit reads—"or if there be no net profit the amount of the insured standing charges less such a proportion of any net trading loss as the amount of the insured standing charges bears to all the standing charges of the business". This apportionment is of benefit to the insured in the event of a claim when the business is showing a net trading loss because it has the effect of slightly increasing the gross profit figure and similarly raising the rate of gross profit payable.

In a "difference" wording no provision is made for an apportionment of this nature and the full amount of any net trading loss is always deducted in arriving at the amount of the insured gross profit. Should any insurable standing charges have been included in the list of uninsured working expenses a lower rate of gross profit would be produced than under the older form of definition. Presumably this anomaly arises through the assumption that under a "difference" wording all insurable charges are included in the gross profit as, in practice, they generally are.

(b) *Other circumstances clause*

There are cases, however, where a net trading loss arises due to a temporary trade recession or change in marketing conditions, a fall in raw material prices necessitating the writing down of stock values, labour troubles, or other exceptional circumstances, or when a business is newly established or is undergoing extensive development which does not immediately produce profitable results. Because the insurance is in respect of future trading possibilities in such conditions the other circumstances clause could be invoked in the event of a claim to give an insured the benefit of an anticipated net profit even though the accounts for the preceding financial year showed a trading loss.

This is notwithstanding the fact that the other circumstances clause does not directly apply, in either the old form or in the "difference" specification, to the definition of gross profit but only to (i) the rate of gross profit (ii) the annual turnover and (iii) the standard turnover. Application of the clause to the standard turnover would answer the problem in many cases. Otherwise if the business would but for the Incident have shown a trading profit in the following year as the result of an increased rate of gross profit the circumstances could be met by an appropriate adjustment of the figures for the rate of gross profit.

Chapter 8

Gross Profit, Gross Earnings or Business Income: Specifications and Definitions (Continued)—United States

97. Meaning of gross earnings or Business Income

The reasons behind the change of wordings in the United States included a realisation that the expression "gross earnings" had no real place in U.S. accountancy but that "Business Income" could be readily understood. However, it is still necessary for the new term to be defined in the policy.

Although the gross earnings basis is being replaced in the United States it is still used extensively elsewhere and detailed comment follows.

(a) *Gross earnings: definition for mercantile and non-manufacturing risks*

As the object of a gross earnings insurance is to indemnify for "actual loss sustained" (paragraph 61) it must take account not only of net profit but also of any expenses of the business (standing charges) which may continue and not be fully earned during either partial or total interruption of business. This requires amongst other things an understanding in the contract between insurer and insured of exactly what is meant by "gross earnings", words which otherwise can mean different things to different insured and their accountants.

The standard definition of gross earnings for this category of business, often called "service risk", is the sum of total net sales and other earnings derived from operations of the business less the cost of merchandise sold including packaging material therefor, materials and supplies consumed directly in supplying the services sold by the insured and the services purchased from outsiders (not employees of the insured) for resale which do not continue under contract. No other costs are to be deducted in determining the amount of gross earnings.

This definition is on similar lines to that used for defining gross profit under a "difference" specification on a U.K. policy, that is turnover ("net sales") less variable expenses, except that in the wording no reference is made to the amounts of opening and closing stocks and work in progress which will affect the figure for gross earnings in any financial year. See paragraphs 81 *et seq.* on gross profit.

The cost of "materials and supplies consumed directly" which may be treated as a deductible expense in arriving at the amount of gross earnings is less specific than the provisions in a U.K. specification of gross profit in which the deductible variable expenses are named individually. The description may leave room for some doubt about a number of charges which may be variable and yet not strictly speaking are "consumed directly" in supplying the services sold or purchased by the insured.

Whilst the words "total net sales" will exclude discounts allowed there are some charges which may be termed borderline or optional which though not "consumed directly" may vary proportionately with sales, for instance, commissions and bonuses to employees and agents (paragraphs 191, 193 and 177–180), travelling expenses (paragraph 125), bad debts on credit given by retailers (paragraph 159(b)), some repairs and renewals (paragraph 172), variable advertising costs (paragraph 120), and entertainment expenses (paragraph 166). See the working definitions of insurable and non-insurable charges in paragraph 104 and the detailed discussion of such charges in subsequent paragraphs.

Because the protection by insurance of the end-product of net profits of a business involves similar problems whatever definitions of terms and methods of calculating losses are employed much of the contents of Chapter 9 will be applicable to consideration of the insurance of gross earnings. Here an important difference in U.K. and U.S. terminology calls for mention. In the former an insurance may refer to "salaries" and to "wages" as separately insurable entities but "payroll" may be used only when all employees' remuneration of both categories is included in certain covers (see paragraphs 204 and 212). The words "ordinary payroll" are not used. The definition of gross earnings does not mention payroll, which is the accepted term for the remuneration of all employees, and so 100 per cent. of such remuneration is included as standard coverage. If any portion of "*ordinary* payroll expense", which is roughly equivalent to "wages" in a U.K. specification, is not required to be insured in full it may be wholly or partially excluded from gross earnings. (See paragraph 217(a)–(c)).

Although the indemnity for gross earnings, without any amendment as above, includes 100 per cent. of the payroll expense this does not mean that all workers will be paid full wages from the insurance throughout a period of interruption. This is because the coverage states only that "due consideration shall be given to the continuation of normal charges and expenses, including payroll expense, to the extent necessary to resume operations etc.". Due to its considerable amount and importance in relation to gross earnings insurances and because in many businesses it may not be necessary to insure the remuneration of all employees for the full period of interruption the matter is discussed in paragraph 217(a)–(c) on Payroll Expenses.

(b) *Gross earnings: definition for manufacturing and mining risks*

The coverage for gross earnings for this category of risks, which in general terms means all businesses that convert raw materials into finished products, embodies practically the same conditions as for non-manufacturing risks. But because the use of raw materials and their conversion to saleable products is involved the standard definition of gross earnings is different from that shown in preceding paragraph 97(a) for non-manufacturing businesses. It is the sum of the total net sales value of production, total net sales of merchandise, and other earnings derived from operations of the business, less the cost of (i) raw stock from which such production is derived; (ii) supplies consisting of materials consumed directly in the conversion of such raw stock into finished stock or in supplying the service(s) sold by the insured; (iii) merchandise sold including packaging materials therefor, and (iv) service(s) purchased from outsiders (not employees of the insured) for resale which do not continue under contract. No other costs shall be deducted in determining gross earnings. Although not mentioned in this definition of gross earnings the normal wording of the worksheets (see paragraph 234(a)) supplied by insurers for computation of the amount to be insured as gross earnings shows discounts, returns, bad accounts and prepaid freight as deductibles from gross sales in the calculation of the net sales value of production and net sales from merchanting.

One difference in the above definition of gross earnings from that for a non-manufacturing business is the addition to the list of deductible working expenses of the cost of raw stock and supplies of materials consumed directly in its conversion to finished stock, these being charges which do not normally apply with a mercantile or non-manufacturing concern. Definitions follow giving the meaning of raw stock, stock in progress, finished stock, merchandise and "normal" (see Appendix R).

An important point arising from another difference in the definition of gross earnings is that it is not the amount of net sales of production but the net sales *value* of production which has to be included in the gross earnings. This will or will not include profit on unsold finished products according to whether or not the view is held that manufacturers have earned their profit when they have converted raw materials into finished stock. There may be grounds for doubt on this matter in view of *the exclusion of finished stock* from the property to which damage by insured perils is the basis of coverage for resulting loss of earnings.

The above exclusion of finished stock comes in the description of coverage in the reference to loss resulting from interruption of business caused by damage to real or personal property "except finished stock" and one of the Exclusions on the policy goes further by stating that the insurer shall not be liable for any loss resulting from damage to or destruction of finished stock nor for the time required to reproduce finished stock.

The exclusion of finished stock in a gross earnings form has been the cause of continuing debate amongst insurers in North America; it gives a more restricted indemnity than is obtained under a U.K. policy. The reason for the exclusion appears to stem from the view that manufacturers differ from wholesalers and retailers who earn their profit when they sell their merchandise. Manufacturers are regarded as earning their profit when they have converted raw materials into finished stock and insurance therefore ends at the point of production.

A normal fire insurance on unsold stock compensates only on the basis of cash value of that damaged or destroyed. In a U.K. policy in the event of a loss of sales resulting because of damage to finished stock by fire the loss of gross profit is treated as covered by the insurance. In a U.S. gross earnings form not only is such loss excluded but the insured is required by the Resumption of Operations condition (paragraph 66) to try to reduce the interruption of business by making use of finished stock at the premises or elsewhere. Extra expense in replacing finished stock is insured under the expediting clause (paragraph 64—Expenses to reduce loss) but this does not compensate for loss of profit on missed sales.

This potential loss is of sufficient importance to some manufacturers for them to effect a separate coverage either on a property damage policy to obtain indemnity based on selling prices less unincurred expenses or on a gross earnings form to cover profit on loss of sales of finished goods.

It may be noted that as the exclusions refer only to "finished" stock any prolongation of the period of interruption necessary to replace raw stock or stock in process to the pre-fire stage of production, even though this is later than the restoration of buildings and machinery, comes within the period of indemnity.

As in the definition for non-manufacturing businesses the whole 100 per cent. payroll is included and the extent to which this can be paid to employees during a period of interruption is left as an open question under the phrase "due consideration shall be given to the continuation of normal charges and expenses, including payroll, to the extent necessary to resume operations, etc.".

The problem of payroll being included in full in the definition of gross earnings mentioned in the preceding paragraph 97(a) regarding non-manufacturing businesses applies with even more importance in connection with manufacturing concerns. With the latter a large proportion of payroll may relate to workers whose services are directly related to production and would be paid for out of it to the extent of its continuation or would be disposed of altogether if work is not available for them during the period of interruption. An "Ordinary Payroll Exclusion endorsement" or an "Ordinary Payroll Limited Coverage endorsement" is necessary if it is required not to insure all "ordinary payroll" (productive wage-earners) in the gross earnings coverage. (See paragraph 217(a)–(c).)

Despite a subsequent definition of "normal" as being the condition which would have existed had no loss occurred other expenses may also be brought into question in the event of a claim because the expression "continuation of *normal* charges and expenses to the extent necessary to resume operations, etc." might be open to different interpretations in respect of, for instance, commission and advertising. See paragraphs 191, 193, 120–124 and 177. Similarly the wording of the deductible expense in the definition of gross earnings—"materials consumed directly in manufacturing processes"—may mean different things in relation to some manufacturing costs such as those mentioned as borderline charges in paragraphs 171 *et seq*.

In the context of the above paragraph "materials" is generally understood to mean materials which become constituents of the finished products and does not include supplies of power, heat and refrigeration. However, it is possible to amend the coinsurance clause to the effect that the cost of heat, power and refrigeration consumed in production operations which do not continue under contract shall be deducted from the gross earnings in the application of the clause provided that the coinsurance percentage is not less than 80 per cent.

(c) *Business Income: non-manufacturing and manufacturing risks*

As already mentioned in paragraph 69, the definition of Business Income is the same for both categories of risk because of the reference to "Net Income" and "continuing normal operating expenses". It thus avoids any mention of the variable charges or non-continuing expenses which differentiates between the two covers under the gross earnings basis. Payroll is included specifically in the cover whereas it was included by non-exclusion under the gross earnings forms. An Ordinary Payroll Limitation endorsement is still available (see paragraph 217(c)).

The new work sheets (see paragraph 234(b)) show a form of calculation very similar to, but much more detailed than, a "difference" basis assessment of insurable gross profit. By deducting direct variable expenses (cost of raw stock, etc., consumed) and adjusting for beginning and end of year inventory balances, a "net" figure is arrived at which is to be the basis of "Net Income and Expenses (Business Income Basis for Coinsurance)". This is very interesting and gratifying for U.K. insurers in that the cover is expressed in "additions" basis terms while the amount insurable is calculated by a "difference" basis method, but there is in all this a discernible narrowing of the gap in philosophy between the U.K. and the U.S. practices.

Finished stock is still excluded from the cover (being defined as "stock you have manufactured") but it is deemed not to include "stock you have manufactured that is held for sale on the premises of any retail outlet insured under this coverage". Stock that is sold by an exclusively non-manufacturing or mercantile insured is clearly not "stock you have manufactured" and is not excluded from the cover.

It may be significant that in both the old and the new work sheets (refer paragraph 234) the difference between opening and closing stock inventory either "of finished stock" (old) or "at sales value" (new) is taken into account in arriving at the amount to be insured either as gross earnings or as Business Income (as it is for the calculation of gross profit on the "difference" basis). Nevertheless having perhaps credited some finished stock "value" to the sum insured, so that it is part of "Net Income", cover in respect of that "value" (for manufacturing risks) is withdrawn. This, however, is a marginal argument—if it has any validity at all—and the insured will not really be paying too much in premium as a result.

98. Costs deducted: mercantile and non-manufacturing risks

Progressing from gross sales to net sales entails the deduction of the cost of prepaid freight, returns and allowances, discounts, bad debts and collection expenses. To arrive at the final gross earnings or Business Income amount the following cost deductions are made on the new work sheets (paragraph 234(b)).

(a) *Cost of goods sold*

This is the difference between the inventory at the beginning of the year and that at the end of the year together with the cost of merchandise sold and other supplies consumed.

(b) *Services purchased from outsiders (not employees) to resell which do not continue under contract*

This is a deduction in the gross earnings definition and remains as a deduction in the new Business Income work sheet.

99. Costs deducted: manufacturing risks

Net sales value of production is achieved on both the gross earnings and Business Income work sheets by taking gross sales, adjusting for finished stock inventory (at sales values) at the beginning and end of the year, and deducting prepaid freight, returns and allowances, discounts (granted), bad debts and (Business Income only) collection expenses. To arrive at the final gross earnings or Business Income amount the following deductions are made.

(a) *Cost of goods sold*

To the inventory (including stock in process) at the beginning of the year are added the costs of raw stock consumed, factory and other supplies consumed (including transportation charges) and merchandise sold so as to provide the cost of goods available for sale. From that amount is deducted the inventory (including stock in process) at the end of the year to achieve the cost of goods sold.

(b) *Services purchased from outsiders, etc.*

The same comment applies as under non-manufacturing risks (paragraph 98).

100. Net Income

This is defined in the new Business Income Coverage form as "Net Profit or Loss before income taxes" and is similar in effect to the old "additions" basis in the United Kingdom where gross profit is made up of either a *positive* amount for net profit added to the insured charges, or a *negative* amount deducted from insured standing charges (to the extent that they represent all the insurable standing charges of the business).

101. Operating expenses

These are qualified in the definition of Business Income to mean "continuing normal operating expenses incurred, including payroll". They are not named and are equivalent in effect to the expenses insured in a U.K. cover on net profit and *all standing charges (less savings)*. They should not include any of the (variable) expenses already deducted in the work sheet but as the latter are not mentioned in the Business Income Coverage form (as they are in the Gross Earnings definition) this is open to doubt. It may be significant that the word "normal" is not defined in the new form whereas in the gross earnings forms it is defined as "the condition which would have existed had no loss occurred".

"Continuing normal operating expenses incurred" are not defined in the same way that standing charges are not defined as such in a U.K. "additions" basis wording, although a list of insured standing charges is usually included in the U.K. specification. The only operating expense mentioned in the Business Income Coverage form is "payroll". (Refer also paragraphs 67(b) and 69.)

However in the Additional Condition—Coinsurance the term "operating expenses" has a wider meaning, including non-continuing expenses in the calculation of adequacy of insurance. The explanation given is that the amount of non-continuing expenses is virtually impossible to determine prior to loss but must be deducted after loss in order to avoid over-indemnity. In the same way it would be impossible under a U.K. form on the "additions" basis to gauge the adequacy of the insurance amount by comparing the sum insured with the total of what would have been the net profit and what would have been the insured standing charges less what would have been savings.

102. Other earnings

To the totals of either net sales (mercantile and non-manufacturing risks) or net sales value of production (manufacturing risks) should be added commissions or rents and cash discounts received from the business operations.

Investment income and rents from other properties are expressly excluded from such other earnings under the Business Income work sheet. In the U.K. "difference" wording, discounts received are usually treated as a reduction in the cost of purchases and are mentioned among the uninsured working expenses as follows—"All purchases (less discounts received)". Again in the United Kingdom receipts in the form of commission or rent would only be included if they were at risk as a result of damage at the premises, and if the business of the insured was suitably additionally defined—as for example "property owners".

103. Trading loss

If there is a trading or net loss being borne by the business at the inception of the year of insurance but a net profit is expected in the year following the year of insurance it would be wise for the insured to base their limit of insurance on that later better year (given that a loss could occur on the last day of the year of insurance) so as to ensure the limit is sufficient to pay the largest possible loss. This would be essential under the coinsurance (or contribution) clause in the gross earnings wording to ensure adequacy of insurance.

However, as the test of adequacy of insurance (coinsurance condition) under the Business Income Coverage form takes as its base the business income for the year of insurance, a projection would not be necessary for losses to be paid in full so long as they did not exceed the limit of insurance.

The same arguments of course apply to any upwards trend in the insured's business. They may not be penalised by the coinsurance condition but the limit of insurance could, in the worst event, prove to be insufficient.

Chapter 9

Standing Charges and Variable Expenses—United Kingdom and United States

104. Working definitions

It is a feature of both the old ("additions") and new ("difference") forms of the U.K. specification that although the one contains several references to standing charges and a list of those insured and the other contains a list of uninsured working expenses which are excluded from the insurance, neither lays down a definition of what is meant by the respective terms or should be included in the lists. This is because an expense which is a standing charge or another which is a variable expense for one business may not be so in the circumstances of a different business, whilst some charges may be termed borderline and some are definitely optional. The persons effecting an insurance have to decide which charges to insure or exclude according to the particular circumstances of their business. In the old form of specification those selected for inclusion in the gross profit are then named in the list of insured standing charges and in the "difference" specification those to be excluded from the cover are shown in the list of uninsured working expenses. On the wisdom of the choice a great deal can depend.

In making a selection of the charges to be insured it is necessary to bear in mind the fundamental principle that in order to protect the net profit of a business it is essential to insure net profit plus those charges which will not fall proportionately with a drop in turnover. From this a working definition can be drawn, namely, that *an insurable standing charge is one which might not diminish proportionately with a reduction in turnover if there is interruption of or interference with the business by any of the contingencies insured against.* To which an important addition must be made—*or any variable charge which it would be desirable to continue in the interests of the business.* Those in the latter category are referred to as optional charges.

Conversely, a working definition for an uninsured working expense in the difference specification would be *an expense which can be reduced, without detriment to the business, proportionately with a reduction in turnover if there is an interruption of or interference with the business by any of the contingencies insured against.*

In day-to-day practice many difficulties arise in applying these definitions, especially when dealing with clients who are not wholly convinced of the value of the insurance or of the necessity for it to be a full one or when the premium cost is a dominant factor. An understanding of the reasons for the inclusion or otherwise of various charges is essential before these can be discussed in detail. The following background is therefore given as the key to the problem, after which individual charges will be considered separately.

105. Practical reasons giving a general principle for insuring charges

A good starting point is the simple position so often put forward by businessmen: if the premises are burnt down there will be neither rent nor rates to pay so why include them in the insurance? It is a fact that many people think solely in terms of a total burn-out and cessation of business activities, an attitude of mind which is all too frequently encountered. Consequently it is advisable when discussing an insurance to make sure that the possibility of partial damage is appreciated and to stress that the damage done by most fires is of a limited nature which, although interrupting a business, probably has little or no effect on the amount payable *inter alia* for rent and rates. This applies particularly when the damage is confined to one small but vital part, such as the power unit, one department in a sequence of operations, or the pattern shop or store in an engineering works or foundry, or a computer, which may bring to a complete standstill the major part of a factory which is nine-tenths undamaged. The burn-out of a roof or of one floor in a storeyed building, fire or explosion in the exhaust system, gas producer plant, air compressors or pumping or cooling plant, damage to regulators and control apparatus, the destruction of the heating unit for either trade processes or space heating, or of the drawing offices, or extensive damage by the fire brigade or automatic sprinklers, are other typical examples of damage which may interrupt a business whilst leaving charges such as rent and rates to be met in full.

A particularly impressive instance of what can happen on the lines mentioned above was a fire at the premises of a major aeroengine manufacturer which severely damaged the main office block and destroyed a high proportion of the records. The resulting claim under the firm's business interruption policy was £2 million, mostly the result of failure to evaluate production due to loss of records.

A further striking demonstration of loss consequent upon damage to a non-producing unit in a manufacturing plant was a fire at a British Aerospace storage depot. Destruction of or damage to hundreds of thousands of spare parts stored for the needs of more than 500 aircraft resulted in interruption of production at the factory to the tune of many millions of pounds for the business interruption claim. It is interesting to note as an illustration of the promptitude of British insurers in dealing with claims that with more than 40 companies and some Lloyd's syndicates involved in the insurance of this fire loss and despite the complicated nature of the same, settlement was made within six months for £70 million in the U.K. insurance market.

That damage can be of such a nature as to slow down production without completely stopping it is shown by the following actual quotations from loss adjusters' reports which are typical of what frequently happens. "Temporary repairs to the plant were carried out forthwith but its efficiency and speed were impaired for the time being and its capacity much reduced. There were a number of breakdowns which meant complete stoppages of short duration and these added to the loss of production." "Disruption of the mechanical conveyor system resulted in reduced output because man-handling materials from point to point in the factory was a much slower process." "Day-by-day difficulties arose in connection with the improvised equipment and break-downs were frequent."

Where there is a completely continuous production flow automated from raw materials, through all processes of manufacture, weighing, filling, wrapping, boxing, labelling and warehousing or loading for delivery, as in very many businesses, damage restricted to only one point in the line may bring the whole factory to a standstill. Should it be possible to feed machines manually or to do other processes or packing by hand there will inevitably be a very severe fall in the tempo of production.

Equally important, but too often overlooked, is the fact that although premises may be razed to the ground charges which on the face of things one might think would cease, such as rent and rates, might still be payable in full. This happens when alternative premises are taken. During the months in which they are being equipped with plant and machinery charges such as rent and rates continue in full, at first with no turnover at all and later with turnover much below the normal level.

It should be noted that if alternative premises are occupied as a result of damage only the *additional* expenditure on rent, rates and similar expenses beyond the normal pre-damage amount of such charges is payable as increase in cost of working. Therefore, unless rent and rates have been included in the gross profit insurance a proportionate loss will be suffered in respect of the normal amount of those expenses during the period when turnover at the temporary premises is at a reduced level.

If suitable alternative premises are not available and those damaged have to be rebuilt a similar position applies in that rent, rates and other charges will have to be paid during the period when the restored buildings are being tooled-up ready for production or fitted up for trading purposes and throughout the running-in period whilst experience is being gained and the final teething troubles are being overcome. Shortage of labour or the necessity to train or retrain employees will often further prolong the period in which a fully equipped factory is producing below capacity.

There is another very important factor to bear in mind. Even when a business is again in a position to handle its pre-fire turnover it does not follow that it will be able immediately to resume its pre-fire sales. Customers and markets may have been lost to competitors or the sales organisation weakened. Several months may elapse before sales are restored to normal and out of the reduced turnover during that period rent and rates will be amongst the standing charges to be met in full.

It is advisable to visualise these different possibilities not only when dealing with clients who find it difficult to understand why they should insure charges which they think would cease after a burn-out but also when considering the problem generally. It will be appreciated that the division into either direct materials, labour and expenses, or indirect labour, materials and expenses, used in standard costing systems is not necessarily a safe guide to decide whether an expense is a variable one or a standing charge for purposes of business interruption insurance: *e.g.* see paragraph 175.

One further point calls for mention. Where an insurance includes an extension of cover to outside premises not in the insured's occupation such as those of suppliers of materials, finished products or components, processors, customers or stores, it postulates that the business can be partly or wholly interrupted without damage of any kind taking place at the insured's buildings. In such circumstances rent, rates and all other standing charges will continue to be payable in full throughout the period of interruption. Similarly when perils such as collapse of boilers, explosion of steam pipes, pressure vessels or bakers' ovens are added to the insurance it is because damage confined to a limited part of the plant can interrupt production and in that event there would be no reduction in rent, rates or similar charges.

106. Inclusion of variable charges

It is necessary also to consider the opposite position in which, rather than run the risk of being penalised following damage because some charge has been omitted which should have been included, an insured wishes to "put them all in". Whilst this is certainly better than omitting a true standing charge it would be a mistake to think that by including a variable charge the insured will recover more in a loss settlement. Its inclusion will certainly increase the rate of gross profit but after this higher rate has been applied to the reduction in turnover, the diminution in the variable (insured) charge will be deducted under the savings clause leaving the insured no better off.

On the other hand the inclusion of a variable charge may mean paying some premium unnecessarily and can involve dissatisfaction or even disadvantage in the event of a claim. To illustrate this consider "carriage", leaving out of the question special cases such as those mentioned in paragraph 156 where it is a true standing charge and taking the general position where it means the payment on a unit cost basis for deliveries made by rail, water, road transport or air carriers or by suppliers of goods to the insured. In general, such charges, whether in the invoice price or charged separately, vary proportionately with the volume of goods going into or out of the premises. Consequently any reduction in turnover will produce an exactly proportionate reduction in charges for carriage whilst the turnover maintained will earn in the normal way the amount of carriage relating to it. This means that carriage is not a standing charge.

Where are the disadvantages if it is insured? Premium will be paid on the annual amount of carriage, which is often a very large item in an insured's accounts; if the maximum indemnity period is for longer than 12 months the amount is further increased to correspond. When the average fire rate is high the premium involved may be very considerable. But when a claim occurs the reduction in carriage which takes place with the fall in turnover is deducted from the loss settlement under the clause which provides for savings in the charges or expenses included in the insurance (paragraph 51(a)). The insured may then find that, perhaps for many years, a considerable amount of premium has been paid unnecessarily and may understandably feel that they have been badly advised in the matter.

It is possible also for the inclusion of a variable charge such as carriage to introduce or add to the incidence of average in the event of a claim. This could arise where the sum insured has not been kept in line with expanding business, which latter would automatically increase the amount of carriage. Alternatively, a rise in freightage charges would have a similar effect.

107. Omission of standing charges—no effect on average

It is sometimes thought that in the old form of net profit plus insured standing charges specification the omission of any charge will automatically introduce average into a claim. This is not so whether the omitted charge be a true standing charge or one such as carriage which is variable with turnover; the insured can leave out of the insurance whatever charges they wish and the omission will not affect the operation of average in any way. The reason is that the average proviso is applied by measuring the sum insured against the net profit and *insured* standing charges without importing any charges which have been omitted.

The comparable position in a "difference" specification would be the inclusion of a non-variable or partially variable charge in the list of uninsured working expenses. In this wording also the average proviso is applied by measuring the sum insured against *the gross profit as defined* in the specification, irrespective of whether certain charges should or should not have been excluded.

108. Omitted charges which increase after damage

It is also frequently and mistakenly thought that if a particular charge is omitted from the insurance no claim can be made under clause (b) in respect of an increase in the amount of that charge during a period of interruption. For example, although carriage may be a variable charge circumstances could arise, such as the destruction of the insured's warehouse, necessitating the goods produced at the factory being sent a considerable distance to temporary warehouse premises with a reluctant heavy increase over the normal pre-damage expenditure on carriage. This does not mean that carriage should have been included in the insurance on gross profit and the fact that it had been omitted should not prevent the insured from recovering under clause (b) the amount of the abnormal carriage arising during the indemnity period as being increase in cost of working. This would leave only the normal transport costs to be borne by the turnover maintained and if such costs are normally variable they would fall proportionately with any reduction in turnover. Hence the insured would not lose anything through the non-insurance of carriage.

109. Loss when insurable charges are omitted

The foregoing is not to say that the insured will not suffer some loss by leaving out an insurable charge; they can do so in two ways. First, the rate of gross profit will be lower because of the omission and when this is applied to the shortage in turnover the resulting amount of the claim will be correspondingly smaller. Secondly, further loss will be sustained if the claim includes an amount for increase in cost of working. By the operation of the uninsured standing charges clause of the specification additional expenditure is apportioned in the ratio of the amount of the insured gross profit to the amount of same plus that of the uninsured standing charges, as explained in paragraph 49. Therefore the omission of an insurable standing charge will mean that the insured have to bear a proportion of this section of the claim. Any variable expense, however, if it is not a true standing charge should not be brought in for the purpose of the uninsured standing charges clause.

110. Borderline charges

As will be explained subsequently in connection with certain charges it is not always possible to reach a clear-cut decision as to the inclusion of all or part of those which might be termed borderline charges. Whenever there is doubt about a charge it is generally advisable to include it, certainly so if the premium involved is not of great moment. But there are so many cases in which premium cost is of paramount importance that considerations of obtaining full security at minimum cost have been kept prominently in mind in drafting the observations in the following detailed examination of charges.

Many insurance brokers use a stereotyped list of charges to facilitate a computation of the amount to be insured on gross profit. A list may also form part of the printed proposal forms issued by some insurance companies, though it is customary in the United Kingdom to waive the use of a proposal form for insurances of any appreciable size since the policy wording does not make a proposal form the basis of the contract.

Lists of this nature can be very useful but no list can give complete guidance on the matter of insurable charges without being too long and involved for practical use. So unless such lists are used with knowledge and discretion misunderstanding may result and lead to future difficulties. Accountants will generally find it preferable to collate the charges direct from their clients' accounts, choosing those to be insured according to the circumstances of the particular business. A list using the same order and designation as in the accounts would then be prepared of either the excluded variables, that is, the uninsured working expenses in a "difference" wording or, alternatively, the charges to be included as insured standing charges in the older form of specification. This method is most helpful when a certificate is required for the return of premium clause (paragraph 225(a)) or when a claim arises.

The co-operation of an insured's accountant in compiling such a list of charges carries the further advantage that he can draw attention to any unusual feature in the accounts. For example, a non-recurring charge which needs to be taken into consideration in computing the future sum insured or materials used for repairs to factory buildings and plant by an insured's own employees and debited in "purchases" which could easily be overlooked if a stereotyped list of charges was being used.

In the following paragraphs 111–188 detailed consideration is given to the majority of charges which appear in business accounts as a help towards deciding whether they are "standing" or "variable" for the purposes of a business interruption insurance.

111. Directors' remuneration and fees

It is obviously desirable that whatever effect the damage may have, the directors of a business shall receive in full the normal amount of their emoluments and this expense should be fully insured.

The remuneration of directors can take various forms and appear in more than one item in the accounts; for example, under salaries, wages, bonus, commission, or directors' emoluments or compensation for loss of office as well as under fees. In a "difference" wording the matter is simply dealt with by no mention of directors' remuneration being made in the list of uninsured working expenses unless in the accounts it constitutes part of any charge in that list such as wages. In such circumstances where wages are separately insured the relevant item in the list would have to be shown as "Wages other than those of directors". Where the specification is on the old wording, if the description "all directors' remuneration and fees" is used in the list of insured standing charges it will be clear that everything the directors receive is to be included but when preferable any other heading to correspond with those in the accounts may be used. It is of course necessary to take care that the amount is not again added in with the figure for any other standing charge of which it might be part, such as salaries or wages, or with the net profit.

Although directors' remuneration may be shown in the accounts as an appropriation of net profit it should be insured as a standing charge when the old form of specification is used because the net profit as defined for purposes of the insurance is the figure "after due provision has been made for all standing and other charges"—which would include directors' remuneration. For the same reason it is still an insurable charge even when it takes the form of a fixed percentage on the amount of net trading profit.

It is sometimes suggested that if the remuneration of the directors has to be agreed and fixed annually at a shareholders' meeting it is not a "standing" charge. This overlooks the fact that any charge which it is in the interests of the business to continue can be insured; almost certainly directors' remuneration is within this category. Moreover, the period of interruption will probably fall between two annual meetings of shareholders, and the remuneration of directors which was authorised at the one preceding the damage will have to be paid however the business is affected. In any event a reduction in directors' remuneration will be balanced by an increase in net profit and leave the amount of gross profit unaffected.

A rather different treatment of directors' remuneration applies for insurances under the dual basis payroll scheme; see paragraph 212 for details. Broadly, under this cover the remuneration of all employees, both salaries and wages, including that of working directors on the staff can be insured in one item separate from that on gross profit. But directors' fees cannot be so included and must continue to be insured in the item on gross profit.

112. Payroll related costs

Largely because of various Acts of Parliament (see paragraphs 202 and 203), direct and indirect beneficial payments to employees in the United Kingdom are now generally brought together by insurers under the broad heading of "payroll" which may be defined as *the whole remuneration, wages as well as salaries (together with employers' per capita pension and national insurance contributions)*.

For this reason the usual procedure in the United Kingdom is to insure "payroll" as a standing charge within gross profit with suitable allowances in premium cost for probable savings in the event of serious loss and a lengthy period of interruption. Nevertheless it is still necessary to examine the possible constituent parts of "payroll", particularly because legislation in other parts of the world where the U.K. system of business interruption insurance is followed is not necessarily so protective. For the sake of dealing with the subject as a whole comment is made in more detail in Chapter 10.

113. Interest payments

These may be of various kinds—interest on debentures, loans or borrowed capital, on bank overdrafts, mortgages, or trade accounts. Some part of such payments may cease after damage if the money obtained from the fire insurance on the property destroyed is used to repay the principal on which interest is payable and the insurers will then obtain the benefit under the savings clause. Nevertheless, all interest payments should be insured, the consideration already set out with regard to charges in general (paragraph 105) applying also in this connection.

Similarly, interest paid on a holiday fund for workers or to a staff savings scheme or workers' thrift club would probably have to be continued and should be included in the gross profit insurance.

114. Rent

Rent was considered in paragraph 105 as an overhead charge which should always be insured and this applies even if there is in the lease a cesser clause for total unoccupancy or an abatement clause for a reduction in rent dependent upon the extent of the damage because other premises may need to be rented. For tenants with no such clause in their lease the need to insure rent in the gross profit is more apparent because they will have to pay rent until the expiry of the lease even though they may have to vacate all or part of the premises because of damage. In such circumstances they will be paying rents for both the damaged premises and the alternative premises, but they will recover the former under the loss of gross profit insurance in ratio to the reduction in turnover and the additional rent under the increase in cost of working provisions of the policy.

Other rental payments such as ground rent, ground annuals, feu duties, rent for railways sidings, rent for room and power, rent for neon signs, rent for office machinery, computer leasing, telephone systems, etc., or for fire or burglar alarm systems, should be similarly insured.

Storage rents introduce another factor; see paragraph 157 with regard to this charge.

The rent or hire of films paid by cinemas for the main pictures and supporting programme is usually an agreed percentage of the actual takings for the performances at which they are shown. This means that in the event of damage at a cinema the charge if on this basis will vary proportionately with turnover, whether the interference with performances is either total or partial and so it is not an insurable standing charge. Where the rental of films is not charged in this way but all or part of it is a fixed amount irrespective of the size of the audiences, as may sometimes be the case, it should be insured in the item on gross profit.

115. Notional rent

Many firms who own all or part of the premises they occupy debit their accounts with notional rent for beneficial tenancy for purposes of costing or of a sinking fund. Under the old form of specification it may then be included as an insured standing charge under some such description as "rental value". If this is done care must be taken to deduct from the figure of net profit the amount which has been credited to balance the charge or it will be brought into the computation of gross profit twice. In fact there appears to be no necessity to mention rental value when it is a nominal entry which is balanced by a credit of the same amount. In such cases the actual financial benefit from there being no physical payment of rent is included in the net profit which if rent were paid would have been correspondingly less. As there is a credit as well as a debit the amount of the net profit shown in the accounts is unaffected and in the event of a claim the insured would be compensated in full.

If other premises had to be occupied following damage at those owned the omission of notional rent from the list of insured standing charges would not prejudice an insured in respect of a claim for increase in cost of working, as the whole rent of the other premises would be additional expenditure, nothing having previously been actually paid for rent.

Any problem about the inclusion of notional rent is avoided when the "difference" definition of gross profit is employed because it leaves out both debit and credit.

116. Double insurance on rent

Difficulty is sometimes experienced with regard to the insurance where the buildings are owned by a member of the insured firm or by an associated company and an insurance is effected by such an owner on Loss of Rent Receivable. (See paragraph 263(b).) It then appears as though premium is being paid unnecessarily by two parties for the same benefit; on the one hand by the owner for rent receivable and on the other hand by the tenant who is practically the same party, to cover the payment of the same rent as a non-variable charge. Is there any necessity for this double insurance?

Take first the position of the tenant. In the event of damage interfering with the business without so damaging the building as to give cause for a reduction in rent loss will be suffered because of the increased ratio of rent to turnover. On the other hand if a building is destroyed or rendered untenantable the payment of rent on it will cease if there is the normal cesser clause in the lease. But the insured will then have to pay rent at alternative premises and until such time as the turnover there reaches the normal figure loss will be suffered because of the increased ratio to it of the rent. Even after that, additional loss will be experienced if the rent of the alternative premises exceeds that of those vacated and if there is no cesser clause the rent of the latter will also have to be met until expiry of the lease. Such loss is recoverable as increase in cost of working. This means that there is a possibility of the tenant suffering loss whether the damage is partial or total and it is essential that rent be insured in the gross profit.

On the other hand whilst the owner may continue to receive full rent if the damage is only partial and the tenant continues in occupation he will lose his revenue if the tenant has to vacate the premises and there is a cesser of rent clause in the lease and possibly even if there is no such provision. In any event the owner will be without rental income after expiry of the lease until such time as the premises are rebuilt and re-let.

Consequently, there is a possibility of loss arising should either party neglect to insure; and whilst there may be some degree of double insurance if each covers the rent this is justifiable because recovery can be made at one and the same time, that is, by both tenant and owner.

117. Internal "rent"

There is another situation where a company owns the freehold of the premises it occupies but charges a "rent" to its subsidiary companies, departments, etc., in respect of that part of the premises which they individually occupy. No money actually changes hands but the "rent" represents the amount of the maintenance, etc., costs for the premises (plus a notional "profit" perhaps). This is simply an internal "discipline" and there should be sufficient overall cover if the company has arranged insurance to pay for the possible increased cost of obtaining alternative accommodation.

118. Taxation—United Kingdom

Under a "difference" specification the question of how taxation on profits is to be dealt with does not arise because only the uninsured working expenses are mentioned as being deducted from the amount of turnover to arrive at the insured gross profit and, consequently, there is no definition of net profit. Therefore any taxation on trading profits is automatically included in the insurance.

In the older form of specification in which gross profit is defined as net profit plus insured standing charges the definition of net profit is "the net trading profit . . . before the deduction of any taxation chargeable on profits" (paragraph 86). Because of this definition taxation on profits must not be included in the list of insured standing charges; to do so would mean insuring it twice over. In the exceptional cases where there is some taxation which should be included as an insured standing charge unless its precise nature is stated the reference must be qualified by using a description such as "taxation other than taxation chargeable on profits". Having to resort to the use of this phrase is, however, deprecated because it can give rise to misunderstanding by an insured. Another drawback to the use of the phrase is that it might be thought to bring in as a standing charge either value added tax or import, export, excise or other revenue duties where applicable.

The phrase might even be considered as bringing into the insurance any charge shown in the profit and loss account for tax suffered by deduction at source, that is, on income from invested money or on other extraneous revenue such as rent. As the income to which this tax is related does not arise from the trading activities of the business and is not included in the computation of gross profit (paragraph 87) the tax which it bears is not an insurable standing charge.

Therefore unless there is a very good reason for not mentioning the specific nature of the taxation it should always be described so as to avoid having to add the qualifying phrase.

The necessity for the inclusion of such taxation on profits is sometimes questioned on the grounds that if there is a diminution in net profit consequent upon damage there will be no taxation payable on the lost portion of profit.

The position is that as the Inland Revenue authorities allow the premiums on business interruption insurances as a business expense for the purpose of tax assessment they will bring into account as earnings of the business any amount recovered under such an insurance. In effect the Inland Revenue authorities are paying part of the premium and in the event of a loss are entitled to the benefit of the insurance for their share of the net profit accruing under it. Unless the amount of taxation has been included in the sum insured the amount of net profit which will be provided by the insurance will be the normal net profit *after* deduction of taxation. On this reduced figure of net profit taxation will be levied in the usual way thereby reducing to less than normal the amount available for distribution to shareholders or for other purposes.

Moreover, as the definition of net profit includes taxation on profits an omission of the amount of the latter from the sum insured could operate to an insured's disadvantage not only in the manner just mentioned but also through the application of the average proviso in respect of a claim for reduction in gross profit or for any increase in cost of working.

The definition of net profit also covers the practice of making an adjustment of taxation in each year's accounts so that the amount charged against profits for tax represents the figure which would have applied had there been no accelerated capital allowance for depreciation, or when adjustment is made for taxation in respect of income and expenditure dealt with for taxation purposes in a different year from that in which it is included for accounting purposes.

Because of the special nature of VAT the position in relation to the insurance of gross profit is made clear by a separate note on all specifications, *viz*.: NOTE: to the extent that the Insured is accountable to the tax authorities for Value Added Tax, all terms in this policy shall be exclusive of such tax.

(See also parallel comment about U.S. taxation on profits—paragraph 188.)

119. Rates

In the preamble to this chapter (paragraph 105) rates were mentioned together with rent in the general illustration of the necessity to insure such charges and no further comment is required.

120. Advertising expenses

Advertising expenses, publicity expenses, fashion show, exhibitions and trade show expenses, sports sponsorship expenses and the like are all, in general, standing charges which should be insured for their full amount because firms will wish to continue the usual expenditure to keep their name and products or brands in public favour although they may temporarily be unable to supply the normal quantity of goods. Moreover much advertising is done by contract and could not be reduced for some considerable time after the occurrence of damage even though for some exceptional reason an insured might wish to do so.

With regard to advertising in newspapers, whilst that in provincial papers may be on a day-to-day basis and can be cut down to correspond with an insured's reduced capacity to meet demand, in national dailies space has to be booked and is "put to bed" long in advance of the date when the advertisement will appear. So whilst the former may be a variable charge the latter, because it would be an expense without commensurate return if the insured could not supply the goods or services as and when the advertisement would be due to appear, might be considered a standing charge for insurance purposes.

Department stores and large retail shops which make a regular practice of advertising special lines in the local daily and evening newspapers on a day-to-day or weekly basis might be an exception to the general rule that advertising should be insured in full as a standing charge. As distinct from advertisements in national newspapers as mentioned in the foregoing paragraph, on cinema screens, theatre programmes, poster sites, in buses, various periodicals and so forth which is often termed prestige advertising and is of a general goodwill or permanent nature and would be continued, advertising in newspapers of different selling lines day by day can be largely controlled according to the goods an insured has for sale at the time. So this might be regarded as a variable charge.

Advertising on commercial television and radio calls for special consideration. In some businesses it is a heavy expense which it might be possible to curtail more or less in line with the degree of interference with a firm's capacity to supply the advertised goods during a period following damage. That is, in the case of advertisements aimed at an immediate response from the purchasing public (as distinct from prestige advertising or promotional activities to enhance their public image which a firm would presumably wish to continue as a long-term measure irrespective of the effects of damage) it might be suggested that this kind of advertising would have to be and could be reduced in frequency to correspond with the reduced capacity to supply goods. If this is demonstrably so, payment to broadcasting companies might be regarded as an expense which is variable with turnover and not an insurable charge; but an insured would need to consider the matter from all angles before deciding to exclude it from the insurance.

The above deals with the cost of buying time on television or radio broadcasting but still leaves for consideration the capital cost payable out of earnings for producing the advertisement video tapes. This expense is a heavy one and it has to be recouped from subsequent sales. The possibility of curtailment of these because of damage at the insured's premises means that advertising production costs must be regarded as an insurable constituent of the gross profit.

It may be questioned whether the expense of advertising of the nature mentioned above which might be incurred one year and not in another is to be included as a standing charge. Its amount should be included in the gross profit sum insured even if it is a non-recurring expense for the reason explained on expenses of that category in paragraph 82(c).

121. Window dressing and display expenses

These are another category of advertising expense, particularly heavy for department stores, which should be insured in the gross profit. Retail shops cannot afford to reduce their normal expenditure on these means of attracting custom if the damage affects only a portion of the premises such as upper floors or basement leaving most or all the ground floor window space undamaged. Alternatively, if the ground floor is badly damaged and the windows are boarded up, temporary display sites will be sought and rented in railway station concourses and other places and so the expense will continue. Similarly, if a shop or department store is completely destroyed temporary accommodation will be obtained wherever possible and though the expenditure on window dressing and display may be less than normal because of the reduced space available the reduction in such expenditure might not be proportionate with the fall in turnover.

122. Mail Order business advertising

In a mail order business specific items of merchandise are despatched by post, public carriers by road or rail, or by a firm's own delivery vans, orders being obtained through advertising in newspapers, magazines and glossies and with radio, television and cinema commercials. It might in some circumstances be possible to reduce the amount and cost of advertising after damage to correspond with the reduced quantity or range of goods which can be delivered during a period of interruption but in many businesses this is uncertain even if advertising is on a day-to-day basis or short term contract. As it is always a substantial proportion of the expenses of a business in this highly competitive industry—and in the United Kingdom and Western Germany the mail order industry accounts for about 10 per cent. of the national non-food retail market—it is an item deserving very careful consideration. (See also paragraph 120 regarding advertising in newspapers.)

Advertising on television may be looked at under two heads, the initial capital cost of producing the commercial and the charges of the television media for screening time. Even if it is considered that the latter can be reduced in line with reduced capability, after damage, to supply the advertised goods the former should be insured. The cost of its production is budgeted to be met from future sales and if these cannot be achieved because of an interruption of business following damage then it is a charge not fully met by turnover.

The preceding remarks about advertising by mail order houses do not include the expense of producing and distributing catalogues; this requires separate consideration and is dealt with in the following paragraph 123.

123. Brochures and catalogues

The cost of producing and distributing brochures and catalogues has like other forms of advertising expense to be earned by turnover subsequent to its being incurred. It is a relatively heavy expense and is of particular importance to mail order houses and clubs, tour operators and travel agents, proprietors of holiday camps and hotels, operators of motor coach tours and pleasure cruises, hirers of holiday boats and yachts, and seed and bulb merchants.

Glossy, illustrated brochures and catalogues are regarded as the shop window for such businesses and a most vital part of their sales organisation.

The cost of such literature could not be curtailed to correspond with a reduction in turnover if damage occurred to interrupt the business after production of the brochures and catalogues, so this expense should be included in full in the insurance on gross profit. This still applies even though the insured's business premises may be only a suite of offices and storerooms. Not only is there the risk of interruption of business resulting from a burn-out of the offices but also from a stock of brochures being destroyed in the stockroom or in process of production at the printers or on the premises of a specialist firm for addressing and mailing.

The fact that if the stock of sales literature is damaged by fire the material loss would be recovered under a fire policy does not necessarily mean that the expense of its production need not be insured as a standing charge under the business interruption insurance. Unless the spoilt brochures or catalogues can be very quickly replaced a considerable loss of orders may result irrespective of any resulting from interruption of business caused by damage to the insured's offices.

Businesses of a seasonal nature are particularly vulnerable and this applies to most of the various types of business mentioned and even to "catalogue mail order" houses and clubs which work through spare-time agents all the year round, because the catalogues issued to such agents are twice-yearly "seasonal" catalogues which are valid only for about six months.

For further points about the production of such literature and dependence on the printers, etc., see paragraph 367.

124. Special advertising campaigns

When manufacturers embark on a major advertising campaign of limited duration, whether in newspapers and magazines, on posters, by television and radio commercials, by direct mail, competitions, sample distribution or other means involving very heavy expenditure the bulk of which will be non-recurring, it may be questioned whether the cost of this should be included in the insured gross profit. If it is and the following year damage causes interference with the business, will the insurers treat the absence of the special expenditure on advertising as a reduction due to the damage and claim the benefit of it under the savings clause? (See paragraph 51(a).)

Although this charge may be non-recurring it should for the reasons explained in paragraph 82(c) on charges of that nature be brought into the computation of gross profit for its full amount. If damage should take place and cause an interference with the business in the year after that of the special campaign, the reduction in the non-recurring portion of the charge for advertising would not be deducted from the claim under the savings clause because it would not be in consequence of the damage. Therefore the insured would be compensated in full for the loss of what would have been net profit had the damage not occurred. This is logical bearing in mind that major advertising campaigns precede the sales they promote and the cost is recouped in the form of net profit on increased sales in the subsequent period.

It is unlikely that difficulty will be experienced in the event of a claim in deciding how far a reduction in advertising expenditure during a period of interruption is the result of deliberate policy and would have been effected had there been no damage and how much comes within the savings clause as being attributable to the damage. The arrangements for major advertising campaigns are fully planned in advance in great detail as to methods, timing and expenditure and adequate evidence should be readily available.

125. Travelling expenses

If there is a shortage of goods coming from a factory or warehouse following damage there, the travellers or representatives who have a round of regular customers will probably find it necessary to call on them just as frequently as before in order to maintain their goodwill or to sell to them a diminished quantity of goods. Consequently, their travelling expenses will not be reduced proportionately with a fall in sales and are an insurable charge.

On the other hand, where salespersons are selling entirely on a raw canvass with no repeat custom their expenses may fall proportionately with a reduction in the volume of goods they have to sell if they can arrange to be off the road for alternate weeks or can work on some similar lines. In such cases consideration might be given as to whether their expenses are necessarily an insurable charge.

When a firm's travelling is done by one or other of the principals or a director along with other duties and the accounts item of travelling expenses also covers their use of motor cars for social and pleasure purposes or journeys for buying, it is obviously a charge to be included in the insurance.

Similarly, when the item refers to the expenditure on travelling of directors, representatives, service specialists, inspectors, buyers, internal auditors and others who go about on the firm's business though not for the purpose of making sales, if it is a charge which would not fall proportionately with a reduction in turnover during a period of interruption it should be insured. The travelling expenses of executives may possibly increase because of their having to make extra journeys to speed up the rehabilitation of the business after serious damage.

Car rentals paid to a national rent-a-car organisation for the use of cars by executives may be regarded as coming into this category of expense as the amount is unlikely to be reduced proportionately with a reduction in turnover.

Should the item of travelling expenses in the accounts include the motor vehicle costs, train, air and bus fares and hotel, etc., allowances of workpeople going to and from jobs away from the factory or workshop and the aggregate is a large enough sum to make it worth while breaking down the item, the portion applicable to their travelling might be looked into to see whether it is a charge which will vary directly with turnover.

126. Airfield and heliport expenses and flying expenses

The expense of maintaining a private airfield or heliport and of flying a firm's own planes or helicopters for the use of directors and executives or other personnel will in most circumstances continue with little, if any, variation during a period of interruption. Similarly with the cost of aircraft charter, rental or leasing services. All these expenses should be included in the gross profit insurance.

127. Motor and motor vehicle expenses

When this item refers to private-type cars it often overlaps in accounts with travelling expenses or alternatively the latter will include the cost of running cars; under whichever heading the expense appears, whether or not it is an insurable charge should be considered on the lines explained in the preceding paragraphs.

Where it refers to goods vehicles, it might be argued that if a firm is running a fleet of delivery vans some of these could be laid up after damage at the premises if there is not sufficient work for all of them and so it is a variable charge which does not need to be insured. Bearing in mind, however, all the various possibilities it seems probable that at any rate so far as licences, garage and maintenance expenses are concerned, as distinct from expenses which vary with mileage, there would not be a saving proportionate with the reduction in turnover. Because of this, to be certain of full protection against possible loss it is advisable to insure the former charges in full.

Petrol or other fuel, oil and tyre costs and to some extent vehicle repairs are in another category. As they do vary in ratio with mileage they could be reduced proportionately with turnover if mileage could be so reduced as, for example, by laying up part of a fleet of vehicles during a period of interruption. In businesses (other than the kind described in paragraph 129) which run a large number of vehicles the delivery by these being a prominent feature of their trade such as laundries, breweries, soft drink factories, dairies and bakeries, laying vehicles off might be a viable proposition but it would depend to a large extent upon the method of working and the areas covered. Where a wide area is covered it might be necessary to run the whole fleet of vehicles with the normal mileage but with each vehicle carrying only a part of its ordinary load; in such circumstances all running expenses would be a non-variable charge. This position would arise in a business such as that of a bakery with vans with a regular round calling on small retailers or used as travelling saleshops; these would have to maintain their regular service to all customers in order to keep out competitors, even though they would have to supply each customer with less than their normal requirements.

But where only one or two delivery vans are owned, whatever the trade may be, the ordinary mileage may have to be run with loads less than the normal, in which case petrol, oil, tyres and repairs would prove to be standing charges.

When the circumstances of a particular case lead to a decision to insure only what is considered the non-variable part of the charge it is inadvisable to insure it by a description such as "50 per cent. of motor vehicle expenses", or "Motor vehicle expenses to an amount of £100,000". That method could in the event of a loss provide only a proportion of each of the non-variable and the variable parts of the charge instead of the insured's intention of the non-variable part in full and none of the variable part. If the savings clause were then to be applied in respect of the variable portion the insured would be left with compensation for only a part of the non-variable expenditure. It is much better to use a specific description in order to avoid possible difficulties under the savings clause. For example, under a "difference" wording the mention of "motor vehicle fuel, oil and tyres" in the list of uninsured working expenses would exclude them and only them from the insurance on gross profit, whilst under the older form of specification the same effect would be obtained by including in the insured standing charges "motor vehicle expenses other than fuel, oil and tyres".

128. Motor cars, trucks, vehicles and trailers

The considerations set out in the foregoing paragraph 127 apply whether the cars or vehicles are owned by the insured or not. But special consideration is required where they are run under one or other of the renting, contract hire or leasing schemes which are increasingly popular in the United Kingdom, involving any number of cars, vans or trucks from one up to fleets of hundreds.

Leasing generally means what is essentially a financial operation. Contract hire and rental packages, however, include other services and may be an all-inclusive transport management scheme providing vehicles, taxing, insurance, tyres, maintenance, repairs and relief vehicle costs, possibly also a driver and relief driver, for a fixed period of years. Therefore the particular circumstances of any individual business, the types of vehicles involved and the scheme and legal agreement under which its fleet is operated must all be considered in deciding whether any part of the overall cost can be regarded as a variable charge in relation to insurance against loss due to interruption of business. In this respect the fact that under some contract hire agreement the monthly rent is, as a safeguard against inflation, fixed for the duration of the lease is of importance.

The costs of renting trailers from a firm specialising in that business requires to be looked at in the light of whether they can be reduced to correspond with a reduction of the insured's turnover and this may depend upon whether the renting is done under short or long term contracts or on a day-to-day request basis.

129. Vehicle operation expenses of transport businesses

Businesses in which the revenue is derived solely from the services given by the operation of transport vehicles are in another category because the vehicles are the productive units of the business and although turnover is the index of loss the real basis is mileage run. So for the insurance of a motor coach or bus operator, haulage or removal contractor, taxi proprietor, or aviation charter freight and taxi services, it would seem unnecessary to include fuel, petrol, oil and tyres in the gross profit insurance since these vary directly with mileage and therefore must vary with revenue. Consideration might also be given as to whether repair costs could be dealt with similarly. As the average heavy lorry runs over 100,000 miles each year it will be appreciated how important running costs can be in considering their inclusion or otherwise in the gross profit insurance.

As licences are a considerable expense in this type of business and a refund can be obtained when a vehicle is laid up or destroyed consideration might also be given as to whether it is necessary to include this expense in the insurance. It should be borne in mind that the refund on licences which are surrendered is not exactly proportionate to the unexpired period which they have to run so that some relatively small loss would be suffered on this account.

130. Insurance premiums

In the same way as with rent and several other expenses, insurance premiums might be reduced to some extent following serious damage but as with those charges there is a greater possibility that there will not be a reduction proportionate with the fall in turnover. In general, therefore, they should be insured in full but an exception might be made for marine insurances on freight, air freight insurances, parcels insurances and export credits guarantee insurance, for which the premium costs usually vary with the value of goods dispatched. For a firm with a large export trade such insurances constitute a heavy item of expenditure and it may be worth while segregating the premiums from those for other insurances and excluding them from the gross profit cover.

The exclusion of employers' liability insurance premiums might also be considered for concerns with a large payroll, particularly those in industries where the accident risk and consequently the employers' liability premium rates are high. The accounts of such firms frequently show this premium separately from those for other insurances as being a productive cost. However, should it be decided that the premium is not a standing charge because it varies directly with the wages paid and therefore with production, the amount applicable to any wages insured should be included with such wages cover. For instance, the amount of employers' liability insurance premium relating to the wages insured in the gross profit item or the whole of such premium if wages are covered under dual basis or payroll cover schemes (paragraphs 205 *et seq.*).

131. Bank charges and credit card facilities charges

Bank charges for interest (see paragraph 113) for loans or overdrafts and any other charges such as those for advisory or miscellaneous services which will not fall proportionately with turnover should be insured.

Charges which are paid by businesses to banks and finance houses for providing financial backing for customer credit card facilities—Visa International, Interbank Mastercharge, Access, Barclaycard, American Express, Diners Club and other providers of plastic money—as a constant percentage of the amounts transacted are not a standing charge as they will reduce proportionately with a fall in turnover.

132. Postages, parcel post and delivery services

For the general run of businesses, although the cost of postage might be less than normal during a period of interruption, the reduction would not be proportionate with the drop in turnover and would be at least partly offset by increased expenditure on postage because of the extra correspondence which is inevitable after serious damage. It would most likely be impracticable to keep a separate record of such postages for the purpose of the claim in respect of both savings in charges and for additional expenditure. So it is in most cases better to include the postage charge shown in the accounts in full in the item on gross profit and recover under clause (a) proportionately with the fall in turnover. This together with the contribution from turnover maintained will make up the amount which postages would have been but for the interruption of business. If the post-damage postages are less than that amount a deduction will be made for savings in charges and if in excess of the amount the additional expense will be paid as increase in cost of working.

An exception to the general rule for insuring this charge might be made in the case of a mail order business, or the delivery of goods by shops, department stores or warehouses by post or parcel service and in similar circumstances where the cost of despatching parcels will vary exactly with sales. In the case of department stores, it is well to bear in mind the long maximum indemnity periods customary for such businesses and that the annual amount of any charge insured has to be multiplied correspondingly. This may mean quite a substantial premium in respect of this particular expense.

Whereas it was once customary for businesses of the foregoing kinds selling goods by mail order not to debit customers with a separate charge for postage or carriage on goods supplied, in America called shipping and handling charges, the steep increases in such charges over recent years has made charging for postage, carriage and packing the current general practice. However, this will not alter the fact that the outgoing postal, etc., charge will vary proportionately with sales and so does not need to be insured. Special consideration in respect of this charge will be needed by firms using the Royal Mail flat-rate contract service or two-part tariff contract.

Publishers of newspapers and periodicals also have a substantial postage bill because of their mailing list to postal subscribers which usually includes many overseas addresses. This expense is directly related to subscriptions and would fall proportionately with a reduction in turnover so there appears to be no necessity to insure it.

In various other classes of business the postage bill is relatively heavy and one which varies more or less with turnover, for instance, merchants with a large export trade dispatching samples by ordinary air mail or by special express air service, manufacturers advertising extensively in newspapers and periodicals with offers of descriptive literature of their products and samples, shade cards, etc., other businesses which issue catalogues and brochures direct to the public and the spare parts departments of manufacturers in industries with a large outgo of small items by parcel post. In such circumstances consideration might be given as to the practicability of excluding from the gross profit insurance the variable content of the postage charge by appropriate nomenclature. An insured offering Freepost facilities to invite enquiries or orders for their merchandise might, depending on the particular circumstances of their business and contract with the Post Office consider that the cost to them of incoming mail is variable with turnover. Regarding postage on return parcels, see paragraph 136.

Where services are used for the highspeed despatch of urgently required goods or samples a decision as to inclusion of this charge in the insurance or otherwise will depend largely on whether it is under a negotiated contract for a regular service over agreed routes or is under an "on demand" service.

133. Telephone, telex, radio and television communications systems, etc.

Rental and where applicable, hire charges for telephones, answering services, telex, view data, visual display systems, and radio communication systems will rank as standing charges to be included in the gross profit insurance.

The position with the expense of calls is similar to that explained in the first paragraph of paragraph 132 regarding the insurance of the charge for postages and on the same grounds it is suggested that the normal expense should be included in full in the gross profit insurance.

An exception might be made regarding telephone calls in the case of firms dealing in perishable commodities, *e.g.* wholesale fruit and fish merchants, who do most of their business over the telephone and have a very heavy bill for long distance calls which might be variable with turnover.

134. Office expenses

It is generally recommended that apart from considerations affecting the charges dealt with in the preceding paragraphs general office expenses should be insured in full. These may include petty cash disbursements, telegrams, cables, cablegrams, rental charges for intercom telephone systems, telephone answering machines, photocopiers, postage meters, maintenance and repair charges for the foregoing and other equipment, and microfilming charges.

The rent for the lease of office computers and micro-computers will rank as an insurable expense but whether charges for the hire of computer time with an outside agency are an insurable or variable expense will depend upon the particular business and the purposes for which computer time is required. Service subscriptions for technical information by computer should be insured.

135. Stationery and printing expenses

An item referring to expenses of this kind will appear in one form or another in the accounts of all businesses and when, as is generally the case, it is not directly related to turnover and appears in the second section of the trading account it will require to be treated as an insurable office expense. But there are exceptions and where any such item is of substantial amount it may need to be looked into to ascertain whether part or all of it is an expense which is variable with turnover.

For instance, part of an accounts item of "stationery and printing" may refer to the cost of labels for bottles or other containers of an insured's merchandise, leaflets giving instructions for their use, address labels for parcels, or order forms and invoices. Similarly with tickets and cards for shop display and pricing purposes. Businesses selling by mail order, particularly those working through agents, may use a large volume of order forms and self-addressed envelopes the quantity and cost of which might fall proportionately with a reduction in sales following damage.

136. Postage: returned parcels

The payment of postage and demurrage on parcels returned by the Post Office is a charge of considerable importance to firms engaged in a certain type of overseas trade in which orders by the general public for goods, generally clothing, are booked by agents, the goods being dispatched by parcel post direct to the customers who are expected to pay immediately on receipt thereof. It is an accepted trade risk that a considerable proportion of these parcels perhaps approaching 10 per cent., are not accepted by the addressees; consequently the recharge by the Post Office to the senders aggregates a substantial amount.

A considerable time is taken over the transit to and from this country in addition to the period during which the parcels are retained at the post offices overseas pending collection by customers. As a result the charges on returned parcels have not to be met and are not debited until some weeks after the goods were invoiced as sales. Should damage occur at the insured's premises and interfere with turnover there will still be parcels coming back and postage and demurrage will have to be paid on them but there will not be the normal turnover to meet the charge. This raises the question as to whether, although such charges are normally variable expenses which do not need to be insured, in view of the peculiar circumstances postal recharges should or should not be regarded as standing charges for purposes of the gross profit insurance.

The answer is that this expense varies with sales and in the normal way is not an insurable charge. The charges which have to be met on returned parcels during a period of interruption relate to sales which were credited in a preceding period and were earned by those sales. Their appearance as a debit in the accounts for the period in which there is a shortage in turnover due to the damage will mean that the ratio of postages and demurrage to turnover in that year will be higher than normal. But this ostensible loss will be balanced by the reduction in the charge after a resumption of normal trading when fewer parcels will be returned since a smaller number was dispatched during the period of interruption. Therefore, the insured will suffer no loss in respect of this item to whatever extent turnover may be affected by the damage, and there is no necessity to include it in the insurance.

Mail order firms which conduct their businesses through part-time, free-lance agents to whom they pay a commission on payments received for completed sales also pay the postage or carriage on goods returned by agents as unsold or requiring to be exchanged. Returned merchandise is a considerable percentage of the overall turnover but for the reason explained above the ratio to sales of postage or carriage on returns during a period of interruption will later be reduced for a time after the return to normal trading. Hence the ratio of returns to sales over the combined periods will be the same as that before the damage and this is not an insurable charge.

137. Lighting, space heating, water charges and meter rents

The necessity to include these charges in full is sometimes questioned but on reference to the general outline in paragraph 105 of what constitutes an insurable standing charge it will be realised that to omit them could leave an insured open to loss in a variety of circumstances. In fact in many cases the costs of lighting and heating increase during a period of interruption because of use at times when they would not normally be necessary.

An exception might be made where water is used extensively for trade purposes and the consumption is measured by meter and charged accordingly, as in laundries, dyeworks and steelworks, textile and paper mills, breweries (for barrel washing) and dairies (for bottle washing). In such circumstances, as the water charge will fall proportionately with a reduction in turnover, only the minimum charge or meter rent, as the case may be, needs to be insured.

Rentals, leasing and service charges for the water softening, purification and desalination plants necessary for industrial processes in some localities and industries and maintenance costs for same will not reduce with a fall in turnover and should be insured. A decision about water pollution prevention and effluent costs will rest on the particular circumstances of each case.

It is a regular practice for the cost of lighting not to be shown separately in trading accounts but to be included with the cost of current for power under the single heading of electricity. If the whole of the latter is not to be insured (see paragraph 173) at any rate the portion of it estimated as being applicable to lighting, for running air-conditioning plant or for space heating and for lifts or elevators should be included by an appropriate description.

138. Subscriptions and donations

Businessmen sometimes say that these expenses would be entirely discontinued following damage mistakenly thinking only of a complete stoppage of business. In actual fact such payments would almost invariably be continued in full, particularly subscriptions to trade associations and trade journals which are essential however low the level of trading may fall, and it is unlikely that a firm would wish charitable, political or social organisations and educational projects to which they normally subscribe to suffer because of damage at their premises. So although the cost of subscriptions and donations may be largely an optional expense it is the general practice to insure it.

139. Trade levies and export promotion levies

Expenses of this kind call for special consideration because there are different methods of charging them and they are frequently of very substantial amounts. Where they are fixed charges irrespective of production they are obviously standing charges for insurance purposes. On the other hand if they are paid at a rate of so much per unit of production or sales as is often the case the annual cost will vary with turnover and is not an insurable charge.

140. Hire purchase or hire contract charges

Hire purchase and hire contract charges do not vary with turnover, but where they arise from the hire of plant and machinery it is sometimes suggested that because its destruction would mean recovery of the value under a fire policy, discharge of the hire agreement and cessation of the charge, it is unnecessary to insure it. Damage may occur, however, which interferes with production without destroying the particular plant or machinery which is the subject of the hiring agreement and to cover this possibility the hire purchase or hire contract charges should be insured in full.

141. Hired transport

In the accounts of some businesses a debit for the cost of hiring motor vehicles may appear as "hired transport"; this is not to be confused with the contract hire of vehicles dealt with in paragraph 128. For example, motor-coach operators and haulage contractors hire vehicles from other operators on a day-to-day basis as a convenient method of dealing with the fluctuating demands of trade which is not sufficiently stable to justify an increase in the size of their own fleet. As this expenditure is paid only as and when such hired transport is required, it varies directly with turnover and is not an insurable charge.

142. Cleaning charges

In most businesses this is an insurable charge, certainly so when it is under a contract for a fixed term for industrial cleaning services. Even in businesses such as printers and engineering works where a considerable sum is spent each year on industrial cleaning cloths for the daily cleaning of plant and machinery, a slowing down or part-time running of the works, as distinct from a complete shut-down, may not produce a reduction in the expense proportionate with the fall in production.

An exception might be made in businesses such as those of operators of motorcoaches, motorbuses, hire cars or haulage vehicles if the cost of materials used in maintaining the cleanliness of the vehicles is in direct ratio to the number in service and the time they are on the road. In such circumstances it is unnecessary to insure this expense as it will reduce proportionately with any fall in revenue.

If the debit under the heading cleaning expenses in an insured's accounts refers to the cost of cleaning employees' working apparel, refer to paragraph 164 on laundry expenses.

143. Expenditure on works' welfare, canteen, outings, sports and social clubs, factory clinics and nurses' services

Each of these items and any of a similar nature such as the rental for radio relay equipment is an insurable charge and the only one calling for comment is that of canteen expenses.

It is sometimes suggested that if a works or even a part of it were closed because of damage the cost of running a work's canteen would be reduced as it represents a loss of so much per meal served and if fewer workpeople partook of meals then the aggregate loss would be proportionately smaller. There is something in this argument in respect of loss arising from the cost of food supplied exceeding the price charged for it and not from the overhead expenses of the canteen. The general overheads of the canteen, however, and any catering consultancy and management charges will be standing charges because they cannot be reduced to correspond with a reduction in the number of meals served.

Should the charge in the accounts be in respect of meal vouchers supplied to workers it would vary directly with the number retained in employment after damage and might be insured as a supplementary part of the cover on wages in the same way as national insurance contributions and other ancillary charges are insured.

144. Cost of production of patterns, swatches, samples, etc.

The reference here to patterns is to those made of cloth, furnishing fabrics, vinyl, paper, or other materials as produced in the textile, clothing, furnishing, floor covering, wallpaper and other trades for the purpose of procuring orders, and not to working patterns as used in a clothing factory, foundry or engineering works.

A charge of this nature sometimes presents difficulty because whilst it is recognised as being an expense of producing articles of no corresponding sale value, it is thought that if they are destroyed the value of materials and the labour which has been expended on them will be recoverable under the fire insurance and there is no need to insure the charge under the business interruption policy. This overlooks the fact that the cost of the production of the patterns and samples already in the hands of customers is normally met out of future sales and if these are reduced because of damage at the factory then the insured will lose correspondingly on the value of patterns and samples already issued. Moreover, the stock of patterns and samples at the factory might be undamaged whilst the productive side is crippled and sales are in consequence reduced. Because of changes in designs or of fashion during the period of interruption some or all of these patterns or samples may be useless when the time to restart production arrives. Hence the expense which went into the making of those now redundant patterns and samples is lost proportionately with the loss of turnover which would have carried their cost. This loss cannot be recovered under a fire policy because they have not suffered material damage. Meanwhile new patterns, etc., must be prepared as far as possible during the period of interruption to solicit orders for the time when production can be resumed. Therefore, where the expense associated with their production is normally debited as a separate item in the trading accounts it should be included in the insurance on gross profit.

When the accounts normally show a separate credit for the cash received from the sale of patterns after they have served their main purpose, only the net cost, that is, the cost of their production less receipts from sales, should be included in the insurance.

If there is no notional debit in the accounts and the cost of materials and labour is part of the general charges for purchases and wages no recovery will be made in respect of materials unless a note is added to the definitions to insure them and recovery will be made for the wages only to the extent to which they are insured in either the item on gross profit or in a separate item on wages. This makes it most advisable for a business in which such circumstances apply to insure fully the wages of all employees engaged in the making of patterns and samples.

145. Reproductive photos and artists' illustrations

The purchase of photos—models, pictorial, views and other subjects—and artists' sketches and paintings by publishers of magazines and periodicals, or by mail order and other businesses for their catalogues or brochures, or by printers for the production of calendars, Christmas cards, showcards and the like, or by clothing, etc., manufacturers, is an expense which has to be earned by subsequent turnover. If the latter is reduced because of damage after the photos, etc., are finished with or if they are undamaged and their value cannot be claimed under the fire insurance then there will be a loss on the amount paid for them proportionate with the reduction in turnover. Hence this item of expense should be included in the insurance on gross profit.

146. Depreciation of buildings, plant, machinery, fixtures, fittings, shopfronts, canteen equipment, motor vehicles, etc.

This is an item which often gives rise to the argument that it is not a standing charge because if buildings and plant are destroyed depreciation will either cease altogether or be reduced in proportion to the amount of damage done. But as explained in the preamble to this chapter turnover can be adversely affected out of proportion to the amount of property destroyed and so the reduction in the depreciation charge will not necessarily be proportionate with the fall in earnings. Also when new buildings and plant replacing those destroyed are still not fully productive depreciation will be taking place in relation to them. The need to insure depreciation is even more obvious when an insurance is extended to include loss of turnover resulting from "other people's fires", that is, damage at the premises of suppliers of goods or components, processors, customers, or storage premises. (See Chapter 17.)

Moreover, depreciation is not necessarily a provision only for wear and tear but may be partly a writing down of values of plant and machinery, or of equipment such as jigs, moulds, lasts, knives, patterns, printers' blocks, dies, etc., due to changes in design of products or to the introduction in the trade concerned of more efficient machinery. It has been said that in the field of composition equipment for newspaper printing, it is prudent to write off investment in a period of five years because of rapid technological advance. This may be an extreme example but obsolescence in some degree applies to all manufacturing concerns and will continue unabated even though the works are stopped entirely, which they may be with only a small part of the plant destroyed.

There is a further reason for insuring depreciation. There is no uniformity in accountancy practice in the method of calculating depreciation. It may be a straight line basis by reference to cost and valuation less government grants, where applicable, and to the anticipated useful lives of the assets concerned; or it may be on some other basis; or the amount which can be claimed for tax allowance may be the deciding factor. In any case the amount written off each year is bound to be an arbitrary figure and may be in excess of the real amount of depreciation. In that event part of it is, in effect, a transfer of profit to capital account or reserve and the insured would wish to be compensated by means of the insurance for a similar allocation if the turnover during a period of interruption were insufficient to earn it.

For these reasons depreciation of buildings, plant, machinery, fixtures, fittings, shopfronts, canteen equipment and motor vehicles is regarded by insurers as an insurable charge and should be included in full. In the "difference" wording the inclusion of depreciation is effected automatically in the definition of gross profit. In the older wording the definition of net profit states that due provision has to be made for depreciation before arriving at the amount of the net trading profit. Depreciation must therefore be included in any list of insured standing charges, the same description being used for that purpose as is shown in the accounts so as to make it clear for the reasons explained in the following paragraph 147 that depreciation of stock is not included. With an insurance for firms which make or sell plant, machinery or vehicles it is customary if depreciation is included in a list of insured standing charges to exclude depreciation of any such property which forms part of their saleable stock.

In cases where allocations are made each year to a "plant and machinery sinking fund" this charge should similarly be insured. Also when an amount is charged against revenue each year for the amortisation of the premium paid for leasehold land and buildings or as occasionally arises for depreciation of freehold land, this should be included in the insurance because the land cannot be destroyed and the annual writing off will continue whatever may happen to the buildings on it.

During a period when exceptionally high profits are being earned a firm may consider it expedient to make a special debit as an increased provision for depreciation. The amount by which this exceeds the normal depreciation allowance is in effect a non-recurring charge and because of this should be included in the insurance in full, as the net profit in the following year would in the ordinary course be correspondingly increased by the absence of this debit. For that reason the reduction in the overall amount of the depreciation charge which would occur in that subsequent year would not be deducted under the savings clause should damage give rise to a claim during that year because the reduction in the excess depreciation allocation would not be due to the damage. (See paragraph 82(c) with regard to non-recurring charges.)

147. Depreciation of stock

Depreciation of stock, whether raw materials, consumable stores, work in progress or finished goods, generally arises through market fluctuations, the ageing of stock, changes in designs and fashions or obsolescence, and in the annual accounts is not debited as a charge but is reflected in the reduced amount of the closing stock figure according to the stock valuation. It is a trading loss attaching to the amount of stock held and in general would arise irrespective of damage occurring. Consequently it is not regarded as insurable in the item on gross profit. When the net profit plus insured standing charges definition is employed it is not permissible to include depreciation of stock in the list of insured standing charges, whilst in the "difference" wording it is automatically excluded by the use of opening and closing stock figures with the Note providing that "due provision be made for depreciation".

Whilst depreciation of stock may be regarded in the normal course of business as a charge in the variable category and therefore outside the scope of a business interruption insurance, special consideration needs to be given to the occasions which do arise when it may be of exceptional severity and a special writing-down of stock values at the year end has to be made in the trading accounts. In such circumstances should a loss of turnover resulting from an insured peril occur in the following year it is possible under the other circumstances clause to adjust, for the purposes of a claim, the rate of gross profit figure for the financial year in which the special writing-down of stock took place to what it would have been but for the damage, as mentioned in paragraph 225(c).

Deterioration of perishable stock which cannot be processed because of damage at the factory is a different matter (see paragraph 269 regarding Spoilage insurance).

148. Depreciation of patents, goodwill, trade marks, and patterns

Patents are a wasting asset as their life is of limited duration. Where an annual provision is made out of revenue for this depreciation in their value, such a charge would require to be continued whatever reduction in turnover might result from damage and it is an insurable standing charge.

The same remarks apply to goodwill for which a purchase price has been paid and to trade marks, as intangible fixed assets for which an annual depreciation charge is debited in the accounts. But should it be a group company's standing practice to write off goodwill arising on the acquisition of interests in subsidiaries by charging an amount direct to reserves instead of through the Profit and Loss Account the amount will not have to be brought into the calculation of gross profit as it is an allocation of profit of previous years. Hence it should not be included in a list of insured standing charges; a "difference" specification will automatically exclude it.

When depreciation of working patterns appears as a debit in the accounts of firms such an engineers, foundries, clothing or textile manufacturers it is a charge which will not decrease proportionately with any shortage in turnover and it should be included in the insurance on gross profit.

149. Balancing charges

When buildings, plant, machinery or vehicles are destroyed by fire the amount recoverable under a fire or motor vehicle insurance will, in all probability, exceed the written-down value; almost certainly so in the case of a fire policy on a reinstatement basis. If the adverse effects of the fire on trading are compensated for by a business interruption insurance the net profit (as insured in the specification, that is, before taxation) will be restored to normal. But the recovery under the fire or motor vehicle insurance if in excess of the written-down value of the assets destroyed could result in corporation tax being levied on a balancing charge up to the extent that capital allowances previously given are found not to have been required. This would result in a proportion of the net profit which has been maintained by the business interruption policy being payable to the revenue authorities if the insured elects to be assessed on a balancing charge.

This ostensible loss is not covered by a business interruption insurance because taxation on a balancing charge would not appear in the previous year's accounts, is not a standing charge and does not arise from a reduction in turnover. Insurance companies hold the view that the taxation on a balancing charge is not really a loss and so is not insurable. The position is that a firm's capital account benefits by recovery under the fire or motor vehicle insurance for the full cost of the new assets without deduction for the benefit received in previous years as tax allowance on depreciation. This writing-down allowance was made to compensate for the loss of capital value due to wear and tear, etc., of fixed assets. Owing to the fire the firm receive under a reinstatement insurance, new plant, etc., in replacement of that which was part-worn, and so have obtained from the revenue authorities in previous years an allowance of tax for wear and tear which events have proved to be unnecessary. The balancing charge is made to rectify this position; but the firm concerned are no worse off because their capital account shows the plant at written-down value whereas they actually have new plant.

An alternative view is put forward that there need be no loss because a taxpayer can avoid assessment on a balancing charge by restricting claims for future capital allowances to the cost of new plant less the amount of the balancing charge attributable to the assets destroyed. This, however, would appear to be only a deferment of taxation and not an actual avoidance of it.

The converse of taxation on a balancing charge must not be overlooked, that is, if the fire or motor vehicle insurance is inadequate and the amount recovered under it is less than the written-down value of the assets destroyed taxation relief can be obtained by a claim for a balancing allowance.

150. Auditors' and accountants' fees and accountancy charges

In general, the accountancy work in connection with a client's audit, taxation and other matters will not be appreciably lessened because of an interference with the business due to damage and the annual fees for such work constitute an insurable charge. This will obviously be so where the amount of the auditors' fees is fixed at a shareholders' annual meeting.

Where separate debits are shown in an insured's accounts for accountancy charges or taxation charges in addition to that for auditors' fees they should similarly be mentioned separately in the list of insured standing charges if the net profit plus standing charges definition of gross profit is being used. If they are combined by name with the charge for auditors' fees the same description should be used in the specification.

The fees for extra accountancy work which will arise in the production of information required by insurers in connection with a claim under a business interruption insurance are payable by the insurers under the terms of the Professional Accountants Clause on the insured's policy as detailed in paragraph 378.

151. Legal and other professional charges

Fees or retainers paid annually for the services of a solicitor, barrister, financial consultant, architect or other professional adviser whether at a fixed amount or according to the actual services involved in connection with the administrative, financial or development aspects of a business are unlikely to decrease with a reduction in turnover. They should therefore be included in the insurance on gross profit. In businesses where a charge for professional services appears in the accounts as an isolated occurrence as distinct from an annual one it should be treated in the manner described in paragraph 82(c) for non-recurring charges.

An exception might be made with regard to legal charges for businesses doing a large retail trade or hire-purchase business which involves a substantial amount of legal work in the attempted collection of instalments or recovery of debts. As this expense will vary proportionately with turnover it may be considered unnecessary to include it in the insurance and it can be shown in the list of uninsured working expenses in a "difference" wording or omitted from the list of insured standing charges in the older wording, as the case may be.

152. Discounts allowed

Whether shown as a debit in the accounts or deducted from the sales figure before this is credited, discounts allowed, being a cash discount allowed to customers for settlement within a credit period, is a charge which will on the average vary in direct ratio to the value of goods sold or services rendered. Therefore, it is not a standing charge.

When the trading accounts are drawn so as to show sales as a net figure after deduction of discounts allowed or when the entry for discounts received (which should be insured in the gross profit—see paragraph 85(b)) or for discounts allowed is the difference either way between the two classes of discount the correct figure for the gross profit insurance will be obtained by taking those accounts figures into the computation as they stand.

153. Discounting charges

Although paid to a third party instead of being allowed to a customer as are discounts allowed, discounting charges are in effect an expense of the same category. They reduce the amount received for goods sold and vary with the volume of trade transacted. Consequently they need not be included in the gross profit insurance.

154. Wrapping materials, packaging, boxes, bottles, sacks and other containers of all kinds, paper and string

These are all items of expense directly related to the quantity of goods sold. Therefore, they may be included as variable charges in a list of uninsured working expenses or omitted from a list of insured standing charges.

It may be suggested that the purchase of these materials is not spread evenly over the year and a considerable quantity may be bought at a time with the result that a new supply may have to be obtained during the period of interruption quite apart from the replacement of those lost in the fire and paid for under a fire policy. This does not alter the position because packing materials will only be used up proportionately with the turnover achieved during the period of interruption and value for the amount expended will be recouped from turnover either during that period or subsequently. So there will in fact be no increased ratio of cost to turnover of materials used during the period of interruption.

155. Packing: making-up and packing costs: containers and pallets

In businesses where an item of "packing charges" or similar descriptions in the accounts means the cost of packing materials or refers to charges paid to an outside firm of specialist packers the annual expenditure will depend upon the quantity of goods dispatched. As it will vary proportionately with a rise or fall in turnover it is not a charge which needs to be insured. On the other hand if it refers to the cost of the maintenance of an insured's own packing departments it is—except for the part of it which relates to the cost of packing materials—a standing charge which should be insured.

The hire of containers, *e.g.* from British Rail for the transport of goods by rail, road or sea, if charged per container used and not at a rental on a time basis, will vary with turnover and may be regarded as a variable charge. Similarly the cost of providing wooden loading pallets or of hiring these from a dock pallet pool may be regarded as variable with turnover.

156. Carriage: shipping, freight container and container base services

Carriage has already been referred to as being in general a charge of a variable nature (see paragraph 106). In some trades what was once a fairly common practice of paying for carriage by contract at a fixed price per month or year irrespective of the quantity of goods carried is now rarely met with. Where it does appertain it is a non-variable charge which should be insured.

Shipping and freight expenses for goods sent overseas—trucking, warehousing, insurance, lighterage to the loading tackle of a ship and shipping charges—including air freight are a form of carriage and if they are a charge which will vary proportionately with any reduction in the quantity of goods transported there is no necessity to include them in the insurance.

Similarly, where the transport of goods overseas is in containers, use being made of the services, equipment, cranes and containers of a container-base firm, if the charges for same relate to the quantity of goods transported they may be regarded as a variable expense.

157. Storage rent

This should be insured in the gross profit if it is paid for space, that is, for specific buildings or portions of warehousing premises. In such conditions the expense will not decrease proportionately with a reduction in the quantity of goods passing in and out of store particularly where the rent is paid on a quarterly or longer basis.

Where the rent is paid according to the quantity of goods stored and the length of time they are there the charge is more controllable but even so the question as to whether it is a standing charge will depend upon circumstances. Should the storage be in respect of goods which are merchanted and which can be sold irrespective of damage at the insured's own premises the charge will vary in the normal way with the amount of goods sold, that is, with turnover, and so is a variable charge. On the other hand, should the goods in store be raw materials or consumable stores waiting transfer to the insured's factory for processing damage at the latter might mean a prolonged period of storage for goods which cannot be taken in at the factory. The aggregate annual charge for storage rent will not increase because of this and there will therefore be no additional expenditure to claim under the increase in cost of working provisions of the policy. But its ratio to the reduced turnover will be higher than normal and from this point of view it is a non-variable charge which should be insured. (See also paragraph 175 regarding the "increased ratio" aspect.)

It may be suggested that as the cost of storage for a specific quantity of goods in store during the period of interruption has in fact increased because of the lengthened time for which the goods have to remain there it is an additional expense which is claimable under the increase in cost of working section of the insurance. This overlooks the provision in clause (b) that the additional expenditure must be incurred "for the sole purpose of avoiding or diminishing the reduction in turnover, etc.". In the circumstances stated the continued storage would not be necessary for the purpose of maintaining turnover unless the goods were in short supply or of a seasonal nature which would necessitate their being kept in order to ensure that the factory had supplies of raw materials available when ready for production again.

158. Storage handling charges

The cost of the manual and mechanical handling by employees at a public warehouse of an insured's goods in store there will vary in ratio to the quantity of goods moved in and out. Consequently it is not necessary to insure this expense in the gross profit cover.

159. Bad debts

(a) *Not an insured standing charge*

Insurers will not permit bad debts to be included as an insured standing charge because bad debts can only accrue on sales transacted or services rendered whereas a business interruption policy is concerned with loss of turnover (sales or services) and bad debts cannot arise on non-existent turnover. But it is sometimes questioned in connection with businesses where bad debts are of irregular frequency and amount or possibly are a purely isolated occurrence as to whether this does not leave an insured open to loss in certain circumstances, for instance, in the case where an exceptional charge for a bad debt appears in the accounts in the financial year preceding the damage reducing correspondingly the net profit shown in that year. It may be thought by an insured that the reduced amount of net profit will be used in the calculation of the gross profit for the business interruption claim whereas during that year they would have had no bad debt to meet and, but for the damage, would have made their normal amount of net profit. Such a view is incorrect. Bad debts appearing as an item in the accounts at irregular intervals constitute a non-recurring charge but because they cannot be included in the list of insured standing charges they can be provided for in a claim only by adjustment to the rate of gross profit under the other circumstances clause and subject to the sum insured on gross profit being adequate as explained in paragraph 82(c) on non-recurring charges. So the insured should include the amount of any such bad debts, less any recovery under an Export Credits Guarantee Department or other credit insurance in the computation of the sum insured on gross profit. This will then be adequate in the event of damage taking place to allow for the rate of gross profit to be appropriately adjusted by means of the other circumstances clause and for the insured to recover as net profit the amount which in the preceding year was taken up by the charge for bad debts.

Where bad debts feature fairly regularly in the accounts but fluctuate in amount considerably from year to year they obviously are not strictly variable with turnover and the amount of them should, for reasons similar to those explained above, be included in the gross profit sum insured. Any necessary adjustment of figures in a claim will then be based on the particular circumstances at the relevant times in order to produce a proper indemnity if the gross profit sum insured is adequate for that purpose.

As insurance companies prohibit the inclusion of bad debts in any list of insured standing charges it would seem that, conversely, when a "difference" wording is used bad debts should be included in the list of uninsured working expenses. In fact, they very often are so included. However as regards bad debts of irregular occurrence which do not vary proportionately with turnover it would seem illogical to include them in a list of variable charges. There seems to be no standard practice in this matter.

The position is different for businesses in which bad debts are an integral feature of the trading activities and year in and year out represent approximately the same percentage of turnover as explained in the following paragraph 159(b).

(b) *Bad debts: retail credit traders*

Whilst the remarks in paragraph 159(a) are applicable where bad debts are of irregular frequency and amount there are some types of business, particularly those which conduct considerable credit trading with the general public such as furniture, television, electrical goods and domestic appliances shops, in which bad debts are numerous but each of relatively small amount. In such businesses the total of bad debts is almost invariably the same percentage of turnover each year and they are looked upon as a trade risk. Because they normally vary proportionately with sales no loss should be experienced in connection with them as a result of a reduction in turnover and generally it will be found unnecessary to include an amount for them in the computation of the sum insured as has to be done for bad debts of irregular occurrence.

The fact that insurers will not allow the insurance of bad debts is immaterial in respect of bad debts of this nature in the case of an insurance under the older definition of gross profit because an insured will not require to include them in a list of insured standing charges. But under a "difference" specification they will have to be included in the list of uninsured working expenses.

(c) *Bad debts reserve: appropriation fund for bad debts*

A charge under one of these or a similar heading in the accounts presents a rather more complex problem influenced to some extent not only by the particular circumstances but also by the form in which the accounts are drawn up.

When such an allocation to reserve is an isolated instance which is charged in a particular year and will not be repeated it could be treated as a non-recurring charge not necessitating mention in a list of insured standing charges.

When the allocation to bad debts reserve is a consistent feature of the accounts each year and corresponds on average over the years fairly closely to the actual bad debts experienced and written off each year it would appear to be a variable charge and so could be omitted from the insurance for the reasons given in the proceeding paragraph 159(b).

When the allocation is simply a prudent business measure to build up a reserve fund against the possibility of an unusually heavy incidence of bad debts at some future date which may in fact never materialise and is always a matter of judgment it is in effect net profit placed to reserve. As such it is insurable and should be included in the sum insured on gross profit and mentioned in the list of insured standing charges if that form of specification is used. Should an exceptional bad debt have to be debited at any time preceding damage this would not have affected the normal total of net profit plus bad debts reserve allocation in the indemnity year. Similarly, if it accrued in the latter period it would arise from pre-damage turnover and be of no consequence in a claim for post-damage shortage in turnover. So by having included bad debts reserve in the insurance on gross profit a proper indemnity would be provided in a claim for the insured's normal net profit plus amount placed to reserve. Should it be omitted from the definition of gross profit it cannot be claimed as a non-recurring charge because it appears consistently year by year in the accounts.

160. Consumer service departments and repair centres: service guarantee expenses and after-sales services

Whether an expense in this category is a variable or a standing charge will depend to some extent upon its particular character and upon its treatment in an insured's accounts.

The sale of consumer goods with or without a guarantee attaching involves the makers in the subsequent expense of repairing or supplying new parts for defective ones. Although not the makers of goods they sell, many large department shops, discount stores and mail order firms maintain their own repair and service maintenance departments in connection with their sale of household domestic appliances, television and electronic consumer goods, etc., in a similar manner to manufacturers. For both makers and retailers the liability to repair or replace will continue even during a period when sales of new goods are reduced or non-existent because of damage either at the insured's own premises or at those of a supplier or processor. During the period of interruption the ratio of this expense may therefore increase and it might be thought that in consequence it should be treated as a standing charge. But as it is an expense which is part of the cost of and variable with the sale of goods it cannot arise in relation to goods not made or sold because of interruption of production, which is what a business interruption policy is concerned with. So because materials, packing and carriage which vary strictly in relation to the amount of guarantee work carried out during a period of interruption, create no actual loss they are not insurable standing charges.

But this may not go quite far enough. The other expenses of a guarantee department—managerial and office salaries and general overheads—will continue unabated throughout the period of interruption and also during the period of reduced guarantee services which follows perhaps for many months after the sales of new goods are back to normal. In other words, although the gap in new production will create a subsequent shortage in free repairs and replacements carried out under guarantees with a correspondingly reduced cost of materials, packing and carriage, the department's overhead expenses will have continued without appreciable reduction throughout the whole period. Hence they are an insurable standing charge.

Where an insured's accounts show a debit for the service guarantee department solely for the administrative cost of running it and charge materials, packing, carriage and wages in the manufacturing section it is a simple matter of including only the former expense in the gross profit insurance. Where the costs of fulfilling liabilities under guarantees are not shown separately from the general charges of the business the administrative salaries and overheads will automatically be included in the gross profit insurance and the variables will similarly be excluded from it. But should all the expenses of the department be debited in one inclusive item in the accounts it will be necessary to break this down and insure by appropriate nomenclature only the fixed overhead element in the charge.

161. Royalties on machinery

This is a good illustration of an expense which is an insurable charge in some cases but not in others. Where royalties are paid in the form of a fixed rental, that is, at an agreed charge per annum for the use of certain machines or parts of machinery the cost will have to be met irrespective of the extent to which the machinery is used and it is a charge of a non-variable nature which should be included in the insurance.

Where the charge is levied on a "user" basis, that is, according to the number of times a machine is operated as recorded by an instrument attached to it the cost to the insured will vary exactly with the amount of use of the machine and also with turnover. Therefore, it is not a standing charge. Similarly, when the royalty is paid as a percentage on sales it will vary with turnover and does not need to be insured.

Where machine royalties are charged on the basis of a fixed minimum to cover up to an agreed number of operations and a "user" charge for any use beyond that limit the minimum charge can be treated as a standing charge and the user charge as a variable one for the purposes of the gross profit insurance.

162. Franchise fees and levies

Another category of royalties are those payable by a business operated under a franchise to the organisation franchisor in the form of a levy or fees as a percentage of turnover. It is reported that in the United States over one-third of all businesses are franchised; the number in the United Kingdom is growing rapidly.

Royalties, advertising and administration services also paid to the franchisor as a percentage of the business turnover will vary proportionately with the latter and in the absence of special terms to the contrary in a contract they are variable expenses not requiring to be insured. A fixed charge, however, for the right to operate in a certain territory and the charge for initial services for the pre-opening public relations exercise and advertising and any subsequent payments for special services will rank for inclusion in the amount to be insured.

163. Uniforms, works overalls, protective clothing, etc.

In a business where the insured provide uniforms or working clothing for employees the expense should be insured at least to the same relative extent that the wages of such employees are similarly covered. This is necessary because the wages of those workers are insured on the grounds that they may be retained on the pay-roll whilst underemployed or whilst turnover is less than normal and in such circumstances it is unlikely that the wear and tear of their uniforms or working apparel will decrease proportionately.

For example, uniforms of commissionaires, porters, lift attendants, theatre and cinema attendants, van drivers and other employees whose wages will probably be fully insured either in the gross profit or under a dual basis wages cover will most likely be worn for the normal working hours during a period of interruption. So far as industrial clothing such as that provided for employees in food factories, shops, garages, etc., is concerned, whilst in theory the wear and tear should vary in strict ratio with the hours worked in practice this may not be so particularly as the normal frequency of laundering might be continued throughout a period of interruption.

In the case of coach and bus undertakings the expense of providing uniforms for drivers and conductors is a considerable item in the accounts and calls for careful consideration in the light of the particular circumstances. When new uniforms are supplied at fixed periods of time off-duty wear is an important factor and it might be that a period of non-employment or of short-time working will not result in any extension of the life of uniforms, particularly having in mind the possibility of extra gardening, household repairs, etc., activities during the employees' enforced leisure! In such cases it would be advisable to include the item in the insurance.

Industrial protective gloves, headgear and clothing are a somewhat different matter and it may be decided that the amount of wear and tear will vary strictly with production in the works and that it is unnecessary to insure this expense. Workwear clothing supplied and serviced under contract by specialist firms will have to be considered in the light of the particular business and terms of the contract in order to decide about inclusion in the insurance.

164. Laundry expenses

Many firms provide a laundering service for the overalls or other working clothes of their employees, particularly in factories handling foodstuffs and in retail stores.

When the laundering is done by outside firms at a charge per garment it may be considered necessary to insure only the portion of the expense which corresponds with the proportion of the employees whose wages are fully insured. The grounds for this are that the rest of the workers will either be dismissed, in which case no laundering will be required for their garments, or, if and when they are working their labour will enable payment to be made for the laundering in the normal way.

Where the laundering is done by contract for a period at a fixed price irrespective of the number of garments cleaned the item should be insured in full as it will not reduce proportionately with a fall in turnover. Similarly, if it is a case of their own laundry being maintained by the insured for cleaning their workpeople's industrial clothing or as in some instances for doing their employee's domestic washing in order to attract married women into employment, that part of the cost which is not a variable charge should be insured.

165. Loss and/or profit on foreign currency exchange

A firm engaged in overseas trade may make a profit or sustain a loss of varying magnitude according to fluctuations in foreign currency rates and the time and nature of the trading or financial transactions concerned. Exchange adjustments on the translation of fixed assets of overseas subsidiaries and associated companies will be taken direct to reserve as a capital gain or loss. Exchange differences arising on trading will be included in the profit and loss accounts.

It is the opinion of insurers that loss on exchange transactions is not an insurable charge but that non-insurance of it does not adversely affect an insured, unless it is in respect of cash balances held overseas in which case it is a capital loss, because losses of this nature can only arise in respect of turnover which has been transacted at some time. Therefore, if a loss on exchange has to be debited in the revenue accounts relating to a period of interruption after damage it either arises from turnover transacted in a period before the damage or from turnover effected during the period of interruption. It cannot result from a shortage in, that is, an absence of, turnover. Consequently, the loss would have occurred irrespective of the damage and so it is not the concern of a business interruption policy the object of which is to provide an indemnity for loss resulting from reduction in turnover.

But a loss on exchange might arise and be debited in the accounts for the financial year preceding the damage thereby reducing the net profit in that year. The fact that it is not named in the insurance need not, however, affect the amount recoverable by an insured during the period of interruption when net profit, but for the damage, would have risen to its normal amount. The position is almost identical to that of bad debts of irregular frequency and amount, with regard to which, reference should be made to paragraph 159(a). Should a debit for loss on exchange be shown in the accounts for the financial year before damage occurs it can be treated as a non-recurring charge and provided that the sum insured on gross profit is adequate, by invoking the other circumstances clause the rate of gross profit could be increased in the claim calculation to give a proper indemnity. Conversely, if it had been a profit on exchange transactions in the year before the damage the insurers could claim an adjustment to reduce the rate of gross profit.

Often firms who are almost entirely dependent on foreign currency payments for goods supplied or services rendered choose to avoid the danger of losing money on exchange by selling the particular currency forward to their bank, who will thereby contract to provide them with a guaranteed sterling sum at a pre-arranged rate of exchange. Should damage occur at their premises, causing an interruption which leads to the non-receipt of the foreign currency, they will not be able to honour their contract with their bank other than by buying the currency at the going rate of exchange. Cover is available from insurers in respect of the extra cost involved. This is a special arrangement and does not alter the comments already made in this paragraph.

166. Music and entertainment: orchestra: dance bands: disc jockeys

Where a charge under one of these or a similar heading arises in the running of hotels, restaurants, holiday camps, seaside concert halls, dance halls, cabarets, theatres, discotheques, night clubs or public houses, etc., and the orchestra or artistes are under contract for a period, it is obviously a standing charge insurable for a period corresponding with the maximum length of the contract.

It should however be insured irrespective of any such contract. Partial damage to the premises may cause a reduction in the accommodation or amenities provided with a corresponding reduction in the number of guests or customers but without reduction in the normal expense for the provision of music and entertainment to correspond with the fall in turnover.

In cases where this charge is equivalent to a very substantial part of the revenue of a business and it is necessary to consider an alternative method of insuring it so as to incur less premium than when it is included in full in the normal way, especially in the case of a long maximum indemnity period, reference should be made to paragraph 262 headed Entertainment Undertakings.

167. Receiving office expenses

The receiving offices of dry-cleaners, dyers, laundries, boot and shoe repairers and other businesses in which goods are received from the public for cleaning, alteration or repairs at the works must be maintained even if those works are completely destroyed and for a time no goods can be accepted there. Site values and liability under leases would generally justify this. But the damage at the works may be only partial and even if it were total arrangements would probably be quickly made to have at least some of the work done by competitors—at considerable increase in costs. So in either case it is probable that some turnover would be maintained but the full expense of maintaining and staffing the receiving offices would continue throughout a period when it might not be possible to accept as much work as usual. Consequently, it should be insured as being a standing charge.

In addition to the above considerations the possibility of damage at one or other of the receiving offices must be kept in mind, as this would involve loss of turnover and increase in cost of working which could be recovered in full only if the standing charges and wages of the receiving offices had been included in the policy.

Where the receiving offices are not staffed by the insured's employees but are agencies held by shopkeepers who are paid a commission on each parcel handled such commission is a variable charge which it is unnecessary to insure except for any minimum which may be payable.

168. Group management charges: central administrative charges: management commission: head office services

Where a number of firms are combined in one financial group or corporation, or their capital is owned by a holding company, the cost of a central office administration and related services may be debited to the various firms in the group under a description of this nature. In such cases the contributions to the expenses of maintaining a group head office made by any member firm will still have to be maintained at normal level despite any reduction in turnover due to damage at the latter's premises. So where an insured is a member of a group its contribution to central administration expenses should be included in its gross profit insurance.

169. Other insurable charges

Typical charges which appear in accounts, on which no special comment is required as they are demonstrably insurable standing charges on the lines already outlined, are ambulance room requisites; apprentice training expenses; benevolent fund; bursary or scholarship expenses; caretaker or janitor services; Christmas gratuities and distribution to customers of gifts, novelties, calendars and diaries; closed circuit television system rent; compensation fund charges (breweries); conference and convention expenses; consultants' fees; contract department expenses; credit data bureaux annual subscriptions; day-study courses for staff; debenture trustees' fees; depot expenses; development expenses (although they are in fact items of regular *capital* expenditure); economic and market research expenses; employees' recreation and sports expenses; entertaining expenses; fashion show expenses; finance costs; garbage disposal costs; hire purchase licence certificates; horse upkeep and stabling costs; hostel expenses for employees; industrial consultants' fees; licenses; London office expenses; management training scheme; market surveys and consumer research expenses; patent fees; progress department charge; public relations functions; refuse collection charges; registrar's fees; railway wagon, tanker and freight car rents;

road repairs; security services charges; servicing charges for weighing and counting machinery; share transfer office expenses; showroom expenses; staff training college; tea money; tests and experimental expenses; towel and soap services; trade mark expenses; training scheme for operatives; visitors' works tour expenses; wayleaves; works fire brigade; works locomotive expenses.

170. Borderline and optional charges

The following paragraphs 171 to 176 deal with charges which might be termed "borderline charges" and paragraphs 177 and 178 with "optional charges" which call for special consideration with regard to their inclusion in whole or in part according to the circumstances of each business. In all these cases the basic principles for including or omitting different charges from the gross profit insurance, set down under "working definitions" in paragraph 104, should be kept prominently in mind.

171. Repairs and renewals

This description covers a wide variety of expenditure in different firms' accounts. The debit is frequently a relatively large one, sometimes very large, and as it may not always be necessary to insure the whole of it as a standing charge it merits careful consideration in every case.

The opinion often expressed that there is no necessity to insure it because the cost of repairs, renewals and decorations will cease if buildings are destroyed can be answered in the same way as in the case of rent (paragraph 105) and depreciation (paragraph 146), and the part of this charge which refers to buildings should undoubtedly be insured in full.

Repairs and renewals of plant and machinery may be regarded similarly but there is often an additional factor to be considered. Those which are the cumulative result of a process of wear or obsolescence over a period of years may have to be undertaken and might involve heavy expenditure in one particular year. These are in effect to a large extent a non-recurring charge and should be included in full in the insurance for the reason explained in paragraph 82(c) about non-recurring charges, that is, net profit will be that much more in the year after the heavy expenditure has taken place. There need be no fear that in the event of a loss occurring insurers would unfairly claim a deduction under the savings clause because comparison would be made with the *normal* amount of repairs and renewals. (See paragraph 51(b).) But although the amount of this item will usually fluctuate from year to year, perhaps very considerably, there will nearly always be some debit in the accounts for repairs and renewals. So in addition to bringing the amount into the computation of the sum insured it is also essential to name it as an insured standing charge when the older form of gross profit definition is used.

Where a firm show a special item in their accounts for a major plant overhaul, spreading the cost equally over a period of possibly five or more years in order to avoid an exceptionally heavy item of expenditure appearing in one year's accounts, the need to insure repairs is perhaps more apparent.

A further point of relevance in some cases is that a repairs charge may have been skilfully stretched to include replacements which are quasi-capital expenditure paid for out of revenue. In such circumstances an insured would expect recompense under the insurance for a corresponding increase in net profit the following year if damage intervened and affected turnover.

Another aspect with some businesses is that if plant and machinery of certain kinds are not in constant use deterioration might cause the cost of repairs and renewals during a year in which the machinery was standing idle for a time because of damage to other plant, to increase beyond the normal. Further aspects of this problem of repairs and renewals are given in the following paragraphs 172(a), (b) and (c).

172. Repairs and renewals: special aspects

(a) *Frequent and regular repairs, etc.*

The problem is different in the case of businesses in which there are various classes of property which require frequent and regular repair, replacement or renewal in direct ratio to the extent to which they are used. The cost of this is sometimes shown in accounts as consumable stores or consumable tools or possibly charged in a separate item such as wastage on containers or indirect material costs but most frequently the debit is shown as repairs and renewals. Typical examples which may be found under this item in the accounts for engineering works are small tools, drills, taps, dies, moulding boxes, moulds, templets, gauges, grinding and buffing wheels and polishing materials, etc., and where woodworking machinery is used, saw blades, cutting tools, etc. In textile mills it may be belting, bobbins, tubes, cases, fallers, shuttles, roller coverings, folding boards, skeps, sheets, tape and band, etc. Similarly with replacements, repairs and cleaning of casks, barrels and bottles at a whisky distillery, brewery or soft drink factory, boxes at a fish or fruit merchant's, drums, kegs and casks at chemical and oil works, sacks in sugar and flour mills, bread and cake tins and trays at a bakery, wagons at iron, steel or chemical works, and the replacement of curing bags at a vulcanisers. In steelworks graphite electrodes and the refractory materials for relining ladles and converters and for rebuilding furnaces and their roofs may be classed either as consumable stores or repairs and renewals. Hotels and catering establishments have a heavy expenditure on the renewal of crockery, cutlery and linen and repairs to furniture and furnishings which depends upon the extent to which such property is used. In general industry trade utensils, cleaning materials and similar items are an expense which usually varies in amount proportionately with the production of the factory.

In cases where it is *certain* that any reduction in turnover would be accompanied by a proportionate fall in the amount spent on repairs and renewals for a specific class of property, on the lines just mentioned, it might be worth while breaking down this item in the insured's accounts and excluding from the insurance that portion which is strictly a variable charge. If this is done it is essential to decide upon an accurate description for the specification, according to whether it is the "difference" wording or the older ("additions") form of definition of gross profit, which will make the insured's intentions perfectly clear.

(b) *Casks, barrels, boxes etc.*

In the list given in the last preceding paragraph of classes of property which might be excluded from the cover in respect of repairs and renewals, some qualification needs to be made, particularly with regard to the repairs and cleaning of casks, barrels, boxes, cases, sacks and other containers. If the insured have their own department for this work equipped with special plant it will probably be impossible to reduce the maintenance costs proportionately with a reduction in the quantity of containers handled for repairs or cleaning. Consequently, if the departmental overheads are debited in the item of repairs and renewals they will have to be treated as an insurable charge. Only the cost of replacements and materials consumed will be variable and so it is only that part of the charge which does not need to be insured. If wages are included in the item these will require to be dealt with according to the particular circumstances of the case.

(c) *Lasts, etc.*

Care must also be exercised with regard to articles such as lasts or press knives in shoe, slipper, games and toy-making, or handbag factories, jacquard cards and designs in mills, jigs in engineering works, iron, prés and paste moulds in glassworks, and patterns in brassworks, iron foundries and various other trades, which have to be replaced periodically because of changes in design or from other causes irrespective of the amount of usage they have had. Therefore, in spite of the fact that they are consumable tools the cost of repairs and replacement of which would otherwise vary directly with the amount of use and similarly of turnover the expenditure in respect of them is governed more by changes in design of the products being manufactured. Hence the advisability in such circumstances of looking at this expense as possibly an insurable charge.

173. Power

This is a heavy expense which may be an insurable charge for one firm but not for another according to the individual circumstances as shown by the following two simple illustrations.

Consider on the one hand a textile mill powered solely by a steam engine with one boiler for the steam supply. If one floor of the mill, or a single weaving shed, is rendered silent by a fire the cost of fuel for steam for the engine whilst it is running light will not be reduced proportionately. Therefore, it is necessary to insure it in full as a non-variable charge.

On the other hand in a clothing or garment factory with every machine driven individually by its own fractional horse-power electro-motor a stoppage of any number of the machines will mean a reduction in consumption of electric current exactly proportionate to the reduction in turnover. So apart from whatever minimum electricity charge might be applicable it would be unnecessary to include power for machines in the gross profit insurance for such a factory.

There are of course many varying circumstances between these two examples and each case must be decided individually the guiding question being—can this charge *always* be reduced proportionately with a reduction in turnover?

An additional factor which has to be kept in mind is that in the accounts the heading "power" may include electricity for running air-conditioning, humidifying or dust extraction plant, passenger and goods lifts, or for heating boilers or other vessels either for space heating or trade processes; the cost of this would be a standing charge.

Where the cost of current for power is considered to be not an insurable charge but there is a fixed minimum charge payable under an electricity board's tariff the latter charge should be insured under an appropriate description. In the case of a "difference" specification this would mean including "electricity-unit charges only" in the list of uninsured working expenses, whilst in the older form of wording it would have to be shown as "electricity—fixed and maximum demand charges only" in the list of insured standing charges.

This form of tariff provides for the annual payment of a Fixed Charge calculated per kilovolt ampere of "service capacity" at the premises plus a Maximum Demand Charge based usually on twice the largest number of units of electricity supplied during a period of 30 consecutive minutes at any time of the year, plus a unit charge on the actual consumption of current metered monthly. The fixed charge and the maximum demand charge, therefore, constitute a substantial minimum charge because if damage at a factory results in partial or total interruption of production these charges could be payable in full however short the period in the electricity board's current "year of account" during which the normal load is taken.

These charges assume serious proportions for large consumers of electricity and whether on the annual demand charge tariff or on the monthly demand charge basis usual with businesses subject to seasonal variations, their annual amount should be insured as being a standing charge.

Supplies of natural gas for power are subject to a minimum charge per quarter per h.p. rating under a gas board's Power Generation Tariff and the annual amount of this is an insurable standing charge.

When power is obtained from an "estate" engine house or power house, or from an adjacent works, the charge may be a fixed amount or included in a composite rent for "room and power"; in either case it is a standing charge.

174. Fuel for trade processes

As with the charge for power two simple illustrations will similarly serve to show that although fuel for trade purposes usually appears in accounts as a productive or manufacturing cost it should in some circumstances be insured as a non-variable charge. Consider first the case of a firm with one boiler to provide steam for trade processes in for example a dyeworks. Stoppage of work in a part of the premises or plant due to damage will reduce the amount of steam required but it is most unlikely that the fuel consumption can be cut down in the same ratio. On the other hand, at works where there is a bank of several boilers for supplying steam if one or more of these can be drawn according to the extent of the interference with works processes resulting from damage fuel consumption may fall roughly in proportion with a reduction in turnover. In the first instance quoted fuel is an insurable charge; in the second instance it might be considered unnecessary to insure it except for the cost of fuel for one boiler which would be an irreducible minimum so long as there is any steam required.

A similar position appertains with furnaces, kilns, ovens, lehrs, annealing furnaces, retorts, forges and other plant consuming solid fuel, oil, gas, electricity or gaseous oxygen. Because the expense is usually shown in the manufacturing section of the accounts it is often too lightly assumed that because it is a working expense it is therefore a variable charge which it is unnecessary to insure. This point can only be decided after careful consideration of the circumstances of each individual case (see paragraphs 175 and 176) and in any event the minimum charges under electricity and gas boards' tariffs dealt with in preceding paragraph 173 must be treated as standing charges.

175. Increased ratio of fuel costs

It must be emphasised that if it is found impossible after damage to reduce the cost of fuel proportionately with the fall in production the increased incidence of this item will mean a loss to the insured unless fuel has been included in the insurance on gross profit. This can be a very serious matter for those trades such as potteries, glassworks, brickworks, iron and steel works, in which the purchase price of raw materials bears a low ratio to the finished product or where there are no purchases because the raw materials are dug from the earth but the fuel expenses are relatively high.

A further point to notice is that when furnaces cease production for a limited period it is customary to maintain heat ready for restarting or to prevent damage to the furnace lining. If the stoppage is of longer duration and the furnaces are allowed to cool the time required for refiring and heating up for production may be considerable. In either event the cost of fuel during the non-productive period will be substantial.

The loss resulting from the *increased ratio* of productive costs when they do not fall in the same proportion as the drop in production is not claimable as increase in cost of working under clause (b). The latter covers only *additional* expenditure as explained in paragraph 46. On the face of it this may seem unfair to the insured who have suffered financial loss in maintaining all or part of the normal production whilst the insurers have benefited through having less to pay for loss of gross profit. The view of insurance companies is that in such a case on the one hand there has been no actual increase in the expenditure on fuel to bring it in as increase in cost of working and on the other hand it has not reduced in ratio to the fall in turnover; so the event has proved the particular expense concerned to be a standing charge which should have been insured. A business interruption policy is based on the idea of insuring non-variable charges because their increased incidence after damage will reduce net profit and if insured omit to include any such charge the resulting loss cannot be treated under clause (b).

This point is not open to doubt since the position was made perfectly clear in analogous circumstances in one of the very few claims under a business interruption insurance which have gone to the courts for a decision. This was the case of *Polikoff Ltd.* v. *North British and Mercantile Insurance Co. Ltd.* (1936) 55 Ll.L.R. 279. Amongst other points in dispute there was a claim in respect of the increased ratio of wages and other expenses as being "increase in cost of working". Mr. Justice Branson pointed out that although there was an increased ratio of wages and other expenses to production there was no additional expenditure on them and he proceeded to disallow the claim in respect of them.

The position is different if the efficiency of steam-raising plant is impaired in consequence of damage and results in an increased ratio of fuel to steam produced. The extra consumption is in such circumstances actual *additional* expenditure and so is claimable as increase in cost of working.

176. Partial insurance of fuel charge

A solution to the problem of the heavy premium which may be required to insure fuel for trade processes when the expenditure on it is relatively very large is sometimes attempted by including only a part of the item as a standing charge, say so many thousand pounds or so much per cent. of the fuel charge. This is often done on the assumption that interruption of production will be only partial and the insured will recover from production maintained augmented by the partial insurance the estimated maximum loss on fuel expenditure. If the reduction in fuel consumption can be so controlled that it is reduced proportionately with a reduction in production, that is, if it is really a variable charge the insured will be covered. In fact in such circumstances there would be no need to include any amount in the insurance for fuel. But if the cost of fuel during the period of interruption does not fall proportionately with a reduction in production after damage the insured will suffer some loss due to there being some degree of under-insurance. This is because whatever amount is insured on this expense is built into the rate of gross profit which is applied to the shortage in production (turnover).

For example, suppose that the item in the accounts for the financial year preceding the damage was £160,000 and £120,000 was estimated to be the variable part of the item, the description in the list of uninsured working expenses in a "difference" wording being either "fuel to the extent of £120,000" or "fuel to the extent of 75 per cent. of the total" (it is immaterial which way—the effect is the same). If the damage caused a 50 per cent. reduction in turnover during the following 12 months but the fuel bill was only reduced to £128,000 the position in that year would be:

	£	£
Cost of fuel	—	128,000
paid for out of turnover maintained (50% of £160,000)	80,000	
paid for out of insurance (50% of £40,000)	20,000	
		100,000
insured's loss due to partial insurance		£28,000

The position would be exactly the same had the definition of gross profit been on the old form of wording and had fuel been shown in a list of insured standing charges either as "fuel to the extent of £40,000" or as "fuel to the extent of 25 per cent. of the total".

Because it is so difficult to make a clear division or an accurate estimate as between the portion of the fuel cost which will vary with turnover and that which will remain static, partial insurance of this nature may involve an insured in some loss.

Another factor enters into the question where the fuel used for trade processes is gas or electricity and there is a minimum charge applicable.

Although the circumstances may be such that consumption of this fuel is controllable and can be reduced proportionately with a fall in production it is necessary to insure in the gross profit the minimum charge applicable. (See paragraph 173.)

177. Agents' (manufacturers' and overseas) commission and expenses

This charge is one which usually comes within the optional category.

In the case of manufacturers' agents whose remuneration is commission on orders booked by them, if goods cannot be delivered to customers because of damage at the factory the agents will have to curtail the booking of orders and the commission paid to them will fall. As the reduction will correspond with the fall in the firm's turnover, agents' commission in such cases, apart from contract to the contrary, is a variable charge.

The insured may wish, however, for reasons of business expediency or possibly of sentiment where an agent of many years' association is concerned, to provide some or all of their agents with their normal commission earnings or at any rate with a substantial minimum during a period of interruption. For example, they might have a sole agent in an overseas country through whom they receive substantial orders; a curtailment of his commission earnings may cause him to change to represent another manufacturer and so a valuable market would be lost to the firm perhaps for all time. Although agents' commission may be a variable charge and one which the firm are legally liable to pay only on orders accepted by them, it can be insured. If it is not to be included in full, being often a very substantial sum, a fixed amount can be stated as the extent to which it is to be insured.

But if it is only partially insured it should be understood that it is not a "first loss" insurance and that recovery will be proportionate with a reduction in turnover. For example, if out of an annual amount of £200,000 commission paid to agents a sum of £40,000 is insured and there is a 75 per cent. reduction in turnover during the year after damage, the insured will receive under the insurance £30,000 (not £40,000) in respect of agents' commission, to add to the £10,000 provided by the £50,000 which the continuing 25 per cent. turnover will provide. Only in the event of there being no turnover whatever in the 12 months after damage would the insurance contribute the full £40,000.

In any case in which the agents have a contract providing for a period of notice of termination or stipulating a minimum amount of remuneration in the event of a reduction in their commission earnings due to circumstances outside their control the appropriate amount of the principal's liability is not an optional charge and should be included in the insurance.

Some businesses issue invoices to their agents, particularly overseas agents, for goods sold through them and deduct the agents' commission on these invoices. In such cases the figures for sales in the trading account may likewise show a net amount and no debit for agents' commission will appear in the accounts. Although such commission is a variable charge the firm might wish for reasons already mentioned to provide for a continuation of its payment to certain agents during a period of interruption by including it in the insurance. The fact that it is not debited as a charge in the accounts does not preclude its being insured in this way but the absence of mention in the accounts means that it might easily be overlooked and whether the "difference" wording or the older form is used, be inadvertently omitted from the gross profit definition and cover. This illustrates how useful it can be for insured to bring their accountant into consultation in negotiations on a business interruption insurance.

When agents are paid an allowance for expenses by a firm, the inclusion of this item in the gross profit insurance will depend upon the circumstances of the particular case and the wishes of the insured. (See paragraph 125 on travelling expenses.)

178. Check trading: collectors' and agents' remuneration

In an entirely different category from the agents referred to in paragraph 177 are those who act as intermediaries or canvassers for the credit business of retailers of various kinds. Clubs, credit check trade and similar schemes are organised with the object of enabling customers to obtain clothing, household goods and other articles on credit, repayment being spread over a period of 20 weeks or more with a 10 per cent. charge added for the facility. A distinction has to be made between firms who run a club of this nature, often as a subsidiary company, for purchases at their own premises only and businesses which provide credit facilities for purchases at a range of shops not owned by them. This paragraph is concerned with the former. In the heavily populated industrial areas and in the mining towns and villages of the United Kingdom there is a very extensive retail trade built on this system and in the accounts of firms whose trade is involved with it the item of agents' commission is naturally a very substantial amount.

These agents or collectors are generally paid by commission on the amount collected by them each week. A fire at an insured's premises—shop, showroom, department store, or warehouse—at which the club checks or cheques are valid or from which the goods are dispatched to customers will interrupt trading. Curtailment of sales will be followed by a corresponding fall in the commission paid to agents or collectors because of the reduced demand for credit facilities by their customers. This reduction will normally correspond to the reduction in the firm's turnover making it a variable charge which it is unnecessary to insure. On the other hand, an insured may include such commission payments as being an optional standing charge if it is desired to do so on grounds of expediency to prevent the loss of agents through their taking an agency with a competitor during a period of interruption.

In some businesses the agents are paid a standing wage plus commission and in such cases an insured may wish to insure at least the basic wages, possibly the whole of the remuneration; either can be done, an appropriate description being used in the definition of gross profit to make the position quite clear.

179. Check trading: commission charged to retailers

Under the check trading system described in the preceding paragraph a check trader grants franchises to selected retailers who then sell their goods or services to the public in exchange for its checks. For this facility the credit check trader charges a commission to the retailer as a percentage of the amount of the check transactions. This charge of commission in the retailer's accounts is therefore variable with turnover and a non-insurable charge.

The word "check" in the foregoing paragraphs is not used as in Northern America to mean "bank cheque" but is the trade name in check trading for "credit note".

180. Mail order clubs—agents' commission

Another extensive agency field is that of the freelance, spare-time agents, usually housewives or women employed in offices or small industrial concerns, who use the illustrated catalogues of mail order firms to obtain orders for sales on a commission basis.

In such businesses a percentage—10 per cent. cash or 12.5 per cent. in goods—is paid to agents on the amount of completed sales only. Therefore the item of agents' commission in the accounts of a mail order firm working on these lines will vary exactly with turnover of sales through agents and is not insurable.

181. Debt collection

"Commission" is sometimes used as the heading in the accounts of shopkeepers for the payments made on a commission basis to the local trade association or debt collector or a solicitor for the collection of outstanding accounts. This charge, more usually shown as debt collection, varies directly with the turnover on which it is paid and so it is unnecessary to insure it.

182. Factoring services

The use of "factoring" services conducted by specialist companies whereby a business firm contracts out to them its sales ledger accounting and payment collection is rapidly extending in the United Kingdom. The service fee charged by factoring companies is generally a percentage, which may be as high as 2 per cent. of their client's turnover and on this basis it is for the latter a variable charge as regards business interruption insurance.

183. Miscellaneous standing charges

With a specification on the "difference" basis the problem does not arise but with the older ("additions") definition of gross profit it is customary to include this item at the end of the list of insured standing charges to provide for any small charges which have not been named individually. When this is done a limit is applied to the aggregation of unspecified charges of 5 per cent. of the total amount of the named charges. It is advisable in view of this to make sure that the total of unspecified charges which it is intended to include in the insurance does not exceed this limit.

Frequently an item on trade expenses or sundries incorporates a considerable number of charges of a miscellaneous nature which in total exceed the 5 per cent. limit. In such cases the particular item in the accounts should be analysed and its main constituents named individually. It should also be noted that the limit is 5 per cent. of the total of the other insured standing charges and not 5 per cent. of the sum insured on gross profit; the latter may be a much higher figure because it includes the amount of net profit.

When providing in connection with an insurance containing this cover for miscellaneous unspecified standing charges a certificate of the gross profit earned in a financial year for the purposes of the return of premium clause (see paragraph 225(a)), some accountants automatically add 5 per cent. to the total of the named standing charges whether there are any others which aggregate that amount or not. This is incorrect because 5 per cent. is the limit and not a fixed percentage to be added; where the premium is substantial the point is important.

The same position applies in connection with a claim; 5 per cent. cannot be added automatically to the total of the other charges brought into the computation of the rate of gross profit but only the amount of any miscellaneous standing charges which have not been specified, up to a maximum aggregate of 5 per cent. of the total of those which are named in the list of insured standing charges.

184. Partial insurance of charges

A note of warning must be given about a practice sometimes adopted of insuring only a portion of a specific standing charge. This procedure was in fact suggested in paragraph 172(a) as being appropriate for some businesses in the case of such charges as repairs and renewals but, conversely, the danger was pointed out in relation to a charge of another kind namely fuel for trade processes (paragraph 172).

In the former case the portion excluded from the insurance would be that relating to repairs and renewals of identifiable classes of property, being those which vary directly with turnover in all circumstances. Consequently, the amount recoverable under the insurance would represent the loss in full of the portion included in the gross profit, according to the reduction in turnover. The uninsured portion would be variable expenditure which would reduce proportionately with the extent to which the machinery was not running and the insured would not lose anything whether the interruption of the business was either total or partial. On the other hand, fuel is generally an indivisible charge and the insurance of only a portion of it could give rise to loss as explained in paragraph 176.

Partial insurance of charges also carries the possibility of loss under the uninsured standing charges clause of the specification, that is, under the apportionment of any increase in cost of working incurred which is made if all the standing charges of the business which should have been insured have not been included. (See paragraph 49.)

The moral, therefore, is that unless it is quite certain that a charge or an ascertainable and identifiable part of it will be variable in all circumstances, bearing in mind the considerations about variable and standing charges mentioned at the beginning of this chapter, it should be insured in full.

185. The United States approach—continuing and non-continuing expenses

Although there has been a change in the forms now promulgated from the basis of net sales value of production, etc., less non-continuing expenses (gross earnings) to net income and continuing normal operating expenses (Business Income), the work sheets take very similar paths to arrive at the basis for an amount to be insured (refer paragraph 234). Both work sheets adopt a kind of U.K. "difference" basis approach involving the deduction from gross income of essential variable expenses (see paragraph 81).

The resultant amount to be used for insurance purposes, *i.e.* subject to coinsurance requirements, includes either a positive net profit or a negative net loss element together with "normal operating expenses". A loss calculation will however take note only of the extent to which these "normal operating expenses" continue, which is similar to the U.K. method of taking all insured fixed costs and deducting savings. No "operating expense" is mentioned other than "payroll" (Business Income Coverage).

186. Payroll related expenses (United States)

As stated more comprehensively in paragraph 217, these expenses in the United States are listed in the Ordinary Payroll Limitation endorsement (to the Business Income Coverage form) as employee benefits, if directly related to payroll, F.I.C.A. payments (paid by the employer) union dues (paid by the employer) and workers compensation premiums.

187. Rental expense (United States)

As with rent in the United Kingdom (refer paragraphs 105 and 114) the United States rental expense must be regarded as an overhead charge which should always be insured. In some cases flat rental building leases contain a provision for cancellation of the lease if the building suffers 25 per cent. or 50 per cent. damage. Of course if the location is regarded as essential to the insured's business it could be advantageous to the business deliberately to continue the lease (and not take what would otherwise be a saving). The *whole* cost of renting any alternative building would then be extra expense and not merely the *increase* in rental expense that might have been incurred if the lease had been cancelled.

Where the renting of machinery, etc., is related to the income derived therefrom the expense may be regarded as variable and deducted in the calculation of net sales value of production.

188. Taxation on profits—United States

(a) *Gross earnings*

A position similar to that in the United Kingdom (refer paragraph 118) applies with the U.S. gross earnings forms in which the definition of gross earnings is total net sales and other earnings derived from operations of the business less the cost of certain named expenses in which there is no mention of taxes. So any property or real estate taxes such as those levied by city and county authorities which have to be paid out of the earnings of a business and will not necessarily be reduced proportionately with a partial interruption of business resulting from an insured peril should be included. They are the same as "rates" in a U.K. insurance (see paragraph 119).

But Sales Tax, which is the counterpart of Value Added Tax in the United Kingdom, Hotel Tax and any provincial or local taxes levied on sales or services which will vary exactly with turnover might be considered as excluded, according to the attitude taken by insurers, because they are not "earnings" of the business for the benefit of the insured and are not precluded from deduction because they are not "costs" within the definition that "no other costs shall be deducted in determining gross earnings". The position under the old Earnings (Short Form) coverage may be held to have been different because it specifically included "taxes" without any qualification in the definition of earnings although this appears to be at variance with the intention to insure only "earnings of the business". (See also paragraph 71(a).)

The reasons for the inclusion of net profit in the insurance are the same as those given in paragraph 118. Insurance premiums are allowed as a deductible business expense under U.S. Federal taxation regulations and any compensation recovered under a business interruption insurance must be declared as income.

(b) *Business Income*

In this currently recommended form it is made clear in the definition of Business Income that the constituent Net Income is equivalent to Net Profit or Loss *before income taxes*. Business Income loss recoveries may be taxed along with the remaining earned income. The "additions" basis definition of gross profit in the United Kingdom refers to "the net trading profit . . . before the deduction of any taxation chargeable on profits" (see paragraph 118).

CHAPTER 10

Insurance of Payroll Cost—United Kingdom and United States

189. Meaning of payroll—salaries, wages, etc., in the United Kingdom

(a) *Salaries*

The remuneration of salaried employees will not as a rule be affected by a reduction in turnover and should be included in full in the gross profit.

There are some businesses where temporary or part-time staff are employed and others where junior typists and office boys and girls might have been working for only a short period at the time of damage occurring. In such cases an insured may consider that in the event of interruption of business they could dispense with the services of such employees, after the expiry of the short period of notice necessary, in line with any reduction in turnover. This attitude might be the result of the fact that as "salary" is not in their case synonymous with a position of much responsibility an insured may regard some salaried employees as being in the same category as ordinary factory workers. This is a dangerous supposition and the omission of any salaries from the insurance on gross profit may lead to some loss in the event of damage.

Businesses where a large mail-order trade is done may be regarded as exceptions to the general rule when they employ more or less casual and unskilled office workers but in order to give the jobs the attraction of prestige employees' pay is treated as "salaries". A similar position applies with some chain stores and department stores in which even the most junior sales assistant is paid a "salary". For example, when a leading chain stores advertises for staff a scale of "salaries" is given for shop assistants aged 16 and upwards.

In any insurance where the insured insist upon the exclusion of any salaried employees the intention should be made perfectly clear by an appropriate description on the specification and care taken to see that the remuneration of the excluded employees is included in any insurance under a separate item on wages. (See paragraphs 205(b) and 213.)

(b) *Distinction between salaries and wages*

Some difficulty may be experienced where the accounts show "salaries and wages" together in one item and a division cannot be obtained because there are no separate book entries for salaries and wages. Frequently an insured cannot say which employees are in either category in spite of the item in the accounts referring to both. There is no infallible guide. In *Polikoff Ltd. v. N.B. & M. Insurance Co. Ltd.* (1936) 55 L1.L.R. 279, one of the very few business interruption claims which, as mentioned before, have gone to the courts for a decision, Mr Justice Branson had to deal with this specific question and said: "The distinction between salary on the one hand and wages on the other hand is quite well understood in every business concern". Unfortunately this dictum does not help very much in those cases where the different terms are used more or less without discrimination and it is not apposite to much present day practice in commerce and industry.

Employees who are engaged on terms of pay of so much per annum and those who are paid monthly are usually classed as salaried staff whilst those paid weekly or hourly are regarded as wage earners. Conversely, in 1969 I.C.I. Ltd., introduced a salary graded scheme for the payment of nearly all its 54,000 manual employees in terms of an annual salary paid weekly. At that time this was a trendsetter for industry which has since been followed by other large companies and in the future may become commonplace and make the traditional distinction between salaries and wages even less of a guide for the purposes of business interruption insurance.

There are so many variations in the treatment of pay by business concerns and by accountants—who sometimes do not discriminate in drawing up the accounts even when their clients have separate records for salaries and for wages—that it is desirable to give the matter special attention whenever salaries and wages are combined in one item in the accounts. One solution of the difficulty (except where wages are insured under the dual basis scheme—see paragraph 205(b)) is to adapt one of the descriptions suggested in paragraph 214(a) for wages to be insured as a standing charge by an appropriate amendment to read "salaries and wages to a combined extent of . . .". Another method is to designate as a standing charge "the remuneration of all employees paid monthly" treating the balance of the payroll as though it were "wages" and of this insuring as a standing charge an appropriate proportion of "the remuneration of all employees paid weekly". For a "difference" wording the converse treatment would be necessary, an appropriate designation being included in the list of uninsured working expenses.

As explained in paragraph 212, under a dual basis payroll cover for large insurances salaries and wages are insured together in one item for a combined amount on remuneration. This may obviate some difficulties but apart from insurances in which 100 per cent. of the payroll is insured as explained in paragraph 204 the necessity remains for a decision to be taken on the percentage of the total remuneration to be covered for the maximum indemnity period, *i.e.* in effect as a standing charge, with the remainder percentage insured for a shorter period.

190. Meaning of salaries and wages (payroll/ordinary payroll expenses) in the United States

In North America also, the distinction between salaries and wages is not always clear cut and indeed, the handbook for guidance under the U.S. Federal Unemployment Tax Act states that "payments made for personal services are wages whether payable on an hourly, daily, weekly, monthly, yearly or other basis" and whether "designated as wages, salaries, bonuses, commissions, profit-sharing etc.". In a gross earnings policy or on the Business Income Coverage form which includes all ordinary payroll, no difficulty arises. Where there is limited coverage, however, as in paragraph 217(c) and the definition of ordinary payroll expense mentions neither salaries nor wages but along with certain categories of employees who would normally be salaried it includes "other important employees" there might be room for disagreement as to the exact meaning of the expression. This vagueness of definition has now been deliberately superseded by reference to "additional exemptions shown in the Schedule or in the Declarations as either Job Classifications or Employees". By 'Employees" it is assumed that what is meant is *specified* "employees" (see also paragraph 217).

191. Bonus or commission to salaried staff

Where bonus or commission is paid to salaried staff it is essential where insured standing charges are listed to add those words after salaries if it is intended (as it usually is) to provide the normal bonus or commission irrespective of a fall in turnover. Should it constitute a separate debit in the accounts it is advisable to show it similarly in the list of insured standing charges and to use the same description, *e.g.* "executives' commission". It may be that under the terms of employment the commission is a percentage of turnover and so would be a variable charge. It can nevertheless be included in the insurance as being an expense which it would be desirable to continue at a normal level in the interests of the business. For example, the manager of a department store may be paid £20,000 a year salary plus a commission on total sales which gives him approximately another £20,000 a year. Such a man is too valuable to lose but should a fire destroy, say, half the premises with a corresponding reduction in sales which will probably continue over a long period, there is an obvious danger that he will seek a job elsewhere if his earnings are similarly reduced. So it would be prudent, in fact essential, to insure his commission in full as a standing charge.

As a rule most retail traders wish to include the buyers' bonus and assistants' commission on sales in respect of those employees whose remuneration is insured in the gross profit because it is regarded as part of their standard pay rather than as an "extra".

In a "difference" specification commission of all kinds, payable to all categories of employee, is automatically included in the gross profit insurance unless specifically excluded in the list of uninsured working expenses or embraced by an item in the accounts, such as wages, which is in the list of variables.

A special loss of personal income policy in the United States provides indemnity on a self-insured basis for managers of department stores and entertainment undertakings, etc., whose remuneration is mainly in the form of commission. Details are given in paragraph 364.

192. Fringe benefits

(a) *General*

Fringe benefits are generally in the provision of a motor car for an employee's private use, mortgage arrangements for house purchase on very lenient terms, free life assurance or accident insurance, low or non-contributory pension schemes, payment of membership subscriptions for B.U.P.A., P.P.P., or a similar medical insurance agency, interest free season-ticket loans, free luncheon vouchers and so on.

In whatever way such benefits are treated in an insured's accounts they should be brought into the computation and definition of gross profit because they are, in effect, part and parcel of employees' salaries. It should be noted, however, that the cost of fringe benefits cannot be included in a U.K. dual basis payroll cover on salaries and wages, as explained in paragraph 212.

In the United States in various trades and businesses, employees can benefit from what are termed "courtesy discounts and mark-downs" on goods supplied by their employers and the cost of these to the business might need to be taken into account, dependent upon the system of bookkeeping, in connection with ordinary payroll coverages.

(b) *Hotel, etc., staff gratuities and fringe benefits*

A peculiar position arises with the insurances of hotels, restaurants, casinos, clubs, hairdressers and beauty salons and other establishments in which a considerable proportion of the earnings of employees consists of gratuities or tips from customers. These emoluments do not pass through the insured's books and so are not insurable with the wages of such employees as they would be if they were a bonus or commission paid by the employer. The latter might wish, however, to provide for the payment to their staff of this portion of their earnings either as a moral obligation or as an act of goodwill with notice wages or, in the case of essential employees, as a necessity to ensure their retention during a period of either partial or total interruption.

The position can be met by adding to the wages cover, on whatever basis this is arranged, either a fixed amount or percentage estimated to be equivalent to that normally earned in the form of gratuities. It would be necessary to append a note to the definition of either gross profit or wages, or both, as the case may be, to the effect that an addition of £ . . . . . . (or . . . . . . per cent.) is to be made to the amount of the wages as insured to provide for the gratuities normally received by employees. The sum insured would be increased correspondingly and in any declaration in connection with the return of premium clause the accountant would have to add the appropriate amount.

Practically all hotel staff from managers to chambermaids receive some fringe benefits the main ones being free meals on duty and sleeping accommodation. If the value of these perks is not accounted for by an appropriate notional or other entry in the hotel accounts the provision mentioned in paragraph 192(a) for the inclusion of fringe benefits in the insurance will be inapplicable. Because these perks are regarded as part of hotel workers' remuneration some such arrangement as that suggested in the foregoing with regard to staff gratuities will have to be made to ensure their inclusion in the insurance.

In hotels where a service charge is added to customers' accounts and subsequently distributed amongst the staff on an agreed basis the amount is sometimes for this purpose paid into what is called a tronc. Generally the service charges collected whether paid into a tronc or otherwise do not appear in the hotelier's trading accounts as revenue although a record is kept and the amount paid to the staff is shown on each individual's income tax return. Where this system operates a position similar to that explained regarding gratuities will apply and the definition of wages and the amounts relative to same should include tronc payments.

On the other hand many hotels, in order to help employees by ironing out fluctuations in their earnings with the volume of trade, themselves take service charges as being part and parcel of the general hotel revenue and pay their staff set rates of wages loaded to include service charges. In such cases it may not be necessary to mention service charges in the definitions of gross profit and/or wages.

193. Travellers', representatives' and salespersons' salaries, commission and bonus

Travellers' remuneration is generally shown under a separate heading in accounts but in any case it is desirable to consider it apart from the salaries of the general staff because frequently special circumstances apply. Moreover commission and bonus are very important factors, often of considerable amount, on which employers hold different views as to the extent to which they would pay them in the event of a reduction in turnover. Representatives and outside salesmen and saleswomen are for present purposes treated as being the same as travellers, but agents are dealt with separately (see paragraphs 177, 178 and 180).

Methods of pay vary from substantial salary and small commission (or none) to small salary (or none) and large commission on sales. Some firms employ some men and women on one basis and some on another. Sometimes there are quotas, guaranteed minimum commissions, or varying rates of commission. If a firm cannot turn out goods for sale because of a fire, the effect on the remuneration of travellers and salespersons will depend upon the terms of their employment. The attitude of the insured on the extent to which they will include such remuneration in the gross profit insurance will not necessarily be circumscribed by those terms and their decision may depend more upon expediency, the size of the sum involved, and whether they are generous or otherwise in outlook. So it is desirable for this matter to be carefully gone into in order that an insured's wishes may be ascertained and accurately expressed in the description used on the specification.

Where there is no liability to pay commission and/or bonus to travellers, etc., it is an optional charge for purposes of the insurance. If included and paid to such employees during a period of interruption no deduction would be made by insurers under the savings clause on the grounds that the insured were not legally liable to pay it.

194. Holiday pay

In some industries there is an agreement between the employers' organisations and the trade unions concerned whereby the employers bank an amount each week in respect of holiday pay and supply an auditor's certificate of the amount at credit. In other industries, whilst some firms credit holiday pay weekly to a special account and show it as a separate amount from wages in their trading account each year end others merely pay it out of their bank account as and when it is due at holiday times. It is then entered as "wages" in the wages book and consequently is within the amount shown as wages in the trading account each financial year end. Whichever procedure is adopted the real position is the same, which is that at any particular date there is due to employees the appropriate amount of holiday pay calculated on the wages earned by them since the last disbursement of it. Even though the money has not been earmarked in any way it has already been earned and the insured has a liability to pay it and should have appropriate assets to meet it.

As a business interruption policy is concerned with charges accruing *after* damage, and not those already earned, it is necessary to insure in the item on gross profit the holiday pay of only those employees whose remuneration is insured in that item. For example, if 25 per cent. of the total wage roll is so insured, then only 25 per cent. of the total annual holiday pay should also be covered and not the holiday pay of all employees. The workers represented by the other 75 per cent. will earn their future holiday pay with their wages if they work after the fire. If they are dismissed there will be no liability to pay them holiday pay beyond that due to them for the weeks worked before the damage, which will have already been earned by them and should be available in the bank, plus a proportion on their notice wage. This latter will be included in the definition of wages in the relevant item on wages (see paragraph 231).

Where wages are excluded entirely from the item on gross profit and insured under a separate item under the dual basis scheme (paragraphs 205 *et seq.*), the holiday pay relating to the wages insured in that item is included with them by appropriate definition as an integral part of the dual basis insurance. But where there is no such item on the specification and part only of the wage roll is included in the insurance on gross profit on a "difference" wording, it must be kept in mind that it is the *uninsured* wages and holiday pay which is mentioned in the list of specified working expenses. So if in that list "30 per cent. of the total wage roll with holiday pay thereon" is mentioned it means that 70 per cent. of the wages, etc., is insured. On the other hand if the net profit plus standing charges definition of gross profit is used, mention of "30 per cent. of the total wage roll with holiday pay thereon" in the list of insured standing charges means that only 30 per cent. of the wages, etc., is insured.

The paid holiday periods of salaried staff are almost invariably treated as salary payments and included in the salaries item in the accounts; in such circumstances no mention of holiday pay is necessary whichever definition of gross profit is used.

195. National Insurance (including State Pension) and Social Security Contributions

(a) *United Kingdom*

Following the decision of Mr. Justice Branson in the *Polikoff* case mentioned in paragraphs 175 and 189(b) that the description "Insurance Premiums" did not include State (now National) Insurance contributions it is necessary to treat the latter separately from insurance premiums in considering them in the terms of business interruption insurance. The employer's portion only is the expense with which the insurance is concerned but over the years it has increased to become an expense of considerable relevant magnitude.

During a period of interruption after damage the insured will have to continue to collect national insurance contributions through P.A.Y.E. income tax arrangements in respect of retained employees and the amount of the employers' concurrent contributions in respect of that portion of the payroll insured in the item on gross profit should therefore be included in that item. Where the definition is on the "difference" wording the national insurance contributions in respect of directors and salaried employees and of any wages not mentioned in the list of uninsured working expenses will automatically be included in the gross profit insurance. Under the older form of definition the list of insured standing charges will have to include an appropriate reference and this is effected by the words "national insurance contributions and holiday pay in respect of the salaries and wages insured".

When there is a separate item on notice wages, see paragraph 231 regarding the inclusion in it of the relevant proportion of national insurance contributions and holiday pay. When the whole of the wage roll is insured under the dual basis scheme the national insurance contributions and holiday pay for all wage earners should be included in the item—see paragraph 196. The national insurance contributions for salaried staff only will then be insured in the gross profit unless salaries are insured with wages in a combined item on remuneration under a dual basis payroll cover (see paragraph 212).

Self-employed persons liable to pay national insurance contributions should insure the amount of their flat-rate Class 2 contributions, as these are a standing charge, in their gross profit insurance. Any Class 4 contributions which are payable to the inland revenue along with Schedule D income tax should also be insured since liability for their payment will attach to any amount received under a business interruption claim as explained about income tax in paragraph 118.

(b) *United States*

A position similar to the foregoing applies to the inclusion in U.S. coverages of the employer's portion of Social Security Contributions paid to the Internal Revenue Service in respect of employees and also regarding the Social Security Contributions made by self-employed persons with their income tax. It is the same with the Payroll Tax paid by employers quarterly or under the Cost Reimbursement scheme for non-profit making organisations under the Federal Unemployment Tax Act.

Within the Ordinary Payroll Limitation endorsement to the Business Income Coverage form, "Ordinary payroll expenses" include (besides payroll) employee benefits (if directly related to payroll), F.I.C.A. payments, union dues and workers compensation premiums.

196. Overtime

It is often considered unnecessary to include overtime payments in the amount insured on wages on the grounds that if workers are to be paid during a period of non-employment or under-employment they cannot expect more than their standard rate of pay. On the other hand, part of the object of insuring wages may be to retain skilled workers and prevent their dispersal to other employers during a period of interruption. If the workpeople concerned are accustomed to drawing their weekly wage plus substantial overtime pay or bonus related to output or performance and find that they can obtain similar financial reward with another employer during the period of interruption many might prefer to take work elsewhere in order to obtain more pay rather than to draw standard rates of pay in return for no work or partial work. So it may be desirable to include overtime wages and bonus payments in the insurance; if it is decided to do this the position should be made clear by an appropriate reference in the definition of wages. (See paragraph 205(b).)

197. Redundancy payments

(a) *Refunds under legislation*

Under the Employment Protection (Consolidation) Act 1978 employers are liable to make lump-sum compensation payments to employees made redundant with at least two years' service after age 18 who become redundant and who also satisfy certain prescribed conditions. The amount of the payments is related to age, pay and length of service with the employer—see paragraph 202(b). A rebate in respect of such redundancy payments is recoverable by an employer through the Department of Employment from the Redundancy Fund which is financed through a supplementary charge incorporated in employers' national insurance contributions.

The cost of these weekly contributions will fall to be dealt with for business interruption insurance purposes as part of an employer's bill for national insurance contributions for employees, as detailed in paragraph 195(a).

So far as *payments under the Act to redundant employees* are concerned the distinction must be appreciated between those made because of circumstances unconnected with an interruption of business due to a fire or other insured peril and those payable to employees who become redundant following and because of such an interruption. The latter are considered in connection with the insurance of wages (paragraph 202(b) and paragraph 203(b)) and in the chapter on claims (paragraph 422). The former, that is, payments made for redundancy unconnected with interference with a business following damage as insured under the policy, are dealt with here.

As payments to redundant employees will arise only when there are actual cases of redundancy, in periods of full employment the cost of payments of this kind is generally unlikely to appear annually as a regular feature in a firm's accounts and will be to some extent in the nature of a non-recurring charge, regarding which see paragraph 82(c). A specification on the "difference" wording, without mention of redundancy payments, will provide automatically for this circumstance so that in the event of a business interruption claim following damage the insured's gross profit and net profit will each be restored to what it would have been but for the damage.

Where the gross profit definition is on the old wording of net profit plus insured standing charges, "Redundancy payments less rebates from the Department of Employment" might be included in the list of the latter in business where redundancy payments arise periodically or, otherwise, as a precaution against the future contingency of such payments having to be made. But in the absence of such mention, recourse could be made, in the event of a claim arising from damage during a year following one in which the net profit had been reduced by redundancy payments which were not a normal feature of the business, to adjustment under the other circumstances clause (see paragraph 55(a)) to provide an insured with a proper indemnity.

In the United States no provision for redundancy pay is made in the Employment Security Law or other Federal legislation but many employers have their own schemes for severance pay as in the next paragraph 197(b).

(b) *Redundancy agreement and severance pay funds*

In addition to payments to the Redundancy Fund (paragraph 197(a)) which they have to make as a supplementary charge in their flat-rate national insurance contributions some firms also maintain a private fund as a voluntary provision for contingent future claims under a redundancy or severance pay scheme for their employees. Annual allocations made to such a fund are obviously a standing charge and as such should be included in the gross profit insurance.

198. Pensions, pension schemes premiums, pension funding, superannuation schemes and annuities (other than National Insurance pensions)

Persons in full-time employment in the United Kingdom included in the National Insurance scheme for a basic pension are also entitled to a second pension which is earnings related. This latter may be either under the State additional pension arrangement or by an approved contracted-out scheme run by the employer generally in conjunction with an insurance company. Payments by employers to the State pension fund are dealt with in paragraph 195(a) on National Insurance contributions.

The annual cost to a business of premiums paid to an insurance company to provide pensions or annuities to employees and directors under a contracted-out scheme will continue to be payable in full irrespective of the effect of damage on the earning capacity of a business. Clearly, therefore, they are standing charges and call for no special comment apart from the position in the year when a firm inaugurates a pension scheme and it is necessary to make a substantial initial payment to provide for back service of their employees. This payment will then be considerably in excess of the annual premium under the scheme but should be included in the computation of the sum insured for the reasons stated in paragraph 82(c) about non-recurring charges.

Workpeople's pension schemes in which an annual premium is paid to an insurance company per capita on the number of workpeople employed should also be included in the item on gross profit. This applies even though the wages of all of them are not insured in that item, because the premium would not be reduced should some of the workpeople be under-employed or even stood off for a time during a period of interruption.

Many large firms operate their own pension schemes embracing the majority of their employees and annual contributions to trustee-administered funds for such schemes are charged against earnings as the payments are made. These payments will be continued irrespective of an interruption of business and so should be included in the insurance on gross profit.

199. Categories of workers

(a) *Key productive workers (United Kingdom and United States)*

There is in most businesses a broad classification of workers identifiable without undue difficulty whose wages should always be regarded as a standing charge. Foremen and forewomen, chargehands, overlookers, supervisors, progress chasers, shop stewards, departmental managers or heads, and similar people whose work includes some supervisory functions, are in this category. Their remuneration is not related directly or entirely to their own productive efforts but rather to that of the employees for whom they are responsible. If work is interrupted or interfered with as a result of damage they will continue to be paid full wages although there may be fewer employees for them to supervise than before the damage and production or turnover is lower than normal.

After serious damage in a factory all new or repaired machinery does not go into full production on the same day but there is a gradual build-up over a period of time as more plant and machinery is brought progressively into use. Throughout this difficult period production may be quite out of balance and an uneven flow of work result. These and other factors generally mean that during the period of return to normal production the "standing charge" portion of the wage roll is not fully earned by the subnormal level of production; and this period may be quite prolonged.

Because the wages of this category of employee generally referred to as "key workers" will not fall proportionately with a reduction in turnover they should be insured for the same maximum indemnity period as the gross profit on the general grounds for insuring any expense which will bear an increased ratio to turnover after damage.

(b) *Administrative, distributive and maintenance workers*

Another broad classification of employees includes those engaged on administrative, distributive or maintenance work such as clerks, warehousemen, skilled packers, storekeepers, inspectors and checkers, boiler and power house staff, works electricians, joiners, bricklayers, mechanics, fitters and other maintenance staff, laboratory and testing house staff, furnace-men, motor drivers, works locomotive and truck drivers, canteen workers, liftmen, stores detectives, reception staff, security staff, commissionaires and gatemen. All such employees will usually have to be retained on full wages even though there is a reduction in the volume of trade during a period of interruption and so their wages should be insured for the same maximum indemnity period as the gross profit. Some employees in the categories mentioned may be paid salaries in which case their remuneration will be included in the insurance on gross profit.

(c) *Skilled workers and craftsmen*

A further category of worker must be considered, especially during an era of full employment. If employees are stood off following a fire because there is no work for them they will seek other employment and may be unwilling to return when wanted. Consequently highly skilled workers in specialised engineering and other trades, craftsmen, pattern makers, moulders and technicians for whose services there is a good demand must be retained as long as possible when there is no work available for them in order to prevent their dispersal to other employers. Many firms consider that their ordinary skilled operatives should be retained similarly. Although the aggregate wages of such workpeople will normally vary in direct ratio to their total productivity and is a variable charge it may well be in the interests of a business to pay them full wages irrespective of the amount of work available. Otherwise they may disperse to employment with other firms. If the insured wish to be in a position to prevent this and to retain them for the time when they can again be fully employed the wages of skilled operatives should be included in the insurance.

There is another important reason for insuring such employees' wages. They will have to be employed during a period when a factory is capable of production but the tempo is slower than normal because of shortages or bottle-necks in the flow of materials and work, slow running or occasional breakdowns of machinery or other results of damage. In any such circumstances the ratio of wages to turnover of this class of employee will rise, probably very steeply. Unless their wages are insured the resulting loss will have to be borne by the insured as subsequently explained in Chapter 20 on Claims (paragraph 424) and is not claimable as increase in cost of working because there is no actual increase in the wage roll (paragraph 425). It should also be borne in mind that a similar position can arise through a reduction in

199

production due to damage at the premises of suppliers, processors, customers or warehousemen to which the insurance may have been extended as explained in Chapter 17.

(d) *Apprentices and trainees*

The wages of apprentices and trainees must be regarded as a standing charge if the insured are bound to continue their pay irrespective of work or training being available for them. Even should there be no agreement to that effect it is prudent to insure their wages in order to be able to retain them with a view to their future employment as skilled men, craftsmen or technicians.

200. Extent of cover in the United Kingdom

Before the general acceptance of 100 per cent. payroll cover (within gross profit), consideration of the effects which interruption of a business following damage may have had upon the deployment of its labour force involved several imponderables and factors beyond those which would have had to be considered in the case of most charges in deciding whether they are variable or standing charges.

In its simplest form the problem was one of deciding which employees or categories of employees would be retained, after damage had taken place, on full wages throughout the indemnity period in whatever manner the turnover of the business might be affected. Wages were once (prior to the introduction of more stringent legislation) looked upon by insurers largely as an optional standing charge; so whilst the views expressed in paragraph 104 on what constitutes an insurable standing charge apply in this connection the emphasis was on what wages should be paid in the best interests of the business rather than on the wages which must unavoidably be paid.

The inclusion of *all* wages in the item of insurance on gross profit has always been the simplest method of dealing with the wages cover. It necessitates no alteration of the normal wording for that item, operates satisfactorily in all respects in the settlement of a claim and gives complete protection. It was, however, generally adopted only for small trade risks, warehouse and shop proprietors and professional men.

It was a more difficult problem for larger, industrial concerns, because the term wages embraced so many different types of employees and was used by some firms where others spoke of salaries, some even including directors in the wages book. One part of the wages item in the insured's accounts may have been a standing charge whilst another part was variable. The matter was further complicated because conditions in relation to employment could change according to the length and progress of the period of interruption.

The main difficulty arose in trying to visualise the different possible effects of damage upon a business and how these would be reflected on the work and earning capacity of employees. Another factor to be taken into account was the general state of the labour market particularly the position in the insured's own trade and locality.

It may have been advisable in some businesses to insure the whole of the wage roll as a standing charge especially when the relative cost was not very heavy. This applied particularly in a highly mechanised factory or one in which most of the machinery was automated and manpower was small in relation to the productive capacity. For general industrial risks, however, the insurance of the whole wage roll might have seemed unnecessary or it might have appeared impracticable to keep all the operatives idle over a period of several months and that, even were this desired, the cost of insurance to enable this to be done would have been prohibitive especially where the fire rate was high, when the maximum indemnity period was a long one, or where the payroll was very large.

Insurers, however, learned by experience following big industrial fires, that insurance of a major part of the wage roll for the same maximum indemnity period as that for the gross profit item was desirable, for even large fires seldom involved all employees being completely workless for very long, under-capacity employment being most often the position. To meet this problem and provide for the unpredictability of what wages cover might be required after a large fire, insurance companies introduced in 1952 a method of insuring wages called the dual basis scheme. By providing a pool of wages insurance this was designed to give almost complete flexibility to the cover, at a reasonable premium cost, as is fully explained in paragraphs 205 *et seq.*

At that time an insured might have been legally liable for the payment of wages in lieu of notice or under trade agreement to all employees for a short period after a fire but not in subsequent weeks. But parliamentary legislation since then placed upon employers an aggregation of liabilities in respect of remuneration—the Redundancy Payments Act 1965, the Contracts of Employment Act 1972 and the Employment Protection Act 1975—which greatly increased the necessity for large businesses to carry an even more extended wages cover. Sections of the first and third of these Acts which were of relevance to wages insurance and the whole of the 1972 Act were repealed by the Employment Protection (Consolidation) Act 1978 but the liabilities on employers were retained by that Act. (See paragraph 202(a).) These liabilities and other considerations led in 1976 to the expansion of the dual basis wages scheme to embrace both salaries and wages in a dual basis payroll cover (see paragraph 212) and to concessions in premium rating for large insurances when 100 per cent. of the payroll (salaries and wages) is insured within the gross profit item. Full details of this are given in paragraph 204 on "100 per cent. payroll cover".

Except in the case of the last mentioned form of cover, however, there still remained the necessity of deciding what proportion of the wage roll should be treated as a standing charge that was to be insured for the maximum indemnity period, and what length of indemnity period should be insured for the remainder.

201. Considerations when damage occurs

Theoretically, in considering the insurance of wages the same possibilities must be envisaged as in the problem of standing charges in general. First, a complete stoppage of relatively limited duration arising from damage to the power unit or to one process or department or a section of a production line which leaves the rest of the works undamaged. Secondly, partial interruption of the business during which the work may be hampered and slowed down due to shortage of materials, slow running of damaged plant, processes having to be done by hand when machinery is out of action, a bottleneck in one department, loss of the packing or dispatch department or warehouse, or one of many other adverse conditions which may follow damage. Thirdly, a complete burn-out at the premises followed by a period during which there is no turnover until other premises are obtained or rebuilding is effected and necessary plant, machinery or stocks installed or until arrangements are made for work to be done by other firms. This will usually be followed by a gradual return to normal turnover in the process of which the labour force will have to be recruited again. Additionally, if an insurance is extended to include loss resulting from damage at the premises of suppliers, processors, customers or outside stores (see Chapter 17) the effect of such potential loss upon employment at the insured's own premises must also be taken into account. Finally, the time required after restoration of the damage at the insured's own premises or of facilities to replace those lost if it has been a case of "other people's fires" and of full productive or trading facilities, for the recovery of custom which has gone elsewhere during the period of interruption.

202. Wages liabilities under United Kingdom Acts of Parliament

(a) *General*

Three Acts of particular relevance to the arrangement of wages insurance under a business interruption policy in the United Kingdom were the Redundancy Payments Act 1965, the Contracts of Employment Act 1972 and the Employment Protection Act 1975. Sections of the first and third of these Acts and the whole of the 1972 Act were repealed by the Employment Protection (Consolidation) Act 1978.

This legislation is of such vital importance to those involved in the arrangement of large insurances that the three categories of liability imposed by it are dealt with individually in the following paragraphs 202(b) to 203 and the points in them of particular importance from the wages insurance angle are given. They are followed by some guidance on the wages insurance which may be necessary to protect insured for the payment of wages in compliance with the Acts in the event of interruption of business necessitating the dismissal of employees.

In considering the insurance necessary to protect an employer against statutory liability for the payment of wages during a period of interruption of business following damage attention should also be given to the possibility of there being additional legal liability. This could be under a special agreement between an employer and employees or between all employers and the trade unions for a particular industry extending wages liabilities beyond the legislative requirements. The statutory liabilities are minimum stipulations and any employer who, from a feeling of moral obligation or other motive, may wish to insure for more than such liability is entitled to do so.

It may be well to mention here, so as not to complicate the issue in the following paragraphs, that when the Redundancy Payments Act was passed in 1965 there were requests from insured for a separate item on a specification to cover liabilities under the Act on a "first-loss" basis with an arbitrary sum insured. Conditions for such an insurance were then formulated, limiting it to an insured's statutory liability, the premium cost being five times the basis rate. But with the subsequent growth of wages liabilities under the later Acts and the improved facilities for covering same, that limited form of cover has fallen into desuetude.

(b) *Employment Protection (Consolidation) Act 1978: redundancy payments*

The Redundancy Payments Act 1965 laid on employers a liability for the payment of wages to workpeople whose employment they terminated. The relevant section of that Act was repealed by and its provisions were incorporated in the Employment Protection (Consolidation) Act 1978 and the liability which is continued under this new Act has to be taken into account in considering the insurance of wages.

To quote the brochure of the Department of Employment (March 1980): "In very general terms the Act requires an employer to make a lump-sum compensation payment called a 'redundancy payment' to an employee under age 65 (man) or 60 (woman) who is dismissed because of redundancy after at least two years' reckonable service since the age of 18". A redundancy payment is calculated with reference to age, length of continuous reckonable service (up to a maximum of 20 years) and weekly pay. The weekly pay is limited and this limit is reviewed annually. Entitlement is reckoned on the following scale:

for each year of reckonable service from age 41 to
65 (man) or 60 (woman) .... 1½ weeks' pay
for each year of reckonable service from age 22 to 40 .... 1 week's pay
for each year of reckonable service from age 18 to 21 .... ½ week's pay

Provisions for calculating the amount of pay and certain limits applicable are laid down and reviewed annually but no question of redundancy payment can arise until an employee has been laid off or kept on short-time, or a mixture of both, either for at least four consecutive weeks or for a broken series of at least six weeks where all the six weeks fall within a thirteen-week period.

It is impossible to lay down any hard and fast rule as to the extent to which wages insurances should be arranged to provide for this liability in the event of workpeople having to be laid off following a fire because this will depend largely upon the composition of each individual firm's labour force having regard to both age and length of service of each of their employees and also the position as regards turn-over of their workpeople. Further, a percentage of the cost of the payments made by an employer can be reclaimed from the Redundancy Fund (subject to periodic review) which is financed by a charge incorporated in employers' national insurance contributions. It is generally regarded that the redundancy payments provisions now incorporated in the 1978 (Consolidation) Act probably added on average up to about seven weeks to the period for which wages cover should be arranged (see also paragraph 203).

(c) *Employment Protection (Consolidation) Act 1978: period of notice of termination of employment*

The period of notice which an employer is required to give to an employee for termination of employment was first laid down in the Contracts of Employment Act 1963 and was progressively increased over the years by an amending Act in 1972 and by Schedule 16 to the Employment Protection Act of 1975. Statutory provision for notification of termination of employment is now contained in Part IV of the Employment Protection (Consolidation) Act 1978. Under this latest Act an employee is entitled to one week's notice (or wages in lieu of notice) after four weeks' continuous service and two weeks' notice after two years' continuous service. He is entitled to an additional week's notice for each year of service, up to a maximum of 12 weeks' notice after 12 years' service. Therefore the overall average period of liability will vary from one firm to another because the period of notice for each employee depends upon the length of his or her continuous employment with the firm.

As regards wages insurance to cover a firm's liability it should be noted that if the average of the notice wages which would be due under the Act is estimated as being say eight weeks it would be inadequate to insure for that length of period. Such cover would provide only for the insured's loss through the payment of wages during the first eight weeks after damage; payments in subsequent weeks in respect of employees entitled to longer periods of notice would not be covered.

On the other hand, the Act deals with notice of termination of employment and under the 1972 Act, the Department of Employment notes for the guidance of employers stated that if a lay-off of employees does not terminate the contract of employment no notice under the Act is required.

The effects of the foregoing on the arrangement of wages insurance along with that in respect of redundancy payments described in preceding paragraph 202(b) will be dealt with in conjunction with the liabilities under the Employment Protection Act 1975 in the following paragraph.

(d) *The Employment Protection Act 1975: prior consultations and notice of redundancy dismissals*

This Act introduced wide legislation regarding industrial relations. The part which has repercussions on business interruption insurance is Part IV which contains provisions for consultations with trade unions about redundancies and for notification to the Secretary of State for Employment and lays down the time limits within which these must take place. Although other sections of the 1975 Act were repealed by the Employment Protection (Consolidation) Act 1978 this part was left to remain in force.

In section 99 of Part IV of the 1975 Act it is stipulated that an employer proposing to dismiss as redundant an employee of a description in respect of which an independent trade union is recognised by him shall consult representatives of that trade union about the dismissal at the earliest opportunity. But if the employer proposes to make 10 or more employees redundant within a relatively short time he must begin consultations within a specified minimum time before the first dismissal takes effect. The minimum times are:

— if 10 to 99 employees may be dismissed as redundant at one establishment over a period of 30 days or less—at least 30 days (originally this was 60 days but was reduced in November 1979)
— if 100 or more employees may be dismissed as redundant at one establishment over a period of 90 days or less—at least 90 days.

Section 100 of the Act (as amended) stipulates that when an employer proposes to dismiss employees as redundant in the numbers indicated above he shall notify the Secretary of State in writing of his proposal at least 30 days (or 90 days as appropriate) before the first dismissal takes effect and give a copy of the notice to the trade union.

If consultations are not commenced within the specified periods as set out in the Act then the trade union may apply for a "protective award" under section 101. If such an award is made it obliges the employer to continue to pay employees from the date of the award or the date when the dismissals take effect, whichever is earlier, for a period which cannot exceed the minimum laid down for consultation.

If during this "protective period" the employer continues to pay wages or damages for breach of contract the amount so paid can be set off against the amount required to be paid under the award and any liability arising under the Employment Protection (Consolidation) Act 1978 will be similarly treated. There is however no reference to redundancy payments due to be made under the same Act and it would appear that these are additional commitments and cannot be set off against the award.

The 1975 Act refers in section 100(6) to special circumstances rendering it not reasonably practicable for the employer to comply with its requirements and requires him in that event to take all such steps towards compliance with the requirements as are reasonably practicable in those circumstances. The Department of Employment has stated that although a fire or other insured peril might constitute a special circumstance rendering it not reasonably practicable for an employer to comply with his obligations to consult a trade union everything would depend on the individual circumstances of the case and it would be up to the Industrial Tribunal to decide. In view of this statement insurers advise policy holders to assume that insured damage is not a special circumstance.

203. Effect of the Employment Protection Acts of 1975 and 1978 on business interruption insurance on wages

It must be assumed that dismissals caused by damage at an insured's premises are not excluded from the application of the foregoing legislation. Similarly it is assumed that the notice periods stipulated under the Employment Protection Act 1975 and the Employment Protection (Consolidation) Act 1978 are not cumulative in effect as there appears to be nothing in the former which would make an employer wait the specified minimum number of days before giving the statutory period of notice under the 1978 consolidating Act. If this is so the employer is not prevented from so timing his actions that the 30 (or 90) days period for consultation and the contractual period of notice expire on the same day.

Nevertheless it will in certain circumstances be necessary to take account of both Acts in fixing the insured period of full wages insurance. The position will be as follows:

(1) Where in the event of damage it is likely to be necessary to pay off 100 or more employees at one establishment within a period of 90 days the period of 100 per cent. wages cover must be sufficiently long to include the time of the compulsory delay in effecting the lay-off of workpeople, *i.e.* 90 days (say 13 weeks) in accordance with the Employment Protection Act 1975. It might be prudent to make this 14 weeks to allow a little more time

for consideration of the problem before starting consultations with representatives of trade unions; it could be that either loss of office records or the general chaos resulting from a serious fire or explosion might mean the elapse of some days before notice of termination of employment can be given.

To this 14 weeks should be added the statutory liability to make redundancy payments less the amount recoverable from the redundancy fund: see paragraph 202(b). This might well mean about seven weeks wages and so periods of around 21 weeks full wages cover may be considered as necessary for large insurances.

(2) When from 10 to 99 employees at one establishment are likely to be dismissed within a period of 30 days, the minimum period of notice for all employees will be 30 days (say 5 weeks) under the Employment Protection Act 1975. However, under the provisions of the Employment Protection (Consolidation) Act 1978 those with 10 years or more service will qualify for a longer period of notice up to the maximum of 12 weeks. The average requirement for all employees being made redundant may therefore be any period up to that maximum.

If it is estimated that this is adequate and the same allowance for time to get organised and for redundancy payments is made as under the previous calculation the period for full wages insurance would be say 18 weeks.

(3) When fewer than 10 employees are likely to be dismissed the provisions of the consolidating Act will apply in establishing the period of notice for individual employees. To this must be added as above a number of weeks to allow for a breathing space and for redundancy payments. With such a small number of workpeople it should not be very difficult to estimate the average requirement likely to be experienced and arrange the wages insurance correspondingly.

The liabilities mentioned in preceding paragraphs can be taken care of by arranging an initial period of 100 per cent. wages cover of appropriate length under a dual basis wages insurance, or by including wages either in a dual basis payroll cover or a 100 per cent. payroll cover.

Before leaving the matter of liabilities under the Employment Protection Acts it should be noted that for a firm having more than one premises it is essential to consider whether one dual basis wages item provides adequate protection, because the 1975 Act refers to liabilities to employees "at one establishment". Where the wages insurance required at their premises varies, averaging out in one item does not provide a satisfactory answer to the problem (see paragraph 215).

Further provisions of the Employment Protection Act 1975 came into force in February 1977 which gave entitlement to its benefits to part-time workers employed for 16 hours or more per week as soon as they have completed the necessary period of continuous employment for the individual right concerned; those working for eight hours or more per week qualify on completing five years' continuous employment. For businesses employing an appreciable number of women workers on a part-time basis this is a matter to be taken into account when considering their wages insurance arrangement; for instance, as many as 20 per cent. of the office and warehouse employees of a mail order house may be part-time workers.

204. 100 per cent. payroll cover

The aggregation of the requirements regarding payments to employees under the various Acts of Parliament, detailed in paragraphs 268 to 272, coupled with the desire of employers to retain staff with special skills or to offer job security to their employees in general in the event of interruption of the business following damage, has resulted in most insured now requiring a much more comprehensive cover on remuneration than would have been necessary in the past. However, even if a long initial period of 100 per cent. cover and a high remainder percentage were arranged some doubt might still remain regarding the adequacy of the insurance to meet all the unforeseen circumstances which could arise following damage at the premises.

With the above in mind it was decided by U.K. insurance companies to offer, subject to certain qualifications, *100 per cent. payroll cover within the gross profit item. That is, to include the whole remuneration, wages as well as salaries (together with employers' per capita pension and national insurance contributions), as being in effect a standing charge for the full maximum indemnity period, at a reduced premium rate.* The latter concession in premium was to compensate insured for the fact that although the whole of the wages were thus insured for the same maximum indemnity period as the gross profit it was virtually certain that insurers would not have to pay a loss in respect of wages proportionate to that on the other components of the gross profit insurance throughout the whole period of indemnity.

The rate reduction applies to the payroll constitutent of the overall sum insured and when cover is arranged on this basis it is necessary, for a calculation of the premium reduction, that the insured provide from the accounts for the last financial year a declaration of (a) the gross profit as defined in the policy including 100 per cent. payroll and (b) the amount included in this which is the payroll element. The special premium charged is reviewed on a regular basis—perhaps every third year.

The normal method of premium rating appears to be complicated but is simple in operation. For an insurance on gross profit including 100 per cent. payroll it is the percentage of the basis rate (paragraph 254(a)) calculated as follows:

   (a) the percentage obtained by taking the aggregate of that proportion of the percentage in normal loadings (*i.e.* 150 per cent. for 12 months etc., as per paragraph 256(a) applicable to the maximum indemnity period which the amount of the gross profit excluding payroll bears to the amount of the gross profit including payroll, and

(b) that proportion of the percentage in the undernoted payroll table applicable to the maximum indemnity period which the amount of payroll bears to the amount of gross profit including payroll.

Payroll table

Maximum indemnity period	Percentage
12 months	112
18 ,,	98
24 ,,	81
36 ,,	63

So taking a 60 per cent. gross profit and 40 per cent. payroll the calculation for a 12 months maximum indemnity period would be (a) 60 per cent. of 150 = 90 plus (b) 40 per cent. of 112 = 44.8 (fractions of 1 per cent. are ignored) = 134 per cent. of basis rate.

One attractive feature of the 100 per cent. payroll cover is that the premium cost compares very favourably with and in some cases may even be less than that which would apply under dual basis with only a percentage of wages insured after the initial period of 100 per cent. full cover.

An additional advantage gained by the arrangement of cover on this basis is the simplification in procedure where some salaries and wages are obscured by being in the accounts under such headings as maintenance, transport and warehousing.

Conditions which are usually applicable to this special cover are:

(a) 100 per cent. of remuneration as defined is insured within the gross profit item
(b) the maximum indemnity period is not less than 12 months
(c) the arrangement cannot be used for insurances under the special schemes at reduced premiums for professional men and hotels, boarding houses and public houses
(d) the premium reduction concession does not apply to water damage, impact and engineering perils and extensions to premises other than an insured's own or to Research Expenditure insurances (paragraph 273) N.B. In the case of all risks covers, the concession applies only to "fire and dry perils".
(e) it is understood that, in view of the reduction in premium rating, in the event of an interruption of business the insured will allow the normal wastage of labour due to retirements, temporary workers, etc., to continue and will not seek to avoid this by taking advantage of the 100 per cent. cover.
(f) not insurable under this cover are directors' fees (paragraph 111) and the cash value of fringe benefits (paragraph 192(a)).

This arrangement for the insurance of wages together with salaries on a 100 per cent. basis for the maximum indemnity period is particularly useful for employers with a labour force which for one reason or another necessitates a high level of insurance in respect of wages. It is essential to keep in mind however that a business interruption policy is drafted to indemnify on the basis of what the position would have been but for the damage during the period of interruption and that the average proviso operates correspondingly. Hence, the greatest care is called for in arranging and in maintaining at all times the combined sum insured on gross profit and wages at an adequate figure with an eye on the future. Wage rolls generally increase proportionately more than, and in advance of, the standing charges and net profit of a business; therefore it is vital to keep the gross profit sum insured always based on future possibilities with the wages position prominently in mind—the position perhaps two or more years ahead—particularly when the maximum indemnity period is longer than 12 months—as explained in paragraph 224 on estimating future gross profit.

205. Insurance of wages on the dual basis

(a) *General principles*

Under the dual basis scheme, wages are removed from the gross profit item and the total wage roll is insured entirely separately under a single item. The insurance then operates on principles similar to and in a manner parallel to that on gross profit. That is to say, the maximum indemnity period is of the same length; the index of loss is shortage in turnover to which is applied the ratio which wages bore to turnover in the preceding financial year; and increase in cost of working is also covered. Where the maximum indemnity period is 12 months (which is the minimum permissible under this scheme) the sum insured is the amount of the total annual wage roll and where it exceeds 12 months the sum insured is the appropriate multiple of that amount. In recognition of the fact that after an "initial period" of 100 per cent. wages cover the insurer's liability is limited to a percentage of the wages for a substantial part of the maximum indemnity period (the "remainder percentage" during the "remaining portion of the indemnity period" as explained in following paragraphs) a lower rate of premium is charged for the dual basis wages item than for the insurance on gross profit.

Provision is made for the trend of the business and for variations in or other circumstances affecting the business by including "the rate of wages to turnover during the financial year immediately before the date of the damage (Incident)" in the bracket against the other circumstances clause. It should be noted that the use of this clause for the wages item in the event of a claim will affect the application of the average proviso similarly to the manner in which adjustments are reflected in the application of average in the gross profit item.

Once the length of the initial period of 100 per cent. cover and percentage limit for the partial insurance thereafter have been agreed upon it is subsequently much easier to keep a check on the sum insured because the comparable figure on which it is based is simply that of the total annual wage roll (allowing for future increases as explained in paragraph 210) or an appropriate multiple of it when the maximum indemnity period exceeds 12 months. For the same reason it is usually a simple matter for accountants to furnish a certificate for purposes of the return of premium clause.

(b) *Definition of wages*

The standard definition of Wages insured under the dual basis scheme reads:

> "The remuneration (including national insurance, bonuses, holiday pay and other payments pertaining to wages) of all employees other than those whose remuneration is treated as salaries in the Insured's books of account".

This makes a definite line of demarcation between employees who are paid wages and those on a salaried basis. The insured's account books, however, may not deal with the payroll so precisely or their terminology may not quite fit in with the original intention of the insurance companies that the dual basis cover was for the insurance only of "wage" earning employees as the term is generally understood and that all salaries should be insured in full as a standing charge for the full indemnity period. Because of divergences from the normal classifications of salaries and wages, which arise in some businesses (as explained in paragraph 189(a) on salaries) it was, until 1976, necessary to provide for the particular circumstances of such businesses by arranging for a variation in the standard definition of wages. But difficulties of this nature may now be dealt with by insuring the combined total of salaries and wages under the nomenclature of "remuneration" in a "payroll cover", for full details of which see paragraphs 204 and 212.

(c) *Initial period*

The item takes its name from the fact that it provides an indemnity for loss due to the payment of wages during two separate periods. *The first of these is an initial period beginning with the occurrence of the damage (Incident) and ending not later than a selected number of weeks thereafter.* The minimum for this is four weeks. During this initial period, 100 per cent. of the rate of wages, that is, the ratio which wages bore to turnover in the last financial year, is applied to the shortage in turnover.

The effect of this is to provide compensation for the payment of all wages, including notice wages and liabilities under parliamentary legislation, throughout the initial period if there is no turnover whatever during that time. If some turnover is maintained such turnover will earn its relative part of the wage bill and the insurance will compensate for the loss in respect of the balance of the wages paid out, that is, for payments made to workers laid off or dismissed and for the portion of the wages of retained employees which is not earned by the reduced amount of turnover.

As the amount payable to the insured for loss due to the payment of wages in the initial period is calculated as being 100 per cent. of the rate of wages applied to the shortage in turnover, allowance must be made for the wages of any employees who could have been paid out of this amount but who are dismissed by the insured or leave of their own volition because of the damage. For instance, if it appears that the interruption of business will be prolonged some employees might be given notice or may leave voluntarily relatively soon after the occurrence of damage. To offset the fact that because of such circumstances the whole of the wages indemnity (100 per cent. of the rate of wages applied to the shortage in turnover) may not be paid out by the insured during the initial period a savings clause is included by the words "less any saving during such period through reduction in consequence of the damage (Incident) in the amount of wages".

It should be noted that this clause operates similarly to the savings clause applicable to the insurance on gross profit (paragraph 51(a)) by confining the savings to those due to the damage, thus giving to the insured the benefit of any reduction in the wage roll which would have taken place had there been no damage, *e.g.* if some employees were due to leave under a reorganisation scheme. But there is an additional advantage in the savings clause in the wages insurance. Any saving in wages in consequence of the damage which is deducted from the basic amount payable in respect of the initial period does not go to benefit the insurers but is held to the insured's credit under the "carry over" provision fully explained in paragraphs 207(a) and (b).

In addition to this provision for carrying a credit forward there is a much more advantageous "carry back" clause incorporated (paragraph 206(a) on the alternative period). Under this clause, generally referred to as the "option to consolidate", the initial period of 100 per cent. wages cover can be very considerably lengthened by compressing the partial insurance— which is defined in the specification as the remainder percentage and is explained in the next paragraph 205(d)—from the later part of the maximum indemnity period.

As already mentioned the minimum initial period of 100 per cent. cover which can be arranged under a dual basis wages insurance is four weeks. This was made a condition when the scheme was introduced in 1952, being at that time accepted as a reasonable and generally adequate minimum period. But since the introduction of legislation from 1963 onwards up to the Employment Protection (Consolidation) Act of 1978 it can no longer be taken as an indication of sufficient initial full cover as fully explained in paragraph 203. Although four weeks remains as the compulsory minimum initial period for dual basis wages insurance much longer periods are now regarded as essential for safety even with the benefit of the option to consolidate. Periods of 20 or more weeks are today common for large firms and with 100 per cent. payroll cover now available the maximum indemnity period of the gross profit item is being increasingly accepted as the prudent length for full cover on wages.

(d) *Remainder of indemnity period*

After the expiry of the initial period the cover continues throughout the remainder of the maximum indemnity period but for a reduced proportion of the wage roll. This is achieved by continuing nominally to provide insurance on the basis of 100 per cent. of the rate of wages applied to the shortage in turnover, as during the initial period. But this nominal basic amount is then subjected to a provision which limits the amount payable to the percentage of the wage roll selected when the insurance is arranged and shown in a definition as the remainder percentage. This percentage should correspond roughly with the wages of the categories of workers described in paragraphs 199 to 201 whose pay had the dual basis not been adopted for the insurance would have been insured in the item on gross profit.

In a claim settlement, before the remainder percentage limit is applied in the calculation of the insurer's liability, a savings clause is operative in terms similar to that applicable to the initial period. The wording of this clause is: "less any saving during such period through reduction in consequence of the damage (Incident) in the amount of wages paid".

The principle is the same as with the savings clause in the item on gross profit (paragraph 51(a)), that is, the claim is calculated as though the insured had disbursed the insured charges (in this case all wages) in full and then offsets the amount of any reduction in them due to the damage. It is only after this deduction of savings in wages (savings limited to those due to the damage, the insured being given the benefit of any which would have accrued had the damage not taken place) that the selected limit (the remainder percentage) is applied. This procedure solves the problem as to how to allocate the savings in the event of a claim, between insured and insurers, a matter which can give rise to difficulties when the dual basis scheme is not employed and partial wages cover is arranged in the gross profit item and described as an amount of £s per annum or as a percentage of the total wage roll.

This method of calculating on the nominal basis of 100 per cent. wages cover and then applying the selected percentage as a limit introduces flexibility. It creates a pool of wages insurance which, although limited to the selected percentage of the total plus any savings carried over from the initial period of full cover, does not restrict the claims upon it to the selected percentage at any part of the indemnity period. It can be more, or less, than that remainder percentage at any time, provided that the total amount claimable at the end of the indemnity period is limited to the total in the pool.

206. The "alternative period" (option to consolidate or carry-back provision)

(a) *General*

The arrangement of wages insurance on the lines described in the two preceding paragraphs 205(c) and (d) does not entirely overcome the difficulty of being unable to foresee what the circumstances and the needs of the business will be throughout a period of interruption after serious damage. It may turn out that the period of serious or possibly total interference with the business is comparatively short, being a matter of weeks rather than months, yet somewhat longer than the initial period which was selected for 100 per cent. wages cover. Consequently, the insured may wish to retain during this longer period all their employees or, at any rate, more than the percentage provided for by the partial cover applicable to the second part of the indemnity period, whilst in later months the insurance nominally provided for the remaining portion of the maximum indemnity period might not be required at all because the business has returned to normal.

To help insured deal with this problem a "carry-back" concession was introduced in 1957 under the name of the "option to consolidate" which allows the partial insurance applicable to the second part of the indemnity period to be compressed so as to increase the number of weeks of 100 per cent. cover. This option, provided under a definition as "the alternative period" (the operation of which is described in the next paragraph, 206(b)) in conjunction with the carry-over provision detailed in paragraphs 207(a) and (b), gives great flexibility to the wages cover by virtually abolishing the distinction between the initial period and the remaining portion of the indemnity period. The division into watertight compartments which was a serious drawback to the now virtually defunct "layer" method is completely absent in the amended dual basis cover. In effect the insured can arrange their wages cover, within limits, after damage has taken place; in fact they can wait until the claim settlement to decide how to utilise their wages insurance and calculate their claim in the manner (again within limits) most advantageous to them.

(b) *How the option to consolidate works*

The effect of the carry-back provision is to give an insured the option, the exercise of which need not be decided upon until after damage and interruption of the business have actually taken place, to compress the partial wages cover from the remaining portion of the maximum indemnity period and use it to lengthen the initial period of 100 per cent. wages insurance. For example, if dual basis wages insurance is arranged to provide 100 per cent. for the first four weeks and 25 per cent. for the remainder of a maximum indemnity period of 12 months then the insured has the option to utilise this as a straight 100 per cent. for the first 10 weeks with no cover thereafter. But with regard to the period after 10 weeks the carry-over of savings provision (paragraphs 207(a) and (b)) would enable the insured by using less than 100 per cent. throughout the full 10 weeks to retain a credit of wages cover to be used later if circumstances proved this to be advisable.

Looking at the combination of cover just mentioned, the value of the option to consolidate will be appreciated if the possibility is visualised of a serious fire occurring in a section of a works which results in total interruption of the whole business but of limited duration estimated to last for about seven weeks. The insured have insurance providing full wages for everyone for an initial period of four weeks but as it appears probable that the business will be ready for normal working at the end of a further three or four weeks it may be considered desirable to continue paying full wages to all workers in order to retain their services until they can be fully employed. The option to consolidate enables the insured to do this. However, even if it should turn out that owing to some unforeseen hitch full production is not achieved by the end of the seventh week the payment of all wages can be continued for another three weeks if necessary, that is, up to the total period of 10 weeks from the date of damage. Alternatively, it is still not too late to lay off the less essential employees and carry forward the savings in wages in the eighth, ninth and tenth weeks to provide during the eleventh and some subsequent weeks the 25 per cent. wages cover originally intended.

Whatever combination of cover is selected under the dual basis scheme the option to consolidate provides a corresponding straight period for the 100 per cent. insurance which is the equivalent in premium value and the increased number of weeks for this 100 per cent. insurance is stated in the definition of alternative period in the description of the wages cover in the specification. (See Appendix H, paragraph 454, for specimen wording.)

(c) Examples of alternatives under the option to consolidate, with premium rates

The table (on page 221) shows the equivalent alternative periods of 100 per cent. wages insurance obtainable under the option to consolidate for various combinations of cover and gives an indication of the very substantial benefit the option confers but any permutation of initial period (subject to a minimum of four weeks) and percentage during the remaining portion of the maximum indemnity period can be arranged. The end column shows the premium rates charged for the different combinations of cover given in the table these rates being so calculated that the premiums resulting from their use are practically the same as those required for insurance of wages for comparable amounts and periods under two items on the older method.

Dual basis wages premium rates are also applicable to dual basis payroll cover (paragraph 212) but not to 100 per cent. payroll cover (paragraph 204) because under the latter scheme, wages are included in the gross profit item and it is in the premium rating for that item that the reduction for insuring the whole of the wage roll applies.

207. The "carry-over of savings" provision

(a) *General*

The circumstances following damage may be of such a nature that if the damage is serious and the period of interruption seems likely to be prolonged all the cover available for 100 per cent. wages during the initial period will not be required.

It is possible that many workers will decide to seek employment elsewhere at once rather than enjoy a few weeks' idleness on full pay with the prospect of unemployment at the end of it because meanwhile jobs available elsewhere have been taken by their workmates. If the insured offer their workers only standard rates of pay whilst there is no work for them those who have been accustomed to earning substantial bonus or overtime and look upon this as their normal earnings will probably seek work under similar conditions with another firm.

The effect of employees leaving from one cause or another in consequence of the damage will be that all the compensation to which the insured are entitled under the insurance for loss on wages during the initial period will not be expended. Therefore a saving will result which the formula states shall be deducted from the amount payable by the insurers in respect of the initial period but, under a special provision, will be carried forward to the insured's credit to be used later in the indemnity period.

Alternatively, an insured may think that the money available for wages in the first few weeks might be more useful towards the end of the period of interruption when the business is being finally organised for a resumption of normal activities. For example, many businesses employ young female workers who have to be given a short period of training during which their labour is non-productive. If damage occurs which is likely to interrupt the business for only a very limited period the insured may wish to pay this class of worker full wages, even though there is no work for them to do, in order to retain their services. On the other hand, if the period of interruption is likely to be prolonged the insured will dismiss them with wages in lieu of notice and when the factory is ready again will have to retrain them or, more probably, engage and train new workers. In that event there may be a greater need for wages cover for such employees towards the end of the period of interruption rather than immediately after the damage.

DUAL BASIS METHOD for insuring
(i) WAGES ONLY or (ii) PAYROLL (salaries and wages)
—SPECIMEN COVERS WITH OPTIONS TO CONSOLIDATE SHOWN

MAXIMUM INDEMNITY PERIOD	INITIAL PERIOD OF 100% INSURANCE	REMAINDER PERCENTAGE INSURED FOR REMAINING PERIOD	ALTERNATIVE PERIOD OF 100% COVER	PREMIUM RATE AS A PERCENTAGE OF THE BASIS RATE	
		%		%	
12 months	4 weeks	15	9 weeks	59	
		25	10 ,,	66	
		50	19 ,,	94	
		75	33 ,,	122	
	8 weeks	15	12 weeks	71	on a sum
		25	15 ,,	81	insured for
		50	24 ,,	104	the annual
	13 weeks	15	16 weeks	86	wage roll
		25	19 ,,	94	
		75	39 ,,	131	
	21 weeks	15	24 weeks	105	
		25	26 ,,	110	
		$33\frac{1}{3}$	29 ,,	115	
18 months	4 weeks	15	12 weeks	46	
		25	15 ,,	54	
		75	58 ,,	111	
	8 weeks	15	15 weeks	54	
		25	19 ,,	64	on a sum
		50	42 ,,	89	insured for
		75	63 ,,	115	$1\frac{1}{2}$ times
	13 weeks	15	19 weeks	64	the annual
		25	26 ,,	73	wage roll
		50	49 ,,	95	
	21 weeks	15	29 weeks	76	
		25	36 ,,	83	
		$33\frac{1}{3}$	42 ,,	90	
24 months	4 weeks	15	12 weeks	35	
		25	17 ,,	46	
		75	74 ,,	99	on a sum
	8 weeks	15	16 weeks	43	insured for
		25	24 ,,	53	twice the
		50	54 ,,	77	annual
	13 weeks	15	22 weeks	51	wage roll
		$33\frac{1}{3}$	42 ,,	67	
		75	76 ,,	103	
36 months	4 weeks	15	16 weeks	28	
		25	29 ,,	38	
		$33\frac{1}{3}$	46 ,,	47	
	8 weeks	15	22 weeks	34	on a sum
		25	39 ,,	43	insured for
		$33\frac{1}{3}$	54 ,,	51	three times
	13 weeks	15	29 weeks	38	the annual
		25	49 ,,	48	wage roll
		$33\frac{1}{3}$	58 ,,	55	
	21 weeks	15	42 weeks	45	
		25	56 ,,	53	
		$33\frac{1}{3}$	65 ,,	60	

A similar need for full wages insurance towards the end of a period of interruption might apply in respect of skilled and semi-skilled workers who have to be re-engaged prior to the resumption of full normal production whose wages, however, will not be fully earned during the period of running-in new or repaired plant and machinery.

In some cases, after damage has occurred, the insured might realise that the percentage limit selected for the remaining portion of the maximum indemnity period is not high enough to cover all the essential workers they want to retain. In such circumstances, they may wish to utilise any saving in wages which takes place in the initial period to increase the amount available for key workers, etc., in the remaining portion of the indemnity period or, in order to increase the amount available under the savings clause, might decide to dismiss ordinary operatives before the end of the initial period.

Provision is made for all or any of these or a similar arrangement by what is termed the "carry-over" clause. This provides that any amount to which the insurers would be entitled under the savings clause applicable to the initial period (as explained in paragraph 205(c) will be carried over into the pool of wages insurance available or the subsequent period. It is included in the specification by the words "increased by such amount as is deducted for savings under the terms of clause (i)" (for the full specification wording see Appendix H). If use is made of the option to consolidate (paragraphs 206(a) to (c)) to extend the initial period to 100 per cent. wages insurance the carry-over provision applies throughout the alternative period.

It should be noted that if it is decided to utilise, under the option to consolidate, the 100 per cent. wages cover available for the longer alternative period then there will be no partial cover (remainder percentage) for wages after expiry of the latter unless there is an amount brought forward under the carry-over provision in respect of savings in wages during the alternative initial period.

(b) *Features of the carry-over provision*

An important feature of any carry-over of savings is that it is brought forward to the second part of the indemnity period as a lump sum and not treated as an increase in the percentage limit applicable to that period. If it were the latter it would then be payable in relation to the reduction in turnover and an insured would lose benefit of it according to the proportion of turnover maintained. Being brought in as an "amount", which is the word used in the carry-over provision, to be added to the amount ascertained after application of the selected limit in the remaining portion of the indemnity period means that it is available in full to offset the loss an insured might otherwise suffer by the retention of under-employed workers beyond the cover provided under that limit.

The specimen loss settlement given in Appendix W, paragraph 469 shows an instance of the beneficial operation of the carry-over provision when the full cover available for the payment of wages in the initial period is not all required during that time and part of it is used later to make good the loss which would otherwise be sustained because the limit in the remaining portion of the indemnity period is exceeded.

Moreover, the carry-over being an amount it can in effect be used in full to pay wages to general operatives, or those in training, during the last weeks before turnover is restored to normal instead of immediately after the damage. (See paragraph 207(a).)

It must be emphasised that the carry-over is of savings in wages out of the amount which the insurers would have been liable to pay during the initial period and not necessarily the difference between the pre-fire and the post-fire wage roll. For example, should 30 per cent. turnover be maintained during the initial period the insurers will be liable for only 70 per cent. of the normal wage roll (100 per cent. of the rate of wages applied to 70 per cent. shortage in turnover). The 30 per cent. for which the insurers are not liable is not a saving for the purposes of the carry-over provision because, in fact, it is not a saving (reduction) in wages but a continuation of wages which are paid for by the turnover maintained and has not been brought into the calculation of the claim. Should the 70 per cent. of wages for which the insurers remain liable not all be paid because employees leave or are dismissed in consequence of the damage the reduction will be a saving for the purposes of the carry-over provision. In other words, "savings" is virtually synonymous with the wages of workers whose employment has been terminated during the initial period because of the interruption of business caused by the damage.

208. Dual basis wages insurance: operation

(a) *When the interference with a business is total*

If an insurance were arranged with, for example, an initial period of eight weeks and a selected limit of 25 per cent. thereafter and there were no turnover whatever during the six months following the date when damage occurred, the compensation provided would be (i) the payment of full wages to all employees during the first eight weeks after the date of damage, and (ii) the payment of wages to the extent of 25 per cent. of the normal wage roll for the following 18 weeks, that is, the remaining portion of the period of interruption.

The insured could disburse the compensation provided by the insurance to whichever employees they chose according to the circumstances at the time and to their liabilities under the legislation dealt with in paragraph 202. The initial period of eight weeks would provide time in which to judge the possible extent and duration of the interference with the business and it would not be necessary to decide upon subsequent wages policy until the end of that initial period. Then, it might be decided to pay less than the insured 25 per cent. in the following three months and more in the fourth month, that is, the sixth since the date of the damage, because steps would then be necessary to recruit a full labour force again. The selected limit of 25 per cent. would be applied to the overall average throughout the second period of the indemnity (the four months mentioned) and provided that the insured had not paid more than the figure produced by applying this percentage of the rate of wages to the shortage in turnover they would be compensated up to the amount of their loss on wages.

Although the option to consolidate would be available it would probably not be particularly advantageous to exercise it in the circumstances used for this example.

(b) *When the interference with a business is only partial*

In these circumstances, which are applicable in the great majority of cases, any turnover maintained after the damage will provide for the direct wages which produce it and also will bear its relative share of the indirect wages which are paid. Towards the unmet portion of the latter the insurance will contribute an amount calculated by applying the 100 per cent. rate of wages to the shortage in turnover, deducting any savings in wages and then applying, as the maximum liability of the insurers during the remaining portion of the indemnity period, the selected limit, say 25 per cent. of the rate of wages applied to the shortage in turnover during that second period.

This would fully reimburse the insured for the payment of the indirect or standing charge wages during the initial period of 100 per cent. cover. During the subsequent period of interruption they would also be fully indemnified provided that the proportion of such wages to the total wage roll did not normally exceed the selected limit of say 25 per cent.; in other words, that the remainder percentage insured was sufficiently high.

It would not be necessary to retain in employment a fixed proportion of indirect wage-earners representing 25 per cent. of the wage roll week by week throughout the second period of the indemnity. A decision could be taken according to the needs disclosed by the circumstances as they arose and the proportion could vary, being more or less than the 25 per cent. limit as time progressed, provided that the overall average throughout the remaining portion of the indemnity period did not exceed that percentage.

The option to consolidate and the carry-over clause would provide for variations required by particular circumstances.

What it amounts to in practice is that in a period following damage the insured conduct their business as well as they can in the circumstances and retain those employees whom they consider it expedient to keep on in the real interest of their business. Loss involved by doing this due to shortage in turnover is met under the insurance up to the extent of the cover arranged by applying the formula already described, modified to the insured's advantage where necessary by the use of the option to consolidate and the carry-over of savings.

A full illustration of a claim settlement showing their advantages is given in Appendix W, paragraph 469.

209. Cover under dual basis for increase in cost of working

An additional advantage attaching to the insurance of wages under an item on the dual basis is the provision it contains for the payment of any excess of the amount recoverable for increase in cost of working under clause (b) of the item on gross profit.

The failure to recover in full under the gross profit item for the additional expenditure incurred may be due to one or more of the following three reasons. First, if it is subject to the provisions of the uninsured standing charges clause; that is, to an appropriate apportionment should any standing charges have not been included in the insurance (paragraph 49). Secondly, it is limited to "the sum produced by applying the rate of gross profit to the amount of the reduction in turnover thereby avoided"; in other words, to the amount of gross profit saved which would otherwise have been lost (paragraphs 47(a) and (b)). Thirdly, the average proviso will operate in the event of underinsurance (paragraph 52(a)).

The dual basis wages item picks up the loss due to any of these three reasons by providing in its own clause (b) for the payment of "so much of the additional expenditure described in clause (b) of item 1 (on gross profit) as exceeds the amount payable thereunder". It is, however, itself subject to a limitation namely the amount which would have been payable for loss on wages had the additional expenditure not been incurred. Further, the wages item is also subject to an average proviso (see following paragraph 210). If neither of these is applicable recovery will be made of any additional expenditure not obtainable under item 1 due to (i) there being some standing charges uninsured, (ii) the £ for £ "economic" limit being exceeded or (iii) the sum insured on gross profit being inadequate. The pick-up can be extremely valuable and the general effect is that in this way insured can receive more from the insurance than they could have done if the same wages cover had been arranged under the two item method. For an actual illustration of this see the claims illustration in Appendix W, paragraph 469.

210. Dual basis—subject to average

The dual basis insurance of wages in common with other methods is subject to average if the sum insured is less than the appropriate figure. The latter is calculated by applying the rate of wages to the annual turnover (proportionately increased if the maximum indemnity period exceeds 12 months) and each of these terms is subject to adjustment under the other circumstances clause to provide for trend and variations. It is essential, therefore, to maintain the sum insured on wages at an adequate amount allowing for possible future increases, using the past or present wage roll only as a basis in a similar manner to that described in paragraph 224 for the insurance on gross profit. A return of premium clause (paragraph 216) provides against the payment of unnecessary premium through overinsurance.

211. Formula for calculating a claim under dual basis

The dual basis wages scheme has been claimed as a simplification of the arrangement and operation of wages insurance giving almost complete fluidity of cover. In broad terms it appears to fulfil this claim but the detailed computation of a loss settlement under its provisions can be rather complicated. So at this point it might be useful to refer to the stucture of a basic claim calculation together with the alternative calculation which has to be made when it is necessary for comparison to ascertain whether the option to consolidate will give the insured a better result.

This will be found in Appendix W in which an illustration is given with figures for a claim calculation for both gross profit and dual wages, the latter showing an alternative with the option to consolidate invoked and also including a pick-up of an amount of uninsured increase in cost of working brought forward from the gross profit item. To avoid making this calculation unnecessarily complicated no adjustments have been shown which might be made to the rate of wages, annual turnover, standard turnover and average proviso through operation of the other circumstances clause.

212. Dual basis payroll

When dual basis wages insurance was introduced it was made a condition that salaries should be included in full in the gross profit item and that the dual basis provisions should apply to wages only, as described in preceding paragraphs. This requirement was made on the premise that employees paid salaries would always be retained in the event of interruption of business due to damage. But for some years past it has become increasingly difficult to relate the traditional concept of salaries and wages to insured's accounts due to a modern tendency for firms to use the term salaries in a much looser way, often as a status symbol or to fit in with computerised accounting systems. The result is that many employees are now called salaried who are not categories of staff as envisaged in the original definition of the dual basis wages item and whom it would not be an insured's intention to retain in the event of lengthy interruption of business. In this connection the information in paragraph 189(b) about the I.C.I.'s salary graded scheme for its manual workers, in the terms of an annual salary paid weekly, is of special interest.

Another factor of increasing future importance is the trend towards the involvement of shop-floor employees as worker–directors on company boards.

The problem of drawing the line between the remuneration of employees in the standing charge category, and others, when the salary–wages position is an insufficient guide has in the past sometimes been dealt with by the use of special definitions of gross profit and wages. However, in 1976 it was decided to regularise the position generally and increase the flexibility of insurance to cope with the problem by making the dual basis wages form of cover freely available for the remuneration of all employees.

Dual basis payroll cover includes the whole of the remuneration paid by an insured including that of working directors but does not include directors' fees and the monetary value of fringe benefits (see paragraph 192(a)) which must continue to be insured as part of the gross profit. To ensure this the definition restricts the cover to gross salaries and wages (which includes holiday pay) paid to all employees and employers' *per capita* pension and national insurance contributions. Remuneration to outworkers paid solely on an output basis, agents or employees paid entirely on a commission basis, casual employees and employees engaged in activities not covered by the policy, can be excluded.

The cover is an optional, alternative way of arranging an insurance which will generally mean simplification and easier negotiation of the terms of the cover. When introduced to an existing policy an appropriate amount will have to be transferred from the gross profit sum insured to the payroll item to provide for the transfer to it of salaries. Further, because salaries are included in the full term of the maximum indemnity period the "remainder percentage" of the pay roll for insurance after the end of the selected initial period of 100 per cent. cover will have to be assessed differently from what would be the procedure if it were a wages only insurance, the remainder percentage being appropriately uplifted so as to maintain the overall insurance of the superseded item. The wording for such an item is the same as that for a dual basis wages item but with the word payroll substituted for wages wherever the latter normally appears, the definition of payroll being the remuneration of all employees including working directors (but excluding directors' fees) together with national insurance contributions, etc.

All the remarks and considerations set out in previous paragraphs on the arrangements of wages on the dual basis are applicable to payroll cover, with the modification that the gross profit item has to exclude in both definition and sum insured all remuneration, etc., as defined in the payroll item.

213. Weekly and annual bases of insuring wages

These older methods present alternative ways of dealing with the problem of wages insurance when the others cannot be employed, *e.g.* if the maximum indemnity period for the gross profit insurance is less than 12 months or if full wages cover is required for less than four weeks. For instance insurance for a period of weeks only, may be all that is necessary for wages of seasonal casual workers; those employed temporarily at the height of the summer season in the catering and entertainment industries at seaside resorts; those taken on as extra labour for the gathering and processing in preserving and canning factories of fruit and vegetables during the short period when the crops are harvested. There are also businesses in which a considerable proportion of the employees are part-time workers as in mail order firms where it may be a quarter of the total. These methods may also be useful for many machinery (accident) business interruption insurances in which maximum indemnity periods are less than 12 months.

The first method is officially termed the "pro rata basis" but more conveniently in everyday use and herein, it is referred to as the "weekly basis". Under this the insurance covers the loss incurred by the payment of wages for a period beginning with the occurrence of the damage and ending not later than a selected number of weeks thereafter which may in some cases be as little as two weeks for wages in lieu of notice to part-time or temporary employees. The sum insured represents the wage roll for the stated number of weeks (not the annual figure) of all employees whose wages are not insured in the item on gross profit. The indemnity payable to the insured is the actual loss sustained by them due to the payment of wages to employees whose services cannot be used at all or cannot be utilised to the full during the stated number of weeks. The method of calculating this loss could possibly be on a straight reference to the wages book or based on a reduction in turnover or output but generally is not stated in the wording for this item.

The second method is known as the "annual basis" and under this the loss is assessed by paying the rate of wages, *i.e.* the percentage which the insured wages bore to turnover in the last financial year, on the reduction in turnover in a manner similar to that in which the loss of gross profit is calculated. The indemnity period is a selected number of months but the sum insured is the annual amount of the wages for the employees so covered.

Thus wages which would be insured under the weekly basis as "Thirteen Weeks' Wages" under the annual basis would be covered as "Wages—maximum indemnity period three months" with a sum insured for the latter four times as large as that for the former because on the annual basis it must represent the annual wage roll. In spite of this difference in sums insured the method of premium rating is such that the actual premium charged for comparable periods is approximately the same under either method.

There are pros and cons to each method but the weekly basis is simpler in wording and more immediate in application through not being tied to shortage in turnover. Also there is less danger than under the annual basis of inadvertent underinsurance arising from a misunderstanding as to the appropriate sum to be insured, for it is important to appreciate that whilst under the weekly basis the sum insured is the amount of wages for the selected number of weeks in the case of an insurance on the annual basis it must be the annual amount of wages even though the maximum indemnity period be less than 12 months.

The annual basis provides a more scientific indemnity by losses being calculated on shortage in turnover. It may, however, leave an insured dissatisfied if after damage productive workers have to be paid notice wages which the insured cannot recover because turnover is maintained from warehouse stocks for a short period and shows no diminution during the first two weeks or so. On the other hand, provision for the payment of increase in cost of working is included in the cover for wages on the annual basis.

Each method is subject to a proviso which applies an average in the event of there being underinsurance at the time when a loss occurs. This can be guarded against by arranging the sum insured with a margin of overinsurance which can be up to 100 per cent. without loss of premium because a return of premium clause can be added to the insurance on whichever basis it is arranged.

A specimen wording for an item covering weekly (notice) wages is given in Appendix I, paragraph 455.

214. Wages insured in the gross profit

(a) *Methods of description*

Except where the insurance of wages is arranged under the dual basis scheme, in which it is dealt with entirely under a separate item on the specification, a decision may have to be reached when preparing a list of the charges to be excluded from or to be included in the item on gross profit (according to the definition being used) and in computing the sum insured for that item, as to the amount of wages to be insured and the description to be employed.

When the definition of gross profit is on the "difference" wording and it is decided to insure the whole wage roll in the gross profit item the matter is dealt with quite simply by making no mention of wages in the list of variables, *i.e.* the uninsured working expenses. If only a portion of the wages is to be insured in the gross profit the uninsured portion must be shown in that list either as a percentage of the total wage roll (100 per cent. if no wages whatever are to be insured in the item on gross profit, *e.g.* if all wages are insured separately on the dual basis), or all wages over a specified amount which latter would represent the standing wages to be kept in the insurance or as all employees other than named categories (such as foremen), the latter being those included in the insured gross profit or specifically as named categories (such as hourly paid employees) to be excluded.

When the definition of gross profit is on the traditional net profit plus standing charges form the wages to be included should be described in the list of insured standing charges in one of the following ways:

(a) The wages of all employees
(b) Wages to the extent of   per cent. of the total wage roll.
(c) Wages to the extent of £   per annum.
(d) Wages to specifically named categories of employees (*e.g.* all employees normally paid on a weekly or hourly basis).

If no wages are to be insured in the standing charges then no mention of this is necessary, except when an "all standing charges" specification is used (see paragraph 389) in which it must be definitely stated that wages are excluded.

(b) *Cover spread over maximum indemnity period*

A mistake frequently made which can result in considerable loss to the insured in the event of a claim is that of assuming that the whole amount insured for wages in that item can be claimed during the period of interruption even if this is only a portion of the maximum indemnity period. For example, if the latter is for 12 months and 25 per cent. of the total annual wage roll is insured it might be thought that in the event of a complete stoppage for three months the insured could during that time pay full wages to all employees and recover in full under the insurance.

Such an assumption is incorrect. The amount included in respect of wages becomes a component of the rate of gross profit which in turn is applied to the reduction in turnover during the indemnity period. Therefore, if there were a complete stoppage for three months only the sum provided by this method would be one-quarter of the annual amount of net profit and charges included in the gross profit item whether the old definition or the "difference" wording be used. As the gross profit insurance would include only 25 per cent. of the wage roll the insured would recover only 25 per cent. of three months' wages. The result would be the same if the wages cover had been described as a fixed amount, say £40,000 (out of an annual wage roll of £160,000); only £10,000 would be recoverable under the insurance if the stoppage were total for a period of just three months, against the insured's disbursement of £40,000 if all employees were paid full wages throughout the stoppage.

This emphasises the necessity to keep in mind that whatever is included for wages in the item, on gross profit will in the event of a claim be recoverable only proportionately to the 12 months' figures because it is a component of the rate of gross profit and so cannot be claimed otherwise than as a relative percentage of turnover applied to the reduction in turnover during the indemnity period. This disadvantage is overcome when the wages insurance is arranged under a separate item on the dual basis scheme, which gives fluidity in the cover or 100 per cent. payroll cover as explained in paragraphs 205 *et seq.*

215. Where there are two or more premises

Where a business occupies two or more premises there is a natural tendency for an insured to think that damage is unlikely to occur at more than one at the same time. From this it is sometimes mistakenly assumed that so far as wages are concerned, particularly notice wages (see paragraph 213) it is sufficient to insure for a sum representing the maximum loss which could arise in respect of wages at any one premises. For example, if there are two factories of equal size it might be thought that cover could be obtained for the payment of wages to all employees at either factory by insuring only half the total wage roll. This, however, would not give the compensation desired because it is one business and the premises and wages paid are treated as one for purposes of the insurance.

If the wages are those insured in the item covering gross profit the position would be on the lines explained in paragraph 214(b). That is, by covering for only 50 per cent. of the total wage roll the insured's recovery under the insurance being calculated on reduction in turnover would be only half of the loss on wages at whichever factory might be affected by the damage.

If the wages concerned are those insured under a separate item for a period of weeks the average proviso applicable (see Appendix I, paragraph 455 wording) stipulates that if the sum insured is less than the aggregate amount of wages, *i.e.* for all the premises the amount payable to the insured shall be proportionately reduced. Thus, in this instance also the insured would recover only half the loss on wages at whichever factory the damage might occur.

The same result would apply even were the insurance under the dual basis scheme if the wages sum insured is inadequate for the total wages at all premises insured because of the average proviso incorporated in the wording (see paragraph 210).

This is equitable because the insurers are carrying the liability for damage occurring at any or all of the premises insured and premium rates are calculated on the supposition of an overall full insurance.

216. All forms of wages insurance—return of premium clause

Whatever method of insuring wages is adopted a clause can be added to the specification to provide for a proportionate return of premium if in any year the wages paid fall short of the relevant sum insured.

The clause for an insurance covering wages on the annual basis is similar to the return of the premium clause for an insurance on gross profit (paragraph 225(a)). In the case of wages insurances under the dual basis and also dual basis payroll cover, the return of premium clause applicable to the gross profit item is slightly amended in order to incorporate the wages item in the same memorandum. In each case the return premium is subject to a limit of 50 per cent. of the premium paid for the item. This permits a margin of up to 100 per cent, overinsurance to allow for fluctuations and possible future increases in the payroll without loss of premium. Recovery in respect of any overinsurance can be made each year when an auditor's certificate is furnished for the same purpose in connection with the insurance on gross profit.

The certificate wording will be the same in whatever manner the wages are insured except under a dual basis payroll cover when the reference will be to remuneration instead of to wages, and generally will be on the lines of:

"I hereby certify that the wages and other payments pertaining thereto as defined under Item No . . . of business interruption policy no . . . in the name of . . . for the financial year . . . amounted to £ . . . ".

If it is not intended to include overtime payments in the insurance and it is worthwhile from a premium point of view to analyse the wages figure in order to exclude overtime the fact that this has been done should be stated on the certificate.

If the certificate is in respect of an item covering wages for a period of weeks only, under the weekly basis, the 12 months' figure should still be given and the insurers will calculate from this the return on the appropriate proportion of that amount in accordance with the wording of the clause. The return of premium provision with such an insurance is shown in the specification in Appendix I, paragraph 455.

When the insurance of wages is on the dual basis auditors sometimes make the mistake of working out a figure for a certificate to correspond with the actual cover in the item. For instance, if the insurance is for 100 per cent. for an initial period of eight weeks and 25 per cent. thereafter they take 8/52nds of the 12 months' wages, for the initial period of full cover, and add 25 per cent. of the balance of 44/52nds for the remaining 44 weeks of partial cover. This is incorrect because the sum insured represents the estimated total annual wages, etc., (multiplied appropriately if the maximum indemnity period exceeds 12 months) irrespective of the particular cover for the initial remaining periods and the premium rating from the dual basis wages scale is applied to that figure. The total annual amount of wages, etc., as defined in the specification should be stated on the certificate and if the maximum indemnity period exceeds 12 months the insurers will multiply this appropriately when calculating the return premium.

For an insurance of 100 per cent. payroll cover no separate certificate of the amount of remuneration is required for return of premium purposes as it is included in the gross profit and will be a component of the amount declared for return of premium under that item.

217. Payroll expenses in the United States

(a) *Full cover*

The standard definition of gross earnings in both non-manufacturing and manufacturing forms includes all payroll of whatever nature as does the definition of Business Income in the more modern wording. This simplifies the arrangement of the insurance and resolves some problems which can arise during a period of interruption following damage. It means that insurance is available to make up to normal full pay the salaries and wages of all retained employees by the proportion of same not being met by whatever production or turnover of the business continues during the period of interruption. But it does leave open one problem inasmuch as indemnity for payroll is subject to the terms of the contractual clause in the gross earnings form that payment by the insurer is subject to "due consideration" as to "the extent necessary to resume operations of the insured with the same quality of service which existed immediately preceding the loss".

In the Business Income Coverage form under "Loss Determination" it is stated that "The amount of Business Income loss will be determined based on . . . the operating expenses, necessary to resume 'operations' with the same quality of service that existed just before the direct physical loss or damage".

This stipulation may give rise to questions as to which workers, for whom full employment is not available, shall be retained; whether any, for whom there is no immediate work, shall be kept on the payroll; whether bonus payments shall be made if target norms are not achieved and similar debatable points. An insured employer with an eye to keeping his labour force available for resumption of full operations after the restoration of the premises may not be of the same opinion as insurers anxious to keep the claim settlement as low as possible. For instance, an insurer may claim that the payment of wages to employees for whom there is no gainful work available is not "necessary to resume operatons". But the insured will have in mind that he has been paying premium for an amount of insurance which includes all his payroll and feels he should therefore be given the option of deciding which workers should be retained in the best interests of his business.

On the other hand there is a possible advantage to an insured through the degree of fluidity which comes from the inclusion of the amount of all ordinary payroll in the sum insured on gross earnings without division. This means that during a period of interruption the less the amount spent on workers' pay the more will be available for the other constituents of gross earnings should this be required because of overall underinsurance and the operation of the coinsurance clause.

Insurance requirements for payroll are different for employers in the United States where there is no onerous liability under legislation (apart from the Federal minimum hourly wage rate) from that of their opposite numbers in the United Kingdom who have to comply with provisions of the employment protection Acts of Parliament. Apart from any such legislative liabilities the factors to be considered at the time of arranging an insurance and during a period of interruption following damage are very similar in all countries, motivation as to the extent of payroll insurance being generally based not on altruism but on hard-headed business considerations for company interests. The reader is therefore referred to paragraphs 199 to 201 and other indexed paragraphs on salaries and wages as containing information of general application.

The following paragraphs 217(b) and (c) deal with the endorsements available for gross earnings insurances for both non-manufacturing and manufacturing businesses and Business Income Coverage when 100 per cent. payroll insurance is not considered necessary.

(b) *Ordinary payroll excluded entirely from the cover*

For a straightforward exclusion of all "ordinary payroll" (which is not the same as excluding all payroll and the distinction must be kept in mind) the appropriate endorsement to the gross earnings form states that the insurer shall not be liable for any ordinary payroll expense. This is then defined as "the entire payroll expense of all employees of the insured except officers, executives, department managers, employees under contract and other important employees". The vagueness of the last category, if it can be regarded as such, may leave room for differences of opinion in the event of a claim.

An alternative definition (now used in the Ordinary Payroll Limitation endorsement to the Business Income Coverage form) with greater scope for selection of categories of employees whose remuneration is to be retained within the cover is as follows—"Ordinary payroll expenses" means payroll expenses for all employees except (1) Officers (2) Executives (3) Department managers (4) Employees under contract and (5) Additional Exemptions, shown in the Schedule or in the Declarations as (a) Job Classifications or (b) Employees.

When ordinary payroll is excluded as above the effect is adjusted accordingly *i.e.* in the new endorsement wording it is stated that in determining the operating expenses for coinsurance purposes, payroll expenses will not include "ordinary payroll expenses". The minimum coinsurance percentage is 50 per cent. (under gross earnings the minimum was 80 per cent.).

(c) *Limited coverage for ordinary payroll*

When an insured wishes to insure the ordinary payroll for a limited coverage the payroll expense included in the gross earnings or Business Income remains unaltered, that is, at 100 per cent. but an endorsement limits the indemnity in respect of ordinary payroll to such expense as must necessarily continue during the interruption of business in a specified number of consecutive calendar days immediately following the date of the damage. The minimum period for this is 90 days but a longer period may be selected and coverages of 180 days are not unusual.

In the gross earnings endorsement the coinsurance clause is amended to make the coinsurance percentage apply to the amount of gross earnings which would have been earned (had no loss occurred) during the 12 months immediately following the date of the damage less the ordinary payroll expense for the portion of that 12 month period which follows the 90 days (or other number of days) specified. If the coinsurance percentage on the policy is less than 80 it must be raised to 80 per cent. of insured earnings.

In the Business Income Coverage endorsement the coinsurance condition relates to operating expenses for the policy year excluding "ordinary payroll expenses", except for those incurred during the number of days shown. If such expenses vary during the policy year, the period of greatest "ordinary payroll expenses" will be used.

CHAPTER 11

CALCULATING THE AMOUNT TO BE INSURED—UNITED KINGDOM AND UNITED STATES

218. Accounts on which to calculate sum insured

When a decision has been reached on the form of specification to be used, that is, either the "difference" wording or the net profit plus standing charges definition of gross profit and how wages are to be dealt with, the next step can be taken towards computing the amount to be insured on gross profit.

In general it is preferable to utilise the accounts for the last completed financial year as these give the most recent figures apart from turnover. However, as the amount thus obtained is only to help in arriving at an estimate of future earnings which are the basis for the sum insured it may be advisable, if there have been exceptional circumstances which affected the results during that period, to use the accounts of a preceding financial year. Sometimes the accounts for two or three years may be necessary to gauge the real position and to make a reliable estimate of future earnings. Where interim accounts are normally prepared these can be a valuable guide and, for instance, if half-yearly accounts are produced the last two will probably be the best basis for computing the annual amount for purposes of the sum insured.

Whichever accounts are used a figure should be computed to represent the estimated *future* annual amount of gross profit in accordance with the particular definition decided upon.

In businesses in which modern techniques of accounting (such as standard costing and budgetary control systems) are employed a correct figure can be extracted provided that the object of the insurance, namely *to protect prospective future earnings*, and the basic principles for computing the sum insured, are kept in mind. When a claim arises under an insurance for such a business in which the accounts are based on a planned budget later corrected by determined variances instead of their being based on historical fact only it should be possible to produce adequate information for the claim negotiations provided that there is a proper understanding of the details required. It is also important to realise how current cost accounting and inflation adjustments for sales, valuation of stocks and work in progress and depreciation allocations may effect the figures for gross and net profit. (See following paragraph 219.)

The usual accounts to study (for firms producing finished stock from raw materials) are Manufacturing, Trading and Profit and Loss accounts. Simple examples are as follows:

Manufacturing Account

Opening stock (raw mat.)	150,000	Closing stock (raw mat.)	120,000
Op. st. (work in prog.)	200,000	Cl. stock (work in prog.)	250,000
Purchases (raw mat.)	750,000	Cost of goods made	2,250,000
Factory direct wages	950,000		
Factory expenses			
Indirect wages	250,000		
General expenses	80,000		
Depreciation (plant, buildings, etc.)	120,000		
Indirect materials	20,000		
Fuel and power	100,000		
	2,620,000		2,620,000

Trading Account

Opening stock (fin. goods)	350,000	Sales	4,800,000
Cost of goods made	2,250,000	Closing stock (fin. gds)	250,000
Gross profit	2,450,000		
	5,050,000		5,050,000

(In fact the above accounts may be merged into one Trading Account.)

Profit and Loss Account

Selling and dist. exp. (1)	630,000	Gross profit	2,450,000
Admin. expenses (2)	850,000	Interest received	30,000
Financial expenses (3)	250,000	Profit on sale of fixed asset	10,000
Net profit (4)	760,000		
	2,490,000		2,490,000

Notes

(1) Selling and distribution expenses—salesmen's salaries, commission, carriage and freight outwards, advertising, entertainment, travelling, etc.

(2) Administrative expenses—administration salaries, office wages, insurance premiums, printing and stationery, rent and rates, etc.

(3) Financial expenses—long term interest, debtors factoring charges, bank overdraft interest, etc.

(4) Net profit—will include provision for taxation and dividends to shareholders.

219. Current cost accounting

The introduction in 1980 by the Institute of Chartered Accountants in England and Wales of a statement of Standard Accounting Practice (SSAP

16) relative to Current Cost Accounting for all large unquoted and all listed Stock Exchange companies led to clarification in respect of business interruption insurances. Although various options exist in the manner of presentation of accounts they may now include data for both current cost and historical cost bases.

Of the various main adjustments to be made to historical cost trading profit to produce current cost operating profit the following are the most pertinent to business interruption insurances:

(i) Depreciation adjustment in relation to fixed assets: this represents the difference between the depreciation charged in the historical cost accounts and a depreciation charge based on the current value of the fixed assets being used in generating the profit for the year. The resulting total depreciation charge thus represents the current value to the business of that part of the fixed assets "consumed" in earning the profit of the year. Where depreciation is insured as a constituent part of gross profit such adjustments would be balanced by corresponding changes in the net profit leaving the overall amount to be insured on gross profit unaffected.

(ii) Cost of sales adjustment in relation to working capital: this recognises that the current value to the business of stock sold may exceed its original cost as charged in the historical cost profit and loss account. The impact of rising prices results in a stock holding gain which is crystallised on the sale of the stock. The resulting total charge for the cost of sales represents the current value to the business of stock consumed in earning the profit for the period. Insured will in general require sums insured and claims to be dealt with on the basis of historical accounts as in the past so that unless special arrangements to the contrary are requested the element of gross profit due to increases in price is included by means of Note 2 on the specification that any adjustment implemented in current costs accounting shall be disregarded.

220. Sum insured in relation to maximum indemnity period

When the maximum indemnity period is 12 months or less, the sum insured should not be less than the annual amount of the gross profit which it is estimated will be earned in the future. (See paragraphs 224 and 225.) Where the maximum indemnity period is for six months the mistake is sometimes made of insuring only half the annual amount of gross profit. But the premium rating table and the average proviso in the specification are based on and designed for the purposes of a method of insurance in which annual figures of gross profit are used when the maximum indemnity period is 12 months or less. As most firms' accounts are 12-monthly and most businesses fluctuate to some extent throughout each year, even if they are not actually seasonal, this is the only practical method.

When the maximum indemnity period exceeds 12 months the sum insured should be not less than the amount of gross profit which it is estimated will be earned in the future during a corresponding length of time. For example, with a maximum indemnity period of 18 months the sum insured should be one-and-a-half times the annual amount and for 24 months it should be twice the annual amount based on an estimate of future earnings as explained in paragraphs 224 and 225. This method is taken into account in the premium rating table (paragraph 256(a)) and in the average proviso in the specification (paragraph 230). An exception arises to the manner of computing the sum to be insured in businesses of a seasonal character in which, for example, two years' gross profit might be earned in 18 consecutive months. In such cases the sum insured for a maximum indemnity period of 18 months would have to be twice the estimated annual amount of gross profit as explained more fully in paragraph 252(a). Another exception arises in the case of Declaration-Linked covers (see paragraph 53).

221. Non-trading revenue and non-recurring charges

When looking at the accounts to calculate the estimated future amount of insurable gross profit it may be found that there are some amounts credited to the profit and loss accounts for moneys received which are not the result of the actual trading of the business. For, example, rents from the letting of property, royalties for the use of machines for patents, profits on the sale of surplus assets, recovery of bad debts, or interest or dividends on invested money. Revenue of this nature will not be affected by interference of the business arising from damage and should not be brought into the computation of the gross profit. With a specification on the "difference" wording the definition automatically omits non-trading revenue. Where the older form of wording is used if the net profit in the accounts includes such extraneous revenue the amount of the latter should be deducted to arrive at the insurable amount of the net "trading" profit. (See paragraphs 86 and 87.)

When the net profit shown in the last available accounts has been reduced by a non-recurring charge such as an unusually large bad debt or legal costs the amount of the insurable gross profit as defined in a "difference" wording will not be affected provided that the particular charge was not in the list of uninsured working expenses. Consequently, the rate of gross profit to be used in a claim if interruption of business resulting from damage takes place in the following year will be the same as it would have been but for the non-recurring charge. If the definition of gross profit is on the older wording then the amount of the non-recurring charge should be added back for the reasons explained in paragraph 82(c) to restore the net profit to its normal amount.

222. Discounts received and sale of scrap

A credit item for discounts received sometimes raises doubts or difficulty. Because discounts allowed on the debit side of the accounts are not insurable in the gross profit as they will vary proportionately with turnover (see paragraph 152) it may be thought, erroneously, that discounts received should similarly be excluded from the computation of gross profit because they also vary with purchases and therefore with turnover. Although it may seem paradoxical the two classes of discount are not so comparable. This will be appreciated when it is considered that the object of the insurance is to provide an indemnity for loss of the normal net profit margin, which will fall proportionately with a reduction in turnover, plus the further loss of net profit due to the payment of any charges which do not diminish in ratio to the fall in turnover. To put it another way, the insurance is not for loss of standing charges but for the loss of the revenue out of which they have to be met as is shown clearly by the "difference" method of insuring turnover less variables.

Discounts allowed are a payment made against the turnover of a business as they will decrease in direct ratio to a reduction in turnover they will not effect the net profit no matter to what extent turnover falls as a result of damage. Therefore, it is unnecessary to include discounts allowed in the gross profit nor, similarly, the cost of giving discounts to customers by means of trading stamps.

Net profit is increased by discounts received and as they vary with purchases and so with turnover net profit will decrease in line with them when they are reduced due to interference with the business. Therefore, to indemnify the insured for loss in respect of them it is essential that they be left in the profit figure and not excluded as is done in the case of non-trading revenue.

The following simple illustration will help to make this quite clear:

Dr.	£		£	Cr
Standing charges	300,000	Gross Profit b/d	400,000	
Discounts allowed	60,000	Discounts received	100,000	
Net Profit	140,000			
	500,000		500,000	

The insurable gross profit is £440,000 (standing charges plus net profit), but if discounts received were to be excluded, as are discounts allowed, it would be only £340,000 leaving the insured to recover under an insurance a reduced amount of net profit dependent upon the extent of the reduction in turnover. So if the interruption of business results in a 50 per cent. loss of turnover the insured will obtain 50 per cent. less in respect of discounts received on purchases (these also being 50 per cent. down) which will not be compensated under the insurance because discounts received have not been included in it. The profit and loss account will show £50,000 less net profit thus:

Dr.	£		£	Cr
Standing charges	300,000	Gross Profit b/d	200,000	
Discounts allowed	30,000	Discounts received	50,000	
Net Profit	90,000	Insurance pays 50% of insurance gross profit £34,000	170,000	
	420,000		420,000	

In the older ("additions") form of specification, discounts received are included automatically in the definition of gross profit (net profit plus insured standing charges) because they increase the net profit figure in the accounts. In a "difference" wording they require to be specially mentioned as explained in paragraph 85(b)

Revenue from the sale of scrap is incidental trading income derived from the operation of the business and as it would reduce in quantity and value following a drop in production because of less scrap being made it should be treated in the same way as discounts received and its amount included in the gross profit insurance (see paragraph 85(c)).

223. Extra profit for buying direct from manufacturers: retrospective discounts

In several trades such as those of tyre factors and tobacco merchants, electrical contractors, motor accessories, television and domestic appliance dealers, and grocers, the very large firms and those not-so-large formed into group-buying pools purchasing supplies direct from manufacturers, receive a turnover bonus or extra discount which is calculated as a percentage on purchases in excess of a stipulated target figure or scale in a six-monthly or yearly period. In petrol sales the trade description for extra bonus is "stepped rebate scheme". Although the amount of this type of bonus will be reduced if there is a reduction in turnover the ratio of the reduction will be higher than that of the drop in turnover if the purchases fall below the prescribed minima or reach the point at which the bonus ceases altogether. In other words the rate of gross profit of the business is not constant and increases as the sales of the goods obtained from certain manufacturers reach set figures.

The peculiar position in such businesses can be provided for, in the event of a claim arising, by making appropriate adjustments to the rate of gross profit at different stages under the provisions of the other circumstances clause. Alternatively, if the bonus is a substantial amount and it is desired to insure it under a separate item this could be arranged. The wording would be drafted to provide that the loss of bonus during the indemnity period be measured by straight comparison between the amount of bonus received during that period and that which was received during the corresponding time in the 12 months preceding the date of the damage—subject, of course, to the provisions of the other circumstances clause. The item covering gross profit would have to exclude revenue obtained from the bonus.

224. Future gross profit to be estimated

The amount of insurable gross profit according to the definition for the particular case, as extracted from the accounts for the last financial year or other convenient period, would be the amount of gross profit on which to base the sum insured if the future trading results were certain to be exactly the same as on those accounts. In practice this is most unlikely to happen and an estimate must be made to allow for possible alterations which may take place in the period ahead.

This, however, does not mean the period of 12 months immediately following. Damage may occur at any time after the decision has been made about the sum to be insured, perhaps 11 months later, and the indemnity will commence on the date of damage and continue in subsequent months throughout the indemnity period. The basis of the loss payment will be the gross profit which would have been earned during the latter period had the damage not occurred, provision for the adjustment of figures necessary to give effect to this being made by the other circumstances clause. (See paragraphs 55(a) to 56.) Also of considerable importance is the fact that it is on this basis—estimated post-damage earnings after adjustment for trends, etc.—that the pro rata average provision is applied (see paragraphs 52(b) to 55(c)).

So, when arranging the sum insured for a policy with a maximum indemnity period of 12 months it is necessary to make an estimate of the gross profit which might be earned in the 12 months from the time when the next revision will be made, that is, a total period up to two years ahead. Similarly, with a longer indemnity the period in the future which must be considered as a possible time during which compensation will be payable is possibly 12 months plus the maximum indemnity period insured and the sum insured must be based on a corresponding estimate.

As explained in the following paragraph 225(a) because of the return of premium clause it is possible to carry a margin of 100 per cent. overinsurance without its costing more in premium than the amount calculated on the gross profit which is subsequently shown to have been actually earned. This margin is considered by insurance companies as adequate for practical purposes and because of difficulties which would be involved if they gave automatic cover for earnings exceeding the sum insured and after the financial year end charged premium on the excess amount of gross profit actually earned, it is a one-way traffic. That is to say, returns are allowed on overinsurance not earned but no excess premium is charged if earnings exceed the sum insured.

In practice this 100 per cent. margin is normally adequate; but not invariably so. Some businesses are subject to violent fluctuations in gross profit earnings in certain periods, whilst developing businesses in particular may show a phenomenal rate of growth in one year and earn gross profits far more than double the preceding year's figures. In any such case it is incumbent upon the insured to keep a close watch on the sum insured and to increase it periodically according to interim trading results and their judgment of likely progress without waiting until each full year's results are available; damage might occur in the interim.

The Declaration-Linked basis (refer paragraph 53) has a different approach, being a non-average cover, and the comments in this paragraph and those that follow do not strictly apply to that form of wording. However, the basic principle is still valid, that it is essential to arrange a cover which is adequate to suit the needs of the insured.

225. Adding a margin of overinsurance

(a) *The return of premium clause*

Because it is impossible to estimate the future amount of gross profit with complete accuracy, as so many unpredictable factors can enter into the matter, it is generally prudent to add a good margin on top of the estimated figure. Insurers encourage such overinsurance as a means to a full indemnity in the event of a claim, for the object of the policy is to protect future earnings. In the event of damage occurring, a reduction in the amount claimed because of the application of the average proviso gives satisfaction to neither insured nor insurers.

Insured are protected against the payment of unnecessary premium through overinsurance by the incorporation of a return of premium clause in all insurances of sufficient size to justify it, in the following terms:

> "The premium paid hereon may be adjusted on receipt by the Insurer of a declaration of Gross Profit earned during the financial year most nearly concurrent with the period of insurance, as reported by the Insured's Auditors.
> If any Incident shall have occurred giving rise to a claim for loss of Gross Profit the above mentioned declaration shall be increased by the Insurer for the purpose of premium adjustment by the amount by which the Gross Profit was reduced during the financial year solely in consequence of the Incident.
> If either declaration (adjusted as provided for above and proportionately increased where the Maximum Indemnity Period exceeds 12 months) is less than the sum insured on Gross Profit for the relative period of insurance the Insurer will allow a pro rata return of premium not exceeding 50% of the premium paid".

It should be noted that the 50 per cent. mentioned as the limit of the return of premium does not mean that only half the premium on the amount of overinsurance will be repaid. A full pro rata return of premium will be made on the amount of overinsurance to a limit of 50 per cent. of the sum insured. For example, on a sum insured of £2 million a full return of premium would be made on the difference between that figure and the certified amount of gross profit earned subject to the limit of 50 per cent. of the former, that is, a full return on any overinsurance not exceeding £1 million.

From this it can be seen that overinsurance to the extent of 100 per cent. of what may prove to be the actual gross profit earned can be effected without any loss of premium. For example, on gross profit of £1 million earned in any year an insured could provide a 100 per cent. margin, that is, could be insured for £2 million without any loss of premium resulting from the 50 per cent. limit in the return of premium clause.

When the date of the end of the financial year of a business is altered there may be a period for which the accounts are made up of either more, or less, than 12 months. Strictly this does not tally with the terms of the return of premium clause—"the accounting period of twelve months most nearly concurrent, etc."—but in practice it is customary to take figures for equivalent periods to compare gross profit earned with sums insured so as to provide for an equitable return of premium.

With the adoption in 1980 by the accountancy profession of current cost accounting as standard practice along with historical cost accounting it is necessary to ensure that declarations furnished for rebate adjustment purposes are made on the same basis as that used in calculating the sum insured.

In general, it may be said that regular returns of premiums year by year are indicative of a well-arranged insurance so far as the sum insured is concerned because they show that a margin of overinsurance is being systematically maintained as a means to adequate protection.

(b) *The main advantage of overinsurance*

Although overinsurance on these lines does not often involve an insured in any loss of premium there is a loss of interest on the premium relating to the overinsurance because the premium is paid in advance and the return is not made until at least 12 months later as the insured is not in a position to furnish an auditor's certificate before that time.

Against this small loss must be set the substantial benefit of having made provision for the settlement of a claim without deduction on the grounds of underinsurance. That it is a benefit to be able to safeguard the future in this way and the wisdom of taking advantage of the arrangement for doing so has been proved with businesses in general on innumerable occasions during years of trade expansion and of inflation as well as by many individual instances of firms with a substantial growth in prosperity from other causes, where claim settlements have been greatly increased under the provisions of the other circumstances clause.

See paragraph 431 regarding requests, after damage has occurred to ante-date an increase in the sum insured.

(c) *Other benefits of overinsurance*

Another advantage to the insured arising from overinsurance is that in some circumstances a certain amount of free insurance is obtained. This arises when there is a progressive increase of gross profit over the years and the sum insured is revised annually on the correct basis of an estimate of earnings for two years ahead as explained in paragraph 224. In such cases the insurers carry a liability under the provisions of the other circumstances clause to pay a claim on the basis of such estimated earnings. However, when an auditor's certificate is furnished each year end, the figure declared is the actual amount earned in that particular year and the return of premium is calculated accordingly. Therefore, the insurers receive no premium for the additional liability carried on the "second year" estimate. Where the maximum indemnity period is longer than 12 months the amount of free insurance obtained by an insured may be correspondingly larger.

Another way in which an insured might benefit arises during a period when there is a steep fall in the price of the basic materials of an industry. The turnover and the profit margin of a business during the year in which this takes place may be about normal but owing to the writing-down of stock values at the year end the gross profit will be substantially reduced. An outstanding example of this was the catastrophic fall in the price of wool, cotton, leather, rubber and other raw materials in 1951, the resultant writing-down of stocks turning what would otherwise have been a net profit into a trading loss for a great many firms. In several industries the need for a special write-down of stock values occurs from time to time as evidenced by the following extract from the published statement of Jeremiah Ambler Ltd., worsted spinners of Bradford.

> "In his review accompanying the accounts for the year ended December 31, 1966, the chairman stated that the profits of the group had fallen very rapidly in the second half of the year, partly due to the credit squeeze and partly due to a fall in the price of raw materials necessitating a write-down of stocks of approximately £100,000. Profits for 1966 were £283,289 against £567,662 in 1965".

If a business sustains damage during such a period and the resulting interference extends into the time when prices have settled down to normal again, the business interruption claim would by means of the other circumstances clause be assessed on the basis of a normal rate of gross profit. This would be the anticipated rate which would have been earned in the post-damage period had the damage not occurred and it would be equitable to pay this and not the depreciated rate obtained from the accounts of the financial year in which the writing-down of stock values took place. The effect of circumstances of this kind is that insurers carry a liability for the full sum insured but by allowing a refund on the actual amount of gross profit shown in the accounts after the writing-down of stock values obtain no premium for the difference due to such writing-down.

(d) *Reduction of sum insured*

When a sum insured has been arranged with a margin of overinsurance the insured is not bound to maintain it at the same figure until the next renewal date. If there is an unexpected adverse development or trend of trade in the interim which indicates that the gross profit for the year in question is going to be much lower than previously anticipated and will probably fall below the 50 per cent. limit in the return of premium clause the sum insured can be appropriately reduced immediately this position becomes manifest. The refund of premium at the year end will then be calculated proportionately with the number of days up to the date of the alteration and again from that date against the respective sums insured during the two periods. In considering any such reduction it should be kept in mind that the sum insured must still be maintained at a figure which is adequate for the gross profit which it is anticipated might be earned during a period considerably ahead. (See paragraph 224 on this latter point.)

226. Return of premium clause

(a) *Claiming a return premium*

The method of claiming under the return of premium clause (paragraph 225(a)) is very simple. Usually, all that is required by the insurers is a letter from the insured's accountants stating: "I/We the Insured's Professional Accountant(s) confirm that the annual gross profit derived from the business and premises as defined in business interruption policy no . . . . . . and as shown in the Insured's accounts for the financial year ended . . . . . . 19 . . . was £ . . . . . . ". Some insurers issue their own stereotyped certificate form with the renewal notice each year which is a convenient reminder to the insured.

When the period covered by an insured's accounts is either less or more than 12 months because of an alteration in the date of the financial year end or other reason this must be stated on the auditor's certificate and an appropriate adjustment will have to be made to give an equivalent 12 months' figure for comparison with the sum insured.

Not all accountants appreciate the serious implications involved in furnishing a certificate when requested to do so for the purposes of the return of premium clause under a client's insurance. Not only must the figures certified be strictly in accordance with the policy definitions and include earnings and wages as insured at all the premises included in the insurance but the certificate must be furnished as early as practicable to enable any increase in sums insured to be arranged should this be considered necessary when the figures are produced.

The onerous responsibility and legal liability which may be involved were highlighted by the court case of *De Meza and Stuart* v. *Apple, Van Straten, Shene and Stone* [1975] 1 Lloyd's Rep. 498 (C.A.) affirming [1974] 1 Lloyd's Rep. 508. Damages were awarded to plaintiffs and upheld in the Court of Appeal in respect of loss suffered by them through being under-insured at the time of a fire. The damages were claimed from their auditors for breach of contract in failing to complete a certificate properly; the earnings from one of the plaintiff's premises had, in error, been omitted from the amount certified by the auditors for the year before the fire and in consequence the sum insured had not been increased as it should have been.

(b) *Maximum indemnity period exceeding or less than 12 months*

If the maximum indemnity period exceeds 12 months the sum insured should be the estimated amount of gross profit for a corresponding length of time because the liability under the policy is for the gross profit of such an extended period. To provide that under the return of premium clause for purposes of comparison the gross profit figure used will be that which would be earned in a similar period the wording of the clause refers to the declaration of earned gross profit being "proportionately increased where the Maximum Indemnity Period exceeds 12 months" (see paragraph 225(a) for the full clause).

Whatever length the maximum indemnity period may be, no alteration is necessary to the certificate provided by an accountant for claiming a return of premium. The certificate should state the amount of gross profit earned in the 12 month period of the accounts and when the maximum indemnity period is longer than this the insurers will multiply the certified amount to correspond. If the maximum indemnity period is less than 12 months the gross profit sum insured is nevertheless on a 12-monthly basis and the certificate has to be for a similar period.

(c) *Proviso regarding claim payments*

There is a proviso within the return of premium clause which reads: "If any Incident shall have occurred giving rise to a claim for loss of Gross Profit the above mentioned declaration shall be increased by the Insurer for the purpose of premium adjustment by the amount by which the Gross Profit was reduced during the financial year solely in consequence of the Incident". This means that where a claim has been made for loss of gross profit the amount paid by the insurers, if not already shown as a credit in the accounts for the year to which it relates and included in the amount of gross profit certified by the auditor, will be added on by the insurers before calculating the return of premium. This is necessary to provide for them to retain the premium in respect of the amount paid by them for the loss of gross profit.

The position is different with regard to any amount paid by insurers in respect of increase in cost of working. Such expenditure will have produced turnover which otherwise would not have been earned and the gross profit resulting from this will automatically have been included in the auditor's computation and certificate. Consequently, the insurers will in this way obtain premium for the amount of insurance to which the payment for increase in cost of working relates and the amount of the latter should not be added into their calculation of gross profit for purposes of the return premium.

Where the specification is on the net profit plus standing charges wording if the accounts show as a credit an amount received under a business interruption claim it is necessary for the accountant to mention in his certificate that such credit is in the accounts and in his computation of the gross profit.

A complicated situation sometimes occurs in respect of policies where the maximum indemnity period exceeds 12 months and there has been a claim with an actual indemnity period in excess of 12 months. There would appear to be no standard formula for dealing with the return of premium calculation in such situations, and a negotiated agreement with the insured is possible whereby he does not need to wait too long for his rebate.

(d) *No time limit and no excess premium*

The return clause does not stipulate a time limit in which a claim for a return of premium must be notified such as one year from the end of the financial year concerned. To do so could involve hardship where the completion of accounts is unavoidably delayed or a certificate is not furnished until later owing to an oversight. In special circumstances insurers generally are willing to allow rebates up to the six-year limit under the Limitation Act 1939 although doing so may possibly involve them in some loss under their reinsurance arrangements. The corresponding return of premium clause in a U.S. insurance (paragraph 70) stipulates that the report form of earnings must be submitted within 120 days of the end of each financial year. (But see paragraph 227 for other situations.)

It is standard practice to include a return of premium clause in the specification but to make no provision for the payment by an insured of an excess premium if the earnings in any year exceed the sum insured because this latter is considered impracticable. This makes it necessary always to maintain the sum insured at a figure which is adequate for any upward trend in gross profit; failure to do so introduces the possibility of loss through the operation of the average proviso should there be underinsurance at the time of a claim. Arrangements for the provisional payment of a percentage of premium may be possible for large insurances as explained in the following paragraph 227(a).

227. Other premium adjustment situations

(a) *Provisional premium payments*

Where the annual premium chargeable on the total of the sums insured is significant (for example not less than £1,000) it is possible to arrange for insurers to accept a premium corresponding broadly to the average of retained premiums over the preceding few years or allowing for the margin built into the sum insured over the budgeted gross profit for the year of insurance but in no case less than 75 per cent. of the current full premium. The period between the expiry date of the period of insurance and the date on which payment of the balance is due has to be kept to a minimum not exceeding six months.

Effect to such an arrangement is given by adding to the specification a clause reading:

> "The first and annual premiums are provisional being 75% of the premiums payable at the commencement of the period of insurance with the balance of 25% to be paid within 6 months of the expiry of that period except that—
>> in respect of any item(s) on Gross Profit the premium paid shall be adjusted on receipt by the Insurer of a declaration of Gross Profit earned during the financial year most nearly concurrent with such period of insurance, as reported by the Insured's auditors
>>
>> if any Incident shall have occurred giving rise to a claim for loss of Gross Profit the above mentioned declaration shall be increased by the Insurer for the purpose of premium adjustment by the amount by which Gross Profit was reduced during the financial year solely in consequence of the Incident
>>
>> if the declaration (adjusted as provided for above and proportionately increased where the Maximum Indemnity Period exceeds 12 months)
>>> (a) is less than 75% of the sum insured on Gross Profit for the relative period, the Insurer will allow a pro rata return of premium not exceeding 33.3% of the provisional premium paid
>>> (b) is greater than 75% of the sum insured on Gross Profit for the relative period, the Insured shall pay a pro rata additional premium not exceeding 33.3% of the provisional premium paid.
>
> In the event that no declaration is received within 6 months of the expiry of such period of insurance the balance of 25% shall be paid".

(b) *Declaration-Linked*

For this policy wording (refer paragraph 53 and Appendix D, paragraph 450) the rule is:
when the amount of insured gross profit or earnings

(a) is less than the Estimated Gross Profit/Earnings a pro rata return of the premium paid may be allowed on the difference but not exceeding 50 per cent. of the premium paid on such Estimated Gross Profit/Earnings,

(b) is greater than the estimated Gross Profit/Earnings a pro rata additional premium shall be charged on the difference.

If any Incident (as defined) shall have occurred giving rise to a claim under the policy then account of such claim shall be taken in arriving at the said difference.

The adjustment clause incorporated in the specification wording is as follows:

"The first and annual premiums (in respect of item no.   ) are provisional and are based on the Estimated Gross Profit.

The Insured shall furnish to the Insurer not later than six months after the expiry of each period of insurance a declaration confirmed by the Insured's auditors of the Gross Profit earned during the financial year most nearly concurrent with the period of insurance.

If any Incident shall have occurred giving rise to a claim for loss of Gross Profit the above mentioned declaration shall be increased by the Insurer for the purpose of premium adjustment by the amount by which the Gross Profit was reduced during the financial year solely in consequence of the Incident.

If the declaration (adjusted as provided for above and proportionately increased where the maximum indemnity period exceeds 12 months)

(a) is less than the Estimated Gross Profit for the relative period of insurance the Insurer will allow a pro rata return of the premium paid on the estimated Gross Profit but not exceeding 50% of such premium

(b) is greater than the Estimated Gross Profit for the relative period of Insurance the Insured shall pay a pro rata addition to the premium paid on the Estimated Gross Profit".

228. Provision for extensions and improvements

The necessity to insure on the basis of anticipated future earnings is also of particular relevance when extensions or improvements in buildings or plant, factory lay-out or productive processes are being made. To provide for the increase in gross profit which will result from such developments the insurance will require to be increased even before they become effective. This is in case damage should occur during the time of preparation which would defer the date when the extensions or improvements will be contributing to the earnings of the business.

A special cover can be arranged where the construction of a complete new factory or major extension to existing premises is involved called "advance profits insurance" details of which are given in paragraph 268(a).

229. New businesses—first year of trading

The principals of a new undertaking may be reluctant to arrange a business interruption insurance before the end of their first 12 months' trading, on the grounds that until then they cannot tell how the business will develop and what profit will be earned. In general this is a mistaken policy. Even though the business has not reached the point of being able to pay all its standing charges and produce a margin for net profit by the time when damage occurs the effects of the damage may be to create a more substantial trading loss. Should a business be paying its way the nearer the time to completion of the first year of trading when damage occurs the more serious will be its effects because the interruption may continue many months into the second year of trading or even longer. This is the time during which fruits of the previous year's efforts would have been gathered in the shape of profits.

When insurance is arranged for an entirely new business, provision has to be made in it for the fact that there are no figures available from a preceding financial year on which to calculate the loss which will arise if damage occurs during the first year of trading. This is dealt with by the addition to the specification of what is termed the "new business clause" of which more details are given in paragraph 383. This clause amends the definitions of rate of gross profit, annual turnover and standard turnover to expand the results from the commencement of the business to the date of the damage to give proportionate figures for a complete 12 months. The other circumstances clause applies to these definitions in the normal manner thus securing to an insured the benefit of any indications of an increase of trade or a higher profit margin which would have resulted as the business became more firmly established.

The inclusion in the specification of the return of premium clause allows for the sum insured to be arranged for an amount which gives a generous margin to provide for anticipated results whilst protecting the insured against the payment of unnecessary premium if the actual earnings prove to be less than the sum insured. In view of this, inability to say in advance what will be the gross profit of a new business is no reason for not insuring on an estimated figure.

230. Indemnity according to formula: no undertaking to pay sum insured

If a critical examination is made of the policy and specification it will be found that in no place is there any undertaking given by the insurer to pay the sum insured. Neither is there any statement that the latter should represent 12 months' gross profit nor in the case of a maximum indemnity period longer than 12 months a corresponding multiple of the annual amount of gross profit.

The explanation of this is that the undertaking to pay is embodied in the wording of the policy schedule and the specification and in brief is an indemnity for loss calculated by the formula in the latter. The only ways in which the amount of the sum insured is brought into the matter are (i) in the schedule, being stated as the limit of the indemnity, and (ii) in the specification where it is shown in the heading as the sum insured which is later referred to in the average proviso as the sum against which comparison is to be made in the application of that proviso.

In connection with the last mentioned it will be seen on reference to the various specimen specifications in the Appendices that where the maximum indemnity period exceeds 12 months a proportionately increased multiple of the annual turnover is used for the purposes of the clause and the sum insured must not be less than the resulting amount to rank as a full insurance.

231. Effect of claims on sum insured; reinstatement

Three other features of business interruption insurance call for mention. One is that the sum insured is automatically reduced by the amount of any loss payment made under the policy because that portion of the contract is thereby fulfilled. Another is that more than one occurrence of damage may take place and give rise to a claim in any one insurance year. Lastly, a period of interruption for which an indemnity is provided in respect of damage occurring during the currency of a policy can extend beyond the renewal date of the policy.

The following hypothetical case will serve to illustrate the effect of these three factors acting concurrently. Assume a sum insured of £1.2 million on gross profit and a maximum indemnity period of 12 months under a policy renewable on December 25. Damage occurs in January causing interference with the business until October with a loss of gross profit of £700,000. The payment of this loss will reduce the sum insured to £500,000 but the insurers are still liable for loss which might arise throughout a maximum indemnity period of 12 months from the date of any further occurrence of damage should this take place before renewal date of the policy on December 25.

Assume a second fire does occur, in November, causing interference with the business until the following September and a loss of gross profit of £800,000. Unless the amount of the first loss has been reinstated, that is, the sum insured has been restored by agreement to the original £1.2 million there will be a balance of only £500,000 insurance available to meet this second loss. This sum will be the insurers maximum liability but the insured might recover even less if the average proviso is strictly applied.

This would reduce the payment to perhaps five-twelfths of the £800,000 loss, that is, to £333,333.

Therefore, when a substantial loss occurs it is advisable to arrange for a reinstatement of the sum insured unless it is certain that there will be an adequate unexpended balance to cover the future possible earnings for a period of 12 months, or longer if the maximum indemnity period exceeds 12 months. Often the actual amount of the loss cannot be ascertained for a considerable time ahead but insurers are willing to reinstate the sum insured and to leave the calculation of the amount of the additional premium due for this reinstatement, which will be for the period up to the next renewal date of the policy, to be made after the loss settlement has been agreed.

Provision for automatic reinstatement of the sum insured is sometimes made by addition to the specification of a memorandum in the following words:

> "Memo: In the event of any claim having occurred under this policy and in the absence of written notice by the Insured to the contrary the amount of insurance cancelled by such claim is to be automatically reinstated as and from the date of the Incident the Insured undertaking to pay the appropriate additional premium as may be required for such reinstatement from that date".

It might be suggested that in the foregoing illustration, because the renewal of the policy on December 25 would have automatically reinstated the cover to a full sum insured there would then be an adequate insurance to make good the second loss. This is not so because the amount available to meet the second loss is the insurance in existence at the date of the second occurrence of damage, in this case £500,000. Subsequent renewal of the policy the following month is really a new contract which cannot affect in any way the liability of the insurers in connection with damage which occurred in the preceding term of insurance.

In this connection it might be pointed out that, if at the renewal date of the case used for illustration the insured for some reason changed to other insurers, the original insurers would still be liable for the loss arising from the damage in November although such loss continues into the following year when they would no longer hold the insurance. Apart from very exceptional circumstances and strong reasons for doing so it would obviously be inadvisable to make such a change during a period of interruption.

When a loss occurs involving a payment under an item on notice wages (paragraph 213) it is particularly important that reinstatement of the amount should be arranged as soon as the dismissed employees resume work, because the sum insured will have been substantially reduced by the loss but the full liability will again attach immediately work restarts.

U.S. policies are more advantageous to the insured as regards reinstatement (see paragraph 238).

232. Position when fire occurs at temporary premises taken after damage

An interesting problem sometimes crops up following damage of a substantial nature which necessitates the occupation of temporary premises—business interruption insurance being then arranged for them—pending the rehabilitation of those damaged. Should an interruption of business occur due to a fire at the temporary premises B during the period of indemnity in respect of the original occurrence at premises A, the insurance on the temporary premises will provide payment for loss of gross profit calculated on reduction in estimated turnover at B. The problem then arises as to which party should benefit from this up to the end of the indemnity period for the original premises A; insured or insurers?

Production was started at premises B in accordance with the insured's duty under the claims condition of the policy (Action by the Insured) to do all things reasonably practicable to minimise the loss. The alternative trading clause of the specification provides that if goods are sold elsewhere than at the premises for the benefit of the business the amount received for same shall be brought into account in calculating any loss of turnover. So the insurers are entitled to offset the loss of turnover at the original premises A by the amount of turnover earned at the temporary premises B. Should they not, therefore, receive the money payable by themselves to the insured in respect of loss due to reduction in estimated *prospective* turnover at premises B?

There is nothing in the policy to say they should and there are two schools of thought with regard to this matter. One viewpoint is that the business is still in the grip of the original damage at premises A and consequently, the failure of measures taken to produce turnover at premises B in mitigation of the shortage at A leaves the position unaffected. That is, the shortcoming in turnover because of the fire at premises B is the insurers' loss whether there is insurance at premises B or not and the insured is entitled to the benefit of an amount recoverable under the business interruption insurance arranged on those premises.

The other view is that after the fire at premises A, steps having been taken to rehabilitate the business in accordance with the claims condition (Action by the Insured) (the insurers fulfilling their part of the contract under the increase in cost of working provisions of the policy) the insurers are entitled under the alternative trading clause of the specification to the benefit of prospective earnings at premises B to set against the loss at premises A. This being so it is only equitable for them to be credited with any amount recoverable under the insurance in respect of loss of turnover at temporary premises B. This may look like the insurers taking money out of one of their pockets to put it in another pocket; actually it is a case of their benefiting from the amount of the claim in respect of damage at premises B to make good what they are losing through the failure of those premises to fulfil the intended help with the loss at premises A. If the insured are given the benefit they will be recompensed twice for what is, in effect, the same loss of turnover at premises A and B, which would be contrary to the principle of indemnity on which the insurance is based. The principle operates in the same way as if the insurance in respect of premises B had been arranged with different insurers from the cover on premises A; the latter insurers would be subrogated to rights of recovery of payments made by the insurers of premises B.

Opinion seems to be divided on this problem. Perhaps, to overcome the difficulty which arises in cases of this kind the insurers might insist on an insured taking out a policy on the temporary premises and in doing so safeguard their own interests by obtaining an agreement from the insured or by an appropriate memorandum on the policy to provide that any indemnity payable under it shall, up to the relevant amount, be paid to the insurers in mitigation of their loss under the original-damage claim. The question as to who should bear the cost of the insurance on temporary premises is dealt with in the following paragraph 233.

233. Need to effect cover at temporary premises

Should damage occur at temporary premises in circumstances such as those described in the preceding paragraph 232 there are two ways in which an insured may suffer loss. If the fire at the temporary premises B happens before they have produced turnover to the amount anticipated when they were occupied the additional expenditure already incurred in respect of them might be more than the economic limit under clause (b) of the cover provided by the insurance on gross profit and wages. That is it might exceed the amount of the loss avoided by the additional expenditure. In such circumstances unless insurance had been arranged for business interruption in respect of premises B the insured would suffer some loss under the increase in cost of working provisions in respect of the insurance at premises A.

Similarly, if the rehabilitation of the original premises is not completed at the time of the expiry of the maximum indemnity period and the interruption of business at the temporary premises at which the second occurrence of damage takes place also continues beyond that date then unless insurance had been arranged in respect of premises B the insured will suffer loss in respect of the turnover which would have been earned at the temporary premises in the months after the end of the maximum indemnity period.

So it seems desirable that in circumstances of this kind the insured should effect business interruption cover in respect of the business at the temporary premises even though the main benefit from this may be reaped by insurers. If such an insurance can be effected at the expense of the insurers under the increase in cost of working provisions of the claim in respect of premises A this would take care of the aspect of cost.

234. Worksheets used in the United States

(a) *For use with gross earnings forms*

A feature in which insurance practice in the United States differs from methods in the United Kingdom is the necessity for an insured to complete a "worksheet" which is provided each year by insurers in a standardised form.

This sets out a detailed schedule of nearly 20 items (see example on page 257), with notes for guidance in its completion, on which are to be shown actual amounts for the previous year of the calculation of the insured gross earnings taking into account ordinary payroll expense as insured and coinsurance percentage applicable. A parallel column for corresponding figures based on an estimate for the next 12 months from the date of the computation makes it appear a rather formidable looking questionnaire and some prospective insured might also consider that it involves divulging too much private information about their business.

The following instructions and explanation notes are found at the foot of each worksheet:

*INSTRUCTIONS: THE COINSURANCE CLAUSE ALWAYS APPLIES TO THE FUTURE (never the PAST). Column 2 is merely a projection of known past values (shown in Column 1) to the next 12 months from the date the computation is prepared.

Do not inadvertently enter Cost of Sales as Cost of Raw Stock under "D" above. Deduction under "D" above should not include any labor. "Freight in" may be considered as a part of the cost of raw stock.

Business interruption values should be checked at regular intervals and the agent or broker notified at once of any actual or impending change that would affect values during the next 12 months from the date such change becomes known.

EXPLANATORY NOTES:

1. To obtain annual net sales value of production from Manufacturing Operations, the following procedure is recommended:

    Net sales of Insured's product during the year (i.e. gross sales less discounts granted, returns, allowances, bad debts, and prepaid freight, if included in sales figures)............... $..............

    DEDUCT—Inventory of FINISHED STOCK at beginning of year, priced at sales value .... $..............
    Balance.. $..............

    ADD—Inventory of FINISHED STOCK on hand at end of year, priced at sales value............ $..............
    TOTAL—Annual Net Sales Value of production during the year............................... $..............

2. To obtain cost of raw stock, merchandise sold, or supplies consisting of materials consumed, the following procedure is recommended:

    Inventory (including stock in process) at beginning of year...................... $..............

    ADD—Cost of raw stock, merchandise and such supplies purchased during the year (including cartage and transportation chages on said incoming purchases)............................. $..............
    TOTAL... $..............

    DEDUCT—Inventory (including stock in process) at end of year............................ $..............
    Amount for deductions 1, 2 and 3 of "D"... $..............

    Note: Adjust for any inventory increase or decrease by price fluctuations.

3. Under deduction 2 of "D", the words "supplies' consisting of materials" are intended to refer only to tangible or physical supplies (i.e. materials), and the deduction of intangible supplies (such as heat and power) is not permitted nor shall intangible supplies which are not "materials" be deemed to be raw stock.

COMBINATION BUSINESS INTERRUPTION WORK SHEET
(For Use With Business Interruption Forms
For Manufacturing, Mercantile or Non-Manufacturing Risks)

COMPANY	POLICY NO.	AGENCY

Name of Insured _____

Location of Risk _____

Date _____

ALL ENTRIES TO BE ON AN ANNUAL BASIS	COLUMN 1 Actual Values for Year Ended.....19__	COLUMN 2 *Estimated Values for Year Ending..........19__
A. Total annual net sales value of production from Manufacturing Operations; and total annual net sales from Merchandising or Non-Manufacturing Operations, (Gross sales less discounts, returns, bad accounts and prepaid freight, if included in sales)	$........................	$........................
B. Add other earnings (if any) derived from operations of the business:		
1. Cash Discounts Received (not reflected in the amounts deducted under D)	....	....
2. Commissions or Rents from Leased Departments.....................	....	....
3.	....	....
C. Total ("A" plus "B")	$........................	$........................
D. Deduct only cost of:		
1. Raw stock from which such production is derived................ $........................		$........................
2. Supplies consisting of materials consumed directly in the conversion of such raw stock into finished stock or in supplying the service(s) sold by the Insured		....
3. Merchandise sold, including packaging materials therefor............		....
4. Service(s) purchased from outsiders (not employees of the Insured) for resale which do not continue under contract		....
5. Total deductions...	$........................	$........................
E. GROSS EARNINGS ("C" minus "D")..	$........................	$........................
IF INSURANCE IS TO BE WRITTEN WITHOUT PAYROLL ENDORSEMENTS:		
F. Take 50, 60, 70 or 80% of "E" Column 2, as amount of insurance required, depending upon percentage Coinsurance Clause to be used (...................%)		$........................
IF INSURANCE IS TO BE WRITTEN WITH ORDINARY PAYROLL EXCLUSION ENDORSEMENT, Deduct From "E" Above:		
G. All Ordinary Payroll Expense..................................	$........................	$........................
H. Business Interruption Basis for Coinsurance ("E" minus "G") ...	$........................	$........................
I. Amount of Insurance—Take 80, 90 or 100% of H, Column 2, depending upon percentage Coinsurance Clause to be used (...................%)		$........................
IF INSURANCE IS TO BE WRITTEN WITH ORDINARY PAYROLL-LIMITED COVERAGE ENDORSEMENT, Complete "G" and "H" and the following:		
J. Select the largest Ordinary Payroll Expense for.............................. .... consecutive calendar days.......................... 90, 120, 150 or 180	$........................	$........................
K. Business Interruption Basis for Coinsurance ("H" plus "J")	$........................	$........................
L. Amount of Insurance—Take 80, 90 or 100% of K, Column 2, depending upon percentage Coinsurance Clause to be used (...................%)	$........................	$........................

234 CHAPTER 11

POLICY NUMBER: COMMERCIAL PROF

BUSINESS INCOME REPORT/WORK SHEET

Your Name _____ Date _____

Location _____

_____

This work sheet must be completed on an accrual basis in conformity with generally accepted accounting principles.

Indicate the inventory valuation method used by your company:

_____ Specific Identification Method   _____ Last-In, First-Out (LIFO) Method

_____ Average-Cost Method   _____ Other (specify):

_____ First-In, First-Out, (FIFO) Method   _____

APPLICABLE WHEN THE AGREED VALUE COVERAGE OPTION APPLIES:

I certify that this is a true and correct report of values as required under this policy for the periods indicated and that the Agreed Value for the period of coverage is $ _____ , based on a Coinsurance percentage of _____ %.

Signature _____

Official Title _____

APPLICABLE WHEN THE PREMIUM ADJUSTMENT FORM APPLIES:

I certify that this is a true and correct report of values as required under this policy for the 12 months ended _____

Signature _____

Official Title _____

Agent or Broker _____

Mailing Address _____

BUSINESS INCOME REPORT/WORK SHEET
FINANCIAL ANALYSIS

	12 Month Period Ending...19__		Estimated for 12 Month Period Beginning...19__	
Income and Expenses	Manufacturing	Non-Manufacturing	Manufacturing	Non-Manufacturing
A. Gross Sales	$	$	$	$
B. DEDUCT: Finished Stock Inventory (at sales value) at Beginning	−		−	
C. ADD: Finished Stock Inventory (at sales value) at End	+		+	
D. Gross Sales Value of Production	$		$	
E. DEDUCT: Prepaid Freight				
Returns & Allowances +				
Discounts +				
Bad Debts +				
Collection Expenses +				
Total	−		−	
F. Net Sales		$		$
Net Sales Value of Production	$		$	
G. ADD: Other Earnings from your business operations (not investment income or rents from other properties):				
Commissions or Rents				
Cash Discounts Received +				
Other +				
Total Other Earnings	+	+	+	+
H. Total Revenues	$	$	$	$

I. DEDUCT: The cost of the following (net of any cash discounts received):
  1. Cost of Goods Sold:
     Inventory (including stock in process) at beginning of year .... $ _____
     ADD: Cost of the following purchased during the year:
     Manufacturing risks only:
        Raw Stock Consumed .... _____
        Factory Supplies Consumed .... + _____
        Merchandise Sold .... + _____
        Other Supplies Consumed (including transportation charges) .... + _____
        Total Purchase Costs .... + _____
     Cost of Goods Available for Sale .... $ _____
     DEDUCT: Inventory (including stock in process) at end of year .... − _____
     Cost of Goods Sold .... $ _____
  2. Services purchased from outsiders (not your employees) to resell, that do not continue under contract .... + _____
  Total (Mining Properties—see next page) .... $ _____

J. 1. Net Income and Expenses (Business Income Basis for Coinsurance if a Coverage Modification does not apply) .... $ _____

J. 2. Combined (for firms engaged in both manufacturing and non-manufacturing operation) .... $ _____

K. Business Income Basis for Coinsurance if a Coverage Modification does apply—see reverse side .... $ _____

L. Amount of Insurance Required (Multiply the amount in J.1, J.2 or K. by the coinsurance percentage specified in the Declarations) .... $ _____

BUSINESS INCOME REPORT/WORK SHEET
COVERAGE MODIFICATION

	12 Month Period Ending...19___	Estimated for 12 Month Period Ending...19___

NET INCOME and EXPENSES (item J.1 or J.2) .... $ _____   _____

1. If Ordinary Payroll Limitation form is attached:
   DEDUCT: All Ordinary Payroll Expenses .... − _____   − _____

   If "90 days" or "180 days" is indicated for Ordinary Payroll Limitation:
   ADD: The largest amount of Ordinary Payroll Expense incurred during the specified number of days .... + _____   + _____
   Total ....

2. If Power, Heat and Refrigeration Deduction form is attached:
   DEDUCT: Power, heat and refrigeration expenses that do not continue under contract .... − _____   − _____

BUSINESS INCOME BASIS FOR COINSURANCE
(Transfer to Line K. on previous page) .... $ _____ $ _____

MINING PROPERTIES: In the Total for Line 1 include the following:
Royalties, unless specifically included in coverage ....
Actual depletion, commonly known as unit or cost depletion (not percentage depletion) .... + _____
Welfare and retirement fund charges based on tonnage ..... + _____
Hire Trucks .... + _____
Subtotal .... $ _____

261

(b) *For use with Business Income Coverage forms*

The business income report/work sheet (see pages 258 to 261) represents a perhaps more logical schedule starting with a gross sales figure, calculating from that either a net sales (non-manufacturing) or a net sales value of production (manufacturing) amount, and then going on to a net income and expenses amount (which corresponds with gross earnings on the older form) to which can be applied the chosen coinsurance percentage. If the cover is modified because an Ordinary Payroll Limitation or a Power, Heat and Refrigeration Deduction endorsement is attached the figures can be suitably amended.

235. Selection of coinsurance percentage (United States)

As stated in paragraph 67(c) the selection may depend on the practice of different insurers and the type of cover required. But generally the choice is at the option of the insured and is based on the following procedure:

(a) Estimate the maximum period of time that the business could be interrupted as a result of the most serious form of damage that could possibly occur following the operation of an insured peril: this period should include not only the time needed to reinstate the buildings, but also any further time required to re-equip them, and provide replacement stock.
(b) Calculate the maximum amount of gross earnings or Business Income that could be lost in any equivalent period.
(c) Estimate the savings that could be made during the interruption.
(d) Subtract (c) from (b).
(e) Calculate the percentage that (d) bears to the projected annual gross earnings or Business Income of the business.
(f) Round up the percentage for added security.

Because of the changing nature of business activities in general, the foregoing procedure should be followed at regular intervals—if necessary, at each renewal.

Another factor to be taken into account is the Additional Coverage now provided by the Business Income Coverage form of up to 30 days income loss beyond the date property (except "finished stock") is actually repaired. This additional period can be extended if the insured wishes.

236. Coinsurance percentage and the period of interruption (United States)

Although the selected percentage may be the result of a calculation which takes into account a probable maximum period of interruption, it is not intended to represent a percentage of 12 months—in other words, a 50 per cent. coinsurance factor does not automatically indicate that a six months period of interruption or restoration is envisaged. Much depends on the seasonal nature of the business and whether significant savings are expected in the event of a loss. The Extended Business Income Additional Coverage relates to a maximum period of 30 days which can be increased by the Optional Coverage of Extended Period of Indemnity to longer stated periods but these are added to a "period of restoration" which is known only in the event of a loss.

237. Premium adjustment (return of premium) endorsement (United States)

(a) *For gross earnings*

A Standard Premium Adjustment Application form is used. On this form detailed figures for the previous 12 months have to be given for the various accounts items corresponding with the definition of gross earnings on the policy. To the amount declared the coinsurance percentage on the insurance is applied and if the resulting figure is less than the amount insured then a pro rata return of premium is allowable on the difference, not exceeding 50 per cent. of the premium paid.

This is in essence the same as the provisions for returns of premium on U.K. policies (see paragraph 225(a)) and like the latter no excess premium is charged if the figure exceeds the sum insured. The adjustment endorsement cannot be used along with an Agreed Amount Endorsement (refer paragraph 68) because with the latter the premiums paid correspond to gross earnings actually achieved.

But the Premium Adjustment endorsement also includes provisions regarding the amount recoverable in the event of a claim under the policy by limiting liability to the smallest of four possible amounts, although only the fourth of these provisions alters existing policy conditions. The first is to limit the insurer's proportion of a loss to that which the amount insured bears to all business interruption insurances on the risk. Secondly, liability is limited to the amount resulting from application of the coinsurance percentage shown on the policy. Thirdly it is limited to the policy's proportion of the coinsurance percentage of gross earnings that would have been earned (had no loss occurred) during the 12 months following the date of the damage. Lastly, liability is limited to the insurer's percentage of that proportion of any loss which the last reported gross earnings prior to the date of damage bear to the actual gross earnings during the period covered by the report. This is a so-called "Honesty clause" the effect of which is to apply pro rata average to a claim if the reported earnings are less than the actual amount which should have been declared.

A report form must be submitted to the insurer within 120 days of the end of each financial year. It will be gathered from the above synopsis that the endorsement is much more comprehensive than the simple wording of the return of premium clause on a U.K. specification (paragraph 225(a)). It goes into great detail in several directions and in fact runs to 19 clauses and approximately 1,000 words.

(b) *For Business Income*

The Business Income Coverage Premium Adjustment endorsement requires the completion of the first column of the business income report/work sheet. If the calculated premium is less than the provisional premium, the excess is repaid to the insured (there is no 50 per cent., or other percentage, of premium paid limit).

There is a limitation of loss payment in the form (as in the gross earnings equivalent) with the smallest of four possible amounts payable. These are in fact exactly the same four amounts as in the gross earnings form with the exception of the first where it is the "Limit of Insurance shown in the Declarations for Business Income Coverage". Examples of loss calculations under the last two alternatives are set out in the endorsement form.

238. Reinstatement of amount insured

Unlike the U.K. practice (refer paragraph 231) where the sum insured stands reduced by the amount of any claims settlement, the U.S. method is to leave the amount insured undisturbed. Under the gross earnings forms there is a Loss Clause which states that "any loss hereunder shall not reduce the amount of this policy". Under the Business Income Coverage form the Limit of Insurance condition provides that the limit applies on a per occurrence basis and remains available after a claim has been settled.

239. Other income

The work sheets also include in the assessment of the basic gross earnings or business income amount "other earnings" from the business operations—commissions or rents (from leased departments), cash discounts received, and any related earnings. The point is made in the Business Income report/work sheet that investment income or rents from other properties are not to be included. These are clearly not items of earnings derived from the operation of the business at the premises described.

240. Extended period of indemnity

This Optional Coverage by which the "30 consecutive days" referred to in the Extended Business Income Additional Coverage is replaced by a (higher) number shown in the Declarations (see also paragraph 63(b)(i)) requires the insured to ensure that the amount insured takes into account the additional income that is potentially at risk.

CHAPTER 12

Risk Management—Analysis, Treatment and Financing (Insurance)

241. Risk analysis—identification and evaluation

The creation of a standardised base has provided U.K. insurers with a more scientific approach to the underwriting of business interruption insurance and decisions on retentions, premium rating and possibilities of improvements in large and other difficult risks. This in turn has accelerated the growing practice for underwriters to require more information through interruption reports for the larger risks. Some insurers use a stereotyped form of questionnaire which, based on their experience, is designed to provide them with the basic information essential for their purposes. These reports are used in conjunction with those of fire surveyors which give the physical features and hazards such as size, height, construction and lay-out of premises, the processes of manufacture and details of materials used, the risks of inception of fire and its spread, and of the fire precautions and extinguishing provisions.

For an underwriter to estimate the potential business interruption risk every factor which may indicate the possible effects of damage by any of the insured perils on production and any feature of influence in the restoration of turnover both in degree and length of time is important. This calls for an investigative turn of mind to seek out and acquire information on any points of special significance beyond those covered by an interruption risk report form such as the specimen given in following paragraph 242(a). Any data on aspects of interruption and rehabilitation whether favourable or unfavourable (including comments on *moral* hazard—housekeeping standards, relationships with workforce, etc.) which might help an underwriter to evaluate a risk will be welcomed by him. Field staff and brokers cannot only give considerable help in that direction but at the same time will increase their own expertise as advisers of insured and may possibly benefit the latter through underwriters granting more favourable rates of premium for risks with specially good features or by suggesting ways of improving the interruption risk of others to their mutual advantage.

Also it must not be forgotten that the investigation, identification and evaluation of the potential business interruption risk is an essential aid to the insured's own risk management procedure. An accurate evaluation may well lead the larger insured to decide to retain part of their own risk—by means of a deductible, perhaps, or a captive company. It may also influence the insured to take certain steps to protect their buildings, plant and machinery, etc., or to segregate parts of their premises so as to reduce or even eliminate a particular interruption risk, with consequent benefits not only of premium saving but also of the safeguarding of the business.

242. Interruption risk

(a) *Specimen basic questionnaire*

1. The Insured: name(s)
   : business(es)
2. a. Situations of all insured premises:
   b. approximate percentage of earnings from each:
   c. extent of dependency between any or all:
3. a. Trade or manufacturing in each range of buildings by plan numbers:
   b. any specialties:
   c. seasonal or steady production or sales:
   d. production flowlines (diagrams)
4. Buildings: a. any special features of relevance:
   : b. estimated time for rebuilding and re-equipping:
5. Raw materials: a. what raw materials are used?
   b. source of supplies: seasonal? restricted?
   c. alternative sources available: how soon?
   d. buffer stocks: for how long? where stored?
6. a. Details of other materials and/or components of importance:
   a. mention any vital to whole production:
   c. what alternative sources are available?
7. Plant, pipe lines, machinery, equipment, conveyor belts:
   a. standard? special? if foreign, which countries?
   b. position regarding repairs or replacement:
   c. any special susceptibility to damage by fire? water?
   d. any key item which can create a bottleneck or stop production entirely?
   e. what duplicate power plant, machines or spares are kept?
8. Power, lighting, heating, air conditioning, humidifying:
   a. main sources of (i) power (ii) electric current
   b. vulnerability of power unit, supply control and distribution areas:
   c. possible alternative temporary arrangements:
9. Computers and mini-computers etc.: usage and importance
10. Sale of finished products:
    a. main marketing outlets: any special contracts:
    b. buffer stocks in separate warehouses: how long supply?
    c. possibilities of having production done outside on commission:
    d. possibilities of buying finished goods from competitors:
    e. how vulnerable to permanent loss of trade in event of serious stoppage:
11. Payroll:
    a. number of productive workers: skilled: semi-skilled:
    b. number of shifts normally worked:
    c. proportion of employees normally on overtime:
    d. local position reemployment of classes of workers required:
12. General conclusions:
    a. likely interruption which may be anticipated:
       (i) total—how long?
       (ii) partial—maximum % how long? : minimum % how long?

b. possible overall effect on earnings: 12 months— %: long %
c. possible action insured might take to reduce effects of damage: contingency planning:
d. possibilities in locality/elsewhere for alternative premises or use of machinery:
e. possible assistance from associated companies or competitors:
f. any likelihood of increase in cost of working being abnormal?

(b) *Estimated maximum loss (E.M.L.)*

There is no universally agreed definition of "estimated maximum loss" (E.M.L.) for business interruption insurance. It could be said to be the maximum *probable* business interruption loss in a maximum *possible* property damage loss situation. The latter occurs when plant protection (sprinklers, etc.) is out of service but competent public or private assistance is available. A reasonably accurate and reliable estimate can be provided for a potential property damage loss in such a situation. For business interruption however other factors come into play which include market forces, seasonal and cyclical business periods, the efficiency of the insured's management, the attitudes of the workforce, etc.

An E.M.L. amount or percentage (of sum insured) for business interruption is essential for an underwriter to function properly—in selecting what gross share of risk he wishes to take and how much he should retain net for his own account. For a broker or risk management specialist it is a useful basis for discussion with his client in determining the extent of the cover and the need for contingency planning, etc.

There are two basic formulae for calculating a gross profit E.M.L. for a U.K. business interruption cover.

Formula 1

(i) From information in report form select key interruption risks.
(ii) Ascertain which key risk contributes the greatest amount to gross profit—express as percentage of total gross profit.
(iii) Estimate maximum *total* interruption—express as percentage of maximum indemnity period.
(iv) Estimate maximum *partial* interruption—convert to equivalent period in total interruption and express as percentage of maximum indemnity period.
(v) Add together (iii) and (iv).
(vi) Emergency measures taken may reduce the interruption—express reduction as percentage of (ii) and subtract from 100 per cent.
(vii) Increased costs may be incurred to maintain turnover—express as percentage of gross profit.
(viii) Add other factors which might affect the loss (market loss, etc.)—express as percentage of gross profit.

(ix) Calculate as follows—

    Multiply (ii) × (v) × (vi) =   %
    Add (vii)   %
    ———
       %
    Add or deduct   %
    ———

    Estimated Maximum Loss   %

Example

Maximum indemnity period—12 months.

  (ii) Greatest contribution to gross profit of key risks   60%
  (iii) Maximum *total* interruption—three months   25%
  (iv) Maximum *partial* interruption—six months at 50%   25%
  (v) Add (iii) and (iv)   50%
  (vi) By emergency measures interruption reduced by 20%   80%
  (vii) Increased costs   10%
  (viii) Loss of markets   5%
  (ix) Calculate as follows—
    (ii) × (v) × (vi) = 60% × 50% × 80%   = 24%
    Add (vii)   = 10%
    Add (viii)   = 5%

    Estimated Maximum Loss   = 39%

Formula 2

(i) Select key interruption risk.

(ii) Estimate maximum period the business could be interrupted (totally plus partially) following damage to key interruption risk.

(iii) Subdivide the estimated period of interruption into months and weeks allocating to each month or week the likely degree of loss.

(iv) Calculate interruption percentage applicable to maximum indemnity period.

(v) Apply interruption percentage in (iv) to the contribution (to total gross profit) percentage of key interruption risk.

(vi) Add increased costs percentage.

Example

Maximum indemnity period—12 months.

(ii) Key risk could be interrupted (totally plus partially) for whole of maximum indemnity period.

(iii) Subdivision—

First two weeks	100%
Third week to end third month	75%
Fourth to end ninth month	50%
Tenth month	30%
Eleventh month	15%
Twelfth month	5%
(iv) 12 months interruption percentage	49%
(v) 49% × 60% (key risk)	29%
(vi) Add increased costs	10%
Estimated Maximum Loss	39%

It must be emphasised that there is a degree of "art" as well as "science" in the calculation of business interruption E.M.L.s and the underwriter in particular (because he is the one who is carrying the risk) must study the information and its application carefully and decide whether to accept the calculated E.M.L. or to amend it suitably in the light of his own experience with such risks.

243. Interruption risk treatment

(a) *Elimination*

In a well-run business enterprise the elimination of a particular interruption risk may be difficult but there are always possibilities. For instance, an alteration in production methods may remove an interruption risk arising out of the use of a particular machine or a particular raw material without adversely affecting the efficiency of the operation.

(b) *Reduction*

This is usually achieved by the resiting of a particular physical hazard away from the production line subject of course to such resiting not interfering with the economies of production flow. Another method is by the duplication of certain processes or the establishment of standby facilities to be used in an emergency situation. Again such procedures must not clash unduly with the operation of the business.

(c) *Transfer*

It is commercial practice now to hold low levels of stocks of raw materials and other supplies at the insured premises and to require suppliers to retain such stocks until the insured actually need them. This is called the "Just in time" method and effectively transfers the stockholding cost from user to supplier. At the same time responsibility for the physical protection of the stock is also transferred. For the business interruption underwriter the stock may be transferred from the premises of the insured but the insured's dependency on that stock remains, albeit under the suppliers' control. Risk transfer for business interruption is difficult and the most enlightened method of transfer must remain the use of insurance cover.

(d) *Acceptance*

If the risk cannot be eliminated, reduced or transferred the insured must decide whether to accept the risk for their own account. It may be that in certain circumstances the retention of what would otherwise have been a business interruption insurance premium (or part of it) is more attractive to the insured (to finance risk improvement, etc.) than the benefits of insurance cover.

(e) *Possible conflict with property damage risk treatment*

On occasion a recommendation to improve a property damage risk (usually by reduction or limitation) may work against the control of the interruption risk at the same premises. For instance, removing all patterns to a separate (but single) building may well reduce the property damage risk but increase the interruption risk. These possible conflicts of interests should be discussed between surveyors and underwriters together with the insured and their risk management advisors.

244. Risk financing

(a) *Captive companies*

The establishment of a captive company is usually restricted to the very large commercial or industrial organisation. Although set up for largely financial reasons—the retention and use of substantial amounts of premium, the possible avoidance of tax, etc.—a captive company can have a significant effect on the control of risk because the impact of a constant flow of claims on its profitability will inevitably stir it to take the action to stem that flow.

(b) *Deductibles*

In 1964 U.K. insurance companies made a radical change in their traditional opposition to arrangements whereby an insured should stand the first amount of any loss, that is, an "excess", under a business interruption policy though still maintaining that such arrangements may not be in an insured's best interests. The change followed a similar concession granted in connection with fire insurances of not less than £2.5 million which in turn arose from the modern trend towards vast concentrations of capital in industrial undertakings. The consequent magnitude of premises and plant often make it uneconomic for such firms to claim on their insurers for the small fire losses which inevitably arise in most large concerns, whilst their financial resources enable them to stand such losses themselves without noticeable effect on their trading results. Fire insurance companies in the United States had for many years accepted this position and allowed insured to have a substantial excess on policies and the increasing extent of American capital investment in British industry no doubt added to the pressure for similar arrangements in this country.

On the face of things insured might consider it illogical and unrealistic when their fire insurers had agreed to such an excess or, to give it the official name imported from the United States, a "deductible" not to be able to have a similar arrangement for their business interruption insurance. But special considerations apply to the latter which are not relevant to deductibles in fire insurances.

Experience shows that it is extremely difficult in many cases, impossible in some, to estimate at the time of damage how much a business interruption claim will amount to and, therefore, whether it will be more than the deductible and become a claim on the insurers. But business interruption insurers must be immediately notified of any damage and appoint a loss adjuster so that the insured shall have the benefit of his skilled advice about steps to be taken to mitigate the interruption as well as to watch their own interest, even though it may be that no adjuster is appointed by the insurers of the material damage because the amount of the latter is demonstrably less than the deductible on the fire policy. Should the ultimate amount of the business interruption loss be less than the deductible no claim will arise under the insurance and yet the insurers will have to pay the loss adjuster's charges. This means that there will be an absence of saving in administrative costs as compared with the fire insurance.

Difficulties may arise where the business interruption loss as envisaged immediately after the damage appears likely to be either just below or just above the amount of the deductible. In such circumstances might not the insured, having to bear the major part or perhaps the whole of the loss, wish to decide upon and control the actions to be taken to restore the business to normality? But it is the traditional practice well founded on a vast experience for insurers to exercise that prerogative themselves. They are entitled to do so should there be any possibility that the loss will exceed the deductible limit and may wish to do so if they foresee actions being taken prejudicial to their interests if they do not have control throughout the period of interruption.

It is possible also to envisage friction with an insured if a loss adjuster's advice is followed to spend money under the increase in cost of working provisions and later it is found that the total of such expenditure combined with the loss of gross profit is less than the amount of the deductible and so is not recoverable under the insurance. Yet although the insurers will have benefited from the outlay on additional expenditure if it has kept the total loss below the amount of the deductible the insured cannot recover anything towards such expenditure.

Extensions to cover loss resulting from damage at the premises of suppliers, processors, customers, contract sites and stores, etc., are a regular feature of business interruption insurances and the insurers' liability is generally limited to an agreed percentage of the sums insured. The effect on such extensions of a deductible introduced into an insurance can produce a contradictory situation by seriously reducing or even nullifying the advantage of an extension for which additional premium has been paid.

The foregoing and other difficulties which may arise in the event of a claim can be a threat to the goodwill which normally exists between insured and insurers and consequently the latter whilst agreeing to make deductibles available do not recommend them. The 1983 U.K. Consequential Loss Committee terms on which deductibles not subject to an annual aggregate limit could be granted were:

(a) a deductible may be granted in the range of £250 to £25,000 regardless of the amount of the annual sum insured (if the annual sum insured does not exceed £50 million, a set table of discounts can be used);

(b) a deductible above £25,000 up to £250,000 may be granted subject to it not being more than one per mille of the annual sum insured or not more than the deductible for the material damage insurance covering the same interests, business and premises—whichever is the greater;

(c) there is an obligatory wording:

"The Insurer shall not be liable for the first £ (amount of deductible) of each and every loss as ascertained after the application of all other terms, conditions and provisions of this policy. Warranted that the Insured shall not effect insurance in respect of the amount specified above".

(d) the application of the deductible is in respect of loss as ascertained under the policy inclusive of any extension to "outside premises".

Because of the demise of the U.K. Tariff organisation it may well be that individual insurers have amended these regulations.

It is permissible, subject to certain regulations, to make the application of the deductible provision subject to an "aggregate limit" during an annual period of insurance. This gives the insured a limit governing the extent to which they contribute towards the cost of their own claims in any one insurance year.

Where a deductible has been authorised for a group of companies the deductible will apply once only in respect of any one occurrence of damage irrespective of whether there is a single group policy or separate policies. This does not apply to a deductible with an aggregate limit.

In any case where there is a deductible on the material damage insurance the customary memorandum is added to the business interruption specification to suspend the operation of the material damage proviso should any loss under the fire policy not be payable because the amount is below the deductible on such policy (see paragraph 16(b)).

Whilst monetary deductibles are normally the result of an insured's request, voluntarily accepted in return for a small discount in premiums, it is possible that in certain circumstances they might have to be imposed by insurers without any allowance of discount in order to mitigate what could otherwise be regarded as an unacceptable insurance. In some cases such as petrochemical complexes where the fire and explosion hazards and the interruption risks are exceedingly high the imposed deductible may be as large as a million pounds.

Up to the present, the "time" deductible under which loss during a stated number of days from the commencement of the period of interruption is excluded has not been generally regarded with favour in the United Kingdom, except in the special circumstances applicable in machinery (accident) business interruption insurances. For instance there are the "technical" difficulties of allocating increase in cost of working which may be incurred during the currency of the time deductible but is of benefit to the business during the remainder of the indemnity period. There is also the "commercial" complication when the impact of the time deductible is rendered non-effective by the utilisation of accumulated stock during the time deductible period.

The fact, however, that this method is operative in some European countries (refer paragraph 78), where the first one or two days (or even weeks, for certain high hazard continuous process industries) of a stoppage are often regarded as the responsibility of the insured rather than of insurers, may mean its ultimate adoption in the United Kingdom as European practice becomes increasingly integrated and perhaps standardised. Continuing high inflation is another factor which may influence a change because it reduces the relative value of monetary deductibles and this may offset their advantage to insurers, as compared with time deductibles, of being deductible from every loss payment. It is to be borne in mind that for a monetary deductible to remain effective while the sum insured is constantly increasing, there must be a review at each renewal which can sometimes lead to protracted and difficult renegotiation.

(c) *Insurance*

This is the traditional method of financing the protection of the business against risk but that can be made subject to the retention by the insured of part of the risk—by deductible, by the exclusion of some premises from the cover or by the deliberate restriction of the maximum indemnity period (see paragraph 249).

245. Definition of indemnity period

(a) *United Kingdom basis*

In the standard U.K. business interruption specification the definition of the indemnity period reads: "The period beginning with the occurrence of the Incident and ending not later than the maximum indemnity period thereafter during which the results of the business shall be affected in consequence thereof" and is completed by a definition of the maximum indemnity period which simply states the number of months selected for the limit to the time element for the payment of compensation. This dual definition is an example of the careful drafting which applies throughout the specification in order to express the exact intention of the insurers.

It is important to note first of all that the indemnity period does not necessarily end when a business is rehabilitated to the point of being able to resume normal trading activities. Subject to the maximum limit selected and stated in the definition the indemnity period continues until the results of the business are restored to normal, which may be many months after the physical damage to buildings, machinery and stock has been made good. It should further be noted that should damage cause an interruption of business the indemnity period is not necessarily the same as the maximum period during which indemnity may be given, that is, the number of months which is selected to be shown in the definition for any particular insurance. It is the period, measured from the date of the damage (or Incident), at the end of which liability ceases because the results of the business are no longer affected by the damage (or Incident), subject to this period not exceeding the insured maximum number of months ("months" means "calendar months", as in all such contracts: *vide* the Law of Property Act 1925, s.61). For example, in the case of an insurance with a maximum indemnity period of 12 months if damage (or an Incident) should occur and cause an interference with the business for 15 weeks the indemnity period will be 15 weeks. This point is also of special relevance in connection with the time limit in the claims condition—Action by the Insured (see paragraph 437).

(b) *United States basis*

With the issue in 1986 of the new U.S. Business Income Coverage form the difference between U.S. and U.K. approaches has lessened somewhat. The "period of restoration" ends on the date when the premises "should be repaired, rebuilt or replaced with reasonable speed and similar quality". The built-in Additional Coverage of Extended Business Income does provide an extra period of up to 30 days during which business income continues to be lost. The Optional Coverage of Extended Period of Indemnity can translate the U.S. cover to an approximate equivalent of what the U.K. cover provides. (See also paragraph 63.)

246. Delayed start of indemnity period

Should damage occur and the turnover of the business not be affected until some weeks later, perhaps due to there being an accumulation of stocks available from which the shortage in production can be temporarily made up, the indemnity period would nevertheless commence with the date of the damage. Its maximum would be the number of months stated in the definition, starting not from the date when the reduction in turnover commenced but from the date of the damage.

This frequently raises the point that circumstances might be envisaged in which a manufacturer holds at the time of damage occurring a substantial stock of finished goods in warehouses or depots which (i) are depleted in keeping down the turnover shortage during the indemnity period (ii) cannot be made good by the end of the maximum term of the indemnity period and (iii) after the end of that term loss is suffered because of a deficiency of finished goods.

Insurers have acknowledged that in such circumstances they will make allowance for the loss under (iii) to the extent of the benefit they have obtained under (i) provided that the maximum indemnity period is not less than 12 months. Requests are sometimes made by insured for an "accumulated stocks" clause to be added to their policy to make this position clear, and such a clause can be added (refer paragraph 386). Insurers, however, hold that to do so would not add anything to what they admit as an equitable interpretation of their undertaking in the policy to provide an "indemnity" for loss due to reduction in turnover.

For the insurance of a business which is temporarily silent the definition of the indemnity period may be amended to make the commencing date coincide with the date on which the business would have restarted and so the insured receive protection for the full period of indemnity for which premium is paid.

247. Increase in turnover during indemnity period

Another important feature of the definition is that it intentionally does not say "the period . . . during which the results of the business shall be *adversely* affected in consequence of the damage" and the following inference can be drawn from the absence of the word "adversely". If the turnover is reduced for a period and then, still as a result of the damage, the sales in subsequent weeks or months exceed the corresponding pre-damage amount the deferred turnover would be brought into the calculation of the claim for benefit of the insurers. This, of course, is provided that the increase accrued within the limit of the maximum indemnity period and would not have arisen had the damage and interruption of the business not taken place. For example, it sometimes happens that due to an accumulation of orders whilst a business is unable to supply them, or because loyal customers agree to wait for delivery, or as a result of measures taken at the insurers' expense under the provision for increase in cost of working, or for other reasons connected with the damage, the turnover temporarily exceeds normal in the weeks or months after a business is ready for full production. That any such increase should be offset against the previous shortage is in accordance with the principle of indemnity which underlies the insurance and the definition was drafted intentionally to ensure this.

248. Other features of the definition of indemnity period

A further point to be noticed is that the maximum number of months for which indemnity is provided is measured from the date of the damage and should this period not be long enough to cover an insured's loss it cannot be construed as being any months subsequently selected by the insured not exceeding in total the maximum stated in the definition. That is to say, an insured could not suspend the cover for a month or months during the period of interruption because trade in such months is normally quiet and extend the maximum limit correspondingly in order to bring within the indemnity period months which normally are busier. The definition specifically states, in effect, the period beginning with the occurrence of the damage and ending not later than . . . months (as shown in the definition of maximum indemnity period) thereafter, that is, after the date when the damage occurred.

On the other hand the definition does not refer to the period during which the turnover is affected but says the period during which the results of the business shall be affected. This benefits an insured in cases in which turnover may be restored to normal but is only maintained at that level by means of continued expenditure on increase in cost of working. The turnover is then no longer affected, but the results of the business are because the continuing payments for additional expenditure will reduce the net profit.

249. Selecting the maximum indemnity period

Any number of months can be selected for the limit inserted in the definition of the maximum indemnity period 12 months being the most usual for small businesses. It is obvious, however, that the more extensive the premises the more difficult it will be and the longer the time required in the event of serious damage to rebuild them or to find adequate and suitable alternative accommodation. Similarly more time will be required for the installation of new plant and machinery and the many ancillary items of a modern industrial undertaking according to its greater size; and the ever increasing size and complexity of works and production lines in many industries is a dominant feature of this modern world.

Other factors will have an effect upon the time necessary for rehabilitation, such as the plant being of a very intricate or specialised nature or manufactured only abroad. Currency and import restrictions can also play a part in this problem. The installation of automated plant in place of numerous individually operated machines, with more and more mechanical and electronic controls in a factory, means that more time is required for replacement and return of full production may be further delayed because of the reduced flexibility.

In this latter regard the vital part which computers play when installed to control production and distribution is of paramount importance in a consideration of the length of the maximum indemnity period required. Catastrophic losses have occurred attributable largely to the destruction of a computer installation, notably that amounting to nearly £9 million at the Mannesmann Steelworks in Germany and £3.5 million at steel rolling mills in France some years ago.

Often it is not appreciated by insured until after their premises are destroyed by fire that not everything is consumed by the flames. Hundreds of tons of twisted steel girders and of concrete, stone or brickwork remain which have to be removed before rebuilding can start, and demolition and site clearance frequently takes many weeks.

Too often business concerns have decided upon insuring for a maximum indemnity period shorter than they would otherwise have covered because they had some old buildings standing empty which they regarded as usable in an emergency. When their working premises have been destroyed by fire they have been disillusioned on finding that the stand-by buildings could not bear the weight and vibration of modern plant and machinery or sometimes even the weight of stocks normally accommodated in larger buildings or perhaps that dry-rot had developed and rendered them unusable.

Similarly, it is frequently too optimistically assumed that in the event of damage to the insured premises alternative buildings can be obtained within a reasonably short time. Undoubtedly, a large fire is very often followed by a number of helpful offers either from owners of vacant property or from somebody willing to vacate premises or from a trader willing to sell his business as a going concern. It often turns out, however, that such offers spring from business opportunism allied to the knowledge that those who have had the fire are in a difficult position and are likely to pay more than the normal market value to get some premises quickly. Often the price demanded for the buildings offered is much too high, or there is an unsuitable lease to be taken up, or stock, goodwill and possibly outstanding book debts have to be bought. Such factors can make the acquisition of buildings, which may only be required until those damaged are rebuilt, an altogether uneconomic proposition involving a capital loss which might exceed the amount of gross profit which would accrue from trading in the temporary premises.

The assistance given by insurers under the increase in cost of working section of an insurance, if the maximum indemnity period insured is reasonably long, may be sufficient to make it worth while for an insured to acquire temporary premises even under such conditions as above. But if the maximum indemnity period is a short one the limitation under clause (b) to the amount of gross profit saved *during the indemnity period* by the additional expenditure (see paragraphs 47 to 48) might leave the insured to bear so much of the cost as to make the purchase uneconomic. They might then still be without premises after the expiry of the indemnity period and without insurance cover for their continuing loss.

A possibility generally overlooked, applicable particularly to shops and offices in large blocks of town property, is the destruction of the whole of such premises in a single fire resulting in a scramble by dozens of expropriated tenants for whatever vacant property there might be available in the town. The inevitable result of this would be that quite a number would not be able to obtain any alternative premises, and those who did might have to pay very dearly for the privilege or take shops in an inferior trading position in lieu of a prime site occupied before the fire.

Possibilities in another direction must be considered by firms such as modest size warehouses and precision engineering workshops and various factories with premises, processes and contents of low fire hazard but with business interruption insurance carrying a dependency extension to the premises of suppliers, processors or customers with a higher fire and interruption hazard. The possibility of a prolonged period of interruption in the event of fire at such outside premises may mean that a longer maximum indemnity period for the extension cover is advisable than would be considered necessary for the insured's own premises risk. (See paragraph 345 on this aspect.)

A very important point of general application for which allowance must be made is that the longer the period of actual interference, the longer will be the time required, after the business is re-equipped and ready for normal trading, to regain customers who have been obliged to go elsewhere in the interim. In highly competitive trades or when it is a buyers' market and everyone is struggling for business a shortage in turnover due to loss of customers can manifest itself for a very long time after reinstatement of the damaged property.

Whilst several of the factors mentioned in preceding paragraphs may have to be kept in mind in reaching a decision upon the number of months to be selected for the maximum indemnity period it is prudent to allow a further margin of time for the unpredictable events which have an unhappy knack of turning up when most inconvenient and delaying still further the resumption of full turnover. Examples of such contingencies are restrictions on rebuilding arising from town planning or other legislative control; a strike in the building industry or ancillary trades, in the transport industry, or at the docks; a shortage of steel, bricks or cement; demarcation disputes of the "who shall do what?" kind between different unions; or exceptionally bad weather which delays building operations. The last mentioned is of importance in the United Kingdom and other countries in temperate zones but in areas of North America and other parts of the world always subject at certain periods of the year to sub-zero temperatures or heavy snowfalls or floods it can be of vital importance.

Even when a factory is rebuilt there may at that time be long delays which were not foreseen in obtaining new plant and machinery especially if this is of a very sophisticated nature or is made overseas. An industrial dispute at the maker's works or in the transport industry or in one of the trades concerned in its installation can prolong the interruption of production by weeks or months. On top of this there may as a result of long closure of works be a shortage of technicians, skilled workers, or sometimes even of unskilled workers, to run it; time may be required to retrain operatives or to train new ones; and a period of teething troubles will generally follow when the various departments and processes have to be integrated to secure a steady flow of production.

If an insured does not own the buildings there is no certainty that in the event of their destruction the landlord will rebuild. This situation frequently arises and causes a serious prolongation of the period of interruption especially when the landlord will not make up his mind for some weeks or months as to whether or not to rebuild.

In view of all these possibilities a maximum indemnity period of 12 months is usually considered inadequate for a concern of any magnitude and experience following serious fires frequently demonstrates the wisdom of indemnity periods up to as long as 36 months.

Sometimes as a feature of risk management and as part of risk acceptance or retention (see paragraph 243(d)) an insured having decided that a prudent maximum indemnity period would be, say, 24 months will take for their own account the final six months of possible exposure. The risk would be relatively minor because, for the majority of losses, the actual indemnity period would not exceed 18 months and even if the whole of the maximum indemnity period were to be involved in a loss, the last six months of loss would be relatively small.

250. Policy an annual contract

Whatever the length of the maximum indemnity period selected, whether less than 12 months, 12 months, or longer, it must not be confused with the term of the insurance. The policy itself is almost invariably an annual contract renewable each year in the same way as a fire policy irrespective of the length of the maximum indemnity period. Should damage occur resulting in a period of interruption overlapping the renewal or expiry date of the policy the indemnity is not affected by the latter and continues up to the limit of the maximum indemnity period from the date of damage whether the policy is meanwhile renewed or lapsed.

251. Standard turnover for periods over 12 months

Another problem sometimes raised in connection with indemnity periods is the method of calculating the standard turnover when the maximum indemnity period exceeds 12 months. The definition of standard turnover once provided for this by stating that it is "the turnover during the period corresponding with the indemnity period in the 12 months immediately before the date of the damage *appropriately adjusted where the indemnity period exceeds 12 months*". In this context it must be kept in mind that indemnity period means the period of interruption and not the insured maximum indemnity period.

There was always an element of vagueness in the words "appropriately adjusted" and the current wording omits this qualification. However, no great difficulty should be experienced in applying the principle. It is possible to compare the turnover during the first 12 months of the period of interruption with that in the corresponding calendar months in the 12 months before the damage. After that the turnover in subsequent months of the indemnity period can be compared with that in the corresponding calendar months in the 12 months before the damage. The fact that the latter have already been used for purposes of measuring the loss of turnover in the first 12 months after the damage does not affect their validity. They are the most up-to-date turnover figures against which comparison can be made. The longer the period of interruption the more likely it is that some variations will have to be allowed for in making a comparison with the standard turnover and, of course, the other circumstances clause is available for that purpose. It is not without significance that its opening words are in the plural—"to which such adjustments shall be made"—which does provide for a different degree of adjustment being made in the second year of the indemnity period from that which might have been made in the earlier months.

This method would appear to provide a more equitable claim payment than would be obtained by simply using the turnover figures for the 12 months before the damage and increasing these by a proportion, say 1/52nd part for each week, for the period of interruption beyond the first 12 months. This would not take account of seasonal or other variations.

252. Seasonal businesses

(a) *General*

Businesses which are predominantly of a seasonal nature such as hotels, boarding houses, holiday camps, fairgrounds, amusement parks, theatres, bingo halls, amusement arcades and other concerns at seaside resorts and inland holiday and tourist centres and businesses in some sports and games and other seasonal trades may earn a year's profit in six months or even less but it does not follow that a maximum indemnity period of six months is adequate for their needs. The deciding factor is the length of time which it would take to restore the earnings of the business to normal. If serious damage were to occur immediately after the end of the busy season a maximum indemnity period of six months would expire before the start of the next season. The turnover during that first six months of the period of interruption, say October to March, would be compared with turnover in the same out-of-season months in the preceding year and little if any diminution would be shown. The premises might still be closed during the following summer season but the maximum indemnity period, *i.e.* six months *from the date of the damage* would have expired. The result would be that although an insured might suffer the loss of a year's earnings the insurance would contribute little or nothing towards that loss.

In fact if damage occured at almost any time in the off-season at least part of the benefit under a six-months maximum indemnity period would be lost because it would relate to a period when there would normally be little or no trading.

In the above context it should be noted that the other circumstances clause (paragraph 55(a)) would not be applicable as there is nothing unusual about the position, the business being always of a seasonal character. The failure of the insurance to recompense the insured would be due entirely to the fact that too short a maximum indemnity period had been selected.

A further important point in connection with a seasonal business is the necessity to see that the sum insured is adequate if a maximum indemnity period of 18 months is selected for a business in which the major part of the year's revenue is earned in a short period, for example, during a summer season. If the sum insured were to be calculated as one-and-a-half times the annual amount of gross profit this would not be adequate to meet the loss which might arise during a period of 18 months' interruption which happened to stretch over two seasons in which gross profit amounting to twice the annual figure would normally be earned.

To meet this situation care should be taken to calculate the sum insured as the maximum amount of gross profit which might be earned in any period of 18 months. This means that where the business has one good season each year the earnings of two good seasons would have to be included. Where it has two good seasons each year the earnings of three good seasons would have to be included in the sum insured. (See paragraph 220 on computing the figure for the sum insured for different indemnity periods.)

This arrangement of what may look like substantial overinsurance, covering 24 months gross profit for an 18 months indemnity, does not cost the insured any unnecessary premium because, when a certificate is furnished each financial year end for the purposes of the return of premium clause (paragraph 225(a)), the figure given will be that for 12 months gross profit. This will then be multiplied by one-and-a-half and a refund of premium will be allowed on the amount by which the resulting figure is exceeded by the sum insured. So the insured will have paid premium only for one-and-a-half times the annual gross profit whilst the insurers have been carrying a potential liability for twice the annual amount. This latter point is balanced however by the fact that there is an equal chance that any claim which might arise would relate to a period of interruption covering only one good season. So on balance it is generally advisable when arranging the maximum indemnity period for the insurance of a business of a seasonal nature to arrange it in terms of a whole year, *i.e.* 12 months, 24 months or 36 months.

(b) *Compensation when period of interruption is in busy season*

The question is sometimes raised as to how compensation will be provided for a seasonal business if damage occurs and the period of interruption is during the busy season. The difficulty in mind is that normally profit is earned during the season which will pay for the standing charges of the whole year, that is, the profit during each month of the season exceeds the monthly average for the year, whereas the insurance provides for the payment of a rate of gross profit calculated on an annual basis. The answer to this problem is that in any business, seasonal or otherwise, it does not matter when the turnover is earned or the standing charges are incurred. Each £ of turnover pays for the same proportion of the year's charges. In the case of a business of a seasonal nature, although practically all the turnover is done during the season it has to provide for the charges for the whole year including the period during which there is no turnover. Therefore, the ratio of gross profit to the turnover which earns it is the average of one annual total to the other. In other words it is the same as the rate of gross profit calculated according to the definition in the specification and when this rate is applied to any shortage in turnover during the season it will give a true measure of the loss sustained. For example, if the whole turnover is normally done in four months of the year and damage causes a complete cessation of business during those four months the rate of gross profit applied to the resulting loss of turnover will provide an amount equal to the normal annual net profit and standing charges of the business.

(c) *Compensation when period of interruption is out of season*

Conversely, it is sometimes asked about seasonal businesses, how will the insurance compensate for the loss if the period of interruption falls during the quiet months of the year when the normal position is that sales are very low and the disbursement on standing charges exceeds the gross profit earned during that time? The answer is that normally the standing charges are not earned and an insured does lose money during the off season each year. Therefore, the insurance cannot provide compensation following damage in respect of loss which would have arisen had the damage not occurred and which is not increased as a result of the damage. The loss is made good by the insured's trading during other months of the year; if interruption continues during that period the insurance will provide a corresponding indemnity provided that the maximum indemnity period insured is sufficiently long.

253. The cost of insurance

A premium is the mathematical end product of the application of a rate to a sum insured. The business interruption (or profits) rate and the gross earnings or Business Income rate are themselves derived from the application of a percentage to a property rate the nature of which can vary but which is taken as representing the degree of vulnerability to physical loss of the particular business carried on in the particular premises. From a purely historical point of view the rating of property damage risks came first and as business interruption insurance was regarded as an extension of property damage insurance it was natural (if not entirely logical) that business interruption rating should be derived from its predecessor. In fact in Germany (see paragraph 78(f)) the rates for business interruption are calculated separately and the mechanics of C.L.O.R.A. (the Consequential loss List of Rating Adjustments of the old U.K. Tariff) tended to make the calculation of "profits" rates a separate process.

It is freely admitted that the use of the average fire insurance rate as a basis of rating for business interruption insurances is not entirely scientific because although it takes the incipient fire risk and the potential destruction hazard into account, these being inherent in the fire insurance rating, it does not make provision for the interruption risk of each individual case. Whilst it would be very desirable to cater for this latter factor the infinite variety of circumstances has in the past meant that there were too many practical difficulties in the way of doing so for all cases. It was done to some extent for certain trades for which the claims experience over a period of years showed that as a class they merited something more favourable than the standard scale of premium rates. Also, where the magnitude of the sums insured for a particular business warranted individual consideration concessions in premium rating may have been given for favourable factors as, for instance, in the number of separate premises, the duplication of plants and processes in different buildings, facilities within their trade for assistance or having work done on commission, availability of new plant, machinery and stocks. On the other hand very large industrial concerns which carried possibilities of frequent, relatively small losses which are nevertheless time consuming and expensive in the negotiation of claims and also carried the risk of a major single loss of almost catastrophic proportions might be required to pay heavier than normal premiums or in some cases to carry an excess to eliminate small claims. Similarly, higher rates of premium have been charged for certain classes of industrial undertakings in which experience over past years has shown that the interruption hazard is abnormally high.

254. Basis rate—United Kingdom: base rate—United States

(a) *Basis rate (United Kingdom)*

Since the inception of business interruption insurance the "basis rate" has for most trades been the average rate of the total annual fire insurances on the contents of the premises of the insured which are included in the policy, that is, total premiums divided by total sums insured or, to be strictly correct, since it is a rate per cent., the total premiums divided by one-hundredth of the total sums insured. It has always been considered that by and large this gives the best indication of the risk involved for the general run of businesses.

The fire insurance on the buildings themselves is omitted from the calculation because often these are not owned by the insured and it would be impracticable to try to ascertain the necessary data. In any case insurance on the contents is generally a better guide to the earning capacity of the different buildings than the insurance on the structure of them. Where the fire insurance is under a valuation-linked scheme only the base values and related premiums are used in any basis rate calculation. In certain cases minimum rates apply.

An exception is made for insurances in respect of wharves and furniture depositories, film production studios, theatres, music halls and cinemas, and the property of public authorities. In these cases the basis rate is derived from the fire insurances on the buildings or structures. Special considerations also apply to the calculation of the basis rate for plastic manufacturers, cold storage warehouses, cotton spinning and weaving mills, lace bleachers, dyers, dressers and finishers, dairy farmers and rent on office premises. (For building contractors, see paragraph 377.)

No charge is made for the inclusion of loss arising from the explosion of boilers and economisers on the insured's premises as this is one of the standard perils included in business interruption policies issued in respect of premises in Great Britain and Northern Ireland. For insurances where additional perils such as those described in Chapter 14 are included in the same policy as that for the standard perils the appropriate charges are added to either the basis rate or the business interruption rate (see paragraph 257).

Of recent years with the benefit of scientific methods of assessing the interruption risk—which is often not really related to the material loss hazard as reflected in the fire insurance rates—more sophisticated methods of premium rating have been introduced. Following the introduction of methods using statistical information (see paragraph 256(a)) an increasing number of insurances of all sizes were being allocated basis rates which were a departure from the traditional method described above. These included a wide miscellany of light and heavy engineering works and other factories the fire insurances of which were dealt with under what was called the Metal Workers Tariff.

(b) *Base rate (United States)*

For a straightforward coverage in the United States the general system of rating is to take as the base rate the 80 per cent. coinsurance direct damage rate applicable to the insured's *building*. These fire insurance rates, with reductions for sprinkler installations also shown, are given for all business premises in the rating handbook published by the Surveying & Rating Bureau of each major city or territory. There are a few variations from this method such as in the New York Metropolitan territory where the base rate is derived from the *contents* direct damage rate of the insured's premises as in most U.K. insurances.

255. Rate of premium

(a) *United Kingdom*

The rate of premium charged varies according to the length of the maximum indemnity period, on a sliding scale, as well as taking into account the hazards arising from the particular perils insured for each individual risk. In general any loss of turnover will be heaviest in the weeks or months immediately after the damage and will gradually grow lighter in subsequent months as steps are taken to restore the facilities for trading. It is equitable therefore to charge relatively higher rates of premium for short indemnity periods and progressively lower ones for longer periods. This is the accepted practice and it is put into effect by means of a rating table (paragraph 256(a)) which prescribes for different maximum indemnity periods a certain percentage of the "basis rate" applicable to any particular case.

Although the rate for a six months indemnity period may appear lower than that for an indemnity of 12 months it is not so. The rates are applied in both cases to an annual figure of gross profit but with the exception of seasonal businesses or the contingency of damage occurring twice in one year the maximum amount recoverable under a six months indemnity is approximately only half of that under a 12 months indemnity period.

(b) *United States*

The rate of premium in the United States varies according to the coinsurance percentage chosen. This is usually in a range of 50 per cent. to 80 per cent. but 100 per cent. or even 125 per cent. is found in certain circumstances (when the period of interruption is likely to be very long).

256. Rating table

(a) *United Kingdom insurances*

Apart from cases to which individual consideration is given inability to make provision for the interruption risk of each business is met to some extent by a method of differential rating according to the length of maximum indemnity period selected. This allows the insured to adjust the premium to suit their own opinion of the interruption hazard of their business, of which they may be presumed to have expert knowledge. In this way they come to be in the position of an underwriter, to some extent, although the privilege also carries the possibility of the insured suffering loss should damage take place and the period of interruption exceed the length of the maximum indemnity period. In U.S. insurances the coinsurance clause fulfils a similar purpose by allowing insured to use their own judgment as to the potential length and degree of the interruption risk for their own business. Because of the much wider experience of insurance brokers and company officials their advice on this matter can often be very helpful although it must be appreciated that any suggestion from them can only be of an advisory nature the final choice being entirely the responsibility of the insured.

The following standard rating table shows the percentage loading of the basis rate for different maximum indemnity periods. This gives the "business interruption rate" or "profits rate" which is applied to the sum insured on gross profit in most insurances, the main exception being engineering business interruption (accident) insurance (see Chapter 15).

RATING TABLE

MAXIMUM INDEMNITY PERIOD	CONSEQUENTIAL LOSS RATE	SUM INSURED REPRESENTING NOT LESS THAN
6 months	110%	the annual amount of gross profit
9 ″	130%	″ ″ ″ ″ ″ ″
12 ″	150%	″ ″ ″ ″ ″ ″
15 ″	145%	$1\frac{1}{4}$ times ″ ″ ″ ″ ″ ″
18 ″	140%	$1\frac{1}{2}$ ″
21 ″	$133\frac{1}{3}$%	$1\frac{3}{4}$ ″
24 ″	125%	twice
30 ″	120%	$2\frac{1}{2}$ times
36 ″	115%	3 ″
48 ″	110%	4 ″
60 ″	105%	5 ″
72 ″	100%	6 ″
exceeding 72 months	95% of a corresponding multiple of the above	

It will be seen from the rating table that the business interruption rates decrease for maximum indemnity periods longer than 12 months. This does not mean that the premiums are also lower. The sum insured has to correspond with the longer period; that is to say, if the insurance provides compensation for up to 24 months after any damage then the sum insured must represent the estimated amount of gross profit for two years. The effect of this is that although the actual rate per cent. is lower than that for a maximum indemnity period of 12 months the premium payable is higher because of the larger sum insured. This can be clearly seen from the following illustration, using a hypothetical sum insured of £1 million and a basis rate of 0·125 per cent.

MAXIMUM INDEMNITY PERIOD	SUM INSURED	CONSEQUENTIAL LOSS RATING	ANNUAL PREMIUM
			£
12 months	£1,000,000	150%—·187	1,870.00
18 months	£1,500,000	140%—·175	2,625.00
24 months	£2,000,000	125%—·156	3,120.00

For purposes of quick calculations to compare the premium cost for different indemnity periods it may be noted from the above that the annual premium for an 18 months maximum indemnity period is one-and-two-fifths of that for a 12 months maximum indemnity whilst for a 24 months period it is one-and-two-thirds the amount of that for a 12 months indemnity.

(b) *United States insurances*

For gross earnings coverages, the rates were calculated as follows:

	Percentage of 80% building rate	
Coinsurance percentage required for gross earnings insurance	Gross earnings— mercantile form	Gross earnings— manufacturing form
50%	80%	90%
60%	70%	80%
70%	65%	75%
80% and over	60%	70%
Pacific coast only—100%	—	64%

For Business Income Coverage the rates are calculated by multiplying the base rates (usually 80 per cent. building rates) by the appropriate factor. The following table sets out rate factors for Business Income (and Extra Expense) Coverage.

Coinsurance percentage	Non-manufacturing rate factor	Manufacturing rate factor
No coinsurance	2.50	2.65
50	1.00	1.15
60	0.90	1.00
70	0.80	0.95
80	0.75	0.90
90	0.70	0.85
100	0.65	0.80
125	0.60	0.70

The apparent increase in rating no doubt reflects the broader automatic cover provided by the Business Income Coverage form.

257. Premium rating for certain extra perils (United Kingdom)

As explained in Chapter 14 the standard business interruption policy can be extended to include loss occasioned by a variety of additional causes of damage called "special perils". In the case of a number of these, notably storm, flood, sprinkler leakage, collapse of boilers, impact of road vehicles, failure of electricity, etc., supplies, and prevention of access it is recognised that the interruption of a business caused by them is unlikely to last very long. Therefore when such special perils are added to an insurance the additional premium charged is the same for any maximum indemnity period less than 12 months as would be charged for a 12 months indemnity.

For a period longer than 12 months the premium rate is so reduced proportionately as to make the actual premium payable the same as it would be were the maximum indemnity period 12 months.

258. Lower rate where automatic sprinklers are installed

A special discount is allowed in the United Kingdom for an insurance relating to a business carried on in buildings protected by an approved system of automatic sprinklers. In the calculation of the basis rate the premium for the fire insurances on the contents of buildings so protected is with certain exceptions brought in net, that is, after deduction of the discount for the sprinkler installation. This discount allowed under a fire insurance is in recognition of the efficiency of sprinklers in extinguishing or at any rate confining many outbreaks of fire. But it has to be recognised that in doing this a considerable amount of damage to machinery and stock often results from the water discharged from the sprinkler heads. The time element saved in respect of interruption of business which accrues from the operation of automatic sprinklers generally outweighs the loss stemming from the damage caused by the discharge of water. This factor is provided for in the calculation of the basis rate for the business interruption insurance by a deduction of a further special discount from the balance remaining after the normal discount has been allowed, subject to a minimum rate limit; it is not applicable to film studios.

When riot, etc., cover is added to the fire insurance in respect of a building or its contents protected by an installation of automatic sprinklers, for most classes of premises the premium otherwise payable for the extension is considerably reduced in recognition of the fact that incendiarism is a major part of the risk of damage by persons taking part in riots or other disturbances or acting maliciously and of the value of a sprinkler installation in this respect. When a business interruption policy for such premises is extended to include riot, etc., risk (see paragraph 289) a similar concession applies to the additional premium.

259. Premium discounts for deductibles

A discount will be granted for deductibles arranged at the insured's request. The size of the discount will vary depending on the extent to which losses will be avoided or reduced but it is influenced by most underwriters' insistence that the effect of a deductible is not necessarily as beneficial for business interruption as it may be for property damage and it may cause difficulties as described in paragraph 244(b). The discount offered may not, therefore, be attractive enough for an insured to accept.

260. Premiums for excess indemnity periods

Excess (maximum) indemnity periods are written by some specialist underwriters as a contingency second "layer" above or beyond the maximum indemnity period stated in the original policy. The premium is based on the calculated exposure (maximum probable loss) for the excess period and much depends on the particular risk.

CHAPTER 13

Special Forms of Insurance—Separate Items or Policies

Most business interruption insurance specifications contain a main item on gross profit with perhaps a further item insuring wages by one method or another as being the essentials of such an insurance. There are, however, a number of other items which can be added or which may sometimes form the sole subject of a specification, and details of the more usual of these are given in this chapter.

261. Contractual liabilities

(a) *Fines or damages for breach of contract*

Although a loss of this nature may be a consequence of damage it is not covered under an insurance on loss of gross profit because it cannot be measured by the reduction in turnover nor is it an increase in cost of working.

In certain trades the delivery of goods to the customer by a due date is a very important feature and in the contract of sale or services a provision is made for the payment of a fine or damages in the event of non-fulfilment by the agreed date. This position often applies in sections of the engineering, printing, textiles, clothing and similar industries, in building construction and in certain Government contracts. Where there is a liability of this kind and there is no *force majeure* clause in the contract providing for its cancellation in the event of fire or other perils covered under an insured's business interruption policy, it is advisable to arrange for the latter to give appropriate protection. This can be effected by a separate item on the specification which under the heading "on fines or damages for breach of contract" reads:

> "The insurance under this item is limited to fines or damages for breach of contract and the amount payable as indemnity thereunder shall be such sums as the Insured shall be legally liable to pay and shall pay in discharge of fines or damages, incurred solely in consequence of the Incident, for non-completion or late completion of orders".

The amount for which a firm may be liable in respect of fines or damages will vary from time to time according to the contracts in hand and their state of completion. The potential loss is not the total of the liability which accrues throughout the course of a year on all the contracts undertaken in that period but the maximum liability which might arise at any one point of time. In estimating what this loss might be, allowance can be made for the possibility of getting work done by other firms in order to fulfil contracts. The additional cost of doing so will be met under the increase in cost of working section of the insurance on gross profit, within the terms and limitations of that section, because it will produce turnover which otherwise would have been lost. But the fines or damages will not rank for payment as additional expenditure because they are not incurred to minimise the interruption of the business.

As any loss under such an item will be most likely to arise in the period immediately after the damage a heavier premium rating applies than for the insurance on gross profit which carries a diminishing incidence of loss over a lengthening period. The sum insured is bound to be an arbitrary figure and so the breach of contract item is not subject to pro rata average.

Where an insured's product is, for instance, machinery to be delivered under a contract with a penalty clause the business interruption policy should be extended to cover the risk during transit of consignments.

The U.S. coverage on gross earnings makes no specific reference to loss due to fines or damages for breach of contract although such loss is excluded by the description of the cover as mentioned in paragraph 61, but the Canadian form makes a point of excluding it as shown in Appendix R, paragraph 464.

(b) *Cancellation charges for components or services under contract*

Manufacturers of motor cars and vehicles, aircraft, refrigerators, washing machines, television sets and various domestic consumer goods do not make all the components which go into the finished products. Supplies of the components made to specific designs are obtained under contracts with firms who specialise in making such goods. Should damage interfere with production at the factory of the principal firm, acceptance of the components on order at the time might possibly be deferred until the restoration of the business is sufficiently advanced for delivery to be accepted. But in these industries there is usually a change in design of their products or at least some parts or fittings for them every year or so and it may be that when the factory is rehabilitated, so much time has elapsed that production of a new model is due. This means that the components ordered before the damage occurred will probably be unsuitable for the new products. Any stock already made by the component manufacturers and still on their premises being unsaleable to other firms for whose products it is not designed, will have to be disposed of as scrap. As this stock was not on the principal's premises where the fire occurred and is undamaged no claim will be possible under a fire insurance policy.

On the other hand, although it is a loss resulting from the damage it is not recoverable under the gross profit item of a business interruption policy. Such an insurance of the principal manufacturer will pay on the loss of turnover the insured rate of gross profit but this will not include the value of the

CONTRACTUAL LIABILITIES   **261**

redundant components because they are not a standing charge. Neither can they be claimed for as increase in cost of working because paying their cost would be an expense which would not contribute towards maintaining turnover after the damage.

So unless there is an escape clause in the contract the loss will fall on the principal manufacturer and should be insured against under an item similar to one covering fines or damages for breach of contract (paragraph 261(a)) appropriately amended to include vendors' cancellation charges as, for example:

> "The insurance under this item is limited to loss, cancellation charges, or fines or damages for breach of contract and the amount payable as indemnity thereunder shall be such sums as the Insured shall be legally liable to pay and shall pay in discharge of contracts to purchase, cancellation charges, or fines or damages for breach of contract, in consequence of the Incident in respect of contracts for the purchase of goods or services which cannot be utilised by the Business during the Indemnity Period less any value to the Insured of such goods or the amount received from the sale of same".

(For a more comprehensive form of cover on depreciation in value of components refer paragraph 269(b)).

A somewhat similar position may apply with clothing and garment manufacturers who purchase cloth and dress materials, etc., under advance contract although in these trades it might be possible to sell such materials on the open market without undue loss.

The organisers of travel tours incur liability for hotel accommodation which is booked by them long in advance of the holiday season. In the event of interruption of their organisation resulting from damage at their own premises or those of the printers of their brochures to which their business interruption insurance has been extended (see paragraph 367) preventing them from filling the accommodation booked, they will have to pay hoteliers for their breach of contract. The risk can be insured against by means of an item of the nature described above.

(c) *Liquidated damages—delay in completion of construction contract*

Liquidated damages for contract delay differ from fines and damages (penalties) in that the amount is agreed upon beforehand as a reasonable estimate of the loss that would be caused by the delay and only liability can be disputed. In U.K. practice a building contractor may be granted an extension to the construction period by the architect and thereby avoid the payment of liquidated damages to the employer. Clause 22D of the current standard J.C.T. (Joint Contracts Tribunal) contract compensates the employer for loss of the liquidated damages in such circumstances but only as a consequence of loss or damage caused by the operation of specified perils. Such compensation is provided by a specialist form of insurance which the employer can elect to have or not to have.

In fact an advance profits cover (refer paragraph 268(a)) might well be more beneficial in that it compensates for ongoing loss of business that might arise as a result of damage and does not confine itself merely to the period of actual delay in construction time.

262. Entertainment undertakings: special position regarding artistes' fees

In the entertainment world the proprietors of a dance hall, night club, discotheque, restaurant, cabaret, theatre or concert hall, and radio and television companies, may be legally liable to a disc jockey, a band leader, or producers of shows, or direct to the artistes for the payment of their fees or for a stipulated minimum if the performances for which they are engaged cannot take place due to fire, water or other damage at the premises.

In these cases it is advisable to consider which is better, to insure the total amount of the fees payable in a year in the item on gross profit as being a standing charge and thereby ensure that the artistes recover the full amount of their fees whether the interruption of the business is either total or only partial, or to insure under a separate item an arbitrary figure to cover only legal liability for non-fulfilment of contracts. Where the total of the fees is small in relation to the annual amount of gross profit, as in the case of an orchestra at an hotel or restaurant it might be considered best to insure them in the gross profit.

However, for theatres, clubs and dance halls such fees may represent a very substantial part of the revenue of the business. Whilst payment is generally in the form of a fixed fee plus a percentage of box office takings it is sometimes arranged in showbusiness solely as a percentage of box office receipts at a rate which may be as high as 50 per cent. The cost of insuring the annual amount of fees as a standing charge, particularly if there is a long maximum indemnity period, might appear prohibitive.

When the fees are solely a percentage of box office takings they will reduce proportionately with any fall in revenue following damage and so are a variable charge which may be thought unnecessary to insure. But the problem is complicated for undertakings in which a variety of productions and artistes are booked in the course of a year under contracts with differing conditions as to fees, some of which will not be within the knowledge of the proprietors when the insurance is arranged.

Furthermore, there is an important point to be considered in all these cases; possible liability under contract for a minimum payment. This might apply to a much shorter period than the maximum indemnity period of the insurance on gross profit or revenue, being limited generally to the notice period in the contract.

Some contracts may contain a *force majeure* clause cancelling the contract in the event of the premises being closed because of fire or other stipulated perils. But such an escape clause may apply only in the event of complete closure and thus leave the proprietors open to loss in respect of fees in the event of partial damage if the premises remain in use but with reduced seating capacity. Damage by fire, water or extinguishing operations might render an area of auditorium seating, some boxes, or a complete circle unusable for a period and the establishment might then remain open to the public and continue its planned programme of entertainment. But apart from fees payable to artistes on the basis of box office takings other fees would have to be paid at normal amounts irrespective of contract although the revenue would be reduced because of the damage.

Because of factors such as the foregoing it is impossible to generalise on insurance and each case must be considered individually in the light of its *modus operandi* and the terms of the contracts entered into. One way to arrange an insurance would be to cover fees under a separate item from that on gross profit and for a shorter maximum indemnity period. Another method would be to insure the fees only for the legal liability under contract under a cover similar to an item on fines or damages for breach of contract explained in paragraph 261(a) with a sum insured representing the maximum amount due under breach of contract at any point of time in the year. The completely safe way is to include the full amount of the fees in the gross profit cover.

263. Rent receivable

(a) *Cover*

Many manufacturing and trading concerns receive revenue from letting buildings or parts of buildings owned by them or from sub-letting those leased by them. This revenue is not part of their trading turnover and although it appears in their profit and loss account it is really revenue obtained from a separate business, that of property owners. In cases where the rents received are, relatively speaking, quite small it may be more convenient and satisfactory to insure against loss resulting from damage by fire and kindred perils by including them in the sum insured and cover in respect of gross profit under a business interruption policy. Otherwise it is advisable to insure rental income either under a fire property damage policy or by means of a separate item or policy on a business interruption form. The pros and cons of the respective covers are discussed in the following paragraph 263(c) and insurance cover for investment companies, etc., is further dealt with in paragraph 267.

Including the amount of rents receivable in the sum insured on gross profit requires also adding "property owners" to the description of the insured's business, including the address of the premises which are let, amending the definition of turnover to include rents received or receivable and adding a form of departmental memorandum (paragraph 380). The last mentioned is to ensure that the rate of gross profit for rents, possibly approaching 100 per cent., will be used for purposes of a claim calculation instead of an average rate calculated over trading gross profit and rental income combined which may be nearer 25 per cent.

In the United States the new Business Income Coverage form has automatic inclusion of loss of rental income (or value) when it is part of the business of the insured (see work sheet—paragraph 234(b)). The form can also be used without amendment to protect those insured whose business income is entirely derived from rentals.

(b) *Rent receivable—details for insurance*

Where rent receivable is the sole subject of a proposal for insurance as in the case of a property investment company it can be insured as the only item under a U.K. business interruption (gross revenue type) policy or under a number of items each in respect of different properties. Where it is only incidental to the main business of a trading concern it can be insured as a separate item on the same specification as that for an insurance on gross profit and wages.

The definition of rent receivable is varied to suit the particular circumstances of each case and the address of the property or description of the portions of the property to which the insurance applies must be stated either in the schedule of the policy or in the specification. The premium ratings are those shown in paragraph 256(a) according to the maximum indemnity period selected, the basis rate being the average fire rate for the property or separate properties which are the subject of the insurance.

The sum insured on rent receivable should be the estimated future gross annual amount expanded to correspond with the number of years in the maximum indemnity period when this exceeds 12 months. Suitable allowance must be made for likely rent reviews (which can be every three years). An average proviso applies to the insurance and in the event of there being underinsurance at the date of damage occurring, based on figures adjusted under an "other circumstances clause", only a proportion of any loss would be recoverable.

A return of premium clause is included on the specification so that a refund of premium can be obtained in the event of any portion of the premises being unlet during the course of an insurance year. This clause also allows a margin of overinsurance to be carried without its costing unnecessary premium to provide for upward trends in the amount of rent receivable.

The rent referred to in the foregoing paragraphs is generally payable to the property owner under a lease running for a fixed period of years. Should the property be destroyed by an insured peril the owner can recover under a loss of rent insurance the amount by which payments to him by the lessor are reduced during the indemnity period. But if the expiry date of the lease falls within that period he will suffer further loss insofar as the rents payable to him would have been increased under the terms of a new lease. This additional loss may be taken care of by the provision in the other circumstances clause in the specification for adjustments to be made to the amounts of rent receivable.

(c) *Advantages of business interruption cover over fire policy on rent*

It is usually a little cheaper to insure against loss of rent under a fire policy rather than under a business interruption policy but the advantages of insuring it under the latter justify the difference in premium. The indemnity under a fire policy is limited to the loss of rents during the time when the damaged premises are unfit for occupation whereas under a business interruption policy the cover extends to the further period after the premises are rebuilt and ready for occupation, but unlet, up to the limit of the maximum indemnity period. The latter need not be limited to 12 months; in fact it is generally considered desirable to insure for a longer period because the possibility of continuing the business in alternative accommodation does not enter into the question in the way it does with a trading concern. The choice of the maximum indemnity period depends almost entirely on the time which it is estimated it would take to to clear the site, obtain permits from the local authorities and planning committees and the period required for actual rebuilding and refurbishing with lighting, heating, lifts, etc., plus—and this is very important—any further time that might be necessary for re-letting.

A further advantage of the cover under a business interruption policy is the provision made for additional expenditure such as temporary repairs, overtime wages for employees of builders and other tradesmen, and advertising, incurred to reduce the period of interference with normal occupation of the premises.

In the case of industrial property in which there is a steam boiler the inclusion of loss resulting from damage caused by boiler explosion, which is part of the cover provided under the standard business interruption policy, is an added point in favour of insuring rent receivable under the latter in preference to doing so under a fire policy.

For insurances where the premium is sufficiently large to justify it, a return of premium clause can be included which is useful for multiple tenancy premises in which some portions are frequently unlet for periods and also during a time of trade depression when buildings may be untenanted.

264. Rent for room and power

In some parts of the United Kingdom notably in the textile areas of Lancashire and Yorkshire portions of what are termed "estate mills" are let to different tenants for manufacturing purposes at an inclusive rent for "room and power". This includes the supply of power and heat and often of lighting from the mill or estate boiler house and power house. A somewhat similar position applies in some of the trading estates or parks in industrial development areas, where factories on such estates are supplied with heat from space heating and for process work, and sometimes also with electricity, from an estate boiler house. In such cases it is advisable for the owners of the premises to insure under a business interruption policy the full amount of the rents receivable and to arrange this with a maximum indemnity period long enough to provide both for rebuilding the premises and the installation of new plant for steam raising and motive power.

The advantageous nature of the cover provided under a business interruption insurance compared with that of a fire policy is enhanced with premises of this kind. In the event of destruction of or damage to the estate boiler and power house heavy expenditure may be necessary on the provision of temporary alternative supplies of heat, power and light or to speed up a restoration of the normal services. Alternatively, considerable reductions in rent may have to be made to tenants during the period when they are deprived of these essential supplies for which they have paid an inclusive rent. As the various tenants' portions of the mill or factories on a trading estate would not be unfit for occupation during that time no claim could be sustained by the landlords for the loss of rent had this been insured under a fire policy nor could they recover under such a policy for the additional expenditure incurred. On the other hand a business interruption policy covering the rent receivable would compensate for both.

265. Municipal authorities—rates insurance

In addition to insuring against loss of rents receivable from property owned by them municipal authorities can also insure against loss of revenue in respect of rates on buildings, whether owned by the municipal authority or not, resulting from damage by fire and other perils to property in a central area or to a large works in the borough. A conflagration in a city centre is always a possibility and the subsequent loss of rates might be really serious; the destruction of a shopping complex, hypermarket area or even of a single very large department store or manufacturing premises could entail a substantial loss of rates.

266. Other covers for property owners and lessors

(a) *Investment value and lease owners' indemnity*

Occasionally a local authority will refuse to permit the reinstatement of a damaged building either at all or as it was before. This can lead to a reduction in the investment value of the property—to nil, if rebuilding is prohibited. Cover is obtainable in respect of this exposure the loss being the whole of the investment value in the event of the absolute refusal by the competent local or government authority to allow the reconstruction of the premises following destruction or damage. In the event of the competent local or government authority allowing partial reconstruction only of the premises after destruction or damage the loss will be the difference between the investment value after such reconstruction and the investment value before the destruction or damage. Any compensation received from the authority and any payment under a material damage policy must be deducted. The investment value must be certified by a competent practising Valuer (who must be a member of the Royal Institution of Chartered Surveyors and agreeable to both sides) as being the open market value of the property full let.

Similarly the owner of a lease can be insured against the loss in value of his asset when the property cannot be reinstated following damage.

(b) *Leasehold interest cover—United States*

Loss may be suffered by a lessee of property in the event of its being damaged or destroyed by fire or other perils if he is obliged under the terms of the lease to continue rent payments even though the property is unusable and is unable to obtain a lease on similar property suitable to his business on comparable terms. The Business Income Coverage form can be used to cover the unavoidable continuing payments.

Under a U.K. policy covering loss of gross profit an insured who has to continue business in other premises at higher rent during the indemnity period will be indemnified for the additional rent under the increase in cost of working provisions of clause (b) up to, but not beyond, the maximum indemnity period insured. Under a U.S. coverage if similar indemnity is obtained by the expenses to reduce loss extension of the policy the period during which this is payable will be limited to such length of time as would be required to restore the damaged property.

Because the damaged property may not be rebuilt or for some reason not reoccupied by an insured and the extra rental at the premises to which the business has removed continue to be payable a special "Leasehold Interest Coverage form" is issued by U.S. insurers to cater for this situation. This undertakes to pay during the unexpired term of the insured's lease the amount by which the intrinsic rental value of the damaged property exceeds the rent which was payable under the lease. That is, it is recognised that the lease was at the time of the damage of more value monetarily than its face value because the insured will have to pay more for another lease elsewhere.

267. Property investment companies, etc.

(a) *Rent insurance on existing property*

In the case of businesses of property owners or the trustees of charities and pension funds with large investments in property the need for an insurance to protect their revenue is obvious and similarly with trading estates and municipal authorities owning large blocks of commercial and industrial properties.

Where the terms of the leases used require tenants to accept liability for the continued payment of rent when premises are damaged and to cover it by insurance for a stated period of months from the date of a fire, the insurance effected by the owners under a business interruption policy on loss of rents receivable can be so arranged that the indemnity will commence to operate only from the end of the tenants' period of liability. For example, the maximum indemnity period considered as adequate by the owners for their insurance on loss of rents might be three years but would not commence until six months from the date of any damage because the tenants had been obliged under the terms of their leases to insure for that initial period. Some reduction in the normal premium for the owners' insurance is given to compensate for this deferment of the commencing date of the indemnity period.

Property leases vary considerably in their terms especially in relation to cesser clauses and provision for a proportionate reduction in rent if due to damage the premises are capable of being only partially used for the purposes of a business. In North America it appears, as in the United Kingdom, that there is no such thing as a standard lease. Leases come in all shapes and sizes, whilst the terminology in some is clear and in others confusing. The terms concerning payment of extra charges such as maintenance, public and private utilities, heating, insurance, etc., may have to be taken into account—they may even be in a separate lease—in arranging a loss of rent insurance. Hence, the negotiation of such cover should not be made without full knowledge of the terms of any relevant lease, which may involve consultation with the lawyer; and the wording of the insurance policy should be scrutinised to ensure that no loopholes are left.

The terms of the normal specification used in the United Kingdom for landlords to insure against loss of rent receivable are very wide in scope and would appear to cater for most contingencies. (For other details see paragraph 263(b).)

(b) *Anticipated income—property development*

Very large sums of money are invested in the construction of multi-storied office and apartment buildings and during the period of construction no rental income can be earned. But payments on account must be made to the building contractors and these mean either loss of interest on the capital outlay or the payment of interest on loans or mortgages. Such loss will be subsequently made good when the property is completed and either sold or leased. If damage occurs during the construction and delays the completion date there will be further loss, not budgeted for, in respect of the extended period of weeks or months before completion of the building to a state ready for sale or letting.

Consequently, it is advisable to insure against the potential loss of rent due to a deferment of the completion date caused by insurable perils (which will not include labour disputes or strikes) whether or not parts of a building have already been leased, on a basis agreed with insurers to cover anticipated rent on lines similar to an Advance Profits Insurance (see paragraph 268(a)). Although during construction such buildings appear to be all incombustible steel, concrete and glass there is always a danger of storm damage and also a high fire risk during the final stages when various trades' workers are operating in the building; serious damage at such times is not unknown. If the property is to be sold, there will be an exposure to loss of use of the money to be obtained from the sale. This money would be used to repay capital borrowed and for further investment. Covers are obtainable which measure the insured's financial loss in terms of the interest which they would have received on the proceeds of the sale of the property during the indemnity period.

Whether the anticipated income is in the form of rents or the proceeds of sale, definitions of terms used in the policy and specification need to be precise. For example, in the event of delay caused by serious damage during the construction period a claim can only be paid after insurers have satisfied themselves that there existed an agreement to let or sell the property to a prospective tenant or purchaser. If no such agreement existed then the services of a Professional Valuer (on the same basis as for loss of investment value (see paragraph 266(a))) must be obtained so as to estimate the rent or selling price the insured would have been paid but for the delay. In the case of an intended sale, indemnity would be based on the application of a percentage of interest per annum (defined in the policy) to the proposed (and agreed) selling price pro rata for the length of the indemnity period.

There are usually three alternative definitions of indemnity period depending on whether at the time of the damage there was a known prospective tenant (or purchaser) or not and whether the construction of the property was complete or not. Commencement of the period of indemnity is usually delayed until the date upon which the property would have been let or sold to a known tenant or purchaser, or until the date upon which the construction contract would have been completed if there is no known tenant or purchaser. However, when construction is complete and there is still no prospective tenant or buyer the indemnity period commences with the occurrence of the damage. (See specimen Interest specification wording—paragraph 462, Appendix P.)

268. Covers for new and extended businesses

(a) *Advance profits insurance (United Kingdom)*

Behind the construction of a large modern factory lie months of research, planning, budgeting, negotiations, obtaining estimates, placing orders and signing contracts for buildings, plant and machinery, the advance engagement of key staff and a hundred and one other matters before the actual work of construction starts. But everything will be geared to a completion date on which the factory is to start ticking over and earning the outlay on the capital invested in it and the loss of interest on that capital or interest paid on loans and the overhead expenses which have been building up during the period of construction.

Any intervention which delays the start-up date means a considerable loss through deferment of production and sales and this could be greatly increased if a competitor engaged on preparations to put a similar product on the market gets into production first and captures part or all of an insured's anticipated share of it. Much can happen to cause delays that is not covered by penalty clauses in contracts. Hence the advisability of insuring against all insurable contingencies which might delay the completion of a new factory or major extension of an existing one, covering loss on the basis of turnover which it is planned to achieve commencing on the date when production should start. In the United Kingdom this is called "Advance Profits Insurance".

The serious implications of new factory construction are well illustrated by the following remarks made by the chairman of the *Daily Mirror* at the annual general meeting following the fire at their new building on February 12, 1960. He said:

> "We have had two pieces of bad luck. Our new building in Holborn Circus was damaged by a fire on the first floor. It is remarkable how much there is to burn in a half-finished concrete building. In our case some £250,000 material damage was done in two hours and, more important for us, the completion of the building was put back six months. Some months afterwards our new photogravure press in Southwark caught fire. The material loss done seems to have exceeded £200,000 and involves a delay of five months before we shall have the use of this important new machine, which with its building and ancillary equipment will have cost £1,000,000".

In general principles and conditions an advance profits policy follows the lines of an ordinary business interruption insurance. But the policy is arranged so as to commence as soon as there is any possibility of an insured contingency causing delay in the start of factory operations which may be as soon as plant and machinery is ordered or construction starts on the site and to end on the estimated date of completion of the first 24 hours of final starting-up test. At that date a normal business interruption policy takes over.

Further, the maximum indemnity period does not commence from the date of interruption taking place during the currency of the policy as it would under a normal policy but commences on the projected starting date of factory operations "the period commencing with the date on which but for the Incident turnover would have commenced . . . ". Should the construction of the factory or the installation of plant and machinery fall behind schedule through causes such as labour disputes not included in the insured contingencies, the policy may be extended at an additional premium to expire on a revised starting-up date, the commencement of the maximum indemnity period being correspondingly deferred.

Reduction of turnover during the indemnity period is used as the index by which the loss is to be measured but because the factory will not have been in production or at any rate not in full production (otherwise a claim cannot arise) it has to be a reduction in anticipated turnover. The rate of gross profit is that "which but for the Incident would have been earned on the turnover during the indemnity period". The standard turnover is that "which but for the Incident would have been earned during the indemnity period" and the annual (or comparative) turnover is "the turnover which but for the Incident would have been earned during the maximum indemnity period immediately following the date on which turnover would have commenced to be earned". An appropriately worded other circumstances clause is bracketed against these definitions commencing: "based upon the estimated production programme of the business and costs and prices relating thereto, to which such adjustments shall be made, etc.".

Increase in cost of working necessarily and reasonably incurred to avoid or diminish a reduction in turnover during the indemnity period is covered as under an ordinary business interruption specification. But because the insured peril must necessarily operate before the commencement of the indemnity period under an advance profits policy the additional expenditure covered can be incurred either prior to or during the indemnity period.

The normal provisions regarding savings in insured charges and expenses and the application of an average proviso are incorporated in the specification wording (refer paragraph 456 Appendix J).

Because of current massive technological developments in industry the introduction of new plant frequently involves unpredictable hazards due to its unique character. In such cases teething troubles are almost certain to arise and insurers may, particularly for chemical works, oil refineries and petrochemical plants, exclude operational and commissioning risks by either the contractors or owners and damage arising from such activities for perhaps a period of seven days after the introduction of feed stocks or until the plant has been satisfactorily operated ready for normal production.

When one considers what contingencies might give rise to a delay in the starting date of a large modern factory it will be realised how wide the scope of a policy of this kind might be. In addition to the ordinary risks of fire, explosion, flood and kindred perils applicable to an established factory is the increased risk to partially fabricated or half-roofed buildings of windstorm damage; the possibility of damage or destruction of plant and machinery while being made at the premises of suppliers or their sub-contractors, which may be overseas and while in transit by land, sea or air; the breakage of plant or machinery during installation or preliminary testing. In fact, the cover generally required is so wide as to combine all the risks normally underwritten separately by the fire, construction, engineering and marine departments of insurance companies. Rating methods vary between insurers but they normally take account of the gradual build up of risk during the construction period, the actual point during the gradual build up when cover is effected, and the application of what is then regarded as a reasonable multiplier to the appropriate basis rate.

Dependent upon the basis on which the premium is calculated for an advance profits insurance insurers may be willing to include a return of premium clause but this will be drafted so as to provide for the fact that during the currency of the cover (which expires on the factory's starting-up date) there will be no gross profit whatever actually earned. Under the clause the amount of gross profit earned during a period commencing with the starting-up of the factory and ending with the number of (working) months in the definition of the maximum indemnity period, *e.g.* 12 or 18, is compared with the sum insured. This differs from the method for a normal business interruption insurance of multiplying the gross profit earned in 12 months by, for instance, one-and-a-half times for an 18 months maximum indemnity period. If the amount earned is less than the sum insured a pro rata return of premium is allowed calculated on the difference, subject to the normal limit of 50 per cent. of the premium paid.

Generally it may be considered unnecessary to add to the specification a separate item on wages because the employees on the payroll prior to completion of the factory and the commencement of a normal business interruption policy will be nearly all key personnel whose remuneration can be included in the item on gross profit. In any case for a large insurance a 100 per cent. payroll cover will almost certainly be arranged.

The basic cover described is capable of being adapted to meet planned phases of development with such circumstances as different sections of a factory being completed and commencing production on different dates with possibly a lengthy period between each successive starting date. But it must be appreciated that if an insured contingency delays the start of production by several months, although during those early months the factory would not have been fully operative irrespective of the damage, the later anticipated full production will be similarly delayed. As a result of such postponement there will be a real loss of full production and the sum insured should be an amount adequate to cover this.

With everything geared for production to start on a certain date supplies of essential raw materials and consumable stores will be arranged well in advance so as to be certain of their availability when required. This may necessitate arranging an advance cover for an extension to the outside premises concerned as is customary with an established business. Similarly insurance may be required against potential loss of turnover due to damage at the premises of customers with whom advance sales contracts have been made (see paragraphs 343 *et seq.*).

Deciding upon the insurance cover for an established industrial unit calls for careful consideration of many relevant factors. In the case of an advance profits insurance the difficulties apparent on gazing in the crystal ball of future possibilities are greatly increased. Hence, more than ordinary care is required to ensure adequate protection and full liaison should take place between a firm's policy makers, financial experts, project controller, works technicians, marketing consultants and others who will be involved in the project, together with their insurance advisers. The last mentioned is vitally important because of the many very special considerations applicable to underwriting advance profits insurance.

A further point to be considered concerns in which department of an insurer an advance profits cover should be written. Because of the breadth of contingencies involved it is possible for a form of advance profits cover to be written in either the fire, construction, engineering or marine departments with a wide range of conditions, exclusions and premium charges. Care must be taken to ensure the insured receives the benefit of the broadest cover necessary and this may entail the sharing of the overall cover between departments.

(b) *Alterations and new building (United States)*

Under this heading a U.S. insurance permits alterations to buildings or the construction of new ones on the described premises and extends the insurance, subject to all its provisions and stipulations, to cover loss due to delay in the commencement of business operations resulting from damage to such buildings during construction or on completion and to building materials, supplies, machinery or equipment incidental to such construction or occupancy whilst on the premises. Loss is calculated from the time when business operations would have commenced had no damage occurred, making it in effect a modified form of Advance Profits insurance (see paragraph 268(a)).

The full wording of the clause used in the gross earnings form is given in Appendix Q. It may be noted that it concludes that it does not waive or modify any of the conditions of the Automatic Sprinkler Clause, if any, attached to the policy. No mention is made of notification to the insurer of any change material to the fire hazard, but it is a condition of the property insurance policy that unless any such change within the knowledge and control of the insured is notified to the insurers the insurance is void.

A further provision of the gross earnings coverage headed Control of Property is that the insurance shall not be prejudiced by any act or neglect of any person (other than the insured) when such act or neglect is not within the control of the insured. It might be deduced from this that an act or neglect of the insured will prejudice the insurance.

This extension is an Additional Coverage under the new Business Income Coverage form (see Appendix S paragraph 465). One difference to be noted is that there is no longer any reference to sprinklers. The Control of Property provision is now found in the Commercial Property Conditions which are in a separate form to be included with the main coverage form (see Appendix S, paragraph 465).

269. Undamaged stock

(a) *"Spoilage" insurance for fruit and vegetable preservers, processors and freezers and for growers*

Special considerations apply to the businesses of fruit and vegetable preservers and processors whose stock being of a perishable nature will depreciate rapidly and probably rot if it cannot be processed due to damage to buildings, plant or machinery at the works.

Unless the stock has been damaged by fire or smoke or by water used in extinguishing operations, which could happen where the stock is in a warehouse, in the open, or in a public warehouse or other storage premises not involved in the fire, the depreciation is not covered by an ordinary fire policy. The business interruption policy applicable to the damaged factory will compensate for the loss of gross profit due to reduction in turnover but the definition of gross profit will not include anything for the loss on unprocessed stock since the stock (purchases) is an uninsured variable expense. This will leave the insured without compensation for the heavy loss in respect of depreciation of the fruit or vegetables which cannot be processed or sold unprocessed at an economic price; it is unlikely that they could rent sufficient cold storage capacity to keep all their stocks until the factory was rehabilitated for normal working.

To meet this contingency a policy can be arranged for the "spoilage risk" to cover the loss sustained in respect of fruit and vegetables which the insured have bought but are unable to use as a result of damage at their premises but excluding any which is itself damaged or destroyed by an insured peril. This latter loss would be compensated under the insured's fire policy. The indemnity provided under the spoilage insurance is limited to:

(i) if a sale is effected of fruit or vegetables which the insured cannot use—the difference between market value and the net price at which they are sold;
(ii) if a sale is not effected—the market value.

From the amount obtained under (i) or (ii) there is deducted any sum saved in respect of transport and handling charges which as a result of the damage are not incurred. Average is applied if the sum insured is less than the total value of all fruit and vegetables which had the damage not occurred would have been delivered to the premises during the 12 months following the date of the damage.

The position is a little different where the stock to be processed is not purchased in the open market but is a crop of fruit or vegetables being grown under contract to the insured. For crops like peas and beans the insured may provide the seed and pay the farmer all other costs of production; for fruit the contract price will probably be an inclusive one. In either case the spoilage insurance will provide an indemnity for the insured's inability to process the crop in the normal way in consequence of damage at the factory the amount payable being the contract price paid for the crop less any savings on handling and transport charges and by sale of the vegetables or fruit.

The need for spoilage insurance applies mainly to fruit and vegetable canners, preserve manufacturers and frozen food businesses but not only to them. For instance, sugar beet factories (and sugar cane factories in areas such as the Caribbean), milk processors and canners, cheese, butter and bacon factories, meat, fish and seafood and similar businesses processing raw materials which are bought under contract and are subject to rapid deterioration are liable to suffer losses of this nature.

In a somewhat similar situation to the foregoing are large-scale growers of fresh vegetables and fruit who do not process their own produce but market it and use sophisticated machinery and processes for packing it for sale. Damage to their premises and plant can mean that they are unable to pack and despatch perishable products to buyers apart from a small proportion which might be packed manually and so growing vegetables and fruit when ready to be harvested will rot. Undamaged by fire the material loss is not recoverable under a fire policy and as the productive costs are a variable working expense not included as part of the grower's gross profit insurance no recovery will be possible under an ordinary business interruption policy. A spoilage insurance should be arranged.

(b) *Depreciation in value of components, etc.*

The insured can also suffer a loss when undamaged stocks of components depreciate in value when their use is delayed or abandoned and they become obsolescent directly as a result of a change in or a cessation of the manufacture of specific types or models of products caused by an interruption of or interference with the business in consequence of insured damage.

The cover which can be obtained relates to:

(i) unused stocks of components on the premises *either* not directly affected by the damage, *or* directly affected by the damage but restored to their pre-fire condition, *or* directly affected by the damage and restorable to their pre-fire condition but not so restored;
(ii) components undelivered at the time of the damage which the insured are under contract to purchase from their suppliers *and* which would

have been utilised by the business during the indemnity period had the damage not occurred *and* which cannot be utilised before or, as far as can reasonably be foreseen, after the expiration of the maximum indemnity period in new or current models as spares.

The amount payable as indemnity under (i) above is the purchase cost of such components less their salvage value, and less (if appropriate) any sums paid or payable in respect of damage under a material damage policy. Under (ii) the amount payable as indemnity is either the purchase cost less salvage or the penalty which the insured is legally liable to pay (see paragraph 261(b)) whichever is the lower.

The same principle can apply to stock other than components which depreciates in similar circumstances.

270. Farming risks

(a) *General*

In 1981, the insurance of farmers' risk in the United Kingdom ceased to be subject to the regulations of the Consequential Loss Committee. It was then possible for those insurers who were members of that Committee to institute their own individual covers and rating bases, and to compete with non-members who were already active in this market.

This led to the creation of a variety of package policies which replaced the previous common methods of insuring farmers—full gross income cover for dairy farmers and additional expenditure only insurance for other farmers—arable, stock, etc. However, it had been realised before package policies emerged that additional expenditure only cover could be inadequate for some modern arable farms where very large, highly specialised machinery was used for harvesting and loading crops and specially designed and constructed buildings, bins and silos were necessary for storage. Such farmers are open to loss of future production not covered by an additional expenditure only policy in the event of fire at certain times of the year. If it is not possible to replace damaged property and machinery in time to avert a failure to harvest or store seasonal crops the sales output of the farm may be seriously affected. In such cases an insurance should be arranged to cover the income from the whole of the farming operations; this will include increase in cost of working in the usual terms to cater for the additional expenditure involved in the resumption of farming operations as quickly as possible.

Where it is considered appropriate to issue an insurance on Increase in Cost of Working only, the customary wording gives an indemnity for:

"the additional expenditure necessarily and reasonably incurred by the Insured during the indemnity period in consequence of the Incident with the object of maintaining during such period farming activities on a scale not exceeding those during the corresponding period in the twelve months immediately preceding the Incident provided that the liability of the Insurer shall not exceed in respect of any one period of three months one quarter of the sum insured".

A typical package policy will provide business interruption cover for the results of damage to buildings, equipment and stock (including growing crops)—reduction in revenue through loss of production, increased expenditure (to hire alternative facilities or other equipment) and the enforced sale of stock. For beef stock, an enforced sale could cause a loss of revenue from anticipated future breeding and rearing. The cover protects against the effect of such losses whether occurring at the farm or other locations such as livestock markets (including transit thereto and therefrom), electricity stations or storage sites. The extension to livestock markets (including transit) is useful as lightning is a standard peril. Cover can also be arranged to insure loss due to electrocution of cattle (see paragraph 304 for details).

A separate section in the package offers optional extra cover relating to business interruption loss following foot and mouth, swine versicular disease (and possibly anthrax), where the indemnity is based upon an agreed percentage of Government compensation.

(b) *Glasshouse complexes*

With more cultivation under glass of all varieties of crops the risk of losing the whole of the crop because of damage caused by severe weather conditions is intensified. If large areas of glass are shattered not only is the crop at the mercy of the wind, rain, etc., and a possible severe drop in temperature but it is also almost certainly going to be ruined by splinters of glass. Recovery from such a disaster could take up to 24 months. More to the point, without the protection of a business interruption policy recovery would be difficult to achieve at all. In addition, the fact that glasshouses are heated by boilers, etc., and their atmospheric conditions often electronically controlled indicates the need for engineering business interruption insurance protection.

(c) *Factory farming, broilers, pig rearers, etc.*

This modern "industry" engaged in the production by intensive methods of eggs, day-old chicks, broiler chickens, turkeys, geese, calves and pigs can be catered for by business interruption policies but the nature of the undertakings and the sensitivity of their stock to a wide variety of perils give cause for several variations in and extensions to the standard policy cover.

Dependence of packing stations, hatcheries and broiler producers upon their own premises and one another and upon electricity supplies and cold stores would normally be insured for business interruption resulting from damage by fire or special perils. But for broiler producers in particular a much more comprehensive form of insurance has been developed by some insurers which provides compensation during a maximum indemnity period of 12 months for loss of revenue and increase in cost of working due to the following contingencies, excluding the wilful act or neglect of the insured and abnormal temperature conditions:

   (a) fortuitous damage by any cause to the buildings, plant, equipment, fuel or feeding stuffs at the premises;
   (b) breakdown of machinery and plant, including lighting and heating equipment at the premises;
   (c) accidental failure of the supply of a public utility;
   (d) violent death of birds (or animals as the case may be) caused by accidental visible external means but excluding loss arising from poisoning or disease;
   (e) loss, destruction or damage caused by theft involving entry to or exit from the premises by forcible and violent means.

There is a limit of compensation calculated per 1,000 bird capacity for broilers, egg production, flock and turkey rearing, per animal capacity for pig rearing and per animal for pig breeding. The amount of any saving in expenses of the business and of any salvage is deductible from the claim and a modest excess is applied to losses other than from contingency (a). The insurance automatically includes costs for removal and disposal of dead birds, etc. The premium is a provisional one adjusted each year end by means of either an additional or return of premium on a declaration of revenue earned.

For intensive rearing industries in general some would advise a maximum indemnity period of 36 months because of the potential long-lasting effects of damage on production and sales.

(d) *Farming in countries outside the United Kingdom*

If no farming risk is standard in the United Kingdom then in countries outside the United Kingdom particularly those subject to extremes of climatic conditions, the diversity of risk is even more complex. Often whole regions, if not whole countries, are dependent for their livelihood on the successful production of certain commodities such as tobacco, tea, sugar, palm oil, coffee, cocoa beans, etc. Basic (if not the whole) production of the commodity from the "harvested" crop is carried out in the vicinity of the growing crop. Destruction of machinery could mean the abandonment of the whole of a season's crop. In some developing countries lack of foreign exchange could delay the replacement of lost machinery for months.

271. Whisky distilleries, wineries, etc.

"Whisky" in Scotland; "Whiskey" produced in Ireland and the United States. Herein spelt as the Scots spell it but its application is universal!

This is an industry which poses its own special problems arising from the feature peculiar to whisky production that after it has been distilled the whisky has to mature for a period which may be as long as 12 years.

To insure for a maximum indemnity period of that order is both impracticable and too costly and as a viable alternative insurers generally recommend, in addition to a normal fire insurance:

(i) a normal business interruption policy on gross profit and payroll with a 24 months maximum indemnity period, applying to both the distillery and the store of maturing whisky;
(ii) an item on accumulated stock value which excludes any whisky which would be due to mature during the 24 months following a fire (loss on such whisky being covered under the gross profit item (i) above) but in respect of other whisky the insurance would pay the difference between the amount paid under the material damage fire policy and the future *matured* value of the whisky destroyed.

To understand how this item would operate assume a warehouse filled with whisky which is to mature for 10 years. If at the end of five years it were destroyed by fire, the fire policy would pay the five-year-old-whisky market value as at the date of the fire. The accumulated stock value item (ii) above would then pay the difference between that amount and the market value of ten-year-old-whisky at the time of the loss. Thus, between the two insurances the distiller would be fully indemnified in respect of loss of the whisky in store. The investment use to which the claims monies can be put will to an extent compensate the insured for a possible loss on the difference between the market value of ten-year-old-whisky at the time of the loss and that at the end of the full 10 year maturing period.

Provision for expenditure on increase in cost of working applies in the normal way to both (i) and (ii) so that if by buying at a premium an insured can replace the partly-matured whisky, which has been destroyed, by a similar aged whisky to continue maturing, the additional expense is paid under the insurance. This expenditure would save the insurers the payment of what would have been an accumulating value over the following years of the whisky destroyed. The insured would receive a stock of partly-matured whisky of the same age as that destroyed and so be assured of continuity of marketing at the date ahead when the lost whisky would have been ready for sale.

Wineries present a similar problem except that provision should be made for the possible declaration of a "vintage" year in which case the value of the wine and the net profit derived from that year will increase considerably. This can be catered for by a special contingency item.

In the United States whiskey and other alcoholic products being aged are included in the definition of "finished stock" in the Business Income Coverage form. This indicates that along with other "finished stock" they are excluded from the cover (refer paragraph 97(c)). However, if there is a coinsurance percentage shown in the Declarations for Business Income they are exempted from the exclusion. The reason given is that the added value of such property will be taken into account when a coinsurance percentage applies. It must be remembered that such products have not really acquired the status of "finished stock" until they have completed their "manufacturing" period and have fully matured.

272. Films, television and radio

(a) *Film production*

This is a specialist area of insurance requiring specialist brokers, underwriters and loss adjusters. A Film Producers' Indemnity policy (known in the United States as Cast Insurance) indemnifies the insured in respect of the additional cost of production consequent upon accident to or sickness of certain named persons—the director and the artistes. An extension is usually available to cover the additional cost of production should fire, etc., damage the studios or the facilities and equipment necessary for production. Certain United Kingdom insurers require a 10 per cent. coinsurance (i.e. a 10 per cent. involvement in the insurance) by the insured in addition to the usual deductible or franchise.

When films are made for the cinema it is often the case that a separate trading company is formed for each film and the cover therefore relates exclusively to that film. Films for television on the other hand are usually less expensive, made more quickly and may be part of a series. In such cases a policy could be issued on an annual declaration basis.

(b) *Commercial television and radio broadcasting companies*

In the United Kingdom broadcasting of television and radio is on a bilateral basis; on the one hand the British Broadcasting Corporation appointed by the Government and financed from licence fees paid by owners of television sets and concurrently the Independent Broadcasting Authority which functions entirely on a commercial basis. Revenue of the IBA is obtained through the ownership of broadcasting stations, masts and equipment in regional areas throughout the country for which they obtain rental for the transmission of programmes produced under a licence by regional independent television companies. The latter, called contractors, obtain their revenue from the sale of viewing and listening time to advertisers for spot advertising (sponsored programmes are prohibited by law) in "natural breaks" in and between programmes and for a limited total of time per day and from selling their productions to other television companies in the United Kingdom and abroad. They may also have a minor source of earnings from videos, records, cassettes and books. Radio broadcasting financed similarly from commercial advertising is carried on by independent radio stations under franchise from the IBA.

The possibilities of serious business interruption loss were shown by the collapse of the transmitter mast at Emley Moor in 1969 which gave rise to claims totalling nearly £1 million under three heads. Yorkshire Television Ltd., lost revenue through lack of facilities for broadcasting, other television companies suffered loss of programme sales to Yorkshire, and the IBA lost rental and incurred increase in cost of working for the erection of a temporary mast.

To meet the special needs of television companies a business interruption policy is issued for fire and normal special perils (or all risks) plus the additional contingency of failure to transmit due to breakdown, collapse of aerial, or failure of the public electricity supply. Depending on the size of the insurance there can be a small excess and in respect of failure to transmit (other than by collapse of aerial) a limit of recovery which may be in excess of £1 million. In addition to the normal policy conditions there are also exclusions of loss due to strikes, rationing of electricity supply, atmospheric conditions, insolvency of the insured or of advertisers, non-appearance of artistes or staff illness and cancellation due to weather.

The insurance is in respect of loss due to damage at the contractors' own studio, office, etc., premises extended to include any IBA transmitter, any telecommunications premises and any other premises used by the insured in connection with the business, this last usually being subject to a limit of 10 per cent. of the sum insured. Gross Profit includes all revenue less discounts and/or rebates, programming expenses and payments to other television companies for programmes. Government levy charges, when chargeable on profits (and not on revenue, as they sometimes are), are in the same category as income tax (paragraph 118) and are included in the cover.

It is generally considered that following the occurrence of any insured contingency a contractor's revenue would be restored to normal in less than 12 months but that increase in cost of working at the insured's own premises (if the damage is at a transmitting site the increase in cost of working would be the responsibility of the IBA) might continue much longer. So it is usual to have a further item on the policy to cover Additional Expenditure beyond that recoverable under the gross profit item, with a maximum indemnity period of 24 months (see paragraph 50). Another item which may be added is on Cancelled Programme Expenses, with an arbitary sum insured, to reimburse money already expended in preparing programmes which owing to an insured contingency cannot be transmitted and would be of no value at a later date.

The operation of television and radio broadcasting services is different in the United States where there are over 1,000 stations, mostly operating on a commercial basis with sponsored programmes, network-affiliated and non-affiliated independent stations, cable television, pay-television, and home video systems, many broadcasting 24 hours a day. Problems and insurance needs however, are similar to those of commercial television companies in the United Kingdom. However, in some areas which are particularly subject to hurricanes, etc. cover in respect of loss following damage to masts, aerials and the like may be excluded. In fact, for Business Income Coverage the Causes of Loss forms (see paragraph 25) carry a special exclusion of "any loss caused by or resulting from direct physical loss or damage to radio or television antennas, including their lead in wiring, masts or towers". Special cover must therefore be arranged for such losses if possible.

It must be remembered that the breadth and detail of cover described in this paragraph are subject to constant review as television broadcasting becomes less subject to complete interruption and further features are introduced such as direct broadcasting by satellite (refer paragraph 274) and cable television.

273. Research and development

Some hundreds of millions of pounds are spent by manufacturers each year on research and development in extensive premises which contain very valuable electronic, laboratory and other equipment, computers, etc., staffed by highly paid scientists, technologists, electronic, design and development engineers and draughtsmen, physicists and chemists. It is indicative of the extent of R. & D. departments that in 1979 the Bayer Group announced that it was employing over 6,000 personnel in such work. Destruction of an R. & D. establishment which may cost many millions could be catastrophic for a business and careful investigation into the possibilities of loss is necessary.

The material cost of rebuilding and re-equipping such premises in the event of its being damaged by fire, explosion or kindred perils will be provided for by a normal fire insurance policy. Such a policy will not, however, give compensation for loss arising from the interruption or suspension of the work carried on and because of the large sums which might be involved the question of how far such loss is or can be insured under a business interruption policy calls for consideration.

In some "R. & D." establishments the work carried out will be mainly the checking of samples of raw materials, work in progress and finished products, or experimental work, quality control and productivity activities of current application. This is an expense which will be borne by the day to day production of the works it serves and because such cost will not reduce proportionately with a fall in turnover following damage by fire at the works it should be included in the insurance on gross profit under the businsess interruption policy applying to the business as a whole. In the event of damage by fire at the works the consequent reduction in the turnover which normally carries such expenditure will then be made good under the insurance on loss of gross profit. Similarly, should damage take place at the research establishment and interfere with factory production the loss of the gross profit out of which the research work is normally paid, or additional expenditure incurred to maintain the laboratory work, will be recovered within the provisions of the business interruption policy of the business provided that the research establishment has been included in the definition of the premises.

The last mentioned is of special importance where prototype plant is being set up because a large volume of future factory production might be dependent upon its results. Destruction in an experimental stage could involve a prolonged delay before restoration of the pilot plant and final application to productive processes; meanwhile a loss of prospective turnover would be sustained. It might possibly be that a competitor engaged on the development of a similar product would gain a lead and be the first to produce it with even greater loss for the insured.

But many extensive establishments are maintained partly or wholly for the purpose of pure or basic research with the object of increasing knowledge in a particular field or of applied research with a view to producing some improved or new product, plant, machinery or process. In addition to this technical research work on the operational side there may be an economic research department engaged in the investigation of markets and long-term forecasting of trends in demand and possibly also a staff college for training personnel. If the cost of maintaining such departments is included, as it should be, in the gross profit insurance either of the policy of the firm which carries the expenditure or of the individual policies of the members of a group organisation where the cost of a central research establishment is debited between them, then, should turnover be reduced because of damage at any of the premises other than the research establishment, an appropriate recovery will be made which will include the cost of continuing the research work.

This still leaves for consideration the problem of loss arising from damage at an actual research establishment in the category described in the preceding paragraph where experimental and pre-production work is done which is unrelated to current work's production. A fire in such premises may seriously interfere with and retard development work of a long-term nature without any adverse effect upon factory production within the customary maximum indemnity period. As a result the loss will not fall within the scope of the business interruption policy of the business. Yet although turnover will continue at its usual level if the works are undamaged and out of this the normal cost of the research establishment and staff will be provided for by turnover in the usual manner the firm may be adversely affected in the following ways.

First, additional expenditure of considerable amount will probably be incurred in obtaining, occupying and equipping temporary premises and in the overtime remuneration of staff. Secondly, if most of the normal costs of maintaining the research establishment continue as they almost certainly will since salaries are a preponderant part but the research work is suspended or retarded, the firm will be paying for unproductive, wasted time and will have to pay again at a later day to achieve the same ultimate results. Lastly, if records of partially or wholly completed research or development projects are lost in the fire further time and labour will have to be expended on making experiments or investigations afresh.

Contingent losses of the foregoing nature not covered by the business interruption insurance of the business can be insured against under a specific item "on research expenditure" (refer paragraph 458 Appendix L for specification wording) or similar descriptive heading appropriate to the particular case, in respect of loss arising from damage at the research establishment as distinct from damage at the factories. The sum insured is the estimated future cost of running the establishment throughout the maximum indemnity period insured. Because the underlying reason for this cover is that such damage will have no measurable effect on sales within a reasonable indemnity period an arbitary method is adopted to arrive at a valuation of the loss. The item undertakes to pay for each working week during which the research work is totally interrupted or totally given over to reworking projects affected by the damage one-fiftieth part of the research establishment expenditure incurred during the financial year before the damage, with an equitable proportion for partial interruption. Suitable adjustment is made where the maximum indemnity period exceeds 12 months.

Additional expenditure necessarily incurred to minimise the interruption is covered on customary lines and similarly an average proviso, a maximum indemnity period and a return of premium clause are included. To provide for new or expanding establishments an "other circumstances clause" is added as on an ordinary business interruption policy, which allows for an adjustment of figures in a claim so as to produce an equitable loss settlement.

274. Satellites—pre-launch

The development of satellite systems circumnavigating the earth is proceeding at an ever increasing pace. Through the agencies of NASA and Arianespace (with probably more to come) we are now able to place complex communications satellites in orbit some 22,000 miles above the surface of the earth where they remain in effect stationary as they keep pace with the earth's revolutions—to the technicians they are therefore geostationary or geosynchronous. The financial outlay of putting them into orbit is enormous but the rewards are equally large, as communications systems become more efficient, in both operation and cost. At the same time the risks involved are daunting, as experience with both Shuttle and Ariane demonstrates.

For the non-aviation business interruption underwriter the cover required relates to the design and manufacture of the satellite, its testing, storage, transit to launchsite, etc., and its immediate pre-launch handling. The premises where damage can cause delay include those of the main manufacturers, the suppliers of components, any storage or testing situations, and the launch-site itself. It is also important that ground stations to be used for tracking, controlling and monitoring the satellites once they are in orbit are functioning at the time of the launch. Transportation of the satellites is a delicate operation, as it can be by road, sea or air, or a combination of all three.

The cover that can be obtained is very much like an advance profits cover (see paragraph 268(a)) the completion date being the precise moment when the satellite in its space vehicle lifts off from the launch pad. The indemnity depends on whether the insured is the maker, the owner or the user of the satellite system and also whether the insured is responsible for the cost of the launch itself, for which there is an increasing penalty exposure as the launch date becomes nearer.

For the manufacturer, the indemnity can be in terms of loss of anticipated income together with a penalty payment if he is responsible for the launch arrangements. For the owner or user the position can be complicated because of possible financial leasing arrangements, government involvement, and the probability that revenue in the early years of the satellite's life will not necessarily cover costs. It may be more relevant to the needs of the owner or user to link the cover to the cost of the project and to relate the indemnity to the additional cost of the project arising out of the delay caused by insured damage. The additional costs can include both the immediate increase in financing charges following damage during the pre-launch period and the payment of fixed charges in what would have been the early post-launch period when income would but for the delay have commenced to be earned. Clearly this is a difficult area of insurance and the underwriter (and broker) must be careful to match the cover to the needs of the insured.

275. Specifications insuring gross revenue

(a) *General*

Whilst the standard form of specification using reduction in turnover as the index by which to measure the after effects of damage is suitable for the majority of businesses there is a simpler form available to insure against loss of earnings which can be recommended for businesses, professional firms, institutions or other concerns in which there is no production and no sale of goods and where all employees' wages are to be included in the insurance. In other words, cases in which the income is derived from the provision of services in which the variable charges are a negligible factor and the insurable gross profit is for practical purposes the same as the turnover and the rate of gross profit can be assumed as being nearly 100 per cent.

The form of specification recommended for such cases adopts as the index of loss reduction in either gross revenue, gross receipts, gross income, gross fees, commission or some similar term.

A specification of this type provides for an insured's loss to be measured by a straight comparison between the amount of the gross revenue, as defined in the specification, earned after the damage with that in the corresponding period in the 12 months before the damage. Provision is made for necessary adjustments by the usual other circumstances clause (paragraph 55(a)) and the cover includes additional expenditure incurred to minimise the loss of revenue. A return of premium clause is added so that the sum insured can be maintained on the top side to provide for anticipated increases in earnings and a refund of premium can be obtained when these fall short of the sum insured. A typical specification is set out in Appendix F, paragraph 452, the references to and definition of gross revenue being altered as may be necessary for any particular case. In all specifications of this kind the usual notes regarding Value Added Tax (see paragraph 118) and Current Cost Accounting (see paragraph 234) are included.

(b) *Specialist services*

A gross income specification might be suitable for almost any concern where the income arises solely from services and not from the sale of goods and where the variable charges are negligible or are excluded in the definition of income. For instance, for consulting engineers and quantity surveyors, the offices of secretarial services, employment bureaux, marketing research specialists, chartered surveyors, realtors, estate agents (with the exclusion of rent collections), auctioneers and valuers, insurance brokers, loss adjusters and appraisers, bond specialists, title companies, analysts, advertising and publicity agencies and travel agents. The last mentioned should have an extension to include loss resulting from damage at the premises of firms producing their travel brochures. (See paragraph 367.)

Dentists, doctors, veterinary surgeons, chiropodists, physiotherapists, clinics and opticians might similarly prefer a gross income specification; it may be advisable in their case to deduct from the income of the practice the cost of materials purchased and to make the definition of gross income correspond.

(c) *Public facilities, etc.*

Other classes of proposer who find the gross revenue form of specification simpler and more suitable than a turnover wording include proprietors of correspondence colleges; art galleries, museums, stately homes and other places of historic or social interest; promoters of exhibitions, trade shows and industrial fairs; conference centres and halls (other than hotels); sports and recreational centres; academies and colleges (hairstyling, beauty, etc.); owners of seaside piers and similar places to which the public pay for admission; schools of ballet, drama and music. In fact almost any concern in which the income is derived solely from services and not from sales. Any cases mentioned above in which some appreciable amount of profit is obtained from the sale of refreshments, guide books, souvenirs, postcards, pictures and other goods are exceptions. In such circumstances sales, the profit on which will not be 100 per cent., like other income would have to be excluded from the definition of gross revenue and if this were done the insurance would not contribute towards any loss of gross profit arising from a reduction in sales. Therefore in such cases a normal turnover specification is necessary to give full protection against loss.

(d) *Commercial or trading businesses*

A gross receipts specification may be issued for commercial or trading businesses in which the earnings are derived entirely from the supply of services; for example, furniture depositories, mini-storage premises, wharfingers, public warehousemen, shipping and forwarding agents, cold stores and bonded stores and possibly bowling alleys and ice rinks. In any case where there are variable expenses of sufficient amount to warrant their exclusion from the insurance, or all wages are not to be insured, this can be effected by an appropriate amendment of the definition of gross receipts.

(e) *Municipal authority departments*

Whilst an additional expenditure only policy is often suggested (see paragraph 278(a)) as suitable for the administrative offices of municipal authorities, more extensive cover is necessary for any revenue earning departments such as those handling public transport, catering, concert and dance halls, swimming pools, abattoirs and seaside entertainments and piers, etc. For these either a normal gross profit specification or one covering gross revenue is advised according to the circumstances, whilst the income received from the ownership of industrial property and public markets should be protected by an insurance on rent receivable (paragraph 263(a)).

(f) *Royalty owners*

A gross revenue specification is the most suitable form of cover for royalty owners who derive income from certain manufacturing processes or products or from the use of machinery incorporating their patents and similarly with lessors of machinery. For such insurances the factory addresses of the firms from whom their income is derived are shown as the premises for purposes of the insurance, as explained in paragraph 363 with regard to manufacturers' agents, for whom incidentally gross commission specifications are recommended.

(g) *Boarding schools*

Gross revenue or gross income policies are also issued to boarding schools but where meals are provided the cost of food for pupils is excluded from the definition as being a variable expense. A special feature of school insurances is that as pupils' fees are paid at the commencement of a school term it is customary to insert a note in the policy stating that should there be any refund of fees in consequence of damage occurring during a school term such refund will be taken into account in arriving at the loss of revenue. In the United States a special coverage is issued for schools and colleges called Tuition and Fees (see paragraph 63(b)).

(h) *Professional men*

For professional men a special "professional men's policy" is provided in a standardised form based on loss of gross fees (or income) with certain additional benefits (see subsequent paragraphs 276(a) and (b)).

(i) *U.S. attitudes*

There is no U.S. coverage on quite the same lines as the gross revenue and other covers described in the foregoing paragraphs and Extra Expense was (and probably still is) usually recommended. The "Earnings (short) form" was in some ways comparable and was suitable for some types of businesses. This is now replaced by the Business Income Optional Coverage of Monthly Limit of Indemnity. The coverage is more restrictive than the U.K. gross revenue insurance inasmuch as recovery is restricted for loss in each consecutive 30 days to a selected fraction of the amount insured. On the other hand the U.K. policies usually incorporate pro rata average whilst the coinsurance condition does not apply to the U.S. coverage.

(j) *Special events—abandonment*

As mentioned in paragraph 275(a) the promoters of exhibitions, trade shows and industrial fairs as well as those running sports and entertainment facilities will find a normal gross revenue form of cover, with a suitable selection of perils, perfectly acceptable. However, there are occasions when a major exhibition in the calendar will represent perhaps 75 per cent. of a promoter's annual income, or a particular sporting event will realise a significant amount of revenue to the organisers. If the exhibition or other event is in the open air a special "pluvius" or "rainfall" policy may be issued (refer paragraph 298), but the cover is by definition narrow and the insured may feel that a wider cover is necessary if the proceeds of the event are to be fully covered. Special contingency covers are available, usually in the Lloyd's market, to protect those proceeds against the abandonment of the event arising out of almost "any cause" other than "war", "nuclear" and other virtually unobtainable perils. As with "rainfall" covers the basis of settlement can be a "valued" amount or a form of gross revenue where there is a measurement of the loss based on the difference between the expected receipts and the actual receipts (if any).

276. Professional men's and other offices policy

(a) *Gross income covered*

Either temporary or permanent loss of a suite of offices and of the records in them can involve accountants, solicitors, lawyers, attorneys, stockbrokers, architects, writers to the signet, consultants and other professional men in serious loss of revenue. Dentists, doctors, opticians, chiropodists and physiotherapists, etc., have been mentioned in paragraph 275(b) with the suggestion of a modified gross income policy because they may supply an appreciable amount of goods as well as their services.

At first consideration it might be thought that work can be carried on in the homes of the staff or at clients' premises or that some facilities will be offered by friends in the same profession and that there will be no loss of gross income. It will be realised on reflection however that the splitting of staffs, the preoccupation of the principals with finding new office accommodation and coping with the disorganisation and the time involved in restoring or replacing lost records as well as the inconvenience of being without them in the interim will all tend to slow down the rate at which work is done for existing clients. Even the lack of office telephones involves delay, if not actual loss of business. All these factors may combine to disrupt perhaps for several months after the damage has occurred, the normal tempo and volume of work on which present earnings and future expansion depend. A glance at paragraph 132 on Office Expenses will bring to mind the wide range of sophisticated equipment, including mini-computers, upon which modern offices are becoming increasingly dependent with a corresponding increase in the potential loss which might result from serious damage.

As blocks of office property increase in area and height the need for this form of insurance increases almost proportionately because a destructive fire could mean that vacant office accommodation available at the time would be quite inadequate to meet the needs of those seeking temporary office suites.

The year or so following damage, while not necessarily recording the loss of any clients will almost certainly show a diminution of earnings if only because everything will be behind time. It will be obvious that the larger the staff the greater will be the dislocation caused by the destruction of the offices. Meanwhile salaries of principals and staff and other overheads have to be met each week or month.

Protection against such a contingency can be obtained by a business interruption policy arranged specifically for professional men to cover loss of gross income—or gross fees if that term is preferred. In general lines it follows a loss of gross profit policy but the specification is simplified by using, instead of reduction in turnover, loss of gross earnings as the yardstick for measuring a loss whilst retaining advantageous features such as the cover for increase of cost in working—which can be very considerable in respect of rent and rates alone when new offices have to be taken in an emergency situation—and the other circumstances clause.

For solicitors in particular a straight comparison of income received in the indemnity period with that in the corresponding months before the damage would not necessarily represent an insured's loss because some work often continues for prolonged periods before being charged to clients. Consequently, the indemnity for loss of gross income is stated as being "the amount by which gross income *earned* during the indemnity period shall in consequence of the damage fall short of the standard gross income". The word "earned" is similarly included in the definitions of annual gross income and standard gross income. This makes it clear that the fees for unbilled work are included in the definition of gross income—"the money paid or payable"— and that it is the reduction in *earnings* for which indemnity is provided.

A useful extension of cover is given without charge to include loss as insured by the policy in consequence of damage (as defined in the policy— except impact) to documents belonging to or held in trust by the insured whilst temporarily at premises elsewhere or in transit anywhere in the country as for instance in hotels or homes or the offices of clients or in the post. Also included without charge is loss due to denial of access to an insured's offices and professional accountants' fees for producing particulars required in the event of a claim.

Another extension of cover available, for which a small extra premium is required, indemnifies for the loss of income or additional expenditure resulting from the temporary loss of telephone and telex facilities due to damage by insured perils at any telephone exchange in a specified area (see paragraph 369).

An item on further additional expenditure beyond that recoverable under item 1, for increase in cost of working, as shown on the usual specification, is an optional item which may be added if it is considered that the cover under clause (b) of item 1, for increase in cost of working, might be inadequate in certain circumstances. (See also following paragraph 276(b) about restoration of records.)

(b) *Professional men—restoration of records*

For most professional men's insurances it is prudent to include an item to cover clerical, legal and other costs (which include materials) incurred in restoring office books, documents, plans, card index sets and similar property which have suffered damage by an insured peril or in extinguishing operations, which latter are often ruinous to the contents of an office.

The wording of this item differs from that for additional expenditure under clause (b) of item 1 on loss of gross income. It does not restrict the payment for expenditure on the restoration of records, etc., to the amount incurred during the indemnity period nor to the expense incurred to prevent loss during that period. In this way it provides for the need which often arises to expend labour on the restoration of documents or records which will not be required during the indemnity period but may be needed in the following year or subsequent years. Such expenditure would not minimise the insured's loss of gross income during the indemnity period but is nevertheless necessary to restore the records and documents which will be needed at some future date. This item generally carries a limit in respect of the charges incurred on any one document, etc., of 5 per cent. of the sum insured by the item and excludes computer systems records.

Similar cover can be added to a fire policy on office contents but the insurance under the item on a business interruption policy is wider in scope because whereas under a fire policy the cover is for materials and labour in rewriting only under a business interruption policy the cost of obtaining the necessary information, that is research, etc., expenses, is included.

277. Architects' and consulting engineers' fees for reinstatement

Following serious damage to premises the services of architects, consulting engineers and quantity surveyors will probably be required in connection with rebuilding and the installation of plant and machinery. Fees for such services do not qualify for payment as additional expenditure under the increase in cost of working provisions of a business interruption policy. Nor are they insurable as are professional accountants' fees in connection with a claim (paragraph 378). Apart from the latter, insurers will not give an undertaking to pay the charges of any other person employed by an insured (as distinct from the fees of loss adjusters appointed by insurers) in connection with the preparation or verification of a claim. The services of architects, etc., are directly related to the material damage reinstatement and if provision for their payment is to be made by insurance this must be by means of appropriate clauses on the fire policy.

278. Additional expenditure only policies

(a) *U.K. policies*

There are many organisations and societies which exist as administrative bodies without engaging in any profit-making activities or are revenue collectors as distinct from revenue earners. For example, such bodies as chambers of trade, chambers of commerce, trade unions, political organisations, municipal authorities and administrative boards, the national headquarters of sports organisations, charitable trusts, animal welfare societies, naturalists' trusts, and various kinds of business, professional, cultural, technological and social organisations.

In the event of serious damage to the offices of such bodies there will usually be little if any loss of revenue; but considerable additional expenditure might be involved in the occupation of temporary premises until those which were damaged are rebuilt or other permanent quarters are obtained and also in the restoration of records. It is customary to insure against loss of this nature the specification being drafted only to cover additional expenditure. This embraces all the various kinds of expense which could arise such as removal expenses, increased rent, rates, lighting and heating, the cost of temporary fixtures, furnishings and decorations and the restoration of records.

The larger the office organisation and accommodation the more essential it is to have cover of this nature because the difficulty and time involved in obtaining a suitable alternative suite of offices increase with the size required. Moreover, it will usually be essential for the administrative work to be continued without break whatever the expense of temporary measures for doing so might be.

The need for similar cover in respect of additional expenditure exists for universities, schools of art, medical and dental schools, colleges of technology, science and further education, state schools, public libraries, art galleries, hospitals, convalescent homes and other institutions. Because the functions of such bodies are much wider than those of administrative offices the insurance should apply not only to their offices but in respect of the whole of their premises and equipment. Should there be any revenue which it is advisable to insure, refer to paragraph 275(a).

The sum insured for a policy covering additional expenditure only is of necessity an arbitrary figure and is not subject to average. In order to ensure that a reasonable premium is obtained for the protection afforded it is customary practice to embody a monthly limit of liability, *e.g.*, where the indemnity period is for 12 months that not more than one-twelfth of the sum insured shall be payable in respect of any one month.

Requests are sometimes received by insurers from firms engaged in commerce or industry for cover of the foregoing nature, that is for additional expenditure only, because they consider that in the event of damage at their premises they can by expenditure on increased working costs in one form or another maintain their turnover at normal level. From their extensive experience of claims over many years insurers believe that there are relatively few businesses where this would apply and that it is a request which is generally motivated by a desire to cut costs and in the event of serious damage such restricted cover may prove "penny wise and pound foolish". So apart from exceptionally soundly based cases insurers are averse to putting clients and their own reputation at risk by the issue of such a policy and prefer to give adequate protection by the proven method of a full gross profit insurance.

With the necessity to operate sophisticated electronic equipment, including computers, insured who previously might have considered additional expenditure to be sufficient should consider some form of full revenue, etc., insurance. Some insurers will in fact make provision in an additional expenditure only policy to reserve up to perhaps 25 per cent. of the sum insured to be used for an *income* loss if such a loss occurs. This cover is usually also subject to a monetary limit.

(b) *United States Extra Expense form*

The suitability of this minimal form of coverage is restricted mainly to organisations, societies and institutions which function as administrative bodies or revenue collectors without engaging in any production, selling or other profit-making activities. In this respect it is similar in application to U.K. Additional Expenditure Only policies (see paragraph 278(a) in which classes of insured for whom it might be suitable are mentioned).

The payment of extra expense is limited to the "period of restoration" of the damaged property and to a limit per month or months in the form of a percentage of the amount insured by the policy. This limit and the actual terms may vary according to the practice of different insurers and may be on a sliding scale with the percentage limit reducing progressively month by month throughout the period of interruption. For instance, 40 per cent. for up to one month, 80 per cent. for up to two months and 100 per cent. when the period of restoration is in excess of two months. There is no coinsurance condition on these coverages.

Most of the general terms, conditions and exclusions follow the lines of those in the full coverage forms. There is a stipulation that any salvage value of property which was obtained for temporary use which remains after the resumption of normal operations shall be taken into account in the claim settlement. For general observations on salvage of this nature see paragraph 419 on Residual Value.

279. Covers written in the marine market

(a) *Stock throughput*

This is a cover recently developed in the U.K. marine market in respect of stock in transit, in store, during processing and while being distributed thereafter—from original producer to eventual customer. It replaces at least three separate covers—marine transit, inland transit and fire policies. The cover is on an "all risks" declaration basis with the stock (wherever it may be) valued at eventual selling price including the insured's profit. Despite the basis of valuation, in order to avoid overindemnification all costs not incurred to date are deducted in arriving at a settlement amount. Underwriters prepared to provide this cover usually refer the non-marine aspects to their fire departments for agreement before a policy is issued. With such cover in force care must be taken to see what changes are necessary to the fire (business interruption) cover on the insured's premises. If the insured's overall business interruption requirements are catered for by more than one policy it is vital that all the relevant policies are maintained at all times. It is important to remember that the stock throughput cover relates solely to a particular consignment of stock and does not protect the insured against the wider effect on their business *as a whole* of the destruction of that stock.

(b) *Advance profits*

As mentioned in paragraph 268(a) a form of advance profits cover can be written in the U.K. marine market in respect of that part of the overall advance profits risk that involves marine perils. For example, a new factory may have ordered plant and machinery from overseas manufacturers and the commencement of the business will obviously be at risk following loss of or damage to such plant and machinery while in transit (including inland transit) from the manufacturers' to the insured's premises. To be certain of full protection the insured must ensure that all other risks—engineering, construction and fire—are also considered. Ideally the overall cover should initially be handled by one "department" with other "departments" accepting their parts in accordance with their own terms and conditions.

(c) *Consequential loss*

Covers can be written by marine (and aviation) underwriters in respect of loss arising out of the operation of a wide range of marine (and aviation) perils, which can include mechanical breakdown of or damage to the vessel (or aircraft), in respect of property whilst in transit (and storage) from manufacturers' to insured's premises. The sum insured can be full gross profit or standing charges only depending on the requirements of the insured. There is usually a deductible equivalent to 30 days delay for an annual cover. Again such covers must be seen in the context of the provision of a comprehensive programme of covers for the insured.

CHAPTER 14

PERILS (UNITED KINGDOM) OR CAUSES OF LOSS (UNITED STATES)

280. Market attitudes

The various markets of the world have different attitudes to the number of perils or causes of loss that can be insured against and their individual scope. Some markets impose restrictions on the extent of cover that can be provided where there are distinct and heavy exposures to particular "elemental" perils—earthquake, flood, volcanic eruption, windstorm, etc. One of the many difficulties confronting an "international" underwriter is the reconciling of one market's interpretation of particular perils with that of another market—the peril of explosion is a notable example.

In the United Kingdom perils wordings are recommended by the Association of British Insurers (A.B.I.) and individual members generally follow them except perhaps where they wish to adapt them to suit their own needs, e.g. to add certain "special" perils to the recommended "standard" perils to form a broader set of "standard" perils of their own.

In the United States the Insurance Services Office (I.S.O.) has three alternative recommended Causes of Loss forms—"Basic", "Broad" and "Special"—which are to be attached to either Property or Business Income Coverage forms. This replaces the older system where the "standard" perils (plus "extended coverage" if required) were to be found on the property damage policy and the gross earnings form was merely an endorsement thereto.

This chapter concentrates on the practices generally employed in the United Kingdom and the United States. Comments about other markets' procedures may be found in Chapter 6.

281. Insurance of "special perils"

(a) *In the United Kingdom*

The normal or "standard" perils from which damage must arise for a claim to be sustainable under a United Kingdom business interruption policy are detailed in paragraph 13(a) and, briefly, are fire, lightning and boiler explosion at the premises of the insured. A policy can be extended at a suitable additional premium or a separate insurance can be arranged to cover loss resulting from a number of other perils which are described in the following paragraphs. These are generally referred to as "special perils".

Except where otherwise stated the material damage proviso of the policy (paragraph 15(e)) applies, that is, there must be an insurance to cover the material damage sustained either by an extension of the fire policy or under an engineering policy or special perils or similar policy and payment must have been made or liability admitted for the damage by the insurers concerned.

A provision common to the memorandum by which any form of special perils is added to a standard fire business interruption policy expressly excludes loss arising from damage occasioned by war, civil war, revolution and the like and any consequential loss arising from nuclear radiation, etc., risks as set out in the General Exclusions on the policy (paragraph 14(a)).

When insurance is arranged by an extension to cover an insured's loss in consequence of damage by fire occurring at the premises of suppliers, processors, customers, warehousemen, etc., as explained in Chapter 17, loss resulting from damage at such premises caused by most of the special perils described in this chapter can generally be included in the extension.

The introduction in 1982 of an Industrial All Risks policy wording—refer paragraph 13(b) and Appendix B, paragraph 448—has given insured in the United Kingdom a choice of selected special perils or *all* risks, at additional cost. Which is better depends largely on the needs of particular insured.

As mentioned in paragraph 12 a feature of the new A.B.I. wordings is the use of the words "CONSEQUENTIAL LOSS" (in capitals to distinguish them from "consequential loss" used to denote consequential damage, etc.). The definition of "CONSEQUENTIAL LOSS" is "loss resulting from interruption of or interference with the Business carried on by the Insured at the Premises in consequence of loss or destruction of or damage to property used by the Insured at the Premises for the purpose of the Business". The intention of this innovation is to avoid repeating the long phrases by which it is defined.

(b) *In the United States*

The standard perils which were normally insured under a gross earnings policy were simply fire and lightning without any definition of these being given. Insurance against loss resulting from damage by other perils was effected by an "Extended Coverage endorsement" which included windstorm or hail; smoke; explosion; riot; riot attending a strike or civil commotion; aircraft or vehicles. The meaning of each of these extra perils was closely defined. The description of the insurance under an extended coverage endorsement limits the property damage to "direct" loss by each specified extra peril.

Under the new Business Income Coverage system "standard" perils are replaced by the Causes of Loss—Basic Form which is made up of fire, lightning, explosion, windstorm or hail, smoke, aircraft or vehicles, riot or civil commotion, vandalism, sprinkler leakage, sinkhole collapse and volcanic action.

The Broad Form includes additionally breakage of glass, falling objects, weight of snow, ice or sleet, and water damage. The Special Form provides causes of loss which mean "risks of direct physical loss" subject to certain exclusions and limitations—a form of "all risks" coverage (see paragraph 308).

282. Explosion

(a) *United Kingdom normal extension*

Whenever a fire policy is extended to include damage caused by explosion it is logical to arrange a corresponding extension of the business interruption insurance to cover loss resulting from such damage. Indeed, in some types of works, where there is very little inflammable material in either the construction of the buildings or in their contents but where explosive gases or chemicals are used, the hazard of business interruption loss resulting from explosion can be greater than that arising from fire damage. The inclusion of gas explosion in the perils covered (usually as standard) is restricted to that "of gas used for domestic purposes only", *i.e.* does not include explosion of gas used for trade processes. In many cases there is the possibility of loss consequent upon damage at an insured's premises caused by an explosion in adjacent works or in say, a chemical or gas works a considerable distance away. The massive explosion at a whisky bond in Glasgow in January 1977 which caused damage over a wide area illustrates the danger to which very many businesses may be exposed without an inkling that there is a potential explosion hazard in their vicinity.

When a business interruption insurance is extended to include explosion risks a memorandum is added to the specification to extend the insurance to include explosion of the same nature as that covered under a similar extension of the fire policy. This memorandum also contains a similar proviso excluding "CONSEQUENTIAL LOSS" caused by the bursting of any vessel, machine or apparatus (other than a boiler or economiser on the premises—loss consequent upon the explosion of these being a normal part of the business interruption cover (see paragraph 13)) under steam pressure and belonging to or under the control of the insured.

The essential part of the A.B.I. recommended explosion wording for business interruption is:

"CONSEQUENTIAL LOSS caused by EXPLOSION excluding
  (a) CONSEQUENTIAL LOSS caused by the bursting of any vessel machine or apparatus (not being a boiler or economiser on the Premises) in which internal pressure is due to steam only and belonging to or under the control of the insured
  (b) CONSEQUENTIAL LOSS by pressure waves caused by aircraft or other aerial devices travelling at sonic or supersonic speeds".

282

It is to be noted (as already stated in paragraph 281(a)) that the words "CONSEQUENTIAL LOSS" in capital letters shall mean "loss resulting from interruption of or interference with the Business carried on by the Insured at the Premises in consequence of loss or destruction of or damage to property used by the Insured at the Premises for the purpose of the Business".

Therefore, for an insurance where there are on the insured's premises any vessels, machines or apparatus (which is understood to include steam pipes) under steam, air, gas or water pressure it is desirable to look into the possibility of loss which might arise from the explosion of such plant.

Certain patent steam generators now made whilst not conforming to the traditional construction of steam boilers are regarded by insurers as ordinary boilers for the purpose of the inclusion of "explosion of any boilers or economisers on the premises" as a standard peril on the face of the policy.

In premises where there are bakers' ovens heated by gas, oil or electricity, the risk of loss resulting from explosion would be included in the normal explosion extension. But that caused by explosion of steam tubes in a steam-heated baker's oven would be excluded by the proviso attaching to the explosion extension wording as these tubes are subject to internal steam pressure. But insurers have put it on record that such ovens are now regarded by them as boilers and as such loss due to explosion in them is covered under the standard policy wording without the need for special insurance.

As stated in paragraph 13(a) the cover for loss resulting from damage caused by the explosion of boilers or economisers on the premises, given on the face of the standard policy, does not include flue gas explosion. Even if the flue or flue space were regarded as part of the permanent structure of the boiler it is not a part "subject to steam or other fluid pressure" which is a requisite under the accepted definition of boiler explosion. However, the normal explosion extension cover detailed above by making no mention of flue gases does include loss resulting from damage caused by the explosion of gases in the flues of boilers and economisers.

In the case of a business which is subject to a specific explosion risk arising from processes peculiar to the trade, *e.g.* dust explosion in a flour mill or explosion in a whisky distillery or bonded store for which cover is provided in the fire insurance without charge, a similar limited extension can be added by memorandum to the business interruption specification without additional premium. A free extension for the explosion risk is not, however, given in respect of plastics factories.

(b) *United States policies*

The standard perils insured under a United States gross earnings policy were simply "fire and lightning". Loss resulting from explosion, including explosion of boilers, was excluded but "spreading fire" resulting from explosion was included. Explosion was one of the extra perils insurable under an Extra Coverage endorsement (see paragraph 281(b)).

Under the new Business Income Coverage system, explosion is included in the Causes of Loss—Basic Form (see Appendix S, paragraph 465) where it includes "the explosion of gases or fuel within the furnace of any fired vessel or within the flues or passages through which the gases of combustion pass". It goes on to say that "this cause of loss does not include loss or damage by (a) rupture, bursting or operation of pressure relief devices, or (b) rupture or bursting due to expansion or swelling of the contents of any building or structure, caused by or resulting from water". Among the general exclusions are (i) rupture or bursting of water pipes (other than Automatic Sprinkler Systems) unless caused by a Covered Cause of Loss; (ii) explosion of steam boilers, steam pipes, steam engines or steam turbines owned or leased by the insured, or operated under the insured's control (but if loss or damage by fire or combustion explosion results, insurers will pay for that resulting loss or damage); and (iii) mechanical breakdown, including rupture or bursting caused by centrifugal force (but if loss or damage by a Covered Cause of Loss results, insurers will pay for that resulting loss or damage).

Explosion of steam boilers, etc., has to be effected by their inclusion as "objects" under a Boiler and Machinery insurance to cover loss resulting from an "accident" to such objects (see Chapter 16).

283. Explosion of steam pipes, vessels and apparatus

Insurance against "CONSEQUENTIAL LOSS" (see paragraphs 281(a) and 282(a)) arising from explosion (*i.e.* loss from explosion other than that of any boiler or economiser on the insured's premises which is included in the cover set out on the face of a standard policy) of steam pipes and of the miscellaneous categories of vessels, machines and apparatus which are excluded under the standard explosion extension (paragraph 282(a), can be arranged at an additional premium according to which of the following items is required, provided that there is in force a normal explosion cover as per paragraph 282(a).

(a) Explosion and collapse of steam pipes.
(b) Explosion of vessels (other than boilers and economisers) under steam pressure.
(c) Explosion of vessels (other than boilers and economisers) under steam pressure and collapse of vessels (other than boilers and economisers) under steam, gas, air or liquid pressure.

In many businesses vessels of this nature such as air compressors and receivers, autoclaves, steam cookers and calorifiers, drying ovens with steam coils, chemical reaction vessels, and pressure filters are a link in the chain of productive processes and the explosion of a vessel of that category, though small in itself, might cause a serious interference with production throughout the factory.

(d) Explosion of machines, as distinct from vessels, is not usually provided for apart from the complete engineering (accident) business interruption insurance dealt with in Chapter 15. The reason is that it is often impossible to distinguish satisfactorily between the damage to plant such as a steam turbine which may be caused by explosion and that due to bursting, rupture or breakdown. Consequently some insurers consider that the only satisfactory manner of dealing with machines that are liable to such damage, which are usually prime movers, is to arrange a full engineering business interruption insurance in respect of them. As explosion comes under a general exception of such a policy special provision has to be made.

284. Collapse and other failures of boilers and economisers

Nearly all types of boilers producing steam for industrial purposes are liable to a "collapse" risk this being defined as the sudden and dangerous distortion caused by crushing stress by force of steam or fluid pressure. Collapse occurs when the structure of a boiler can no longer withstand the difference between greater external pressure and lesser internal pressure; there is then a sudden and dangerous distortion of the plant. If this involves a rupture and ejectment of the contents of the boiler it may constitute an explosion; if there is no rupture it is collapse.

Collapse often involves repairs lasting only a few days but sometimes a much longer period. In either event there may be a complete standstill during the time when the boiler is out of commission of whatever part of a works is dependent upon it for the supply of steam for motive power or trade processes. This might for that time mean a considerable loss of production and where this contingency is a possibility the additional cover provided by an appropriate extension of the insurance is well worth the premium cost.

Other contingencies which will put a boiler or economiser out of commission and can be included in the cover are overheating or cracking of the boiler shell and failure of oil-firing apparatus, water supply feeds and circulating pumps.

Factories and warehouses heated by a central heating system supplied from a separate boiler for that purpose can sustain loss if such a boiler is out of service due to failure from some cause. Should this happen during a spell of severe weather employees might be unable or refuse to work until the central heating was restored or portable gas, electric or oil heaters were installed. Such temporary measures would entail considerable additional expenditure and this is covered under the increase in the cost of working clause on the specification.

During winter months the risk of interruption of business due to the failure of steam and hot water supplies is heightened because that is the period when boiler makers and heating engineers are at their busiest because of heavy seasonal demands. Hence, repairs or replacements may be subject to longer than normal delay, whilst bringing portable steam boilers into the premises may not be feasible for practical difficulties of space, etc.

285. Overheating of tubes consequent upon general deficiency of water in boiler

This is another type of damage which may put out of action for a time the boiler upon which a part or the whole of a works is dependent with a consequent temporary but serious loss of production. In certain types of boiler for which the supply of water has to be treated by a softening process the risk of overheating may be very severe because of the increased possibility of a failure of the supply of water.

When required an appropriate extension of the insured perils can be arranged to include the overheating of boilers or tubes consequent upon general deficiency of water either in conjunction with the collapse of boiler cover (paragraph 284) where this is applicable or on its own in the case of boilers where there is no collapse risk to insure.

286. Cracking and fracturing of pipes and boilers and nipple leakage

In the same category of extension are the risks of cracking and fracturing of steam and feed pipes and of boilers and supply pipes and nipple leakage of heating boilers. Loss consequent upon such contingencies can be added to an insurance at an extra premium.

This cover, together with that described in the preceding paragraph 285 is particularly important for nurserymen, chicken breeders and producers of table poultry where heat is obtained from a boiler and a regulated temperature has to be constantly maintained, because even a short stoppage of the heating supply could mean serious business interruption loss through plants, chickens or poultry dying. It is also of interest to hoteliers and motel owners for whom a shortage of hot water for culinary and sanitary purposes and for room heating might mean having to close the premises for a period, for example, Christmas time.

287. Aircraft and other aerial devices or articles dropped therefrom

(a) *United Kingdom*

As the volume of air traffic increases and the aircraft used grow in size and speed the possibility of serious damage to industrial premises being caused by a falling plane becomes of increasing importance especially in the case of factories in the vicinity of an airport or situate near regular air lanes. Even though there may be a reasonable prospect of recovering compensation from the aircraft operators or the insurers of their third party liability circumstances could arise in which such compensation might not be obtained in part or whole. For instance the amount available under the operator's insurance might be inadequate or the policy might be voided by breach of a condition or it might be a hijacked plane.

There is also the possibility of damage by space rockets or falling debris from spent satellites and at present there is no international law covering compensation for this. In 1978 a Soviet satellite fell in Canada and in 1979 a United States sky-lab came down partly in Australia. By the end of 1980 there were over 5,000 satellites circling the earth which in the form of space debris may eventually present a hazard.

A standard fire policy contains no exclusion of destruction or damage by *fire* caused by aircraft and, similarly, loss resulting from fire so caused is covered by a standard business interruption policy. It is possible to add a memorandum to include insurance against the contingency of damage, other than fire damage caused by aircraft and other aerial devices or articles dropped therefrom which reads:

> "DAMAGE (by fire or otherwise) caused by AIRCRAFT or other aerial devices or articles dropped therefrom excluding DAMAGE by pressure waves caused by aircraft or other aerial devices travelling at sonic or supersonic speeds".

For businesses which have such cover added to their fire policy, a similar extension should logically be arranged for the business interruption insurance; the additional premium required for this is very small. The words "CONSEQUENTIAL LOSS" replace the word "DAMAGE".

In fact the need for the addition of aircraft perils is greater under a business interruption policy than with a fire policy because the liability imposed on aircraft operators under section 40, Part IV, of the Civil Aviation Act 1949 refers only to "material loss or damage". Liability for business interruption is, therefore, left open to proof of negligence, default or other cause of action. Even though liability may be admitted or proved, the amount of loss remains to be established, which might be a difficult and costly proceeding and much less rewarding than substantiating a claim for the same loss under a business interruption policy with a firm's own approved insurers.

The specific wording of an aircraft cover extension should be noted because the results of damage by meteors, asteroids or other celestial bodies, should such ever unfortunately fall on industrial buildings, are not included.

(b) *United States*

A similar coverage to the above applies when aircraft perils are added to United States policies, this being described as direct loss resulting from actual physical contact of an aircraft or by articles falling therefrom (this rules out damage by sonic booms without mentioning them) with the insured premises or contents. The United Kingdom inclusion of aerial devices in the cover is taken by the United States definition of aircraft including self-propelled missiles and spacecraft.

288. Earthquake

(a) *United Kingdom*

This hazard may fortunately be lightly regarded in Great Britain because earthquakes which have reached destructive intensity are rare. But there are on average about a dozen earth tremors in the British Isles recorded annually, certain areas being recognised as earthquake centres where a settling of rock strata can be expected at intervals. Such an occurrence caused widespread damage in the Midlands in 1957 and there were serious tremors in Cheshire and Lancashire in 1976, in Scotland in 1979, and in North Wales in 1984.

Standard fire and business interruption policies exclude from the meaning of fire that occasioned by or happening through earthquake; non-fire damage caused by earthquake is not an insured peril under either policy. However, cover is available at an additional premium the risk being dealt with in two parts either or both of which may be added to the insurance:

(a) loss resulting from damage by fire only caused by earthquake (fire so caused being excluded by the wording on the face of the policy) and termed "earthquake fire risk";
(b) loss resulting from damage (other than by fire) caused by earthquake, called "earthquake shock risk".

Composite insurances for hotels, guest houses and public houses combine the risks of earthquake and subterranean fire along with those of fire, explosion, aircraft, riot, storm, flood and malicious damage at a special inclusive premium rate.

(b) *United States*

In the United States the possibilities of earthquakes in various regions are such that this risk was not included in the standard extended coverage endorsement for extra perils on a United States gross earnings coverage, being regarded as a risk not normally insurable nationwide. It is similarly excluded from all the Causes of Loss Forms—Basic, Broad and Special—except where "loss or damage by fire or explosion results" when payment will be made for "that resulting loss or damage".

289. Riot, etc.

(a) *United Kingdom—Riot, civil commotion, strikers, locked-out workers or persons taking part in labour disturbances or malicious persons acting on behalf of or in connection with any political organisation*

Loss by fire or explosion occasioned by or happening through riot and civil commotion is specifically excluded in standard fire business interruption policies but there is no exclusion of loss resulting from fire or boiler explosion caused by strikers or the other persons mentioned in the heading to this paragraph. Loss arising from other forms of damage caused by strikers, etc., such as, for instance, breakage of machinery, the cutting of supply pipes or electricity supplies and any other malicious damage, is not included in the standard policy cover.

Policies can be extended on payment of additional premium to include "CONSEQUENTIAL LOSS" caused by riot and civil commotion and persons as mentioned in the paragraph heading. It should be noted that "CONSEQUENTIAL LOSS" is excluded where it "is caused (other than by fire or explosion) by malicious persons (not acting on behalf of or in connection with any political organisation) in respect of any building which is empty or not in use".

It should also be noted that as regards strikers and locked-out workers, whilst the extension would cover business interruption resulting from material damage caused by such persons it would not include any loss due to their absence from work, staging sit-ins or occupying a factory. A proviso in the extension memorandum makes this quite clear by the exclusion of loss due to "cessation of work". This proviso also excludes loss "from confiscation or requisition by order of the government or any public authority".

The above mentioned exclusion of loss due to industrial disputes is because insurers have in the past always considered that from an underwriting viewpoint it would be impracticable and would also be contrary to the public interests to insure employers against loss due to withdrawal of labour. Such insurance would enable employers to adopt a hardline attitude and perhaps encourage them to prolong the period before settlement with strikers or locked-out workers, all at the insurers' expense. However, the change in the frequency, extent and tactics of industrial action throughout the 1970s led the Confederation of British Industry (C.B.I.) to try in 1979 to secure the co-operation of the major industrial companies amongst its members to persuade insurers to underwrite a strike insurance fund for cover against business interruption due to industrial disputes. When insufficient support was forthcoming the idea was shelved in 1980 although there are sources where it may be possible for smaller companies to obtain such insurance on an individual basis.

The destructive activities by fire and explosives in Great Britain in recent years by members of the IRA and of other politically motivated individuals claiming allegiance to organisations with aims of national independence or other objectives, and even damage at their own works by striking or locked-out workers, emphasise the need for insured to consider the advisability of an extension of cover for "R. & C.C." as in the heading to this paragraph. The extra premium required may seem heavy during a long spell of industrial and political calm. But it must be borne in mind that if at some future time a situation developed in which civic disturbances with destructive action appeared to be imminent or actually started, on a widespread scale, premium rates for new insurances might rise very steeply or insurers might even decline to accept new proposals. The extensive damage caused by rioting in London, Liverpool, Manchester and other cities in recent years may well lead to this.

The extra cover under an R. & C.C. extension can be confined to business interruption resulting from fire only, caused by riot and civil commotion only but as the difference in premium rates between this and the much wider cover outlined in previous paragraphs is very small the latter is normally arranged.

The conditions attached to the memorandum by which the riot, etc., cover is incorporated in an insurance contain a stipulation to the effect that details of any damage caused by the insured perils must be furnished to the insurer within seven days of the event. This is in order to facilitate inquiries as to the parties responsible for the damage and the exercise of any rights the insurer may have to claim compensation under the Riot (Damages) Act 1886 or the amending Police Act 1964 and Local Government Act 1972. (It is interesting to note that the Public Order Act 1986, applying to England and Wales, redefined the offence of "riot" to mean the participation of at least 12 (previously three) persons using or threatening unlawful violence for a common purpose, and introduced the new offence of "violent disorder" meaning the participation of at least three persons using or threatening unlawful violence and not necessarily with a common purpose. Subject to the new definition of "riot", compensation continues to be available under the 1886 Act.)

Because persons of the kind described in the heading to this paragraph if deliberately causing damage by fire or otherwise to premises or their contents would aim to inflict the maximum financial loss, the interruption risk is regarded as proportionately heavier than that of material damage. Consequently, the basis rate for the extension on the fire insurance is usually loaded in the calculation of the additional rate for the business interruption insurance.

When riot, etc., cover is added to the fire insurance in respect of a building protected by an installation of automatic sprinklers, for most classes of premises the premium otherwise payable for the extension is often substantially reduced in recognition of the fact that incendiarism is a major part of the risk of damage by rioters and of the value of a sprinkler system in this respect. When a business interruption policy for such premises is extended to include riot risks a similar concession usually applies to the additional premium.

(b) *Riot, etc.—United States*

On a U.S. gross earnings form an Extended Coverage endorsement (paragraph 282(b)) includes with other extra perils direct loss by riot, riot attending a strike or civil commotion and acts of striking employees of the owner or tenants of the insured premises and from pillage and looting.

Under the new Causes of Loss forms riot and civil commotion includes "(a) acts of striking employees while occupying the described premises, and (b) looting occurring at the time and place of a riot or civil commotion".

290. Northern Ireland

The insurance available against loss resulting from damage as set out in the foregoing paragraph 289 on riot and civil commotion, etc., does not apply in Northern Ireland, where for many years damage by fire and explosion has been caused on a huge scale, because of statutory provisions for recovery by victims from the government for losses so caused.

Following a bomb explosion compensation for business interruption as well as the material damage was recovered in the case of *Bairnswear Knitwear Co. Ltd.* v. *Armagh County Council* in the Northern Ireland Court of Appeal in 1970 under the Criminal Injuries Acts (N.I.) 1956 and 1957. These Acts were repealed and replaced by the Criminal Injuries to Property (Compensation) Act 1971. It is said that in order to reflect the decision in the *Bairnswear* case and to clear up any uncertainty for the future, this Act deliberately changed the wording of the previous Acts by stating that where damage has been unlawfully, wilfully or maliciously caused to property (a) by any three or more persons, unlawfully, riotously or tumultuously assembled together or (b) as a result of any act committed maliciously by a person acting on behalf of or in connection with an unlawful association, then compensation may be awarded by the Secretary of State for Northern Ireland for "*loss from that damage*". This is taken to include business interruption.

The 1971 Act was subsequently repealed and the question of compensation was included in the Criminal Damage (Compensation) (N.I.) Order 1977. This repeats the above conditions for the payment of compensation, again using the word "loss". This 1977 Order adds a new proviso that where the Chief Constable is of the opinion that any act was committed maliciously by a person acting on behalf of or in connection with an unlawful association he shall issue a certificate for the purposes of an application for compensation for *loss resulting from damage* alleged to have been caused by an act so committed. Again business interruption loss is inferred.

If no certificate is issued by the Chief Constable a claim may be considered under the terms of the insurance policy applicable only if the insured can prove that the loss arises from damage not excluded under the Northern Ireland Overriding Exclusion Clause (now embodied in the wordings for current standard policies). This clause was applied by insurers as from April 1, 1978 as a result of the 1977 Order, and excludes from all fire and business interruption insurances of commercial and industrial premises in Northern Ireland damage or loss caused by civil commotion or acts committed maliciously by anyone acting in connection with an "unlawful" organisation. For the precise wording see General Exclusion 3 of the policy form in Appendix A, paragraph 447, or Exclusion 12 of the all risks policy form in Appendix B, paragraph 448.

Legal advice obtained confirms the opinion received from the Northern Ireland Office that compensation under the Government scheme is not available unless a legally enforceable interest in the damaged property can be established. Hence, a firm's financial loss arising from terrorist damage at the premises of their suppliers or customers in Northern Ireland is not recoverable under either the Government scheme or their insurance, the latter being made clear in the original wording of the overriding exclusion that it "applies to the policy and to any extensions thereof".

291. Malicious damage

Fire caused by malicious persons is within the meaning of fire in the normal cover of fire and business interruption policies but physical damage of other kinds may be done by malicious persons and this is not covered except by an extension of the insurances for which an additional premium is required. Insurance in respect of damage by malicious persons which is included in the riot and civil commotion extension (paragraph 289 is restricted to that done by such persons "acting on behalf of or in connection with a political organisation". Damage can be done by persons acting simply out of personal malice and insurers are prepared to cover loss consequent upon such damage but this extension will only be given when the risks of riot and civil commotion, etc., are covered because of the difficulties which would be experienced in ascertaining the exact cause of damage arising in the course of a civil disturbance.

In works where there is a power unit or some vital machinery or plant or computers which can be relatively easily damaged the malicious damage risk may be a serious one for it can be assumed that a person wanting to injure the productive capacity of the works would choose to damage the most vulnerable part.

When the risk of malicious damage is added to a business interruption policy the wording used does not define the meaning of malicious. The existence of the material damage proviso (paragraph 15(e)) on the face of the policy, however, has the effect of giving malicious damage the same meaning as under a similar extension on the fire policy plus that provided by a theft policy if one is held by the insured. The latter point is important because the extension on a fire policy for malicious damage specifically excludes damage by theft.

When malicious damage cover is added to a fire policy, claims for trifling occurrences are often excluded by a proviso stating that the insured must stand the first £250, perhaps, of any loss. This exclusion is considered to be unnecessary for a business interruption policy as such minor material damage is unlikely to give rise to a loss of turnover. The waiving of the exclusion means that the cover under the business interruption policy is to that extent wider than that under the fire policy. To bring this into conformity with the material damage proviso on the face of the policy an additional clause is added to the extension memorandum suspending the operation of that proviso so far as the amount deducted from the material loss is concerned. (For the wording of this clause, see paragraph 16(b).)

292. Spontaneous fermentation or heating

Damage to property by fire arising from these causes (but not damage to other property to which such a fire might spread) is excepted from the definition of damage on the face of the business interruption policy in line with the similar exclusion under a standard fire policy. This contingency may be included at an appropriate additional premium according to the particular circumstances of any business in which such an extension of the normal cover is considered necessary. For example, it is customary for tar distillers who hold bulk quantities of material which is liable to ignite spontaneously and gas works holding stocks of coal for the production of coal gas to effect this extra cover.

When manufacturers hold stocks of coal in the open for their factory boilers an extension is given without charge under the fire policy to cover loss due to spontaneous heating and the business interruption insurance is often regarded as attaching in a similar manner without the necessity of a specific memorandum being placed on the specification.

293. Hot metal or break-out risk (United Kingdom): molten material clause (United States)

This is a contingency which is largely confined to iron and steel works. It relates to the accidental discharge of molten metal from blast furnaces, other furnaces or similar plant on the premises. In some instances this ignites inflammable material in the vicinity of the furnace and the business interruption loss due to the "spreading fire" damage is within the normal provisions of a business interruption policy. Interruption of the business not caused by any actual fire but due to the molten metal solidifying in different parts of the furnace house and having to be removed before work can proceed or caused by intense heat from the escaping hot metal damaging plant and equipment in the vicinity is outside the terms of the policy.

To meet possible occurrences of the latter kind an appropriate extension of a business interruption insurance can be arranged, at an additional premium, to cover "loss as insured by the policy resulting from interruption or interference with the business in consequence of accidental discharge of molten metal from the furnaces". To use A.B.I. phraseology, the cover would be in respect of "CONSEQUENTIAL LOSS (refer paragraph 12) caused by an accidental discharge of molten metal from the furnaces".

Similar coverage can be given on United States policies by the "Molten Material clause" and this also makes specific mention that the cost of removing the material or repairing any fault which caused the break-out is not insured. Under the Additional Coverage Extensions in the Causes of Loss—Special Form the extension relating to Water Damage, Other Liquids, Powder or Molten Material Damage states that "if loss or damage caused by or resulting from covered water or other liquid, powder or molten material damage loss occurs, we will also pay the cost to tear out and replace any part of the building or structure to repair damage to the system or appliance from which the water or other substances escapes". This would appear to refer to "preventative" repair.

294. Storm and flood (excluding subsidence or landslip)

(a) *United Kingdom*

Our increasing urbanisation and industrialisation today make businesses more and more vulnerable to the vagaries of the weather and the question of insurance against storm and flood consequently merits very careful consideration.

Businesses holding a material damage insurance against these perils may require similar protection in respect of a business interruption loss arising from the same contingencies. Although the interruption of business which would arise from damage by storm, tempest or flood might not in the majority of businesses be of prolonged duration a serious loss can be sustained. As pointed out in paragraph 7, reduction of turnover for a relatively short period during which all the standing charges of a business continue to be payable in full can result in a loss equivalent to the net profit normally earned over a much longer period.

However, the general assumption that in the majority of cases the period of interruption will not be of prolonged duration does not hold good for all industrial concerns and certainly not so far as the flood risk is concerned. Cases are on record where factories covering many acres and not considered particularly vulnerable have been flooded to a depth of several feet and had not only their stocks but also key plant, machinery and electronic equipment ruined. There have been a number of instances where the period of interruption lasted over 12 months and the business interruption loss ran into six figures.

The glass houses and growing plants of nurserymen and market gardeners are particularly susceptible to storm damage and as a considerable period is necessary for the growth of plants up to the time when they or their fruits are ready for sale a business interruption insurance is a vital necessity for such businesses (refer paragraph 270(b)).

Business interruption policies can be extended, where the material damage cover for the same perils has been arranged, to insure loss resulting from destruction or damage either by storm only or by storm and flood. They follow the general practice in connection with the material damage insurance in giving no definition for the meaning of storm or flood. In the event of damage taking place, if there were any question of whether the damage was or was not insured not resolved by the wording, the material damage proviso of the business interruption policy (paragraph 15(e)) would make for concurrency with the interpretation of the cover given under the material damage insurance. But when storm only is insured without the flood risk there is generally an exclusion in the business interruption policy of "CONSEQUENTIAL LOSS":

> "(a) (i) caused by the escape of water from the normal confines of any natural or artificial water course lake reservoir canal or dam
> (ii) caused by inundation from the sea
> whether resulting from storm or otherwise
> (b) attributable solely to change in the water table level
> (c) caused by frost subsidence ground heave or landslip
> (d) in respect of movable property in the open, fences and gates".

When flood is insured only exclusions (b), (c) and (d) apply.

The exclusion of loss "attributable solely to change in the water table level" was included only in the late 1980s because of the general rise in the levels of water tables in the United Kingdom. The word "solely" is important.

It is customary to make the material damage insurance for these perils subject to a proviso that the insured must themselves bear the first £250 perhaps, or some higher amount, of any loss. This excess is generally waived in the case of a business interruption insurance, a clause being added to the description of the perils covered to suspend the operation of the material damage proviso so far as the uninsured excess of the material loss is concerned. (See paragraph 16(b).)

(b) *United States*

Because of the very different climatic and geographical conditions in North America the cover available against the vagaries of the weather differs in terms and conditions from the foregoing U.K. business interruption insurances; understandably flood risks are not included in insured perils. Extra perils of Windstorm and Hail can be insured under an Extended Coverage endorsement of a U.S. gross earnings policy (or the current Causes of Loss forms) but this excludes, *inter alia*, frost or cold weather or ice (other than hail), snow or sleet whether driven by wind or not but does not mention cyclones or hurricanes.

295. Bursting or overflowing of water tanks, apparatus or pipes

Business interruption resulting from these perils is, from the point of view of interruption of business, generally of less importance than loss due to storm and flood. But relatively serious loss can be sustained, generally in the smaller type of businesses such as warehouses and shops with high-value stocks susceptible to damage by water, hairdressers' and beauty salons, fashion boutiques and the like, and substantial claims do arise under business interruption insurances. As previously mentioned closure of a business for a few days can, because all standing charges and wages continue unabated, cause a loss equal to the net profit earned over a much longer period.

The premium charged for adding these perils to those covered under a business interruption policy is usually small and whenever storm and flood are insured it is the general practice to include burst pipes, etc. Loss resulting from damage caused by water discharged or leaking from an installation of automatic sprinklers is always excluded, as this is a heavier risk involving separate consideration and premium rating (see paragraph 297). Damage by water used in extinguishing a fire is treated as fire damage without its being mentioned on the policy (see paragraph 13).

Material damage covers include a small deductible (perhaps £250), the same comments applying to business interruption insurance as for storm, etc., (paragraph 294).

296. Impact

(a) *Damage caused by road vehicles, horses or cattle*

For shops, hairdressers' salons, restaurants, hotels and similar trading establishments fronting onto streets through which heavy motor traffic passes, or which are situated on a corner or at the foot of a steep road the possibility of business interruption arising from impact damage can be a matter of some importance. Not only has the loss of publicity value arising from damage to a shop front to be considered but also the more serious loss of trade which would result if the ground floor and upper floors had to be closed to the public because of damage at street level to supporting walls and pillars or access to a business in basement premises was blocked. The very small premium charged for insurance against business interruption following impact damage makes the cover well worth while, particularly when the great size, weight and speeds of modern juggernauts of the road and the increasing number of accidents with them are taken into account.

Although there may be a possibility of claiming damages at common law against the owner of a vehicle there is a definite risk that such a course could be a very lengthy process involving loss of time and money before a satisfaction is obtained or for one of various possible reasons may prove completely abortive. It is a risk not worth taking when the several advantages of cover with one's own business interruption insurers, at low cost, are considered.

In the extra perils included in an Extended Coverage endorsement on a United States gross earnings policy is that of damage by vehicles to the property covered or to buildings containing it. This excludes loss by any vehicle owned or operated by the insured or by any tenant of the described premises or to any vehicle including contents other than vehicles in process of manufacture or for sale.

The current Causes of Loss—Basic and Broad Forms exclude loss or damage caused by or resulting from vehicles owned by the insured or operated in the cause of business.

(b) Damage in works by own vehicles

In some factories or works damage caused by impact of road vehicles or more especially by the works' own locomotive engines, wagons, runabout trolleys or fork-lift trucks at a vital point such as the power house, gas producer plant or pipe lines could result in a serious interruption of production. In such cases cover against loss resulting from impact damage is advisable. As the normal wording for impact cover is limited to damage by road vehicles, horses or cattle "not belonging to or under the control of the insured or their employees" it has to be amended by the deletion of this restriction whilst at the same time it is extended to include works vehicles of all kinds in addition to road vehicles.

It should be noted that the foregoing means loss resulting from damage caused *by* vehicles, because impact cover is not included in any business interruption insurance of loss due to damage *to* vehicles or property in transit. This is of special relevance to the extensions of cover detailed in paragraphs 375 and 376.

Material damage covers usually include a small deductible, the same comments applying as for storm, etc., (refer paragraph 294).

297. Sprinkler leakage

Damage by water released by the opening of sprinkler heads due to fire is treated as damage by fire within the meaning of a standard fire policy and business interruption resulting from such water damage would similarly be within the cover provided, under a standard business interruption policy. Damage or loss, however, resulting from the accidental operation of sprinkler heads or leakage from the installation is not covered under either class of policy unless specially insured and is specifically excluded from an insurance on the bursting or overflowing of water tanks, apparatus or pipes (see paragraph 295).

Although material damage to stock, plant and machinery due to sprinkler leakage may be considerable it is sometimes considered that normal working would be interfered with for only a short period and because of this assumption protection against business interruption is not always arranged concurrently with the material damage insurance covered under a sprinkler leakage policy. To be consistent, an extension of the business interruption insurance should be arranged for any business in which the plant and machinery is vulnerable to water damage especially where there is any plant involved in a heating process which if fractured by a sudden douche of water would take an appreciable time to restore to working condition. Factories using or producing materials which on contact with water become glutinous or solidify and prevent machinery being used until a lengthy process of cleaning is completed, as happens in flour mills and premises processing farinaceous powders, are particularly open to business interruption loss. Also, where there are stocks of essential raw materials or of finished goods of a seasonal nature which are susceptible to water damage and are not quickly replaceable, whether in factories, warehouse or shops, substantial loss of trade might result from damage by water. For such businesses and for theatres and cinemas, cover should certainly be arranged under a business interruption insurance.

298. Rainfall

Rain without doing any material damage or destruction can cause serious business interruption loss for the organisers of outdoor functions such as gymkhanas, riding competitions, cricket and tennis matches, sports and athletics meetings, galas, charity fêtes and garden parties. Rain falling during a period shortly before or perhaps during the time of the function may result in a considerable drop in the anticipated attendances and receipts. Because arrangements have to be organised a considerable time in advance the official weather forecasts seldom help.

This is a type of business interruption requiring very specialised knowledge and experience and there is a very limited number of insurers catering for it by what are termed "pluvius" or "rainfall" policies. These offer a wide choice of alternative covers, compensation being paid if rainfall reaches a stipulated measurement during a specified period of hours or days insured. The simplest form is an "agreed value" policy under which there is an arbitrarily agreed sum insured which is payable irrespective of the financial result of the insured function. Where more substantial amounts are involved there is an "indemnity basis" policy in which the sum insured is based on estimated receipts and payment is made of any adverse difference between this amount and the actual gross receipts. A further alternative form of policy operates if the function is prevented from taking place because of rain (irrespective of measurement) or if required other adverse weather conditions such as fog, frost, snow or flood. Under this the amount payable is the net loss, that is the total of the expenses incurred less any refunds or retained income but anticipated profit is not insurable.

There are also policies with conditions suitable for an undertaking which extends over a long period in which a promoter is prepared to carry the risk of a normal number of wet days by having an excess on the policy in the form of an agreed number of days, and there are policies with a wide variety of options to meet the circumstances peculiar to cricket and tennis matches.

In all cases the insurance must be completed at least 14 days before the commencement of the risk. Whilst not providing an exact indemnity because the effects of the weather on attendances are not capable of precise measurement these insurances do give promoters of outdoor events compensation for what may be regarded as the major factor of risk.

In the United States coverage of the foregoing nature is known as Rain Insurance and insures against loss due to rain, hail, sleet or snow.

299. Sunshine deficiency

A "sunshine deficiency" insurance can be arranged with U.K. insurers who underwrite pluvius policies (see preceding paragraph 298) a cover which is particularly suited to enterprises such as swimming pools, chair hire, hotels and restaurants whose summer trade is dependent to a considerable extent upon a bright season. The sum insured is paid in proportion according to the extent to which the officially recorded number of sunshine hours falls short of the average shown by Meteorological Office statistics during the period insured which can be from one to six months.

300. Food poisoning risk: food processors and distributors

As a sequel to the serious effects on sales and fears of manufacturers of future possibilities which arose from an outbreak of food poisoning in the United Kingdom in 1979 attributed to the products of a firm of salmon canners with a worldwide reputation, insurers evolved a scheme of business interruption insurance for manufacturers, canners and preservers of food products. Because this type of risk is not a very attractive one for insurers there was at first no standard form of cover and terms and conditions varied between different insurers. In general the insurance was restricted to loss due to consumption of the insured's products either on or away from their premises following closure of same by a competent Public Authority.

From 1989 a standard form of cover has been available in the United Kingdom as part of the A.B.I. recommended wording for Notifiable disease, vermin, defective sanitary arrangements, murder and suicide (see following paragraph 301 and Appendix O, paragraph 461) which extends the business interruption policy to include loss following the occurrence of a notifiable disease (as defined) at the premises or attributable to food or drink supplied from the premises, any discovery of an organism at the premises likely to result in the occurrence of a notifiable disease, the discovery of vermin or pests at the premises or any accident causing defects in the drains or other sanitary arrangements at the premises, any of which events causes restrictions on the use of the premises on the order or advice of the competent local authority. The indemnity period starts with the application of the restrictions: it is likely that the maximum indemnity period granted by insurers will not in general exceed three months. There is also a monetary limit of liability. A form of material damage cover can also be provided, subject to a monetary limit, in respect of the cost of cleaning and decontaminating the insured's property and of removal and disposal of contaminated stock in trade.

Two other features have appeared recently which affect food manufacturers. The first is the increasing influence of biotechnology by which, for example, fungi and other bacteria are produced for additives used in foods and drink preparations. This is an important dependency exposure involving severe contamination risks. The second is that of criminal contamination which has shown itself in extortion threats to both food manufacturers and saleshops leading to actual or potential reduction in sales. This a difficult area for insurers.

301. Infectious or contagious diseases: murder, suicide, food or drink poisoning, vermin, pests or defective sanitary arrangements

The risk of business interruption loss arising from any of these contingencies is of particular concern to owners of hotels, boarding houses, guest houses, public houses, holiday camps, caravan sites, exhibition halls, private hospitals, nursing homes and schools and especially as regards food poisoning restaurateurs and catering contractors are also interested. Cover can be provided under a business interruption policy at a premium which will depend upon the individual circumstances; the material damage proviso of the policy (paragraph 15(e)) does not apply to these contingencies because they cannot be the subject of a material damage insurance other than the limited cover now provided.

In 1989 the A.B.I. issued a recommended wording (see Appendix O, paragraph 461) which with certain variations can be applied to three categories of insured—(a) hotels, restaurants and public houses, (b) schools, private hospitals, etc., and (c) food processors and distributors. This replaces and to an extent widens the various forms of cover previously issued by different insurers. The business interruption policy can be extended for categories (a) and (b) to include loss in consequence of:

(a) *Hotels, restaurants and public houses*

"1 (a) Any occurrence of a Notifiable Disease (as defined below) at the Premises or attributable to food or drink supplied from the Premises
   (b) any discovery of an organism at the Premises likely to result in the occurrence of a Notifiable Disease
   (c) any occurrence of a Notifiable Disease (in the town/borough of . . .) (within a radius of 25 miles of the Premises)
2 the discovery of vermin or pests at the Premises which causes restrictions on the use of the Premises on the order or advice of the competent local authority
3 any accident causing defects in the drains or other sanitary arrangements at the Premises which causes restrictions on the use of the Premises on the order of the competent local authority
4 any occurrence of murder or suicide at the Premises".

(b) *Schools, private hospitals, etc.*

"1 (a) any occurrence of a Notifiable Disease (as defined below) at the Premises or attributable to food or drink supplied from the Premises
   (b) Any discovery of an organism at the Premises likely to result in the occurrence of a Notifiable Disease
   (c) any occurrence of a Notifiable Disease (in the town/borough of . . .) (within a radius of 25 miles of the Premises)
2 the discovery of vermin or pests at the Premises
3 any accident causing defects in the drains or other sanitary arrangements at the Premises which causes restrictions on the use of the Premises on the order or advice of the competent local authority
4 any occurrence of murder or suicide at the Premises".

Maximum indemnity periods granted by insurers are not likely to exceed 12 months for category (a) and three months for category (b).

Category (c)—food processors and distributors—is described on the preceding paragraph 300.

Notifiable Disease is defined as meaning "illness sustained by any person resulting from (a) food or drink poisoning, or (b) any human infectious or human contagious disease an outbreak of which the competent local authority has stipulated shall be notified to them".

Acquired Immune Deficiency Syndrome (AIDS) must receive special underwriting treatment because of the particular element of fear attached to it. Legionnaires Disease which was not in the list of notifiable diseases either under the Public Health (Control of Disease) Act 1984, or under the Public Health (Infectious Diseases) Regulations 1988, but which a "competent local authority" may include in their "local" list, must also be treated with care if the premises contain a potential source (*e.g.* air-conditioning equipment using "wet" cooling towers) of the disease and it is known that the local health officers have added it to their list of notifiable diseases.

Requests by seaside hotel proprietors which arose at the time of the *Torrey Canyon* disaster in March 1967 for the inclusion with the foregoing special contingencies of the further risk of business interruption due to oil pollution of beaches were not acceded to by insurers and this risk has only recently been included in the general run of composite hotel policies (refer paragraph 391).

But hoteliers and other business proprietors at coastal resorts who may suffer business interruption arising from such a cause do have the possibility of recovering compensation from the shipowners responsible. When the Amoco Cadiz supertanker went down off Britanny in March 1978 spewing 220,000 tons of crude oil into the English Channel and onto French beaches the actual cost of compensation paid according to the book "Black Tide Rising" was £58 million. And there are large funds upon which an hotelier sustaining loss of this nature can claim which are administered at the headquarters in London of the International Oil Pollution Compensation Fund.

Another very serious risk of business interruption for businesses at seaside resorts or harbour towns for which there appears to be at present no insurance generally available is the possibility of evacuation of an area following an accident to a ship transporting liquefied natural gas, ethylene, creosote, naphthalene or butane. (See also paragraph 302.)

302. Pollution and contamination

Because of growing worldwide concern about the effect on the environment of the discharge, for whatever reason, of poisonous chemicals, etc., from industrial premises, insurers both in the United Kingdom and in the United States have introduced exclusions into their policies with regard to pollution or contamination.

In the United Kingdom the General Exclusions in the new standard fire (business interruption) policy (see Appendix A, paragraph 447) now include the exclusion of "loss resulting from pollution or contamination" which is then qualified by the statement:

> "but this shall not exclude loss resulting from destruction of or damage to property used by the Insured at the Premises for the purpose of the Business, not otherwise excluded, caused by (a) pollution or contamination at the Premises

which itself results from a peril hereby insured against, or (b) any peril hereby insured against which itself results from pollution or contamination".

In the All Risks wording (refer Appendix B, paragraph 448) the original exclusion of "contamination" has been widened to refer also to "pollution". There is a similar qualification (as in previous paragraph) but it relates only to "Defined Perils", *i.e.* those risks which can be covered in a standard fire and special perils policy. The question of "accidental damage" caused by or causing pollution or contamination is a matter of ongoing debate.

As has been described in the context of Notifiable Diseases, etc., cover (refer paragraphs 300 and 301) certain limited forms of contamination and pollution can be offered by U.K. insurers but the effects of widespread "area" pollution are too horrific to be contemplated.

In the United States neither the Basic nor the Broad forms of Causes of Loss refer to pollution or contamination but the Special form (equivalent to an "all risks" cover) deals with the exclusion of the "release, discharge or dispersal of 'pollutants' " with similar qualification as in the United Kingdom. All Risks form with "specified causes of loss" (those provided by the Broad form) being similar to "Defined Perils".

Under the new Business Income Coverage form the "period of restoration" definition stipulates that it does not include any increased period required due to the enforcement of any ordinance or law that requires any insured or others to test for, monitor, clean up, remove, contain, treat, detoxify or neutralise, or in any way respond to, or assess the effects of "pollutants" (any solid, liquid, gaseous or thermal irritant or contaminant, including smoke, vapor, soot, fumes, acids, alkalis, chemicals and waste— materials to be recycled, reconditioned, reclaimed, etc.).

303. Theft

In industry generally where electronic equipment is used and in certain trades where processes depend upon scientific or photographic apparatus there is a risk of serious interference with production if such equipment is stolen or wantonly smashed by thieves. Such damage is often done by intruders suffering disappointment in their search for cash or other property. Replacement may take an appreciable time if the apparatus is of an extensive nature or is obtainable only from abroad or has to be specially made. Businesses in which precious stones or metals attractive to thieves such as industrial diamonds, platinum anodes, gold, silver, cadmium and chromium are used in manufacturing or plating processes might sustain a loss of production should their stock of the metal or tools in which it is incorporated be stolen and not be immediately replaceable.

Antique dealers could suffer serious subsequent loss if their stock were badly depleted by thieves because not only would they lose profit through lack of goods to sell until the slow process of replacement had been effected, perhaps at considerable increase in cost of working through having to travel abroad to make purchases, but the sparsity of their stock during that period would mean less attraction for customers to call and inspect what goods they might have for sale.

Where there are special circumstances such as those mentioned above which make a business vulnerable to a loss of production or of turnover in the event of a burglary it is advisable to effect insurance under an appropriate business interruption policy. The word damage is defined as including "loss, destruction or damage caused by theft involving entry to or exit from the premises by forcible or violent means"; loss resulting from the action of any person lawfully on the premises or from the connivance of any member of the staff is usually excluded. It should however be noted that where a business is insured against business interruption loss through malicious damage as described in paragraph 305 such cover includes malicious damage (but not taking away of property) done by thieves.

Business interruption resulting from theft is a risk which may apply also to businesses which produce materials for the clothing or dress goods trades, etc., and have to work considerably ahead of the seasons in which their products will be sold as finished garments. Patterns to show the materials and designs are prepared in advance for the use of a firm's representatives and the booking of orders may depend almost entirely on the showing of these patterns to prospective customers. If they are lost or destroyed it may not be possible owing to the seasonal nature of the trade to produce new patterns in time to avoid the loss of a substantial part of a normal season's orders. Consequently, if these patterns are of a nature to make them attractive to thieves it is prudent to insure against the loss which might follow from their being stolen, the description of the insured's premises being worded to include their representatives' cars, homes and hotels and other places where they might stay or show their samples (refer paragraph 361).

304. Electrocution of cattle

Where the fire insurance held by a dairy farmer is extended to include the risk of electrocution of cattle, a similar addition may be made to the perils covered in the farmer's business interruption policy. The word damage is then extended to include the death of any animal which occurs as a direct result of electrocution.

The risk is relatively heavy on farms where a number of pedigree cows are tied up to one head harness, a short circuit on which might result in several deaths, and the additional premium required corresponds.

305. Abnormal current or self-heating of electrical plant

It has been the practice of some insurers to place a clause on a U.K. fire policy specification for the insurance of an industrial risk where electrical plant or apparatus is used, in the following or similar terms:

> "Electrical Clause—The Company will not be liable for any destruction of or damage to any portion of electrical plant, installation or appliances directly due to its own excessive pressure, overrunning, short-circuiting or self-heating".

The exclusion applies only to the incipient outbreak and not to damage caused by the spreading fire. It has the effect of similarly restricting the meaning of damage on the business interruption policy for the same business, even though there is no electrical clause on the policy, through the operation of the material damage proviso (paragraph 15(e)).

There is a similar exclusion in the U.S. Causes of Loss forms—

> "We will not pay for loss or damage caused by or resulting from artificially generated electric current, including electric arcing, that disturbs electrical devices, appliances or wires. But if loss or damage by fire results, we will pay for that resulting loss or damage".

306. Disablement of refrigerating plant by fire: rise in temperature risk

It is held by some but not all insurers that the destruction or damage caused to food or other goods in a cold store as the result of a change of temperature due to the disablement of the refrigerating plant by fire or lightning would not be covered under a standard fire policy. This view is based on the long-established legal doctrine of proximate cause under which the dominant effective cause of a loss (said in these circumstances to be the disablement of the refrigerating plant) and not the remote cause (the fire or lightning) is to be considered.

If this should be the position the business interruption loss arising from the destruction of or damage to the contents of the storage chambers would similarly be outside the cover of a business interruption policy, because of the material damage proviso on the latter (paragraph 15(e)).

It is customary to mention on a fire policy which insures goods in public cold stores that this "rise in temperature" risk is included so any business interruption policy which has been extended to cover loss resulting from damage to an insured's goods whilst in such premises (as described in paragraph 355) is entitled to benefit similarly.

In cases where insured own their own refrigerating plant and cold storage for their goods a similar extension to cover loss occasioned by a rise in temperature due to fire or lightning can be arranged for both the fire policy and the business interruption insurance. If the contents of the cold store are food-stuffs of a seasonal nature such as fruit, vegetables, fish or poultry which are not immediately replaceable its spoilage can mean a substantial business interruption loss especially for preservers and canners, etc. So when negotiating a business interruption insurance it is essential to clarify with insurers the position with regard to the rise in temperature risk. A U.S. Boiler and Machinery insurance can be extended to cover consequential damage (refer paragraph 338).

307. All risks covers

The so-called "all risks" cover is a varied and variable form of insurance fulfilling the needs of insured (and their advisors) but not necessarily benefitting insurers. It exists in many markets (refer Chapter 6) but is not generally regarded with favour by insurers because of the ever-present possibility of an unforeseen contingency operating notwithstanding the lengthy list of exclusions and restrictions.

308. "All Risks" (United Kingdom)

Industrial all risks policies were first issued officially by U.K. insurers in 1982. They provided cover against the results of accidental loss or destruction of or damage to the insured property subject to the exclusion of certain defined categories of property and to the exclusion of certain prescribed causes some of which can be "bought back" at additional premium. The current A.B.I. recommended wording in Appendix B, paragraph 448 is an updated version (see also paragraph 13(b)).

Other forms of "all risks" covers are to be found in the U.K. market some including cover in respect of book debts, research and development, computers, etc.

309. Causes of Loss—Special Form (United States)

Before 1980 a form of all risks cover could be obtained by adding together a Fire and Extended Coverage policy and a Difference in Conditions policy (which was itself a form of "all risks" cover). The new Special Form issued first in 1983 provides a form of "all risks" cover in one document. Covered Causes of Loss means "risks of direct physical loss" subject to exclusions or limitations—property and causes (see also paragraph 25(c)).

310. Worldwide all risks policies

These are usually one-off, specially constructed "master" covers based either on a U.S. or a U.K. format with U.K. or U.S. alternative bases of cover, etc., included where necessary. They are intended to suit almost any and every possible situation but because of the inclusion of large deductibles (per event and annual aggregate) relatively modest losses are often excluded. It is essential that insurers are fully aware of the scope of cover provided. (Refer also paragraph 382(c).)

CHAPTER 15

ENGINEERING BUSINESS INTERRUPTION INSURANCE—UNITED KINGDOM

311. Accidents to and breakdown of plant and machinery

Many of the factors and problems calling for consideration in the negotiation of an insurance against business interruption following fire and kindred perils, generally dealt with by an insurer's fire department, apply similarly to insurance against loss resulting from the contingencies which are the preserve of insurance companies' engineering departments and specialist engineering insurance companies. But the material damage accident or breakdown risks handled by them call for extremely specialised knowledge and surveys and as a result they also generally deal with what was originally called consequential loss engineering or consequential loss breakdown and is now termed Engineering Business Interruption insurance.

The cover under current policies is much wider than the one-time "breakdown" insurance and applies to loss resulting from "accident", this being defined as sudden and unforeseen damage from an accidental cause to "the machinery" or "the property".

In the United States the corresponding insurance is called Boiler and Machinery business interruption coverage and is dealt with in Chapter 16, paragraphs 328 to 339.

312. Daily payments "time loss" insurance

The original practice was to issue a restricted form of protection against consequential loss by what was known as a "time loss" policy as a supplement to the cover under a breakdown material damage insurance policy. A time loss policy provided for the payment of an agreed fixed amount per day in the event of a complete stoppage due to the breakdown of the plant or machinery concerned and, generally, a proportionate part of this amount for each day of partial interruption.

While a time loss policy has the merit of simplicity it cannot provide a true indemnity and the loss consequent upon breakdown of plant or machinery may considerably exceed the limited amount usually provided under such an insurance, the sum insured being of necessity an arbitrary figure. It is rigid in application, makes no satisfactory provision for increase in cost of working, no allowance for seasonal fluctuations in earnings, cannot adequately meet the complications of wages losses and fails to indemnify for any loss after the plant is operating again.

An engineering business interruption policy arranged so that an insured's loss is determined on more flexible lines similar to those under an insurance against business interruption through fire is to be preferred in order to secure a full indemnity and is now regarded as the normal practice except for a limited range of small businesses. These latter include such retail trade risks as butchers, fried fish shops, launderettes, dry cleaners' shops, hairdressers and beauty salons, and motor garages in which the only vulnerable plant comprises small electric motors, refrigerators, boilers, air compressors and the like and the period of interruption is likely to be very short. For this type of business a policy providing compensation of an agreed amount per working day of stoppage seems the most practical way of insuring.

313. Engineering business interruption—reasons for insuring

Much plant and machinery runs for years free from serious breakdown and this coupled with the fact that the premiums charged for business interruption accident insurance relating to it can appear to be heavy may be a deterrent to the negotiation of appropriate cover. But the premiums charged are relatively higher than those for policies covering business interruption through fire because the overall incidence of accident or breakdown is high. Insurance companies' records show that about one in every five policies covering engineering business interruption gives rise to a claim each year.

Some firms hold the view that such insurance is unnecessary because they have duplicate standby plant which could be quickly brought into use in the event of an accident or breakdown. Unfortunately, in actual practice this opinion is not always fully substantiated. It may be that only the main power units are duplicated or that the standby plant is old or less efficient and probably more expensive to run or being the predecessor of the current plant is incapable of carrying the present full works' load.

Even where there is a modern and self-contained standby plant capable of meeting the whole of the factory's needs there is still a strong case for insurance. The running machine may be out of use for a lengthy period of repairs following breakdown and during that time the works will be wholly dependent upon the standby plant which in turn may suffer breakdown. Should the two units normally be situate side by side a breakage in the running plant might also damage the standby machine and so render them both inoperative simultaneously. Moreover, the reliability and efficiency factor of standby plant is always taken into account when fixing the premium for an insurance of this nature and may result in a very substantial reduction.

Experience of losses due to electricity supply cuts and power reductions by public supply undertakings during the 1970s led many industrial concerns to install standby generating plant as a precautionary measure against future occurrences but because of either oversight or overconfidence they sometimes omit to include it in their schedule of plant for business interruption insurance. Breakdown of such plant if ever called into use is possible, particularly so if it had not been run over a prolonged period. Insurers recognise that its purpose is only as a reserve power unit which will be called upon on very infrequent occasions, if ever, and as it is a minimal risk the premium charged for such standby generators is generally a nominal one which makes inclusion in the insurance worthwhile.

Another mistake is often made in thinking that repairs or replacements can be effected within a matter of hours or at most a day or two. In practice it is all too frequently found that unforeseen delays occur because the makers or repairers are out of stock of replacement parts or units, or are fully engaged on urgent orders, that temporary plant cannot be bought or hired locally, or that some extraneous contingency such as holidays, illness or a strike at the repairers coincides with the breakdown. Often the repairs effected are to some extent an experiment because even experts cannot be certain of their efficacy until they are tried; if such work proves unsuccessful then the period of breakdown is further prolonged. In fact the whole problem of plant and machinery repairs is fraught with difficulties and the only way for a firm to be adequately protected is to arrange business interruption insurance with a good margin for unforeseen complications.

314. Sudden and unforeseen damage—"accident" cover

Until around 1970 an engineering business interruption insurance was the subject of a closely defined and restrictive definition of "breakdown" and some other causes of damage and detailed schedule of items of plant and machinery. But the march of progress saw the evolution of a multi-perils contract embracing in the one definition "accident" any sudden and unforeseen damage. This is much wider cover than the previous definition gave and also can be applied to any part of an overall description of the insured plant which might include process machinery as well as prime movers. In circumstances where this inclusive cover is not required definitions are stated in the policy of the risks insured such as breakdown, extraneous (accidental) damage, explosion, collapse and overheating of boilers.

Cover is ordinarily applicable to steam, gas or oil engines and turbines, electric generators, motors, transformers, rotary converters, rectifiers, switchgear, etc., pumps, fans, compressors, boilers, heat exchangers, hydraulic machinery, air conditioning plants, calorifiers and piping, passenger and goods lifts, cranes and other lifting and handling plant, and to numerous types of process machinery. An insured can select for business interruption insurance key machines essential to production and is not required to insure all machines. (For insurance of computers see paragraph 328.)

315. The engineering business interruption policy

A typical engineering business interruption policy undertakes to indemnify the insured against the amount of loss resulting from interruption of or interference with the business in consequence of "the Accident". The meaning of the latter is not usually given in the policy wording but in the specification (see following paragraph 316). The general terms and conditions of the policy are similar to those of a fire business interruption policy but the contingencies insurable under such a policy are excluded—that is, loss resulting from fire, lightning, explosion, aircraft, storm, flood and water damage or sprinkler leakage (and sometimes earthquake, subterranean fire and volcanic eruption) is not insured. Also normally excluded are any consequences of loss or damage consisting of wearing away, wasting, erosion, corrosion, slowly developing deformation or distortion or any other gradual deterioration or failure of any part requiring periodical review (but insurers are liable for loss in consequence of damage resulting from such causes and otherwise insured by the cover). Loss resulting from riot, strike, lock-out or civil commotion is another common exclusion. The insured is also usually required to take certain precautions—to keep the machinery (or "property") in a proper state of maintenance and repair, to prevent accident or loss, and to retain in efficient working condition and available for immediate use any standby or spare machines which were in existence when the insurance was effected. Another possible condition is that the insured must discontinue the use of any damaged machine (or "property") until it is satisfactorily repaired. Engineering business interruption policy wordings are not standard in the United Kingdom with terms, conditions, exceptions, etc., varying in some respects between insurers and appearing either in the policy itself or in the specification (where reference is made at times to the terms, conditions, exceptions, etc., in the relevant material damage policy or material damage section where the policy is a combined one). An example of a policy wording is set out in Appendix M, paragraph 459.

316. The specification for engineering business interruption insurance

A specimen specification is set out in Appendix N, paragraph 460. The specification sets out the formula for calculating the amount of an insured's claim on a turnover basis on the same lines as for a fire business interruption insurance except that the word "accident" is substituted for the word "damage" (or "Incident") and there is an exclusion of the first 24 hours or other period stated in an excess or exclusion provision as per paragraph 317. Professional accountants' charges for preparing details required for a claim are included free as in paragraph 378.

"Accident" is defined in the specification as "sudden and unforeseen damage from an accidental cause to the property whilst at the situation" (both "property" and "situation" being defined in the schedule which is part of the policy document). "Accident" also means failure of the supply of an Insured Public Utility as stated on the schedule, this cover being in effect that described in paragraph 319.

Concurrency of the fire and the engineering business interruption specifications facilitates periodic revisions and alterations to the sums insured; in the engineering business interruption policy the sum insured is termed the "amount of indemnity". The shorter maximum indemnity periods which are a regular feature of business interruption accident insurances may mean differences in the sum insured for gross profit and particularly for wages as compared with the corresponding business interrupton fire policies.

For some businesses a loss of gross revenue or a takings specification may be more suitable than one based on loss of turnover because the effects of a stoppage on income might be total but the stoppage may be for a short period only as quick repair or replacement of the equipment is possible, and also it is unlikely that there would be any savings in standing charges, for instance, theatres, cinemas and floodlit evening entertainments such as professional football, cricket and baseball matches and dog racing stadiums. For such insurances the indemnity is made subject to a condition that if the cancelled event is held on a subsequent date any money received for it shall be brought into account to offset the loss.

317. The indemnity period: 24 hours', etc., exclusion (period of excess)

The maximum indemnity period chosen is frequently shorter than that covered under the insurance against business interruption through fire because the question of the time necessary for rebuilding premises does not normally enter into the question; in appropriate circumstances a period as short as seven days might be arranged. Because the effects on production of machinery impaired by accident differ so radically from those following damage by fire and allied perils the method of calculating premium charges is different from the standardised percentage loadings on a basis rate used in business interruption fire insurances. In addition it is more necessary and practicable to give special consideration to individual cases and make allowance for circumstances such as a store of spare parts, standby motors or machines, whether plant is made in the home country or abroad, the speed of service for repairs from the makers, the qualifications of the insured's own maintenance staff, and so on.

An important feature of the indemnity period is that liability for a minimum period of the first 24 hours etc., after an accident is excluded. The purpose of this exclusion is to eliminate claims arising from stoppages of short duration which may occur from time to time as a result of minor occurrences. If policies were to include these small losses the expense of investigating and handling them would be disproportionately expensive and the higher premiums required would nullify the benefit of the extra cover. Nevertheless, it is possible where very special circumstances apply to obtain cover even for the first 24 hours after the accident but considerable additional premium is required for this.

On the other hand when desired a time excess of 48 hours, 96 hours or even longer can be arranged with a corresponding reduction in the rate of premium. An arrangement of this nature would probably suit the needs of a firm which always carries a stock of finished goods large enough to maintain turnover for at least the length of the chosen time exclusion, though it might be advisable even in such cases to limit the period to 24 hours for the wages insurance. As an underwriting requirement, *e.g.* in respect of foreign made machinery which could involve long delays in obtaining replacement parts, insurers might want a longer excess period than 24 hours.

It will be noticed that there is no reference to "24 *working* hours" and if the insured contingency occurred shortly before a factory closed down for the weekend the indemnity would be fully effective from the normal starting time on the following Monday morning.

Accidents frequently occur in which although the stoppage for repairs would in the ordinary way exceed the excluded first 24 hours after the accident thanks to special measures the repairs are completed and the machinery is running again within the excepted period. These special measures may involve considerable additional expenditure on overtime wages, air freightage on replacement parts from abroad, or temporary repairs. Increased cost of working incurred in the first 24 hours or longer excess period immediately following an accident which is excluded from the insurance is not recoverable under clause (b) even though it may avert some loss of turnover after the expiry of the excess period. This is because the exclusion is of "*loss of gross profit* insured during any excess period" and in the operative clause the "loss of gross profit" insured is defined as that due to reduction in turnover and increase in cost of working, that is, the two combined.

318. Items of plant included for business interruption insurance but not insured for material damage

While many firms wish to exclude certain items of plant from their business interrruption cover some may wish to include items which are not insured under an engineering direct damage insurance. The reason for this may be that a firm have their own engineering staff to maintain the plant or certain items of it in running order and are also large enough financially to stand the cost themselves of any repairs should breakdown occur. But although the cost of such repairs may be of limited amount the potential loss of production may be entirely disproportionate should the particular plant be a key factor in their manufacturing process. Hence their wish to insure the business interruption risk attaching to certain plant for which there is no breakdown cover.

Insurers will generally accept a proposition of this nature provided that they are satisfied that the plant concerned is adequately serviced and is inspected regularly by a competent engineer. Their attitude will be more favourable if the inspections are carried out by the engineering surveyor under their own or a specialist company's inspection service contract.

Should there be a material damage proviso on the policy—this is not the invariable practice—like that on a business interruption fire policy it would be necessary to amend or delete it in respect of any plant on which there is no material damage insurance.

319. Failure of electricity, gas and water supplies

The majority of manufacturing business and also those in the entertainment industry such as theatres and cinemas, sports, etc., grounds operating in evenings with floodlighting, and racecourses using totalisators and dependent upon electricity supplies are faced with a loss of revenue should there be a failure of supply for even a limited period. The crops of nurserymen whose glasshouses are dependent upon electricity for temperature control are very vulnerable to a failure at night particularly in the winter (refer also paragraph 309). Chicken, etc., breeders are similarly liable to sustain severe loss but in their case the risk is included in a composite policy for "factory farming" (paragraph 270(c)). Some manufacturers are also dependent upon public utility supplies of gas or water as mentioned later.

It is usual for an engineering business interruption policy to include as a second meaning of "accident" the failure of supply of a public utility at the terminal point of the undertaking's feed to the insured's premises, subject to the exclusion of certain defined occurrences of deliberate act or scheme of rationing by the supply undertaking. For details see the wording in the specification in Appendix N. "Public Utility" includes electricity, gas and water supplies. There is usually an initial 30 minute Period of Franchise so that if there is a failure of supply for at least that period the insurance cover will operate from the start of the failure.

A special policy can be issued independently of any engineering business interruption insurance in respect of an insured's plant or the risk of failure of electricity, etc., can be included in such a policy as above. The policy generally issued gives an indemnity in respect of any stoppage up to 30 days in duration; sometimes a short indemnity period of only 10 days is arranged. There is no initial time exclusion but a 30 minute franchise is included, that is, if there is total cessation of supply for at least 30 consecutive minutes the cover operates from the start of the failure. A 24 hour excess can be substituted for the 30 minute franchise in which case the premium rate is reduced to about a quarter of the normal charge.

The premium charge depends upon which of the three supplies—electricity, gas and water—is included in the cover, whether they are from public authorities or from independent sources and whether there are alternative means of supply available, as well as on the nature of the insured's business.

Thanks to the national electricity grid the failure of the power supply in any area may not be of long duration in normal conditions. But even grid systems can fail as 25 million people found in the record United States electricity breakdown in November 1965 which affected nearly all New York, Boston, most parts of nine north-western states and two provinces in Canada. And as all standing charges and probably all wages will continue to be payable in full during a stoppage of short duration when there may be no production whatever the resulting loss of net profit can be quite disproportionate to the length of the stoppage.

A greater risk attaches when gas from the public supply is used for industrial processes essential to the production at a factory although the distribution of natural gas through a national transmission grid considerably reduces the risk. But a serious fire or explosion at the terminal plant where the natural gas is converted for commercial use or at a distribution point could have widespread effects. As illustrated by the explosion and fire at the liquified natural gas regasification plant at Cove Point terminal on Chesapeake Bay, United States in 1979 which closed down operation of the transmission system for two weeks and, also, the destruction of the pump station at Forchheim near Munich in October 1980 which disrupted the supply of natural gas through the Soviet pipeline to West Germany. Many works are wholly dependent upon gas which is used for furnaces, lehrs or other process plant; steelworks, wireworks, glassworks, potteries, the motor industry and engineering works of various kinds, bakeries and biscuit factories, are typical examples. In a variety of other trades many factories have gas-heated appliances on a production line thereby making the flow of work dependent upon a continuous supply of gas.

In a similar manner certain trades, notably laundries, breweries, soft drink factories, dairies, steelworks, paper mills, textile dyers and the like may be dependent upon the public water supply. Although a waterworks is not associated in the public mind with the danger of fire, that or explosion or a breakdown of plant can occur at a waterworks pumping station, or pumping operations can be stopped by a failure of the electricity supply, causing an interruption of supplies. Experience shows that in such an event any emergency supplies obtained from neighbouring towns have to be conserved for domestic use; and were the damage to take place during a period of severe drought as for instance that in 1976 or in 1990 the difficulties would be even more acute. Many water companies carry a business interruption insurance to cover the loss which they would suffer as a result of interruption caused by damage or breakdown at their pumping and filtration plants which indicates that for businesses substantially dependent on public water supplies an appropriate extension of their business interruption policy is a wise precaution.

It should be noted that the loss covered by insurance against failure of public utilities is that due to reduction in turnover and any loss of materials which are spoilt whilst in process because of the failure of electricity, gas or water supplies is not insured beyond the part of their value which constitutes the gross profit on any turnover lost. This may be of considerable importance where loss of power or heat or water can cause the spoilage of valuable materials or where solidification might set in and damage the plant itself (see paragraph 321 for United Kingdom insurance of such loss and paragraph 338 for United States coverage).

320. Special simplified schemes for engineering business interruption

To cater for certain classes of businesses in which the machinery used is to a very large extent standardised throughout their particular trade special simplified schemes are provided by some insurers. These may eliminate the need for an inspection survey of the machinery to be included in the insurance which may be described as being "all machinery and plant permanently at the premises used directly by the insured in (a) the manufacture of the products of or (b) providing the services rendered by the insured's business". Machinery excluded from the cover may be office machinery, computer installations and other data processing equipment, machinery and plant which is prototype or experimental or otherwise not proven under normal operating conditions or known by the insured not to be in current production by the manufacturer at the time of inception of the insurance or at any renewal of it; tools, dyes, moulds or parts of any machinery or plant which require periodical renewal; and refractory materials.

Otherwise the terms of the usual policy and specification are the same as in a normal engineering business interruption insurance covering sudden and unforeseen damage from accidental cause. There is a 24 hour excess period and an extension to the public utilities supply of electricity, gas and water with a 30 minute franchise. Any consequences of damage resulting from fire or kindred perils insurable under such policies are excluded as well as those from wear and tear, overloading, strikes, etc. The amount of indemnity to be insured is the total annual gross profit of the whole of the business. Premium charges are according to trade categories based on the types of plant and machinery normal in such trades. Typical of these are, in ascending order of premium rating, (i) bakers, breweries, cold stores, dry cleaners, laundries, clothing and textiles (ii) cardboard factories, meat processors, printers (iii) cement, glass, glue, plastics and rubber manufacturers.

A scheme aimed at small to medium-sized firms (with a maximum annual gross profit sum insured of perhaps £3 to £5 million) is also available with a minimum of information required covering all the insured's plant and machinery that is less than 25 years old at the time of the "accident". Cover may be included in respect of spoilage of products in process subject to a monetary limit (of perhaps £25,000).

321. Spoilage of materials due to failure of electricity, etc., supplies

Processes in quite a number of industries are dependent upon the maintenance of a continuous, regulated temperature and if this is interrupted the materials being processed may be ruined. Although public utility undertakings' employees try to give advance warning when a cut in supplies is imminent this may not always be in sufficient time or, in an emergency situation due to damage at an undertaking's works, it may not be possible.

Spoilage from this cause may happen in bread and confectionery bakeries, biscuit factories, dyehouses for textile fabrics, pharmaceutical or other chemical works, chocolate and candy makers dependent on cooling equipment in hot weather, porcelain, glassware and ceramic annealing tunnels, dyeing of leather in tanneries, injection moulding machines or articles being plated with nickel, zinc or chrome in light engineering works, and so on. Certain types of high tensile steel products which have to be subjected to very high temperatures produced by electricity will fragment and be ruined if the current is suddenly cut off.

Although the above is consequential loss in the sense that it is loss consequent upon an insurable peril whether machinery accident or interruption of public utilities when these are insured, the value of the material as at the time of the spoilage is outside the terms of a U.K. business interruption policy on loss of gross profit due to reduction in turnover. Similarly it is not covered by a U.S. policy which is concerned solely with loss of income as is defined and specifically excludes any consequential loss.

It is possible, however, to insure against such material loss by means of an additional item, with a separate sum insured, on a U.K. engineering accident business interruption policy in respect of process plant and machinery the stoppage of which might give rise to spoilage of materials, extended to include such loss due to failure of public utility supplies. Similarly in the United States, insurance is available by means of a specific coverage under what is termed a "consequential loss" insurance.

322. Advance profits (machinery accident) insurance

Business interruption insurance giving advance cover of an "all risks" nature in connection with the construction of new factories or major extensions to existing premises is dealt with in paragraph 268(a). Machinery accident risks are included as part of such cover from its inception at a machine maker's works through the stages of loading, transit, unloading, installation and testing at the new location.

But even where there is no new building construction or alteration of existing factory premises there may be times when an insured is open to loss resulting from accident to a machine not in his works. This can arise in connection with the purchase of a new machine whilst under construction and after completion at the maker's premises and during transit and installation. Similar risks may attach to an existing machine whilst removed from the insured's works for overhaul or repair.

Extra hazard is entailed when a purchase of new machinery is made to replace existing plant. Before it can be installed the plant and machinery to be replaced, which may be an individual item of a key nature or possibly a whole factory floor, must be removed to make room for the replacement and might already have been scrapped or sold before the latter arrives at the insured's factory. This is a period of maximum risk with the firm exposed to the danger that if any damage occurs to the new plant before it is installed they will be left with both old and new out of commission without any business interruption insurance operative.

Hence the need in any circumstances of the above nature to arrange in good time beforehand with the insurers of the firm's engineering insurance an advance profits cover on somewhat similar lines to that described in paragraph 268(a) for the new factory premises. For such an insurance it is usually required that there be appropriate material damage cover in force from the time the risk commences at the maker's works until the machinery is installed and tested at the insured's factory.

323. Disablement of refrigerating plant by accident

Loss due to reduction in turnover (as distinct from the material loss of fruit, vegetables, fish, seafood, meat or other perishable commodities which is termed the "spoilage risk" and is a matter for special insurance (see paragraph 324) consequent upon the disablement of refrigerating plant due to accident) can be insured under a normal engineering business interruption insurance either as a separate policy or as an addition to the policy in respect of the material damage.

But in arranging such cover it should be borne in mind that although the actual period of disablement may probably be quite short, the business interruption loss arising from shortage of food for processing or from increased costs of obtaining new supplies, due to the damage to the perishable goods in the cold stores, might extend over a period of weeks or months during which they would normally have been taken into the factory for processing. Where they constitute a seasonal supply and cannot be replaced until the next season the loss of such goods could, according to the time when the breakdown occurred, affect turnover for up to 12 months—longer if customers are lost permanently.

In a business interruption policy solely in respect of the refrigerating plant in an insured's cold store the exclusion of the first 24 hours after the accident which is normally applied to an engineering business interruption policy is waived. It is considered unnecessary because it is unlikely that the contents of a cold store would deteriorate within that time.

324. Deterioration of stock in refrigerators and cold stores

The insurance described in the preceding paragraph 323 is in respect of the continuing interruption of business which may result from a serious breakdown of refrigerating plant. In such an event the policy would operate to measure the insured's loss by the reduction in turnover of the business in subsequent months. But this would not compensate for any loss due to deterioration of stock, that is, the loss of material value. For manufacturers, processors and wholesalers of perishable foods this is a serious risk. A fuller discussion of this is given in paragraph 269 about "spoilage insurance" in connection with fire, etc., damage.

To provide against such loss due to an "accident" a cover can be arranged to indemnify an insured in respect of reduction of value of stored goods and increase in cost of working. Accident is defined as (a) a rise or fall in temperature in cold chamber(s) in which the stored goods are contained as a direct result of sudden and unforeseen damage from an accidental cause to a machine or to the permanent structure and (b) the action of refrigerant fumes escaping from any accidental cause. (See also paragraph 338 and 339 for United States practices.)

The reduction in value insured is the amount by which the money realised from the sale of the stored goods falls short of the estimated selling price in consequence of the damage. The estimated selling price is that which would have been obtained at the market(s) selected by the insured on the date(s) on which he would have sold the stored goods had no accident occurred, with due allowance for all material factors which would have affected the price had the accident not occurred. A pro rata average proviso is applied on that basis and loss of value of stored goods due to faulty packing or storage or inherent defects or diseases is excluded.

It is possible for such an insurance to be extended to include loss of value of goods which at the time of the accident are not in the cold store but are at the situation and would in the normal course be placed in a refrigerated chamber.

325. Frozen food in cabinets in shops and in specialist frozen food stores

An insurance similar to that in respect of deterioration of food in refrigerating plants described in the preceding paragraph 324 is provided to compensate for loss or damage to food whilst in frozen food cabinets in retail shops, e.g. butchers, fish, fruit and poultry dealers, grocers, etc. The sum insured is the maximum full value of the stock in the cabinet and the insurance is granted irrespective of any breakdown policy, but is subject to the exclusion of loss or damage occasioned by the wilful act or neglect of the insured.

A similar cover is available for specialist frozen food shops and stores in which food from freezers is the sole commodity handled.

326. Computer installations

The ownership of computers, on-line computer systems, computerised data-banks and data-processing equipment by commercial and industrial concerns, banks, building societies, credit unions, insurance companies and other large office organisations, universities, institutions and administrative bodies of all kinds, involves the necessity for some form of business interruption insurance. In some cases it may be considered adequate if the insurance covers only increase in cost of working which may consist largely of the additional expenditure on hiring time at a computer centre and the overtime and travelling expenses of staff in the operation. But the possibility must be considered that it may not be possible to hire computer time just when needed.

A policy provided for non-manufacturing concerns with computerised functions such as office organisations mentioned above may be inadequate if it insures only increase in cost of working and not loss of revenue. A bank for instance, as with any financial institution today, is heavily dependent on computer-based systems for its operations particularly in the area of international currency dealing, etc., where income lost cannot be "clawed back" at a later stage (see also paragraph 392 on Financial Institutions).

Ownership of computers and minicomputers is now widespread throughout industry and commerce in all kinds of businesses and increase in cost of working insurance alone may not be adequate, particularly for on-line working systems which can include many small installations because it is the immediacy of the information it can supply which is a very important feature. For instance, a firm which sells electronic components may use a computer which enables them to put up a stock list immediately and so they can handle many more phone calls which might increase their sales by as much as 25 per cent. If the computer is out of action the effect on turnover will be immediate and severe. The business of organisations of all kinds connected with tourism and travel which use computers would be greatly handicapped without their facilities.

Once a computer becomes part of the daily functioning of any business the increasing dependency upon it, whether a small desk model or a large installation, spells loss if it is out of action for more than a very short period. The fully automated factory will soon be with us and sophisticated new computer equipment will be needed to assist in the organisation, control and monitoring of the new production and assembly methods and systems. A maintenance contract will not pay for loss of revenue or additional expenditure resulting from damage to a computer from external causes, accident or negligence.

A special Computer Policy is generally in two sections, one insuring material damage and the other covering business interruption corresponding in general conditions and exclusions with the direct damage section but possibly being wider in scope in respect of perils insured. Where the computer operations are an integral part of a commercial or industrial undertaking a fire and named perils business interruption insurance of the business will include loss resulting from the damage to the computer installation by fire, boiler explosion and any other insured perils. But because such insurances do not cover loss due to accidental damage or breakdown, to which risks computers are specially vulnerable and may not include water damage (other than that arising from fire extinguishing operation) which can be very serious should the computer room be flooded, a special Computer Policy is worthwhile. Even where the main business interruption cover is on an all risks basis, a separate computer policy is probably still preferable.

Because the ownership or leasing of computers is now widespread and normal throughout all types of businesses there has been of recent years a rapid development of the provision of insurance by package policies and by individually tailored covers. Many include novel features with practically all risks protection. The introduction of silicon chips and microcomputers into small factories and computerised individual machines such as drills and lathes in engineering works has increased the range of insurance possibilities. Machines which are solid state computers are usually dealt with as being included in a normal business interruption policy but in some businesses, *e.g.* in the clothing industry, it may be found best to cover the machines under a separate computer policy. So there is no hard and fast rule and the scope and terms of insurance now on the market vary from insurer to insurer, competition being a spur for the provision of better value to insured. But the provisions of specifications used for calculating the loss of gross profit or revenue and increase in cost of working are generally in the standard form.

A typical definition of a computer in a policy is that it means all parts of the electronic data processing installation at the situation stated in the policy schedule, excluding tapes, cards, disks and disk packs or any other data-carrying material other than fixed disks and any air conditioning plant. So it automatically includes peripherals such as readers, visual display units, punches, printers, tape decks, sorters, terminals and disk drives, all a matter of importance for a large installation.

The insurance refers to loss consequent upon interruption of or interference with the business caused by "Accident" which is then defined as accidental damage or breakdown or failure of distribution equipment together with failure of the public supply of electricity, denial of access to the use of the computer caused by damage to property in the vicinity, and also the erasure of data.

Erasure of data is defined as the accidental or malicious erasure, destruction, distortion or corruption of data or programmes contained on the property resulting from an identifiable cause but excluding the permanent or temporary loss of or loss of use of or inaccessibility of data or programmes directly resulting from pre-existing faults in or unsuitability of programmes or computer systems software and also excluding losses caused by a malicious act and discovered later than 12 months after the loss was initiated.

Additional benefits usually available include cover against the results (costs of modification, etc.) of incompatibility of computer records following a loss, the increased risk of temporary removal (within the United Kingdom), consulting engineers' fees, the additional expense of temporary repairs, removal of debris costs and the costs of protecting the property from further damage. Limitations of liability are applied where practicable.

Insurance of additional rental charges is usually included in the policy without a separate sum insured. That is, if as a direct result of an accident the lease or hire contract in force is cancelled and has to be replaced by a new one at a higher rental or charge, the insurance pays the additional amount during the two year period commencing from the time when the business is no longer affected by the contingency, subject to a limit of 25 per cent. of the gross profit or increased costs sum insured.

To eliminate claims for short periods of stoppage which could probably be made good by subsequent longer working there is a time excess in respect of accidental damage or breakdown or erasure of data or failure of distribution equipment and a time franchise in respect of failure of electricity supply. The cost of reinstatement of data or programmes on to data carrying media can be insured provided that the loss of the data is directly caused by an "Accident".

This includes the often considerable expenses of collecting the data again from its various sources. A monetary excess may be applied to this cover. Also for an additional premium loss resulting from damage to the air conditioning plant, motor generators, etc., at the installation can be insured.

In certain circumstances dependence on land line connections of computers to terminals can carry serious risk of interruption of business in the event of damage to British Telecom land lines. If an extension of cover is added for this contingency a time excess is incorporated but cover cannot be provided against loss due to deliberate withdrawal of facilities by the telecommunications authorities.

Charges payable to professional accountants for producing particulars of a claim are paid as described in paragraph 378, a return of premium clause is included as detailed in paragraph 225(a) and automatic reinstatement of the amount payable under a claim is provided for on the lines of the memo, in paragraph 231 (with the insured possibly paying an additional premium only when the reinstatement exceeds a certain amount, *e.g.* £25,000).

Automatic cover is given in respect of property similar to that insured which is installed after the inception of the insurance, generally up to a limit of perhaps £25,000 and subject to its being in satisfactory working order when installed and to the insurer being notified within 200 days of commencement of use and the insured paying any additional premium required.

With the increasing dependence of business in general on electronic data processing equipment, there is the need for disaster planning. An insurance policy, however wide it is in the cover it provides, will only compensate for a financial loss; it will not guarantee the maintenance of the service provided by the equipment. Recent years have seen the emergence of so-called "disaster clubs", professional computer recovery services, reciprocal arrangements between firms with similar installations, and the establishment of in-house standby computer rooms or even standby computers. Such is the exposure to severe disruption in some circumstances that it is more important to *manage* the risk as a whole than merely to insure it (refer also paragraph 241).

The rapidly increasing sophistication of computer installations and of those using them has given rise to a number of new "perils" which are computer-related. There are "bugs" or "viruses" with which computer systems can be 'infected" and which can cause chaos particularly if they are deliberately introduced by persons who have malicious or criminal motivations. We now hear of "Trojan Horses" and "logic bombs" which some insurers may accept as forms of malicious damage. Insurers must be aware of the risks they are facing and underwrite accordingly.

327. Electronics industry

Parallel with the growth of the use of computers throughout industry and commerce is that of the electronics industry in general and on its heels follows the provision of insurance designed specifically for protection against the many risks involved. In particular those associated with the manufacture and supply of small but valuable items of electronic equipment of which speedy delivery is of great importance and delay may mean considerable consequential loss by a customer.

Package covers have been devised to provide insurance against practically all risks for goods in transit which include business interruption insurance for loss of gross profit and additional costs resulting from the damage by insured perils at the premises of the makers or intermediate suppliers anywhere in the world. It extends to give what in this industry can be very useful cover for fines or damages for breach of contract in respect of non-completion or late completion of orders resulting from an insured contingency (refer also paragraph 261(b)).

CHAPTER 16

BOILER AND MACHINERY COVERAGE—UNITED STATES

328. General observations

As with U.K. engineering business interruption accident insurance practice which has largely changed from "time loss" insurance to the more flexible cover provided by using reduction in turnover as the basic yardstick for measuring a loss, in the United States the traditional "U & O" methods have been superseded by a more modern form on similar lines to fire business interruption coverages.

The form is an "actual loss" coverage on net profit and fixed charges. It is applied in the form of an endorsement on the direct damage insurance of a Boiler and Machinery Coverage form to the general conditions and exclusions of which they are subject along with the Common Policy Conditions. A primary condition of the insurance is that loss must result from direct damage to a unit by an "accident" insured under the Boiler and Machinery Coverage form. On the other hand all items insured by the latter need not be included in the business interruption insurance.

Because conditions for the operation of plant and machinery and problems involved in interruption of their functioning are similar in industry worldwide the various comments on the necessity for insurance in Chapter 15 on U.K. engineering business interruption insurances apply equally to B. & M. coverages in the United States. But the wordings for the latter are much longer and more involved than U.K. policies and include some onerous conditions not featured in U.K. insurances.

An anomaly in fire gross earnings forms which has produced problems in claim settlements over past years was obviated in the pre-1987 B. & M. forms in which the meaning of "business" is broadly defined. For a mercantile business it was gross sales on the premises; for a manufacturing risk it was production on the premises of finished goods ready for packing, shipment or sale; for service businesses such as entertainment undertakings, garages, offices, hotels, etc., it was gross income; and for rent insurances it was rents collectible from the premises.

The new form evolved by the I.S.O. (Insurance Services Office) in 1988 is in line with the new fire Business Income Coverage forms in its use for instance of "you" and "we" instead of "insured" and "insurers", etc. However, it remains an endorsement to the Boiler and Machinery Coverage form and cannot stand alone as a separate policy. There is no definition of the meaning of "business".

329. Material damage insurance

The contractual clause of a Boiler and Machinery direct damage policy insures loss from an "accident" to an "object"—the counterpart of "accident" to a "machine" in a U.K. policy. The current definitions of the U.S. terms in general use are as follows: "accident" means a sudden and accidental breakdown of the object or a part of the object. At the time the breakdown occurs it must manifest itself at the time of its occurrence by physical damage to the object that necessitates repair or replacement of the object or part thereof. Then customary exclusions such as depletion, deterioration, corrosion, erosion, wear and tear, etc., follow.

"Object" means the equipment shown in the Declarations. Full descriptions of specific object categories are found in the Object Definitions endorsement attached to the Boiler and Machinery Coverage form. There are several such endorsements ranging from specific objects such as mechanical or electrical objects to a comprehensive coverage.

330. Period of indemnity

Similarly to a U.K. insurance the coverage does not normally start until a specified time after the occurrence of an accident. This "time deductible" may be a minimum of 12 time-hours or any longer period in multiples of 12 hours. In lieu of a waiting period expressed in this way there may be substituted a "dollar deductible" calculated by converting the number of hours to a monetary figure.

As in a fire business interruption coverage, no indemnity period is stated as such but instead of the time necessary for rebuilding and restoration of damaged premises being the time element during which compensation is payable the boiler and machinery insurance uses the "limit of loss" stated in the schedule as the maximum amount of payment for any one accident. The "limit of loss" is not part of the "limit of insurance" (the overall amount insured), it is a separate limit. The period during which compensation is paid is not limited to the expiry date of the policy.

331. Actual loss sustained form: insuring agreement

This policy form undertakes to indemnify for total or partial interruption of business though it does not, as a fire business interruption coverage form does, refer to loss of gross earnings or Business Income. Instead, whilst similarly providing for payment based on the actual loss sustained it goes straight to a definition of such loss. This is defined as meaning loss of net profits and that part of the following fixed charges and expenses which the business did not earn because of the accident but which it would have earned had the accident not occurred: (i) manufacturing, selling, administrative expenses and any other items contributing to the overhead expenses of the insured (ii) salaries and wages of officers, executives, employees under contract and other essential employees, pensions and directors' fees but not including the insured's ordinary payroll expense. When insurance on ordinary payroll expense is required this may be added and the exclusion is deleted in the definition. The definition of "actual loss" concludes with a provision for trends of business and special circumstances informing the insured that consideration shall be given to the actual experience of the business before the accident and probable experience thereafter.

The description of Coverage undertakes to pay, in addition to the amount of actual loss sustained, reasonable extra expense incurred by the insured or the insurer to reduce or avert interruption of business but only to the extent that the total amount that would otherwise have been paid for actual loss sustained is thereby reduced. In other words, additional expenditure is covered not exceeding X dollars to save X dollars. The combined total of actual loss sustained and the extra expense incurred is subject to the limit of loss on the policy and all such extra expense is thus part of and not in addition to the limit of loss.

332. Commencement of liability

The insured is required to give immediate notice of an accident (to be confirmed later in writing) to any address of the insurer and commencement of liability is either 24 hours before this notice is received or the time of the accident whichever is later. No mention is made of any particular method which will not be accepted as notification of an accident.

If a policy contains a time deductible this applies for the stated number of hours immediately following the commencement of liability. If it is a dollar deductible this is to be subtracted from the total amount of the loss sustained and extra expenses for which the insurer would be liable under the insuring agreement. Therefore, under either category of deductible, an insured has to stand any loss accruing during the period prior to commencement of liability as well as the actual deductible.

The statement is made that insurers "will not pay for any loss or expense due to the interruption of business that would not or could not have been carried on if the accident had not occurred". This will exclude payments by the insurer for periods when production would normally have ceased, such as closure at weekends and holidays or due to shortage of orders or by strikes or by partial stoppages for installing new plant and machinery.

333. The amount of indemnity: coinsurance

The limit of loss is stated in the policy schedule as an amount of dollars. This may be a percentage, from 25 per cent. to 100 per cent. of the "estimated annual value" and is the maximum amount recoverable under the policy. The amount of the "estimated annual value" is also shown in the schedule with a definition of its meaning which is the amount for the following 12 months, as estimated in the most recent annual report, of net profit, fixed charges and expenses as referred to in the definition of actual loss. This excludes ordinary payroll.

The amount of the "estimated annual value" (the amount that would have been earned in the same period) comes into the coinsurance condition. This differs from the similar condition on a fire business interruption coverage by not stating any coinsurance percentage. The condition reads:

> "If the Business Interruption 'annual value' at the time of loss is greater than the 'estimated annual value' shown in your latest report or if your report was received by us more than three months after the due date, or if your report is overdue, we will not pay the full amount of any loss. Instead, we will determine the most we will pay using the following steps:
>
> a. Divide the 'estimated annual value' last reported to us by the 'annual value' at the time of the 'accident';
> b. Multiply the total amount of the covered loss by the figure determined in paragraph a. above;
> c. Subtract the applicable deductible from the amount determined in paragraph b. above;
> d. The resulting amount or the Limit of Loss for Business Interruption, whichever is less, is the most we will pay. We will not pay for the remainder of the loss.
> e. If more than one 'location' is shown in the Schedule for this coverage, this Coinsurance Condition applies separately to each 'location'.".

This means that the coinsurance requirement is 100 per cent. and becomes a straight application of "average", namely that the insurer will pay only such a proportion of the actual loss that the amount insured on estimated annual value bears to the annual value, *i.e.* the sum of net profit, fixed charges and expenses as in the definition of actual loss that would have been earned, had no accident occurred, after adjustments for probable experience. In other words, the insurer is liable to pay:

$$\frac{\text{estimated annual value}}{\text{annual value}} \text{ up to the limit of loss}$$

It is interesting to note that the basis of comparison is no longer the amount that would have been earned in the 12 months following the accident. It is thus effectively the same as the fire form which relates back to the 12 months following the inception, or last previous anniversary date, of the policy. (See the following paragraph 334 regarding the provision by the insured of annual reports with an estimate of future earnings.)

334. Annual reports

The place of the worksheet used for fire business interruption purposes is taken by an Annual Report which must be furnished on an Approved Report Form not later than three months after the effective date of the policy and at 12-monthly intervals thereafter. This must show the amount of net profits, fixed charges and expenses as referred to in the definition of actual loss sustained actually earned during the preceding 12 months and estimated for the following 12 months and, also, the actual number of working days in the preceding 12 months and the estimated number of working days in the following 12 months.

The figures shown on the form will be used for the application of the co-insurance clause in the event of a claim. (See preceding paragraph 333.)

335. Reduction of loss

This is a condition that as soon as possible after an accident the insured shall continue or resume business in whole or in part and shall make up lost business within a reasonable period of time (not to be limited to the period during which business is interrupted) through use of every available means including surplus machinery, duplicate parts, equipment, supplies, surplus or reserve stock, owned or controlled or available from other sources and through working extra time or overtime at the premises or at such other premises acquired for the purposes, all to the extent that the amount for which the insurer would otherwise be liable is reduced.

Under the relevant provision in the description of Coverage the extra expense resulting from actions for the speedier restoration of business will be reimbursed to the insured (paragraph 331). The Reduction of Payment condition under the old wording further provided that the insurers may take such means as will in their opinion reduce the interruption of business or the loss, but this is not repeated in the current wording.

336. Premium adjustment condition

Provision is made by a condition (previously an optional endorsement) for an adjustment of premium to be allowed should the amount of net profit, fixed charges and expenses as in the definition of actual loss, which are actually earned and declared in the annual report for any 12 months, be less than, or more than, the amount of insurance for which premium has been paid. The return is limited to 75 per cent. of premium paid but the additional premium is unlimited.

337. Interruption of facilities power, etc., supplies

Coverage for loss due to prevention of business caused by failure of supplies from public utility companies can be arranged and this is more extensive than the insurance under a U.K. business interruption extension (paragraph 319) for failure of electricity, gas and water supplies because in many cities in the United States central heating plants furnish heat to buildings used for industrial purposes and there are also refrigeration facilities available. Some typical classes of business for which this coverage is specially advisable are mentioned in paragraph 319.

338. Consequential damage: spoilage

An extension of cover can be added by endorsement to a B. & M. business interruption insurance to insure against loss due to spoilage of specified property resulting from lack of power, light, heat, steam or refrigeration caused by an accident to boilers or plant as insured under the policy. This provides compensation on the basis of the cash value of the spoilt materials. In addition it undertakes to pay any amounts for which the insured may be legally liable to other parties for loss by spoilage. This is similar to the cover provided by U.K. engineering departments (refer paragraph 324).

339. Small businesses

Two Boiler and Machinery Coverage forms developed by the I.S.O. in the 1980s relate to small businesses. They are in fact property damage forms with coverage extended to expediting expenses (regarded as a property damage cover) and to business interruption and extra expense.

(a) *Basic form*

The extension wording for business interruption and extra expense opens with the following statement—"Coverage always applies to Boilers and Pressure Vessels. It also applies to Air Conditioning and Air Compressing Units if—COVERED—is indicated for both Property Damage and Business Interruption and Extra Expense for these 'objects' in the Declarations".

Loss following explosion relates only to steam boilers, electric steam generators, steam piping or moving or rotating machinery caused by centrifugal force or mechanical breakdown and to other "objects" covered by the insurance and described on an Object Definitions endorsement.

The limit of liability for business interruption and extra expense loss arising out of any "one accident" is equal to 25 per cent. of the Limit of Insurance and is additional thereto.

"One accident" means that if an initial "accident" causes other "accidents" all will be considered "one accident". All "accidents" at any one location that manifest themselves at the same time and are the result of the same cause will be considered "one accident".

(b) *Broad form*

The business interruption and extra expense coverage extension relates to losses caused solely by an accident to:

1. an object; or
2. any transformer or electrical apparatus that is:
    (i) located on or within 500 feet of the "location";
    (ii) owned by a public utility company; and
    (iii) used to supply electrical power solely to that "location".

A property damage extension in this form which is not in the "Basic" form is in respect of spoilage where payment will be made for loss of perishable goods due to spoilage resulting from lack of power, light, heat, steam or refrigeration caused solely by an "accident" to the same property as is described under business interruption and extra expense. Payment will be determined on the basis of the actual cash value of the damaged goods at the time of the "accident".

Besides the addition of spoilage cover, the "Broad" form is wider than the "Basic" form mainly in respect of the definition of "Object" where for example any boiler is included (as against selected types of boiler). In other respects the "Broad" form is essentially the same as the "Basic" form.

CHAPTER 17

Dependence on Other Businesses and Premises—United Kingdom and United States

340. Interdependence of businesses: motor industry

The dependence of one business upon another which arises from the growth of specialisation and integration in modern industry is of special relevance in the arrangement of business interruption insurances. The motor industry furnishes probably the best illustration of this.

Motor manufacturers obtain many different components and accessories for their cars from other, mostly specialist, firms who make their particular product to the car manufacturer's exact requirements. Consequently if there is a serious fire at the premises of any one supplier the assembly of cars will be entirely stopped as soon as the maker's reserve stock of that particular component is used up. The stoppage will continue until an alternative source of supply can be contracted for and, as this may involve the special tooling-up of a factory floor the period involved may be a very prolonged one.

The extent of this dependency is well illustrated by a statement in February 1980 that for every worker on British Leyland car assembly lines there were five other workers in over 4,000 firms of suppliers, some totally committed.

As a matter of general interest regarding interdependency the fire at the General Motors' Works at Detroit which occurred in 1953 might be cited. This modern factory, only four years old and covering 34 acres, was the sole producer of hydromatic automatic gears for the Cadillac, Oldsmobile and Pontiac cars of General Motors Ltd., and for cars of the Nash and Hudson Companies. Although the factory was almost entirely only one storey in height, was partly protected by automatic sprinklers and was considered by the owners to be so invulnerable against fire that only a partial fire insurance and no business interruption insurance was carried, it was completely razed to the ground. The material damage was estimated at 50 million dollars and the business interruption loss must have been on a similar scale. The point of special relevance here is that it was subsequently reported that an immediate result was the slowing down of production throughout a great part of the American automobile industry.

Generally speaking it may be said that where a motor manufacturer is buying components and accessories from other works there may be 100 per cent. dependency upon the safety of the premises of each of the suppliers. It becomes essential in such circumstances to arrange for an extension of the business interruption insurance of the motor manufacturer to include the risk of loss which would result from damage by fire or kindred perils at the premises of any one of the component and accessory makers.

In the United Kingdom an extension of cover of this nature is a normal feature of the business and generally only a relatively modest additional premium rate is charged for it although the potential risk shouldered by the insurers can be very substantial. For example, in the case of a motor manufacturer if there is total dependency on each of a dozen component suppliers the insurers will carry the risk of a corresponding loss if damage occurs at the premises of any one which means a 1,200 per cent. potential liability, even though the insured cannot claim more than the sums insured.

The reverse of this position applies to the firms who make the components and accessories. They are faced with the risk of losing valuable orders, probably irreplaceable, if the car works are badly damaged by fire. To meet this eventuality each of these firms can have their business interruption insurance extended to include loss consequent upon damage at the premises of the motor manufacturer and those of any other customers who take an appreciable proportion of their products.

The vital nature of this reciprocal dependency of suppliers and customers has been demonstrated repeatedly during recent years by strikes in one section or another of the motor industry. Such strikes have meant a stoppage of work within a day or two for sometimes thousands of non-striking employees on the one hand because the motor factory was short of some component or on the other hand because of a temporary stoppage in the acceptance of deliveries of such components because of a strike at the car factory. Loss due to strikes is not usually insurable but if fire was the cause of such stoppage the result would arise just as quickly and be of much longer duration and such loss is insurable.

A third category of business which might be involved in the risk of loss as a result of fire at other firms' premises due to specialisation in the motor industry comprises the firms who do process work such as chromium plating. In their case also an extension of their business interruption insurances is necessary to protect them against loss due to reduction in turnover which may result from damage at the premises of any of their customers.

Awareness by industrialists of the serious nature of this interdependency is underlined by the fact that the scheme formulated in 1980 by the Confederation of British Industry to set up a mutual strike fund to insure against business interruption losses included indemnity against loss when production at an insured's premises was injured as a result of strikes by employees of direct suppliers and customers.

Finally, the ubiquitous motor garage rounds off the illustration, underlined by the statement of Sir William Lyons at the annual general meeting of Jaguar Cars Ltd., on June 26, 1958, apropos their works fire in February 1957—"I am afraid the set-back occasioned by the fire resulted in many disappointed customers throughout the world". Motor dealers with an agency for the sale of certain makers' cars stand to lose a substantial part of their profits if the delivery of new cars is interfered with by a fire or other damage at the motor factory. They can be protected by an appropriate extension of their business interruption policy to include loss resulting from damage at the premises not only of specified makers but also at those of unspecified suppliers of those firms. (See paragraph 359.)

341. Extension of insurances to cover interdependence of businesses

Whilst the motor industry furnishes a good illustration of the problem of interdependency similar circumstances apply, for example, to the aircraft industry, where finding alternative sources can be a lengthy and complicated business, to the chemical and petrochemical industries and to many other trades in large or small degree. Where they do apply a business interruption insurance is not complete unless it provides protection in respect of the contingent loss attaching to "other people's fires".

Many firms are confident that because their premises and trade processes are of a non-hazardous nature and the fire prevention and extinguishing arrangements are so efficient the risk of serious damage is very remote. But their Achilles' heel may be the possibility of a serious fire at the premises of a substantial supplier of materials or components, a sub-contractor or processor or even an important customer. This contingency can in many cases carry a much more serious risk of business interruption for them than that of damage at their own premises. For instance, a merchant occupying a fire resisting and sprinklered warehouse may be dependent for supplies of a substantial proportion of the goods he sells upon a manufacturer whose factory fire risk is a very heavy one.

Whilst most businesses are to some extent dependent for their normal functioning upon some outside concern there is great variety in the form and extent of this dependency and in the effects on turnover which would result from damage by fire or kindred perils at another firm's premises. Imagination as well as considerable thought and inquiry may be necessary to decide upon the potential risk involved and the best arrangement to make for adequate protection. This feature of business interruption insurance is not only extremely interesting but when a loss occurs as a result of damage at outside premises if it is insured under an extension of the policy there is a rewarding sense of satisfaction for both the insured and for the person who recommended and negotiated the cover.

Often this problem is too lightly dismissed, but large fires do bring serious financial loss to many business firms who had never even thought of the possibility of such loss. A striking example of this was the destruction by fire of the pre-cooling sheds in the Duncan and Victoria Docks, Cape Town in 1958. Western Province fruit growers, who in 1957 exported

341

£9·5 million of fruit from these docks, depended on the pre-cooling stores for their livelihood and the loss of these export facilities was a disaster for the economy of the whole province. The port authorities estimated at the time that it would take at least three years to restore the damaged cold stores and Mr. Joel le Roux, Paarl representative on the Deciduous Fruit Board said that meanwhile the export fruit industry of the Western Province would cease to exist.

Some insured are apt to think that the contingency is not worth insuring if they cannot suffer to a really substantial degree of, say, more than 10 per cent. through damage at any one outside firm's premises, overlooking the possibility that a 10 per cent. loss of turnover may result in a 50 per cent. loss of *net* profit. In this respect it might be useful to mention that very many firms consider it well worth while and do insure extensions with limits at some locations as low as 1 per cent.; at any rate for large insurances even 1 per cent. is not an inconsiderable amount. In fact in a U.S. old style Contingent Business Interruption coverage, the limit allowed in respect of unnamed situations was only 0·5 per cent. of the amount insured by the policy for any month of the period of interruption whereas in the current Business Income from Dependent Properties endorsement it is 0·03 per cent. of the Limit of Insurance per (working) day. (See paragraph 347.)

Generally speaking large firms will experience more difficulty in obtaining new sources of supply or processors capable of doing their work than will small businesses. Nobody wishes to go to the expense of laying out factory space and installing plant and machinery in order to meet a temporary need knowing that the orders may well dry up when the burnt-out supplier whose place they are taking is once more back in production.

A further point to be kept in mind is that whilst alternative arrangements might be made within a certain length of time for new suppliers, processors or customers, as the case may be, they cannot necessarily be made on terms as favourable to the insured as those which they were previously enjoying. This difference in terms can amount to a substantial sum which if an extension cover is operative can be claimed under clause (b) as increase in cost of working.

Finding new customers to make up for the loss of trade which will result if the premises of a sizeable customer are badly damaged by fire will often present greater difficulties than obtaining new suppliers or processors. In this matter of finding new customers large firms will generally be in a more unfavourable position than small ones.

The foregoing reasons for an established business insuring against loss due to "other people's fires" may apply equally to firms having new or extended premises constructed for a major project who arrange their supplies and sales outlets in advance of the planned date for the start of production. In such circumstances an extension to their Advance Profits insurance (paragraph 268(a)) is a necessity. At the same time, consideration must be given to extending the cover to the suppliers of new plant and machinery (see also paragraph 322).

342. Cost and factors to be considered for extensions of cover

The additional premium which will be charged for an appropriate extension of an insured's policy to take account of other people's fires will depend partly upon the degree of fire hazard at the "outside" premises. Another factor which governs the additional charge is the proportion of the sums insured under gross profit and wages items, etc., which can be fixed as the limit of the insurer's liability in respect of a claim arising from damage at one or other of the outside locations. Of prime importance in deciding upon these limits is the insured's intimate knowledge of their own business; its dependency upon different outside firms and the extent to which business could be interrupted by a single incident of damage by fire or other insured perils at such premises, and for how long; whether any alternatives are available and if so the time necessary to get them into full operation and the extra cost above normal of such alternative supplies or processors; the seasonal nature of supplies or sales; the extent to which specialised materials of limited availability are used; and what buffer stocks, if any, are held; and similar factors. The effect of "Just in time" deliveries of supplies (mentioned in paragraph 243(c)) where almost total reliance is placed on suppliers for the holding of stocks of materials, components, etc., is also an important consideration.

Although in the United Kingdom a percentage of the total of the sums insured under the different items of the specification is the normal manner in which the limit of the insurer's liability is stated, there are circumstances in which it is considered more suitable to show the limit as a fixed amount in £s. For example, where the products sold are diverse, each with its own supplier dependency, a percentage of the total sum insured could easily become inaccurate when the mixture of products sold changes. On the other hand a fixed amount in £s needs to be re-evaluated on a regular basis.

343. Categories of dependency extensions

Extensions to insure loss resulting from reduction in turnover due to damage at other firms' premises fall into the following broad categories:

(a) suppliers, processors and sub-contractors: paragraphs 346 to 349 (also 359 and 363 to 370);
(b) suppliers of the insured's suppliers: paragraph 350;
(c) customers: paragraph 351;
(d) suppliers of the insured's customers: paragraph 352;
(e) the insured's own goods in store, and public or private warehouses, cold stores, etc.: paragraphs 354 to 356;

(f) the insured's own property temporarily on other firm's premises for processing, finishing or other services: paragraphs 357 to 360;
(g) motor traders and garage proprietors: paragraph 359;
(h) the insured's vehicles whilst away from their premises: paragraph 375;
(i) premises where a contract is being carried out by the insured: paragraph 377;
(j) suppliers of electricity, gas, water or steam: paragraphs 371 and 372 (also 319); telephone exchanges: 369;
(k) the insured's goods whilst in transit or in showrooms, exhibitions, etc.: paragraphs 376, 361 and 362;
(l) prevention or denial of access because of damage at adjacent premises: paragraph 373; loss of attraction and leader locations: 374;
(m) reciprocal extensions for interdependency within a group of associated companies: paragraph 382.

344. Method of effecting a dependency extension

If so required most of the categories set out in the preceding paragraph 343 can be included in the same extension of cover. This is effected by a memorandum on the specification which states in effect that for the purposes of the insurance damage (as defined in the policy) at any of the situations or property specified thereunder shall be regarded as being damage at the premises of the insured. The names of the firms and addresses of the premises or description of the property to which the extension applies are then stated together with the respective limits applicable, either as percentages of sums insured or as amounts.

The material damage proviso (paragraph 15(e)) is not mentioned in this memorandum because, as it is obviously inapplicable to premises outside the insured's control where they have no insurable interest, it is considered to be inoperative with regard to such premises and property in them.

345. Perils, indemnity period and locations insurable under extensions: United Kingdom and abroad

The perils to be insured under a dependency extension need not necessarily be the same as those covered in respect of the insured's own premises. The risks insured at the latter may be only the standard perils (paragraph 13(a)) stated on the face of the policy but generally any of the special perils described in Chapter 14 which are relevant in respect of an extension to premises other than those of the insured can be included. For example, such wider cover might be desirable in an insurance where it is considered unnecessary to insure against explosion at the insured's own premises but those of a supplier to whose premises the extension applies, are known to carry an inherent risk of explosion because of the materials used or the manufacturing processes. In such circumstances the insurance should be arranged so that the extension memorandum includes the peril of explosion in the definition of damage as applied to the supplier's premises.

Similarly, it is possible to arrange for a longer maximum indemnity period for an extension than that applying to an insured's own premises. This would be advisable if the insured is a wholesaler with only warehouse premises and the supplier's are a large factory and there is no alternative source of supply for the insured's needs. The position would then be that rehabilitation of the supplier's business and resumption of normal supplies to the insured would exceed the maximum period of interruption to be anticipated following damage at the insured's own premises.

Dependency extensions are normally limited to premises in the United Kingdom but cover attaching to insured's premises here can be extended to insure loss resulting from damage at factories abroad from which supplies of goods or components are obtained. As the fact that a firm is purchasing supplies or services abroad postulates difficulty in obtaining them in the home country on comparable terms, if at all, the risk is regarded by insurers as meriting premium rating higher than the normal scale for suppliers extensions because of the added difficulty likely to be experienced, in the event of a claim, in finding a suitable alternative source of supply.

The range of perils for extensions to situations overseas may not be as wide as those covered in respect of the insured's own premises in the United Kingdom because of the differences in geographical and political conditions in various countries as, for instance, cover for storm, tempest, flood, earthquake and riot.

It should be noted in relation to the above that the Northern Ireland Exclusion in the policy (paragraphs 14(b) and 290) applies fully to all extension covers. Legal advice obtained confirms the opinion received from the Northern Ireland (Government) Office that compensation under the Government scheme is not available unless a legally enforceable interest in the damaged property can be established. Thus financial loss suffered by a firm arising from damage excluded by the above clause at the premises of their suppliers, processors or customers in Northern Ireland is not recoverable under the Government scheme either. This does not preclude an insured having an extension to the premises of suppliers, etc., in Northern Ireland to insure against loss resulting from fire and other perils not caused by civil commotion or terrorism (or against what is provided by an all risks policy (refer paragraph 14(b)).

346. Suppliers, processors and sub-contractors: extension details

The expression "suppliers extension" embraces various kinds of dependency of insured upon other firms for supplies or services. For instance, the dependence of manufacturers upon the suppliers of materials or components and sub-assemblies for their products, upon processors and sub-contractors and for packaging materials and containers for the finished goods. Or the dependence upon manufacturers by wholesalers and retailers for the goods they sell; and similarly that of retailers upon wholesalers.

As mentioned in a preceding paragraph, the memorandum which is added to the specification to give effect to the extension of cover states the names of the outside firms and addresses of the premises to which the extension applies. Here it might be useful to emphasise the need for an insured always to state *the situation* of those premises. The address shown on the letter paper of a firm of suppliers might be only its head office or main factory address and it may have factories in various other situations to which the extension should apply, but will not unless the addresses of such locations are stated in the extension endorsement.

But the potential loss of turnover for the insured is not necessarily 100 per cent. in respect of any one premises for which an extension is required and the smaller the percentage limit of the sums insured which can be shown in the extension memorandum the lower will be the additional premium charged. An insured has therefore to estimate the maximum percentage of the combined total of the sums insured on gross profit and on wages which can be applied as the limit of the insurer's liability for loss arising from damage at any one situation to be named in the extension.

Whatever limit is selected is then inserted in the extension memorandum. Different limits can be arranged for the various locations when variations between the degree of dependence upon them are wide enough to justify this and these will be taken into account by the insurers in calculating the additional premium to be charged for the extension.

The rates of additional premium charged for such extensions are governed not only by the percentage limit chosen but also by the fire hazard at each of the premises not in the insured's occupation to which the insurance is extended.

347. Business Income from Dependent Properties—United States

The potential loss which a business can sustain as a result of "other people's fires" is identical in all countries and the general factors appertaining and the specific circumstances in which protection by insurance is required, as discussed throughout this chapter, are of universal application. But the actual terms and conditions of the insurance protection available will vary from country to country; those current in North America are dealt with in this paragraph the contents of which should be read in conjunction with those relating to the specific category of coverage required.

Under the previous gross earnings system the cover was called Contingent Business Interruption and could be effected either by endorsement of a gross earnings insurance or by a separate policy. Under the new system it is effected by one of two endorsements to the Business Income Coverage forms—"(And Extra Expense)" or "(Without Extra Expense)". The Broad Form endorsement is used if coverage is subject to the same Limit of Insurance, coinsurance percentage and coverage options (other than Agreed Value, see paragraph 68, or Premium Adjustment, see paragraph 237). The Limited Form endorsement is used when the basic own premises cover is not provided, or when separate Limits of Insurance are selected for "contingent business properties" which differ from the direct Business Income Limit of Insurance or differ from the Limits of Insurance of other "contingent business properties". Individual limits per Location are set out in the Limited Form.

The coverage is for the actual loss of Business Income sustained during the necessary suspension of "operations" during the "period of restoration". The suspension must be caused by direct physical loss of or damage to "contingent business property" at the premises described in the Schedule caused by or resulting from a Covered Cause of Loss.

"Contingent business property" means property operated by others whom the insured depends on to:

(a) deliver materials or services to the insured, or to others for the insured's account (*Contributing Locations*)
(b) accept the insured's products or services (*Recipient Locations*)
(c) manufacture products for delivery to the insured's customers under contract of sale (*Manufacturing Locations*)
(d) attract customers to the insured's business (*Leader Locations*).

Coverage in respect of all unnamed properties within the Continental United States is incorporated in both endorsements by adding to the Additional Coverages provided by the Business Income Coverage form (see paragraph 30) cover in respect of Miscellaneous Locations. Insurers will pay for the actual loss of Business Income sustained due to direct physical loss or damage at the premises of a "contingent business property" not described in the Schedule caused by or resulting from any Covered Cause of Loss. However, such payment will not exceed 0·03 per cent. of the Limit of Insurance (Broad Form) or the sum of all Limits of Insurance shown in the Schedule (Limited Form) for each day's suspension of "operations" due to loss arising from any one location.

Because the two forms are endorsements they are subject to the same Covered Causes of Loss forms and to the same exclusion of any increase of loss (to the insured's business) caused by or resulting from delay in rebuilding, repairing or replacing the "contingent business property" or resuming "operations" due to interference at the location of the rebuilding, repair or replacement by strikers or other persons.

In addition other endorsement forms are available which extend Business

Income Coverage to cover loss at the described premises caused by direct physical loss of or damage to "off-premises"—properties providing water, communications or power supply services and overhead power transmission and communications lines—on a similar basis to the covers described in paragraphs 369 and 371.

348. Arranging the limits for a suppliers extension

When a suppliers extension involves only one percentage limit provision for this is made in the extension memorandum in the following words:

"provided that after the application of all other terms conditions and provisions of the policy the liability under this memorandum in respect of any one occurrence shall not exceed
 (a) the percentage of the total of the sums insured by the policy
   or
 (b) the amount
shown below against such situations or property as the limit."

When different limits apply to different locations the proviso is amended appropriately.

It must also be noted that when the Declaration-Linked wording is used (refer paragraph 53 and Appendix D, paragraph 450) a percentage limit relates to the limit of liability under the overall cover and not to the estimated gross profit amount.

The manner in which the limits operate can be illustrated by the case of an insurance shown on the specification as follows (with wages insured as a separate item):

ITEM NO.		SUM INSURED £
1.	On Gross Profit	800,000
2.	On Wages	700,000
		£1,500,000

An extension to named outside suppliers with a limit of 20 per cent. in respect of any one would provide cover for loss as described up to the following amounts in respect of any one occurrence or up to double those figures if damage occurred at two places in the course of a year, and so on.

Item No. 1.	Gross Profit	} combined limit of £300,000 being 20% of £1,500,000
Item No. 2.	Wages	

Should a loss occur the amount of the limit would be reduced by the amount of the claim and may therefore require to be reinstated immediately (see paragraph 231).

Whatever length the maximum indemnity period may be, provided it is not less than 12 months, recovery could be made under items 1 and 2 jointly for loss resulting from damage at any one extension premises up to the above figure of £300,000 even though the loss were sustained entirely during the first few months after the damage. This means that the limit to be selected is the percentage which the estimated maximum total loss bears to the combined sums insured on gross profit and dual basis wages or payroll.

For example, the insured might obtain all their supplies of a certain raw material from certain premises of one particular firm and so be 100 per cent. dependent upon that situation. However, if they were certain that within say three months of damage occurring they could obtain full normal supplies from another source, at no greater cost, they might think in terms of an extension subject to a 25 per cent. limit if their maximum indemnity period were for 12 months or with a 12·5 per cent. limit if it were for 24 months. To provide a margin of safety they could arrange the percentage rather higher, although this might be thought unnecessary if they always endeavour to carry three or four weeks' reserve supply of the particular raw material.

But in arranging percentage limits other factors which might have a bearing on the period during which lack of supplies of materials or components or goods could adversely affect an insured's business must be borne in mind. For instance, in the foregoing example a three months' shortage of supplies at certain periods of the year might in a business subject to seasonal variations entail a loss of turnover substantially greater than 25 per cent. of their annual amount or might involve a loss of customers' trade which would take several months to make good. They may have been too optimistic in deciding that they could obtain alternative supplies after three months at no greater cost than they would have paid for their normal supplies. If after considering all relevant factors an insured considers that an extension to suppliers' premises would be adequately covered by a maximum indemnity period shorter than that for their own premises it is unnecessary to arrange for a separate, shorter period because the point is taken care of by the percentage limit selected, as already explained. This in turn means that the cost of premium for the added risk is adjusted correspondingly.

349. Extensions to unspecified suppliers and storage sites

While extensions to suppliers' premises normally require the locations to be stated in the memorandum giving effect to the extension circumstances may arise in which it would be an advantage to an insured to include also unspecified suppliers. This would apply where there are a considerable number of such firms each responsible for a very small proportion of the insured's total supplies and they are subject to change from time to time. In such circumstances insurers are willing to add to the list of named principal suppliers an extension to unspecified firms, subject normally to a top limit lower than any of those specified and in any case not usually exceeding 10 per cent. or a stipulated monetary amount, whichever is the less, although this limit may be increased for very large insurances. In 1983, it was agreed by the United Kingdom Tariff insurers that an unspecified suppliers extension could be granted provided that the sum insured or estimated gross profit—Declaration-Linked (see paragraph 53) or earnings exceeded £25 million, and subject to a limit of one per cent. or £500,000, whichever was the less. Not unnaturally the extra premium required for an extension to unspecified suppliers is relatively higher than for an extension to named suppliers.

To give effect to an extension to unspecified suppliers the definition of the situations of the specified suppliers is extended to include the premises of any other of the insured's suppliers, manufacturers or processors of components, goods or materials, and premises not in the occupation of the insured where property is stored, all in Great Britain or Northern Ireland. The wording excludes the premises of public utilities, that is, electricity, gas and water works as these have to be covered under a separate extension endorsement.

Should a loss occur the amount of the limit would be reduced by the amount of the claim and may therefore require to be immediately reinstated (see paragraph 231).

350. Extensions to suppliers of suppliers

In many businesses the extension of a business interruption insurance to cover the insured's dependency upon suppliers would not reach back sufficiently far in a chain of production to give adequate protection inasmuch as the insured may be open to serious loss in the event of damage at the premises of their suppliers' supplier.

A simple example of this is the interdependence throughout the motor industry, taken a stage further back than already discussed in the opening paragraphs of this chapter, a particular case in point being the serious loss of sales experienced by motor garages throughout the country as the result of a stoppage in production at the works of motor manufacturers with whom they held agencies whose supply of car bodies was curtailed by a fire at the premises of the Pressed Steel Co. Ltd. in 1959. (For details of a special scheme for motor dealers to cover this contingency which was introduced as a result of their experience in 1959, see paragraph 359.)

A similar dependency attaches where insured obtain from another manufacturer materials for their own productive processes which that manufacturer has already processed from raw or basic materials. If the latter are specialised products, perhaps made exclusively by another manufacturer as is the case with many synthetic fibres and materials, or production at the premises of the insured's supplier depends upon the use of special catalysts or silicones, damage at the factory of any such supplier of the insured's supplier would in turn affect the business of the insured.

This aspect of dependence in modern industry is of increasing importance as more and more use is made of chemicals, plastics and synthetic fibres and fabrics and the products of biotechnology the manufacture of which tends to be concentrated in perhaps only one or two multimillion pound plants in this country or abroad and often involves secret manufacturing processes. Dependence upon supplies from such factories is fairly obvious but often overlooked is the tenuous nature of supplies of products upon which *they* depend. Consider, for instance, propylene oxide, a highly specialised *intermediate* of restricted manufacture used mainly in the production of other chemicals which are in turn used in the manufacture of polyurethane foams, resins, pharmaceuticals, cosmetics and, directly or indirectly, in a wide range of other products.

Hence, where an insured has a normal suppliers extension, it is advisable to give careful consideration to the further protection available against loss resulting from damage by fire, explosion and other perils under a "suppliers of suppliers" extension. The scope of such an extension is defined by simply adding to the list of specified suppliers under the heading "situations" in the suppliers extension the words "and the premises situate in Great Britain or Northern Ireland of any manufacturer supplying them with materials or components" followed by the insertion of the agreed percentage limit of the combined sums insured which is to be applied in respect of loss due to damage at any one location. This wording makes it clear that the premises of public utilities, that is, electricity, gas and water works, are not included in the cover.

A business interruption claim amounting to £4·5 million was paid to an insured under a suppliers extension to the premises destroyed in the great Flixborough disaster of June 1974. One wonders how many customers of that prudent insured who received this large amount suffered business interruption losses through lack of supplies from that intermediary link in their chain of production because they had not been alert to the possibilities of loss in the event of damage at the source of supplies and were not insured for a "suppliers of suppliers" extension to the Flixborough works.

351. Extensions to customers' premises

The reverse of a suppliers extension is one to cover an insured's dependence for trade upon customers, the insurance under a "customers extension" providing an indemnity for loss through reduction in turnover due to damage at the premises of named customers.

The possibilities of very serious losses of this nature are well illustrated by the 1974 Flixborough disaster mentioned above in connection with extensions to suppliers of suppliers. The Flixborough firm were not only large suppliers of products to other businesses but were themselves large buyers; in other words, they were also some other firms' *customers*. It is on record that one such firm which should have had a customers extension on their policy but had not, suffered in consequence a loss said to be approaching a million pounds.

The expression "customers" does not mean only those to whom goods are sold but also includes the sale of services. Firms engaged in process work or as sub-contractors are open to a loss of orders should the business of one of their customers or principal contractors be interrupted by damage. Service industries may be similarly dependent upon customers; for instance laundries with regular work for certain large hotels, hospitals or other institutions. Or the dependency may be that of a haulage contractor working solely for one or two manufacturing concerns and so placed that a factory burn-out would leave him without alternative haulage work available.

From an insurer's point of view there is a greater risk involved in a customers extension than in a suppliers extension largely but not entirely due to the fact that there is in most trades and at nearly all times more competition to sell than to buy. But also, in the case of a suppliers extension, when an alternative source of supply is found the benefit is automatically reflected in some restoration of the insured's turnover and there is no question but that this benefits the insurers. However, in the case of a loss under a customers extension if a new customer is found it is always open to an insured to think (and perhaps overstress in the claim negotiation) that such a customer would have been acquired even had there been no loss of the one at whose premises the damage occurred. The larger the number of customers and the smaller the proportion each takes of an insured's sales, the more likely is this latter problem to arise; whilst the fewer the customers and the larger the trade of each one, the more difficult will it be to find replacements.

Because of these factors, extensions to customers were until 1981 treated as warranting somewhat higher premium charges than are those to suppliers. But the number of customers extensions requested is far fewer than that of suppliers and the rating and wording are now the same as for suppliers extensions.

Similarly, as for a suppliers extension, the insurer's limit of liability is expressed as a percentage of the combined sums insured under the policy and, as explained in paragraph 348, the insured may elect to cover a percentage lower than the actual proportion of their annual sales to any particular

352. Extensions to customers' suppliers

Just as an insured might suffer loss resulting from a shortage of supplies because of damage at the premises of a supplier's supplier (see paragraph 350) an insured can similarly sustain loss through a reduction in sales because of damage at the premises of a customer's supplier. Here again the motor industry serves as a useful illustration. If a serious fire at a car component maker cuts supplies to a motor manufacturer the latter will turn out fewer cars and will require fewer ancillary parts, fittings and furnishings. To makers of this latter type of equipment the motor manufacturer is a "customer" and any loss they, the equipment maker, suffer through a reduction in orders will be due to damage at the premises of the component manufacturer, that is, of a *customer's supplier*. Hence the need for an appropriate extension of cover similar to that to the premises of suppliers of suppliers when circumstances show this to be necessary.

353. Extensions with various limits

As already mentioned the potential loss of turnover is not necessarily 100 per cent. in respect of each or all of the premises included in an extension insurance. On the other hand the total dependency covered under a suppliers extension may greatly exceed 100 per cent., because the insured might be using several materials or components on the supply of each of which they are wholly dependent (as already instanced in the case of a motor-car manufacturer). For example, an insured's position might be:

SUPPLIERS			DEPENDENCY
Firm A supply	100% of certain materials used for making 25% of the Insured's finished products		25%
Firm B ,,	60% of certain materials used for making 50% of the Insured's finished products		30%
Firm C ,,	40% of certain components used in making 50% of the Insured's finished products		20%
Firm D ,,	100% of certain materials used for making 20% of the Insured's finished products		20%
Firm E ,,	50% of certain components used in making 40% of the Insured's finished products		20%
PROCESSORS			
Firm F	30% of the Insured's production passes through the factory of F for specialised processes		30%
Firm G	25% of the Insured's production passes through the factory of G for specialised processes		25%

CUSTOMERS
  Firm H take 22% of the Insured's total sales................................. 22%
  Four other specified firms each take between 10% and 15% of the
    Insured's total sales.. 15%
                                                                                any one

STORAGE
  Property of the Insured whilst stored anywhere in Great Britain or Ireland—
  limit 2½% any one location.

In circumstances of this nature an appropriate extension might be arranged with a limit in respect of the insured's loss resulting from damage at any one of the suppliers' or processors' premises, of 30 per cent. of the total sum insured under the specification or to allow a margin of say 33⅓ per cent. subject to any further uplift necessary for factors such as those mentioned in paragraph 348. Yet the extra cover given for those categories of dependency totals 170 per cent., which is the potential liability carried by the insurers, who will be responsible for loss resulting from damage at any one, or more than one, of the premises named even though the insured cannot actually recover more than the sums insured shown on their specification.

354. Property of the insured stored

Another possibility of loss consequent upon damage at premises other than those occupied by the insured arises when their goods are stored in public or private warehouses, cold stores or bonded stores. The seriousness of this risk is highlighted by the fact that in 1980 over half the number of fires costing over £1 million were in storage and warehousing premises. In 1983, there were 59 major warehousing fires, costing over £200 million, and in 1984 a fire in a London trading estate warehouse was estimated to have caused a loss in excess of £100 million (some early reports said in excess of £150 million). Here a distinction must be drawn between a business interruption loss resulting from damage to the *insured's property* in store, dealt with in this paragraph, and that due to damage to the storage *premises* which may be a continuing loss and is dealt with in paragraph 356.

If the goods in store are finished products awaiting sale the insured's business interruption loss due to their destruction will normally be limited to the profit which would have been earned on their sale. It will also be of a limited nature if they are materials or components which are quickly and easily replaceable.

Premises not in the occupation of an insured where property is stored are included in an extension to unspecified suppliers but this latter is normally only given together with an extension to specified suppliers (paragraph 346). An insured may, however, have no need for such an extension and consider it adequate to have an insurance restricted to goods in store only. There is usually no additional premium for an extension of this nature if the value of the property has been included at the appropriate rate in the calculation of the basis rate. Alternatively, where an insured has an unspecified suppliers extension the limit in respect of goods in store of 10 per cent. or a stipulated monetary amount, whichever is the less, might be inadequate and necessitate being increased, in which case the excess amount only is to be insured under a separate extension. It is well, therefore, to consider in detail the question of possible loss consequent upon destruction of goods in store.

The additional premium charged for an extension of this nature is related to the limit of loss applied to the cover given and, therefore, the difference between the limited loss consequent upon the destruction of easily replaceable raw materials, components or finished stock, and the continuing loss consequent upon the impairment of productive or selling capacity, should be clearly understood when deciding upon the appropriate limit to be placed on the insurer's liability. Although a low limit is generally adequate for an extension in respect of goods in store it is not invariably so.

For example, the insured may at any time of the year have a maximum of say 20 per cent. of their total finished stocks in a public warehouse. This may not necessitate a limit as high as 20 per cent. for the extension to cover their potential loss because if they normally turn their stock over a number of times in the course of a year, the loss of turnover which would arise from the destruction of goods which constituted 20 per cent. of their total stock at any specific date would be considerably less than 20 per cent. of their total annual turnover. For instance, if their stock-turn is four times yearly then the loss of 20 per cent. of stock in any one fire might not affect their annual turnover by much more than 5 per cent.

The position would be different however if the goods destroyed were raw materials, components or packing materials essential to the insured's business which would take some considerable time to replace; and in some cases the manufacture of goods may be 100 per cent. dependent upon an indispensable material or part which constitutes as little as perhaps 5 per cent. of the finished products. In circumstances where the loss of the insured's property in store would interrupt the manufacture or sales of their products, an estimate would have to be made of the possible maximum effect on the annual turnover of the business (see paragraph 355).

For a "property stored" extension it is not necessary to inform insurers of the storage addresses because the cover applies to property of the insured whilst stored anywhere in Great Britain or Northern Ireland elsewhere than at premises in the insured's occupation. If raw materials, components or manufactured goods are held in store abroad a property stored extension can be arranged but details of the location will have to be furnished.

Premises or a part of premises rented by insured for their exclusive use for storage purposes, that is, rented storage space open to access of their employees at will, are not regarded as "extension" premises as would be those in which their goods are stored at a charge according to the quantity and time stored. In the former circumstances the address of the rented premises or space is included in the definition of the insured's premises in the policy schedule and the amount of the annual fire insurance on the stock kept there will be brought into the calculation of the basis rate for the business interruption insurance; thus no property of the insured stored extension is necessary.

In the memorandum for a property stored extension the selected percentage limit is inserted as the maximum liability of the insurers for loss consequent upon damage at any one location and the indemnity is restricted to loss resulting from interference with the business caused by damage to property *of the insured*. This means that subsequent trading loss, due for example to a shortage of storage capacity for an insured's goods because of the destruction of the premises where they are normally warehoused, would not be covered by this form of extension. For insurance of such continuing loss (see paragraph 356).

355. Seasonal raw materials in public storage

In the preceding paragraph the statement that the loss consequent upon destruction of an insured's goods in a storage warehouse or other premises is not a continuing one was qualified in respect of the position where the goods destroyed are the insured's raw materials which it would be difficult to replace. This qualification is very necessary in relation to certain trades, notably those which are dependent upon seasonal supplies. For example, brewers buy the hops for their year's brewing before or when harvested and may store large quantities in outside warehouses until required in subsequent months. Fruit preservers and suppliers of frozen vegetables and fruit may put a large part of their year's supply into public cold storage warehouses until such time as they require it for manufacturing purposes or to put it into packs for sale. If such stocks are lost by fire shortly after the seasonal intake it may be almost impossible to replace them and turnover for several months could be seriously affected. Where circumstances of this kind apply it is essential that when an extension is arranged in respect of the insured's stock in outside warehouses not in their occupation the limit of the insurer's liability is fixed sufficiently high to allow for a continuing loss of turnover on the lines just described.

A rather similar position applies with the import of raw materials by sea if their supply is restricted to certain months of the year, due either to their growth being seasonal—as with grain, seed, cereals, dried fruit, etc.,—or because shipments from the Baltic and northern ports are restricted to months when the ports are free from ice—as with timber from Finland and the Soviet Union. The loss of an insured's stock of such commodities or materials in outside warehouses might not be replaceable for several months and could mean the loss of a substantial part of a year's turnover. A further point about imports by sea is that the insurances of merchants importing such commodities should be extended to include loss resulting from their destruction not only whilst in dock warehouses but also whilst on the quay and on board any ship or craft alongside and whilst in transit to their premises.

356. Loss of storage facilities

In stating in paragraph 354 that an insured's loss consequent upon the destruction of goods in store is not a continuing one it was mentioned that the position might be different where the loss of warehousing *facilities* is important. In certain trades the destruction of the warehouse premises normally used by insured for the storage of their goods can involve them in a continuing loss. For example, the provision of cold storage facilities is limited and the needs of the frozen food industry are continually expanding. The destruction of a large cold store could mean that firms using it regularly might suffer serious interference with their business in the future through lack of storage facilities. Even should accommodation be obtained at a cold store in another town the extra costs of transport and possibly higher rentals could be considerable.

A striking example of the importance of this feature is given in paragraph 341 and further stressed by a fire at a refrigerated warehouse in south Wales in December 1979 where the damage was said at the time to be estimated at over £9 million. Destruction of premises of that size must mean a shortage of storage accommodation for frozen foods for a considerable period afterwards.

Of recent years the increasing development of sophisticated stacker cranes, equipment and pallets has made possible the storage of a wide range of goods in high bay racking in fully automated, computer controlled, warehouses. This has led to the formation of specialist companies which combine the roles of traditional public warehousemen and those of a wholesaler and a haulage contractor functioning for the storage and small-scale distribution of their customers' products. This service is economically beneficial to manufacturers but because of its specialised nature and that of the premises and automated equipment it creates a high degree of dependency upon it for businesses integrated to its use. Hence damage by fire or other perils at such premises can mean a substantial continuing loss for manufacturers dependent on its services.

In any such or other cases where insurance is required to cover the insured's loss which might result from the destruction of storage *premises* (which is really a suppliers extension, *i.e.* of services) as distinct from and in addition to that due to damage to the insured's goods in those premises, care must be exercised to see that this is clearly understood by the insurers and that the extension memorandum is appropriately worded.

357. Textile manufacturing industry: goods at processors' premises

In a number of trades, mainly in the textile industry, in which it is customary for manufacturers to send either raw materials or partly finished goods to outside firms for various specialist processing work a limited form of extension was at one time given by insurers without charge. This covered loss arising from damage (as defined in the policy) to the insured's goods whilst temporarily deposited on the premises in Great Britain or Northern Ireland of bleachers, dyers, textile printers, finishers, weavers, cotton cloth manufacturers, artificial silk cloth manufacturers, worsted mills, burlers, menders, makers-up and packers, and yarn processors and in railway, canal, dock or other public warehouses or whilst in transit.

An extension applying to an insured's goods temporarily on the premises of named firms in trades such as the above can be arranged at an additional charge dependent on the individual circumstances of each case and the percentage limit adopted. This will normally be a low one if the extension cover is limited to the loss on the particular consignment of the insured's goods which are at risk of damage. If more extensive cover is required to insure against subsequent loss, if the insured's production is hampered because it is impossible to have work done elsewhere which was previously carried out by the processor whose premises have been damaged, a suppliers extension as per paragraphs 346 to 349 is necessary.

358. Engineers' patterns at other firms' premises

Another possibility of a continuing loss is that which attaches to a variety of machinery and machine tool makers and engineers who send patterns, models, drawings, etc., to firms in associated trades to have castings made or parts processed or finished. Should any of these patterns, etc., be destroyed whilst on the premises of such firms or in transit, especially if the castings etc., are required for current use the insured may suffer a considerable interference with their production until new ones can be made quite apart from any loss which may arise due to difficulty in finding another firm to do the required work. To provide against this possibility the insured can have an extension to include loss consequent upon damage (as defined in the policy) to patterns, jigs, models, templets, moulds, dies, tools, plans, drawings and designs, the property of the insured or held by them in trust or on commission for which they are responsible whilst at the premises in Great Britain or Northern Ireland of any machine makers, engineers, founders or other metal workers (excluding any premises wholly or partly occupied by the insured) and while in transit, all in Great Britain or Northern Ireland.

No additional premium is normally required for such an extension provided that in the calculation of the basis rate the value of the said property is included at the appropriate rate. The maximum limit of the insurer's liability is normally 10 per cent. This relatively small limit underlines the fact that the cover is loss resulting from damage to "the property of the insured", that is, the patterns, etc., only and does not include any continuing loss due to lack of processing facilities—the premises risk. If the latter is wanted the limit required will probably exceed the 10 per cent. maximum of the rating scale and this will draw attention to the necessity for a full suppliers extension.

Should the insured have a suppliers extension already on their policy which includes either specifically all the firms to whom they send patterns, etc., or unspecified suppliers with an adequate limit in respect of any one location, then the foregoing general extension will not be necessary.

359. Motor traders and garage proprietors extensions

Prior to 1959 it was a general practice for motor traders to carry a suppliers extension on their business interruption policies in order to include loss resulting from fire, etc., at the premises of named motor manufacturers with whom they held agencies. But in that year a serious fire occurred at the works of the Pressed Steel Co. Ltd., which caused a complete interruption of the output of steel motor bodies, which in turn resulted in a serious reduction in the production of cars by a leading manufacturer due to the lack of car bodies. But the effects did not finish there and passed on to the motor dealers holding agencies with that manufacturer whose normal allocation of new cars did not come through.

These motor traders throughout the country quickly experienced a reduction in sales and claimed upon their business interruption insurers who had the unpopular job of pointing out that as the fire had not occurred at the premises of the motor manufacturer there was no liability under the extensions. Following this a request from the motor dealers' association was met by the introduction of a new scheme by insurance companies to include in a motor trader's extension the premises not only of named motor manufacturers but those also of any supplier of materials or components to such manufacturers, these latter suppliers' suppliers not being specified by name.

This scheme gives a standard form of extension, additional rates of premium being charged according to the percentage limit of the total of the sums insured which is selected in respect of loss arising in consequence of damage at any of the premises of any named motor manufacturer. The cover under the policy is extended to:

" . . . The premises of . . . (and any manufacturer supplying them with components or materials) all in Great Britain or Northern Ireland".

It will be noticed that the standard form of extension limits its scope to locations in Great Britain or Northern Ireland and this is inadequate for dealers holding agencies for motor cars and vehicles manufactured abroad or assembled in the United Kingdom with parts made overseas. For such dealers provision can be made to insure their dependency in most cases at an appropriate additional premium on submission of specific details. Moreover, today even British makes of cars and vehicles ostensibly produced in the United Kingdom are in many cases made with some components imported from abroad. Therefore any motor trader desiring complete protection in respect of loss of car sales will have to look closely at this aspect and the possible need for an extension of the territorial limits.

It is not always appreciated that when motor dealers sell new cars they frequently sell a number of accessories, or bodywork treatment, at the same time and that the loss of gross profit in respect of these extras can be included in a claim for loss of sales of new cars under a standard motor traders extension.

Although this scheme of extensions for motor traders is officially called the "motor vehicle manufacturers" extension similar cover can be arranged applicable to motorcycle and scooter dealers and also for firms having agencies for agricultural tractors and machinery.

360. Extensions to outworkers for clothing, etc., manufacturers

It is customary with many makers of clothing, outerwear, mantles and costumes, shoe manufacturers and some others to have part of their manufacture carried out by out-workers, usually in small workrooms, flatted workrooms or dwellinghouses. Although the amount of the insured's materials on any one such outworker's premises at any point of time may be relatively small the specialised nature of the work done by each might mean interference with the insured's production if an outworker's premises were burnt out, particularly if this should happen at a busy season, and this potential loss can be covered by an appropriate extension.

It is customary in these trades for frequent changes in the list of outworkers employed by different manufacturers so to avoid having constantly to make alterations in a list of named outworkers on the extension memorandum of a manufacturer's policy insurers will give an extension to include loss resulting from damage at any outworkers, without specifying each individual outworker's premises provided that the limit of liability in respect of any one location is a low one, as it generally is.

361. Seasonal displays of samples, etc.

Special consideration is required in respect of an insured's property temporarily deposited in other premises when this consists of samples and designs which are there for purposes of seasonal display for the booking of orders. This may be a stockroom display for buyers at an hotel or a trade exhibition or show. Should the insured's goods be destroyed by fire at such a time it might be impossible to obtain new samples and showing facilities in time to book orders for the particular season's trade and this would involve a loss of sales out of all proportion to the value of the property destroyed.

To meet such a contingency an extension of the manufacturer's business interruption policy should be arranged to include any hotel or other premises at which displays for buyers are held with an appropriate limit in respect of the loss of gross profit which might result from damage at any one location. The latter should also include representatives' cars and this aspect of potential loss brings in the advisability of arranging cover for business interruption arising from the theft of samples and patterns, regarding which see paragraph 303.

362. Exhibitions and trade fairs

Somewhat similar circumstances may arise where a firm takes a stand each year at an industrial exhibition, trade fair, or one which caters for the general public like the Ideal Home Exhibition. Substantial orders may normally be booked either at the exhibition itself or subsequently as a result of the firm's display there and the loss of at any rate a part of those orders might be anticipated if the exhibition could not be held because of fire damage particularly where overseas buyers are concerned. The risk with trade fairs may attach for quite a long period before the opening date because buildings of the size and type suitable as a temporary venue for an exhibition pending the rebuilding of those destroyed are not readily available.

That there is a very considerable potential loss attaching will be appreciated when one considers that orders worth many millions of pounds are booked at trade exhibitions such as the Motor Show, the International Toy Fair, Antique Fair and others each year, a large proportion of these orders being from buyers from overseas who have come specially for the particular exhibition. The risk of fire is illustrated by the £40 million damage to the building and contents of the McCormick Place exhibition hall in Chicago in January 1967. Consider the effect on prospective exhibitors' order books should a similar disaster occur at the National Exhibition Centre near Birmingham. The provision of adequate alternative exhibition space and facilities or the rehabilitation of the premises would require a very considerable period of time if this enormous multimillion pound complex with over 100,000 square metres of roof covering, were destroyed.

Although there would obviously be difficulty in assessing the amount of trade lost by an insured if an exhibition had to be cancelled because of fire damage the results obtained from similar previous exhibitions should provide sufficient evidence for an estimate to be made of the loss sustained. To provide an indemnity for such loss the business interruption policy in respect of the exhibitor's own premises can be extended to include the possible loss of turnover which would result if an exhibition hall was damaged by fire or other perils. For such an extension a monetary limit is sometimes inserted in lieu of the customary percentage limit as being more practicable.

If compensation is required for loss not of gross profit but only in respect of expenditure incurred and appertaining to a stand, which might be money wasted if the exhibition could not be held because of a fire, insurance can be arranged as part of a composite "exhibition policy". A policy of this kind also covers loss of or damage to the insured's property at the exhibition and liability to the public for personal injuries, etc.

In the case of firms holding catering, display construction, decor, or other contracts or selling goods at an exhibition appropriate provision to cover their loss of prospective gross profit should the hall be damaged can be made by an extension of their business interruption policy to include loss resulting from damage at the exhibition premises. The additional premium required will depend upon the limit which is decided by the insured and stated as a percentage of the total sums insured under their policy up to which the cover given by the extension is to apply.

363. Manufacturers' agents (United Kingdom) and selling agents (United States)

With this class of businessmen who usually have no premises except an office and sample room and who carry no stocks, the potential loss of earnings which would follow from damage at their own premises is slight but they can suffer serious loss if damage occurs at the factory or mill of the firm for whose products they are agents. The fewer the number of agencies held the larger the possible loss whilst in cases where only one agency is held there is the possibility of a total loss of income.

A business interruption policy can be arranged to provide a manufacturers' agent with an indemnity for the loss which might result from damage at the premises of the firms for whom agencies are held and a simplified form of specification is used for the purpose. In this either "commission" or "gross income" is adopted as the subject-matter of the insurance instead of gross profit and also as the index of loss in lieu of turnover to which it would bear a ratio of 100 per cent. (See paragraph 275(a).)

"The premises" referred to in the schedule of the policy are those of the firms with whom agencies are held and the premium charged depends upon the fire risk at those premises and the relative percentage of the insurance applied as the limit in respect of the different premises. Small alterations are made to the preamble on the face of the policy because the insured does not occupy the premises and part (c) of General Condition 2 (Alteration) on the policy is deleted. The material damage proviso is inapplicable.

If it is considered desirable for the insurance to apply also to the agent's office and sample rooms this can be arranged in the normal manner. These then become the premises defined in the policy and the cover in respect of the manufacturers' premises is provided by means of an extension as for a supplier (paragraph 346).

Loss arising from damage at the premises of specified customers of a manufacturers' agent can be arranged on the lines similar to the foregoing, if required.

In the United States a coverage similar to the above was provided by a standard form called Commissions of Selling Agents. This was in respect of actual loss sustained if a selling agent, factor or broker lost income because of damage by an insured peril at named factories, warehouses or depots, a specified amount of insurance being applicable to each location and a coinsurance clause applying separately to each. The cover was described as the actual loss sustained by the insured due to reduction in gross selling commissions under contracts for the sale of products less charges and expenses which do not necessarily continue. This cover is now provided by the Business Income from Dependent Properties endorsement forms by extension to Manufacturing Locations.

364. Personal business interruption insurance—United States: managers, etc.

In general the practice in the United Kingdom differs from that in the United States with regard to the remuneration of managers of business enterprises. In the former they may be managing directors of limited companies, owners of the company or employees under annual contract or remunerated solely by salary or by salary and commission. Almost invariably their income will be assured by its inclusion in the cover on gross profit in the business interruption insurance of the business.

In the United States it is quite usual for managers of entertainment, sports and amusement enterprises, department stores, etc., to be paid a comparatively modest salary and a substantial rate of commission or bonus in order to encourage initiative and dollar results. To cater for the needs of such individuals, whose remuneration would be seriously reduced if their place of employment were badly damaged by fire or other perils and their employer had for one reason or another no business interruption insurance which included the manager's normal earnings, a standard form of coverage has been available throughout must of the United States to managers which is known as Loss of Income Insurance for Individuals.

In broad terms this insures their net loss of personal income resulting from interruption of their employer's business, "income" being the total of salary, commissions, bonus and other earnings accruing to the insured from the operation of the named business less any income guaranteed to the insured by the owners.

There is no time limit for the period of indemnity apart from the usual restriction to the time required for physical restoration of the damaged property and there is an 80 per cent. coinsurance clause on the policy.

In the current system of simplified coverage bases, no particular provision has been made for this form of cover, possibly because it is not often called for. However, it would be possible to adapt the Business Income Coverage form suitably by showing, in the Declarations, an appropriate description of the intended coverage.

365. Concessionaires and sole distributors, etc.

A dependency similar to that described in paragraph 363 exists for concessionaires and distributors of various manufactured goods particularly where they have a monopoly for a certain territory. Contracts of this nature are usually much sought after and very valuable and it is unlikely that alternative selling lines of an equally profitable nature could be obtained even should the contract permit such action if damage at the source of manufacture interferes with the supply of goods.

The holders of such contracts have often built up an extensive sales organisation which they would wish to maintain throughout a period of interruption resulting from fire at the manufacturer's premises. In such cases an extension of the distributor's own premises business interruption insurance should be arranged to include the factory or factories producing the goods they sell whether they actually handle those goods or have them dispatched direct to their customers. The need for business interruption insurance is the same in respect of contracts for selling rights in the United Kingdom held with manufacturers overseas and an extension should be arranged to include the maker's premises.

366. Manufacturers without plant

Many trading firms style themselves as "manufacturers" when in fact they have no manufacturing plant. In some cases they are merchant converters; others may be simply a marketing organisation carrying on the selling arrangements for goods made under their patent by a manufacturer at an agreed price. Often the real manufacturer dispatches the goods under the principal's name direct to customers of the latter.

The risk of business interruption in these circumstances is one of complete dependency upon the works of the actual manufacturer with a relatively small risk attaching to the concern's own premises according to the size of their office accommodation and organisation and whether they themselves do any warehousing or dispatching of finished goods. An appropriate cover can be arranged to meet these circumstances with a specification on a turnover basis and at a premium basis rate which is substantially the fire insurance rate applicable to the premises of the actual manufacturer.

Other self-styled "manufacturers" may buy materials and have these processed and made-up on commission to their own requirements. Sometimes more than one process is involved, each carried out by a different firm, up to the finished state when the products enter the warehouse of the self-styled manufacturer ready for merchanting. Sometimes there may be no warehouse, only an office organisation, the packing and dispatching being done on commission by an outside firm.

When the arrangements are such that a fire at the premises of any of these other firms might have an adverse effect upon the so-called manufacturer's trading a suitable business interruption policy is advisable. This would include the various premises upon which there is dependency. If this dependency is not total in respect of each of the outside premises a percentage of the sum insured could be arranged as the maximum liability of the insurers in respect of loss resulting from damage at any one location, with a corresponding reduction in the premium.

367. Publishers and producers of literature printed elsewhere

Publishers of books of all descriptions, periodicals, journals, magazines, trade directories, brochures and catalogues, in fact any reading matter, who do not themselves print their publications are another category of businesses which are liable to suffer a serious loss of turnover in consequence of damage at some other firm's premises. They are dependent primarily on printers and binders for production of their publications possibly also upon engravers and block makers for illustrations and sometimes upon paper manufacturers for covers, especially hardbacks, or when special qualities of paper are used. It may not be possible to secure publication until a considerable time after serious damage at the premises of one of these links in their chain of production.

A business interruption policy suitably drafted to include loss resulting from damage at the premises of printers upon whom they will be mainly dependent and other processors according to the particular circumstances of their methods of production, will be necessary for security against the potential loss. The very considerable amount of printwork which is done on the Continent for British firms indicates the seriousness for publishers of this aspect of business interruption. When the cover necessary for protection has to extend to include premises overseas then it will be given special consideration by insurers.

In this category of firms for which an extension to the premises of printers, suppliers and processors can be of vital importance might also be included mail order houses and clubs, package holiday firms, operators of motor coach tours and pleasure cruises, hirers of holiday boats and yachts, seed and bulb merchants, proprietors of holiday camps and hotels, and various other businesses which depend for their trade very largely upon illustrated brochures or catalogues. If the business is a seasonal one failure to issue their literature at the appropriate time might result in the loss of a substantial part of a year's revenue. Such businesses should also have an extension of their business interruption insurance to include loss should their brochures be destroyed whilst on the premises of a firm specialising in packing and despatching literature of that nature.

In cases where publication date must be maintained if at all possible even if it involves expenditure beyond the limit in clause (b) of the increase in cost of working section of the cover it is advisable to arrange for an item to be added to the specification to insure against loss in respect of such additional expenditure. (See paragraph 50.)

368. Catalog sales merchants—United States

In the United States there are businesses the sole function of which is to act as intermediaries for "catalog shopping" by the public who obtain from them goods purchased by ordering from the catalogues of firms such as Sears, Roebuck & Co. These goods are delivered to the premises of the Catalog Sales Merchant for collection in person by the purchaser. The catalog sales merchants carry no stock of their own but as intermediaries handling the goods they have a direct dependence upon the operation of the principal supplier's premises and upon the production of the catalogues for which protection by a Business Income from a Dependent Properties form (Contributing Locations) (paragraph 347) is advisable.

369. Telephone exchanges: extensions to

Travel agents are particularly dependent upon telephone facilities for obtaining information about air, sea, rail, cruise and package holiday reservations and in receiving and making bookings. This applies especially in the London area and other large cities where the lack of such facilities would mean customers telephoning to a firm in another part of the city or an adjacent suburb. To meet this contingency an extension can be arranged to insure against loss resulting from damage by fire, explosion and aircraft at any telephone exchange in a specified area.

Equally dependent upon the telephone service are theatre agents a large part of whose income is derived from telephone bookings by customers and for such businesses an extension to cover loss resulting from damage at their area telephone exchanges also merits consideration. For bookmakers and betting offices it might be thought a "must".

Most professional offices would experience hindrance to their work with a consequent postponement of income and in many cases actual loss of fees and some additional expense if deprived for some time of telephone and telex facilities. Because in their circumstances the incidence and extent of loss would not be as great as for trading concerns such as those mentioned above the extra premium required for this extension for professional offices is about half the normal charge.

It is not possible to know how many businesses in New York sustained loss due to the interruption of communications caused by the $60 million fire at a telephone exchange there in February 1975 but it was very considerable and the incident illustrates the ever present hazard.

International currency dealing at major banks is another activity which is dependent on telecommunications and an extension to telephone exchanges and other premises of the United Kingdom (and possibly overseas) telecommunications authorities is vital.

The United States Off-Premises Services Time Element endorsement specifically extends cover to Communication Supply Services, meaning property supplying communication services, including telephone, radio, microwave or television services, to the described premises, such as communication transmission lines, coaxial cables and microwave radio relays except satellites. It does not include overhead communication lines, cover for which is provided by the Off-Premises Overhead Transmission Lines endorsement. (Refer paragraph 371 for the extension wording used in the United Kingdom.)

370. Packaging and containers for goods

Packaging of goods is a highly specialised and substantial industry with its own annual exhibition. Because the production of wrappings and containers for all kinds of goods has been brought to such a high level it has created for the firms who use these products a degree of dependency upon them which will involve a loss of turnover if the source of supply is interrupted by fire or kindred perils.

Hygienic standards demand specialised pre-packing or wrapping of certain kinds of goods, and particularly of foodstuffs. Competitive selling likewise calls for attractive containers with distinctive designs, and the growth of self-service stores and supermarkets has increased the importance and value of compulsive buying appeal. Jars, bottles, plastic "bouncing bottles", cans, cartons, tubes, tins, caps, closures, aerosols, flexible packs, decorative wrappings and boxes are often the outcome of a lengthy preparation of designs and the adaptation of machinery to make them. Modern containers are usually a precision-made product manufactured on high-speed automatic machinery; and to withstand the stringencies of processing and to allow them to flow through high-speed filling and closing machinery it is necessary to be made to an accuracy of thousandths of an inch. If a factory making such containers or packaging materials to particular designs is seriously damaged it may be a considerable time before customers can find an alternative suitable source of supply. In the interim the sale of the latter's goods will be seriously interfered with and an interruption of their packaging supply would be particularly harmful at a time of a seasonal build-up or heavy delivery of stocks for such a period as Christmas. It was said at one time that there was only one British company manufacturing the PVC stretch film which is essential for wrapping polystyrene food packaging trays.

Where dependence of this nature exists an appropriate extension can be arranged for the business interruption policy of a firm using the containers for its products, to cover loss resulting from damage at the premises of the manufacturer in the same manner as explained in paragraphs 344 *et seq.* for dependence upon suppliers.

Conversely, the packaging maker has a particular dependence upon each of the customers because if one of them can no longer take supplies owing to damage at their own premises the containers made to their individual design and specification will not be saleable on the open market. To insure against this potential loss of turnover a customers extension (paragraph 351) is indicated.

371. Public utilities

The possibilities of a business sustaining a business interruption loss as the result of failure of the public supply of electricity, gas or water is fully discussed in paragraph 319 in the chapter on engineering business interruption insurances in which it is explained that a special policy can be issued to cover loss resulting from failure of supplies due to almost any cause. Because the contingencies included in such a policy are very much wider than those which can be covered under a "public utilities" extension of a normal fire business interruption policy the former may be preferred.

An appropriate extension can, however, be added to a standard fire business interruption policy, if desired, at less premium and without the 30 minute franchise which applies to the special (engineering department) policy. It applies to loss as insured by the policy resulting from damage to property at any:

1. generating station or sub-station of the public electricity supply undertaking.

2. land-based premises of the public gas supply undertaking or of any natural gas producer linked directly therewith.
3. waterworks or pumping stations of the public water supply undertaking.
4. land-based premises of the public telecommunications undertaking

from which the insured obtain electric current, gas, water or telecommunications all in Great Britain or Northern Ireland.

The perils insured are usually restricted to fire, lightning, aircraft and explosion; but the perils of riot, malicious damage, earthquake, storm and flood can be added even though they are not covered in respect of the insured's own premises.

It is interesting to note that the arrival on the scene of the space communications satellite has not gone unnoticed on either side of the Atlantic. In the U.S. extension wording (refer paragraph 369) satellites are expressly excluded; and in the U.K. wording, reference is made to (and thereby limited to) "land-based premises".

Under the premium rating table for extensions to public utilities, provision can be made for any one, or more, of the utilities to be insured. Insurers recognise that any stoppage is likely to be of limited duration because public utility undertakings must be restored as quickly as possible after damage and there are national electricity and gas grids and telecommunication networks. Consequently the additional premium charged for an extension of this nature is comparatively small and does not vary with the length of the maximum indemnity period for the insurance on gross profit.

The production of chemical manufacturers and tar distillers who obtain supplies of crude tar from a local gasworks or steelworks' coking plant might be seriously interfered with in the event of a lengthy stoppage of those supplies resulting from fire or explosion at such premises. For such businesses a suitable suppliers extension could be arranged to insure against loss consequent upon an interruption of supplies of crude tar resulting from damage at the source of supply.

372. Process steam, space heating, power or lighting current from an "estate" boiler and engine house; waste heat from electricity works

A business which obtains light, heat or power from the boiler and engine house of an industrial trading estate on which its premises are situate or that of the landlords of a multiple tenancy mill or factory or of another firm in adjacent works, may be in danger of a serious interruption of production in the event of damage by fire or other perils to its source of supply. Even though there may in some cases be transformer equipment installed at the trading estate so that electricity can be taken from the public supply when needed, no independent alternative supply of steam for process work or space heating will be available.

Where there is dependence of this kind an appropriate extension should be made to the insured's business interruption policy to cover the loss which would arise from a failure of their supply of light, heat, power or process steam due to damage in the boiler or engine house.

If a firm of nurserymen is obtaining waste heat from an electricity power station to heat their glasshouses they should consider the question of dependency and an extension of their insurance for protection against loss in the event of damage by insurable perils to the source of their heat supply. (Refer also paragraph 270(b).)

373. Prevention (denial) of access

The necessity for the various forms of extension already described in this chapter arises from the fact that a business interruption policy in its normal terms covers loss resulting from damage only at the premises occupied by the insured. The possibilities of loss as a result of damage at other premises which have already been dealt with are those arising from dependency due to some trading or servicing relationship. But there can be forms of dependency upon the safety of other parties' property in which there is no such relationship involved; what might broadly be termed the adjacent premises risk.

In many towns there are shopping arcades. A fire in one part of an arcade might leave a tangled mass of steel girders and insecure walls, making it necessary in the interest of public safety to close some or all of the undamaged part of the arcade until completion of the work of demolition and clearance and this would apply particularly where the arcade is a cul-de-sac. This would result in an immediate reduction, perhaps total for some days, in the turnover of the undamaged shops but there would be no compensation under the respective shopkeepers' business interruption policies because no material damage had occurred at their premises. (See paragraph 15(b).)

A somewhat similar situation may arise in public markets or city or regional shopping centres and malls in which closure of some parts of the premises following a serious fire could adversely affect trading in undamaged shops through restriction of access.

When a serious fire takes place in a shopping thoroughfare of tall buildings and unsafe walls make it necessary to close part of the street to the public for a time the inevitable result is a temporary loss of trade by shops and theatres, etc., in the prohibited area. Over the years there have been many occasions in which fires in city centres have resulted in the temporary cordoning off of parts of streets or the closure of shopping arcades. An example of this was the closure of Church Street in Liverpool for about 10 days following the fire at Henderson's Store in June 1960. Loss of turnover for businesses to which the public are denied access is inevitable in such cases and if this occurs at a seasonal time of peak sales for instance shortly before Christmas the loss can equal what would normally be earned over a much longer period.

For any business with premises so situate that similar circumstances could arise it is simply ordinary prudence to insure against the possible business interruption loss, the additional premium required being very small and, because the period of interruption is unlikely to be prolonged, the premium does not vary with the length of the maximum indemnity period. In "compact" insurances for retail shops it is included as a standard part of the policy. Otherwise any necessary extension of cover is made under what is termed the "prevention of access" or "denial of access" clause, which reads (after the common extension preamble):

> "Property in the vicinity of the Premises, loss or destruction of or damage to which shall prevent or hinder the use of the Premises or access thereto, whether the Premises or property of the Insured therein shall be damaged or not, but excluding loss or destruction of or damage to property of any supply undertaking from which the Insured obtains electricity, gas or water, or telecommunications services which prevents or hinders the supply of such services, to the Premises".

It is interesting to note that the clause does not restrict the indemnity to damage which prevents actual use of or access to the insured's premises but includes loss in consequence of damage which shall "hinder the use" thereof; in some circumstances "hinder" might have wider connotations. Even so the wording leaves an insured shopkeeper open to the possibility of serious loss. If damage in one part of a shopping centre or the destruction of a major attraction in it such as a cinema, theatre, leisure centre, multistorey car park or a particularly popular supermarket or departmental store reduces the incentive for the public to visit the centre there may be a very substantial reduction in the insured's turnover, although there is neither prevention of nor hindrance to the use of or access to his own shop. The insured will have no control over steps to be taken to rehabilitate the damaged premises and his loss may continue for a long period. To safeguard against this contingency an insured should obtain from insurers an agreement that not the shop address but the overall description of the shopping centre or market is accepted by them as being the definition in the policy schedule of The Premises, even if doing this involves additional premium.

Under the "Additional Coverage of Civil Authority" U.S. business interruption policies are extended to include loss for a period up to two weeks sustained by the insured as a result of direct physical loss of or damage to property other than that of the described premises when access to the said described premises is prohibited by order of a civil authority. It is not stated specifically whether this extension operates whether or not the insured's premises are damaged (see paragraph 65(a)) but either way it does not approach the protection given under a U.K. prevention of access cover.

A sinister development over the past few years has been the bomb scare. Bombs have been planted in shopping areas and have either exploded or have been found and made harmless. Sometimes there has been only a false alarm with no bomb present. In these situations, areas have been cleared by the police authority which has led to shops losing business. Covers are available for such situations where the prevention or hindrance of the use of the premises arises directly from the actions of the police or other statutory body. There is usually a 24 hours excess.

374. Loss of attraction (United Kingdom): Leader locations (United States)

The point made in paragraph 373 above might be pursued further to the dependency position of shops in the vicinity of, but not actually in, a shopping centre or near a large department store (in major cities in the United States these may have 150 or more separate departments) which are magnets drawing potential shoppers to the immediate area. Such shops in the vicinity benefit from the spin-off effect of people passing their premises en route and making purchases. In the event of the premises which are the prime attraction for shoppers to go to the area being destroyed smaller shops around would suffer a reduction in their catch-trade turnover because of the reduction in the number of people who normally go to the shopping centre or department store. This loss might continue for many months.

Such loss is not covered under a prevention of access extension on a U.K. insurance because the damage does not prevent or hinder the use of the insured's premises or access to them. However, cover is obtainable as an extension to a prevention of access cover, although it may be restricted to losses arising from damage to a named "attraction," and the "area of attractiveness" may be defined as being within a prescribed radius of a few hundred yards of the insured's own premises. There may also be a monetary limit and a short (say six months) maximum indemnity period. Some special schemes for shops incorporate loss of attraction as an integral part of the overall cover (refer paragraph 390).

In the United States this possibility of loss is recognised and specially catered for by the issue of a Business Income from Dependent Properties coverage as an extension of shopkeepers' Business Income policies with Details of the Leader Locations inserted.

It might be argued that the destruction of a large department store, *e.g.* the complete destruction by a £17 million fire in December 1980 of "Minion", the biggest store in Athens, Greece, covering a whole block, would mean more trade available to other shops in the vicinity because of the temporary elimination of a major competitor. On balance, however, the likelihood would appear to be that fewer shoppers coming on their regular pre-fire customary routes would result in reduced turnover.

375. Road risks: motor vehicle operators, etc.

When motor vehicles are in an insured's own garage business interruption resulting from fire damage is covered provided that the garage premises have been included in the description of premises on the policy schedule and the vehicle insurance covers fire risks. But when they are away from the insured's premises on the road or in parking grounds or in garages for repair or other reasons business interruption resulting from damage by fire is not covered unless an appropriate extension of the insurance has been effected.

Whether an extension of this category is worth the additional premium involved will depend upon the particular circumstances of each case. If a vehicle is damaged by fire it will often be possible to hire another until the damaged vehicle is either repaired or is replaced by a new one. But the cost of hiring may be heavy especially if a driver has to be hired with it; this would be payable (up to the "economic limit"—paragraph 47(a)) under the increase in cost of working section of the specification if the extension had been added to the insurance. Where the vehicles are of a special type it may not be possible to hire others of the same suitability.

It may be suggested that if a vehicle of standard design is burnt out a new one can be purchased and put on the road in a very short time and therefore the additional cover is unnecessary. This overlooks the fact that vehicles can be and frequently are seriously damaged by fire without being total losses. In such cases the motor insurers will insist upon the repair of the damaged vehicle if this is less costly than the purchase of a new one and the repairs may take several weeks. During that period the loss of use or the cost of hiring can involve an insured in a substantial loss.

A "road risk extension" may be seen as divided into two categories. The first is for haulage contractors, motor coach and bus proprietors, taxicab proprietors, private hirers, furniture storers and removers and others whose turnover is dependent wholly or mainly on the operation of motor vehicles. The larger the fleet of vehicles the more likelihood there is of one taking fire on the road because the possibility of this increases with every additional vehicle in service. On the other hand, the amount of loss which can arise from a single vehicle being out of use is proportionately less as the size of a fleet increases and is further minimised if, as is customary with large fleets, there are spare vehicles always available.

The premium rate charged for the extension depends upon the percentage limit chosen and because the potential loss in any one occurrence is minimised according to the number of vehicles owned and their dispersal the cost can generally be modified by opting for a low limit.

The risk is much more serious for hauliers and truckers owning only two or three vehicles as these are probably the sole source of income of the business and it is not impossible for more than one vehicle away from an insured's premises to be damaged at the same time, especially should they be in a local garage for repairs.

Owner–drivers with only one vehicle and heavy interest charges on it to be met each month are especially vulnerable to loss through fire damage to a truck away from their own garage.

Because of the seriousness of the risk for haulage contractors in general and to make insurance against it attractive to them some insurers issue a simplified policy providing cover against business interruption at flat rates of premium. This insurance is in respect of loss resulting from damage by fire, lightning, explosion or aircraft to the insured's premises or vehicles therein and extends to vehicles elsewhere with a limit of 10 per cent. of the sum insured. The latter is the amount of gross income of the business less the cost of fuel, lubricants, tyres and bad debts, so includes all drivers' wages.

Where the vehicles concerned are "travelling saleshops" and the trade from them constitutes a major part of an insured's business (sometimes it is the whole of it), the loss consequent upon even one being out of commission can be substantial, and the premium required for the road risk cover is well worthwhile.

The other category under a "road risk extension" comprises businesses not mainly dependent upon the operation of motor vehicles. In this category the cover is appropriate for firms which use vehicles as revenue earning units ancillary to their main business. It is particularly useful when the vehicles are of special type or construction and it can be anticipated that repairs of a damaged vehicle or the purchase of a new one will take a long time and that meanwhile it will be difficult to hire a suitable temporary replacement.

Among the types of vehicle for which road risk (fire) cover should be considered are tankers, especially those with special alloy linings, used by chemical works for the transport of acids and highly inflammable or dangerous chemicals or by dairies, breweries and oil works for the collection or delivery of liquids; similar vehicles constructed for the bulk transport of flour, glucose, sugar and so forth; insulated vans used in the meat trade and ice cream trade; refrigerated vans for carrying fish; and pantechnicons and large capacity vans used in the furniture and similar trades for the conveyance of bulky goods. Another vulnerable class of vehicle is that of the giant, multi-wheel trucks and articulated tractors incorporating advanced technology and highly sophisticated mechanical and bodywork design, some with sleeper cabs with cooker, refrigerator, etc., for long-distance transcontinental hauls, which are now a normal feature of our roads. The five-figure capital cost of such vehicles alone means that the *per diem* loss in standing charges can be a considerable amount. There is the possibility of considerable loss of turnover or heavy expense on hiring if a vehicle of special type such as those mentioned is off the road for any length of time.

Travelling saleshops upon which insured are wholly or mainly dependent have already been mentioned as in the first category but for road risk extensions there are others which come within the second class. These latter are mobile shops which are only ancillary to the shop trade, and although their weekly turnover may be a very considerable amount it still constitutes only a relatively small part of the total trade of the business. Nevertheless the business interruption loss can be substantial when one such vehicle is damaged by fire and is off the road.

It must be clearly understood that the only contingencies giving rise to damage to a motor vehicle which are insurable under a road risk extension on a business interruption policy are specifically those insured under the general cover of such a policy, *e.g.* fire and such special perils as explosion and aircraft. Accidental damage and impact cover for vehicles will be regarded by many insurers as not to be included in the extension, the usual wording for which is (after the usual extension preamble): "motor vehicles of the insured in Great Britain or Northern Ireland elsewhere than at premises in the insured's occupation".

376. Goods in transit

As distinct from the loss resulting from damage to an insured's vehicles as discussed in the preceding paragraph 375 that arising from damage by fire and similar perils to "property of the insured whilst in transit in Great Britain or Northern Ireland" can be covered under a "transit extension". Firms who send goods of high value away for process work or send machinery or plant from one factory to another or to trade exhibitions might suffer a considerable loss of gross profit or be involved in additional expenditure in the event of a consignment being destroyed by fire whilst in transit. If in the course of transport to a customer an important machine sustains damage which might mean a long period for repair or replacement payment under a penalty clause for late delivery may be incurred, regarding which see paragraph 261(a).

The destruction of goods in transit from a factory or warehouse to branch shops or depots or to customers will involve insured in the loss of their profit margin unless the goods are already sold and invoiced and recovery of the full sale price is made under the fire or transit policy by which they are insured. For launderers and dry cleaners a free extension is given for the risk of business interruption arising from an insured peril during collection and delivery of customers' goods.

Loss arising from accidental damage (impact) to the goods can now be included in the perils covered by a transit extension; if insurers do not wish to provide this cover for the conveying road or rail vehicle or waterborne craft the wording should be amended to say so. If transit is by air, additional cover is necessary. Accidental damage to machinery whilst loading, in transit and unloading can be insured in an Advance Profits cover of an almost "all risks" nature as per paragraphs 268(a) and 322.

The extension should not apply to the insurances of the business of any haulage contractor, bus, coach or taxi proprietor, private hirer, furniture storer or remover, or any other business where the turnover is dependent wholly or mainly on the operation of motor vehicles of any kind. The motor vehicles extension should be used for such businesses.

377. Premises where a contract is being carried out

The risk of loss in the event of damage by fire at other people's premises is a normal feature of those businesses which engage in carrying out large-scale contracts in connection with the construction, maintenance or repair of large properties, public buildings or industrial undertakings. Public works and building contractors, constructional engineers, electrical engineers, heating and ventilating engineers, glaziers, tilers, joinery contractors, sanitary engineers, refrigeration engineers, painting contractors and shopfitters are all in this category.

Should a building to which a contract relates be seriously damaged by fire the contractors' work on it will cease and it may be a considerable time before it can be recommenced; the structure may have to be demolished, the site cleared and a fresh start made. The disastrous fire in November 1958 at the partially completed Brussels National Airport doing damage amounting to nearly £2 million—one of many cases over the years of serious fires at buildings in course of erection—well illustrates what can happen at contract sites. In the meantime it may not be possible to obtain alternative work because contracts of this nature are usually let by tender and this is a lengthy process. Unless the contractors have other contracts in hand to which they can divert their workmen and plant there will then be a period when a reduction in turnover will take place even though the contract which has been interrupted is subsequently resumed. Skilled workers may have to be paid redundancy pay, or wages during enforced idleness, and other standing charges will continue unabated during this period of interruption involving the contractors in considerable financial loss.

If the insured undertake work of this nature and the individual contracts are of such a size in relation to a year's turnover that stoppage on one would have an appreciable adverse effect on their gross profit, the business interruption policy in respect of damage at their own premises should be suitably extended. The extension would cover loss resulting from damage as defined in the policy occurring at any premises in Great Britain or Northern Ireland not in the occupation of insured where they are carrying out a contract, subject to an agreed limit such as 10 per cent. of the sum insured applying in respect of loss at any one location. The additional premium required for an extension of this nature is modest and the lower the percentage limit selected the smaller will be the charge.

The problem of possible loss on overseas contracts is highlighted by the magnitude of building construction now being carried out in oil rich countries of the Middle East. This calls for consideration by contractors of many nationalities involved regarding the possibilities of business interruption loss in the event of destruction of buildings in course of erection.

Many builders and contractors manufacture on their own premises the joinery work required on their building contracts and their fire insurance then includes the woodworking machine shop for which the fire rate is usually comparatively high. But it would be inequitable to adopt the normal method of making the average fire rate for their premises the basis rate for a business interruption insurance because most of the gross profit is earned on building sites where the fire hazard is very low. To meet these circumstances a special scheme is available for builders and contractors in the building and ancillary trades which gives cover for business interruption resulting from damage at either their own premises or at any contract site but uses a method of rating which takes into account the proportion which the gross profit dependent on their own premises bears to the total gross profit of the business. This makes allowance for the reduced fire risk at building sites where most of the earnings are derived, the result generally being a very moderate premium for an insurance which combines business interruption resulting from damage at either the firm's own premises—offices, drawing offices, machine shop and stores, etc.,—or at any contract site. But this specially reduced premium rate cannot be applied to wages insurance restricted to employees at the insured's premises only.

CHAPTER 18

Miscellaneous Clauses and Covers

378. Professional Accountants clause

In the event of damage causing interference with business activities the normal service of auditing the firm's books and preparing accounts will continue generally without any substantial diminution in the work involved except in the rare cases when damage results in the complete closing down of the business. Consequently, the annual charge for this work is a standing charge and should be included in the insurance on gross profit. But accountants' charges of another kind will become payable as a result of the damage which are not a standing charge and which cannot be measured by the reduction in turnover. These are the charges to which an insured's accountants will be entitled for the work involved in the preparation of such information as may be required by the insurers for the purposes of the claim; this work may extend over a prolonged period.

Such charges are payable by the insured on whose behalf the services are rendered and it is made quite clear in Claims Condition 1 (Action by the Insured) of the policy (see paragraph 435) that the details required by the insurers shall be furnished at the insured's "own expense".

Provision for the above is made by an addition to the specification of the Professional Accountants Clause the first part of which reads:

> "MEMO. Any particulars or details contained in the Insured's books of account or other business books or documents which may be required by the Insurers under Claims Condition 1 of this policy for the purpose of investigating or verifying any claim hereunder may be produced by professional accountants if at the time they are regularly acting as such for the Insured and their report shall be prima facie evidence of the particulars and details to which such report relates".

The memo does not mention computerised data but no doubt this comes within its intention and will be included in due course.

It should be noted that the scope of this clause is limited to the acceptance as prime facie evidence by the insurers of details required by them and is not an undertaking to accept the accountants' formulation of the claim. Neither does the clause bind insurers to accept the opinion of the insured's accountants as to whether certain items in the accounts are or are not insurable standing charges.

It does, however, guarantee to insured that in the event of a claim it will be unnecessary for a loss adjuster to go through their books of account and so precludes the possibility of private information not relevant to the claim being seen. This aspect is of particular importance in the case of public companies whose shares are quoted on the Stock Exchange who have additional reason for wishing to be sure that no outside party acquires confidential information about their business.

To provide for the reimbursement to an insured of the cost of their accountants' services it was necessary until 1978 in the United Kingdom to have a separate item and sum insured on the specification. Then in that year insurers decided to dispense with the requirement for a separate item of insurance and to include automatically for the payment by them to the insured of such accountants' charges by an extension of the cover provided in the item on gross profit.

Effect is given to this by the second part of the Professional Accountants Clause on the specification which reads:

> "The Insurers will pay to the Insured the reasonable charges payable by the Insured to their professional accountants for producing such particulars or details or any other proofs, information or evidence as may be required by the Insurers under the terms of Claims Condition 1 of this policy and reporting that such particulars or details are in accordance with the Insured's books of account or other business books or documents.
>
> Provided that the sum of the amount payable under this clause and the amount otherwise payable under the policy shall in no case exceed the liability of insurers as stated.".

The amount to be included for the possible cost of accountants' fees in the event of a claim, when calculating the sum to be insured on gross profit, is an arbitrary figure because it is impossible to know in advance how much work will be involved. A firm's auditors can give the best estimate. But as it is not shown on the specification as a separate amount, it does not entail any specific premium payment and is limited only as stated in the proviso at the end of the memorandum. If the gross profit sum insured is maintained as advocated in paragraph 225(a) the inclusive amount can be decided upon with a good safety margin. Allowance must be made for an extension of the time element when the maximum indemnity period is longer than 12 months.

Two further points should be noted about this clause. First, the compensation provided is restricted to the charges payable for producing particulars and reporting thereon; that is, it does not cover the cost of any time spent by an insured's accountants in negotiations with a loss adjuster. Secondly, the particulars referred to are such "as may be required by the insurers"; this precludes the cost of accountants' time spent unnecessarily in producing figures to substantiate a claim on lines not contained in the policy formula. In practice it is customary for insurers to place a generous interpretation on the clause when requested to meet a reasonable charge for work necessarily incurred by accountants.

In certain businesses the work of supplying the details required in the event of a claim would not be done by the insured's auditors. For example, there may be a group of companies each of which has a different auditor with the holding company employing for the affairs of the whole group a firm of accountants as consultants, whom it would wish to act in the event of a loss by any member. In such cases it can be arranged for the name of the accountants who would produce details for the claim to be inserted in the wording of the clause in lieu of "their professional accountants".

379. Payments on account in claims

Requests are sometimes made for a memorandum to be inserted in the specification to the effect that payments on account of a claim will be made to the insured monthly if desired. It is considered by insurance companies in general that this clause is unnecessary because the concluding words of Claims Condition 1 of the policy postulate such payments. In practice payments on account are made on request according to the circumstances of claims and, indeed, generally benefit the insurer as well as the insured by providing means to rehabilitate the insured's business as quickly as possible, thereby reducing the loss of gross profit and also saving possible additional expenditure in the form of interest on borrowed money. Because of this, as it is desirable to avoid adding any unnecessary clauses to a specification which is in any event a fairly lengthy document, it is not the general practice to add this particular clause.

380. Departmental clause

Many businesses have two or more revenue earning departments and because they produce or sell different commodities or supply different services their respective rates of gross profit to turnover may differ. After meeting out of its earnings the expenses debited to it each department's profit will be carried to a combined profit and loss account. The rate of gross profit earned by the different departments may vary considerably but in the event of damage affecting the turnover of one or more of them the business interruption claim will in the normal terms of the specification be based on the rate of gross profit, that is the average rate of the whole business.

Consequently, if the damage were to interfere solely or mainly with a department earning a low ratio of profit the insured would be over indemnified. On the other hand, if it affected a department with a high profit ratio the insured would not receive a full indemnity. Even if it is argued that the construction of the premises and situation of the department in them is such that any damage would affect all departments equally it must not be overlooked that some departments may have a seasonal trade. So the damage could whilst doing the same material injury to each department have an entirely different effect on one from that on another according to the time of year when it took place. Moreover, after damage has occurred efforts will be made to rehabilitate the business as quickly as possible and trading may be re-established in some departments—possibly in temporary premises elsewhere before it is in others with the result that the shortage in turnover due to the damage will not be uniform throughout the different departments. Therefore, wherever there are sections of a business earning different profit ratios it is advisable to make provision to meet those circumstances.

It is held by some insurers that the other circumstances clause takes care of this matter but a careful reading of it will show that it does not provide for a division of the rate of gross profit or of the annual turnover or standard turnover into departmental figures. The fact that separate sections earn different rates of gross profit is a normal and permanent feature of the business. It does not constitute "a trend of the business or a variation in or other circumstance affecting the business either before or after the damage". Moreover the turnover referred to directly or indirectly in the clause is by definition the turnover of the business and not the turnover of "part of the business".

The method laid down in the specification for calculating the claim is legally binding. This does not mean that the insurers and the insured could not mutually agree, in order to provide a true indemnity, to settle the claim on a departmental basis but it would be inequitable if the position were such that an insured, with a greater knowledge than the insurers of the circumstances of the business, could elect to do this only when advantageous. Experience shows that ambiguities and loopholes may sometimes be used to an insurer's disadvantage.

In view of the foregoing, where a business is conducted in departments, sections, branches or divisions, the following "departmental clause" is often added to the specification with the object of ensuring a true indemnity whichever part of the business is affected by the damage.

"MEMO. If the Business be conducted in departments the independent trading results of which are ascertainable, the provisions of clauses (a) and (b) of the item on Gross Profit shall apply separately to each department affected by the Incident, except that if the sum insured by the said item be less than the aggregate of the sums produced by applying the Rate of Gross Profit for each department of the Business (whether affected by the Incident or not) to its relative Annual Turnover (or to a proportionately increased multiple thereof where the Maximum Indemnity Period exceeds 12 months), the amount payable shall be proportionately reduced".

The last part of the clause starting with "except that . . . " is omitted when the insurance is on the Declaration-Linked basis (see paragraph 53).

When the specification includes an item on wages under the dual basis scheme the above memorandum is amended to apply its terms, including the application of average, separately to the gross profit item and the wages item.

It will be noticed from the wording of the memorandum that when it is added to the specification the insured cannot elect to have it applied in a loss settlement only when that would be in their favour. It must be applied in every settlement even though separate departmental accounts are not kept, provided that the independent trading results of each department, that is the turnover and gross profit figures, can be ascertained.

For an illustration of a claim settlement under a policy with the clause applicable, where there are three departments interfered with for varying periods each with a different rate of gross profit, see Appendix Y, paragraph 470.

There are some businesses for which this clause would be appropriate in which the word branch, or division, being the expression in day-to-day use in the business itself, would be more suitable than department and corresponding alterations are made in the clause. If necessary in some cases a note might be added giving the actual descriptions used in the business or the addresses of premises or alternatively a note that "department" means "any activity of the insured for which separate Manufacturing or Trading and Profit & Loss Accounts are kept".

381. Departments of a business with different indemnity periods

The departmental clause described in the preceding paragraph 380 does not meet the circumstances of a business where maximum indemnity periods of different lengths are required for different sections of the business. For instance, one comprising a bakery and several retail shops may want an 18 months maximum indemnity period for the bakery but only 12 months for the shops. Or a hardware business with three warehouses and several shops might want only six months maximum indemnity period for the warehouses and 12 months for the shops. Or a business with three divisions, one manufacturing, one factoring and another retailing, might want three different maximum indemnity periods. Because of the dependence of one section of such businesses upon another section it may seem illogical to have different maximum indemnity periods; but sometimes circumstances justify this.

If in such cases the manufacturing or warehousing sections supply goods only to their own retail outlets and trading and profit and loss accounts are drawn up separately for each section of the business, charges between the different sections being fixed arbitrarily, it may be possible to deal with the matter by incorporating them with separate sums insured on one specification and with a separate maximum indemnity period applicable to each. Alternatively separate policies might be issued for each section of the business.

If the former method is adopted loss arising from interdependence between the sections is covered automatically; if separate policies are issued it would have to be provided for by an appropriate extension on each policy.

382. Methods of arranging insurance for group companies

(a) *United Kingdom*

•The departmental clause (paragraph 380) can also be used in a specification for a policy issued in the joint names of a holding company and subsidiaries. With one overall sum insured and an appropriate note to show the name of each constituent firm in the group as being a "department" for the purposes of the clause each firm included in the policy would be treated as an independent unit for purposes of a claim settlement.

This method of issuing one policy in joint names with the departmental clause incorporated has the advantage that an extension of cover for dependency of the kind described in the preceding chapter of any of the firms within the group upon the premises and business of one or more of the others, whether the relationship be suppliers, processors or customers, is included automatically. If separate policies were issued for each firm it would be necessary to arrange for the appropriate cover by means of an extension memorandum on each policy to provide reciprocal dependency insurance throughout the group.

Cover for interdependency within a group is especially desirable where there is intra-group trading by different companies purchasing from or processing for one another and the price paid between them for goods or services is an artificial one for financial reasons of the group. Interruption of the business of one firm following damage might have a serious effect on another member of the group which was obtaining from it goods or services below the market price. In such circumstances if the interdependency is provided for and there is adequate business interruption insurance for all members of the group in the event of damage at the premises of any member of the group those whose business was affected would be indemnified for their respective losses.

Another aspect of this matter to be considered is the possibility of fire or other damage occurring at a group's administrative head office separate from manufacturing premises. If there is any possibility of damage at the central administrative offices having an adverse effect on turnover, or causing increase in cost of working, at any group member's premises it is essential to include the head office premises in the overall business interruption insurance of the group and obtain cover for the interdependency. The serious nature of the loss which such a contingency can cause is illustrated by a Press report in January 1977, " . . . Mr. Robert Maxwell yesterday reported a massive profits increase for his Pergamon Press Company. He said that but for a serious fire at the head office in July the total for both sales of £11 million and profits of £2,350,000 would have been even higher". Even where damage at the head office would appear to have no discernible effect on the business of the group, insurers agree that reasonable increased costs are payable as a claim under the group policy (including the head office premises), because it is accepted that the central administrative function is a necessary part of the overall group activities. This is known in the United Kingdom as the "Blundell Spence" agreement.

The overall premium cost for a single policy in joint names may be more, or less, than the total premium cost of separate policies for the different firms. The question depends upon the relative amounts of the fire insurances, of the fire insurance rates, and of the sums insured for business interruption. It is, therefore, impossible to generalise.

A joint or blanket policy may hold an advantage as regards the operation of the average proviso in the event of a claim because a combined sum insured will give some elasticity, allowing increased profits of one firm to be offset by the reduced profits of another should such a position apply. On the other hand it could operate to an insured's disadvantage if the overall sum insured is inadequate.

The same element of variation in profit earning as between different members of the group might in the case of a combined policy result in a smaller return of premium under the return of premium clause than if separate policies were issued. Moreover the operation of this clause can present difficulties if the financial years of firms within a group end on different dates.

Should the cover in respect of wages required by the firms in the group be materially different, as may be the case where a group has gone in for diversification, a single policy might be inappropriate unless the wages insurance is arranged to give sufficient scope for the differing needs of the individual firms, possibly by stating the wages cover separately for each constituent firm in the group. With 100 per cent. payroll cover this problem does not arise.

A decision as to which method should be adopted will generally be influenced to some extent by the insured's administrative and accountancy arrangements; for the purposes of debiting premiums to each firm for costing purposes separate policies are generally preferable. Large groups, combining a considerable number of subsidiary companies, often in a diversity of trades, with different requirements in lengths of maximum indemnity periods, extensions to suppliers and customers, etc., and other items of cover, particularly if some of the companies are overseas, may find it more practicable to have an individual policy for each firm within the group.

Some groups prefer to have one policy in joint names but with a separate sum insured for each constituent firm. This can be provided for by the use of a specification which sets out at its head the sum insured for each firm as a separate item and then uses the normal wording for the specification preceded by a statement making each item separately but similarly subject to its provisions. This facilitates reference to all the members' insurances by one responsible individual such as a holding company secretary or group insurance manager and enables him to keep an eye on sums insured.

A complication (but one which can be overcome with a little thought) arises when the constituent firms are perhaps a mixture of manufacturers, on-site contractors, service providers (*e.g.* plant designers, etc.) and computer operators: the definitions of gross profit or gross revenue for each will probably need to be different for each type of operation, with differing uninsured working expenses, etc.

Reference should be made to paragraph 23(a) regarding the description of the insured when there are associated and subsidiary companies to be included in the same policy.

(b) *Blanket coverage—United States*

Problems of arranging business interruption insurances for holding and group corporations and companies in North America are similar to those mentioned in paragraph 382(a) preceding. One solution is to issue a Blanket Coverage but as with United Kingdom insurances there are pros and cons to be considered in determining whether this method is in a group's best interests. Whilst a blanket coverage will give protection for interdependency within a group the rate of premium charge, which is an average one over all the premiums of the group, may mean that the insurance will be more costly than for individual policies with the appropriate dependent properties insurance. Blanket coverage may be written using either (i) an average base rate (80 per cent. coinsurance building rate—see paragraph 256(b)) weighted by floor area unless otherwise specified, or (ii) the highest 80 per cent. coinsurance building rate for each cause of loss as the base rate if no average base rate is available. Hence, the particular circumstances of each group must be considered in order to decide whether a blanket coverage is advisable. Blanket insurance may be written only if there is substantial common ownership, actual management or operating control by the insured.

(c) *Worldwide*

Because of the factors mentioned in paragraph 80, group companies operating on a worldwide scale with subsidiaries in other countries or as part of a binational or multinational combine introduce serious extra difficulties in the arrangement of business interruption insurance. In the absence of provisions for a global cover it becomes a matter of considering each unit's individual requirements and arranging appropriate insurance according to the facilities for the country where it is situate. A "Difference in

Conditions" policy can then be issued to make good shortcomings in each individual policy issued, usually a matter of dependency extensions and special perils.

Even greater difficulties may stem from the vast financial resources of industrial giants operating on a global scale which enable them to switch production from a factory in one country to that in another, to alter their pricing policies for purchases of components, etc., between factories in different countries and to transfer money from one currency to another. By such means they may seek to maximise their overall profit by taking advantage of low tax areas, government investment grants and changes in currency rates or to outflank labour troubles, in the countries in which they operate. The effect is to complicate considerably the arrangement of a business interruption insurance or the settlement of a claim under it.

Nevertheless, the trend (in both the United Kingdom and the United States) is towards the establishment of "master" combined material damage and business interruption policies for international or multinational concerns. The intention is to ensure that there is central control and that there is uniformity of cover wherever in the world the insured operates. Local policies are retained so as to take advantage of local tax deductibility for premiums, to conform to local regulations, to facilitate local claims adjustment, and to deal with special local hazards (*e.g.* earthquake). The "master", however, is the policy to which the insurance or risk manager at head office will refer for a basic description of the cover his group enjoys worldwide.

383. New business clause

The formula in the turnover specification for measuring the loss of gross profit resulting from damage uses the rate of gross profit, annual turnover and standard turnover figures from a period of at least 12 months prior to the date of the damage. In the case of a new business such information cannot be obtained until the first year of trading is completed. To provide for the possibility of damage occurring during that first year an appropriate memorandum is added to the specification.

The operation of this memorandum involves taking the trading results for the period from the inception of the business to the date of the damage in order to ascertain the rate of gross profit and rate of wages and also to expand the turnover realised during that period by means of a proportional equivalent to give the annual turnover and the standard turnover. The other circumstances clause is then applied to make any reasonable adjustments which may be necessary in the light of the progress of the business up to the date of the damage and of its future prospects. The wording of the New Business clause follows:

"MEMO. For the purpose of any claim arising from damage occurring before the completion of the first year's trading of the Business at the Premises the terms Rate of Gross Profit, Annual Turnover and Standard Turnover shall bear the following meanings and not as within stated.

Rate of Gross Profit—The Rate of Gross Profit earned on the Turnover during the period between the date of the commencement of the Business and the date of the Incident

Annual Turnover—The proportional equivalent, for a period of twelve months, of the Turnover realised during the period between the commencement of the Business and the date of the Incident

Standard Turnover—The proportional equivalent, for a period equal to the Indemnity Period, of the Turnover realised during the period between the commencement of the Business and the date of the Incident

to which such adjustments shall be made as may be necessary to provide for the trend of the Business and for variations in or other circumstances affecting the Business either before or after the Incident or which would have affected the Business had the Incident not occurred, so that the figures thus adjusted shall represent as nearly as may be reasonably practicable the results which but for the Incident would have been obtained during the relative period after the Incident."

384. Salvage sale clause

In the event of a saleshop, department store or factory outlet being damaged without being completely destroyed the opportunity is sometimes taken to hold a salvage sale if the commodities dealt in are of suitable nature for this. Such a sale enables a quick disposal to be made of stock which has been damaged by smoke or water on the value of which agreement has been reached with the insurers under the fire policy. At the same time the publicity and appeal of the special circumstances and possible bargains provide a welcome opportunity to put in the sale undamaged stock of which a firm may be anxious to clear its shelves. It is not unknown for out-of-date stock to be bought cheaply from other shopkeepers and job lines purchased and brought into the premises where the damage has occurred, for sale as "salvage".

The effect of a salvage sale is to stimulate turnover during the early days of the indemnity period but the margin of profit earned on the goods sold may be considerably lower than the normal percentage. If the insured are only recompensed under their business interruption policy by a payment based on the shortage in turnover during the indemnity period they will lose the difference between the average rate of profit obtained on goods sold at reduced prices and their normal rate, on the amount of goods disposed of in the salvage sale.

To provide for an appropriate adjustment to be made should such circumstances arise a special "salvage sale clause" can be included in the specification (although insurers generally recognise that the provisions of the clause are now sufficiently well known to render the use of the wording unnecessary unless specifically asked for). Laying down in advance in this way the lines on which the adjustment will be made avoids difficulties which might otherwise arise if a method of adjustment had to be devised within the terms of the other circumstances clause, after damage had taken place. The clause reads:

> "If, following an Incident giving rise to a claim under this policy, the Insured shall hold a salvage sale during the Indemnity Period, clause (a) of the item on Gross Profit shall for the purpose of such claim read as follows:
> a. IN RESPECT OF REDUCTION IN TURNOVER: the sum produced by applying the Rate of Gross Profit to the amount by which the Turnover during the Indemnity Period (less the Turnover for the period of the salvage sale) shall, in consequence of the Incident fall short of the Standard Turnover, from which sum shall be deducted the Gross Profit actually earned during the period of the salvage sale".

Put briefly, the clause states that the insurers agree to disregard turnover obtained from a salvage sale provided that any gross profit which may accrue from such a sale is credited to them.

The method is to deduct the turnover during the salvage sale from the total turnover of the indemnity period. This produces a corresponding increase in the figure for the shortage in turnover during the indemnity period and the rate of gross profit (as under the policy definition) is applied to this adjusted shortage in the normal way. This really means calculating the insured's loss as though there were no turnover whatever resulting from the salvage sale; but in the calculation the amount of the gross profit actually earned in the sale is then credited to the insurers, leaving the insured with a true indemnity.

Should there be an item insuring wages on either the annual basis or the dual basis, under which the calculation of a loss is made by applying the rate of wages to the shortage in turnover, a similar provision for the eventuality of a salvage sale can be made by a slightly amended clause.

385. Subrogation waiver clause

Claims Condition 4 of a U.K. business interruption policy is known as the subrogation condition and is the counterpart of that of similar purpose printed on all fire insurance policies. Under it insurers are entitled on paying the business interruption claim, to exercise the rights of their insured deriving from third parties whether under contract, remedy for tort, or any other benefit, legal or equitable (paragraph 441).

In the case of insurances for members of a group of companies it is possible that insurers on paying the business interruption claim of one firm in the group might become entitled by subrogation to recover from another member of the group. In certain special circumstances it may be necessary to suspend in relation to a group of companies the normal operation of the subrogation condition and to do this a clause on the following lines may be added to the specification.

> "MEMO. In the event of claim arising under this policy the Insurers agree to waive any rights, remedies or relief to which they might become entitled by subrogation against
> (a) any Company standing in the relation of Parent to Subsidiary (or Subsidiary to Parent) to the Insured as defined in section 154 of the Companies Act 1948
> (b) any Company which is a Subsidiary of a Parent Company of which the Insured are themselves a Subsidiary in each case within the meaning of section 154 of the Companies Act 1948".

386. Accumulated stocks clause

As mentioned in paragraph 246 an indemnity period can be effectively delayed because of the insured's use of finished stock to maintain turnover. To clarify this possibly disadvantageous situation insured sometimes ask for an "accumulated stocks" clause to be added to their business interruption policy. The clause reads as follows:

> "In adjusting any loss account shall be taken and an equitable allowance made if any reduction in Turnover due to the Incident is postponed by reason of the Turnover being temporarily maintained from accumulated stocks of finished goods in warehouses or depots".

Insurers regard this clause as inoperative unless the following combination of circumstances occurs:

(a) if a manufacturer's stock of finished goods
  (i) be depleted in keeping down the reduction in turnover during the indemnity period and
  (ii) cannot be made good by the end of the maximum indemnity period.
(b) after the end of the period the manufacturer suffers loss because of the deficiency.

387. Discontinuance of business clause

It may be that following severe damage and a potentially long and difficult period of interruption and recovery the insured will decide that the business should be discontinued. As described in paragraph 436 it is necessary to obtain the permission of insurers for this course of action to be followed. In certain circumstances where such an eventuality may be foreseen it is possible for a clause on the following lines to be added to the policy:

"If the Business is discontinued after the occurrence of the insured event, the indemnity will be paid for the period (up to the Maximum Indemnity Period) which would normally have been required to bring the Business back to normal. In the event that the Insured controls the circumstances because of which the Business is discontinued, the said indemnity, will not be payable in full. Insurers will only indemnify the Insured for that part of the said indemnity which equals unavoidable insured expenses actually incurred".

To an extent the restrictive terms of the above clause demonstrate the benefit of having no clause and allowing insurers to "indemnify" the insured in the full light of the actual circumstances.

388. Material damage proviso waiver

The new A.B.I. policy wordings contain in the preamble a rider to the material damage proviso to deal with situations where "payment would have been made or liability admitted therefor but for the operation of a proviso in such insurance excluding liability for losses below a certain amount".

In earlier versions of the standard fire business interruption form such a rider did not exist and the following "waiver" should be added to those versions:

"It shall not be a condition precedent to liability in respect of interruption or interference in consequence of destruction or damage (as within defined) that payment shall have been made or liability admitted under the insurance covering the interest of the insured in the property at the premises against such destruction or damage if no such payment shall have been made nor liability admitted solely owing to the operation of a proviso in such insurance excluding liability for losses below a specified amount".

389. "All standing charges" specification

A form of specification which embraces the principle of the traditional net profit plus insured standing charges definition of gross profit (described in paragraphs 37 *et seq.*) is one in which the standing charges insured are not named individually but are included in the definition of gross profit by use of the word "all". Hence, this once popular form of specification was generally referred to as "the all standing charges specification".

Because *all* standing charges are embraced within the definition of gross profit in the way mentioned above the whole definition of insured standing charges, describing them individually by name, is left out of the specification. This constitutes the fundamental difference between the two forms of specification.

The most obvious advantage of the all standing charges specification is its simplicity because it does away with the necessity to select for mention on the specification the various charges to be included in the insurance. Over the years difficulties of interpretation have arisen in claims and insurers generally do not recommend it though some think it suitable for retail shops and small businesses. Since the introduction of the simplified specifications for such risks described in the following paragraph 390 it is now seldom used.

390. Retail shops and small businesses

A simplified form of specification is usually recommended for small businesses in general where the amount of variable charges is negligible and all wages are to be insured. Gross profit may be defined on the lines of the "difference" wording principle as being "the money paid or payable for goods sold and delivered and services rendered in the course of the business less the cost of purchases relative thereto". This definition is easy to understand and the calculation of the sum insured is also straightforward.

Even greater simplicity is achieved in the wording given in Appendix G, paragraph 453 which can sometimes be used in composite policies for shops. Instead of the traditional nomenclature of gross profit the expression "trading profit" is used. This is defined very simply as "the takings less the cost of goods or materials relative thereto". "Takings" replaces the customary "turnover" and is defined as "the money paid or payable to the insured for goods sold and delivered and for work done in the course of the business at the premises".

This wording automatically includes in the insurance all wages and all charges except purchases. It goes further than an ordinary "difference" specification in the way of simplification by not bringing the amounts of opening and closing stocks into the definition of trading profit. Generally speaking in a small shop the amount of stock will vary little from one year end to another. However, it should be noted that for a shop where workpeople are employed wholly on tradesmen's work away from the premises and this would be little affected by damage at the shop, *e.g.* plumbers, both the revenue from such work and the wages paid to those employees may need to be specifically excluded from the definition of gross profit.

Apart from textual adjustments which follow from these changes such as the use of "rate of trading profit", "annual takings" and "standard takings" the only other variation is a shortened version of the other circumstances clause and the addition to it of a provision for the possibility of damage occurring before the expiry of the first financial year of a business. In such an event the results of the business to the date of the damage are to be used as a basis upon which to assess any loss.

Because trading profit is practically synonymous with a shopkeeper's gross margin on his sales and he generally has a fair idea of the annual amount of both, this wording makes it easier for him in the initial arrangement of a business interruption insurance and in keeping an eye on the sum insured in the future than trying to think in terms of net profit and standing charges or of the full "difference" definition.

There has been a trend for composite "traders" policies for small retail shops to include business interruption insurance as an integral part of the package either without any specific amount being shown as the sum insured or with cover up to a standard limit such as twice the sum insured on contents, the maximum indemnity period being selected by the insured. The assumption is that the gross profit of such businesses is within certain limits related to the amount of the direct damage insurance on contents of the shop and the trade concerned, premium being assessed accordingly.

Whilst it might be suggested that this method may not provide an adequate indemnity for a business with a turnover of stock much quicker than the average it will generally be that this is achieved by cutting overheads and profit margins and that the final result in gross profit will be about the same as the average for normal trading. The automatic inclusion of cover for loss of profit without need for an insured to have to work out figures and make estimates for future trading is a great convenience and facilitates the selling of business interruption insurance; no doubt the practice will increase and possibly spread to larger risks.

Another useful feature of the U.K. combined policies is that when an insured shopkeeper occupies and operates warehouse premises, whether owning or renting them, solely for the purpose of supplying merchandise for sale in the insured shop(s) any loss resulting from damage to the warehouse premises by an insured peril may be included in the business interruption section of the insurance.

In 1981, the rules of the Consequential Loss Committee ceased to apply to shop premises used by retailers, and this led to the formulation of new and varied specialist covers. One particular business interruption policy (also capable of being used for restaurateurs, cafe proprietors, farmers, market gardeners and nurserymen) offered a cover without a sum insured, without an average provision, and with a built-in maximum indemnity period of 36 months within which losses could be paid provided that the liability of insurers did not exceed

   (a) in respect of each period of 12 months, or part thereof, during the indemnity period: twice the annual gross profit;
   (b) nor in total: five times the annual gross profit.

Annual gross profit is defined in the usual way but is not subject to the other circumstances clause (refer paragraphs 55 to 56). Premium is charged on the basis of the insured's estimate of his gross profit/revenue for the year of insurance, and at the end of the year there is an adjustment procedure (on declaration of actual earnings) with rebate restricted to 50 per cent. but with no limitation to the additional premium payable. There are obvious disadvantages to this basis of cover but it does indicate the extent to which United Kingdom insurers have been prepared to go in recognising the need to be commercial and innovative. Other covers for shops now include loss of attraction (refer paragraph 374), prevention of access (refer paragraph 373), notifiable diseases, food poisoning and defective drains (refer paragraph 301), and failure of gas, water and electricity (refer paragraph 319) as standard features.

391. Hotels, private hotels, guest and public houses: composite policies

For the business interruption section of a composite policy for these businesses a specially drafted specification is used adapted to meet their particular needs. Whilst following the standard form of a turnover, "difference" wording, the normal term of gross profit, is replaced by "trading profit". This is defined as the turnover less the cost of food and drink relative thereto and goods bought for resale. Turnover is defined as being the money paid or payable to the insured for accommodation provided, services rendered and goods sold in the course of business at the premises. (Alternatively the cover may be in terms of "revenue" with the definition being the combination of the two foregoing definitions.) A result of these definitions is that the sum insured will include all wages and every other charge except purchases of food, drink and goods bought for resale and Value Added Tax which is excluded by the standard clause.

Amongst the charges which are automatically included in the insurance are wages of part-time and temporary seasonal workers, which may be considerable in these trades, laundry expenses, breakages of crockery and renewals of linen, etc. In insurances for large hotels such charges might be excluded as being variable with turnover. No mention is made of opening and closing stocks in the definition of trading profit, presumably because as these composite policies are intended primarily for small and medium sized establishments it is assumed that variations in stock values between one year end and another are likely to be relatively unimportant.

Payments received by hotels for incidental services for customers such as laundering and dry cleaning of garments and from telephone calls from bedrooms through the hotel switchboard are included in full in the trading profit by the definition of turnover. Where the total amount is substantial the charges paid by the hotel to the launderers, cleaners and telephone undertaking might be specifically excluded (the same as are goods bought for resale) so as to leave only the hotel's actual profit on such services in the insurance and avoid paying premium on variable charges which could be deducted under the savings clause in a claim settlement.

This type of composite policy gives wider cover than the standard perils and includes fire, subterranean fire, explosion, aircraft, riot, malicious damage, earthquake, storm, flood, impact and other minor contingencies at a special inclusive rate of premium. Prevention of access cover (paragraph 373) is usually included as well as an extension of the insurance to include loss due to the contingencies of infectious disease, etc., and pollution of beaches within a 10 mile radius as set out in paragraph 301.

A further benefit may be the inclusion of an item to cover the additional expenditure in excess of that recoverable under the increase in cost of working clause, entailed in the provision of alternative accommodation and food for the insured, his family and staff normally living in the premises and in removal costs and incidental expenses.

As with insurances for shopkeepers some insured may include as standard cover in composite policies for small hotels, guest houses and public houses business interruption insurance for an amount of trading profit related to the sum insured on contents, such as twice the amount of the latter, the maximum indemnity period being selected by the insured.

392. Financial institutions

As stated in paragraph 326 on computer installations, banks and other financial institutions are insured for different risks today than they were a few decades ago when the payment of increased costs would have guaranteed the almost unbroken maintenance of full business activities.

The steady increase in dependence on computer-based systems, in filing, processing, communication, etc., means that the "office" risk at the end of the twentieth century has become very similar to that of a modern factory. Any failure of the systems can result in a quick (in many cases, immediate) reduction in business income. Banks, stockbrokers, commodity brokers, insurance companies and the larger insurance brokers all possess extensive and complicated computer systems dependent on a central processor and data base. Interruption may entail a loss of cashflow from which the profits of the enterprise may be drawn.

Many covers that were previously for increase in cost of working only with a maximum indemnity period of anything up to 36 months have been transformed into full income insurances for the first 12 months (the heaviest part of the interruption), with an additional increase in cost of working cover (see paragraph 50) for 24 or 36 months providing funds for *uneconomic* expenditure in the first 12 months and for any *ongoing* expenditure for the period beyond that of full cover.

Specialist policies will include cover against the consequences not only of damage to property at the insured's premises but also of failure of the public electricity supply and of telecommunications networks (other than satellite services). Failure of telecommunications due to strikes (withdrawal of labour only) is usually excluded. Some policies will include cover against a broad range of "computer related risks" such as bugs, viruses, etc., but such covers are usually only provided if there is an initial and thereafter regular specialist survey of the insured's facilities on behalf of the insurers.

For large firms, risk management is imperative with contingency plans for emergency action such as the establishment without undue delay of alternative computer facilities ("recovery centres" can by prior arrangement be set up in car parks or other nearby open spaces within a matter of hours with computer rooms ready to receive the necessary equipment), the relocation of personnel, the re-equipment of those personnel, etc.

Chapter 19

Insurance of Outstanding Debit Balances—Book Debts (United Kingdom): Accounts Receivable (United States)

393. Outstanding accounts—the risk of loss

If a firm's ledgers and other accountancy records are destroyed by a fire at their premises the collection of accounts which are outstanding at the time will depend upon any duplicate records or information as to the balances due which they may have in a separate place or upon the memories of their staff and the goodwill or honesty of their customers. Consequently apart from those businesses in which complete duplicate records are kept in another premises—and even then there may be risk during a time-lag of a day or two between preparation of the duplicates and their transfer elsewhere—loss of accounts records will almost inevitably entail some loss. This will be greatest in businesses selling goods on instalment systems or with a large number of credit accounts with small tradesmen or direct with the public.

In this respect hire purchase finance companies are particularly vulnerable as also are department stores, retailers of furniture, television and radio sets, refrigerators, washing machines and other electrical appliances and domestic durable goods, suppliers of clothing, furnishings, central heating, timber buildings and also mail-order clubs selling through spare-time agents—in fact all who sell to the public with facilities for deferred payments; a very wide field! Similarly manufacturing or factoring firms with a large number of customers amongst retail shopkeepers, small tradesmen and garages or farmers, etc., are open to sustain loss if their records of outstanding debits are destroyed by fire or kindred perils. Should the loss of their records become known to Press reporters at the time of a fire and be publicised in local or national newspapers and on television as has unfortunately occurred upon occasion—as happened about Debenham's loss at their Southampton branch department store in December 1980 following the theft of account records in a hold-up raid—the risk of default by small debtors is greatly increased.

Loss consequent upon destruction of records is in respect of goods sold and delivered or services rendered before the damage occurred and as it has no connection with sales in the period after the damage it will not be recoverable under an insurance on gross profit. The latter covers loss arising from, and assessed on, the reduction in the amount of turnover which but for the damage would have been transacted in the period after the date of the damage, that is, loss on post-fire sales or services. On the other hand the loss cannot be recovered under a policy of fire insurance either because that covers only material loss and does not provide indemnity to an insured in respect of the *information* on outstanding debits contained in accounting records.

394. The insurances available

(a) *United Kingdom—Book Debts*

There is a gap between the protection afforded by fire and business interruption policies. To bridge this gap between the covers given by fire and business interruption policies insurance can be arranged under a separate "loss of book debts" policy.

A separate policy for this form of insurance is the general practice because the terms and conditions appropriate to it differ in several respects from those of both fire and business interruption policies. To incorporate the cover in either would involve a cumbersome and impracticable document. Loss of book debts insurance is generally handled by the business interruption underwriters of insurance companies as being loss consequent upon, and not happening at the time of, a fire.

(b) *United States—Accounts Receivable*

In the United States there is a gap between the coverage under a property damage policy and that of a business interruption insurance on earnings similar to that mentioned above in United Kingdom insurances. Similarly provision can be arranged to bridge this gap by a special coverage called an Accounts Receivable policy.

Monthly declarations of outstanding accounts are not required as they are under a United Kingdom policy and consequently the last declaration before a loss cannot be made the basis of settlement. Instead the monthly average of accounts receivable during the previous 12 months is used and adjustments to this figure are made for normal fluctuations and changes during that period and in the month involved. Deductions are made for probable bad debts which would not have been collected and also unearned interest and service charges from deferred payment accounts receivable.

A condition stipulates that the insurers be allowed to inspect the insured's books at any time up to three years after the policy period ends to verify the statement of losses of accounts receivable and any recoveries of same made by the insured. Another provision in some United States policies which is not in standard United Kingdom insurances, and a useful one, is that if the insured has to borrow finance whilst waiting for payment of the indemnity for loss of accounts receivable the insurers will pay interest charges on the loan.

395. Loss of book debts policy form—United Kingdom

The printed policy is a standardised form incorporating a schedule and a separate specification, the latter being altered as may be necessary to suit the particular circumstances of each individual case. A specimen specification is given in Appendix K, paragraph 457.

Whilst the policy terms and conditions are similar to those in a business interruption policy, two main differences should be noted. First, there is no material damage proviso (see paragraph 15(e)) to stipulate that the property to which the insurance relates, in this case the insured's books of account or other business books or records at the premises, must be insured against damage by the perils covered in the book debts insurance. Secondly, the perils included in the standard book debts policy are fire, lightning and explosion but the limitations imposed in the standard fire and business interruption policies in respect of these perils (apart from the usual exclusions of earthquake, riot, war, nuclear radiation, etc.) are not mentioned. The main benefit from this is that explosion peril is included in full in the policy and, there being no material damage proviso, is operative even though the fire and business interruption policies do not include such full explosion cover.

A further advantage of the absence of a material damage proviso is that additional perils such as aircraft, riot and civil commotion, malicious damage, earthquake, storm and flood, burst pipes, sprinkler leakage and impact can all be included in a loss of book debts policy irrespective of whether there is such cover on the insured's fire or business interruption policies. Because the premium rates charged for such additional perils are very low, as also are the rates charged for the basic fire, lightning and explosion perils, it is customary practice to include them all and, also, theft. The latter is restricted to theft involving entry to or exit from the premises by forcible and violent means and so would not include extraction of records by a dishonest employee legally on the premises wishing to destroy evidence of embezzlement. But destruction of accounting records by a dishonest employee deliberately setting fire to office contents is covered. It is unlikely that burglars who have opened a safe in a search for cash will spend time destroying account records but there is a risk of destruction of papers by explosives used to open a safe.

396. Loss of book debts—the specification

The specification takes over the task of describing the indemnity provided by the policy, which is limited to "the loss sustained by the insured in respect of outstanding debit balances directly due to the damage". Provision is made for the possibility of more than one loss occurring in any current term of insurance by the added words "and the amount payable in respect of any one occurrence of damage shall not exceed:—". Then follows the operative clause describing how the loss will be calculated, which is (i) the difference between the outstanding debit balances and the total of the amounts received or traced in respect thereof; (ii) the additional expenditure incurred with the previous consent of the insurers in tracing and establishing customers' debit balances after the damage.

397. Basis for claims—monthly declarations

With the accounting records partly or wholly damaged or destroyed, as they must be to give rise to a claim, establishing the amount of the current outstanding debit balances becomes the crux of any claim under the policy. Therefore a basis for calculating the amount of the outstanding debit balances, at any point of time, is laid down through a memorandum on the specification that "the insured shall within 30 days of the end of each month deposit with the insurers a signed statement showing the total amount outstanding in customers' accounts as set out in the insured's accounts as at the end of the said month". In practice "the end of the said month" can be altered by the substitution of some other fixed monthly date, say the fifteenth, to fall in line with an insured's particular methods of dispatching accounts or collating figures. To facilitate the rendering of these monthly declarations a pad of printed forms is issued to each insured. In exceptional cases where declarations at monthly intervals are quite impracticable insurers might possibly agree to statements being furnished quarterly.

398. Adjustments to declaration for purposes of a claim

The amount of the outstanding debit balances to be used as the basis for calculating an insured's loss is stated as being "the total declared in the statement last given", that is, the last monthly declaration preceding the damage. Provision is then made for adjustments for both normal and abnormal conditions which may be necessary "so that the figures thus adjusted shall represent as nearly as reasonably practicable those which would have been obtained at the date of the damage had the damage not occurred". The adjustments to be made are for:

(i) bad debts;
(ii) amounts debited (or invoiced but not debited) and credited (including credit notes and cash not passed through the books at the time of the damage) to customers' accounts in the period between the date to which said last statement relates and the date of the damage;
(iii) any abnormal condition of trade which had or could have had a material effect on the business.

399. Provision for additional expenditure

Because insured are required both under the doctrine of good faith and under the claims condition of the policy to do everything possible to reduce the amount of the potential loss, they may incur considerable expense in trying to trace debtors and in establishing the amounts owed by them. To complete the insurance indemnity, therefore, a similar provision to that for increase in cost of working in a normal business interruption policy is included for the payment of such additional expenditure incurred with the previous consent of the insurers.

400. Underinsurance—average proviso

The total amount of the claim for loss in respect of unrecovered outstanding debts and the additional expenditure incurred is then subject to an average proviso. Under this, "if the sum insured be less than the outstanding debit balances the amount payable shall be proportionately reduced". This simply introduces the normal principle that if the sum insured is less than it should be in the circumstances applicable at the time of a loss the insured must bear a proportionate part of the claim.

Because the insurance is subject to pro rata average, when arranging the sum insured it is essential to make a forward projection up to at least the time of the next revision or generally 12 months ahead, to allow for possible business growth and inflationary tendencies, etc., in the interim. Protection against unnecessary expenditure of premium is provided by the incorporation of a return of premium clause in respect of overinsurance (see paragraph 401).

Destruction or damage may occur after any one of the subsequent monthly declarations and as that declaration would then become the basis of the loss calculation special care must be taken in the case of businesses subject to seasonal fluctuations, such as department stores which do extra trade each December, to arrange the sum insured at an amount adequate to cover the abnormally high total of outstanding debits during the busy period and in the months immediately following.

401. Return of premium clause

No wastage of premium is entailed through carrying a sum insured which may be much too high for most months of the year because the specification incorporates a return clause whereby at the expiry of each period of insurance the premium actually earned is calculated on the average amount insured, *i.e.* the total of the sums declared divided by the number of declarations. If the premium so calculated is less than the premium paid, the difference is repaid to the insured provided that such repayment shall not exceed half of the premium which had been paid.

A further memorandum states that if the amount of a monthly declaration exceeds the sum insured then, for the purposes only of the repayment of premium calculation, the sum insured shall be taken as the declaration amount. Consequently, as with the return of premium clause for normal business interruption policies on gross profit and wages it is a one-way traffic—returns allowed but no excess premium is charged. This makes it essential to maintain a sum insured adequate for any month of the year ahead in order to avoid loss under the average proviso.

402. Definition of customers' accounts

The specification provides for a definition of customers' accounts, details being inserted to suit the particular circumstances of the insured business. This is generally a straightforward matter but there may be cases in which it is considered unnecessary to include the outstanding debit balances of certain definable categories of customer. For instance, a firm's own subsidiary companies might be their customers. Or an insured might have a limited number of very large firms as customers whose size and standing is such that there would be no question of their not meeting their outstanding debits from their own records, in addition to a large number of smaller firms in relation to whose accounts insurance might be desirable. Or a firm might supply both wholesalers and retailers and wish to insure the outstanding debit balances of the latter category only. If the insurers concerned are willing to cover only a part of the total of an insured's debit balances in order to cater for special circumstances of the nature mentioned the definition of customers' accounts must be worded correspondingly.

403. Warranty regarding safe keeping of records

There is a wide degree of variation between businesses in the safe keeping of accounting records but the standard definition contains a warranty—a warranty being a condition which must be strictly complied with at all times—that "the insured's books of account or other business books or records in which customers' accounts are shown shall be kept in . . . when not in use", a description such as "fire-resisting safes or fire-resisting cabinets" being inserted appropriate to the particular circumstances.

This warranty can be amended to include, for instance, a fire-resisting strong-room, or ordinary metal cabinets, or in special circumstances even an open office but this aspect of the risk is investigated and agreed when the insurance is negotiated, premium rates being adjusted according to the extent of hazard involved. If at anytime subsequently the insured wish to alter the agreed arrangements stated in the warranty their insurers must be informed.

404. Reinstatement of amount of claim

A further memorandum on the specification provides for the automatic reinstatement in the sum insured from the time of any loss of the amount by which it may be reduced, subject to the payment of the proportionate extra premium calculated on the amount of the loss from the date thereof to the end of the current term of the insurance.

405. Time limit for claims

No indemnity period is mentioned in the specification because the time taken for the rehabilitation of a business after damage does not affect the collection of outstanding debts which accrued prior to the damage. Consequently, the claims condition cannot include a stipulation like that in the corresponding condition in a business interruption policy that a statement of claim must be furnished within 30 days after the expiry of the indemnity period. But it does, in addition to making provisions for the notification of claims and the furnishing of various information, stipulate that the insured shall deliver a statement of the claim "as soon as is reasonably possible".

406. Professional accountants' charges

A memorandum on the specification provides that any particulars or details in the insured's books which the insurer may require for checking any claim under the policy can be produced by the insured's professional accountants whose report thereon will be accepted as prima facie evidence. Reimbursement of the expenses to the insured of such professional accountants' services is provided by the same memorandum without any separate sum insured being stated, in line with that discussed in paragraph 378.

407. Loss of records away from the insured's premises

Another extension of cover which may be added to the specification without additional charge includes loss due to (i) damage at premises to which records are temporarily removed and (ii) any peril insured by the policy (except theft) whilst the records are in transit, as described in memorandum 4 of the specification in Appendix K.

408. Value added tax

Any liability of a business to the Customs and Excise for the payment of Value Added Tax on sales already made and debited at the time of a loss of records will have to be met irrespective of recovery of outstanding debts from customers. Therefore the amount of VAT must be included in the sum insured on Outstanding Debit Balances and in the monthly declarations.

409. Premium rates

As might be expected the premium rates for book debts insurances are generally very low because the basic risk of damage to records by fire, etc., is small when they are kept in fire-resisting cabinets or safes and particularly so when these are in a building occupied solely as offices. Also there is no risk of a total loss of the sum insured because even if all the records were destroyed and there were no means of tracing debtors there would still be a proportion of customers who of their own volition would make payment of their outstanding indebtedness.

The rating scale adopts as a basis the normal rate for fire and explosion perils of the building in which records are kept and of this a small percentage only is charged, subject to a minimum rate, according to whether the records are kept in (a) a fire-resisting safe or strong-room or (b) ordinary metal cabinets, etc. A fire-resisting cabinet built and tested to withstand a duration test or complying with a fire-fall test as approved by insurers is regarded as a fire-resisting safe.

As the aspect of recovery of outstanding balances depends very largely on the particular circumstances of each case, substantial concessions in premium rating are made for favourable features, subject to certain minimum rates and a minimum premium per policy. The favourable features for which concessions in premium are given may be summarised as:

(i) Duplicate records which would enable customers and the amounts of their outstanding debits to be traced, kept in a different building from that where the original records are kept; particularly if lodged with the insured's bank or auditors.
(ii) A note of the outstanding debits of customers called on being supplied monthly to each of the insured's travellers or representatives.
(iii) Original hire purchase or instalment agreements, being kept at the insured's bank.
(iv) A significant proportion of hire purchase or instalment accounts being paid by banker's order or by cheque each month.
(v) Recourse agreements, under which an intermediary dealer or agent accepts liabilities.
(vi) A substantial proportion of the insured's customers being of a particularly favourable class such as large concerns of national standing.
(vii) Magnitude of sums insured, which are generally indicative of more stringent precautions against loss and a reduced possibility of any

loss being more than a proportion of the total at risk. Discounts are allowed on a sliding scale increasing with the size of the insurance and exceeding 50 per cent. when sums insured run into millions of pounds.

In addition to the foregoing concessions for favourable features, long term agreements can be entered into (see paragraph 21) and a suitable discount deducted from the net premium.

410. Dentists, etc., and the Department of Health

Dentists, chemists and opticians all might suffer loss if their records of work done for patients or prescriptions dispensed under the national health scheme are destroyed before they have submitted their monthly statement to the Department of Health. Although in such circumstances the Department might as an act of grace make payment on say the average of the preceeding three months' figures, there is no legal requirement for them to do so. To cover this contingency an insurance can be effected against loss of outstanding accounts on the normal lines but somewhat simplified.

Fire-resisting safes or cabinets are not insisted upon an insured being required only to keep his business records in steel cabinets when they are not in use. No monthly declaration of the total of outstanding debits is required but the insured must keep at a place other than that where he keeps his records a note of the amount paid to him by the Department the preceding month. Presumably records of his in-payments to the bank would in most circumstances meet this stipulation.

In addition to providing an indemnity for the shortage in the amount received from the Department for the accounts destroyed the policy covers the extra expenses incurred in collecting such amount. The outstanding accounts insured are defined as being "the amount due from the Department of Health in respect of work done and services rendered at the premises". An average proviso is included for application in the event of under-insurance at the time of a loss. Should a dentist or optician wish to include in the insurance the outstanding accounts of private patients this can be arranged on normal terms and conditions.

CHAPTER 20

CLAIM SETTLEMENTS

411. Action upon damage occurring

(a) *Appointment of the loss adjuster (United Kingdom)*

Immediately damage has taken place which is likely to result in an interruption of the business the insurers should be informed and they will then instruct a qualified, independent loss adjuster to handle the matter on their behalf and supply him with details of the insurance. At the same time a formal check will be made to ascertain that the policy is in force, whether there is any record of other insurances also applicable, that the business and the premises where the damage took place are included in the insurance, that the cause of it is a peril covered under the business interruption insurance and whether liability for the material damage is admitted under a fire or similar policy. On this latter see paragraph 16(a) regarding the material damage proviso and *ex gratia* payments.

Until satisfied on all these points the claim will be handled without prejudice to the rights of insurers. The adjuster appointed must then ascertain from the insured whether there are any other insurances in force relative to the loss and if there are he will immediately contact the insurers for details of their policies and suggest the benefits of his representing their interests in the matter.

It will be readily appreciated that the interests of the insured and of their insurers are identical; each desires a restoration of normal business as quickly as possible. Although insured will often be in a better position to formulate steps towards that objective, close collaboration with the loss adjuster is desirable throughout the period of interruption. Whilst insured will have only a limited experience, or none, of a serious fire a loss adjuster has a very extensive knowledge of such matters, for handling the after-effects of fires is his business. Often he can from his experience suggest steps to be taken to minimise the interference with the business which might otherwise never occur to the insured.

It should here be noted that the services of an impartial *loss adjuster* are provided and paid for by insurers for the mutual interests of themselves and their insured and, though doubtless it is in that order, insured can have every confidence when a claim is handled by Fellows or Associates of the Chartered Institute of Loss Adjusters who are qualified members of an association with very high standards of integrity. However, if insured wish to employ on their own behalf a *loss assessor* to look solely after their interests they are at liberty to do so but the fees for his services are payable by themselves and are not recoverable under the business interruption insurance. A specific cover to reimburse to insured payment of loss assessors' fees has been available in other European countries for many years but not in the United Kingdom although in 1979 a Loss Assessor Fee Insurance scheme was introduced by one insurance company against the general opinion of insurers that giving such cover is not in the best interests of the business. It is interesting to note that in some European countries it is the practice for both sides, insurers and insured, to have their own "experts" to represent them in the often difficult negotiations that need to be entered into (see paragraph 78).

(b) *The United States claim representative*

In the United States the opposite number of the United Kingdom loss adjuster representing insurers is known by the same title or as a "claim representative" but may be either an independent individual or firm working on a fee basis or a salaried member of the staff of an insurance company. Often when the loss is very complicated the services of a certified public accountant are called upon. The counterpart of a United Kingdom loss assessor is known as a public adjuster and represents insured on a fee basis.

The adjuster will meet the insured as soon as possible and present his credentials including a letter of appointment from insurers. He must then remind the insured of their immediate obligations under the loss conditions, *i.e.* to provide a description of the nature of the damage, take all reasonable steps to protect the property from further damage, keep a record of expenses incurred, permit insurers (or their representatives) to inspect the property and records proving the loss, and if requested permit insurers to question them under oath about any matter regarding the insurance and the claim. He should also ask the insured to provide details of all insurances that relate to the insured's claim.

Thereafter the relationship between insured and adjuster is very much the same as in the United Kingdom with both sides seeking a mutually acceptable settlement based on a necessary degree of trust and co-operation.

(c) *Action by the insured*

It is likely that immediately after the time of the Incident (the new A.B.I. term which is defined as "Loss or destruction of or damage to property used by the Insured at the Premises for the purpose of the Business"—refer paragraph 38) the insured, whatever the size of the organisation, will suffer a degree of shock. When this wears off, however, the insured will need to know what action is to be taken which is of most benefit to them in the circumstances.

The United States Business Income Coverage form includes in its Loss Conditions under Duties in the Event of Loss the following instructions to the insured:

"Take all reasonable steps to protect the Covered Property from further damage by a Covered Cause of Loss. If feasible, set the damaged property aside and in the best possible order for examination. Also keep a record of your expenses for emergency and temporary repairs for consideration in the settlement of the claim".

The United Kingdom Claims Condition—Action by the Insured—does not give such precise practical instructions but states that "the Insured shall with due diligence carry out and permit to be taken any action which may reasonably be practicable to minimise or check any interruption of or interference with the Business or to avoid or diminish the loss".

It is often said that the insured should act as though uninsured and in this context the following generalised points of action are recommended:

1. Talk to employees, reassure them and obtain their co-operation for the period of interruption
2. Communicate with and reassure customers (if possible)
3. Plan what to do with the business, (*e.g.* increased sales effort, sub-contracting, relocation, etc.) to ensure recovery
4. Expedite rebuilding, reequipping, etc.
5. Establish a system of recording all emergency and other expenditure
6. Establish accounting systems to monitor all cancelled or delayed orders, to amend budgets or forecasts, etc.

It is to be hoped however that the insured are fully covered and that they can arrange the foregoing and any other necessary and beneficial action with the co-operation of the loss adjuster.

The task of restoring a business to normal after damage is made much easier and the expense and time necessary for this are reduced if the insured firm has planned in advance ways and means to minimise an interference with production. The importance of damage control planning is becoming increasingly recognised in the United Kingdom and specialist advice is readily available from insurers, risk management specialists and fire brigade officials.

In some large organisations a "start-up" committee is ready to act in the event of a serious loss leading to a lengthy period of interruption. Regular practices are carried out so as to ensure an efficient performance when an emergency actually happens (see also paragraph 243 on interruption risk treatment).

412. Incurring additional expenditure

Although the standard U.K. business interruption policy does not stipulate that the consent of the insurers must be obtained before the insured embark upon additional expenditure it is clearly desirable that there should be adequate consultation on this between the insured and the loss adjuster. In the first place, it is the duty of the latter to satisfy himself that all practicable measures are being taken to restore the turnover and to perform this function he must be aware what steps the insured are taking whether or not his views are sought on the matter. In a manufacturing risk it is fundamental to explore immediately the possibilities of restoring some production as quickly as possible by bringing into use any spare machinery, hiring plant or equipment, by overtime working or by having work done elsewhere on commission. In a saleshop or warehouse business he must pursue any opportunity to obtain alternative accommodation, temporary or permanent, and even consider buying out an existing business, provided that the proposition is a viable one and the extra cost will be within the economic limit of the provisions for additional expenditure. New stock must be purchased as quickly as possible and possibly a salvage sale organised. The need to retain customers and keep out competitors by public relations methods, telephone calls and visits, circularising and advertising optimistic reassurances of a speedy return to normal trading, is of paramount importance. Secondly, the loss adjuster must give the insured the benefit of his experience so as to obtain the maximum benefit to which they are entitled under the policy. In advising an insured about both the scope and the limitations of the indemnity for additional expenditure he may possibly avert any overspending which might otherwise take place.

A reminder might be useful here of the precise words of the relevant clause providing for payments by insurers in respect of increase in cost of working, italics being used to emphasise the strict conditions governing such payments, *viz.*: "the additional expenditure *necessarily* and *reasonably* incurred for the *sole* purpose of avoiding or diminishing the reduction in turnover which *but for that expenditure* would have taken place *during* the indemnity period *in consequence of the damage*, but not exceeding"—then follows the limitation that insurers will not contribute in respect of such expenditure an amount greater than that which it saves them in respect of loss of gross profit and wages.

In connection with the above, paragraphs 46 to 48 and 209 about the limitations on additional expenditure are of particular relevance, and paragraphs 245 to 247 similarly regarding shortage, or increase, of turnover during the indemnity period or later, as the points raised in them may have to be taken into account when figures are finally formulated for the settlement of a claim.

Under the terms of the United States Business Income Coverage form insurers promise to pay any necessary expenses incurred by the insured to reduce the loss (subject to the same kind of "economic limit" imposed in United Kingdom policies). When Extra Expense is also covered insurers will pay other necessary expenses to avoid or minimise the suspension of business including relocation expenses.

413. Book-keeping during period of interruption

An insured's normal system of book-keeping and accounting should be continued to whatever extent is practicable throughout the period of interference following damage. This in conjunction with the accounts and records for the trading in preceding years will provide most of the information subsequently required for formulation of the claim calculation. But all day books, books of account and payroll records should be ruled off and restarted as from the time of the damage occurring and it is advisable to earmark in some way, or keep a separate analysis or note of, any additional expenditure incurred which may rank for payment under clause (b) as increase in cost of working.

This is particularly necessary when overtime work is done by the insured's employees, to enable a detailed statement of the appropriate amount of any overtime pay to be furnished when required. Similarly it is advisable to keep a record, with dates, of any abnormal transactions, the loss of orders, and changes in prices of raw materials, fuel and power costs, wage rates and selling prices, etc., which may arise.

Information can be gleaned by the loss adjuster through periodic contact with the insured and sometimes from the columns of newspapers, business and trade journals or figures and forecasts in government and chambers of commerce publications. Such knowledge might subsequently be very useful if adjustments are required under the other circumstances clause. Friendly contacts with persons in the same trade as the insured might provide information on past, present and future trends which also could be useful in discussions with an insured. Notes should be made of any extraneous events such as strikes or abnormal weather conditions which might have affected the insured's business in either the pre-damage or post-damage periods.

If in order to avoid unnecessary delay in rehabilitating a business it is considered advisable to order stock replacements before the actual extent of the interference with the business and requirements for the continuation of trading can be fully established arrangements for this should be worked out between loss adjuster and insured, specific records being kept. This, if a calculated risk, is justifiable and if it turns out that it has resulted in some overstocking, rectification can no doubt be subsequently arranged.

414. Records destroyed in a fire

Should the insured's books of account and other records be destroyed in the fire it is generally possible to obtain from other sources sufficient information for purposes of the ordinary business interruption claim. (This does not apply to any loss of outstanding accounts, regarding which see Chapter 19 on Loss of Book Debts.) The firm's auditors will have a copy of the accounts for the last financial year which will contain most of the figures required. The insured's bank will be able to supply a record of the amounts paid in and of withdrawals during the preceding 12 months. From these together with copies of invoices obtained with the co-operation of customers of goods supplied prior to the damage and not paid for at that time, turnover figures up to the date of the damage can be calculated with reasonable accuracy.

The Extra Expense cover in the current United States policy states that the extra expense necessary to research, replace or restore the lost information on damaged valuable papers and records will be paid.

415. Payments on account

If the period of interruption is likely to be lengthy an insured may after a certain time wish to receive payments on account of the claim which will ultimately be formulated. In some cases this may be essential to maintain cash flow for trading or to pay wages or for additional expenditure. On production to the loss adjuster of sufficient data to substantiate the request and subject to the circumstances of the claim being in order insurers will make such an interim payment and subsequent payments on account as the period of interruption continues, the amounts so paid being offset against the final settlement. (See paragraph 379.) At this stage the insured's accountants will probably be brought into the negotiations, if they have not already been consulted, to formulate provisional figures.

416. Statement of claim

When the effects of the damage on the turnover of the business have ceased and there is no need for further additional expenditure in order to maintain turnover, the insured should ask their accountants to prepare a statement of claim on the lines of the formula in the specification in respect of the loss suffered within the terms of the specification and the policy. It might be deemed profitable to have a joint consultation with the loss adjuster regarding the specific application of principles to the particular case. There may be problems which are difficult to reconcile and very possibly he will previously have met and negotiated similar difficulties. These remarks may be particularly relevant where an insured uses accounting techniques such as standard costing and budgetary control with resulting differences between figures compiled under such systems and those which would be produced by the traditional method of actual costs. When accounts are based on a planned budget later corrected by determined variances instead of their being based on historical fact only, or when a system of inflation accounting is employed, adequate information for the claim negotiations can be extracted provided that there is a proper understanding on both sides of the details required. The guidance of an experienced loss adjuster can be very helpful but it is essential for him to have full information on the method of accounting employed and to know whether he is being given historic or inflation adjusted figures and to give effect to the Note on the specification to disregard any adjustment implemented in current cost accounting. Paragraphs 219 and 220 are of special relevance to this matter. Because the present "difference" specification stipulates that in calculating the gross profit the amounts of the opening and closing stocks are to be "arrived at in accordance with the insured's normal accountancy methods" but makes no provision for amending the amount of gross profit to allow for a cost of sales adjustment, it may be necessary to have recourse to the other circumstances clause to arrive at a proper indemnity.

The adjuster must also have regard to the respective quantities of opening and closing stocks because any substantial difference in these can have an effect on the gross profit during a period of economic inflation or of declining values. Similarly, the question should be looked into as to whether the amounts were determined by methods of computation consistent with those for the previous year, which might be by valuing stocks at the lowest of cost (including direct labour and other manufacturing overheads), replacement cost or net realisable value, whether on a first-in-first-out basis, and whether arrived at by a physical or a book-stocktaking method.

Another accountancy matter to which the loss adjuster must pay special attention is an insured's normal practice in regard to the charging of depreciation on the assets of the business and how this relates to the terms of the insurance cover and to the claims under both the material damage insurance and the business interruption policy. (See paragraph 146.)

417. Information required for formulation of claim

Whilst the details and figures necessary for the calculation and negotiations of the settlement of a claim will vary with each particular case the following itemises the information which will generally be required.

1. The date which can be agreed as the end of the indemnity period ("the period beginning with the occurrence of the Incident and ending not later than the maximum indemnity period thereafter during which the results of the business shall be affected in consequence of the Incident"). That is, when the turnover was no longer affected either adversely *or beneficially* (see paragraph 247) and expenditure on increase in cost of working ceased (see paragraph 48) for a period limited to the maximum indemnity period insured.

2. A detailed statement of the amount of the insured gross profit, showing its computation as defined in the specification, from the accounts for the last financial year preceding the Incident.

417

3. Details of names and amounts of any charges in those accounts which should have been, but may not have been, included in the definition of gross profit.

4. The amount of turnover, as defined in the specification, in the accounts for the last financial year preceding the Incident.

5. The amount of turnover in the 12 months immediately preceding the date of the Incident.

6. The shortage in turnover, ascertained by comparing the turnover achieved during the period of interruption (monthly or weekly figures required)—limited to the number of months in the definition of maximum indemnity period—with that in the corresponding period in the 12 months immediately before the Incident.

7. Details of all additional (*i.e.* abnormal) expenditure incurred to minimise the interference with the business.

8. Details of any property included in 7 above as additional expenditure which remains of some use after the end of the period of interruption and residual value of same (paragraph 419).

9. Details of any reduction due to the Incident in the amount of any charges or expenses of the business which are included in the definition of gross profit.

10. Wages: the information required will depend upon the method under which they are insured. Assuming this is the dual basis scheme:

   (a) The amount of the wages, holiday pay, national insurance contributions and the like (as defined in the specification) shown in the accounts for the last financial year preceding the Incident.
   (b) The shortage in turnover during
       (i) the initial period;
       (ii) the remaining period;
       (iii) the extended initial period (alternative period) available under the option to consolidate;
       (iv) the remaining period after (iii).
   (c) The respective amounts of any saving in wages in consequence of the damage during each of the above periods under (b).

The figures obtained under (b) and (c) above will enable alternative calculations to be made to decide whether it is to the insured's advantage to exercise the option to consolidate

11. Any grounds for adjustment of the preceding 2 to 6 and 10 under the terms of the other circumstances clause.

> "NOTE: i. production of the trading and profit and loss accounts for the last three years preceding the Incident for the loss adjuster's perusal will often be helpful as an indication of trends of business and special circumstances;
> ii. for the purposes of calculating the claim under an item on wages on the dual basis in the manner most beneficial to the insured the

amount of the wages for each week after the Incident and similarly of the turnover each week if possible, if not each month, would be required".

Loss determination is set out in the Loss Conditions of the new United States form where it states that:

"the amount of Business Income loss will be determined based on: (1) the Net Income of the business before the direct physical loss or damage occurred; (2) the likely Net Income of the business if no loss or damage occurred; (3) the operating expenses, including payroll expenses, necessary to resume 'operations' with the same quality of service that existed just before the direct physical loss or damage; and (4) other relevant sources of information, including: (a) your financial records and accounting procedures; (b) bills, invoices and other vouchers; and (c) deeds, liens or contracts".

Where Extra Expense is also covered, the condition goes on to state that:

"the amount of Extra Expense will be determined based on: (1) all expenses that exceed the normal operating expenses that would have been incurred by 'operations' during the 'period of restoration' if no direct physical loss or damage had occurred. We will deduct from the total of such expenses: (a) the salvage value that remains of any property bought for temporary use during the 'period of restoration,' once 'operations' are resumed; and (b) any Extra Expense that is paid for by other insurance, except for insurance that is written subject to the same plan, terms, conditions and provisions as this insurance; and (2) all necessary expenses that reduce the Business Income loss that otherwise would have been incurred".

Specimen calculations of loss settlements to show the operation of the claims formula (paragraph 57) and the effect of the different clauses and factors relevant to it which are dealt with in preceding chapters, are given in Appendix X Paragraph 470 and Appendix Y paragraph 471 whilst a specimen calculation for a claim under a dual basis wages item is given in Appendix W paragraph 469. A specimen of a claim calculation under a United States Business Income Coverage form is shown in Appendix Z, paragraph 472.

418. "Finished stock" exclusion in United States gross earnings (manufacturing risks) and Business Income coverages

In a claim under a United States gross earnings policy for a manufacturing business the loss adjuster is faced with special problems in addition to the points mentioned in preceding paragraph 417. These arise because (i) loss resulting from damage to finished stock is excluded (ii) the definition of gross earnings gives specific meanings to raw stock, stock in progress and finished stock the respective amounts of which must therefore be sorted out (iii) the condition about resumption of operations stipulates that an insured must make use of stock—raw, in process or finished (iv) the expediting expenses clause covers expenses in excess of normal incurred in replacing any finished stock used to reduce the loss (v) due consideration has to be given to the experience of the business before the damage and probable experience thereafter had no loss occurred.

The situation is in essence the same under a Business Income Coverage form and special attention is therefore required by the loss adjuster to the various factors which may influence the effects of the damage at various stages of production particularly where seasonal production is involved.

419. Residual value

One feature of claim settlements which frequently arises in practice but is not mentioned in the specification concerns what is termed "residual value". Additional expenditure incurred under the provision for increase in cost of working often takes such forms as the construction of temporary buildings, roofing, floors, gangways or partitioning, electric wiring, etc., the temporary installation of secondhand machinery, or possibly the complete fitting up of other premises and the installation of electric motors, cables, switchgear, etc., a boiler and other plant, pipe lines, conveyors, etc., purely as a temporary measure. Provisional office, canteen and washroom facilities may be required with portable space heaters; or perhaps temporary fencing might have to be erected for the security of unprotected buildings and contents. When such buildings or property are no longer required because the permanent reconstruction and re-equipping of the damaged premises has been completed and the temporary buildings, plant or fittings, etc., are sold, the net amount realised will be deducted from that which was incurred on them, only the difference being claimable as increase in cost of working.

It may be, however, that the period of interruption extends beyond the maximum indemnity period covered by the insurance and the insured wish to continue to use the temporary structures or plant and equipment in order to benefit turnover for a period after that for which the insurers are liable under the policy. Alternatively, whether the maximum indemnity period insured is too short or otherwise the insured may wish to retain some of the temporary buildings or plant because of their future value to the business. In any such circumstances the insurers are entitled to some compensation for relinquishing their right to sell the property for which they are paying under the heading of increase in cost of working. The policy limits the insurer's liability to the expenditure incurred "for the sole purpose of avoiding or diminishing the reduction in turnover which but for that expenditure *would have taken place during the indemnity period in consequence of the Incident*". So agreement must be reached on a suitable contribution from the insured for the benefit of retaining such property, that is, for its residual value. This is comparable with salvage in a claim for loss under a fire policy and is simply an application of the principle of indemnity. In assessing what the insured's contribution should be, they should be given the benefit of the fact that if they did not retain the temporary installations the sale value of these would be considerably reduced by the costs of dismantling and removal.

The position under a United States Business Income Coverage form is the same as the foregoing. Unlike the United Kingdom policy specification the form states that insurers will deduct from Extra Expenses necessarily incurred "the salvage value that remains of any property bought for temporary use during the 'period of restoration' once 'operations' are resumed".

420. Period of interruption prolonged or amount of loss increased by external causes

(a) *United Kingdom covers*

A matter of very considerable importance is the attitude which insurers might adopt to the effect on the time taken to rehabilitate a business after damage, of external influences which prolong the period of interruption. For example, such external influences might include delays in rebuilding or re-equipping premises or in obtaining alternative accommodation caused by town planning or other legislation, Government restrictions on building activities, adverse weather conditions, the reluctance of a landlord to rebuild, a scarcity of steel, bricks, cement or other materials or of machinery, the effects of war here or abroad, or of strikes or lock-outs in the building, engineering or transport industries.

It may rightly be contended that the loss sustained by an insured in such circumstances has been increased by the intervention of a contingency not covered by the insurance, the policy being a contract of indemnity for loss due to certain specified perils. Under a policy of fire insurance the long-established doctrine of proximate cause applies, that is, the immediate cause of loss, and not the remote cause, is to be considered.

The traditional practice in the United Kingdom has always been to accept increase of business interruption loss due to extraneous causes outside the control of the insured which delay rehabilitation of a business but which would not have affected the business had it not been already subject to interruption following damage, as being within the scope of the intended indemnity. This was substantially proved during the war of 1939–45 and the years immediately following. During that period, delays in or complete prohibition of rebuilding prolonged the period of interruption in nearly every case of a large fire, but it was never claimed by insurers that the additional loss entailed thereby was not their liability. Their attitude in arranging insurances provides further evidence. For example, although in the post-war period the destruction of a cinema or theatre by fire meant that there was no possibility of rebuilding for several years, due entirely to Government restrictions, insurers freely offered to give cover for indemnity periods as long as five years thereby proving that they accepted all the loss, the bulk of it due to rebuilding restrictions, as being within the meaning of "in consequence" of the fire damage.

If the intention of insurers was to compensate only for loss that stems directly from damage to an insured's property by an insured peril and to exclude an aggravation of that loss due to the intervention in rehabilitation of a non-insured contingency, *e.g.* a strike in the building industry, they would presumably have given effect to this in the policy wording. This is done in the case, and only in the case, of the material damage proviso which by the expedient of stipulating that the material damage must be covered by insurance excludes loss due to an insured's inability to rehabilitate a business resulting from lack of financial means. At least that appears to be part of the reason for the proviso although it does not stipulate that the insurance must be adequate for rebuilding and re-equipping. An insured only partially covered for material damage sustained might appear nominally to fulfil the requirements of the proviso but through shortage of capital as well as underinsurance might be unable to rehabilitate the business as quickly as would otherwise have been possible. In such circumstances a strict interpretation of "an insurance covering the interest of the insured in the property at the premises against such damage, etc.," might prove to mean an *adequate* insurance. Or it might be held that the prolongation of the period of interruption was caused not by an external factor beyond the control of the insured but that the proximate cause was the lack of adequate material damage insurance which is an insured's responsibility. In either view it would be outside the scope of the business interruption insurance.

But factors which increase the loss during the indemnity period *which would have affected the insured's trading results had there been no damage* are outside the scope of the insurer's liability. For example, a trade depression, an increase in wage rates, new taxation on purchases or sales, changes in import duties, or a strike or lock-out. Because such events would have affected the insured's business had the damage not taken place, allowance must be made for them in the claim settlement and specific provision for this is made by the other circumstances clause.

Further it must not be overlooked that after damage there is an onus imposed on insured by the Claims Condition—Action by the Insured—of the policy that they shall "with due diligence carry out . . . all things which may be reasonably practicable to minimise or check any interruption of or interference with the business or to avoid or diminish the loss". Should they allow their essential employees to disperse during a period of interruption without due regard to subsequent needs and later find that they cannot restart production or can achieve only partial production because they cannot obtain the necessary key workers, it might be questioned whether the resulting loss is the liability of their insurers.

(b) *United States covers*

The attitude of United States insurers is much less sympathetic to the effect of outside influences. Until 1943 the extra loss attributable to wartime delays was amongst the excluded contingencies. In the current Business Income forms the contractual clause would appear to show some easing of the situation in that it no longer contains a phrase limiting the indemnity to "the actual loss sustained by the Insured resulting *directly* from such interruption of business" (gross earnings wording) but instead limits the indemnity to the actual loss sustained "due to the necessary suspension of the Insured's 'operations' during the 'period of restoration' ". However, in the definition of the latter expression it is stated that the "period of restoration" does not include any increased period required due to the enforcement of any ordinance or law that regulates the construction, use or repair, or requires the tearing down of any property, or that requires any insured or others to test for, monitor, clean up, remove, contain, treat, detoxify or neutralise, or in any way respond to, or assess the effects of "pollutants".

Further, in the Special Exclusions in the Covered Causes of Loss forms insurers state that they will not pay for:

"any increase of loss caused by or resulting from: (a) delay in rebuilding, repairing or replacing the property or resuming 'operations,' due to interference at the location of the rebuilding, repair or replacement by strikers or other persons; or (b) suspension, lapse or cancellation of any licence, lease or contract—but if the suspension, lapse or cancellation is directly caused by the suspension of 'operations,' we will cover such loss that affects your Business Income during the 'period of restoration' ".

(Refer paragraph 65.)

The only area where some allowance is made is in respect of the action of civil authority: an Additional Coverage pays for loss:

"caused by action of civil authority that prohibits access to the described premises due to direct physical loss of or damage to property, other than at the described premises, caused by or resulting from any Covered Cause of Loss. This coverage will apply for a period of up to two consecutive weeks from the date of that action".

(Refer paragraph 65(a).)

421. Injury or death of personnel

Another feature which occasionally arises and may have a very important, perhaps all-important, bearing upon the amount of the insured's loss is the injury or death of one or more of their staff or workpeople caused by fire or explosion. The temporary or permanent loss of key personnel of one kind or another may result in a serious delay in the rehabilitation of a business and a diminution of turnover for a longer period or of greater degree than would otherwise have been the case.

If reference is made to the contractual clauses of the policy it is apparent that loss attributable to personal injuries is outside the terms of the insurance even though such injuries are directly caused by an insured peril. The indemnity is in respect of loss resulting from interruption of or interference with the business in consequence of destruction or damage by the insured perils of "any building or other property or any part thereof used by the insured at the premises for the purpose of the business". Consequently, any loss resulting from absence from work of injured employees which can be segregated from that arising from damage to the buildings, plant, machinery or stock, would not be the liability of the insurers.

In many cases in which this situation arises it is not practicable to separate the amount of such loss nor is it usually of serious extent in relation to the total claim. In such instances insurers will probably adopt a generous view and accept the total amount of the loss as being their responsibility particularly if the employee's injuries were sustained in fighting a fire.

It might be, however, that the fire or explosion or other contingency causes the injury or death of an insured, or of a working partner or director, a works or shop manager, chief engineer, production manager, chief chemist, or other person of vital importance to the conduct of the business, whose absence would have a most serious, and ascertainable, effect on turnover. In the case of a professional practice, the absence of a partner, legal executive or managing clerk could make a substantial difference to revenue whilst the loss of a sole principal could be calamitous. Unfortunately these things do happen.

In such circumstances an insured might claim that the casualties which have resulted in an aggravation of loss are the intervention of an extraneous cause in line with those mentioned in paragraph 420(a) and accepted by insurers as their liability. Which raises the problem of proximate cause of the loss; was it the damage to property or was it the injury to and absence from work of personnel of the insured? Whilst the personal injuries would not have been sustained but for the fire or other contingency they took place simultaneously with the damage to property; had there been no such event and the personnel been absent from work from other causes their absence would have affected turnover; their absence did not originate during the period of rehabilitation as an external factor but was concurrent with the period of interruption from its commencement. From these considerations it might be decided that although the loss resulting from the absence of personnel is attributable to an insured peril giving rise to a claim for business interruption arising from that damage, the effect on turnover of such absence of personnel cannot be construed as resulting from *damage to property*. If this view is taken any loss of turnover resulting from personal injuries or death caused by the same occurrence and at the same time as the damage is not the liability of insurers.

However, there is a difference between the position discussed in the foregoing and circumstances such as, for instance, the following. Say the managing director of a company who was not present at the premises during the time when the damage was taking place but some weeks later during the period of interruption suffered a heart attack as the direct result of the strain, worry and overwork involved in his efforts to rehabilitate the business as quickly as possible. If as a consequence of his subsequent absence through incapacity or death, the restoration of the business to normality was seriously delayed would not this be on a par with the examples quoted in paragraph 420(a)? That is, would it qualify as an intervening influence, which arose during the period of interruption and which would not have arisen had the damage not occurred, and establish the proximate cause of the increase in the amount of business interruption loss as resulting from the damage and therefore be the liability of the insurer? There might, of course, be grounds for the legal profession to bring another case for the courts to decide on the issue of proximate cause if the said individual had a pre-damage history of heart trouble!

The introduction of Key Man insurance in the life market has helped to clarify the insurance situation. Insured who have key employees are now encouraged to take out such insurance which will compensate the insured for the financial effects of the temporary or permanent loss of an employee because of death, injury, etc.,. The sum insured is a fixed amount based on the cost of replacement of such an individual and the effect on the (net) profit of the business of his or her temporary or permanent loss.

422. Decision on retention of employees

When arranging an insurance much care may be taken over the cover relating to wages in trying to provide for the various situations which are at that time visualised as possible consequences of damage but when damage does occur there is frequently doubt in the minds of insured as to the extent to which they can retain employees during the period of interruption without involving themselves in financial loss. This is a real problem, especially when the damage is serious and insured are without any prior warning faced with a hundred-and-one other problems each demanding an immediate answer and possibly the major one of the complete reorganisation of their business from a heap of smouldering ruins.

This latter possibility is highlighted by the following quotation from a Press report of a dinner given by the managing director of a firm to 90 employees, 12 months after a disastrous fire at the works, to celebrate the firm's survival. "Mr. Lawton said: We didn't have so much as a piece of typing paper left. I worked at a desk in the middle of rubble. Typists shivered in caravans and our factory hands worked at nights on machinery rented at other factories".

Amidst all the other preoccupations, nearly every one of which is urgent, there is the crucial one of deciding which employees shall be retained and who shall be given dismissal notices and what will be required to comply with current legislation.

It was with the knowledge born of long experience of this type of situation and its attendant problems that insurers formulated the dual basis scheme for insuring wages, subsequently improved by the option to consolidate. In the event of a serious fire it is a great boon for the insured to know that if they wish to do so they can without financial loss pay all employees full wages throughout the initial period insured or longer if the option to consolidate is invoked. This gives a most welcome breathing space during which they will have time to explore the possibilities of rehabilitating their business and to reach a considered decision on the staffing and labour problem in a calmer atmosphere than would be possible in the days immediately following the fire. Their position and that of the loss adjuster are a great deal easier if the whole payroll is insured under a 100 per cent. payroll cover.

The problem of a continuation of most other charges solves itself because they either have to be paid as they arise or are no longer payable in part or whole. Some part of the wages bill may fall within this category but at the same time part or all of it may become an optional charge. It is not always easy for the insured to grasp the significance of this or to appreciate exactly how the insurance is going to operate; yet a decision must be made about retaining employees, possibly with no certain knowledge as to when or to what extent their services can be utilised. The wages bill is generally a major part of the total costs of running a business and if the insured is involved in a loss on wages beyond the amount recoverable under the insurance it may have a serious effect on the net profit.

Liabilities of insured during a period of interruption for compulsory periods of consultation with trade unions and periods of notice for termination of employment and for redundancy payments under the two employment protection Acts of 1975 and 1978 (see paragraphs 202 and 203) call for action without delay. This legislation is of relevance even though payments due to be made under it are not mentioned in the definition of wages or payroll.

Whilst the rehabilitation of the business must be the primary consideration in any decisions about the retention of employees, information as to the extent and the ways in which the wages insurance can be used towards that end with the greatest advantage is one of the many services which the loss adjuster can render the insured as the outcome of his wide experience. It is generally the case that after a serious fire employees are strenuous in their help in the work of reinstatement either out of loyalty to their employers or with an eye to the main chance so that they can get back to full-time employment as soon as possible, even if this involves bending trade union rules. But one factor which must not be overlooked by loss adjusters is the necessity to consult and secure the co-operation of workers, their shop floor stewards and trade union officials in order to avoid or iron out any problems about temporary, substandard working conditions, inconvenient time schedules and questions of trade demarcations which may arise through steps proposed to obtain speedy rehabilitation of the business.

Similarly in the United States where legislation is a little easier on employers, there may still be union rules which bind the insured. Business Income includes, beside Net Profit, "continuing normal operating expenses incurred, including payroll". Ordinary payroll expenses as defined in the Ordinary Payroll Limitation endorsement are "payroll expenses for all employees except: officers, executives, department managers, employees under contract, and additional exemptions, shown in the Schedule or in the Declarations as to job classifications or employees". Such expenses are regarded as potential "savings" in the event of a prolonged interruption. Retention of employees earning Ordinary Payroll is a matter for discussion with the loss adjuster taking into account both short-term and long-term views of the interruption.

423. Operation of the wages cover in the United Kingdom

Decisions must necessarily depend upon the probable extent and duration of total stoppage and of partial interruption and upon other factors affecting the retention or subsequent recruitment or training of employees, local labour conditions and so on.

No difficulty arises with regard to employees who are direct producers whose work is not affected by the damage; they will be retained and their labour will produce turnover out of which their wages will be paid as normal. Regarding the rest of the workers, the primary problem is to decide who shall be retained throughout the whole period of interruption. These employees can then be informed that, although there might be no work for them for a time and possibly insufficient work to provide them with full employment for several weeks thereafter, if they remain with the firm their wages will be made up to normal during the whole period. The wages paid to these employees will be met partly by any turnover maintained and partly from the insurance according to the adequacy of the extent to which the latter had been arranged.

The insured can temporarily lay off or can give notice of dismissal to any of the remainder of their workpeople for whom there is no work immediately available and whom they do not wish to retain. The wages payable in this respect will be the amounts for which they are liable under the Employment Protection Act 1975 and the Employment Protection (Consolidation)

423

Act 1978, but they can pay more if the insurance provides 100 per cent. wages for a longer period and the insured wish to utilise this cover. Any credit for holiday pay for the number of weeks of employees' dismissal wages will be given in addition and national insurance contributions deducted throughout any period during which they are retained by the insured. As steps are taken in subsequent weeks to restore turnover some of these dismissed employees will have to be re-engaged or new workers recruited. The work done by these people will, in the main, be producing turnover which should carry their wages in the normal way except where training or retraining is necessary. Regarding liability for redundancy payments under the Employment Protection (Consolidation) Act 1978 see paragraph 202(b).

To summarise the position under the different methods of wages insurance: the insured may pay without loss to themselves (being reimbursed from any turnover maintained plus the contribution from their insurance), assuming the terms of the insurance are adequate:

1 with wages insured part in the gross profit and part in a separate wages item (not dual basis):

   (a) full wages to all employees during the short period covered under the separate wages item;
   (b) full wages thereafter to the proportion of the total wage roll or categories of employee included in the gross profit item.

2 with wages insured on the dual wages or dual payroll basis;

   (a) full wages to all employees during the initial period;
   (b) full wages thereafter to the percentage of the total wage roll which is shown as the limit for the remaining portion of the indemnity period; and
   (c) utilise during that remaining portion of the indemnity period, to augment the payment under (b), any saving in wages due to the damage which accrued during the initial period (a);

alternatively:

   (d) extend the initial period for full wages to all employees up to the maximum number of weeks shown on the policy as the alternative period available for 100 per cent. wages cover under the option to consolidate whilst retaining throughout this extended period any benefit provided by the carry-over of savings provision;
   (e) utilise during the remaining portion of the indemnity period any savings in wages carried over from the extended initial period (d).

3 with the whole of the wage roll included in the gross profit item in a 100 per cent. payroll cover;

   (a) full wages to all employees throughout the whole period of interruption within the maximum indemnity period.

424. Where production drops but wages bill does not

Circumstances sometimes arise following damage in which the tempo of production in a factory is slowed down due to one or other of many possible causes. It may be that machinery has to be run more slowly or is subject to periodic breakdowns because of its damaged condition or that interruption in one department results in a shortage of material in other departments. A bottleneck at one point may reduce the rate of flow along a whole production or assembly line. Three men may be needed to work a machine ordinarily worked by two. Possibly some work has to be done by hand whilst the machinery with which it is normally done is being repaired or replaced, or the slowing down of production may merely be the result of general disorganisation caused by the damage. The running-in period and teething troubles usually experienced with new or repaired plant can have the same effect. In circumstances of the above or similar nature the total wages paid to ordinary productive workers may remain at the normal amount but owing to the reduction in the volume of goods produced they will bear a higher ratio to turnover than they did before the damage.

A similar position can arise in department stores, supermarkets, hypermarkets, cash-and-carry and discount stores, factory outlets and various wholesale and retail businesses during repairs to the premises and equipment or the occupation of temporary premises following damage in which time the full complement of employees is required to maintain less than the normal volume of sales. Damage to product coding computers can substantially increase the ratio of wages to sales.

The insured's loss due to an increased incidence of wages in this way will be recovered by them in full if all wages are insured for the full length of the maximum indemnity period. If 100 per cent. of the wage roll is covered for only a shorter period full compensation will be obtained only during that time or, if the cover is on the dual basis, during the extended initial period (the alternative period) provided under the option to consolidate. After this recovery under the insurance will be made only in proportion to the extent to which wages are insured in the item on gross profit or when wages are covered on the dual basis up to the limit of any insurance applicable to the remaining portion of the indemnity period, that is, the amount provided by the remainder percentage plus any amount brought forward under the carry-over provision. Consequently, in such abnormal—though not unusual—circumstances some loss may be sustained in connection with the uninsured portion of the wage roll which will not be recoverable under the policy.

425. Increased ratio of wages is not increase in cost of working

It is sometimes mistakenly thought that loss of the foregoing nature due to an increased ratio to turnover of wages which normally vary directly with turnover, is recoverable under "the increase in cost of working" clause of the item on gross profit. That this is not so was clearly stated by Mr. Justice Branson in the case of *Polikoff Ltd.* v. *North British and Mercantile Insurance Co. Ltd.* (1936) 55 Ll.L.R. 279 when he pointed out that there was no *additional* expenditure on wages and proceeded to disallow the claim in respect of that item. (But see paragraph 426.)

When the insured sustain loss in circumstances of this kind it may seem a hardship particularly as the labour out of which the loss has arisen has benefited the insurers by producing turnover. Had the insured not retained so many employees to keep the business functioning they would not have sustained the loss arising from the increased incidence of wages to turnover, whilst the loss of gross profit on the resulting shortage in turnover would be claimable under the insurance. In this matter insurance companies hold the view that it is incumbent upon the insured under the Claims Condition—Action by the Insured—of the policy (see paragraph 435) to do all things reasonably practicable to minimise the loss of turnover and that, in doing so, if a loss arises in the way described it is because events have proved that an insufficient part of the wage roll has been insured for the full period of interruption. Insurers cannot be expected to meet a loss which could have been covered by the insurance but has not been insured, although their practice in this respect may be to treat insured generously.

426. "Additional" expenditure on wages of insured's employees

A loss due to the increased ratio of wages to turnover must not be confused with the expense of paying overtime wages or with payments for additional labour with the object of maintaining turnover after the damage. In such circumstances the amount of wages paid would exceed the normal wage roll and would constitute additional expenditure as provided for under the increase in cost of working section of the specification.

It must be clearly understood that if overtime wages are paid in connection with the production or sale of goods to obtain turnover which would otherwise be lost, only the difference between normal rates and overtime rates of pay will be the insurer's responsibility as increase in cost of working. The reason is that ordinary wage rates would have had to be paid to produce that turnover had there been no need to have employees on overtime to do so and the sale of the goods will provide for the normal ratio of wages. Hence, the insured's loss is the difference between ordinary rates of pay and the overtime wage rates and it is this difference only which ranks as increase in cost of working.

See also paragraph 428 regarding overtime wages in connection with rebuilding operations.

427. Recovery of wages paid during period of interruption

Misconception sometimes arises from the knowledge that the loss resulting from an increased ratio of wages to turnover is not recoverable as increase in cost of working and so it is suggested that even with a 100 per cent. wages cover, an insured could sustain loss. For example, if damage occurs and only 50 per cent. of normal turnover can be maintained and to do so requires 70 per cent. of the labour force on full wages whilst the remaining non-employed 30 per cent. are paid full wages for the period of interruption, will not the insured suffer loss to the extent of the increase in the normal wages ratio?

In such circumstances the insured would recover the whole of their wages expenditure; from (i) the money they receive on the sale of the goods manufactured together with (ii) payment under their insurance of the normal rate of gross profit, which includes 100 per cent. wages, applied to the shortage in turnover, as in the following illustration.

Assume a turnover of £1.2 million a year and a wage roll of £400,000 included in full in the insurance on gross profit with a maximum indemnity period of 12 months. Following damage there is a 50 per cent. reduction in turnover, that is, a shortage of £600,000 during the following 12 months. The position then becomes—

	£
Wages paid to produce the 50% turnover maintained (70% of normal labour force)	280,000
Wages paid to non-employed workers (30% of normal labour force)	120,000
Actual expenditure on wages	400,000
Provided by the turnover maintained: in respect of wages—50% of the normal total	200,000

Recovered under the insurance:

$$\text{ratio of wages } \frac{£400{,}000}{£1{,}200{,}000} = 33\tfrac{1}{3}\%$$

applied (as a component of the rate of gross profit) to the shortage in turnover (£600,000)	200,000
Total received in respect of wages	400,000

428. Claim for overtime wages on rebuilding

In addition to the question of overtime wages paid to an insured's employees to maintain turnover discussed in paragraph 426, it is necessary to consider the position with regard to a claim as increase in cost of working of overtime wages paid either to the insured's employees or to those of builders and other tradesmen in the rehabilitation of the premises when these are owned by the insured.

Overtime wages necessarily incurred to speed up work of repairs or rebuilding of a temporary nature which has to be subsequently replaced by the permanent repairs or rebuilding will rank in full, together with the wages paid at standard rates, as additional expenditure. On the other hand, when overtime wages are paid in connection with the permanent repairs or rebuilding and fitting up of damaged premises to speed up work in order to reduce the period of interruption, only the difference between standard rates and overtime pay will be claimable as additional expenditure. The reason for overtime being treated in two different ways is that the cost of repairs of a temporary nature is wholly the responsibility of the business interruption insurer, whereas permanent repairs are at the expense of the insured as owners of the building and so are claimable under the material damage insurance. In the latter connection, if men did not work overtime the same total number of hours would be worked for which the material damage insurers would have to pay at standard wage rates. Therefore the "additional" expenditure which is the business interruption insurer's liability is confined to the difference between the pay at standard rates and that at overtime rates, on the number of hours of overtime worked.

429. Overlap with indemnity under a material damage policy

(a) *Cleaning up after damage*

One of the first tasks put in hand after damage by fire, explosion, storm or flood, etc., is that of cleaning up and of protecting any plant and machinery either undamaged or worth repairing and the salvaging of such equipment and stock as remains of any value, followed when necessary by the removal of debris and clearing of the site for rebuilding. Apart from major fires or where the height of the buildings or the heavy nature of construction and plant call for demolition and removal by specialists with appropriate plant and experience, an insured's own employees are sometimes put on to do such work when they cannot do their normal jobs.

Work of the kind described has to be carried out as a necessary stage in the reinstatement of the material damage and payment for it is therefore the responsibility of the insurers under the material damage policy and under a removal of debris memorandum on such a policy. So when the insured's own employees have been engaged on such work it is the general practice to reimburse the insured for their wages as part of the claim under the material damage insurance.

To this extent there is an overlap between the cover under a material damage policy and that under a business interruption policy. Under the material damage policy, payment of the amount which would otherwise have been paid to an outside contractor will be made as wages to the insured's employees for cleaning up operations. There could be a concurrent claim under the wages insurance of the insured's business interruption policy calculated in accordance with the terms of the wages cover. But this would mean the insured's recovering their payments for wages twice and the established method of dealing with such a situation is to deduct from the claim under the business interruption policy the amount paid for wages under the material damage insurance, as follows:

(a) where wages are insured under the dual basis or dual payroll cover; as a saving in wages to be held to the insured's credit under the carry-over provision and available for use later in the indemnity period;

(b) where the wages concerned are insured for 100 per cent. in the item on gross profit (as 100 per cent. payroll or otherwise): as a saving in a charge or expense of the business under the savings clause, for the benefit of the insurers;

(c) where the wages involved are insured under a separate item on the annual basis; as a saving in wages under the relevant clause, for the benefit of the insurers;

(d) where the wages concerned are insured in a separate item on the pro rata or weekly basis: since the wording of the item confines the indemnity to "the insured's *loss* by the payment of wages" the weekly amount paid under the item will be after deduction from the payroll of the wages paid for by the material damage insurers.

If overtime wage rates have to be paid to either the insured's own workpeople or those of demolition contractors in order to hasten the work of clearance and so bring forward the resumption of production or turnover, the material damage insurance will be responsible only for the standard rates of wages and the overtime element of these will rank for payment under the business interruption policy as increase in cost of working, as explained in the foregoing paragraph 428.

(b) *Damaged stock*

An overlap between the indemnities provided by fire and business interruption policies sometimes arises through the basis on which the claim under the fire insurance is settled. The accepted practice is that the insured must be indemnified for the stock destroyed according to its value at the time and place of its destruction. In the case of a wholesaler or shopkeeper this may include the cost in wages and other overhead expenses incurred in sorting, recording, pricing, ticketing and putting the stock on the shelves.

In the case of a manufacturer the value at the time of damage may include not only prime costs but also an appropriate amount for fixed and variable overhead costs, dependent upon the stage of manufacture reached at the time of damage.

If damaged stock cannot be replaced shortly afterwards the resulting loss of sales may constitute part of the shortage in turnover on which a claim is calculated for loss of gross profit under a business interruption policy. This apparently means that an insured recovers twice for the loss of any expenses incurred on stock up to the date of damage which are recouped both under the material damage insurance claim and, as charges which are components of the rate of gross profit, under the business interruption claim.

However, there are two schools of thought about this problem, particularly with regard to the wholesaler or shopkeeper. One maintains that appearances are deceptive and that there is in fact no double indemnity because the costs of reshelving were incurred on stock at the inception of the business, before trading commenced, and the time-lag between expenses and sales continued up to the date of the damage. Before trading can start again after the damage the same procedure must be adopted in order to put goods on the shelves. Hence, there is a double loss of such expenses and recovery of them under both the fire insurance (which pays pre-fire expenditure) and a business interruption insurance (which pays post-fire expenditure) is no more than an indemnity. The other view is that if the idea of looking back to the inception of a business is conceded it must also be applied hypothetically into the future and the time when the business ceases trading. The same time-lag will be present with the reverse effect, the insured having goods for sale without having to incur expense in putting them on the shelves. Hence, there is double indemnity.

It is, however, for manufacturing risks that the problem has become so important particularly over the last few decades. The reason for this is largely because accountancy systems have developed with regard to the costing of stock (at its various stage of manufacture) and more "overhead" costs are being included in the insured's valuation of their stock than before. Hence the possibility of an overlap, which has always been present but which in the past was regarded as not significant enough to concern insurers, is now a sufficient threat (in terms of financial strain) for insurers (and their representatives, the loss adjusters) to take what they consider to be fully justifiable action.

The theory connected with those who merely stock and restock shelves does not enter into the more complex field of manufacturing. The overlap is more immediate and obvious and the current practice among loss adjusters, particularly when the losses on both stock and business interruption are large, is to settle the stock loss and then, if possible, to take account of whatever overlap can be demonstrated of insured fixed costs by suitable deduction from the business interruption settlement.

430. Fire extinguishing expenses

One of a loss adjuster's duties will be to apportion between the business interruption insurers and the material damage (fire, etc.,) insurers the amount of any fire extinguishing expenses. The normal procedure for apportioning such expenses between insurers of property damage alone is based on sums insured according to their relative covers on buildings and contents and it is the accepted practice for business interruption policies to be brought into the calculation for an amount equivalent to 20 per cent. of the total sum insured on contents ranking for contribution by all fire policies effected by or standing in the name of the insured under the business interruption policies but in no case exceeding the total sums insured by the latter.

431. Increase of sum insured after damage

It was mentioned in paragraph 52(c) that many firms make a regular practice of consulting their accountants when the accounts for each financial year are completed and then instructing their broker or insurers with regard to any alteration required in the sum insured. When such a practice has been carried on for several years there is a danger that it may be wrongly assumed by the insured that in the event of damage taking place between the end of a financial year and the time when the annual revision is made the insurers will accept a figure subsequently extracted from the accounts for that financial year as being the sum insured at the time when the damage occurred. This assumption is especially likely if the practice (incorrectly) has been to review the cover to correspond exactly with the actual amount of insurable gross profit revealed by the preceding year's accounts.

Alternatively, it could happen that in such circumstances instructions would be given and accepted during the period of interruption to increase the sum insured and it be subsequently claimed that for purposes of applying the average proviso in the settlement the revised figure should be taken as the relevant sum insured at the time of the damage or, more plausibly, at any rate as from the date when instructions were given for the increase.

In circumstances of this kind the insured have no legal right to the benefits of an increase in the sum insured after damage has taken place because the contract applies according to its terms at the date of damage. Subsequent alterations in those terms or in the sum insured, even though they are made by endorsement of the existing policy, constitute a new contract and cannot be applied retrospectively. Insurers may rightly point to the provisions of the other circumstances clause combined with the return clause, whereby the protection of a margin of 100 per cent. overinsurance can be obtained without any unnecessary payment of premium (see paragraphs 224 and 225(a)). Insurers encourage such overinsurance and it would be unreasonable to ask them to ante-date an increase to benefit insured who have not taken advantage of those provisions.

432. Other circumstances clause—United Kingdom: loss determination—United States: variations in application

Because of the endless variety of circumstances which can effect business earnings either before or during a period of interruption following damage the other circumstances clause is invoked in probably a majority of claim settlements; almost inevitably so in a period of inflation. Its importance does not end with the adjustment of figures to be used in a computation of an insured's loss; it can seriously affect the application of the average proviso to the subsequent amount of the insured's claim. The general reasons for and effects of the clause are dealt with in paragraphs 55 and 56 but the following paragraphs are given as being of special relevance in the negotiation of claims and as indications of variations from the normal method, or less obvious ways, in which the clause may have to be applied in order to secure a proper indemnity in a claim settlement or an equitable application of the average proviso.

Although the United States insurance form does not stipulate that reduction in turnover must be used as the yardstick for measuring "the amount of Business Income loss", this is one possibility and whether it or any other method is used, similar considerations to the following may apply if an analysis of the Net Income the business had earned prior to the loss, and would have earned if no loss had occurred, is used, as referred to in the Loss Determination condition.

When the figures for standard turnover are adjusted for trends it is logical, and normal practice, to apply a corresponding adjustment to the amount of the annual turnover. The former alters the standard for measuring the amount claimable and the latter brings the figures for the application of average into line. For example, if the standard turnover figure is increased by 20 per cent. then the annual turnover figure is normally increased by 20 per cent. But this method of equal adjustments is not invariably equitable and each case needs to be considered in the light of the particular circumstances. An adjustment of the amount of Business Income in a United States coverage will directly affect the figure used for application of the coinsurance condition particularly when the loss occurs early in the period of insurance (*i.e.* the basis of the coinsurance standard).

As an instance take the case of damage occurring at one shop belonging to a firm of multiple retailers with shops in several different parts of the country and an overall sum insured on gross profit. Unusual circumstances of purely local relevance might warrant a substantial increase in the standard turnover figure for that particular shop but, because a comparable increase could not possibly accrue to the other shops, it would not be equitable to apply the same percentage increase to the annual turnover of the whole business for the purposes of the average proviso. Thus, an 80 per cent. uplift for reasons applying only to the turnover of the shop where the damage occurred might mean only 0.5 per cent. increase in the combined turnover of 150 shops and whilst it would be correct to increase the standard turnover figure of the individual shop by 80 per cent. for the claim calculation, the annual turnover of the whole business would have to be increased by only 0.5 per cent. for comparison with the overall sum insured on gross profit as required by the average proviso.

Another instance is a claim in which exceptional circumstances of limited duration warrant a substantial increase in the standard turnover of a business for a period corresponding with a short period of interruption, say three months. If the exceptional circumstances are applicable only during a short period of that kind it would be wrong to adjust for purposes of the average proviso the annual turnover figure for a full 12 months by the same percentage uplift. For example, if the adjustment for the three months turnover figures was agreed at 60 per cent., then the appropriate increase in the annual turnover amount might be only 15 per cent.

Provisions included in both United Kingdom and United States business interruption insurances for the adjustment of figures to compensate for the probable future trading results which would have been achieved had no damage occurred, whilst necessary if a proper indemnity is to be obtained, do give rise to many difficult problems for loss adjusters. A typical case is where a manufacturer has made costings for future production based on certain improvements in plant lay-out and new, more modern machinery, computer controlled, which are calculated to produce a greater quantity of goods at less cost per item or unit of measurement. The alterations are duly put in hand but before completion a fire damages the factory. A claim is submitted on the basis of projected increased earnings but there is no positive evidence that the improved factory conditions would have produced the anticipated results. The utmost skill of a loss adjuster and a willingness by both insurers and insured is then required to reach a satisfactory claim settlement. For instance, in such a case it might be possible to arrange for a payment on account to be made of less than the insured's claim and to leave a final settlement until the factory is restored and the new plant and machinery is in full production. Estimated costings in the claim can then be checked by actual results and any further necessary payment made.

Variations in the amounts of opening stocks and closing stocks as between one financial year end and another affect the amount of gross profit shown in the accounts. Should there have been at the end of the last financial year before damage occurred a change in the basis of valuing stocks from that adopted in previous years there will be in that year's accounts a variation one way or another from the normal profit ratio of the business shown in the preceding year which is not related to trading and similarly it will be at variance with that in the accounts for the following year. It will be necessary therefore to make an appropriate adjustment to the rate of gross profit used in the calculation of a claim to give a true picture of gross profit which would have been earned in the year following the damage.

Businesses using as their raw materials cotton, wool, grain, cocoa beans or metals and dealing in "futures" or making speculative advance purchases can make substantial profits or losses in any particular year resulting from the rise or fall of prices on commodity markets. In handling a claim in respect of a business where this has occurred, if it affects the trading accounts and profits of the year before the damage an adjuster must eliminate the financial results of speculations which have nothing to do with the regular production and turnover of the business. This can be done by means of the other circumstances clause to adjust the rate of gross profit.

433. Contra adjustments where turnover figures are increased under the other circumstances clause

When an increase is made by means of the other circumstances clause to the figure for standard turnover it may be necessary to make also a deduction from the resulting extra gross profit, under the "savings clause". This is to allow for the fact that there would have to be an increase in standing charges in order to achieve the extra turnover but no such expense had been incurred because it was only hypothetical extra turnover.

Consider for example the position if the actual standard turnover is £2 million and by agreement this is adjusted to £2.6 million to allow for an increased volume of sales which it is considered would but for the damage have been achieved during the period of interruption. The turnover realised during that period is the same as in the comparable period before the damage, namely £2 million but because of the adjustment for projected results a shortage of £600,000 is brought into the claim calculation.

To this hypothetical increase of 30 per cent. in sales the rate of gross profit of say 25 per cent. (20 per cent. standing charges and 5 per cent. net profit) is applied, producing a figure of £150,000. But it is not possible that 30 per cent. turnover could be achieved without some expense on standing charges being incurred. So in allowing for the hypothetical £150,000 increase of gross profit a reasonable deduction will have to be made for the fact that no amount has been actually paid for standing charges. Otherwise the insured would receive an amount of *net* profit calculated as 25 per cent. (instead of a normal 5 per cent.) on the fictitious £600,000 turnover.

Under the Loss Determination condition in the Business Income Coverage form the adjustment for probable experience relates solely to Net Income (Net Profit or Loss). As regards operating expenses, only those necessary to resume "operations" with the same quality of service *that existed just before the direct physical loss or damage* are taken into account.

434. Savings clause: can increased charges be offset?

Another aspect to be considered is when some charges are reduced whilst others show an increase during the period of interruption above their normal amount. It may then be suggested by the insured that the extra amount over normal charges which are not new forms of additional expenditure should be offset against the reductions and that the insurers should take credit only for the difference, that is, for the overall reduction. In considering this problem, increases in charges arising from causes other than the damage can be ignored for a reason similar to the exclusion from the savings clause of reductions in such charges. That is, such increases would have arisen irrespective of the damage and would then have automatically produced a corresponding reduction in net profit; therefore they are the insured's loss.

This leaves for consideration increases both in insured charges and in uninsured charges due solely to the damage. Increases in either category of charge rank for payment by the insurers as additional expenditure under clause (b) covering increase in cost of working. So if the amount of such increases were offset against any savings in charges included in the cover on gross profit there would be the possibility of a subsequent oversight and of the insured being compensated twice, that is, by a deduction from the amount due to insurers under the savings clause and also by payment as additional expenditure. This can be avoided if the application of the savings clause is confined to reductions in insured charges whilst increases in charges are dealt with separately in the computation of additional expenditure.

435. Claims Condition: Action by the Insured

Although in practice it is seldom necessary for a loss adjuster to inform or remind insured of their obligations under the conditions which are effective subsequent to damage occurring the need to do so does sometimes arise. Insurances based on the legal doctrine of *uberrima fides*, "the utmost good faith", are underwritten on the understanding that in the event of damage the insured will take all reasonable steps to minimise the resulting loss; in broad terms, they will act as though they were not insured. Whilst this would be expected as the normal action of insured reinforced by self-interest with an eye to successful trading after the expiry of the indemnity period; it does not always happen that way.

So this Claims Condition of the policy sets down in black and white an insured's obligations following the occurrence of damage and reference is made in the following paragraphs to matters arising. The condition is no. 1

of the policy Claims Conditions; for the actual wording see Appendix A. For United States insurances see Appendices Q, R and S.

436. Discontinuation, liquidation or sale of business

The winding up or liquidation or permanent discontinuation of a business before the occurrence of damage is dealt with by the General Condition—Alteration—of the policy, regarding which see paragraph 17. But discontinuance of a business after damage has taken place has to be considered in the light of the Claims Condition—Action by the Insured—of the policy (where it is not catered for by a special clause—see paragraph 387).

Occasions may arise when on account of their policy being arranged on an inadequate basis in respect of either the amount insured, the charges included in the gross profit or the length of the maximum indemnity period covered, the insured find that the cost of the additional expenditure necessary to continue the business above that provided under their policy would be heavier than they may be willing, or perhaps able, to undertake. Cases are on record where liquidation has resulted from the additional expenditure incurred under such circumstances. It may be that reconstruction of a business could be only partially effected within the limit of the maximum indemnity period and the loss of customers during that period would create such a permanent loss of business that it would be uneconomic for an insured to attempt rehabilitation. On the other hand, an elderly insured faced with serious damage to his business is possibly reluctant or perhaps physically incapable of undertaking the hard and worrying task of its restoration. The incentive to retire from business is then very strong.

Legally an insured must in the words of the Claims Condition—Action by the Insured, "with due diligence carry out and permit to be taken, any action which may reasonably be practicable to minimise or check any interruption of or interference with the business or to avoid or diminish the loss". Liquidation of a business would be a failure to take action to minimise the interruption of business, though not necessarily a failure to take action which could be considered "reasonably practicable". It will also be noted that the condition states "*or* to avoid *or* diminish the loss"—not "*and* to avoid, etc.". From this it might be argued that by early liquidation of the business, so saving the amount of most of the standing charges, the insured would be taking the most practicable steps to diminish the loss which would otherwise fall on the insurers.

In practice, in circumstances following damage which incline an insured to discontinue the business, insurers are not given to treating respected policy-holders harshly by a strict interpretation of the clause and prefer to use the scope of "reasonably practicable" to consider a proposition for a compromise settlement. Approximate figures can generally be agreed of the loss of gross profit and wages and the amount of additional expenditure which the insurers would have had to meet if steps were taken to restore the business and alternatively of the saving which would accrue through early liquidation. In such cases in the negotiation of a compromise settlement account will also have to be taken of the amount which the insured might earn, during the balance of the estimated period of interruption within the maximum indemnity period, by investment of the money paid to them.

A more complicated situation may arise where the business is sold following a loss, *i.e.* within the period of interruption. The adjuster must first ascertain whether the insured had indicated their intention before the loss occurred to sell the business and had even perhaps found a potential buyer. In such circumstances the insured's claim must be pursued under the requirements of the Claims Condition until actual sale: thereafter, if ownership of the business is transferred with no other effect on the "would have been" business then the outstanding claim estimate is shown in the balance sheet and is a factor in the purchase of the business being part of future projected turnover. Insurers may be prepared in such circumstances (refer also the Alteration General Condition) to continue to deal with the claim despite the change of ownership provided that the Claims Condition will continue to be complied with and their interests safeguarded.

However, should the insured have decided after the loss to sell the business the adjuster must discover whether the sale is being made as a result of the loss or whether the business would probably have been sold because of the insured's reorganisation plans, etc. Whatever the reasons for the sale the adjuster must ensure that the requirements of the Claims Condition are met and that an equitable settlement is obtained.

437. Time limit for statement of claim

A point in the Claims Condition of special importance to accountants is the stipulation that a statement of claim must be furnished within 30 days after the expiry of the indemnity period or within such further time as the insurers may allow. As the provision of the statement of claim generally devolves upon the insured's accountants this imposes upon the latter a definite responsibility to act promptly, within the prescribed time limit, in the interests of their client.

It is particularly important in this connection to remember that the indemnity period is not necessarily the number of months shown in the definition of maximum indemnity period. It is the actual period of interruption within a limit of the number of months stated in that definition. (See paragraph 245(a).) This means that the time allowed for presentation of the detailed statement of claim is not 30 days after the end of the number of months stated as the maximum indemnity period, calculated from the date of the damage, but 30 days from the date, within that maximum, when the results of the business ceased to be affected by the damage. There may be many months difference between the two.

The duty placed on insured to furnish written details of the claim within 30 days of the end of the period of interruption is regarded by insurers as necessary and reasonable. But it is recognised that this period will not always be long enough and in the Claims Condition provision is made for an extension of the time allowed for presentation of the claim statement, at the option of the insurers, and this will be granted when there are reasonable grounds for it though it cannot be assumed that it applies automatically.

The above limit under United Kingdom policies seems generous to insured by comparison with its counterpart in United States insurances. In these the Loss Condition—Duties in the Event of Loss—imposes on an insured the obligation of providing a signed, sworn statement of loss, containing the information insurers request to investigate the claim, within 60 days after their request.

438. Information to be furnished for claim

The Claims Condition—Action by the Insured—gives a comprehensive list of the kind of information and documents the insured may be required to produce. From this part of the condition arises the value of the professional accountants clause (see paragraph 378) by which the insurers agree to accept figures produced by the insured's professional accountants as prima facie evidence without the insured's books of accounts being made open to the loss adjuster's examination.

The stipulation that information which may be required must be produced at the insured's expense is met in respect of accountants' charges by the undertaking under the Professional Accountants clause for the insurer to pay those charges provided that the sum insured on gross profit is adequate for their inclusion.

From the above Claims Condition it is clear that if insured employ a loss assessor to act on their behalf his charges must be paid for by them and cannot be included in the claim under the policy. It might also be mentioned here that insurers will not agree to the addition of an item on a policy to pay for claims assessors' charges. They regard their own appointment of a qualified loss adjuster as adequate, providing independent advice and help to the insured as well as themselves with a view to a speedy rehabilitation of the business and amicable conclusion of the claim.

The importance of the above Claims Condition is emphasised by the provision in it for a statutory declaration, if demanded by the insurers, and by the final clause which makes compliance with the condition a prerequisite for payment of a claim even to the extent that in the event of non-compliance in any respect any payment on account of the claim already made shall be refunded by the insured.

439. Claims Condition: Fraud

The next condition is the same as the so-called fraud condition in fire policies and reads:

"If a claim is fraudulent in any respect or if fraudulent means are used by the Insured or by anyone acting on his behalf to obtain any benefit under this policy or if any loss destruction or damage to property used by the Insured at the Premises for the purpose of the Business is caused by the wilful act or with the connivance of the Insured all benefit under this policy shall be forfeited".

Its meaning is quite clear, though it might be mentioned that the established position with fire insurances is that an overstatement in a claim due to a mistake does not of itself constitute fraud (*Park* v. *Phoenix Assurance Co.* (1859) 19 U.C.R. 110 (Canada)) although if it is so greatly in excess as to make it clear that it could not be regarded as an honest estimate then it could be taken as evidence of fraud (*Worsley* v. *Wood* (1796) 6 Term Rep. 710). Presumably the same position would apply in regard to a claim under a business interruption policy.

It might be noted that the scope of the condition extends beyond acts of the insured and includes those of anyone acting in their behalf. Should there be a commission of fraud all benefit under the policy is forfeited and the insured cannot withdraw a falsified claim and submit an honest one.

The United States Commercial Property Conditions contain a similar condition in respect of Concealment Misrepresentation or Fraud.

440. Claims Condition: Contribution

This condition states that the insurer's liability under the policy shall be limited to an ascertained proportion if the insured has other policies covering the whole or a part of the same loss. Because the policy is a contract of indemnity an insured could not by insuring with more than one insurer legally recover in total more than the amount of the loss actually sustained but, nevertheless, could select which of the insurers should meet the claim. The contribution condition is inserted as in all material damage policies to prevent an insured selecting which insurer or insurers shall meet the claim and to provide for an equitable sharing of any loss between all the insurers according to their respective insurances.

To enable insurers to act on this condition, if necessary, it is a duty of the loss adjuster to ascertain details of all insurances applicable to the loss.

The condition of similar purposes on United States policies is called the Other Insurance condition and simply states that the liability under the policy shall not exceed that proportion of any loss which the limit of insurance bears to all the limits of insurance covering in any manner the loss insured against by the policy.

441. Claims Condition: Subrogation

By virtue of the legal doctrine of subrogation an insurer can recover from an insured the value of any benefit relating to the latter's loss paid under the insurance. This condition states the position where the insured has a right of recovery from a third party which might for instance arise on grounds of negligence or nuisance as in the case of *S.C.M. (United Kingdom) Ltd.* v. *W.J. Whittal & Son Ltd.* [1970] 2 All E.R. 417 in which a business interruption loss was sustained due to interruption of production caused by a Whittall's workman damaging an electric cable to S.C.M.'s factory and cutting the electricity supply for seven hours.

It is interesting to note in relation to the discussion on proximate cause in paragraph 44 that in this case Mr. Justice Thesiger held that the action of the contractor's workman was the proximate cause of the business interruption loss.

A business interruption policy is a contract of indemnity and any means open to an insured of diminishing a loss must be brought into account. For this purpose an insurer is subrogated to the rights of the insured deriving from third parties whether under contract, remedy for tort or any other benefit, legal or equitable. The insurer can insist upon an insured taking any necessary steps against a third party and this is provided for in the subrogation condition but according to the decision in *Andrews* v. *Patriotic* (1886) 18 L.R.Ir. 355 only after the insurer has paid the loss. The condition goes further than this by stipulating in its final sentence "before or after any payment is made by the insurer".

As many fires are caused by the negligence of outside contractors' workmen, often by the careless use of blow torches, claims by insurers against such contractors under their rights of subrogation are frequent. But as the contractor almost invariably has a third party liability insurance of adequate amount to meet the claim—and such claims sometimes run into six or seven figures—which is then settled between the respective insurers, such cases rarely come before the courts.

For information regarding a Subrogation Waiver clause for companies standing in the relationship of parent and subsidiary companies within a group, see paragraph 385.

Subrogation clauses appear on United States and Canadian property damage policies in slightly differing terms but with the same intent. On the United States standard Commercial Property Conditions it is called the Transfer of Rights of Recovery Against Others to Us condition (see Appendix S, paragraph 465). As with the subrogation condition in Canadian forms it includes both rights and waiver in a composite condition.

442. Claims Condition: Arbitration

The terms of this condition are similar to those in the corresponding condition on fire policies. The wording in use up to 1957 precluded the insured from resorting to a court of law on any difference—either of liability or of amount—arising out of the policy until the matter had first been submitted to arbitration. In that year in deference to the views of the Law Reform Committee—Fifth Report, Comnd. 62—insurers agreed (in respect of insurances in the United Kingdom) to allow an insured wishing to do so to have questions of liability, as distinct from those of amount, determined by the courts.

The following year a new arbitration condition was adopted by insurers providing that if any difference shall arise as to the amount to be paid (liability being otherwise admitted) such difference shall be referred to an arbitrator. Under this revised condition (see specimen policy in Appendix A) where any difference about the amount to be paid is referred to arbitration the making of an award is to be a condition precedent to any right of action against the insurer.

The statutory provisions referred to in the condition are those of the Arbitration Act 1950 as amended by the Arbitration Act 1979. These are of particular relevance if, for instance, agreement cannot be reached on the appointment by the parties of a single arbitrator. In such a case each party has to appoint an arbitrator and this necessitates the appointment also of an umpire. This procedure considerably increases the costs which is contrary to one main object of the arbitration condition namely to minimise the expenses of a settlement.

The precise wording of the condition should be noted in that it applies solely to the amount to be paid under a claim. Therefore, if insurers assert that the insurance is void or if they contend that they have no liability for the particular claim on other grounds they cannot invoke the condition and the insured can proceed to legal action immediately. Further, when an award is made by an arbitrator an insured dissatisfied with its amount cannot then start an action in the courts although legal steps could be taken if the insurers refused to pay the amount of the award.

443. Loss Condition: Appraisal (United States)

The United States "arbitration" condition is found not in the Commercial Property Conditions but in the Loss Conditions on the Business Income Coverage form (see Appendix S, paragraph 465). This appraisal condition differs considerably from the arbitration condition in United Kingdom policies (paragraph 447) and is longer and more detailed, referring to conditions for the appointment and payment of appraisers and an umpire. Like a United Kingdom business interruption arbitration condition its application is confined to the amount of loss and does not include any question of liability but an insured may sue directly on the policy after an appraisal award as to amount has been made.

444. Practical application of the claims formula

In conclusion of the foregoing information in this chapter on the settlement of claims the statement in paragraph 5 may be repeated that in practice a rigid application of the specification formula may not be insisted upon when the interference with a business is of relatively small degree or of very short duration. In such circumstances a quicker and less exacting method of calculating an insured's loss may be acceptable to both parties provided that a claim for such a short period can be sustained at all. But this in no way detracts from the value of the formula which is the normal method for settling claims of any consequence.

445. Loss payment

The new Business Income Coverage form carries a Loss Payment condition by which insurers undertake to pay for covered loss within 30 days after they have received the sworn statement of loss subject to the insured having complied with all the terms of the coverage and insurers having reached agreement with insured on the amount of loss, or an appraisal award has been made. No such time limit appears in a United Kingdom policy, although a time limit of 30 days is imposed on the insured to present their claim after the expiry of the indemnity period (Claims Condition—Action by the Insured).

If for whatever reason insurers in the United Kingdom delay payment of the claim the insured may request the additional payment of the "interest" lost on the delayed payment. This can create a situation of acute embarrassment to insurers and loss adjusters. Payment of claims is almost invariably made very promptly after agreement of the amounts.

446. Companies with multinational operations

This chapter of specific interest to claims adjusters cannot be concluded without reference to what may be for some of them at some time their biggest headache. In paragraph 382 mention is made of the aggravation of normal problems and difficulties in the realm of business interruption insurance which attach to industrial organisations operating on a global scale. It can easily be appreciated what involved accountancy work and difficult negotiations must result from a major interruption of business at one or other unit in an insured's international network of operations.

The best advice to loss adjusters for action when confronted with a case of this nature if they do not have professional accountants on their staff is to enlist help by engaging without delay the services of a top-ranking firm of chartered accountants with experience and expertise in the financial and accountancy practice of industrial giants.

In fact the largest firms of loss adjusters are now truly international in their own right with offices and subsidiary or associated companies in most parts of the world. Local expertise is thus available to be drawn on, which is essential given the complicated and sometimes delicate nature of the claims negotiations.

Where worldwide business interruption programmes are set up with centrally appointed loss adjusters a "claims co-operation" condition can be added to any necessary reinsurance arrangements made for particular territories whereby the "local" adjusters will be "assisted" by the central adjusters.

It is important to remember that whereas interdependency is a factor to be catered for in any international business interruption insurance arrangement, so, in the event of losses, interassistance can be of benefit with a factory, say, in Spain providing products which a damaged factory (owned by the same group) in, say, Germany is unable to manufacture. However, because of local legislation, fiscal difficulties, etc., the switching of production and supply may not be as easy as it appears on paper. This is but one of the problems confronting the international business interruption insurance underwriter whether he be United Kingdom or United States based.

APPENDICES

NOTE: *The United Kingdom wordings are those recommended by the A.B.I., except where the word "Example" is shown when the wording is based upon that of an individual United Kingdom insurer. The United States wordings are those recommended by the I.S.O.*

447.—APPENDIX A

STANDARD UNITED KINGDOM FIRE POLICY FORM (BUSINESS INTERRUPTION)

The Insurer agrees (subject to the terms, definitions, exclusions and conditions of this policy) that if after payment of the first premium any building or other property used by the Insured at the Premises for the purpose of the Business be lost destroyed or damaged by

1. FIRE but excluding loss destruction or damage caused by
    (a) explosion resulting from fire
    (b) earthquake or subterranean fire
    (c) (i) its own spontaneous fermentation or heating, or
        (ii) its undergoing any heating process or any process involving the application of heat

2. LIGHTNING

3. EXPLOSION
    (a) of boilers used for domestic purposes only
    (b) of any other boilers or economisers on the Premises
    (c) of gas used for domestic purposes only

    but excluding loss destruction or damage caused by earthquake or subterranean fire

during the period of insurance (or any subsequent period for which the Insurer accepts a renewal premium) and in consequence the business carried on by the Insured at the Premises be interrupted or interfered with then the Insurer will pay to the Insured in respect of each item in the Schedule the amount of loss resulting from such interruption or interference provided that

1. at the time of the happening of the loss destruction or damage there shall be in force an insurance covering the interest of the Insured in the property at the Premises against such loss destruction or damage and that
    (i) payment shall have been made or liability admitted therefor, or

(ii) payment would have been made or liability admitted therefor but for the operation of a proviso in such insurance excluding liability for losses below a specified amount

2. the liability of the Insurer under this policy shall not exceed
    (i) in the whole the total sum insured or in respect of any item its sum insured at the time of the loss destruction or damage
    (ii) the sum insured remaining after deduction for any other interruption or interference consequent upon loss destruction or damage occurring during the same period of insurance, unless the Insurer shall have agreed to reinstate any such sum insured

This policy incorporates the Schedule, Specification and Endorsements which shall be read together as one contract. Words and expressions to which specific meaning is given in any part of this policy shall have the same meaning wherever they appear.

Signed on behalf of the Insurer.

DEFINITION

The words "CONSEQUENTIAL LOSS", in capital letters, shall mean loss resulting from interruption of or interference with the Business carried on by the Insured at the Premises in consequence of loss or destruction of or damage to property used by the Insured at the Premises for the purpose of the Business

GENERAL EXCLUSIONS

This policy does not cover

1. CONSEQUENTIAL LOSS occasioned by riot civil commotion war invasion act of foreign enemy hostilities (whether war be declared or not) civil war rebellion revolution insurrection or military or usurped power.

2. loss destruction or damage occasioned by or happening through or occasioning loss or destruction of or damage to any property whatsoever or any loss or expense whatsoever resulting or arising therefrom or any consequential loss directly or indirectly caused by or contributed to by or arising from
    (a) ionising radiations or contamination by radioactivity from any nuclear fuel or from any nuclear waste from the combustion of nuclear fuel
    (b) the radioactive toxic explosive or other hazardous properties of any explosive nuclear assembly or nuclear component thereof

3. CONSEQUENTIAL LOSS in Northern Ireland occasioned by or happening through
   (a) civil commotion
   (b) any unlawful wanton or malicious act committed maliciously by a person or persons acting on behalf of or in connection with any unlawful association

   For the purpose of this exclusion

   "unlawful association" means any organisation which is engaged in terrorism and includes an organisation which at any relevant time is a proscribed organisation within the meaning of the Northern Ireland (Emergency Provisions) Act 1973

   "terrorism" means the use of violence for political ends and includes any use of violence for the purpose of putting the public or any section of the public in fear

   In any action suit or other proceedings where the Insurer alleges that by reason of the provisions of this exclusion any CONSEQUENTIAL LOSS is not covered by this policy the burden of proving that such CONSEQUENTIAL LOSS is covered shall be upon the Insured.

4. loss resulting from pollution or contamination but this shall not exclude loss resulting from destruction of or damage to property used by the Insured at the Premises for the purpose of the Business, not otherwise excluded, caused by

   (a) pollution or contamination at the Premises which itself results from a peril hereby insured against
   (b) any peril hereby insured against which itself results from pollution or contamination.

GENERAL CONDITIONS

1. **Policy Voidable**
   This policy shall be voidable in the event of misrepresentation misdescription or non-disclosure in any material particular.

2. **Alteration**
   This policy shall be avoided if after commencement of this insurance
   (a) the Business be wound up or carried on by a liquidator or receiver or permanently discontinued or
   (b) the interest of the Insured ceases other than by death or
   (c) any alteration be made either in the Business or in the Premises or property therein whereby the risk of loss destruction or damage is increased unless admitted by the Insurer in writing.

CLAIMS CONDITIONS

1. **Action by the Insured**
   (a) In the event of any loss destruction or damage in consequence of which a claim is or may be made under this policy the Insured shall
       — notify the Insurer immediately
       — with due diligence carry out and permit to be taken any action which may reasonably be practicable to minimise or check any interruption of or interference with the Business or to avoid or diminish the loss.
   (b) In the event of a claim being made under this policy the Insured at his own expense shall
       — not later that 30 days after the expiry of the Indemnity Period or within such further time as the Insurer may allow, deliver to the Insurer in writing particulars of his claim together with details of all other insurances covering property used by the Insured at the Premises for the purpose of the Business or any part of it or any resulting consequential loss
       — deliver to the Insurer such books of account and other business books vouchers invoices balance sheets and other documents proofs information explanation and other evidence as may reasonably be required by the Insurer for the purpose of investigating or verifying the claim together with, if demanded, a statutory declaration of the truth of the claim and of any matters connected with it.
   (c) If the terms of this condition have not been complied with
       — no claim under this policy shall be payable and
       — any payment on account of the claim already made shall be repaid to the Insurer forthwith.

2. **Fraud**
   If a claim is fradulent in any respect or if fraudulent means are used by the Insured or by anyone acting on his behalf to obtain any benefit under this policy or if any loss destruction or damage to property used by the Insured at the Premises for the purpose of the Business is caused by the wilful act or with the connivance of the Insured all benefit under this policy shall be forfeited.

3. **Contribution**
   If at the time of any loss destruction or damage resulting in a loss under this policy there be any other insurance effected by or on behalf of the Insured covering such loss or any part of it the liability of the Insurer hereunder shall be limited to its rateable proportion of such loss.

4. **Subrogation**
   Any claimant under this policy shall at the request and expense of the Insurer take and permit to be taken all necessary steps for enforcing rights against any other party in the name of the Insured before or after any payment is made by the Insurer.

5. **Arbitration**
   If any difference arises as to the amount to be paid under this policy (liability being otherwise admitted) such difference shall be referred to an arbitrator to be appointed by the parties in accordance with statutory provisions. Where any difference is by this condition to be referred to arbitration the making of an award shall be a condition precedent to any right of action against the Insurer.

Policy No

THE SCHEDULE

THE INSURER	
THE INSURED	
THE BUSINESS	
THE PREMISES	
ITEMS	As detailed in the attached Specification
TOTAL SPECIFICATION ESTIMATED GROSS PROFIT/ SUM INSURED	£
THE ESTIMATED GROSS PROFIT/SUM INSURED BY THIS POLICY	£ being % of the total Specification sum insured
INSURER'S LIABILITY	The Insurer's liability under this policy is limited to % of the amount otherwise payable under the provisions of the Specification
PERIOD OF INSURANCE	From to
RENEWAL DATE	
FIRST PREMIUM	£
ANNUAL PREMIUM	£
AGENCY	

Note:
For insurances solely on a Sum Insured basis references to Estimated Gross Profit (refer Declaration—Linked—paragraph 450, Appendix D) should be deleted.

448.—APPENDIX B

STANDARD UNITED KINGDOM "ALL RISKS" POLICY FORM
(BUSINESS INTERRUPTION)

The Insurer agrees (subject to the terms, definitions, exclusions and conditions of this policy) that if after payment of the first premium any building or other property used by the Insured at the Premises for the purpose of the Business be accidentally lost destroyed or damaged during the period of insurance (or any subsequent period for which the Insurer accepts a renewal premium) and in consequence the business carried on by the Insured at the Premises be interrupted or interfered with then the Insurer will pay to the Insured in respect of each item in the Schedule the amount of loss resulting from such interruption or interference provided that

1. at the time of the happening of the loss destruction or damage there shall be in force an insurance covering the interest of the Insured in the property at the Premises against such loss destruction or damage and that
   (i) payment shall have been made or liability admitted therefore, or
   (ii) payment would have been made or liability admitted therefor but for the operation of a proviso in such insurance excluding liability for losses below a specified amount

2. the liability of the Insurer under this policy shall not exceed
   (i) in the whole the total sum insured or in respect of any item its sum insured or any other limit of liability stated in the Schedule at the time of the loss destruction or damage
   (ii) the sum insured (or limit) remaining after deduction for any other interruption or interference consequent upon loss destruction or damage occurring during the same period of insurance, unless the Insurer shall have agreed to reinstate any such sum insured (or limit).

This policy incorporates the Schedule, Specification and Endorsements which shall be read together as one contract. Words and expressions to which specific meaning is given in any part of this policy shall have the same meaning wherever they appear.

Signed on behalf of the Insurer

DEFINITIONS

1. The words "CONSEQUENTIAL LOSS", in capital letters, shall mean loss resulting from interruption of or interference with the Business carried on by the Insured at the Premises in consequence of accidental loss or destruction of or damage to property used by the Insured at the Premises for the purpose of the Business.

2. The words "Defined Peril" shall mean fire, lightning, explosion, aircraft or other aerial devices or articles dropped therefrom, riot, civil commotion, strikers, locked-out workers, persons taking part in labour disturbances, mali-

cious persons, earthquake, storm, flood, escape of water from any tank apparatus or pipe or impact by any road vehicle or animal.

EXCLUSIONS

This policy does not cover

1. CONSEQUENTIAL LOSS caused by or consisting of
   1.1 inherent vice, latent defect, gradual deterioration, wear and tear, frost, change in water table level, its own faulty or defective design or materials
   1.2 faulty or defective workmanship, operational error or omission, on the part of the Insured or any of his employees
   1.3 the bursting of any vessel machine or apparatus (not being a boiler or economiser on the Premises or a boiler used for domestic purposes only) in which internal pressure is due to steam only and belonging to or under the control of the Insured
   1.4 pressure waves caused by aircraft or other aerial devices travelling at sonic or supersonic speeds
   but this shall not exclude subsequent CONSEQUENTIAL LOSS which itself results from a cause not otherwise excluded

2. CONSEQUENTIAL LOSS
   2.1 caused by or consisting of corrosion, rust, wet or dry rot, shrinkage, evaporation, loss of weight, dampness, dryness, marring, scratching, vermin or insects
   2.2 caused by or consisting of change in temperature colour flavour texture or finish
   2.3 arising directly from theft or attempted theft
   2.4 consisting of joint leakage, failure of welds, cracking, fracturing, collapse or overheating of boilers, economisers, superheaters, pressure vessels or any range of steam and feed piping in connection therewith
   2.5 consisting or mechanical or electrical breakdown or derangement in respect of the particular machine apparatus or equipment in which such breakdown or derangement originates
   2.6 caused by the deliberate act of a supply undertaking in withholding the supply of water, gas, electricity, fuel or telecommunications services

   but this shall not exclude
   (a) such CONSEQUENTIAL LOSS not otherwise excluded which itself results from a Defined Peril or from any other accidental loss destruction or damage
   (b) subsequent CONSEQUENTIAL LOSS which itself results from a cause not otherwise excluded

3. loss resulting from pollution or contamination but this shall not exclude loss resulting from destruction of or damage to property used by the Insured at the Premises for the purpose of the Business, not otherwise excluded, caused by
   (a) pollution or contamination at the Premises which itself results from a Defined Peril
   (b) a Defined Peril which itself results from pollution or contamination

APPENDIX B

4. CONSEQUENTIAL LOSS caused by or consisting of
   4.1 subsidence ground heave or landslip unless resulting from fire explosion earthquake or the escape of water from any tank apparatus or pipe
   4.2 normal settlement or bedding down of new structures
   4.3 acts of fraud or dishonesty
   CONSEQUENTIAL LOSS arising directly or indirectly from
   4.4 disappearance, unexplained or inventory shortage, misfiling or misplacing of information
   4.5 erasure or distortion of information on computer systems or other records:
      (a) whilst mounted in or on any machine or data processing apparatus, or
      (b) due to the presence of a magnetic flux,
   unless caused by accidental loss destruction or damage not otherwise excluded, in respect of the machine or apparatus in which the records are mounted, used by the Insured at the Premises for the purpose of the Business

5. loss resulting from destruction of or damage to a building or structure used by the Insured at the Premises caused by its own collapse or cracking unless resulting from a Defined Peril in so far as it is not otherwise excluded

6. CONSEQUENTIAL LOSS in respect of movable property in the open, fences and gates caused by wind rain hail sleet snow flood or dust

7. CONSEQUENTIAL LOSS
   7.1 caused by fire resulting from its undergoing any heating process involving the application of heat
   7.2 (other than by fire or explosion) resulting from its undergoing any process of production packing treatment testing commissioning servicing or repair

8. CONSEQUENTIAL LOSS
   8.1 caused by freezing
   8.2 caused by escape of water from any tank apparatus or pipe
   8.3 caused (other than by fire or explosion) by malicious persons not acting on behalf of or in connection with any political organisation
   in respect of any building which is empty or not in use

9. CONSEQUENTIAL LOSS in respect of
   9.1 fixed glass
   9.2 glass (other than fixed glass) china earthenware marble or other fragile or brittle objects
   9.3 computers or data processing equipment
   9.4 vehicles licensed for road use (including accessories thereon) caravans trailers railway locomotives rolling stock watercraft or aircraft
   9.5 property or structures in course of construction or erection and materials or supplies in connection with all such property in course of construction or erection
   9.6 land roads pavements piers jetties bridge culverts or excavations
   9.7 livestock growing crops or trees
   other than in respect of such CONSEQUENTIAL LOSS caused by a Defined Peril in so far as it is not otherwise excluded

10. CONSEQUENTIAL LOSS occasioned by war invasion act of foreign enemy hostilities (whether war be declared or not) civil war rebellion revolution insur-

STANDARD UNITED KINGDOM "ALL RISKS" POLICY FORM   448

rection military or usurped power nationalisation confiscation requisition seizure or destruction by the government or any public authority

11. loss destruction or damage occasioned by or happening through or occasioning loss or destruction of or damage to any property whatsoever or any loss or expense whatsoever resulting or arising therefrom or any consequential loss directly or indirectly caused by or contributed to by or arising from
    (a) ionising radiations or contamination by radioactivity from any nuclear fuel or from any nuclear waste from the combustion of nuclear fuel
    (b) the radioactive toxic explosive or other hazardous properties of any explosive nuclear assembly or nuclear component thereof

12. CONSEQUENTIAL LOSS in Northern Ireland occasioned by or happening through
    (a) riot civil commotion and (except in respect of CONSEQUENTIAL LOSS by fire or explosion) strikers locked-out workers or persons taking part in labour disturbances or malicious persons
    (b) any unlawful wanton or malicious act committed maliciously by a person or persons acting on behalf of or in connection with any unlawful association

    For the purpose of this exclusion

    "unlawful association" means any organisation which is engaged in terrorism and includes an organisation which at any relevant time is a proscribed organisation within the meaning of the Northern Ireland (Emergency Provisions) Act 1973

    "terrorism" means the use of violence for political ends and includes any use of violence for the purpose of putting the public or any section of the public in fear

    In any action suit or other proceedings where the Insurer alleges that by reason of the provisions of this exclusion any CONSEQUENTIAL LOSS is not covered by this policy the burden of proving that such CONSEQUENTIAL LOSS is covered shall be upon the Insured.

DEDUCTIBLES

This policy does not cover the amounts of the deductibles stated in the Schedule in respect of each and every loss as ascertained after the application of all other terms and conditions of the policy.

GENERAL CONDITIONS

1. **Policy Voidable**
   This policy shall be voidable in the event of misrepresentation misdescription or non-disclosure in any material particular.

448   APPENDIX B

2. **Alteration**
   This policy shall be avoided if after the commencement of this insurance
   (a) the Business be wound up or carried on by a liquidator or receiver or permanently discontinued or
   (b) the interest of the Insured ceases other than by death or
   (c) any alteration be made either in the Business or in the Premises or property therein whereby the risk of loss destruction or damage is increased
   unless admitted by the Insurer in writing.

CLAIMS CONDITIONS

1. **Action by the Insured**
   (a) In the event of any loss destruction or damage in consequence of which a claim is or may be made under this policy the Insured shall
      — notify the Insurer immediately
      — deliver to the Insurer at the Insured's expense within seven days of its happening full details of loss destruction or damage caused by riot civil commotion strikers locked-out workers persons taking part in labour disturbances or malicious persons
      — with due diligence carry out and permit to be taken any action which may reasonably be practicable to minimise or check any interruption of or interference with the Business or to avoid or diminish the loss.
   (b) In the event of a claim being made under this policy the Insured at his own expense shall
      — not later than 30 days after the expiry of the Indemnity Period or within such further time as the Insurer may allow, deliver to the Insurer in writing particulars of his claim together with details of all other insurances covering property used by the Insured at the Premises for the purpose of the Business or any part of it or any resulting consequential loss
      — deliver to the Insurer such books of account and other business books vouchers invoices balance sheets and other documents proofs information explanation and other evidence as may reasonably be required by the Insurer for the purpose of investigating or verifying the claim together with, if demanded, a statutory declaration of the truth of the claim and of any matters connected with it.
   (c) If the terms of this condition have not been complied with
      — no claim under this policy shall be payable and
      — any payment on account of the claim already made shall be repaid to the Insurer forthwith.

2. **Fraud**
   If a claim is fraudulent in any respect or if fraudulent means are used by the Insured or by anyone acting on his behalf to obtain any benefit under this policy or if any loss destruction or damage to property used by the Insured at the Premises for the purpose of the Business is caused by the wilful act or with the connivance of the Insured all benefit under the policy shall be forfeited.

3. **Contribution**
   If at the time of any loss destruction or damage resulting in a loss under this policy there be any other insurance effected by or on behalf of the Insured

covering such loss or any part of it the liability of the Insurer hereunder shall be limited to its rateable proportion of such loss.

4. **Subrogation**
Any claimant under this policy shall at the request and expense of the Insurer take and permit to be taken all necessary steps for enforcing rights against any other party in the name of the Insured before or after any payment is made by the Insurer.

5. **Arbritation**
If any difference arises as to the amount to be paid under this policy (liability being otherwise admitted) such difference shall be referred to an arbitrator to be appointed by the parties in accordance with statutory provisions. Where any difference is by this condition to be referred to arbitration the making of an award shall be a condition precedent to any right of action against the Insurer.

Policy No

THE SCHEDULE

THE INSURER	
THE INSURED	
THE BUSINESS	
THE PREMISES	
ITEMS	As detailed in the attached Specification
TOTAL SPECIFICATION ESTIMATED GROSS PROFIT/ SUM INSURED	£
	LIMIT OF
LIMIT OF LIABILITY AND DEDUCTIBLE	LIABILITY DEDUCTIBLE

In respect of:

(i) CONSEQUENTIAL LOSS by fire lightning explosion aircraft or other aerial devices or articles dropped therefrom riot civil commotion strikers locked-out workers persons taking part in labour disturbances malicious persons or earthquake

the sum insured or as detailed in the Specification   the first £

APPENDIX B

(ii) CONSEQUENTIAL LOSS by storm flood escape of water from any tank apparatus or pipe or impact by any road vehicle or animal   £

(iii) Other insured CONSEQUENTIAL LOSS   £

} the first £

THE ESTIMATED GROSS PROFIT/SUM INSURED BY THIS POLICY   £ being   % of the total Specification estimated gross profit/sum insured

INSURER'S LIABILITY   The Insurer's liability under this policy is limited to   % of the amount otherwise payable under the provisions of the Specification and this Schedule

PERIOD OF INSURANCE   From
to

RENEWAL DATE

FIRST PREMIUM   £

ANNUAL PREMIUM   £

AGENCY

Note: For insurances solely on a Sum insured basis references to Estimated Gross Profit (refer Declaration—Linked—paragraph 450, Appendix D) should be deleted.

449.—APPENDIX C

UNITED KINGDOM BUSINESS INTERRUPTION ("DIFFERENCE" BASIS) SPECIFICATION
"GROSS PROFIT" WORDING—SUM INSURED BASIS

Item No.		Sum Insured
1	On Gross Profit	£ _____
	Total Sum Insured	£ _____

The insurance under Item No. 1 is limited to loss of Gross Profit due to **(a) Reduction in Turnover and (b) Increase in Cost of Working** and the amount payable as indemnity thereunder shall be:—

(a) **in respect of Reduction in Turnover:** the sum produced by applying the Rate of Gross Profit to the amount by which the Turnover during the Indemnity Period shall fall short of the Standard Turnover in consequence of the Incident

(b) **in respect of Increase in Cost of Working:** the additional expenditure (subject to the provisions of the Uninsured Standing Charges Clause) necessarily and reasonably incurred for the sole purpose of avoiding or diminishing the reduction in Turnover which but for that expenditure would have taken place during the Indemnity Period in consequence of the Incident, but not exceeding the sum produced by applying the Rate of Gross Profit to the amount of the reduction thereby avoided

less any sum saved during the Indemnity Period in respect of such of the charges and expenses of the Business payable out of Gross Profit as may cease or be reduced in consequence of the Incident

provided that if the sum insured by this item be less than the sum produced by applying the Rate of Gross Profit to the Annual Turnover (or to a proportionately increased multiple thereof where the Maximum Indemnity Period exceeds twelve months) the amount payable shall be proportionately reduced.

DEFINITIONS

Notes:
1. To the extent that the Insured is accountable to the tax authorities for Value Added Tax, all terms in this policy shall be exclusive of such tax.
2. For the purpose of these definitions, any adjustment implemented in current cost accounting shall be disregarded.

Incident: Loss or destruction of or damage to property used by the Insured at the Premises for the purpose of the Business.

Indemnity Period: The period beginning with the occurrence of the Incident and ending not later than the Maximum Indemnity Period thereafter during which the results of the Business shall be affected in consequence thereof.

Maximum Indemnity Period: months.

Turnover: The money paid or payable to the Insured for goods sold and delivered and for services rendered in course of the Business at the Premises.

Gross Profit: The amount by which—
  (i) the sum of the amount of the Turnover and the amounts of the closing stock and work in progress shall exceed
  (ii) the sum of the amounts of the opening stock and work in progress and the amount of the Uninsured Worked Expenses.

Note: The amounts of the opening and closing stocks and work in progress shall be arrived at in accordance with the Insured's normal accountancy methods, due provision being made for depreciation.

Uninsured Working Expenses:

(*Appropriate list to be inserted*)

Note: The words and expressions used in this definition (other than wages) shall have the meaning usually attached to them in the books and accounts of the Insured.

Rate of Gross Profit:—The Rate of Gross Profit earned on the Turnover during the financial year immediately before the date of the Incident

Annual Turnover:—The Turnover during the twelve months immediately before the date of the Incident

Standard Turnover:—The Turnover during that period in the twelve months immediately before the date of the Incident which corresponds with the Indemnity Period

to which such adjustments shall be made as may be necessary to provide for the trend of the Business and for variations in or other circumstances affecting the Business either before or after the Incident which would have affected the Business had the Incident not occurred, so that the figures thus adjusted shall represent as nearly as may be reasonably practicable the results which but for the Incident would have been obtained during the relative period after the Incident.

Alternative Trading Clause: If during the Indemnity Period goods shall be sold or services shall be rendered elsewhere than at the Premises for the benefit of the Business either by the Insured or by others on his behalf the money paid or payable in respect of such sales or services shall be brought into account in arriving at the Turnover during the Indemnity Period.

Uninsured Standing Charges Clause: If any standing charges of the Business be not insured by this policy (having been deducted in arriving at the Gross Profit as defined herein) then in computing the amount recoverable hereunder as Increase in Cost of Working, that proportion only of any additional expenditure shall be brought into account which the Gross Profit bears to the sum of the Gross Profit and the uninsured standing charges.

Premium Adjustment Clause: The premium paid hereon may be adjusted on receipt by the Insurer of a declaration of Gross Profit earned during the financial year most nearly concurrent with the period of insurance, as reported by the Insured's Auditors.

If any Incident shall have occurred giving rise to a claim for loss of Gross Profit the above mentioned declaration shall be increased by the Insurer for the purpose of premium adjustment by the amount by which the Gross Profit was reduced during the financial year solely in consequence of the Incident.

If either declaration (adjusted as provided for above and proportionately increased where the Maximum Indemnity Period exceeds 12 months) is less than the sum insured on Gross Profit for the relative period of insurance the Insurer will allow a pro rata return of premium not exceeding 50 per cent. of the premium paid.

Professional Accountants Clause: Any particulars or details contained in the insured's books of account or other business books or documents which may be required by the Insurer under Claims Condition 1 of this policy for the purpose of investigating or verifying any claim hereunder may be produced by professional accountants if at the time they are regularly acting as such for the Insured and their report shall be prima facie evidence of the particulars and details to which such report relates.

The Insurer will pay to the Insured the reasonable charges payable by the Insured to their professional accountants for producing such particulars or details or any other proofs, information or evidence as may be required by the Insurer under the terms of Claims Condition 1 of this policy and reporting that such particulars or details are in accordance with the Insured's books of accounts or other business books or documents

provided that the sum of the amount payable under this clause and the amount otherwise payable under the policy shall in no case exceed the liability of the Insurer as stated.

Note: Where the Uninsured Working Expenses are recognised variable charges, the Uninsured Standing Charges Clause and the reference hereto under paragraph (b) of Item No. 1 should be deleted.

450.—APPENDIX D

UNITED KINGDOM
BUSINESS INTERRUPTION ("DIFFERENCE" BASIS)
SPECIFICATION
"GROSS PROFIT" WORDING—DECLARATION—LINKED BASIS

Item No.		Estimated Gross Profit
1	On Gross Profit	£

The insurance under Item No. 1 is limited to loss of Gross Profit due to **(a) Reduction in Turnover and (b) Increase in Cost of Working** and the amount payable as indemnity thereunder shall be:—

(a) **in respect of Reduction in Turnover:** the sum produced by applying the Rate of Gross Profit to the amount by which the Turnover during the Indemnity Period shall fall short of the Standard Turnover in consequence of the Incident

(b) **in respect of Increase in Cost of Working:** the additional expenditure (subject to the provisions of the Uninsured Standing Charges Clause) necessarily and reasonably incurred for the sole purpose of avoiding or diminishing the reduction in Turnover which but for that expenditure would have taken place during the Indemnity Period in consequence of the Incident, but not exceeding the sum produced by applying the Rate of Gross Profit to the amount of the reduction thereby avoided

less any sum saved during the Indemnity Period in respect of such of the charges and expenses of the Business payable out of Gross Profit as may cease or be reduced in consequence of the Incident

Notwithstanding proviso 2 on the face of this policy
 (i) the liability of the Insurer shall in no case exceed, in respect of Gross Profit 133·3 per cent. of the Estimated Gross Profit stated herein, in respect of each other item 100 per cent. of the sum insured stated herein, nor in the whole the sum of 133·3 per cent. of the Estimated Gross Profit and 100 per cent. of the sums insured by other items, or such other amounts as may be substituted therefor by memorandum signed by or on behalf of the Insurer
 (ii) in the absence of written notice by the Insured or the Insurer to the contrary the Insurer's liability shall not stand reduced by the amount of any loss, the Insured undertaking to pay the appropriate additional premium for such automatic reinstatement of cover.

DEFINITIONS

Notes:
 1 To the extent that the Insured is accountable to the tax authorities for Value Added Tax, all terms in this policy shall be exclusive of such tax.
 2 For the purpose of these definitions, any adjustment implemented in current cost accounting shall be disregarded.

Incident: Loss or destruction of or damage to property used by the Insured at the Premises for the purpose of the Business.

Indemnity Period: The period beginning with the occurrence of the Incident and ending not later than the Maximum Indemnity Period thereafter during which the results of the Business shall be affected in consequence thereof.

Maximum Indemnity Period: months.

Turnover: The money paid or payable to the Insured for goods sold and delivered and for services rendered in course of the Business at the Premises.

Gross Profit: The amount by which—
  (i) the sum of the amount of the Turnover and the amounts of the closing stock and work in progress shall exceed
  (ii) the sum of the amounts of the opening stock and work in progress and the amount of the Uninsured Working Expenses.

Note: The amounts of the opening and closing stocks and work in progress shall be arrived at in accordance with the Insured's normal accountancy methods, due provision being made for depreciation.

Uninsured Working Expenses:

(Appropriate list to be inserted)

Note: The words and expressions used in this definition (other than wages) shall have the meaning usually attached to them in the books and accounts of the Insured.

Estimated Gross Profit: The amount declared by the Insured to the Insurer as representing not less than the Gross Profit which is anticipated will be earned by the Business during the financial year most nearly concurrent with the period of insurance (or a proportionately increased multiple thereof where the Maximum Indemnity Period exceeds twelve months).

Rate of Gross Profit:—The Rate of Gross Profit earned on the turnover during the financial year immediately before the date of the Incident

Standard Turnover:—The Turnover during that period in the twelve months immediately before the date of the Incident which corresponds with the Indemnity Period

to which such adjustments shall be made as may be necessary to provide for the trend of the Business and for variations in or other circumstances affecting the Business either before or after the Incident or which would have affected the Business had the Incident not occurred, so that the figures thus adjusted shall represent as nearly as may be reasonably practicable the results which but for the Incident would have been obtained during the relative period after the Incident.

Alternative Trading Clause: If during the Indemnity Period goods shall be sold or services rendered elsewhere than at the Premises for the benefit of the Business either by the Insured or by others on his behalf the money paid or payable in respect of such sales or services shall be brought into account in arriving at the Turnover during the Indemnity Period.

Uninsured Standing Charges Clause: If any standing charges of the Business be not insured by this policy (having been deducted in arriving at the Gross Profit as defined herein) then in computing the amount recoverable hereunder as Increase in Cost of Working that proportion only of any additional expenditure shall be brought into account which the Gross Profit bears to the sum of the Gross Profit and the uninsured standing charges.

Renewal Clause: The Insured shall prior to each renewal provide the Insurer with the Estimated Gross Profit for the financial year most nearly concurrent with the ensuing year of insurance.

Premium Adjustment Clause: The first and annual premiums (in respect of Item 1) are provisional and are based on the Estimated Gross Profit.
The Insured shall provide to the Insurer not later than six months after the expiry of each period of insurance a declaration confirmed by the Insured's auditors of the Gross Profit earned during the financial year most nearly concurrent with the period of insurance.
If any Incident shall have occurred giving rise to a claim for loss of Gross Profit the above mentioned declaration shall be increased by the Insurer for the purpose of premium adjustment by the amount by which the Gross Profit was reduced during the financial year solely in consequence of the Incident.
If the declaration (adjusted as provided above and proportionately increased where the Maximum Indemnity Period exceeds 12 months.)
  (a) is less than the Estimated Gross Profit for the relative period of insurance the Insurer will allow a pro rata return of premium paid on the Estimated Gross Profit (but not exceeding 50 per cent. of such premium)
  (b) is greater than the Estimated Gross Profit for the relative period of insurance the Insured shall pay a pro rata addition to the premium paid on the Estimated Gross Profit

Professional Accountants Clause: Any particulars or details contained in the Insured's books of account or other business books or documents which may be required by the Insurer under Claims Condition 1 of this policy for the purpose of investigating or verifying any claim hereunder may be produced by professional accountants if at the time they are regularly acting as such for the Insured and their report shall be prima facie evidence of the particulars and details to which such report relates.
The Insurer will pay to the Insured the reasonable charges payable by the Insured to their professional accountants for producing such particulars or details or any other proofs, information or evidence as may be required by the Insurer under the terms of Claims Condition 1 of this policy and reporting that such particulars or details are in accordance with the Insured's books of account or other business books or documents
provided that the sum of the amount payable under this clause and the amount otherwise payable under the policy shall in no case exceed the liability of the Insurer as stated.

Notes: Where the Uninsured Working Expenses are recognised variable charges, the Uninsured Standing Charges Clause and the reference thereto under paragraph (b) of Item No. 1 should be deleted.

451.—APPENDIX E

UNITED KINGDOM BUSINESS INTERRUPTION ("ADDITIONS" BASIS) SPECIFICATION— "GROSS PROFIT" WORDING—SUM INSURED BASIS

(**Note:** No longer in general use in the United Kingdom but still used elsewhere.)

Item No.		Sum Insured
1	On Gross Profit	£ _____

The insurance under Item No. 1 is limited to loss of Gross Profit due to (*a*) Reduction in Turnover and (*b*) Increase in Cost of Working and the amount payable as indemnity thereunder shall be:

(*a*) **In respect of Reduction in Turnover:** the sum produced by applying the Rate of Gross Profit to the amount by which the Turnover during the Indemnity Period shall, in consequence of the Incident, fall short of the Standard Turnover

(*b*) **In respect of Increase in Cost of Working:** the additional expenditure (subject to the provisions of the Uninsured Standing Charges Clause) necessarily and reasonably incurred for the sole purpose of avoiding or diminishing the reduction in Turnover which but for that expenditure would have taken place during the Indemnity Period in consequence of the Incident but not exceeding the sum produced by applying the Rate of Gross Profit to the amount of the reduction thereby avoided

less any sum saved during the Indemnity Period in respect of such of the Insured Standing Charges as may cease or be reduced in consequence of the Incident
provided that if the sum insured by this item be less than the sum produced by applying the Rate of Gross Profit to the Annual Turnover (or to a proportionately increased multiple thereof where the Maximum Indemnity Period exceeds twelve months) the amount payable shall be proportionately reduced.

DEFINITIONS

NOTES: 1 To the extent that the Insured is accountable to the tax authorities for Value Added Tax all terms in this policy shall be exclusive of such tax.
2 For the purpose of these definitions any adjustment implemented in current cost accounting shall be disregarded.

Incident—Loss or destruction of or damage to property used by the Insured at the Premises for the purpose of the Business.

Gross Profit:—The sum produced by adding to the Net Profit the amount of the Insured Standing Charges, or if there be no Net Profit the amount of the Insured Standing Charges less such a proportion of any net trading loss as the amount of the Insured Standing Charges bears to all the standing charges of the business.

APPENDIX E

Net Profit:—The net trading profit (exclusive of all capital receipts and accretions and all outlay properly chargeable to capital) resulting from the Business of the Insured at the Premises after due provision has been made for all standing and other charges including depreciation, but before the deduction of any taxation chargeable on profits.

Insured Standing Charges:
          (*Appropriate list to be inserted*)

Indemnity Period: The period beginning with the occurrence of the Incident and ending not later than the Maximum Indemnity Period thereafter during which the results of the Business shall be affected in consequence thereof.

Maximum Indemnity Period: months.

Turnover: The money paid or payable to the Insured for goods sold and delivered and for services rendered in course of the Business at the Premises.

Rate of Gross Profit:—The Rate of Gross Profit earned on the Turnover during the financial year immediately before the date of the Incident

Annual Turnover:—The Turnover during the twelve months immediately before the date of the Incident

Standard Turnover:—The Turnover during the period corresponding with the Indemnity Period in the twelve months immediately before the date of the Incident

to which such adjustments shall be made as may be necessary to provide for the trend of the Business and for variations in or other circumstances affecting the Business either before or after the Incident or which would have affected the Busines had the Incident not occurred, so that the figures thus adjusted shall represent as nearly as may be reasonably practicable the results which but for the Incident would have been obtained during the relative period after the Incident.

Alternative Trading Clause: If during the Indemnity Period goods shall be sold or services shall be rendered elsewhere than at the Premises for the benefit of the Business either by the Insured or by others on the Insured's behalf the money paid or payable in respect of such sales or services shall be brought into account in arriving at the Turnover during the Indemnity Period.

Uninsured Standing Charges Clause: If any standing charges of the business be not insured by this policy then in computing the amount recoverable hereunder as increase in cost of working that proportion only of the additional expenditure shall be brought into account which the sum of the Net Profit and the Insured Standing Charges bears to the sum of the Net Profit and all the standing charges.

Return of Premium Clause: In the event of the Gross Profit earned (or a proportionately increased multiple thereof when the Maximum Indemnity Period exceeds twelve months) during the accounting period of twelve months most nearly concurrent with any period of insurance as certified by the Insured's auditors being less than the sum insured thereon, a pro rata return of premium not exceeding 50 per cent. of the premium paid on such sum insured for such period of insurance will be made in respect of the difference. If any Incident shall have occurred, giving rise to a claim under this policy, such return shall be made in respect only of so much of the said difference as is not due to such Incident.

Professional Accountants Clause: Any particulars or details contained in the Insured's books of account or other business books or documents which may be required by the Insurer under Claims Condition 1 of this policy for the purpose of investigating or verifying any claim hereunder may be produced by professional accountants if at the time they are regularly acting as such for the Insured and their report shall be prima facie evidence of the particulars and details to which such report relates.

The Insurer will pay to the Insured the reasonable charges payable by the Insured to their professional accountants for producing such particulars or details or any other proofs, information or evidence as may be required by the Insurer under the terms of Claims Condition 1 of this policy and reporting that such particulars or details are in accordance with the Insured's books of account or other business books and documents

provided that the sum of the amount payable under this clause and the amount otherwise payable under the policy shall in no case exceed the total sum insured by the policy.

452.—APPENDIX F

UNITED KINGDOM BUSINESS INTERRUPTION SPECIFICATION
GROSS REVENUE WORDING—SUM INSURED BASIS

Item No.		Sum Insured
1	On Gross Profit	£
	Total Sum Insured	£

The insurance under Item No. 1 is limited to **(a) Loss of Gross Revenue and (b) Increase in Cost of Working** and the amount payable as indemnity thereunder shall be:—

(a) **in respect of Loss of Gross Revenue:** the amount by which the Gross Revenue during the Indemnity Period shall fall short of the Standard Gross Revenue in consequence of the Incident

(b) **in respect of Increase in Cost of Working:** the additional expenditure necessarily and reasonably incurred for the sole purpose of avoiding or diminishing the reduction in Gross Revenue which but for that expenditure would have taken place during the Indemnity Period in consequence of the Incident, but not exceeding the amount of reduction in Gross Revenue thereby avoided

less any sum saved during the Indemnity Period in respect of such of the charges and expenses of the Business payable out of Gross Revenue as may cease or be reduced in consequence of the Incident

provided that if the sum insured by this item be less than the Annual Gross Revenue (or a proportionately increased multiple thereof where the Maximum Indemnity Period exceeds twelve months) the amount payable shall be proportionately reduced.

DEFINITIONS

Notes:
 1 To the extent that the Insured is accountable to the tax authorities for Value Added Tax, all terms in this policy shall be exclusive of such tax.
 2 For the purpose of these definitions, any adjustment implemented in current cost accounting shall be disregarded.

Incident: Loss or destruction of or damage to property used by the Insured at the Premises for the purpose of the Business.

Indemnity Period: The period beginning with the occurrence of the Incident and ending not later than the Maximum Indemnity Period thereafter during which the results of the Business shall be affected in consequence thereof.

Maximum Indemnity Period: months.

Gross Revenue: The money paid or payable to the Insured for services rendered in the course of the Business at the Premises.

Annual Gross Revenue:—The Gross Revenue during the twelve months immediately before the date of the Incident

Standard Gross Revenue:— The Gross Revenue during that period in the twelve months immediately before the date of the Incident which corresponds with the Indemnity Period

} to which such adjustments shall be made as may be necessary to provide for the trend of the Business and for variations in or other circumstances affecting the Business either before or after the Incident which would have affected the Business had the Incident not occurred, so that the figures thus adjusted shall represent as nearly as may be reasonably practicable the results which but for the Incident would have been obtained during the relative period after the Incident.

Alternative Trading Clause: If during the Indemnity Period goods shall be sold or services rendered elsewhere than at the Premises for the benefit of the Business either by the Insured or by others on his behalf the money paid or payable in respect of such sales or services shall be brought into account in arriving at the Gross Revenue during the Indemnity Period.

Premium Adjustment Clause: The premium paid hereon may be adjusted on receipt by the Insurer of a declaration of Gross Revenue earned during the financial year most nearly concurrent with the period of insurance, as reported by the Insured's Auditors.

If any Incident shall have occurred giving rise to a claim for loss of Gross Revenue the above mentioned declaration shall be increased by the Insurer for the purpose of premium adjustment by the amount by which the Gross Revenue was reduced during the financial year solely in consequence of the Incident.

If either declaration (adjusted as provided for above and proportionately increased where the Maximum Indemnity Period exceeds 12 months) is less than the sum insured on Gross Revenue for the relative period of insurance the Insurer will allow a pro rata return of premium not exceeding 50 per cent. of the premium paid.

Professional Accountants Clause: Any particulars or details contained in the Insured's books of account or other business books or documents which may be required by the Insurer under Claims Condition 1 of this policy for the purpose of investigating or verifying any claim hereunder may be produced by professional accountants if at the time they are regularly acting as such for the Insured and their report shall be prima facie evidence of the particulars and details to which such report relates.

The Insurer will pay to the Insured the reasonable charges payable by the Insured to their professional accountants for producing such particulars or details or any other proofs, information or evidence as may be required by the Insurer under the terms of Claims Condition 1 of this policy and reporting that such particulars or details are in accordance with the Insured's books of account or other business books or documents

provided that the sum of the amount payable under this clause and the amount otherwise payable under the policy shall in no case exceed the liability of the Insurer as stated.

453.—APPENDIX G

UNITED KINGDOM BUSINESS INTERRUPTION SPECIFICATION—TO INSURE TRADING PROFIT (EXAMPLE)

(POSSIBLE WORDING FOR RETAIL SHOP BUSINESS)

Item No.		Sum Insured
1	On Trading Profit	£

The insurance under Item No. 1 is limited to loss of Trading Profit due to (a) Reduction in Takings and (b) Increase in Cost of Working and the amount payable as indemnity thereunder shall be

(a) **In respect of Reduction in Takings:** the sum produced by applying the Rate of Trading Profit to the amount by which the Takings during the Indemnity Period shall in consequence of the Incident fall short of the Standard Takings

(b) **In respect of Increase in Cost of Working:** the additional expenditure necessarily and reasonably incurred for the sole purpose of avoiding or diminishing the reduction in Takings which but for that expenditure would have taken place during the Indemnity Period in consequence of the Incident but not exceeding the sum produced by applying the Rate of Trading Profit to the amount of the reduction thereby avoided

less any sum saved during the Indemnity Period in respect of such of the charges and expenses of the Business payable out of Trading Profit as may cease or be reduced in consequence of the Incident

provided that if the sum insured by this item be less than the sum produced by applying the Rate of Trading Profit to the Annual Takings (or to a proportionately increased multiple thereof where the Maximum Indemnity Period exceeds twelve months) the amount payable shall be proportionately reduced.

DEFINITIONS

Notes:
1 To the extent that the Insured is accountable to the tax authorities for Value Added Tax, all terms in this policy shall be exclusive of such tax.
2 For the purpose of these definitions, any adjustment implemented in current cost accounting shall be disregarded.

Incident: Loss or destruction of or damage to property used by the Insured at the Premises for the purpose of the Business.

Trading Profit: The takings less the cost of goods or materials relative thereto.

Takings: The money paid or payable to the Insured for goods sold and delivered and for work done in course of the Business at the Premises.

Alternative Trading Clause. If during the Indemnity Period goods shall be sold or work done elsewhere than at the premises for the benefit of the Business either by the Insured or by others on his behalf the money paid or payable in respect of such sales or work shall be brought into account in arriving at the Takings during the Indemnity Period.

Indemnity Period: The period beginning with the occurrence of the Incident and ending not later than the Maximum Indemnity Period thereafter during which the results of the Business shall be affected in consequence thereof.

Maximum Indemnity Period: months.

Rate of Trading Profit:—The Rate of Trading Profit earned on the Takings during the financial year immediately before the date of the Incident

Annual Takings:—The Takings during the twelve months immediately before the date of the Incident

Standard Takings:—The Takings during the period corresponding with the Indemnity Period in the twelve months immediately before the date of the Incident

adjusted as may be necessary to provide for variations in or other circumstances affecting the Business so that the adjusted figures shall represent as far as possible the results which but for the Incident would have been obtained during the relative period after the Incident.
In the event of an Incident occurring before the expiry of the first financial year of the Business, the results of the business to the date of the Incident shall be used as a basis upon which to assess any loss subject otherwise to all the conditions of the policy.

Premium Adjustment Clauses: In the event of the Trading Profit earned (or a proportionately increased multiple thereof where the Maximum Indemnity Period exceeds twelve months) during the accounting period of twelve months most nearly concurrent with any period of insurance as certified by the Insured's auditors being less than the sum insured thereon, on a pro rata return of premium not exceeding 50 per cent. of the premium paid on such sum insured for such period of insurance will be made in respect of the difference. If any Incident shall have occurred, giving rise to a claim under this policy, such return shall be made in respect only of so much of the said difference as is not due to such Incident.

454.—APPENDIX H

UNITED KINGDOM
BUSINESS INTERRUPTION SPECIFICATION—
ITEM INSURING WAGES UNDER
THE DUAL BASIS SCHEME

(**Note:** No longer in general use in the United Kingdom but still used elsewhere.)

Item No.		**Sum Insured**
2	**On Wages**	£_____

The insurance under Item No. 2 is limited to loss in respect of Wages and the amount payable as indemnity thereunder shall be:

(a) **In respect of Reduction in Turnover:**
   (i) during the initial period
      the sum produced by applying the Rate of Wages to the Shortage in Turnover during such period
      less any saving during such period through reduction in consequence of the Incident in the amount of Wages paid;
   (ii) during the remaining portion of the Indemnity Period
      the sum produced by applying the Rate of Wages to the Shortage in Turnover during such period
      less any saving during such period through reduction in consequence of the Incident in the amount of Wages paid
but not exceeding
      the sum produced by applying the remainder percentage of the Rate of Wages to the Shortage in Turnover during the said remaining portion of the Indemnity Period,
      increased by such amount as is deducted for savings under the terms of clause (i);
      Note—At the option of the Insured the alternative period may be substituted for the initial period provided that the amount arrived at under the provisions of clause (a)(ii) shall then be limited to such amount as is deducted under clause (a)(i) for savings effected during the alternative period.

(b) **In respect of Increase in Cost of Working:**
   so much of the additional expenditure described in clause (b) of Item No. 1 on Gross Profit as exceeds the amount payable thereunder
   but not more than the additional amount which would have been payable in respect of reduction in turnover under the provisions of clauses (a)(i) and (ii) of this item had such expenditure not been incurred;

provided that if the sum insured by this item be less the sum produced by applying the Rate of Wages to the Annual Turnover (or to a proportionately increased multiple thereof where the Maximum Indemnity Period exceeds twelve months) the amount payable under this item shall be proportionately reduced.

Definitions of Incident Indemnity Period, Maximum Indemnity Period, Turnover, Annual Turnover, Standard Turnover and Alternative Trading Clause are those applicable to and shown in the item on Gross Profit—see Appendix C.

DEFINITIONS

Wages: The remuneration (including national insurance, bonuses, holiday pay and other payments pertaining to wages)* of all employees other than those whose remuneration is treated as salaries in the Insured's books of account.

Rate of wages: The Rate of Wages to Turnover during the financial year immediately before the date of the Incident. (*This definition is included after that of rate of Gross Profit—see Appendix C—within the bracketed provisions of the Other Circumstances Clause.*)

Shortage in Turnover: The amount by which the Turnover during a period shall in consequence of the Incident fall short of the part of the Standard Turnover which relates to that period.

The Return of Premium Clause for the item on Gross Profit is amended to include the Wages item in the provisions for a return of premium.

*This definition my be amended as required.

455.—APPENDIX I

UNITED KINGDOM BUSINESS INTERRUPTION SPECIFICATION— ITEM INSURING NOTICE WAGES ON THE "PRO RATA" BASIS

(**Note:** No longer in general use in the United Kingdom but still used elsewhere.)

Item No.		Sum Insured
2	On Wages	£ _____

The insurance under this item is limited to the loss incurred by the Insured by the payment of Wages for a period beginning with the occurrence of the Incident and ending not later than the Period of Wages Liability thereafter.

The amount payable as indemnity under this item shall be the actual amount which the Insured shall pay as Wages for such period to employees whose services cannot in consequence of the Incident be utilised by the Insured at all and an equitable part of the Wages paid for such period to employees whose services cannot in consequence of the Incident be utilised by the Insured to the full

provided that if the sum insured by this item shall be less than the aggregate amount of the Wages that would have been paid during a period equal to the Period of Wages Liability immediately following the Incident, had the Incident not occurred, the amount payable shall be proportionately reduced.

For the purpose of this item the term Wages shall mean wages, national insurance and holiday pay of all employees other than those whose remuneration is insured in the Gross Profit as defined under Item No. 1.

DEFINITIONS

Period of Wages Liability: weeks.

Return of Premium Clause: In the event of that proportion that the Period of Wages Liability bears to twelve months of the Wages (as defined herein) paid by the Insured during the accounting period of twelve months most nearly concurrent with any period of insurance as certified by the Insured's auditors being less than the sum insured thereon, a pro rata return of premium not exceeding 50 per cent. of the premium paid on such sum insured for such period of insurance will be made in respect of the difference. If any Incident shall have occurred giving rise to a claim under the said item no such return of premium shall be made.

456.—APPENDIX J

UNITED KINGDOM BUSINESS INTERRUPTION SPECIFICATION—FOR ADVANCE PROFITS (EXAMPLE)

Item No.		Sum Insured
1	On Gross Profit	£

Item No. 1. The Insurance under Item 1 is limited to loss of Gross Profit due to **(a) Reduction in Turnover** and **(b) Increase in Cost of Working** and the amount payable as indemnity thereunder shall be—

(a) **In Respect of Reduction in Turnover;** the sum produced by applying the Rate of Gross Profit to the amount by which the Turnover during the Indemnity Period shall, in consequence of the Incident, fall short of the Standard Turnover,

(b) **In Respect of Increase in Cost of Working;** the additional expenditure necessarily and reasonably incurred for the sole purpose of avoiding or diminishing the reduction in Turnover which but for that expenditure would have taken place during the Indemnity Period in consequence of the Incident but not exceeding the sum produced by applying the Rate of Gross Profit to the amount of the reduction thereby avoided

less any sum saved during the Indemnity Period in respect of such of the charges and expenses of the Business payable out of Gross Profit as may cease or be reduced in consequence of the Incident

provided that if the sum insured by this item be less than the sum provided by applying the Rate of Gross Profit to the Comparative Turnover the amount payable shall be proportionately reduced.

DEFINITIONS

Notes:
1. To the extent that the Insured is accountable to the tax authorities for Value Added Tax all terms in this policy shall be exclusive of such tax.
2. For the purpose of these definitions any adjustment implemented in current cost accounting shall be disregarded.

Incident—Loss or destruction of or damage to property used by the Insured at the Premises for the purpose of the Business.

Gross Profit: The amount by which
  (i) the sum of the amount of the Turnover and the amount of the closing stock and work in progress
      shall exceed
  (ii) the sum of the amount of the opening stock and work in progress and the amount of the Uninsured Working Expenses.

N.B. The amounts of the opening and closing stocks and work in progress shall be arrived at in accordance with the Insured's normal accountancy methods, due provision being made for depreciation.

Uninsured Working Expenses:

(Appropriate list to be inserted)

N.B. The words and expressions used in this definition (other than wages) shall have the meaning usually attached to them in the books and accounts of the Insured.

Turnover: The money (less discounts allowed) paid or payable to the Insured for goods sold and delivered and for services rendered in course of the Business at the Premises.

Indemnity Period: The period beginning with the date upon which but for the Incident Turnover would have commenced to be earned and ending not later than the Maximum Indemnity Period thereafter during which the results of the Business shall be affected in consequence thereof.

Maximum Indemnity Period: months.

Rate of Gross Profit:—The Rate of Gross Profit that but for the Incident would have been earned on the Turnover during the Indemnity Period

Comparative Turnover:—The Turnover which but for the Incident would have been earned during the Maximum Indemnity Period immediately following the date on which Turnover would have commenced to be earned

Standard Turnover:—The Turnover which but for the Incident would have been earned during the Indemnity Period

based upon the estimated production programme of the Business, and costs and prices relating thereto, to which such adjustments shall be made as may be necessary to provide for the trend of the Business and for variations in or other circumstances affecting the Business either before or after the Incident or which would have affected the Business had the Incident not occurred so that the figures thus adjusted shall represent as nearly as may be practicable the results which but for the Incident would have been obtained during the relative period after the Incident.

Alternative Trading Clause: If during the Indemnity Period goods shall be sold or services shall be rendered elsewhere than at the Premises for the benefit of the Business either by the Insured or by others on their behalf the money paid or payable in respect of such sales or services shall be brought into account in arriving at the Turnover during the Indemnity Period.

Uninsured Standing Charges Clause: If any standing charges of the Business be not insured by this policy (having been deducted in arriving at the Gross Profit as defined herein) then in computing the amount recoverable hereunder as Increase in Cost of Working that proportion only of any additional expenditure shall be brought into account which the Gross Profit bears to the sum of the Gross Profit and the uninsured standing charges.

Professional Accountants Clause: It is understood and agreed that any particulars or details contained in the Insured's books of account or other business books or documents which may be required by the Insurers under Claims Condition 1 of this policy for the purpose of investigating or verifying any claim hereunder may be produced by professional accountants if at the time they are regularly acting as such for the Insured and their report shall be prima facie evidence of the particulars and details to which such report relates.

The Insurers will pay to the Insured the reasonable charges payable by the Insured to their professional accountants for producing such particulars or details or any proofs, information or evidence as may be required by the Insurers under the terms of Claims Condition 1 of this policy and reporting that such particulars or details are in accordance with the Insured's books of account or other business books or documents

provided that the sum of the amount payable under this clause and the amount otherwise payable under the policy shall in no case exceed the total sum insured by the policy.

457.—APPENDIX K

UNITED KINGDOM BUSINESS INTERRUPTION SPECIFICATION— FOR THE INSURANCE OF LOSS OF BOOK DEBTS (EXAMPLE)

Item No.		Sum Insured
1	On Outstanding Debit Balances	£

The insurance under Item No. 1 is limited to the loss sustained by the Insured in respect of Outstanding Debit Balances directly due to the Incident and the amount payable in respect of any one occurrence of an Incident shall not exceed:

(i) the difference between
    (a) the Outstanding Debit Balances
    and
    (b) the total of the amounts received or traced in respect thereof

(ii) the additional expenditure incurred with the previous consent of the Insurer in tracing and establishing customers' debit balances after the Incident

provided that if the sum insured by this item be less than the Outstanding Debit Balances the amount payable shall be proportionately reduced.

DEFINITIONS

Incident: Loss or destruction of or damage to property used by the Insured at the Premises for the purpose of the Business.

Outstanding Debit Balances: The total declared in the statement last given under the provisions of Memo. 1 adjusted for:—
    (a) bad debts,
    (b) amounts debited (or invoiced but not debited) and credited (including credit notes and cash not passed through the books at the time of the Incident) to customers' accounts in the period between the date to which said last statement relates and the date of the Incident, and
    (c) any abnormal condition of trade which had or could have had a material effect on the Business,
so that the figures thus adjusted shall represent as nearly as reasonably practicable those which would have obtained at the date of the Incident had the Incident not occurred.

Customers' Accounts: *Here is inserted a description of the nature of the accounts to which the insurance applies, e.g., hire-purchase accounts, all credit accounts, retail customers accounts only, etc.*

Warranty: It is warranted that the Insured's books of account or other business books or records in which customers' accounts are shown shall be kept in—*here is inserted a description such as fireproof safes, fire-resisting cabinets, etc.*

Memo. 1. The insured shall within thirty days of the end of each month deposit with the Insurer a signed statement showing the total amount outstanding in customers' accounts as set out in the Insured's accounts as at the end of the said month.

Memo. 2. On the expiry of each period of insurance the actual premium shall be calculated at the rate per cent. per annum on the average amount insured, *i.e.*, the total of the sums declared divided by the number of declarations. If the actual premium shall be less than the first premium (or in the case of the second and subsequent periods of insurance the annual premium) the difference shall be repaid to the Insured, but such repayment shall not exceed one-half of the first or annual premium respectively.
If the amount of a declaration exceeds the sum insured applicable at the date of such declaration, then for the purposes of this memorandum only, the Insured shall be deemed to have declared such sum insured.

Memo. 3. In consideration of the insurance not being reduced by the amount of any loss the Insured shall pay the appropriate extra premium on the amount of the loss from the date thereof to the date of the expiry of the period of insurance.

Memo. 4. Subject to the terms and conditions of this policy this insurance extends to include the amount of any loss resulting from an Incident
  (i) in any premises in Great Britain, Northern Ireland or the Republic of Ireland occupied by persons acting on behalf of the Insured to which records are temporarily removed
  (ii) occurring to the Insurers books of account or other business books or records whilst in transit within Great Britain, Northern Ireland or the Republic of Ireland.

Memo. 5. Any particulars or details contained in the Insured's books of account or other business books or documents which may be required by the Insurer under the policy for the purpose of investigating or verifying any claim hereunder may be produced by professional accountants if at the time they are regularly acting as such for the Insured and their report shall be prima facie evidence of the particulars and details to which such report relates.
The Insurer will pay to the Insured the reasonable charges payable by the Insured to their professional accountants for producing such particulars or details or any other proofs, information or evidence as may be required by the Insurer under the terms of this policy and reporting that such particulars or details are in accordance with the Insured's books of account or other business books or documents
provided that the sum of the amount payable under this clause and the amount otherwise payable under the policy shall in no case exceed the total sum insured by the policy.

458.—APPENDIX L

UNITED KINGDOM BUSINESS INTERRUPTION SPECIFICATION—FOR THE INSURANCE OF RESEARCH EXPENDITURE (EXAMPLE)

Item No.		Sum Insured
1	On Research Expenditure	£

The indemnity under Item No. 1 is limited to the loss sustained by the Insured in consequence of the Incident in respect of (*a*) **Research Expenditure** and (*b*) **Increase in Cost of Working,** and the amount payable as indemnity thereunder shall be:

(*a*) **In Respect of Research Expenditure:** for each working week in the **Indemnity Period** during which the activities of the Business are, in consequence of the Incident
  (i) **Totally Interrupted** or totally given over to the re-working of projects affected by the Incident: the **Insured Amount** per week;
  (ii) **Partially Interrupted** or partially given over to the re-working of projects affected by the Incident—an equitable portion of the **Insured Amount** per week based upon the time rendered ineffective by reason of the Incident

(*b*) **In Respect of Increase in Cost of Working:** the additional expenditure reasonably and necessarily incurred solely in consequence of the Incident in order to minimise the interruption but the amount payable under this heading shall not exceed the additional amount payable under (*a*) for loss of **Research Expenditure** if no such **Increase in Cost of Working** had been incurred,

less any sum saved during the **Indemnity Period** in respect of such of the **Research** expenses as may cease or be reduced in consequence of the Incident,

provided that if the Sum Insured hereby is less than the **Annual Research Expenditure** the amount payable under (*a*) and (*b*) hereof shall be proportionately reduced.

DEFINITIONS

Notes
  1 To the extent that the Insured is accountable to the tax authorities for Value Added Tax all terms in this policy shall be exclusive of such tax.
  2 For the purpose of these definitions any adjustment implemented in current cost accounting shall be disregarded.

Incident: Loss or destruction of or damage to property used by the Insured at the Premises for the purpose of the Business.

Research Expenditure: The total expenditure on research by the Insured at the Premises less the relative cost of raw materials consumed.

Indemnity Period: The period beginning with the occurrence of the Incident and ending not later than the Maximum Indemnity Period thereafter during which the results of the Business shall be affected in consequence thereof.

Maximum Indemnity Period: months

Insured Amount Per Week:— One fiftieth part of the Research Expenditure incurred during the financial year immediately before the date of the Incident

Annual Research Expenditure:— The aggregate amount of the Research Expenditure incurred during the twelve months immediately before the date of the Incident

} to which such adjustments shall be made as may be necessary to provide for the trend of the Business and for variations in or other circumstances affecting the Business either before or after the Incident or which would have affected the Business had the Incident not occurred, so that the figures thus adjusted shall represent as nearly as may be reasonably practicable the results which but for the Incident would have been obtained during the relative period after the Incident.

Premium Adjustment Clause: In the event of the Research Expenditure during the accounting period of twelve months most nearly concurrent with any period of insurance being less than the respective sum insured thereon a pro rata return of premium not exceeding 50 per cent. of the premium paid on such sum insured for such period of insurance will be made in respect of the difference. If any Incident shall have occurred, giving rise to claim under this policy, such return shall be made only in respect of so much of the said difference as is not due to such Incident.

459.—APPENDIX M

UNITED KINGDOM ENGINEERING BUSINESS INTERRUPTION POLICY (EXAMPLE)

In consideration of the Insured named in the Schedule paying to the Insurer the First Premium mentioned in the Schedule, the Insurer agrees to insure in the manner and to the extent provided for in the Schedule in respect of events occurring during the Period of Insurance set out in the Schedule or any subsequent period for which the Insured shall pay and the Insurer shall accept the premium required.

GENERAL CONDITIONS

Identification
1 This Policy Schedule and Endorsements shall be read together as One Contract and unless specifically stated to the contrary any word or expression to which a specific meaning has been given shall bear such meaning wherever it may appear.

Precautions
2 The Insured shall comply with all statutory requirements concerning safety use and inspection of the Property and shall take precautions to keep the Property in a proper state of maintenance and repair and to prevent accident or loss. The Insured shall immediately notify the Insurer of any changes which materially alter the risks covered by the Policy. The Insurer may at any time by notice in writing to the Insured suspend the insurance provided in connection with any item of Property until the requirements of the Insurer have been fulfilled and in such event the Insurer will return a proportionate part of the premium.

Right to inspect
3 The Insurer shall have the right at all reasonable times to inspect and examine any Property Dismantling and re–assembling in connection with any examinations shall be carried out by the Insured on such date or dates as the Insurer and the Insured shall mutually agree for the making of such examinations.

Cancellation
4 The Insurer may cancel the Policy by sending seven days notice by registered letter to the Insured at his last known address and in such event will return to the Insured a proportionate part of the premium for the unexpired Period of Insurance

Arbitration
5 If any difference shall arise as to the amount to be paid under this Policy (liability being otherwise admitted) such difference shall be referred to an arbitrator to be appointed by the parties in accordance with the statutory provisions in that behalf for the time being in force. Where any difference is by this condition to be referred to arbitration the making of an Award shall be a condition precedent to any right of action against the Insurer.

Premium adjustment

6 If any part of the premium for this Policy is based on estimates furnished by the Insured the Insured shall as soon as possible after the expiry of each Period of Insurance furnish such information as the Insurer may reasonably require to adjust the premium. Any refund of premium resulting from such adjustment is subject to the retention by the Insurer of the amount specified in the Schedule as the Minimum Premium for this Policy.

Observance of Conditions

7 The due observance and fulfilment of the terms provisions and conditions so far as they relate to anything to be done or complied with by the Insured and the truth of the statements in the proposal made by the Insured (which shall be the basis of the contract and held to be incorporated herein) shall be conditions precedent to any liability of the Insurer.

GENERAL EXCEPTIONS

This Policy excludes

War etc.

1 any consequence of war invasion act of foreign enemy hostilities (whether war be declared or not) civil war rebellion revolution insurrection military or usurped power.

Radioactivity

2 a loss or destruction of or damage to any property whatsoever or any loss or expense whatsoever resulting or arising therefrom or any consequential loss
 b any legal liability of whatsoever nature
  directly or indirectly caused by or contributed to by or arising from
   i ionising radiation or contamination by radioactivity from any nuclear fuel or from any nuclear waste from the combustion of nuclear fuel
   ii the radioactive toxic explosive or other hazardous properties of any explosive nuclear assembly or nuclear component thereof.

Sonic Bangs

3 loss damage or liability directly occasioned by pressure waves caused by aircraft or other aerial devices travelling at sonic or supersonic speeds.

Overloading

4 loss damage or liability caused by the application of a loading to an item of Property in excess of that stipulated in the report of the last examination of the item by a competent person or in the certificate of a subsequent test of the item by a competent person (whichever is the lower) or where an examination or test by a competent person has never been carried out in excess of the manufacturer's design loading of the item or in excess of that stipulated by the Insurer in writing but this Exception shall not apply when the application of the excess loading is completely outside the control of the Insured.

Testing

5 loss damage or liability directly caused by and occurring during testing.

CLAIMS CONDITIONS

Action by Insured
1 On the happening of any occurrence which might result in a claim under this Policy the Insured shall

Notice of Claims
a give immediate notice thereof to the Insurer and send written confirmation to the Insurer within forty-eight hours of the occurrence and in the case of Property stolen or lost or wilfully damaged give immediate notice to the police

Admission of Liability
b make no admission of liability or offer promise or payment without the Insurer's written consent

Minimising Loss
c do and concur in doing and permit to be done all things which may be reasonably practicable to minimise or check any interruption of or interference with the Business or to avoid or diminish any loss or damage and at the request and expense of the Insurer do and concur in doing all such acts and things as the Insurer may reasonably require

Prevention of Further Loss
d discontinue the use of any damaged Property unless the Insurer authorises otherwise until such Property shall have been repaired to the satisfaction of the Insurer Any damaged parts which are replaced shall be kept for inspection by the Insurer.

Evidence of Loss
2 In the event of a claim being made under this policy the Insured shall when called upon to do so furnish to the Insurer at his own expense in writing all details of the claim together with such evidence vouchers proofs and explanations as the Insurer may reasonably require.

Insurer's Rights

Entry & Possession
3 On the happening of any occurrence which might result in a claim under this Policy the Insurer and every person authorised by the Insurer may without thereby incurring any liability enter any premises where the occurrence has happened and may take and keep possession of and deal with any salvage.

Control of Claims
4 The Insurer shall be entitled at its discretion to take over and conduct in the name of the Insured the defence or settlement of any claim and to prosecute at its own expense and for its own benefit any claim for indemnity or damages against any other persons whether or not any payment has been made by the Insurer and the Insured shall give all information and assistance required.

Other Insurances

5 If at the time any claim arises under this Policy there is or but for the existence of this Policy would be any other policy of indemnity or insurance in favour of or effected by or on behalf of the Insured applicable to the same loss or damage the Insurer shall not be liable under this Policy to indemnify the Insured in respect of such loss or damage except in respect of any excess beyond the amount which would be payable under such other indemnity or insurance had this Policy not been effected.

Settlement

6 In the event of loss of or damage to any item of Property for which indemnity is provided under this Policy the Insurer may at its option reinstate replace or repair the item or may pay in cash the amount of the loss or damage. The Insurer shall not be liable for the cost of any reinstatement replacement or repair undertaken without its written consent.

460.—APPENDIX N

UNITED KINGDOM ENGINEERING BUSINESS INTERRUPTION SPECIFICATION (EXAMPLE)

The Insurer will indemnify the Insured against loss of Gross Profit due to reduction in turnover and increase in cost of working and the amount payable as indemnity shall be

    a in respect of reduction in Turnover: the sum produced by applying the Rate of Gross Profit to the amount by which the Turnover during the Indemnity Period shall in consequence of an Accident fall short of the Standard Turnover

    b in respect of increase in cost of working: the additional expenditure necessarily and reasonably incurred for the sole purpose of avoiding or diminishing the reduction in Turnover stated above which but for that expenditure would have taken place but not exceeding the sum produced by applying the Rate of Gross Profit to the reduction thereby avoided

less any sum saved during the Indemnity Period in respect of such of the charges and expenses of the Business insured hereunder as may cease or be reduced in consequence of the Accident

The insurance extends to include the reasonable charges payable by the Insured to their professional accountants/auditors for producing any particulars or details or any other proofs information or evidence as may be required under the Claims Conditions and reporting that such particulars or details are in accordance with the Insured's books of account or other business books or documents Provided that the sum of the amount payable hereunder and the amount otherwise payable under this Policy shall in no case exceed the Amount of Indemnity

DEFINITIONS

Note:
    1 To the extent that the Insured is accountable to the tax authorities for Value Added Tax all terms in this Policy shall be exclusive of such tax
    2 For the purpose of these definitions any adjustment implemented in current cost accounting shall be disregarded

Accident means:
a sudden and unforeseen damage from an accidental cause to the Property whilst at the Situation
b failure of the supply of an Insured Public Utility at the terminal point of the supply undertaking's feed to any Situation which is not caused by a deliberate act of the supply undertaking unless performed for the sole purpose of safeguarding life or protecting a part of the supply undertaking's system or not caused by a scheme of rationing unless necessitated solely by physical damage to a part of the supply undertaking's system

Gross Profit: means the amount by which the sum of the Turnover and the value of the Closing Stock and work in progress shall exceed the sum of the value of the Opening Stock and work in progress and the amount of all Purchases (less discounts received) Carriage Packing and Freight and any Uninsured Working Expenses specified by endorsement to this Policy

The values of the Opening and Closing Stocks and work in progress shall be arrived at in accordance with the Insured's normal accountancy methods due provision being made for depreciation

The words and expressions used in this Definition shall have the meaning usually attached to them in the books and accounts of the Insured

Turnover: means the money paid or payable to the Insured for goods sold and delivered and for services rendered in the course of the Business at the Situation If goods shall be sold or services shall be rendered elsewhere than at the Situation for the benefit of the Business either by the Insured or by others on his behalf the money paid or payable in respect of such sales or services shall be brought into account in arriving at the Turnover

Indemnity Period: means the period beginning with the occurrence of the Accident and ending not later than the Maximum Indemnity Period shown in the Schedule thereafter during which the results of the Business shall be affected in consequence of the Accident

Rate of Gross Profit:—Means the rate of Gross Profit earned on the Turnover during the financial year immediately before the date of the Accident

Standard Turnover:—Means the Turnover during that period in the twelve months immediately before the date of the Accident which corresponds with the Indemnity Period

Annual Turnover:—Means the Turnover during the twelve months immediately before the date of the Accident

to which such adjustments shall be made as may be necessary to provide for the trend of the Business and for variations in or other circumstances affecting the Business either before or after the Accident or which would have affected the Business had the Accident not occurred so that the figures thus adjusted shall represent as nearly as may be reasonably practicable the results which but for the Accident would have been obtained during the relative period after the Accident

EXCEPTIONS

This Policy excludes
1 any consequence of

Fire etc.
a damage at a Situation resulting from fire lightning explosion aircraft and other aerial devices or articles dropped therefrom storm tempest flood inundation bursting or overflowing of water tanks apparatus or pipes or the operation of or discharge or leakage from a sprinkler installation

Wear etc.
b loss or damage consisting of wearing away wasting erosion corrosion slowly developing deformation or distortion or any other gradual deterioration or failure of any part requiring periodical renewal but the Insurer shall be liable for loss in consequence of damage resulting from such causes and otherwise insured by this Policy

460 APPENDIX N

Chipping and Scratching
c loss or damage consisting of chipping of painted surfaces or scratching of any surfaces

Foundations, Expendable Parts etc.
d loss of or damage to
    i foundations brickwork masonry chimneys or underfloor heating equipment
    ii belts trailing cables flexible hoses non-metallic linings electric elements or filaments cathode ray or X-ray tubes or cutting edges
unless such loss or damage is attributable to an occurrence causing loss or damage to the Property for which liability is admitted by this Policy

Riot etc.
2 loss resulting from riot strike lock-out or civil commotion

SPECIAL CONDITION

Precautions
The Insured shall at all times take precautions to retain in efficient working condition and available for immediate use any standby or spare machinery or any other loss minimising factors in existence when this insurance was first effected

SPECIAL CLAIMS CONDITIONS

Excess
1 The Insurer shall not be liable in respect of each and every claim for
    i loss of Gross Profit incurred during any Excess Period (Sudden and Unforeseen Damage) shown in the Schedule immediately following the occurrence of sudden and unforeseen damage to the Property
    ii loss of Gross Profit incurred during any Excess Period (Failure of Public Utilities) shown in the Schedule immediately following the occurrence of failure of an Insured Public Utility
    iii loss of Gross Profit incurred as a consequence of failure of an Insured Public Utility the duration of which is less than any Franchise Period (Failure of Public Utilities) shown in the Schedule

Underinsurance
2 In the event of a claim for which liability is admitted under this Policy if the Amount of Indemnity be less than the sum produced by applying the Rate of Gross Profit to the Annual Turnover (or to a proportionately increased multiple thereof where the Maximum Indemnity Period exceeds twelve months) the amount payable shall be proportionately reduced

REBATE CLAUSE

In the event of the Gross Profit earned (or a proportionately increased multiple thereof where the Maximum Indemnity Period exceeds twelve months) during the financial year most nearly concurrent with any Period of Insurance as certified by the Insured's Auditors being less than the Amount of Indemnity thereon a pro rata return of premium not exceeding 50 per cent. of the premium paid on such Amount of Indemnity for such Period of Insurance will be made in respect of the difference If an Accident shall have occurred giving rise to a claim under this Policy such return shall be made in respect only of so much of the said difference as is not due to such Accident

461.—APPENDIX O

UNITED KINGDOM BUSINESS INTERRUPTION EXTENSION WORDING IN RESPECT OF NOTIFIABLE DISEASE, VERMIN, DEFECTIVE SANITARY ARRANGEMENTS, MURDER AND SUICIDE

(For Use with Standard Policy—Refer Appendix A)

Use Part A of the Master Wording and incorporate the Special Conditions from Part B as indicated in Part C.

MASTER WORDING

Part A

The insurance by (item(s). . . . of) this policy shall subject to all the Exclusions and Conditions of the policy (except in so far as they may be hereby expressly varied) and the Special Conditions set out below extend to include loss resulting from interruption of or interference with the Business carried on by the Insured at the Premises in consequence of:—

Here insert the wording(s) from Part C appropriate to the peril(s) selected

Part B

SPECIAL CONDITIONS

1 Notifiable Disease shall mean illness sustained by any person resulting from—
   (a) food or drink poisoning, or
   (b) any human infectious or human contagious disease [excluding Acquired Immune Deficiency Syndrome (AIDS)], an outbreak of which the competent local authority has stipulated shall be notified to them.

2 For the purpose of this memorandum
   Indemnity Period shall mean the period during which the results of the Business shall be affected in consequence of the occurrence discovery or accident, beginning—
   (a) in the case of 1 and 4 above, with the date of the occurrence or discovery
   (b) in the case of 2 and 3 above, with the date from which the restrictions on the Premises are applied
   and ending not later than the Maximum Indemnity Period thereafter.
   Maximum Indemnity Period shall mean . . . months.
   Premises shall mean only those locations stated in the Premises definition; in the event that the policy includes an extension which deems loss destruction or damage at other locations to be an Incident such extension shall not apply to this memorandum.

3 For the purpose of this memorandum
   Indemnity Period shall mean the period during which the results of the Business shall be affected in consequence of the occurrence discovery or accident,

beginning with the date from which the restrictions on the Premises are applied (or in the case of 4 above, with the date of the occurrence) and ending not later than the Maximum Indemnity Period thereafter.
Maximum Indemnity Period shall mean . . . . months.
Premises shall mean only those locations stated in the Premises definition; in the event that the policy includes an extension which deems loss destruction or damage at other locations to be an Incident such extension shall not apply to this memorandum.

4 The Insurer shall not be liable under this memorandum for any costs incurred in the cleaning, repair, replacement, recall or checking of property.

5 The Insurer shall only be liable for the loss arising at those Premises which are directly affected by the occurrence discovery or accident.

6 The Insurer's liability under this memorandum shall not exceed £ . . . . . . in any one period of insurance, after the application of all other terms and conditions of the policy.

Part C

Hotels, Restaurants and Public Houses

1 (a) any occurrence of a Notifiable Disease (as defined below) at the Premises or attributable to food or drink supplied from the Premises
   (b) any discovery of an organism at the Premises likely to result in the occurrence of a Notifiable Disease
   (c) any occurrence of a Notifiable Disease (in the town/borough of . . .) (within a radius of 25 miles of the Premises)

2 the discovery of vermin or pests at the Premises which causes restrictions on the use of the Premises on the order or advice of the competent local authority

3 any accident causing defects in the drains or other sanitary arrangements at the Premises which causes restrictions on the use of the Premises on the order of the competent local authority

4 any occurrence of murder or suicide at the Premises.

and Special Conditions 1, 2, 4 and 5.

Schools, Private Hospitals etc.

1 (a) any occurrence of a Notifiable Disease (as defined below) at the Premises or attributable to food or drink supplied from the Premises
   (b) any discovery of an organism at the Premises likely to result in the occurrence of a Notifiable Disease
   (c) any occurrence of a Notifiable Disease (in the town/borough of . . .) (within a radius of 25 miles of the Premises)

2 the discovery of vermin or pests at the Premises

461 APPENDIX O

    3 any accident causing defects in the drains or other sanitary arrangements at the Premises

which causes restrictions on the use of the Premises on the order or advice of the competent local authority

    4 any occurrence of murder or suicide at the Premises.

and Special Conditions 1, 3, 4 and 5.

Food Processors and Distributors

    1 (a) any occurrence of a Notifiable Disease (as defined below) at the Premises or attributable to food or drink supplied from the Premises
       (b) any discovery of an organism at the Premises likely to result in the occurrence of a Notifiable Disease

    2 the discovery of vermin or pests at the Premises

    3 any accident causing defects in the drains or other sanitary arrangements at the Premises

which causes restrictions on the use of the Premises on the order or advice of the competent local authority

    4 any occurrence of murder or suicide at the Premises.

and Special Conditions 1, 3, 4 and 6.

Notes:
    1. Use only those parts of the wordings as are appropriate.

    2. Where cover is to be given for decontamination etc. add the following memorandum:—

Notwithstanding Special Condition 4 the insurance by this memorandum extends to include the costs and expenses necessarily incurred with the consent of the Insurer in—
    (i) cleaning and decontamination of property used by the Insured for the purpose of the Business (other than stock in trade),
    (ii) removal and disposal of contaminated stock in trade,
at or from the Premises, the use of which has been restricted on the order or advice of the competent local authority solely in consequence of the loss as defined above, provided that the Insurer's liability in respect of (i) and (ii) above shall not exceed £ . . . . in any one period of insurance after the application of all other terms and conditions of the policy.

462.—APPENDIX P

UNITED KINGDOM BUSINESS INTERRUPTION SPECIFICATION— TO INSURE LOSS OF INTEREST (EXAMPLE)

(For Property Developers—Refer Paragraph 267(b))

Item No.		Sum Insured
1	On Interest	£
	TOTAL	£

The insurance under Item no. 1 is limited to the financial loss suffered by the Insured in consequence of the Incident and the amount payable as indemnity thereunder shall be

(a) the loss of Interest incurred during the Indemnity Period but not exceeding the amount produced by applying the Percentage Rate of Interest to the Proposed Selling Price of the Premises calculated pro rata for the length of the Indemnity Period

(b) the additional expenditure necessarily and reasonably incurred for the sole purpose of avoiding or diminishing the loss of Interest which but for that expenditure would have taken place during the Indemnity Period but not exceeding the amount of the loss of Interest thereby avoided

Provided that if the Sum Insured by this Item be less than (*multiple*) the sum produced by applying the average Percentage Rate of Interest during the Indemnity Period to the Proposed Selling Price of the Premises the amount payable hereunder shall be proportionately reduced.

DEFINITIONS

The Business:

The Premises: The site of the Contract and/or the completed buildings at. . . . .

Incident: Loss or destruction of or damage to property at the Premises.

The Contract: The erection and/or reconstruction and/or redevelopment of buildings at the Premises.

Interest: The money that would have been payable to the Insured in respect of the Proposed Selling Price of the Premises were that money invested at the Percentage Rate of Interest.

Indemnity Period: (*if evidence is provided of an agreement with a prospective purchaser*): The period beginning with the date upon which but for the Incident the premises would have been sold and ending not later than the Maximum Indemnity Period thereafter during which the premises remain unsold in consequence of the Incident.

Indemnity Period: (*if evidence is not provided of an agreement with a prospective purchaser and the Premises are ready for sale*): The period beginning with the occurrence of the Incident and ending not later than the Maximum Indemnity Period thereafter during which the Premises are untenantable in consequence of the Incident.

Indemnity Period: (*if evidence is not provided of an agreement with a prospective purchaser and the Contract is not complete*): The period beginning with the date upon which but for the Incident the Contract would have been completed and ending not later than the Maximum Indemnity Period thereafter during which the Completion of the Contract is delayed in consequence of the Incident.

Maximum Indemnity Period: months

Percentage Rate of Interest: The actual rate of Interest payable by the Insured during the Indemnity Period in respect of Capital borrowed to finance the Contract and/or purchase the Premises adjusted in respect of the non-borrowed portion of the Proposed Selling Price of the Premises to the ninety-day money market rate pertaining during the Indemnity Period

Proposed Selling Price of the Premises: The money that would have been paid or payable to the Insured in respect of the sale of the Premises at the commencement date of the Indemnity Period as negotiated between the Insured and a purchaser before the date of the Incident or as assessed by the Professional Valuer if no such negotiations have taken place.
N.B. the amount thus arrived at shall be reduced by such charges of the Business payable out of the Proposed Selling Price of the Premises as are deferred until after the expiry of the Indemnity Period.

The Professional Valuer: A practising member of the Royal Institution of Chartered Surveyors whose appointment shall be satisfactory to both the Insured and the Insurer or otherwise by nomination of the President for the time being of the Royal Institution of Chartered Surveyors.
Note—The fees payable to the Professional Valuer shall be paid by the Insurer.

Other Circumstances Clause: In the settlement of any loss under this Policy account will be taken of any factor which might affect the trend of the Business and consideration will be given to any variations in or other circumstances affecting the Business either before or after the Incident or which would have affected the Business had the Incident not occurred so that the final settlement of the loss shall represent as nearly as may be reasonably practicable the results which but for the Incident would have been obtained during the Indemnity Period in accordance with the terms of this policy

Auditors Clause: Any particulars or details contained in the Insured's books of account or other business books or documents which may be required by the Insurer under the Claims Condition of this policy for the purpose of investigating or verifying any claim hereunder may be produced and certified by the Insured's Auditors and their certificate shall be prima facie evidence of the particulars and details to which such certificate relates

The Insurer will pay to the Insured the reasonable charges payable by the Insured to their Auditors for producing such particulars or details or any other proofs information or evidence as may be required by the Insurer under the terms of the Claims Condition of this policy and reporting that such particulars or details are in accordance with the Insured's books of account or other business books or documents provided that the sum of the amount payable under this clause and the amount otherwise payable under the policy shall in no case exceed the total sum insured by the policy

463.—APPENDIX Q

UNITED STATES BUSINESS INTERRUPTION INSURANCE OF GROSS EARNINGS FOR MERCANTILE AND NON-MANUFACTURING BUSINESSES

Note—No longer in general use in the United States but still used elsewhere.)

Location of premises
                  Co-insurance clause   Limit of
                           percentage   Liability
                                                    $

1. Interruption of business: This policy insures against loss resulting directly from necessary interruption of business caused by damage to or destruction of real or personal property by the peril(s) insured against during the term of this policy on premises occupied by the Insured and situate as above described.

2. Contract to indemnify:
(a) **Actual loss sustained**—in the event of such damage or destruction this Company shall be liable for the actual loss sustained by the Insured resulting directly from such interruption of business but not exceeding the reduction in Gross Earnings less charges and expenses which do not necessarily continue during the interruption of business, for only such length of time as would be required with the exercise of due diligence and dispatch to rebuild, repair or replace such part of the property herein described as has been damaged or destroyed, commencing with the date of such damage or destruction and not limited by the date of expiration of this policy. Due consideration shall be given to the continuation of normal charges and expenses, including payroll expense, to the extent necessary to resume operations of the Insured with the same quality of service which existed immediately preceding the loss,
(b) **Expenses to reduce loss**—this policy also covers such expenses as are necessarily incurred for the purpose of reducing loss under this policy (except expense incurred to extinguish a fire) but in no event shall the aggregate of such expenses exceed the amount by which the loss otherwise payable under this policy is thereby reduced. Such expenses shall not be subject to the application of the Co-insurance Clause.

3. Extensions of coverage:
(a) **Alterations and new buildings**—permission is granted to make alterations in or to construct additions to any building described herein and to construct new buildings on the above premises. This policy is extended to cover, subject to all its provisions and stipulations, loss resulting from damage to or destruction of such alterations, additions or new buildings while in course of construction and when completed or occupied, provided that in the event of damage to or destruction of such property (including building materials, supplies, machinery or equipment incident to such construction or occupancy while on the described premises or within 100 feet thereof) so as to delay commencement of business operations of the Insured the length of time for which this Company shall be liable shall be determined as otherwise provided herein but such determined length of time shall be applied and the loss hereunder calculated from the date that business operations would have begun had no damage or destruction occurred.

This clause does not waive or modify any of the conditions of the Automatic Sprinkler Clause, if any, attached to this policy.

(b) **Interruption by civil authority**—this policy is extended to include the actual loss sustained by the Insured resulting directly from an interruption of business as covered hereunder during the length of time not exceeding two consecutive weeks when as a direct result of damage to or destruction of property adjacent to the premises above described by the peril(s) insured against access to such described premises is specifically prohibited by order of civil authority.

4. Resumption of operations: It is a condition of this insurance that if the Insured could reduce the loss resulting from the interruption of business (a) by complete or partial resumption of operation of the property herein described whether damaged or not or (b) by making use of merchandise or other property at the location(s) described herein or elsewhere, such reduction shall be taken into account in arriving at the amount of loss hereunder.

5. Co-Insurance clause: This Company shall not be liable for a greater proportion of any loss than the amount of insurance specified for this policy bears to the amount produced by multiplying the Gross Earnings that would have been earned (had no loss occurred) during the 12 months immediately following the date of damage to or destruction of the described property by the co-insurance percentage applicable as specified on this policy.

6. Definitions:

Gross Earnings: For the purposes of this insurance Gross Earnings are defined as the sum of
   the total net sales and other earnings derived from operations of the business less the cost of
   i. merchandise sold including packaging material therefor,
   ii. materials and supplies consumed directly in supplying the service(s) sold by the Insured, and
   iii. service(s) purchased from outsiders (not employees of the insured) for resale which do not continue under contract.
No other costs shall be deductible in determining Gross Earnings.

Normal: Normal shall mean the condition that would have existed had no loss occurred.

7. Adjustment for probable experience: In determining Gross Earnings due consideration shall be given to the experience of the business before the date of damage or destruction and the probable experience thereafter had no loss occurred.

8. Limitations and exclusions:
   a. The Company shall not be liable for any increase of loss resulting from
      i. enforcement of any ordinance or law regulating the use, construction, repair or demolition of property, or
      ii. interference at the described premises by strikers or other persons with rebuilding, repairing or replacing the property or with the resumption or continuation of business, or
      iii. the suspension, lapse or cancellation of any lease, license, contract or order unless such suspension, lapse or cancellation results directly from the interruption of business and then the Company shall be liable for only such loss as affects the Insured's earnings during and limited to the period of indemnity covered under this policy.

b. The Company shall not be liable for any other consequential or remote loss.
c. The Company shall not be liable for any loss resulting from any electrical injury or disturbance to electrical appliances, devices, fixtures or wiring caused by electrical currents artificially generated unless fire as insured against ensues and then the Company shall be liable for only its proportion of loss caused by the ensuing fire.
d. With respect to loss resulting from damage to or destruction of media for or programming records pertaining to electronic data processing or electronically controlled equipment including data thereon by the peril(s) insured against, the length of time for which the Company shall be liable hereunder shall not exceed 30 consecutive calendar days or the length of time that would be required to rebuild, repair or replace such other property herein described as has been damaged or destroyed, whichever is the greater length of time.
e. The word "fire" in this policy or endorsements attached hereto is not intended to and does not embrace nuclear reaction or nuclear radiation or radioactive contamination, all whether controlled or uncontrolled, and loss by nuclear reaction or nuclear radiation or radioactive contamination is not intended to be and is not insured against by this policy or said endorsements, whether such loss be direct or indirect, proximate or remote, or be in a whole or in part caused by, contributed to, or aggravated by "fire" or any other perils insured against by this policy or said endorsements; however, subject to the foregoing and all provisions of this policy, loss by "fire" resulting from nuclear reaction or nuclear radiation or radioactive contamination is insured against by this policy. This clause is not applicable in New York.
f. In respect of insurance in New York this policy does not cover loss or damage caused by nuclear reaction or nuclear radiation or radioactive contamination, all whether directly or indirectly resulting from an insured peril under this policy.

9. Other provisions

a. Control of Property: This insurance shall not be prejudiced by any act or neglect of any person (other than the Insured), when such act or neglect is not within the control of the Insured.

b. Divisible Contract Clause: If this policy covers two or more buildings or the contents of two or more buildings, the breach of any condition of the policy in any one or more of the buildings covered or containing the property covered shall not prejudice the right to recover for loss occurring in any building covered or containing the property covered, where at the time of loss a breach of condition does not exist.

c. Inspection of Property and Operations: This Company and any person or organization making inspections on this Company's behalf shall be permitted but not obligated to inspect the Insured's property and operations at any time. Neither the right of this Company and any person or organization to make such inspections nor the making thereof nor any report thereon shall constitute an undertaking, on behalf of or for the benefit of the Insured or others, to determine or warrant that such property or operations are safe or healthful, or are in compliance with any law, rule or regulation.

d. Liberalization Clause: If during the period that insurance is in force under this policy, or within 45 days prior to the inception date thereof, on behalf of this Company there be adopted, or filed with and approved or accepted by the insurance supervisory authorities, all in conformity with law, any changes in the form attached to this policy by which this form of insurance could be extended or broadened without increased premium charge by endorsement or substitution of form, then such extended or broadened insurance shall insure to the benefit of the Insured hereunder as though such endorsement or substitution of form had been made.

e. Loss Clause: Any loss hereunder shall not reduce the amount of this policy.

f. Pro Rata Clause: The liability under this policy shall not exceed that proportion of any loss which the amount of insurance hereunder bears to all insurance, whether collectible or not, covering in any manner the loss insured against by this policy.

g. Protective Safeguards: It is a condition of this insurance that the Insured shall maintain so far as is within his control such protective safeguards as are set forth by endorsement hereto. Failure to maintain such protective safeguards shall suspend this insurance, only as respects the location or situation affected, for the time of such discontinuance.

h. Requirements in Case Loss Occurs: The Insured shall give immediate written notice to this Company of any Business Interruption loss and protect the property from further damage that might result in extension of the period of interruption; and within 60 days following the date of damage to or destruction of the real or personal property described, unless such time is extended in writing by this Company, the Insured shall render to this Company a proof of loss, signed and sworn to by the Insured, stating the knowledge and belief of the Insured as to the following:
    i the time and origin of the property damage or destruction causing the interruption of business,
    ii the interest of the Insured and of all others in the business,
    iii all other contracts of insurance, whether valid or not, covering in any manner the loss insured against by this policy,
    iv any changes in the title, nature, location, encumbrance or possession of said business since the issuing of this policy, and
    v by whom and for what purpose any building herein described and the several parts thereof were occupied at the time of damage or destruction,
and shall furnish a copy of all the descriptions and schedules in all policies, and the actual amount of business interruption value and loss claimed, accompanied by detailed exhibits of all values, costs and estimates upon which such amounts are based.

The Insured, as often as may be reasonably required, shall exhibit to any person designated by this Company all that remains of any property herein described, and submit to examinations under oath by any person named by this Company, and subscribe the same; and, as often as may be reasonably required, shall produce for examination all books of account, bills, invoices and other vouchers, or certified copies thereof if originals be lost, at such reasonable time and place as may be designated by this Company or its representative, and shall permit extracts and copies thereof to be made.

i. Subrogation Clause: This insurance shall not be invalidated should the Insured waive in writing prior to a loss any or all right of recovery against any party for loss occurring to the property described.

464.—APPENDIX R

UNITED STATES BUSINESS INTERRUPTION INSURANCE OF GROSS EARNINGS FOR MANUFACTURING AND MINING BUSINESSES

(Note—No longer in general use in the United States but still used elsewhere.)

Location of premises

| | Co-insurance clause percentage | Limit of Liability $_____ |

The only differences in the policy wording for manufacturing risks from that given in preceding Appendix Q for mercantile and non-manufacturing risks are:—

para. 1. **Interruption of business:** *this is amended by addition of the words "except finished stock" so as to read . . .*
This policy insures against loss resulting directly from necessary interruption of business caused by damage to or destruction of real or personal property, except finished stock, by the perils insured against during the term of this policy on the premises occupied by the Insured and situate as above described.

para. 2. (b) **Expenses to reduce loss:** *a sentence is added extending this by the inclusion of* . . . "such expenses, in excess of normal, as would necessarily be incurred in replacing any finished stock used by the Insured to reduce loss under this policy."

para. 4. **Resumption of operations:** *a third stipulation is added . . .*
"or (c) by making use of stock (raw, in process or finished) at the location(s) described herein or elsewhere."

para. 6. **Definitions:** *"Gross Earnings" is amended by additions which make it read . . .*
For the purposes of this insurance Gross Earnings are defined as the sum of
   i. total net sales value of production
   ii. total net sales of merchandise, and
   iii. other earnings derived from operations of the business, less the cost of
   iv. raw stock from which such production is derived,
   v. supplies consisting of materials consumed directly in the conversion of such raw stock into finished stock or in supplying the service(s) sold by the Insured,
   vi. merchandise sold including packaging materials therefor, and
   vii. services purchased from outsiders (not employees of the Insured) for resale which do not continue under contract.
No other costs shall be deducted in determining Gross Earnings.

The following definitions relating to stock are added . . .
"Raw stock" means material in the state in which the Insured receives it for conversion by the Insured into finished stock.
"Stock in process" means raw stock which has undergone any ageing, seasoning, mechanical or other process of manufacture at the location(s) herein described but which has not become finished stock.

"Finished stock" means stock manufactured by the Insured which in the ordinary course of the Insured's business is ready for packing, shipment or sale.

"Merchandise" means goods kept for sale by the Insured which are not the product of manufacturing operations conducted by the Insured.

para. 8. **Limitations and exclusions:** *to these are added* . . .
- g. The Company shall not be liable for loss resulting from damage to or destruction of finished stock nor for the time required to reproduce such finished stock.
- *h. The Company shall not be liable for loss due to fines or damages for breach of contract for late or non-completion of orders or for any penalties of whatever nature.

* Canadian form only.

465.—APPENDIX S

UNITED STATES BUSINESS INCOME COVERAGE FORMS

(**Note**—The following Coverage and Causes of Loss forms are examples of what can be provided. They are issued in combination with the Commercial Property Conditions (text shown), the Common Policy Conditions, a Schedule and a Declaration page (with or without a Property Damage Coverage form). Refer paragraphs 24 to 34.)

COMMERCIAL PROPERTY

BUSINESS INCOME COVERAGE FORM (AND EXTRA EXPENSE)

Various provisions in this policy restrict coverage. Read the entire policy carefully to determine rights, duties and what is and is not covered.

Throughout this policy the words "you" and "your" refer to the Named Insured shown in the Declarations. The words "we," "us" and "our" refer to the Company providing this insurance.

Other words and phrases that appear in quotation marks have special meaning. Refer to SECTION G - DEFINITIONS.

A. COVERAGE

We will pay for the actual loss of Business Income you sustain due to the necessary suspension of your "operations" during the "period of restoration". The suspension must be caused by direct physical loss of or damage to property at the premises described in the Declarations, including personal property in the open (or in a vehicle) within 100 feet, caused by or resulting from any Covered Cause of Loss.

1. Business Income

Business Income means the:

a. Net Income (Net Profit or Loss before income taxes) that would have been earned or incurred; and

b. Continuing normal operating expenses incurred, including payroll.

2. Covered Causes Of Loss.

See applicable Causes of Loss Form as shown in the Declarations.

3. Additional Coverages

a. **Extra Expense.**

Extra Expense means necessary expenses you incur during the "period of restoration" that you would not have incurred if there had been no direct physical loss or damage to property caused by or resulting from a Covered Cause of Loss.

(1) We will pay any Extra Expense to avoid or minimize the suspension of business and to continue "operations":

(a) At the described premises; or

(b) At replacement premises or at temporary locations, including:

(I) Relocation expenses; and

(II) Costs to equip and operate the replacement or temporary locations.

(2) We will pay any Extra Expense to minimize the suspension of business if you cannot continue "operations".

(3) We will pay any Extra Expense to:

(a) Repair or replace any property; or

(b) Research, replace or restore the lost information on damaged valuable papers and records;

to the extent it reduces the amount of loss that otherwise would have been payable under this Coverage Form.

b. **Civil Authority.** We will pay for the actual loss of Business Income you sustain and necessary Extra Expense caused by action of civil authority that prohibits access to the described premises due to direct physical loss of or damage to property, other than at the described premises, caused by or resulting from any Covered Cause of Loss. This coverage will apply for a period of up to two consecutive weeks from the date of that action.

c. **Alterations and New Buildings.** We will pay for the actual loss of Business Income you sustain due to direct physical loss or damage at the described premises caused by or resulting from any Covered Cause of Loss to:

(1) New buildings or structures, whether complete or under construction;

(2) Alterations or additions to existing buildings or structures; and

(3) Machinery, equipment, supplies or building materials located on or within 100 feet of the described premises and:

(a) Used in the construction, alterations or additions; or

(b) Incidental to the occupancy of new buildings.

CP 00 30 07 88   Copyright, ISO Commercial Risk Services, Inc., 1983, 1987   Page 1 of 6

APPENDIX S

If such direct physical loss or damage delays the start of "operations", the "period of restoration" will begin on the date "operations" would have begun if the direct physical loss or damage had not occurred.

d. **Extended Business Income.** We will pay for the actual loss of Business Income you incur during the period that:

(1) Begins on the date property (except "finished stock") is actually repaired, rebuilt or replaced and "operations" are resumed; and

(2) Ends on the earlier of:

(a) The date you could restore your business, with reasonable speed, to the condition that would have existed if no direct physical loss or damage occurred; or

(b) 30 consecutive days after the date determined in (1) above.

Loss of Business Income must be caused by direct physical loss or damage at the described premises caused by or resulting from any Covered Cause of Loss.

4. **Coverage Extension**

If a Coinsurance percentage of 50% or more is shown in the Declarations, you may extend the insurance provided by this Coverage Part as follows:

Newly Acquired Locations

a. You may extend your Business Income Coverage to apply to property at any location you acquire other than fairs or exhibitions.

b. The most we will pay for loss under this Extension is 10% of the Limit of Insurance for Business Income shown in the Declarations, but not more than $100,000 at each location.

c. Insurance under this Extension for each newly acquired location will end when any of the following first occurs:

(1) This policy expires;

(2) 30 days expire after you acquire or begin to construct the property; or

(3) You report values to us.

We will charge you additional premium for values reported from the date you acquire the property.

This Extension is additional insurance. The Additional Condition, Coinsurance, does not apply to this Extension.

B. **EXCLUSIONS**

See applicable Causes of Loss Form as shown in the Declarations.

C. **LIMITS OF INSURANCE**

The most we will pay for loss in any one occurrence is the applicable Limit of Insurance shown in the Declarations.

The limit applicable to the Coverage Extension is in addition to the Limit of Insurance.

Payments under the following Additional Coverages will not increase the applicable Limit of Insurance:

1. Alterations and New Buildings;
2. Civil Authority;
3. Extra Expense; or
4. Extended Business Income.

D. **LOSS CONDITIONS**

The following conditions apply in addition to the Common Policy Conditions and the Commercial Property Conditions.

1. **Appraisal**

If we and you disagree on the amount of Net Income and operating expense or the amount of loss, either may make written demand for an appraisal of the loss. In this event, each party will select a competent and impartial appraiser.

The two appraisers will select an umpire. If they cannot agree, either may request that selection be made by a judge of a court having jurisdiction. The appraisers will state separately the amount of Net Income and operating expense or amount of loss. If they fail to agree, they will submit their differences to the umpire. A decision agreed to by any two will be binding. Each party will:

a. Pay its chosen appraiser; and

b. Bear the other expenses of the appraisal and umpire equally.

If there is an appraisal, we will still retain our right to deny the claim.

2. **Duties In The Event Of Loss**

You must see that the following are done in the event of loss:

a. Notify the police if a law may have been broken.

b. Give us prompt notice of the direct physical loss or damage. Include a description of the property involved.

Copyright, ISO Commercial Risk Services, Inc., 1983, 1987   CP 00 30 07 88

UNITED STATES BUSINESS INCOME COVERAGE FORMS

c. As soon as possible, give us a description of how, when, and where the direct physical loss or damage occurred.

d. Take all reasonable steps to protect the Covered Property from further damage by a Covered Cause of Loss. If feasible, set the damaged property aside and in the best possible order for examination. Also keep a record of your expenses for emergency and temporary repairs, for consideration in the settlement of the claim. This will not increase the Limit of Insurance.

e. Permit us to inspect the property and records proving the loss.

Also permit us to take samples of damaged property for inspection, testing and analysis.

f. If requested, permit us to question you under oath at such times as may be reasonably required about any matter relating to this insurance or your claim, including your books and records. In such event, your answers must be signed.

g. Send us a signed, sworn statement of loss containing the information we request to investigate the claim. You must do this within 60 days after our request. We will supply you with the necessary forms.

h. Cooperate with us in the investigation or settlement of the claim.

i. Resume all or part of your "operations" as quickly as possible.

3. **Limitation - Electronic Media And Records**

We will not pay for any loss of Business Income caused by direct physical loss of or damage to Electronic Media and Records after the longer of:

a. 60 consecutive days from the date of direct physical loss or damage; or

b. The period, beginning with the date of direct physical loss or damage, necessary to repair, rebuild or replace, with reasonable speed and similar quality, other property at the described premises due to loss or damage caused by the same occurrence.

Electronic Media and Records are:

(1) Electronic data processing, recording or storage media such as films, tapes, discs, drums or cells;

(2) Data stored on such media; or

(3) Programming records used for electronic data processing or electronically controlled equipment.

This limitation does not apply to Extra Expense.

Example No. 1:

A Covered Cause of Loss damages a computer on June 1. It takes until September 1 to replace the computer, and until October 1 to restore the data that was lost when the damage occurred. We will only pay for the Business Income loss sustained during the period June 1 - September 1. Loss during the period September 2 - October 1 is not covered.

Example No. 2:

A Covered Cause of Loss results in the loss of data processing programming records on August 1. The records are replaced on October 15. We will only pay for the Business Income loss sustained during the period August 1 - September 29 (60 consecutive days). Loss during the period September 30 - October 15 is not covered.

4. **Loss Determination**

a. The amount of Business Income loss will be determined based on:

(1) The Net Income of the business before the direct physical loss or damage occurred;

(2) The likely Net Income of the business if no loss or damage occurred;

(3) The operating expenses, including payroll expenses, necessary to resume "operations" with the same quality of service that existed just before the direct physical loss or damage; and

(4) Other relevant sources of information, including:

(a) Your financial records and accounting procedures;

(b) Bills, invoices and other vouchers; and

(c) Deeds, liens or contracts.

CP 00 30 07 88 Copyright, ISO Commercial Risk Services, Inc., 1983, 1987

b. The amount of Extra Expense will be determined based on:

   (1) All expenses that exceed the normal operating expenses that would have been incurred by "operations" during the "period of restoration" if no direct physical loss or damage had occurred. We will deduct from the total of such expenses:

      (a) The salvage value that remains of any property bought for temporary use during the "period of restoration", once "operations" are resumed; and

      (b) Any Extra Expense that is paid for by other insurance, except for insurance that is written subject to the same plan, terms, conditions and provisions as this insurance; and

   (2) All necessary expenses that reduce the Business Income loss that otherwise would have been incurred.

5. **Loss Payment**

   We will pay for covered loss within 30 days after we receive the sworn statement of loss, if:

   a. You have complied with all of the terms of this Coverage Part; and

   b. (1) We have reached agreement with you on the amount of loss; or

      (2) An appraisal award has been made.

6. **Resumption Of Operations**

   We will reduce the amount of your:

   a. Business Income loss, other than Extra Expense, to the extent you can resume your "operations", in whole or in part, by using damaged or undamaged property (including merchandise or stock) at the described premises or elsewhere.

   b. Extra Expense loss to the extent you can return "operations" to normal and discontinue such Extra Expense.

E. **ADDITIONAL CONDITION**

   Coinsurance

   If a Coinsurance percentage is shown in the Declarations, the following condition applies in addition to the Common Policy Conditions and the Commercial Property Conditions.

   We will not pay the full amount of any loss if the Limit of Insurance for Business Income is less than:

   a. The Coinsurance percentage shown for Business Income in the Declarations; times

   b. The sum of:

      (1) The Net Income (Net Profit or Loss before income taxes), and

      (2) All operating expenses, including payroll expenses,

      that would have been earned (had no loss occurred) by your "operations" at the described premises for the 12 months following the inception, or last previous anniversary date, of this policy (whichever is later).

   Instead, we will determine the most we will pay using the following steps:

   1. Multiply the Net Income and operating expense for the 12 months following the inception, or last previous anniversary date, of this policy by the Coinsurance percentage;

   2. Divide the Limit of Insurance for the described premises by the figure determined in step 1; and

   3. Multiply the total amount of the covered loss by the figure determined in Step 2.

   The amount determined in step 3 is the most we will pay. For the remainder, you will either have to rely on other insurance or absorb the loss yourself.

   Example No. 1 (Underinsurance):

   When: The Net Income and operating expenses for the 12 months following the inception, or last previous anniversary date, of this policy at the described premises would have been $400,000
   The Coinsurance percentage is   50%
   The Limit of Insurance is $150,000
   The amount of loss is $ 80,000

   Step 1: $400,000 x 50% = $200,000 (the minimum amount of insurance to meet your Coinsurance requirements)

   Step 2: $150,000 ÷ $200,000 = .75

   Step 3: $ 80,000 x .75 = $60,000

   We will pay no more than $60,000. The remaining $20,000 is not covered.

Example No. 2 (Adequate Insurance):

When: The Net Income and operating expenses for the 12 months following the inception, or last previous anniversary date, of this policy at the, described premises would have been $400,000
The Coinsurance percentage is 50%
The Limit of Insurance is $200,000
The amount of loss is $ 80,000

Step 1: $400,000 x 50% = $200,000 (the minimum amount of insurance to meet your Coinsurance requirements)

Step 2: $200,000 ÷ $200,000 = 1.00

Step 3: $ 80,000 x 1.00 = $80,000

We will cover the $80,000 loss. No penalty applies.

This condition does not apply to the Extra Expense Additional Coverage.

F. **OPTIONAL COVERAGES**

If shown in the Declarations, the following Optional Coverages apply separately to each item.

1. **Maximum Period Of Indemnity**
   a. The Additional Condition, Coinsurance, does not apply to this Coverage Form at the described premises to which this Optional Coverage applies.
   b. The most we will pay for loss of Business Income is the lesser of:
      (1) The amount of loss sustained during the 120 days immediately following the direct physical loss or damage; or
      (2) The Limit of Insurance shown in the Declarations.

2. **Monthly Limit Of Indemnity**
   a. The Additional Condition, Coinsurance, does not apply to this Coverage Form at the described premises to which this Optional Coverage applies.
   b. The most we will pay for loss of Business Income in each period of 30 consecutive days after the direct physical loss or damage is:
      (1) The Limit of Insurance, multiplied by
      (2) The fraction shown in the Declarations for this Optional Coverage.

Example:

When: The Limit of Insurance is $120,000
The fraction shown in the Declarations for this Optional Coverage is 1/4

The most we will pay for loss in each period of 30 consecutive days is:

$120,000 x 1/4 = $30,000

if, in this example, the actual amount of loss is:

Days 1-30 $40,000
Days 31-60 20,000
Days 61-90 30,000
              $90,000

We will pay:

Days 1-30 $30,000
Days 31-60 20,000
Days 61-90 30,000
              $80,000

The remaining $10,000 is not covered.

3. **Agreed Value**
   a. To activate this Optional Coverage:
      (1) A Business Income Report/Work Sheet must be made a part of this policy and must show financial data for your "operations":
         (a) During the 12 months prior to the date of the Work Sheet; and
         (b) Estimated for the 12 months immediately following the inception of this Optional Coverage.
      (2) An Agreed Value must be shown in the Declarations or on the Work Sheet. The Agreed Value should be at least equal to:
         (a) The Coinsurance percentage shown in the Declarations; multiplied by
         (b) The amount of Net Income and Operating Expenses for the following 12 months you report on the Work Sheet.
   b. The Additional Condition, Coinsurance, is suspended until:
      (1) 12 months after the effective date of this Optional Coverage; or

(2) The expiration date of this policy; whichever occurs first.

c. We will reinstate the Additional Condition, Coinsurance, automatically if you do not submit a new Work Sheet and Agreed Value:

(1) Within 12 months of the effective date of this Optional Coverage; or

(2) When you request a change in your Business Income Limit of Insurance.

d. If the Business Income Limit of Insurance is less than the Agreed Value, we will not pay more of any loss than the amount of loss multiplied by:

(1) The Business Income Limit of Insurance; divided by

(2) The Agreed Value.

Example:

When: The Limit of Insurance
is $100,000
The Agreed Value is $200,000
The amount of loss is $ 80,000

Step (a): $100,000 ÷ $200,000 = .50

Step (b): .50 x $80,000 = $40,000

We will pay $40,000. The remaining $40,000 is not covered.

4. **Extended Period Of Indemnity**

Under paragraph A.3.d., Extended Business Income, the number "30" in subparagraph (2)(b) is replaced by the number shown in the Declarations for this Optional Coverage.

G. DEFINITIONS

1. **"Finished Stock"** means stock you have manufactured.

"Finished stock" also includes whiskey and alcoholic products being aged, unless there is a Coinsurance percentage shown for Business Income in the Declarations.

"Finished stock" does not include stock you have manufactured that is held for sale on the premises of any retail outlet insured under this Coverage Part.

2. **"Operations"** means your business activities occurring at the described premises.

3. **"Period of Restoration"** means the period of time that:

a. Begins with the date of direct physical loss or damage caused by or resulting from any Covered Cause of Loss at the described premises; and

b. Ends on the date when the property at the described premises should be repaired, rebuilt or replaced with reasonable speed and similar quality.

"Period of restoration" does not include any increased period required due to the enforcement of any ordinance or law that:

(1) Regulates the construction, use or repair, or requires the tearing down of any property; or

(2) Requires any insured or others to test for, monitor, clean up, remove, contain, treat, detoxify or neutralize, or in any way respond to, or assess the effects of "pollutants".

The expiration date of this policy will not cut short the "period of restoration".

4. **"Pollutants"** means any solid, liquid, gaseous or thermal irritant or contaminant, including smoke, vapor, soot, fumes, acids, alkalis, chemicals and waste. Waste includes materials to be recycled, reconditioned or reclaimed.

COMMERCIAL PROPERTY

CAUSES OF LOSS - BASIC FORM

A. COVERED CAUSES OF LOSS

When Basic is shown in the Declarations, Covered Causes of Loss means the following:

1. **Fire.**
2. **Lightning.**
3. **Explosion,** including the explosion of gases or fuel within the furnace of any fired vessel or within the flues or passages through which the gases of combustion pass. This cause of loss does not include loss or damage by:
   a. Rupture, bursting or operation of pressure relief devices; or
   b. Rupture or bursting due to expansion or swelling of the contents of any building or structure, caused by or resulting from water.
4. **Windstorm or Hail,** but not including:
   a. Frost or cold weather;
   b. Ice (other than hail), snow or sleet, whether driven by wind or not; or
   c. Loss or damage to the interior of any building or structure, or the property inside the building or structure, caused by rain, snow, sand or dust, whether driven by wind or not, unless the building or structure first sustains wind or hail damage to its roof or walls through which the rain, snow, sand or dust enters.
5. **Smoke** causing sudden and accidental loss or damage. This cause of loss does not include smoke from agricultural smudging or industrial operations.
6. **Aircraft or Vehicles,** meaning only physical contact of an aircraft, a spacecraft, a self-propelled missile, a vehicle or an object thrown up by a vehicle with the described property or with the building or structure containing the described property. This cause of loss includes loss or damage by objects falling from aircraft.

   We will not pay for loss or damage caused by or resulting from vehicles you own or which are operated in the course of your business.
7. **Riot or Civil Commotion,** including:
   a. Acts of striking employees while occupying the described premises; and
   b. Looting occurring at the time and place of a riot or civil commotion.
8. **Vandalism,** meaning willful and malicious damage to, or destruction of, the described property.

   We will not pay for loss or damage:
   a. To glass (other than glass building blocks) that is part of a building, structure, or an outside sign; but we will pay for loss or damage to other property caused by or resulting from breakage of glass by vandals.
   b. Caused by or resulting from theft, except for building damage caused by the breaking in or exiting of burglars.
9. **Sprinkler Leakage,** meaning leakage or discharge of any substance from an Automatic Sprinkler System, including collapse of a tank that is part of the system.

   If the building or structure containing the Automatic Sprinkler System is Covered Property, we will also pay the cost to:
   a. Repair or replace damaged parts of the Automatic Sprinkler System if the damage:
      (1) Results in sprinkler leakage; or
      (2) Is directly caused by freezing.
   b. Tear out and replace any part of the building or structure to repair damage to the Automatic Sprinkler System that has resulted in sprinkler leakage.

   Automatic Sprinkler System means:

   (a) Any automatic fire protective or extinguishing system, including connected:
      (i) Sprinklers and discharge nozzles;
      (ii) Ducts, pipes, valves and fittings;
      (iii) Tanks, their component parts and supports; and
      (iv) Pumps and private fire protection mains.
   (b) When supplied from an automatic fire protective system:
      (i) Non-automatic fire protective systems; and
      (ii) Hydrants, standpipes and outlets.

CP 10 10 07 88   Copyright, ISO Commercial Risk Services, Inc., 1983, 1987   Page 1 of 3

APPENDIX S

10. **Sinkhole Collapse**, meaning loss or damage caused by the sudden sinking or collapse of land into underground empty spaces created by the action of water on limestone or dolomite. This cause of loss does not include:
    a. The cost of filling sinkholes; or
    b. Sinking or collapse of land into man-made underground cavities.
11. **Volcanic Action**, meaning direct loss or damage resulting from the eruption of a volcano when the loss or damage is caused by:
    a. Airborne volcanic blast or airborne shock waves;
    b. Ash, dust or particulate matter; or
    c. Lava flow.

    All volcanic eruptions that occur within any 168-hour period will constitute a single occurrence.

    This cause of loss does not include the cost to remove ash, dust or particulate matter that does not cause direct physical loss or damage to the described property.

B. EXCLUSIONS

1. We will not pay for loss or damage caused directly or indirectly by any of the following. Such loss or damage is excluded regardless of any other cause or event that contributes concurrently or in any sequence to the loss.

    a. **Ordinance or Law**

    The enforcement of any ordinance or law:
    (1) Regulating the construction, use or repair of any property; or
    (2) Requiring the tearing down of any property, including the cost of removing its debris.

    b. **Earth Movement**
    (1) Any earth movement (other than sinkhole collapse), such as an earthquake, landslide, mine subsidence or earth sinking, rising or shifting. But if loss or damage by fire or explosion results, we will pay for that resulting loss or damage.
    (2) Volcanic eruption, explosion or effusion. But if loss or damage by fire or volcanic action results, we will pay for that resulting loss or damage.

    c. **Governmental Action**

    Seizure or destruction of property by order of governmental authority.

    But we will pay for acts of destruction ordered by governmental authority and taken at the time of a fire to prevent its spread, if the fire would be covered under this Coverage Part.

    d. **Nuclear Hazard**

    Nuclear reaction or radiation, or radioactive contamination, however caused.

    But if loss or damage by fire results, we will pay for that resulting loss or damage.

    e. **Power Failure**

    The failure of power or other utility service supplied to the described premises, however caused, if the failure occurs away from the described premises.

    But if loss or damage by a Covered Cause of Loss results, we will pay for that resulting loss or damage.

    f. **War and Military Action**
    (1) War, including undeclared or civil war;
    (2) Warlike action by a military force, including action in hindering or defending against an actual or expected attack, by any government, sovereign or other authority using military personnel or other agents; or
    (3) Insurrection, rebellion, revolution, usurped power, or action taken by governmental authority in hindering or defending against any of these.

    g. **Water**
    (1) Flood, surface water, waves, tides, tidal waves, overflow of any body of water, or their spray, all whether driven by wind or not;
    (2) Mudslide or mudflow;
    (3) Water that backs up from a sewer or drain; or
    (4) Water under the ground surface pressing on, or flowing or seeping through:
        (a) Foundations, walls, floors or paved surfaces;
        (b) Basements, whether paved or not; or
        (c) Doors, windows or other openings.

    But if loss or damage by fire, explosion or sprinkler leakage results, we will pay for that resulting loss or damage.

2. We will not pay for loss or damage caused by or resulting from:
   a. Artificially generated electrical current, including electric arcing, that disturbs electrical devices, appliances or wires.

   But if loss or damage by fire results, we will pay for that resulting loss or damage.

   b. Rupture or bursting of water pipes (other than Automatic Sprinkler Systems) unless caused by a Covered Cause of Loss.

   c. Leakage or discharge of water or steam resulting from the breaking or cracking of any part of a system or appliance containing water or steam (other than an Automatic Sprinkler System), unless the system or appliance is damaged by a Covered Cause of Loss.

   d. Explosion of steam boilers, steam pipes, steam engines or steam turbines owned or leased by you, or operated under your control.

   But if loss or damage by fire or combustion explosion results, we will pay for that resulting loss or damage.

   e. Mechanical breakdown, including rupture or busting caused by centrifugal force.

   But if loss or damage by a Covered Cause of Loss results, we will pay for that resulting loss or damage.

3. **Special Exclusions**

   The following provisions apply only to the specified Coverage Forms.

   a. **Business Income (And Extra Expense) Coverage Form, Business Income (Without Extra Expense) Coverage Form, or Extra Expense Coverage Form.**

   We will not pay for:

   (1) Any loss caused by or resulting from:
       (a) Damage or destruction of "finished stock;" or
       (b) The time required to reproduce "finished stock".

       This exclusion does not apply to Extra Expense.

   (2) Any loss caused by or resulting from direct physical loss or damage to radio or television antennas, including their lead-in wiring, masts or towers.

   (3) Any increase of loss caused by or resulting from:
       (a) Delay in rebuilding, repairing or replacing the property or resuming "operations", due to interference at the location of the rebuilding, repair or replacement by strikers or other persons; or
       (b) Suspension, lapse or cancellation of any license, lease or contract. But if the suspension, lapse or cancellation is directly caused by the suspension of "operations", we will cover such loss that affects your Business Income during the "period of restoration".

   (4) Any Extra Expense caused by or resulting from suspension, lapse or cancellation of any license, lease or contract beyond the "period of restoration".

   (5) Any other consequential loss.

   b. **Leasehold Interest Coverage Form**

   (1) Paragraph B.1.a., Ordinance or Law; does not apply to insurance under this Coverage Form.

   (2) We will not pay for any loss caused by:
       (a) Your cancelling the lease;
       (b) The suspension, lapse or cancellation of any license; or
       (c) Any other consequential loss.

   c. **Legal Liability Coverage Form**

   (1) The following Exclusions do not apply to insurance under this Coverage Form:
       (a) Paragraph B.1.a., Ordinance or Law;
       (b) Paragraph B.1.c., Governmental Action;
       (c) Paragraph B.1.d., Nuclear Hazard;
       (d) Paragraph B.1.e., Power Failure; and
       (e) Paragraph B.1.f., War and Military Action.

   (2) **Contractual Liability**

   We will not defend any claim or "suit", or pay damages that you are legally liable to pay, solely by reason of your assumption of liability in a contract or agreement.

   (3) **Nuclear Hazard**

   We will not defend any claim or "suit", or pay any damages, loss, expense or obligation, resulting from nuclear reaction or radiation, or radioactive contamination, however caused.

COMMERCIAL PROPERTY

COMMERCIAL PROPERTY CONDITIONS

This Coverage Part is subject to the following conditions, the Common Policy Conditions and applicable Loss Conditions and Additional Conditions in Commercial Property Coverage Forms.

A. CONCEALMENT, MISREPRESENTATION OR FRAUD

This Coverage Part is void in any case of fraud by you as it relates to this Coverage Part at any time. It is also void if you or any other insured, at any time, intentionally conceal or misrepresent a material fact concerning:

1. This Coverage Part;
2. The Covered Property;
3. Your interest in the Covered Property; or
4. A claim under this Coverage Part.

B. CONTROL OF PROPERTY

Any act or neglect of any person other than you beyond your direction or control will not affect this insurance.

The breach of any condition of this Coverage Part at any one or more locations will not affect coverage at any location where, at the time of loss or damage, the breach of condition does not exist.

C. INSURANCE UNDER TWO OR MORE COVERAGES

If two or more of this policy's coverages apply to the same loss or damage, we will not pay more than the actual amount of the loss or damage.

D. LEGAL ACTION AGAINST US

No one may bring a legal action against us under this Coverage Part unless:

1. There has been full compliance with all of the terms of this Coverage Part; and
2. The action is brought within 2 years after the date on which the direct physical loss or damage occurred.

E. LIBERALIZATION

If we adopt any revision that would broaden the coverage under this Coverage Part without additional premium within 45 days prior to or during the policy period, the broadened coverage will immediately apply to this Coverage Part.

F. NO BENEFIT TO BAILEE

No person or organization, other than you, having custody of Covered Property will benefit from this insurance.

G. OTHER INSURANCE

1. You may have other insurance subject to the same plan, terms, conditions and provisions as the insurance under this Coverage Part. If you do, we will pay our share of the covered loss or damage. Our share is the proportion that the applicable Limit of Insurance under this Coverage Part bears to the Limits of Insurance of all insurance covering on the same basis.

2. If there is other insurance covering the same loss or damage, other than that described in 1. above, we will pay only for the amount of covered loss or damage in excess of the amount due from that other insurance, whether you can collect on it or not. But we will not pay more than the applicable Limit of Insurance.

H. POLICY PERIOD, COVERAGE TERRITORY

Under this Coverage Part:

1. We cover loss or damage commencing:
    a. During the policy period shown in the Declarations; and
    b. Within the coverage territory.
2. The coverage territory is:
    a. The United States of America (including its territories and possessions);
    b. Puerto Rico; and
    c. Canada.

CP 00 90 07 88   Copyright, ISO Commercial Risk Services, Inc., 1983, 1987   Page 1 of 2   □

UNITED STATES BUSINESS INCOME COVERAGE FORMS **465**

I. TRANSFER OF RIGHTS OF RECOVERY AGAINST OTHERS TO US

If any person or organization to or for whom we make payment under this Coverage Part has rights to recover damages from another, those rights are transferred to us to the extent of our payment. That person or organization must do everything necessary to secure our rights and must do nothing after loss to impair them. But you may waive your rights against another party in writing:

1. Prior to a loss to your Covered Property or Covered Income.
2. After a loss to your Covered Property or Covered Income only if, at time of loss, that party is one of the following:
   a. Someone insured by this insurance;
   b. A business firm:
      (1) Owned or controlled by you; or
      (2) That owns or controls you; or
   c. Your tenant.

This will not restrict your insurance.

466.—APPENDIX T

UNITED KINGDOM OVERSEAS ("HOME FOREIGN") STANDARD CONSEQUENTIAL LOSS POLICY FORM

(**Note**—This is a wording of very long standing and is the subject of discussion between insurers to make it more relevant to contemporary circumstances.)

In consideration of the Insured paying to the Company the first premium

The Company agrees (subject to the Conditions contained herein or endorsed or otherwise expressed hereon) that if any building or other property or any part thereof used by the Insured at the premises for the purpose of the business be destroyed or damaged by
  (1) Fire
  (2) Lightning
  (3) Explosion in a building in which gas is not generated and which does not form part of any gasworks of gas used therein for illuminating or domestic purposes

(destruction or damage so caused being hereinafter termed Damage) at any time after payment of the premium and before the time specified in the schedule on the last day of the period of insurance or of any subsequent period in respect of which the premium required for the renewal of this policy shall have been paid to and accepted by the Company and the business carried on by the Insured at the premises be in consequence thereof interrupted or interfered with

Then the Company will pay to the Insured in respect of each item in the schedule hereto the amount of loss resulting from such interruption or interference in accordance with the provisions therein contained

Provided that at the time of the happening of the damage there shall be in force an insurance covering the interest of the Insured in the property at the premises against such damage and that payment shall have been made or liability admitted therefor under such insurance

And that the liability of the Company shall in no case exceed in respect of each item the sum expressed in the said schedule to be insured thereon or in the whole the total sum insured hereby or such other sum or sums as may hereafter be substituted therefor by memorandum signed by or on behalf of the Company.

Signed on behalf of the Company ....

CONDITIONS

1. If there be any material misdescription of the business or premises to which this insurance refers or any misrepresentation as to any fact material to be known for estimating the risk or any omission to state such fact the Company shall not be liable upon this policy.

2. No payment in respect of any premium shall be deemed to be payment to the Company unless a printed form of receipt for the same signed by an official or duly appointed agent of the Company shall have been given to the Insured.

3. The Insured shall give notice to the Company of any insurance or insurances already effected, or which may subsequently be effected covering any of the loss hereby insured against and unless such notice be given and the particulars of such insurance or insurances be stated in or endorsed on this policy by or on behalf of the Company before the occurrence of any damage all benefit under this policy shall be forfeited.

4. Immediately upon any fall or displacement
   (a) of any building damage to which might give rise to a claim under this policy
   (b) of any part of such building
   (c) of the whole or any part of any range of buildings or of any structure of which such building forms part

the insurance under this policy shall cease in respect of loss resulting from damage to such building or property therein

PROVIDED THAT—
   (1) Such fall or displacement is of the whole or a substantial or important part of such building or impairs the usefulness of such building or any part thereof or leaves such building or any part thereof or any property contained therein subject to increased risk of damage or is otherwise material
   (2) Such fall or displacement is not caused by damage loss resulting from which is covered by this policy or would be covered if such building, range of buildings or structure were included in the premises to which this policy refers.

If any claim be made upon this policy in consequence of damage whether occurring before, during or after such fall or displacement the Insured shall produce such proof as may reasonably be required that the loss was not, either in origin or in extent, directly or indirectly, proximately or remotely, occasioned by or contributed to by any such fall or displacement and did not either in origin or extent, directly or indirectly, proximately or remotely, arise out of or in connection with any such fall or displacement.

In any action, suit or other proceeding, the burden of proving that any fall or displacement is caused by damage shall be upon the Insured.

5. This insurance does not cover:
   Loss occasioned by or happening through or in consequence of—
   (a) The burning of property by order of any Public Authority
   (b) Subterranean fire
   (c) Explosion except as stated on the face of this policy
   (d) The burning, whether accidental or otherwise, of forests, bush, prairie, pampas or jungle and the clearing of lands by fire
   (e) Damage to property occasioned by its own fermentation, natural heating or spontaneous combustion or by its undergoing any heating or drying process
   (f) Loss or damage directly or indirectly caused by or arising from or in consequence of or contributed to by nuclear weapons material
   (g) Loss or damage directly or indirectly caused by or arising from or in consequence of or contributed to by ionising radiations or contamination by radioactivity from any nuclear fuel or from any nuclear waste from the combustion of nuclear fuel. For the purpose of this Condition 5(g) only, combustion shall include any self-sustaining process of nuclear fission.

6. This insurance does not cover any loss resulting from damage occasioned by or through or in consequence, directly or indirectly, of any of the following occurrences, namely:
   (a) Earthquake, volcanic eruption or other convulsion of nature
   (b) Typhoon, hurricane, tornado, cyclone or other atmospheric disturbance
   (c) War, invasion, act of foreign enemy, hostilities or warlike operations (whether war be declared or not), civil war
   (d) Mutiny, riot, military or popular rising, insurrection, rebellion, revolution, military or usurped power, martial law or state of siege or any of the events or causes which determine the proclamation or maintenance of martial law or state of siege.

Any loss resulting from damage happening during the existence of abnormal conditions (whether physical or otherwise) which are occasioned by or through or in consequence, directly or indirectly, of any of the said occurrences shall be deemed to be loss which is not covered by this insurance except to the extent that the Insured shall prove that such damage happened independently of the existence of such abnormal conditions.

In any action, suit or other proceeding where the Company alleges that by reason of the provisions of this condition any loss is not covered by this insurance, the burden of proving that such loss is covered shall be upon the Insured.

7. The insurance by this policy shall cease if:
   (a) the business be wound up or carried on by a liquidator or receiver or permanently discontinued
   or
   (b) the Insured's interest cease otherwise than by death
   or
   (c) any alterations be made either in the business or in the premises or property therein whereby the risk of damage is increased

at any time after the commencement of this insurance unless its continuance be admitted by memorandum signed by or on behalf of the Company.

8. Notice shall be given to the Company and if required an additional premium paid if the rate of premium payable in respect of the insurance covering the interest of the Insured in the property at the premises against damage shall be increased.

9. This insurance may be terminated at any time at the request of the Insured in which case the Company will retain the customary short period rate for the time the policy has been in force. This insurance may also at any time be terminated at the option of the Company on notice to that effect being given to the Insured, in which case the Company shall be liable to repay on demand a rateable proportion of the premium for the unexpired term from the date of the cancelment.

10. On the happening of any damage in consequence of which a claim is or may be made under this policy the Insured shall forthwith give notice thereof to the Company and shall with due diligence do and concur in doing and permit to be done all things which may be reasonably practicable to minimise or check any interruption of or interference with the business or to avoid or diminish the loss, and in the event of a claim being made under this policy shall, not later than thirty days after the expiry of the indemnity period or within such further time as the Company may in writing allow, at his own expense deliver to the Company in writing a statement setting forth particulars of his claim together with details of all other insurances

(if any) covering the damage or any part of it or consequential loss of any kind resulting therefrom. The Insured shall at his own expense produce, procure and give to the Company such books of account and other business books, vouchers, invoices, balance sheets and other documents, proofs, information, explanation and other evidence as may reasonably be required by or on behalf of the Company for the purpose of investigating or verifying the claim together with a declaration on oath or in other legal form of the truth of the claim and of any matters connected therewith. No claim under this policy shall be payable unless the terms of this condition have been complied with and in the event of non-compliance therewith in any respect any payment on account of the claim already made shall be repaid to the Company forthwith.

11. If the claim be in any respect fraudulent, or if any false declaration be made or used in support therof or if any fraudulent means or devices are used by the Insured or anyone acting on his behalf to obtain any benefit under this policy; or if the damage be occasioned by the wilful action or with the connivance of the Insured; or, if the claim be made and rejected and an action or suit be not commenced within three months after such rejection, or (in case of an arbitration taking place in pursuance of the 14th condition of this Policy) within three months after the arbitrator or arbitrators or umpire shall have made their award, all benefit under this policy shall be forfeited.

12. If at the time of any loss under this policy there be any other subsisting insurance or insurances whether effected by the Insured or by any other person or persons covering such loss or any part of it the Company shall not be liable to pay or contribute hereunder more than its rateable proportion of such loss.

13. The Insured shall at the expense of the Company do and concur in doing and permit to be done all such acts and things as may be necessary or reasonably required by the Company for the purpose of enforcing any rights and remedies or of obtaining relief or indemnity from other parties to which the Company shall be or would become entitled or subrogated upon its paying for any loss under this policy whether such acts and things shall be or become necessary or required before or after his indemnification by the Company.

14. If any difference arises as to the amount of any loss such difference shall independently of all other questions be referred to the decision of an arbitrator to be appointed in writing by the parties in difference, or, if they cannot agree upon a single arbitrator, to the decision of two disinterested persons as arbitrators, of whom one shall be appointed in writing by each of the parties within two calendar months after having been required to do so in writing by the other party. In case either party shall refuse or fail to appoint an arbitrator within two calendar months after receipt of notice in writing requiring an appointment the other party shall be at liberty to appoint a sole arbitrator; and in case of disagreement between the arbitrators the difference shall be referred to the decision of an umpire who shall have been appointed by them in writing before entering on the reference and who shall sit with the arbitrators and preside at the meetings. The death of any party shall not revoke or affect the authority or powers of the arbitrator, arbitrators or umpire respectively; and in the event of the death of an arbitrator or umpire another shall in each case be appointed in his stead by the party or arbitrators (as the case may be) by whom the arbitrator or umpire so dying was appointed. The costs of the reference and of the award shall be in the discretion of the arbitrator, arbitrators or umpire making the

award. And it is hereby expressly stipulated and declared that it shall be a condition precedent to any right of action or suit upon this policy that the award by such arbitrator, arbitrators or umpire of the amount of the loss if disputed shall be first obtained.

15. In no case whatever shall the Company be liable in respect of claim under this policy after the expiration of
    (a) one year from the end of the indemnity period or, if later,
    (b) three months from the date on which payment shall have been made or liability admitted by the insurers covering the damage giving rise to the said claim,

unless the claim is the subject of pending action or arbitration.

16. This policy and the schedule annexed (which forms an integral part of this policy) shall be read together as one contract and words and expressions to which specific meanings have been attached in any part of this policy or of the schedule shall bear such specific meanings wherever they may appear.

17. Every notice and other communication to the Company required by these conditions must be written or printed.

467.—APPENDIX U

SPECIMEN SETTLEMENT OF A SIMPLE LOSS CLAIM UNDER A UNITED KINGDOM BUSINESS INTERRUPTION POLICY

to illustrate the four basic stages of the specification formula for settling claims under an item on **Gross Profit** (para. 54)

The Policy—sum insured on Gross Profit—£450,000.
           all insurable charges are included.
           Maximum Indemnity Period—12 months.

Last Financial Year preceding the Incident—ended December 31.
    accounts show—Turnover £2,000,000.
                  —Gross Profit as defined in specification £500,000,
            therefore Rate of Gross Profit = 25%.
Annual Turnover (for the twelve months immediately preceding the Incident) = £2,000,000.

An Incident occurs on March 11 and the business is not restored to normal until November 20 of same year.

Reduction in turnover totals £900,000.

Calculation of Claim

clause (a)—
    rate of gross profit applied to reduction in turnover: 25% of £900,000 .   £225,000

clause (b)—
    increase in cost of working: additional expenditure incurred ....   £ 21,500

                                                                                      £246,500

savings in insured charges:
    reductions due to the damage ....   £ 8,900

actual loss sustained by the Insured £237,600

average proviso:
$$\frac{\text{sum insured}}{\text{rate of gross profit} \times \text{annual turnover}} = \frac{450{,}000}{25\% \text{ of } 2{,}000{,}000} = 90\%$$

therefore the policy pays 90% of £237,600 = £213,840

468.—APPENDIX V

REDUCTION IN TURNOVER—EFFECT ON ACCOUNTS (UNITED KINGDOM)

ILLUSTRATION of the effect on variable charges, standing charges and net profit respectively when the turnover of a business is reduced in consequence of an Incident.

Specimen Accounts on which the illustration is based

TRADING ACCOUNT AND PROFIT & LOSS ACCOUNT
YEAR ENDED DECEMBER 31, 1989

tha1.

Dr.	£		Cr. £
Stock January 1, 1989	708,000	Sales	3,000,000
Purchases	1,410,000	Stock December 31, 1989	708,000
Productive wages	630,000		
Fuel	24,000		
Power	60,000		
Consumable stores	15,000		
Gross profit c/d	861,000		
	£3,708,000		£3,708,000

Dr.	£		Cr. £
Salaries	201,000	Gross profit b/d	861,000
Warehouse wages	63,000		
National Insurance	120,000		
Rent	12,000		
Rates	9,000		
Carriage	18,000		
Packing materials	9,000		
Traveller's salary	48,000		
Travelling expenses	9,000		
Motor expenses	15,000		
Advertising	24,000		
Insurance premiums	6,000		
Pension scheme	30,000		
Bank charges	3,000		
Interest	—		
Postages, telephone and office sundries	33,000		
Lighting, heating and water	18,000		
Trade sundries	12,000		
Repairs and renewals	18,000		
Agents' commission	36,000		
Trading profit c/d	177,000		
	£861,000		£861,000

Dr.	£		Cr. £
Directors' fees	12,000	Trading profit b/d	177,000
Auditors' fees	6,000		
Depreciation:			
machinery and plant	30,000		
vehicles	6,000		
Net Profit	123,000		
	£177,000		£177,000

APPENDIX V

Figures extracted from the preceding accounts to show the different categories into which the charges fall for business interruption insurance purposes

Sales £3,000,000

Percentage to Turnover %		£	£	
47·0	Purchases	1,410,000		
·5	Consumable stores	15,000		variable charges not
·6	Carriage	18,000		requiring to be insured
·3	Packing materials	9,000		
			1,452,000	
21·0	Productive wages	630,000		insurable or not according to circumstances of the business dependent upon salaries and wages insured
2·0	Power	60,000		
·8	Fuel for trade purposes	24,000		
			714,000	
4·0	National Insurance	120,000		
			120,000	
6·7	Salaries	201,000		
2·1	Warehouse wages	63,000		
·4	Rent	12,000		
·3	Rates	9,000		
1·6	Traveller's salary	48,000		
·3	Travelling expenses	9,000		
·5	Motor expenses	15,000		
·8	Advertising	24,000		
·2	Insurance premiums	6,000		
1·0	Pension scheme	30,000		
·1	Bank charges	3,000		
	Interest	—		insurable charges
1·1	Postages, telephone and office sundries	33,000		
·6	Lighting, heating and water	18,000		
·4	Trade sundries	12,000		
·6	Repairs and renewals	18,000		
·4	Directors' fees	12,000		
·2	Auditors' fees	6,000		
1·2	Depreciation of plant, machinery and vehicles	36,000		
			555,000	
1·2	Agents' commission	36,000		
			36,000	optional charge
			2,877,000	
4·1	NET PROFIT (before taxation)	123,000		
			123,000	
100%			3,000,000	

REDUCTION IN TURNOVER—EFFECT ON ACCOUNTS

DATA FROM PRECEDING ACCOUNT

It is assumed that an Incident causes a reduction in annual turnover from £3,000,000 to £1,500,000; the following might then be the position for the twelve months during which the turnover is affected.

	Year before Incident £	Ratio to turnover before the Incident %	Year after Incident £	Ratio to reduced turnover after the Incident %	Loss in consequence £
Purchases	1,410,000	47·0	705,000	47·0	—
Consumable stores	15,000	·5	7,500	·5	—
Carriage	18,000	·6	9,000	·6	—
Packing materials	9,000	·3	4,500	·3	—
Productive wages	630,000	21·0	435,000	29·0	120,000
Power	60,000	2·0	30,000	2·0	—
Fuel for trade purposes	24,000	·8	12,000	·8	—
National Insurance	120,000	4·0	75,000	5·0	15,000
Staff salaries	201,000	6·7	201,000	13·4	100,500
Warehouse wages	63,000	2·1	63,000	4·2	31,500
Rent	12,000	·4	9,000	·6	3,000
Rates	9,000	·3	6,000	·4	1,500
Traveller's salary	48,000	1·6	48,000	3·2	24,000
Travelling expenses	9,000	·3	7,500	·5	3,000
Motor expenses	15,000	·5	10,500	·7	3,000
Advertising	24,000	·8	24,000	1·6	12,000
Insurance premiums	6,000	·2	4,500	·3	1,500
Pension scheme	30,000	1·0	30,000	2·0	15,000
Bank charges	3,000	·1	3,000	·2	1,500
Interest payments	—	—	—	—	—
Office expenses, postages, etc.	33,000	1·1	31,500	2·1	15,000
Lighting, heating & water	18,000	·6	15,000	1·0	6,000
Trade sundries	12,000	·4	12,000	·8	6,000
Repairs and renewals	18,000	·6	15,000	1·0	6,000
Directors' fees	12,000	·4	12,000	·8	6,000
Auditors' fees (*including work in connection with claim)	6,000	·2	*10,500	·7	7,500
Depreciation of plant and vehicles	36,000	1·2	30,000	2·0	12,000
Agents' commission	36,000	1·2	18,000	1·2	—
	2,877,000	95·9	1,828,500	121·9	390,000
Net profit	123,000	4·1	—	—	61,500
Net loss	—	—	328,500	21·9	—
	£3,000,000	100%	£1,500,000	100%	£451,500

The above shows how a 50 per cent. reduction in turnover in twelve months can turn a pre-Incident annual net profit of £123,000 into a net loss of £328,500 that is, an actual loss consequent upon the Incident of £451,500 over 3½ times the annual net profit normally earned.

Reconciliation Statement

for the twelve months following the date of the Incident.

	£
Costs and charges (including accountants' fee of £4,500* for producing figures for the claim)	1,828,500
less proportion paid for by turnover maintained, *i.e.*, on normal basis as prior to the Incident (50% of £2,877,000)	1,438,500
loss attributable to the Incident, in respect of costs and charges	390,000
add loss of net profit on 50% shortage in turnover	61,500
Total business interruption loss due to the Incident	£451,500

HAD THERE BEEN A BUSINESS INTERRUPTION INSURANCE the above loss of £451,500 would have been made good as follows (to simplify the illustration all wages have been included in the gross profit insurance and increase in cost of working has not been brought into the illustration):

Gross Profit sum insured £1,800,000 computed from previous accounts:—

	£
Productive wages	630,000
National Insurance	120,000
Insurable charges	555,000
Net profit before tax	123,000
	1,428,000
margin of over-insurance	372,000
	£1,800,000

Rate of Gross Profit— $\frac{1,428,000}{3,000,000}$ = 47.6% applied to £1,500,000

	£
reduction in turnover	714,000
less savings in insured charges	267,000
	447,000
*Professional accountants' charges re claim details	4,500
	£451,500

The insurance on Gross Profit (£1,800,000) is adequate so average does not apply and the amount claimed is payable in full.

469.—APPENDIX W

ILLUSTRATION OF SETTLEMENT OF A CLAIM UNDER A UNITED KINGDOM BUSINESS INTERRUPTION POLICY WITH WAGES INSURED ON THE DUAL BASIS

The illustration of the settlement of a claim set out in the following pages gives a summary from the insured's accounts for the financial year before the Incident and another from the accounts for the year in which it occurred. These accounts show how payments under a business interruption policy covering gross profit and dual basis wages restore the net profit of the business to what it would have been had the Incident not occurred.

It also gives details of the wages paid throughout those two years to enable the alternative calculations of the claim under the dual basis wages item to be followed.

To avoid making this claim calculation unnecessarily complicated, no adjustments have been made which might be applied to the rate of wages, annual turnover, standard turnover and average provision through the operation of the other circumstances clause.

	£
On Gross Profit—12 months maximum indemnity period	1,400,000
On Wages—100% first 6 weeks, 25% remaining portion of the indemnity period or 100% for 13 weeks under the alternative period (option to consolidate)	2,600,000
	£4,000,000

SUMMARY OF ACCOUNTS FOR THE YEAR (TO DECEMBER 31) BEFORE THE INCIDENT

Dr.	£		Cr. £
Stock	289,000	Sales	5,180,000
Purchases	1,187,200	Stock	179,000
Production charges	516,400		
Factory wages	2,019,200		
Gross Profit c/d	1,347,800		
	£5,359,600		£5,359,600
Wages	260,000	Gross Profit b/d	1,347,800
Standing charges	832,200		
Net Profit	255,600		
	£1,347,800		£1,347,800

An Incident occurs on February 1 and causes interference with the business until October 31 inclusive, and results in a reduction of turnover and wages in the year in which the Incident occurred, as shown below.

APPENDIX W

Increase in cost of working amounts to £185,000
Savings in insured charges and expenses total £52,200
The sums insured on Gross Profit and Wages are adequate.

Month	Weeks	Turnover in the year before the Incident	Turnover in year in which the Incident occurred	Reduction in Turnover due to the Incident	Wages in the year before the Incident	Wages in year in which the Incident occurred	Savings in Wages due to the Incident
		£	£	£	£	£	£
January	4½	420,000	420,000	nil	186,200	186,200	nil
February	4	390,000	nil	390,000	172,060	167,670	4,390
March	4½	410,000	nil	410,000	182,320	85,240	97,080
April	4½	460,000	nil	460,000	201,850	65,150	136,700
May	4	440,000	40,000	400,000	191,500	68,250	123,250
June	4½	410,000	80,000	330,000	182,330	76,830	105,500
July	4½	390,000	130,000	260,000	174,530	85,550	88,980
August	4½	350,000	190,000	160,000	158,900	96,850	62,050
September	4	460,000	330,000	130,000	199,310	150,020	49,290
October	4½	470,000	420,000	50,000	205,700	204,280	1,420
November	4	490,000	490,000	nil	211,000	211,000	nil
December	4½	490,000	490,000	nil	213,500	213,500	nil
	52	£5,180,000	£2,590,000	£2,590,000	£2,279,200	£1,610,540	£668,660

Recovery under the Insurance

ITEM 1—ON GROSS PROFIT £
    clause (a)

$$\text{rate of gross profit } \frac{832,200 + 255,600}{5,180,000} = 21\%$$

    applied to the reduction in turnover—£2,590,000 543,900
    clause (b) Increase in cost of working:
        additional expenditure incurred = £185,000.
        Application of limit. Rate of gross profit (21%) applied to loss of turnover avoided by the expenditure—agreed at £750,000 157,500
        (balance of £27,500 carried forward to be claimed under clause (b) of Item 2 on Wages).

                                                                                             701,400
less savings in insured charges 52,200
(full insurance under Item 1—average not applicable) £649,200

ITEM 2—ON WAGES (**first calculation**) £ £
    clause (a)

$$\text{rates of wages } \frac{2,019,200 + 260,000}{5,180,000} = 44\%$$

  (i) First 6 weeks of indemnity period (initial period):
        44% of shortage in turnover £480,000 211,200
        less savings in wages during this period (i) 24,550
                                                                                                              186,650

ILLUSTRATION OF SETTLEMENT 469

	£	£
(ii) Remaining portion of indemnity period:		
44% of shortage in turnover (mid-March to end of October inclusive) £2,110,000	928,400	
less savings in wages during this period (ii)	644,110	
	284,290	

LIMIT under (ii)
25% of the rate of wages (44%), *i.e.*, 11% of the shortage in turnover (mid-March to end of October inclusive) £2,110,000 232,100
★INCREASED by the amount of the savings during period (i) as above, *i.e.*, on wages in first 6 weeks 24,550
                                                                            256,650

The limit (£256,650) is less than the formula figure (£284,290) for period (ii), and is therefore the amount recoverable under clause (a) (ii) of Item 2 256,650

clause (b) increase in cost of working.
    balance of amount from Item 1 (agreed as being less than the limit under clause (b) of Item 2) 27,500

(full insurance under Item 2—average not applicable) £470,800

★ "Carry-over clause."

ITEM 2—ON WAGES (**alternative calculation utilising the alternative period— the option to consolidate**)

	£	£
clause (a)		
rate of wages = 44% (as before)		
(i) First 13 weeks of indemnity period (alternative period):		
44% of shortage in turnover £1,260,000	554,400	
less savings in wages during that time	238,170	316,230
(ii) Remaining portion of indemnity period:		
44% of shortage in turnover (beginning of May to end of October) £1,330,000	585,200	
less savings in wages during that time	430,490	
	154,710	

LIMIT under (ii) is the amount of savings during (i) above, *i.e.*, on wages during first 13 weeks, brought forward under the carry-over clause = £238,170. As the claim under (ii) is less than this limit, it is brought into the calculation in full 154,710
                                                                            470,940

clause (b) increase in cost of working:
    balance of amount (not recovered) under Item 1 27,500

(full insurance under Item 2—average not applicable) £498,440

469   APPENDIX W

NOTE —This alternative calculation, utilising the option to consolidate (the alternative period of 100 per cent. cover), provides recovery in full for the loss on wages and is, therefore, put forward for the claim under the policy.

PROFESSIONAL ACCOUNTANTS' CHARGES AS INSURED IN THE POLICY

Account for £3,150 submitted to the Insured by their accountants for producing reporting figures for the claim—payable in full £3,150

SUMMARY OF ACCOUNTS FOR THE YEAR (TO DECEMBER 31) IN WHICH THE INCIDENT OCCURRED

Dr.	£		Cr. £
Stock	179,600	Sales	2,590,000
Purchases	593,600	Stock	124,900
Production charges	258,200		
Factory wages	1,350,540		
Gross Profit c/d	332,960		
	£2,714,900		£2,714,900
Wages	260,000	Gross Profit b/d	332,960
Standing charges	780,000	Recovery under insurance:	
Additional expenditure resulting from the Incident	185,000	Item 1	649,200
		Item 2	498,440
		Accountants' charges	3,150
Accountants' charges in connection with the claim	3,150		
Net Profit	255,600		
	£1,483,750		£1,483,750

NOTE —The above claim settlement illustrates the need to insure gross profit and wages in order to protect net profit. The accounts show that an insurance contribution of £1,150,790 was required to maintain the net profit at £255,600. It also shows how a wages insurance under the dual basis scheme (i) can pick up a loss in respect of increase in cost of working under the Gross Profit item (ii) by the exercise of the "carry-back" option can provide a larger amount for the Wages item claim than would otherwise be obtained, and (iii) the "carry-forward" of savings clause can be of benefit to an insured after the expiry of the initial period of 100 per cent. wages insurance.

470.—APPENDIX X

SPECIMEN SETTLEMENT OF A MORE COMPLICATED LOSS CLAIM UNDER A UNITED KINGDOM BUSINESS INTERRUPTION POLICY

DATA

An Incident takes place—April 1.
Business interrupted for seven months (April 1 to October 31).
Turnover in last financial year—December 31—was £6,000,000
Gross Profit as defined in the specification for the same period totalled £1,320,000 therefore the Rate of Gross Profit in the last financial year was 22 per cent.

Sum insured on Gross Profit—1,250,000. Maximum Indemnity Period—12 months.
"Standing" charges amounting to £100,000 are not insured.
Standard Turnover (April to October in year before the Incident)—£2,800,000.
Turnover during period of interruption—£520,000, therefore reduction in turnover—£2,280,000.
Annual Turnover (twelve months immediately before the damage)—£6,500,000.
Increase in Cost of Working incurred—£110,000.
Savings in insured charges and expenses—£130,000.

In consequence of increased production at lower labour cost, resulting from the installation of new machinery since the end of the last financial year and an expansion of sales it is agreed to make two adjustments under the provisions of the other circumstances clause:
  (i) to increase the rate of gross profit from 22 per cent. to 25 per cent.
  (ii) to increase the standard turnover by 10 per cent.

CALCULATION OF CLAIM

	£	£
Clause (a) Loss of Gross Profit		
standard turnover (seven months—April to October year before the damage)	2,800,000	
agreed increase of 10% under other circumstances clause	280,000	
adjusted standard turnover	3,080,000	
less turnover maintained during the indemnity period (April to October)	520,000	
reduction in turnover	2,560,000	
rate of gross profit after agreed adjustment (25%), applied to reduction in turnover 2,560,000		640,000
Clause (b) Increase in Cost of Working		
additional expenditure incurred—£110,000		
apportionment under uninsured standing charges clause:		
$\dfrac{\text{gross profit as defined in specification}}{\text{gross profit + uninsured standing charges}} \times \text{increase in cost of working}$		
$= \dfrac{£1,320,000}{£1,420,000} \times £110,000$		102,250
Total of (a) and (b)		742,250
less savings in insured charges and expenses which have ceased or been reduced because of the damage		130,000
		£612,250

application of average proviso:

$$= \frac{\text{sum insured}}{\text{adjusted rate of gross profit} \times \text{adjusted annual turnover}} = \frac{£1{,}250{,}000}{25\% \text{ of } (£6{,}500{,}000 + £650{,}000)} = 69\cdot93\%$$

therefore the amount payable under the policy is 69·93% of £612,250 =   £428,140

NOTE 1.—Had no adjustments been made to the rate of gross profit and the standard turnover, the claim calculation would have been:

	£
clause (a)—22% of £2,280,000	501,600
clause (b)	102,250
	603,850
less savings in insured charges	130,000
	£473,850

average proviso:

$$\frac{£1{,}250{,}000}{22\% \text{ of } £6{,}500{,}000} = 87\cdot41\% \text{ of } £473{,}850 = \quad £414{,}190$$

From this it will be seen that because the upward adjustments also increased the amount of under–insurance and consequently the incidence of average the insured was only £13,950 better off as a result of the application of the other circumstances clause.

Had there been a full insurance, the benefit from the adjustment would have been £138,400.

NOTE 2.—The loss in respect of increase in cost of working not recovered under clause (b) was:

	£
(i) apportionment under the uninsured standing charges clause because some insurable standing charges were not included in the definition of gross profit (£110,000 less £102,250) =	7,750
(ii) application of the average proviso because of under-insurance: 30·07% of £102,250 =	30,680
	£38,430

Should there be an item insuring wages under the dual basis scheme this loss of £38,430 would be carried forward to be dealt with under clause (b) of that item. (See para. 209 and illustration in Appendix W, para 469.

471.—APPENDIX Y

ILLUSTRATION OF A CLAIM SETTLEMENT UNDER A UNITED KINGDOM BUSINESS INTERRUPTION SPECIFICATION INCLUDING A DEPARTMENTAL CLAUSE

Data

The sum insured on gross profit is £12,000,000 and the maximum indemnity period insured is 24 months.
All insurable charges are included in the definition of gross profit.
An Incident takes place on April 1 and the period of interruption ends:

Department A—November 30
Department B—October 31 } in the same year.
Department C—September 30

Increase in cost of working is incurred and agreed as being within the terms and limits of clause (b).
There is a saving in some of the insured charges and expenses.
It is agreed that no adjustment of figures under the other circumstances clause is required.
Departmental figures from the accounts for the financial year ended December 31 preceding the Incident are as follows:

	Turnover £	Gross Profit £	Rate of Gross Profit
Department A	10,000,000	2,500,000	25%
,, B	6,000,000	900,000	15%
,, C	4,000,000	1,200,000	30%
	£20,000,000	£4,600,000	

Annual Turnover (12 months immediately before the date of the Incident)—
April 1 to March 31

Department A	£10,030,000
,, B	£6,025,000
,, C	£4,010,000

Turnover in the different departments fluctuated from month to month both before and after the Incident but the following amounts were agreed with the loss adjuster as being the
Reduction in Turnover due to the Incident—

Reduction in Turnover due to the Incident—
Department A	£2,525,000
,, B	£365,000
,, C	£1,700,000

Calculation of Claim for Loss of Gross Profit on the Departmental Basis

	£
clause (a)	
Department A rate of gross profit (25%) applied to reduction in turnover (£2,525,000)	631,250
Department B rate of gross profit (15%) applied to reduction in turnover (£365,000)	54,750
Department C rate of gross profit (30%) applied to reduction in turnover (£1,700,000)	510,000
	1,196,000
clause (b)	
increase in cost of working—all departments	223,000
	1,419,000
savings in insured charges:	
sundry savings in all departments totalling	67,500
	£1,351,500

	£
average proviso:	
Department A rate of gross profit (25%) applied to twice the annual turnover (£10,030,000)–£20,060,000	5,015,000
Department B rate of gross profit (15%) applied to twice the annual turnover (£6,025,000)–£12,050,000	1,807,500
Department C rate of gross profit (30%) applied to twice the annual turnover (£4,010,000)–£8,020,000	2,406,000
	£9,228,000

This amount is less than the sum insured on gross profit of £12,000,000 (24 months maximum indemnity period) and therefore the amount of the loss, namely, £1,351,500 is payable in full.

Note—Had the departmental clause not been applicable, the loss under clause (a) would have been calculated as:
overall rate of gross profit (23 per cent.) applied to the total reduction in turnover for all three departments (£4,590,000) = £1,055,700. As the insured's loss under clause (a), calculated separately for the three departments, was £1,196,000 the application of the departmental clause benefits the insured to an amount of £140,300.
Had the Incident caused a greater degree of interruption and loss of turnover in Department B (which has a low rate of gross profit) and a less amount in Department C (which has a high rate of gross profit), the effect of the clause would have been reversed.

472.—APPENDIX Z

SIMPLIFIED SPECIMEN CLAIM SETTLEMENT—UNITED STATES BUSINESS INCOME (AND EXTRA EXPENSE) COVERAGE

Data

THE COVER (as shown in the Declarations)

Insurance period: 12 months from January 1 to December 31

Limit of Insurance: $120,000,000

Coinsurance percentage: 80 per cent.

THE LOSS

Damage occurred: April 1

"**Period of restoration**": seven months (April 1 to October 31), during which time all operations suspended and no sales achieved.
Loss of Business Income: continued (totally) for a further 45 days to December 15. (But under Extended Business Income Additional Coverage 30 days limit restricts insured period of interruption to end of November = eight months.

Extra Expenses incurred: $ 5,000,000

Calculation of Claim

	Apr 1 to Nov 30 previous year (Actual) (A)	8 months after loss (Anticipated) (B)	8 months after loss (Actual) (C)
Net Income	10,000,000	12,000,000	nil
Operating expenses			
Direct labour costs	70,000,000	76,000,000	57,000,000
Heat, light, power	700,000	750,000	600,000
Depreciation	500,000	550,000	550,000
Rent	5,000,000	6,000,000	6,000,000
Salaries costs	28,000,000	30,000,000	30,000,000
Maintenance	250,000	300,000	300,000
Advertising	400,000	500,000	600,000
Insurance	4,000,000	4,500,000	3,800,000
Telephone	200,000	250,000	300,000
Donations	250,000	300,000	300,000
Travel	500,000	600,000	300,000
Interest	200,000	250,000	250,000
Total (Op. ex.)	110,000,000	120,000,000	100,000,000

Claim

Net Income (B)	$ 12,000,000
Operating expenses (C)	100,000,000
Business Income loss	$112,000,000
Extra Expenses	$ 5,000,000

Application of Coinsurance Condition

Net sales value of production 12 months from January 1	$300,000,000
less cost of goods, etc.	120,000,000
	$180,000,000
Net Income and operating expenses for 12 months following last anniversary date	$180,000,000
Coinsurance percentage	80 per cent.
Limit of Insurance	$120,000,000
Business Income loss	$112,000,000

Application of condition:
1. $180,000,000 × 80 per cent. = $144,000,000
2. $\frac{\$120,000,000}{\$144,000,000}$ = 0·834
3. $112,000,000 × 0·834 = $ 93,408,000

Claim Payable

Business Income	$93,408,000
Extra Expense	5,000,000
	$98,408,000

INDEX

(References are to paragraph numbers, those in heavier type being the principal paragraphs on the particular subject. Paragraphs dealing specifically with U.S. business interruption coverages are all listed individually under the heading United States of America and not elsewhere in the index).

Abandonment, 275(j)
Abattoirs, revenue from, 275(e)
Abnormal electrical current, 305
Academies, 275(c)
Access, loss due to prevention of, 373
Accidental damage to machinery, Chapter 15: 311–327, Appendix N, 460
Account books destroyed in fire, 39(b), 414, Chapter 19: 393–410
Accountancy methods, 218, 219
Accountant's certificate for return premium, 216, 226(a)–(c)
Accountants' charges or fees
  as a standing charge, 150
  for work in respect of claims, 378, 406
Accountants, policy for, 276(a) (b)
Accounts, 218
Accumulated stocks clause, 246, 386
Additional expenditure after damage—*see* increase in cost of working
Additional expenditure, extra item for, 47(b), **50**, 367
  special policy for, 278(a)
"Additions" basis definition of gross profit, 6, 35–59, **81**, 82, 86, Appendix E, 451
Adjacent premises risks, 373
Adjustment of figures for claims—*see* other circumstances clause
Adjustment of premiums, 216, **225(a)**, 225(b)–226(d), 227
Administrative boards, policy for, 278(a)
Advance profits insurance, 15(b), 23(c), **268(a)**, 279(b), 456
  machinery (accident) insurance, 322
Advance rent, 267(b), 268(a)
Adverse trading conditions, 55(d), 95
Advertising and publicity agents, 275(b)
Advertising as a standing charge, 120–124
Aerial devices, damage by, 287(a)–(b)
Africa, 76
Agents' commissions and expenses, 177–181
Agents, manufacturers', policy for, 353
Agricultural tractor and machinery agencies, 50, 359
AIDS, 301
Air compressors, explosion of, 283
Air conditioning plant, 314
Aircraft manufacturers, 94, 261(b), 341
Air freight
  expenses, 129, 156
  insurance premiums, 130

Air transit of goods, 376
Aircraft, damage by, 287(a)–(b)
Airfield and flying expenses, 126
All risks, 12, **13(b)**, 281(a), 307–310, Appendix B, 448
"All standing charges" specification, 389
Alterations to premises or business, 17
Alternative trading clause, 58
Alternatives to turnover basis, 5
Ambulance room requisites, 169
American insurance methods, *see* **United States of America**.
Amusement arcades, 252(a)–(c)
  parks, 252(a)–(c)
Analysts, policy for, 275(b)
Animal welfare societies, 278(a)
Annual turnover, **52(b)–(c)**, 55(a), 55(c)
  for new businesses, 383
Annuities, 198
Answering services, 133
Ante-dating increase in sum insured, 431
Antique dealers, 303
Apprentices and trainees, 199(d)
  training expenses of, 169
Appropriation fund for bad debts, 159(c)
Arbitration condition, 442
Arcades (shopping), 373
Architects' fees
  for rebuilding after fire, 277
  in accounts, 82(c), 151
Architects, policy for, 276(a)–(b)
Argentina, 74(a)
Art galleries, policy for, 275(a), 278(c)
Artistes' fees, 166, 262
Artists' sketches etc., for printers, 145
Asia, 77
Assets, sale or appreciation of, 86, 221
Associated companies, 23(a), 80, **168**, 382
Attraction, loss of, 374, 390
Auctioneers and valuers, policy for, 275(b)
Auditors—*see* accountants
Australia, 75(a)
Austria, 78(a)
Autoclaves, explosion of, 283
Automatic sprinkler installations, 258, 289(a)–(b), **297**
Automobiles—*see* motors
Average proviso for gross profit insurance, **52(a)–(c)**, 54, **55(c)**, 57, **107**, 209, 230
  for wages insurance, 210, 213, 215
Aviation charter services, 129, 173

571

INDEX

Bacon factories, 50, 269
Bad debts, 159(a)–(c)
  appropriation fund or reserve for, 159(c)
  recovery of, 221
  withdrawals from reserve, 87
Bakeries, 50, 127, 172, 282(a), 319–321, 381
Bakers' ovens, 282(a)
Balancing charges, 149
Ballet schools, policy for, 275(c)
Bank charges and interest, 51(b), 113, 131
Banks, policy for, 326, 392
Barrels; repairs, renewals and cleaning, 172(a)–(b)
Baseball stadiums, 319
Basis of U.K. business interruption insurance, 1–8
Basis rate for premiums, 254(a), 358
Beauty salons, 192(b), 295, 311
Beer allowances, 196
Belgium, 78(b)
Benevolent fund, 169
Bingo halls, 252(a)–(c)
Biotechnology, 300
Biscuit works, 282(a), 319, 321
"Blundell Spence" agreement, 382(a)
Boarding houses, 252(a)–(c), 288, 301
Boarding schools, 50, 275(a)
Boilers and economisers
  collapse of, 284
  cracking and fracturing of, 286
  explosion of, **13**, 254(a), **282(a)**
  nipple leakage, 286
  overheating of boilers and tubes, 285
Bomb scare, 373
Bonded stores
  insured's stock in, 354
  policy for owners, 275(d)
Bonus
  buyers', 191
  employees', 92, **191**, **196**
  travellers' and salespersons', 193
Book debts, loss of—*see* loss of book debts
Bookmakers (turf accountants), 369
Books of account destroyed
  compiling claims information, 414
  loss of outstanding accounts—*see* loss of book debts
Boot repairers, 167
Borderline charges, 104, 110, **170–176**
Bottles not a standing charge, 154
Bowling alleys, 319
Boxes: repairs, renewals and cleaning, 154, 172(a)–(b)
Branches of a business, 23(b), 380–382(a), (c)
Brassworks, 172(c)
Brazil, 74(b)
Breach of contract, 261, 262, 327, 376
Breach of warranty on fire policy, 16(a)
Breakdown (engineering)—*see* machinery (accident) insurance
Break-out (hot metal) insurance, 293

Breweries, 127, 137, 169, 172(a)–(b), 319, 320, 355, 375
Brickworks, 50, 175
Bridge building engineers, 94
Brochures and catalogues
  cost of production, 123
  dependence on printers, etc., 367
Broiler producers, 270(c)
"Bugs," 326
Building contractors and trades, 377
Building societies, policy for, 326
Bulb merchants, 123, 367
Burglar alarm systems, rent of, 114
Burlers and menders, pieces at, 357
Bursary expenses, 169
Bursting or overflowing of water tanks and pipes, 295
Business (insured's)
  description of, 15, 23(b)
  discontinuance of, **17**, **18**, 21, **387**, **436**
  new, 229, 245(a), 268(a), 383
  running at a loss, 7, 95–96
Business Income Coverage—*see* **U.S.A.**
Butchers' shops, 311, 325
Butter factories, 269

Cabarets, 166, 262
Cables and cablegrams, 134
Calendar month, meaning of month, 245(a)
Calendars, complimentary gifts of, 169
Calorifiers, explosion of steam, 283
Canada, 73(a)
Canal warehouses, insured's property in, 354, 355, 357
Cancellation charges re components, hotel accommodation etc., under contract, 261(b)
Canteen expenses, 143
Capital outlay, receipts, etc., 86
Captive companies, 244(a)
Caravan site owners, 301
Car radio-telephones, 133
Car (rent-a-car) rentals, 125
Cardboard factories, 320
Carriage, **106**, 108, **156**, 433
Caribbean, 73(c), 269(a)
"Carry-back" clause in wages insurance, **206(a)–(c)**, 423
"Carry-over" clause in wages insurance, **207(a)–(b)**, 423
Cartons for packaging, 154
Cash-and-carry discount stores, 424
Casinos, 192(b)
Casks at whisky distilleries, 172(a)–(b)
Catalogues and brochures
  cost of production, 123
  dependence on printers, 367
Catering contractors, 301, 362
Catering consultancy and management services, 143
Catering establishments, 172(a), 301

572

INDEX

Cattle
  electrocution of, 304
  loss from damage by, 296(a)
Cement manufacturers, 320
Central America, 73(b)
Central office administration charges, 168
Certificate for return of premium clause, 216, 226(a)–(d)
Cessation of insured's interest, 17, 21
Chambers of Trade and Commerce, 278(a)
Change of insurers, 20, 231
Charitable trusts, policy for, 267, 278(a)
Check (credit club) agents' commission, 178
Check trading; charges to retailers, 179
Cheese factories, 50, 269
Chemical works, 172, 321, 351, 371, 375
Chemists' shops, 410
Chicken breeders, 270(c), 386
Chile, 74(c)
Chiropodists, policy for, 275(b)
Chocolate manufacturers, 321
Christmas gratuities, gifts, calendars, diaries, etc., 169
Chromium platers, 321, 340
Cinemas, 39(a), 114, 163, 297, 319
City Tailors Ltd. v. *Evans* (1921), 58
Civil Aviation Act 1949, 287(a)
Civil commotion, 13, 289
Civil war, policy exclusion, 13, 281(a)
Claims
  account books destroyed, 39(b)–(c), 414
  accountant's certificate and charges for work in respect of, 378, 438
  action on damage occurring, 411(a), 412–413, 422–423
  amount received in respect of, 118, 226(c), 231
  condition (action by insured), 18, 411(c), 435–438
  conditions for validity of, **15, 16(a)**, 17–19, 411(a)
  employees: employment after damage, 422–429(a)
  formulation of, 54, 55(a), 57, 59, **211, 417**, 444
  fraudulent, 16(a), 439
  illustration of claim settlement calculations, 4(b), 7, 467–471
  increase in cost of working, 50, 412, 419, 424–428
  increase of sum insured after damage, 431
  injury or death of personnel, 15(d), 421
  interim payments on account, 415
  loss increased due to external causes, 43, 44, 420(a)
  miscellaneous standing charges, 183
  other circumstances clause, 55–57, 432, 470
  overlap with fire insurance, 429–430
  procedure following damage, 411 *et seq.*
  purchases from competitors, 50
  reduction in sum insured by, 231
  residual value, 419

Claims—*cont.*
  savings in standing charges and wages, 433, 434: *see also under* "savings clause"
  settlements, Chapter 20: 411–446
  temporary premises after damage, 232–233, 419
  time limits for statement of claim, overseas policies, 79
  U.K. policies, 245(a), 437
  U.S. policies, 437
  wages during period of interruption, 208(a)–(b), 422–429(a)
Cleaning charges and materials, 142, 164, 172
Clinics, policy for, 275(b)
Clinics (factory) and nurses, 143
CLORA, 253
Clothing manufacturers, 144, 145, 173, 261(b), 320, 360
Closed circuit t.v. rental, 169
Club agents and collectors, 178, 180
Clubs, social, political, etc., 192(b)
Coal in the open, spontaneous heating, 292
Cold stores
  insured's goods in, 306, 323, 324, 355
  owners of, 39(a), 275(d), 306, 320
Collapse of boilers and steam vessels, etc., **283, 284**, 314
"Collective" policies, 22, 23(d)
Collectors for credit trade, 178
Colleges, policy for, 278(a)
Colombia, 74(d)
Commission as a standing charge
  agents', 177, 178–180
  debt collectors', 181
  employees', 191
  retail shops, 179, 181
  travellers' and sales persons', 193
Commission, policy for—*see* gross revenue
Commission received, 87
Commission, work done on, 85(d)
Commodity exchanges, dealings in futures, 40(a), 432
Compensation fund charges (breweries), 169
Component manufacturers, 261(b), 340, 341
Computers, increasing the interruption risk, 17, 249
Computer leasing, 114
Computer owners, policy for, 326
Computer-time rent, 134
Concert halls, 166, 262, 275(e)
Concessionaires, policy for, 365
"Consorcio" perils, 78(m)
Conditions of policy, 17, 18, 439–442, 447, 448
Conference and convention expenses, 169
Conference centres, policy for, 275(c)
Confidential information, 82(a)
"CONSEQUENTIAL LOSS", **12**, 281(a), 289(a)
Conservation societies, 278(a)
Constructional engineers, 94, 377
Consultants' fees, 82(c), 151, 169

573

INDEX

Consultants, policy for, 276(a)
Consulting engineers' fees, for rebuilding after fire, 277
Consulting engineers, policy for, 275(b)
Consumable stores and tools, 172
Consumer service departments, 160
Contagious diseases, loss due to, 301
Containers, 154, 155, 172(a)
Container base charges, 156
Contamination, 14(c), 300, 301, 302
Contingencies insured—*see* perils
Contingency planning, 242, 326
Contract department expenses, 169
Contract hire of vehicles, 128
Contract price clause, 39(a)
Contractors, loss at outside sites, 377
Contracts
    extension of cover to sites and premises where carried out, 377
    damages for breach of, 261, 262
    profit not credited until completion, 94
Contracts of Employment Act 1972, 202(a)
Contractual liabilities, 261
Contribution condition, 440
Convalescent homes, policy for, 278(a)
Cookers, steam, explosion of, 283
Corporation Tax, 86, 118
Correspondence colleges, 275(c)
Cost of insurance, 253
Cotton industry, 137, 144, 172, 173, 303, 357
Cracking etc. of pipes and boilers, 286
Credit card facilities—charges for, 131
Credit data bureaux, subscriptions to, 169
Credit transactions, 39(a)–(b), 40(b)
Credit unions, policy for, 326
Cricket clubs, policy for, 298, 316, 319
Criminal Damage (Compensation) Northern Ireland Order 1977, 290
Cumulative preference share dividends, 86
Current cost accounting, 219
Curling risks, 319
Customers' premises, extensions to, 341, 351
Customers' suppliers, extensions to, 352

Dairies, 50, 127, 137, 375
Dairy farmers, 270(a), 304
Damage, conditions for valid claim, **15**, **16(a)**, 17–19, 411(a)
    at temporary premises during period of interruption, 232, 233
    meaning of, 13, 15, 281(a)
    occurring twice in one year, 231
Damages for non-completion of contracts, 261–262
Dance,
    bands, 166, 262
    halls, 39(a), 166, 262, 275(e)
Day-study courses for staff, 169
Days of grace for renewal, 20
Death of insured or employees after damage, 15(d), 421

Debenture interest, 113
Debenture trustees' fees, 169
Debris, removal after damage, 45
Debt collection charges, 181
Declaration-Linked, **53**, 224, 227(b), 348, Appendix D, 450
Decor specialists, 377
Decoration expenses, 171
"Deductibles," 16(b), 73(a)–(c), 74(a)–(g), 75(a)–(b), 76(a)–(c), 77(a)–(d), 78(a)–(o), 244(b), 259, 317, 330
Defective sanitary arrangements, 301
Deferment of start of indemnity period, 245(a), 267, 268(a)
Defined perils, 13, 302
Delays in restoration of business, 44
De Meza and Stuart v. *Apple, van Straten, Shene and Stone* (1975), 226(a)
Demolition costs, 45
Demurrage on returned parcels, 136
Denial of access to premises, **373**
Denmark, 78(c)
Dentists, policies for, 275(b), 410
Department stores, 120, 121, 132, 135, 160. 178, 189(a), 191, 380, 384, 393, 471
Departmental clause, 380, 471
Dependency upon outside firms and premises, 340–377
Depots, 23(c), 169
Depreciation
    as an insurable charge, 86, **146**–148
    deduction under savings clause, 146
    of components, 269(b)
    of stock, 147, 225(c)
    special allocation for, 146
Deterioration of undamaged stock, 269, 324
Development expenses, 169
Diaries, distribution of, as gifts, 169
"Difference" basis definition of gross profit, 37, 49, **81–85**, 104, 449
"Difference in conditions" policies, 80, 382(c)
Directors' remuneration, 82(a), 86, **111**, 212
Disaster planning, 242, 326
Disc jockeys' fees, 166
Discontinuance of business, **17**, **18**, 21, 387, 436
Discotheques, 166, 262
Discounting charges, 153
Discounts
    allowed, 84, 152, 222
    received, 84, 85(b), 222, 223
Discounts, premium, for deductibles, 259
Discount stores, 160
Diseases, infectious, loss due to, 301
Display expenses, 121, 135
Distributors, sole, policy for, 365
Dividends
    on investments, 86
    on trade, to club federations, 87
Divisions of a business, 23(b), 380–382(a), (c)
Dock warehouses, 354, 355, 357

574

INDEX

Docks, goods on quays and vessels, 355
Doctors, policy for, 275(b)
Dog racing stadiums, 316, 319
Domestic appliance manufacturers, 261(b) saleshops, 159(b), 223, 393
Donations and subscriptions, 138
Drawing offices (building contractors), 377
Drink poisoning, loss due to, 301
Dry cleaners, 39(a), 50, 167, 320
Dual basis payroll, 111, 112, 189(b), **200, 201**, 423
Dual basis wages insurance—*see under* wages insurance
Dyers and dyeworks, 137, 167, 174, 319, 321, 357

Earthquake, 13, 75, 288
"Economic limit" in increased cost of working, 49(a)–(b)
Economiser explosion—*see* boilers
Egg packing stations, 270(c)
Electric generators, motors, switchgear, etc., loss due to accident, 311–317
Electrical contractors, trade bonus, 223
Electrical engineers, 377
Electrical goods saleshops, 159(b), 393
Electrical installations, self-heating, 305
Electricity
 as a standing charge, 137, 173
 failure of supply extension to electricity works, 319, 371
Electrocution of cattle, 304
Electronics industry, 327
Employee share scheme, 93
Employees' recreation expenses, 169
Employers' liability insurance premiums, 130, 196, 205(b)
Employment bureaux, policy for, 275(b)
Employment Protection Act 1975, 202(a), (c), **(d)**, 203
Employment Protection (Consolidation) Act 1978, 202(a), **(b), (c)**, (d), **203**, 422, 423
Engine breakdown, loss due to, 314
Engineering
 business interruption insurance Chapter 15: 311–327
Engineering trade, 172, 319, 320, 321, **358**
 heavy engineering, 94
Entertaining expenses, 169
Entertainment businesses, 262
Epidemics at seaside resorts, 301
Erasure of data, 326
Estate agents, policy for, 275(b)
Estate boiler and engine house, 173, 264, **372**
Estate mills, rent receivable, 264
Estimated Maximum Loss (EML), 242(b)
European Community, 80
European countries—insurance methods, 78(a)–(o)
Exceptional circumstances—*see* other circumstances clause

Excess (deductible) on policy, 244(b)
Excess indemnity periods, 260
Excess on material damage policy, 16(b)
Excess premium not charged/charged, 226(d), 227
Exchange, loss on currency, 165
Exclusion of first 24 hours in machinery accident: insurance, 317
Exclusions, General, 13, 14(a)–(c)
Executives' commission, 191
Ex gratia payments, 16(a)
Exhibition expenses, 120
Exhibitions
 cover for exhibitors at, 361, 362
 policy for promoters of, 275(c), 301
Expanding businesses, 82(d), 224, 228
Experimental and test expenses, 169, 273
Explosion, 13, **282(a)**, 283, **314**
 of boilers and economisers, 13, 282(a)
 of flue gases, 282(a)
 of gas, 13
 of machines, steam pipes, vessels, apparatus, etc., 282(a), 283, 314
 of steam ovens, 282(a)
Export Credits Guarantee Dept. recoveries, 159(a)
Export credits guarantee insurance premiums, 130
Exporters Increased Tax deduction—New Zealand, 75(b)
Export promotion levies, 139
Exporters, 130, 132, 136
Extension of insurance
 Chapter 17: 340–377
 general considerations, 15(b), 340–345
 to adjacent premises risk, 373
 to associated companies, 382(a)
 to cold stores, 354, 355, 356
 to contract sites, 377
 to customers' premises, 351, 353
 to customers' suppliers, 352
 to electricity works, 319, 371
 to estate boiler and power house, 372
 to exhibition halls, 351, 352
 to gasworks, 319, 371
 to motor manufacturers, 359
 to motor vehicles on the road, 375
 to premises abroad, 345, 359
 to processors' premises, **346–350**, 353, **357**, **358**, 360, 367
 to property stored, 354, 355, 356
 to samples on display, 361
 to stock on another's premises, 354, 355
 to storage facilities, 356
 to suppliers' premises, 23(c), **346–349**, 353, 363–370
 to suppliers of suppliers, 350
 to telephone exchanges, 369
 to waterworks, 319, 371
Extinguishing operations, damage by, 13
Extraneous revenue, 86, **87, 88**, 95, 221

575

INDEX

Fabricating engineers, 94
Factoring services, 182
Factory extensions, 15(b), 228, 268(a)
Factory farming, policies for, 270(c)
Failure of public utilities, 316, 319, 371
Fairgrounds, 252(a)–(c)
Fairs, trade and industrial, 361, 362
Farmers, policies for, 270, 304
Fashion show expenses, 120, 169
Feu duties, 114
Film production, 272(a)
Film rent or hire charges, 114
Finance costs, 169
Financial institutions, 326, **392**
Fines for breach of contract, 261–262
Finishers for textile trade, goods at, 357
Finland, 78(d)
Fire alarm systems, rent of, 114
Fire damage, excepted origins of, 13, 14(a), 37, 287, 288, 289, 292, 305
Fire extinguishing expenses, 430
Fire insurance overlap with b.i. insurance after damage, 429–430
Fish canners, 269, 323
Fish friers' shops, 311
Fish merchants, 132, 172, 375
Flood, loss due to, 294
Floor covering manufacturers, 144
Flour mills, 172, 282(a), 375
Food cabinets in shops, 325
Food poisoning, loss due to, manufacturers, reservers, canners, 300
  hotels, public houses, restaurants, etc., 301
Football clubs, 319
Foreign currency losses/profits, 165
Forges, fuel for, 174
Forward sales and contracts, 39(a)
Foundries, 174, 293, 358
France, 78(e)
Franchise fees and levies, 89, 162
Fraudulent claims, 16(a), 439
Freepost expenses, 132
Freightage charges, 84
Fringe benefits, 192(a)–(b)
Frozen food trade, **269**, 306, 323, **354–356**, 375
Frozen food stores, 325
Fruit and poultry shops, 325
Fruit and vegetable growers, 269
Fruit and vegetable preservers and processors, **269**, 306, 323, **354–356**
Fruit in cold stores, 306, 323, **354–356**
Fruit merchants, 132, 172
Fuel consumption increased due to damage to plant, 175
Fuel costs for cooling and reheating kilns and furnaces, 50, 175
Fuel for trade purposes, 174–176
Furnaces, 50, 174, 175
Furnishing trade, 144
Furniture
  depositories, 275(d)
  manufacturers, 85(a)

Furniture—*cont.*
  removers, 129, 375
  shops, 393
  trade vans, 375
"Futures" on commodity exchanges, 40(a)

Games manufacturers, 172(c)
Garage for insured's vehicles, 23(c)
Gas
  engine breakdown, 314
  explosion, 13
  for space heating, 137
  for trade processes, 173, **174**, **319**, 371
  works, 292
Gasworks, extensions to, 319, 371
General Exclusions, 13, 14(a)–(c)
Germany, 78(f)
Glasshouse complexes, 270(b)
Glassworks, 50, 174, 175, 319, 320, 321
Glaziers, 377
Good faith, principle applicable, 15, 18, 435
Goods in railway, canal, dock or public warehouses, 60(a), 349, 354, 357
Goods in transit, 376
Goodwill; purchase, depreciation, 148
Grain and seed importers, 354, 355
Gratuities; hotel, etc., employees, 192(b)
Greece, 78(g)
Greyhound racing stadiums, 319
Grocers' shops, 223, 325
Gross profit, 4(a), 6, 37, Chapter 7: 81–96
  "difference" specification, 6, 37, **81**, 82, 86–96, Appendix C, 449
  net profit plus insured standing charges specification, 6, 37, **81**, 82, 86–95, Appendix E, 451
  "shopkeepers'" specification, 390, 453
  meaning of, 4(a), 81, 82, 224
  when a net trading loss, 95
  sum insured on, 45, 52(c), Chapter 11: 218–240
Gross revenue (or commission, fees, income, receipts)—policy for loss of, **275**, **276(a)**, Appendix F, 452
Ground annuals or rent, 114
Group companies, **23(a)**, 80, **168**, **382(a)**, 385
Group management charges, 168
Group purchasing pools, 223
Guest houses, 301, 391
Gymkhanas, 298

Hairdressers' salons, 23(c), 231, 295, 311
Handbag factories, 172(c)
Handling charges for storage, 158
Haulage contractors, 39(a), **129**, 141–143, 351, **375**
Head offices of group companies—covers available, 382(a)
Head office service charges, 168
Heating engineers, 377

Heating
 for trade processes, 174–176, 372
 space, 137, 284, 372
Heliport expenses, 126
Hire car businesses, 129, 142, 375
Hire contract charges, 140
Hire purchase
 businesses, 39(a)–**(b)**, 40(b), 393
 licence certificates, 169
 payments, 140
Hired plant and machinery, 140
Hired transport, 141
Holding company, **23(a)**, 80, **168**, **382(a)**
Holding company's expenses, 168
Holiday camps, 123, 166, 252(a), 301
Holiday fund, interest on, 113
Holiday pay, **194**, **196**, 205(b), 423
Holland, 78(h)
Hong Kong, 77(a)
Hops in store, 354, 355
Horse upkeep and stabling costs, 169
Hospitals, policy for, 278(a), 301
Hostel for employees, 23(c), 169
Hotels, 123, 166, 172, **192(b)**, **252(a)–(c)**, 286, 288, 296(a), **301**, **391**
Hot metal risk, 293
Hypermarkets, 424

Ice-cream trade, 50, 375
Ice factories, 50
Ice rinks, 319
Ice hockey rinks, 319
Impact damage by road vehicles, 296(a)
Impact damage in works by own vehicles, 296(b)
Import duties, 118
Import merchants, 60(a), 355
Incident, 15, **38**, 43, 226(c)
Income from extraneous sources, 86, **87**, **88**, **89**, 95, 221
Income policy—*see under* gross revenue
Income tax, 118
Increase in cost of working, 8, 39(a), **45–49**, 50, 54, 57, 109, **209**, 419, 425, 426
 after end of indemnity period, 50
 "economic limit" 47(a), 57
 expenditure which is not covered, 45, 46
 item on additional, 47(b), 50
 limitations on amount recoverable, 47–49, 50
 omitted charges increased after damage, 108
 partial conversion to full revenue cover, 278(a)
 policy solely for, 278(a)
 residual value in claims, 419
 turnover benefited after expiry of maximum indemnity period, 48
 uninsured amount picked up by wages item, 209, 211, 469

Increase in cost of working—*cont.*
 "uninsured standing charges" clause, 49, 51(a), 109, 209
Increase in charges after damage, 108
Increase in sum insured after damage, 431
Increase in turnover during indemnity period, 247
Increased ratio after damage of
 charges, 7, 46, 175
 wages, **46**, **424**, **425**, 426, 427
Increasing trade, 55(b), 82(d), 224, 228
Indemnity, description of, 23(d), 38, 230
Indemnity period, 41, 245–251
 deferred commencement, 246, 267, 268(a)
 excess, 260
 maximum indemnity period—*see under that heading*
 meaning of, 41, 245(a), 247, 248
 prolonged by extraneous causes, 44, 420(a), 421
 seasonal businesses, 252(b)–(c)
Indemnity, principle of, 19, 230
India, 77
Indirect material costs, 172(a)
Industrial All Risks, 12, **13(b)**, 281(a), Appendix B, 448
Industrial cleaning cloths, 142
Industrial clothing, 163
Industrial consultants' fees, 169
Industrial fairs and exhibitions, 361, 362
Infectious diseases, loss due to, 301
Injury to or death of personnel, 15(d), 421
Inland revenue authorities, attitude to premiums and claim payments, 118
Instalment credit, sales on, 39(a)–**(b)**, **40(b)**, **393**
Insurable interest, 15, 19
Insurable perils, **13**, Chapter 14: 280–310, Chapter 15: 311–327
Insurance brokers, policy for, 275(b)
Insurance premiums, as a standing charge, 130
 taxation deductible, 118, 188(a)
Insured
 cessation of interest, 17
 death or injury of, 15(d), 421
 description of, 23(a)
 joint, 23(a), 382(a)
Insured standing charges, Chapter 9: 104–188
 partial insurance of, 184
 reduction after damage, **51**, 433
Intercom telephone systems, 134
Interdependence of businesses
 associated companies, 382(a)
 general considerations, 340, 341
 insurances for—*see* Chapter 17 extensions of insurance
Interest, loss of, 267(b), Appendix P, 462
Interest payments, 113
Interest on investments, 86, 221
 interim payments in claims, 379, 415
Internal telephone systems, 134

577

INDEX

Interruption of business
   increased by external causes, 420(a), 421
   postponement of, 246
Interruption risk, 17, 241, 249
Interruption risk reports, 241, 242(a)
Interruption risk treatment, 243
Investment grants, 88
Investment value, 266(a)
Ireland, Republic of, 78(i)
Ironworks, **50**, 172, 174, **175**, **293**, 358
Italy, 78(j)

Jacquard cards and designs, 172(c)
Janitor service, 169
Japan, 77(b)
Jigs in engineering works, 172(c)
Joinery contractors, 377
Joint insured, 23(a), 382(a)
"Just in time" 243(c), 342

Kenya, 76(b)
Key man insurance, 421
Key productive workers' wages, 199(a)
Kilns, fuel for, 50, 174, 175
Knives in manufacturing processes, 172(c)
Korea, South, 77(c)

Labels, printing costs, 135
Labour disturbances, loss due to, 289(a)
Landlords, rent receivable insurance, 116, **263(a)**, **(b)**, **264**, **267**
Laundries, 39(a), 50, 127, 137, 167, 319, 320, 351, 375
Laundry expenses, 164
Law cases—*see also* legal decisions
Leader properties (U.S.), 374
Leasehold, premium amortisation, 146
Leasing and contract hire of vehicles, 128
Lease owner's indemnity, 266(a)
Legal costs or expenses, 151
Legal decisions
   City Tailors Ltd. v. *Evans* (1921), 58
   De Meza and Stuart v. *Apple, Van Straten, Shene & Stone* (1975), 226(a)
   Park v. *Phœnix Assurance Co.* (1859), 376
   Polikoff Ltd. v. *North British & Mercantile Insurance Co. Ltd.* (1936), 46, 175, 189(b), 195(a), 425
   SCM (UK) Ltd. v. *W.J. Whittal Ltd.* (1970), 441
   Worsley v. *Wood* (1796), 439
Legionnaires Disease, 301
Lessors of machinery, policy for, 275(a)
Levies, 139
Liability, insurer's, 23(d)
Libraries, policy for, 278(a)
Licences, 129, 169
Lighting expenses, 137
Lightning, damage caused by, 13

Liquidated damages, 261(c)
Liquidation of a business, **17**, 21, **436**
Lloyd's Underwriters, 12, 60(a)
Loans, interest on, 113
Locked-out workers, damage by, 289(a)
Lodging allowances to workers, 196
"Logic bombs," 326
London offices, showrooms and depots, 23(c), 169
Long term agreements (contract), 21, 22
Loss adjusters, 411 *et seq.*
Loss assessors, 411
Loss due to extraneous causes other than "damage," 43, 44, 420(a)
Loss of attraction, 374, 390
Loss of book debts (outstanding accounts) insurance—Chapter 19: 393–410
   specification, Appendix K, 457
Loss of rent insurance, 23(b), 89, 116, **263(a)–(c)**, 264, **267**
Loss of use and access clause, 373
Loss on currency exchange, 165
Loss settlements—*see* claims
Loss, business trading at a, 7, 95–96
Luncheon vouchers, 192(a)

Machinery and Business interruption insurance—Chapter 15: 311–327
   policy, Appendix M, 459
   specification, Appendix N, 460
Machinery
   engineers, 358
   lessors of, 275(f)
   rental of, 114
Machine tool makers and engineers, 358
Mail order businesses, **122**, **123**, 132, 135, 136, 160, **180**, 189(a), 203, **367**, **393**
Makers-up and packers, goods at, 357
Making-up and packing costs, 155
Malicious damage, 16(b), 289(a), **291**, 303
Management training schemes, 169
Managers—personal b.i. insurance (U.S.), 364
Mantle and costume manufacturers, 360
Manufacturers' agents, policy for, 363
Manufacturers without plant, 366
Manufacturing account, 218
Marine insurance premiums, 130
Marine market, covers written in, 279
Market gardeners, 286, 294(a)–(b)
Market research expenses, 169
Market research specialists, 275(b)
Markets
   insurance of rents from, 275(e)
   shops or stalls in, 373
Master policies, 382(c)
Material damage proviso, 15(e), 16(a), (b), 78(e), (f), 281(a), 420(a)
   waiver, 16(b), 388
Maximum indemnity period, **41**, 220, **245(a)**, **249**, 255, 256, 256(a), 257

578

INDEX

maximum indemnity period—*cont.*
  choice of length of, 249, 256
  different periods in same policy, 381
  extended for additional expenditure only, 50
  in machinery accident b.i., 317
  premium rates, 255, 256, 257
  relevant sums insured, 220
  seasonal businesses, 252(a)
Meat canners and processors, 269, 320
Meat trade vans, 375
Medical insurance subscriptions, 192(a)
Merchant converters, 366
Metal foundries, 358
Meter rents, 137
Microfilming services, 134
Middle East, 77
Milk processors and canners, 50, 269, 375
Miscellaneous standing charges limit, 183
Mobile shops, 375
Molten material clause, 293
Month, meaning of, 245(a)
Moral hazard, 16(a), **241**, 439
Mortgage interest, 113
Motels, 286
Motor accessory and component makers, 340, 351, 352
Motor accessory dealers, 223
Motor coach and bus operators, 123, 129, 141, 142, 163, **375**
Motor, motor cycle and scooter dealers, special cover for, 359
Motor garages, 312, 359
Motor haulage contractors, **129**, 141, 142, **375**
Motor manufacturers, 132, **261(b)**, 340, 359
Motor running expenses, 127, 128, 129
Motor vehicles
  damage in insured's garage, 23(c)
  damage whilst away, 375
  damage to buildings caused by, 296(a)
  hiring and leasing, 128
  licences, 127, 129
  running expenses, 127, 128, 129
Moulds in glassworks, etc., 172(c)
Multi-national companies, 80, **382(c)**, 446
Municipal authorities, policy for
  administrative offices, 278(a)
  markets and abattoirs, 275(a)
  loss of rates, 265
  loss of rents, 267
  revenue from catering, entertainment and transport departments, 275(e)
Murder on premises, loss of trade, 301
Museums, policy for, 275(c)
Music halls, 39(a), 166, 262
Music, provision of as a standing charge, 166

National Insurance Contributions, **195(a)**, 196, 205(b)
Natural catastrophes, 78(e), 78(m)
Naturalists' trusts, policy for, 278(a)

Neon signs rental, 114
Net profit, 82, **85(e)—94**, **118**
  general principles, 3–7
  meaning of, 86–87
  not credited until completion of contract, 94
Net trading loss, 7, 95–96
New business clause, 229, 383
New businesses, 229, 245(a), 383
New factories, 228, 268(a)
Newspaper advertising, 120, 122
Newspaper publishers, 50, 132
New Zealand, 75(b)
Night clubs, 262
Nipple leakage of heating boilers, 286
Non-average covers—*see* Declaration Linked
Non-completion of contracts, 261, 262
Non-recurring charges, 82(c), 221
Non-revenue earning concerns, 278(a)
Non-trading revenue, 86, **87**, **88**, **89**, 95, 221
Northern Ireland, 12, 14(b), **290**
Norway, 78(k)
"Notice wages"—*see under* wages
Notional rent, 115
Nuclear fuel risks exclusion, 14(a), 281(a)
Nurserymen, 286, 294, 372
Nursing homes, 301

Obsolescence of plant, etc., 146, 172(c)
Office
  computers rent, 134
  equipment, hire of, 114
  expenses, 132–135, 168, 169
  machinery, servicing of, 114, 134
  stationery and printing, 135
Offices, inclusion in "the premises," 23(c)
Offices, professional and business, policy for, 276(a)–(b)
Official Receiver, 17, 21
Oil engine breakdown, 314
Oil pollution of beaches, 301
Oil works, 172, 375
Operatives' wages, 199(c)
Opticians, policy for, 275(b), 276(a), 410
Option to consolidate in wages insurance—*see under* wages
Optional standing charges, 104, 170, 177, 178
Orchestra, remuneration of, 166, 262
"Other circumstances clause," **55–56**, 96(b), 383, 432, 433
  claim illustration, Appendix X, 470
  double adjustment under, 56
"Other people's fires"—*see under* extensions of insurance
Output basis, etc., specifications, 5
Outstanding accounts—*see* loss of book debts
Outworkers for clothing, etc., manufacturers, 85(d), 360
Overflowing of water tanks, 295
Overheating of boilers and tubes, 285

579

INDEX

Overseas business interruption insurance, Chapter 6: 72–80
  specification "Home Foreign", Appendix T, 466
Overseas suppliers, extensions to, 345, 359
Overtime wages
  claimable as increase in cost of working, 45, 426, 428
  to be insured, 196, 231
Owner's wages or salary, 90

Packaging of goods
  packing dept. costs, 154, 155
  dependence upon; extensions, 370
  manufacturers, 370
Packing expenses, 152, 153
Packing plant for vegetables, 269, 323
Painting contractors, 377
Pakistan, 77
Pallets for dock loading, 155
Paper manufacturers, 137, 319
Paper (wrapping materials), 154
Parcels insurance premiums, 130
Parcels
  post and delivery services, 132
  returned; postage on, 136
Park v. *Phœnix Assurance Co.* (1859), 439
Partial insurance of standing charges, 184
Partners' drawings, salaries, wages, 91
Patent fees, 169
Patents, depreciation of, 148
Patterns
  debited in repairs and renewals, 172(c)
  depreciation of, 148
  expense of production, 144
  on foundry premises, 358
"Pay as paid" policies, 60(b)
Payment on account for claim, 379, 415
Payments in advance, stage or progress payments, 39(c)
100 per cent. payroll insurance (U.K.), **200, 201**, 423
Pension fund trustees; property rents insurance, 267
Pensions, pension and superannuation scheme premiums, etc., 198
Percentage of fire loss policies, 60(a)
Perils, defined, 13
Perils insured
  additional ("special")—Chapter 14: 280–310
  standard, 12, **13(a)**, 15(a), 447
Period of interruption
  commencement postponed, 246
  exceeding maximum indemnity period, 233, 419
  extending over renewal date, 231
  prolonged by extraneous causes, 44, 420(a), 421
Personal b.i. insurance for managers (U.S.), 364

Personal injuries of personnel; "damage to property" 15(d), 421
Peru, 74(e)
Pests on hotel, etc., premises, 301
Petrochemical works, 94, 244(b)
Petrol, oil and tyre costs, 127
Petrol sales bonus, 223
Petty cash, 134
Photocopiers rent, 134
Photographs (reproductive) for printers, 145
Physiotherapists, policy for, 275(b)
Piers, seaside, 275(c)
Plant and machinery sinking fund, 146
Plastics manufacturers, 320, 350
Pluvius (rainfall) policies, 298
Policy, the, 12–23, 35, 250, Appendix A, **447**
  all risks, 13(b), Appendix B, 448
  collective, 22, 23(d)
  conditions—*see under* conditions
  overseas ("Home Foreign"), 79, Appendix T, 466
  renewal date and terms, 20
  schedules, **23(a)–(d)**, 447
  specification—*see under* specification
  world-wide, 80, 310
Polikoff Ltd. v. *North British & Mercantile Insurance Co. Ltd.* (1936), 46, 175, 189(b), 195(a), 425
Political organisations, 278(a), 289, 290
Pollution, 14(c), 301, 302
Portugal, 78(l)
Postage meters rent, 134
Postages, 132
  on returned parcels, 136
Potteries, 50, 175, 319
Power expenses, 173
Power house of "estate mill" or trading estate, 173, 264, 372
Preference share dividends, 86
Premises
  description of the, 15(b), (c), 23(c)
  other than the insured's—*see* extensions of insurance
  temporary after damage; damage at, 232, 233
Premium on issue of share capital, 86
Premium rates for insurance
  gross profit, 254–258
  100 per cent. payroll, 204
  wages, 206(c), 213
Preserve manufacturers, 269
Press knives, 172(c)
Prevention of access clause, 373
Printers, 50, 320, 367
Printing and stationery expenses, 135
Private warehouses, insured's goods in, 354, 356
"Pro rata basis" for insuring wages—*see under* wages
Processors' premises, extensions to, 340–342, **346–350**, 353, **357**, 360, 367
Product coding computers, 424

INDEX

Production bonus on wages, 92, 196
Professional accountants' charges, 378, 406
Professional men's policies, 276(a)–(b)
Profit and loss account, 218
Profit and loss appropriation account, 86
Profit sharing schemes, 92
Profits form—Canadian, 73(a)
Progress department charges, 169
Prolongation, 44, 420
Property, meaning of, 15(d), 421
Property investment companies, 267
Property owners, rent insurance, 23(b), 89, 263(a), (c), 264, **267**
Property stored extension, 355
Proposal form, 110
Proprietors' drawings, 90
Protective works clothing, 163
Provisional premiums, 227
Proximate cause, 44, 420(a), 421
Public authorities, policies for—*see* municipal authorities
Public libraries, policy for, 278(a)
Public houses and inns, 301, 391
Public Order Act 1986, 289(a)
Public relations functions, etc., 169
Public warehouses
  insured's goods in, 60(a), 354–357
  policy for, 39(a), 275(d)
Public works' contractors, 94, 377
Publicity agencies, policy for, 275(b)
Publicity expenses, 120
Publishers, 50, 132, 367
Purchases, 84

Quantity surveyors, policy for, 275(b)
Quarry owners, 23(c)

Racetracks, 319
Radioactive contamination, 14(a)
Radio broadcasting companies, 50, 262, **272**
Radio communication systems, 133
Radio relay equipment, hire of, 143
Railway sidings, rent of, 114
Railway wagon, tank and freight car rents, 169
Railway warehouses, insured's goods in, 60(a), 354–357
Rainfall insurance, 298
Rate of gross profit, 4(a), 38, **40**
  adjustments to, **55(a)–(d)**, 57, 470
  for different departments, 380
  for new businesses, 229, 383
Rates, as a stanging charge, 119
Ratio of wages increased after damage, 424–427
Raw materials prices, fall in, 225(c)
Receipts, policy for—*see* gross revenue
Receiver, business carried on by, 17, 21
Receiving office expenses, 167
Records, rewriting of office, 276(a)–(b)

Recovery of bad debts, 221
Reduction in charges after damage—*see* savings clause
Reduction in turnover, 4(a), **38**, 43, 54, 55(d)
Redundancy agreement fund (voluntary), 197(b)
Redundancy payments to dismissed workers, **202(a)–(d)**, **203**, 422
Redundancy Fund rebates, 197(a), 422
Refrigerated warehouses—*see* cold stores
Refrigeration plant, breakdown of, 323, 324
  disablement of by fire, 306
Refrigeration engineers, 377
Refrigerator manufacturers, 261(b)
Refrigerator sales shops and dealers, 393
Regional development grants, 88
Registrar's fees, 169
Reinstatement of sum insured after loss, 231, 232
Removal contractors, 39(a), 129, 375
Renewal of policy, 20, 231
Rent
  advance, 267(b), 268(a)
  as a standing charge, 105, 114–116
  internal, 117
  receivable, insurance against loss of, 23(b), 89, 116, **263**, 264, **267**
  storage, 157
Rental value or nominal rent, 115
Repair and service departments, 160
Repairs and renewals, 171, 172, 184
Representatives, **125**, 177, 178, **193**, **303**, **361**, 363
Research and development (R & D), 273, Appendix L, 458
Reserve for bad debts, 159(c)
Residual value in claim, 419
Restaurateurs, 166, 172(a), 192(b), 262, 296(a)
Restoration after damage, delays in, 44
Retirement from business, 18, 436
Re-training employees, 207(a)
Retrospective discounts, 223
Return of premium clause
  for gross profit, **225(a)**, 225(b)–226(d)
  for wages, 216
Returned parcels, demurrage on, 136
Revenue, policy for loss of, 275, **276(a)**
  specification—Appendix F, 452
Revolution, risk excluded, 13, 281(a)
Riot and civil commotion
  insurance against, 289(a)
  policy exclusion, 13
Riot (Damages) Act 1886, 289(a)
Riot (South Africa), 76(a)
Rise in temperature risk at cold stores, 306, 323
Risk analysis, 241
Risk financing, 244
Risk management, 241, 326
Risk, interruption, treatment, 243, 249

581

Road repairs charges, 169
Road risk, insurance of
  goods in transit, 376
  motor vehicles, 375
Roofing contractors, 377
Room and power
  policy for landlords, 264
  tenants' rent, 114, 173
Royalties
  payable, 161, 162
  revenue from, 89, 221, 275(f)
Rubber manufacturers, 320

Sacks; repairs, renewals and cleaning of, 172(a), (b)
Salaries, **189–193**, 199(b), **204**, 205(b), **212**
Salaries and wages combined, 189(b), 204, 212
Sale of assets, 86, 221
Sale of business, 436
Sale of scrap, 85(c), 222
Salespersons, 125, 193, 303
Salvage sales clause, 384
Salvage value of temporary property, 419
Samples
  cost of production of, 144
  loss of seasonal, 303, 361
Sanitary arrangements, defective, 301
Sanitary engineers, 377
Satellites, 274, 287
"Savings clause"
  in gross profit insurance, **51(a)–(b)**, 54, **82(c)**, 433, 434, 470
  in wages insurance, 205(c)–(d), 207(a), 469
Schedule of the policy, **23(a)–(d)**, 447, 448
Scholarship expenses, 169
Schools, 50, 275(g), 301
Schools of art, dentistry, medicine, technology, etc., policy for, 278(c)
Schools of ballet, music and drama, 275(c)
S.C.M. (U.K.) Ltd. v. W.J. Whittall & Son Ltd. (1970), 441
Scrap, income from sale of, 85(c), 222
Seafood canners and bottlers, 269, 323
Seaside piers, 254(a), 275(c)
Seaside resorts, 252(a)–(c), 301
Seasonal business, 252(a)–(c)
Seasonal supplies of raw materials, 355
Secretarial services, policy for, 275(b)
Security services charges, 169
Seed and bulb merchants, 123, 367
Self-heating of electrical installations, 305
Service charges at hotels, 192(b)
Service charges for weighing and counting machinery, 169
Service guarantee expenses, 160
Severance pay schemes, 197(b)
Share transfer office expenses, 169
Shipbuilders, 95
Shipping and forwarding agents, 275(d)
Shipping expenses, 156
Ships in dock, goods on board, 355

Shoe factories, 172(c)
Shop assistants' bonus and commission, 191
Shopfitters, 377
Shopfronts, depreciation of, 146
"Shop within a shop," 23(c)
Shopping arcades and streets, 373
Shops, 120, 121, 132, 135, 154, 178, 181, 249, **295**, **296(a)**, 325, **373**, 384, **390**, 393
  specification—Appendix G, 453
Showroom expenses, 169
Showrooms to be included, 23(c)
Sick pay schemes for workpeople, 262
Silent businesses, 245(a)
Singapore, 77(d)
Sinking fund, 146
Skilled workers' wages, 199(c)
Slipper factories, 172(c)
Social Security contributions—*see* National Insurance contributions
Soft drink manufacturers, 127, 128, 172(a), 319
Sole distributors and concessionaires, 365
Solicitors, policies for, 276(a)–(b)
Sonic bangs exclusion, 282(a), 287(a)
South Africa, 76(a)
South America, 74
South Korea, 77(c)
Space heating, 137, 173, 284, 372
Spain, 78(m)
Special circumstances—*see* other circumstances clause
Special perils insurable, 281–306, 345
Specification
  as part of policy, 12, 23(d), **35**, 36, 37
  "difference" basis, 6, 35–39, Appendix C, 449
  gross revenue, etc., basis, 275, Appendix F, 452
  loss of book debts, 395, Appendix K, 457
  net profit and standing charges ("additions") basis, 6, 35–59, Appendix E, 451
  offices (professional men's), 276(a)–(b)
  rent receivable, 263(a), (c), 267
  retail shops "trading profit " 324, Appendix G, 453
  various other bases, 389–391
Specified working expenses—*see* uninsured working expenses
Spoilage of
  fruit, meat, vegetables, etc., 269, 323, 324
  materials in process due to electricity, etc., failure, 321
Spontaneous fermentation, heating or combustion, 13, 292
Sports and recreation centres, 275(c)
Sports clubs (works) expenses, 143
Sports events—weather insurance, 298
Sports organisation offices, policy for, 278(a)
Sports sponsorship expenses, 120
Sprinkler installations
  discount in premium rates, 258

INDEX

Sprinkler installations—*cont.*
 leakage, loss consequent on, 297
Stabling costs, 169
Staff salaries, 189(a)–(b), 191
Staff training college, 169
Standard turnover, 42, 247, 251
 adjustments to, 43, 55(a), 57, 433
 for new businesses, 229, 383
Standing charges, 3–7, Chapter 9: 104–188
 definition of, 104
 general principles for insuring, 3, 4(a), 105
 miscellaneous unspecified, 183
 omitted—*see* uninsured standing charges
 partial insurance of, 184
 reduction after damage—*see* savings clause
 specified—*see* insured standing charges
 unearned, 95
 ininsurable, 147, 159(a)
 uninsured—*see* uninsured standing charges
Stately homes, policy for, 275(c)
Stationery and printing expenses, 135
Statistics, for rating, 254(a)
Statutory declaration in a claim, 438
Steam engine breakdown, 313, 314
Steam pipes, explosion of, 282(a), 283
 cracking and fracturing of, 286
Steam raising plant, damage to, 175, 372
Steam turbines breeakdown, 313, 314
 explosion of, 283(d), 314
Steelworks, 50, 137, 172(a), 174, 175, 293, 319
Stepped rebate scheme—petrol sales, 223
Stock depreciation, **147**, 225(c), 269, 323, 324
Stock in outside warehouses, 60(a), 354-356
Stock reserves, withdrawals from 87
Stock throughput covers (marine), 279(a)
Stock, variations and closing accounts affecting claims, 432
Stockbrokers, policy for, 276(a)–(b)
Storage handling charges, 158
Storage premises, 349, 354–356
Storage rent, 119
Storm, tempest and flood, 16(b), 294
Strikers and locked-out workers, 289
Strikes, indirect effect of, 43, 44, 340, 420(a)
 insurance against, 289
String and wrapping materials, 154
Sub-contractors, extensions to premises of, 346
Subrogation, 385, 441
Subrogation waiver clause, 385
Subscriptions and donations, 138
Subsidence, loss due to, excluded, 294
Subsidiary companies, 23(a), 85(b), 382(a), 385
Sugar beet factories, 269
Sugar mills, 172, 375
Suicide on the premises, 301
Sum insured on gross profit, 45, 218–233
 annual revision of, 52(c)
 based on estimated future earnings, 52(c), 55(c), **224**, 225(a)

Sum insured on gross profit—*cont.*
 increased after damage, 431
 in relation to maximum indemnity period, 220
 reduced by claim payments, 231
Sundries (trade), 183
Sunshine deficiency insurance, 299
Superannuation schemes, 198
Supermarkets, 424
Suppliers of insured's customers, extensions to, 352
Suppliers of insured's suppliers, extensions to, 350
Suppliers' premises, extensions to, 23(c), 281(a), **346–349**, 359, 363–370
Suspension of part of indemnity period, 248
Sweden, 78(n)
Swimming pools, 275(e)
Switzerland, 78(o)

"Takings" substituted for "turnover," 390
 specification—Appendix G, 453
Tanneries, 321
Tar distillers, 292, 371
Tax deduction, incentive schemes, 75(b), 78(i)
Taxation, **118**, 149
Taxi proprietors, 129, 375
Tea money, 169
Telegrams, 134
Telephone answering machines, 134
Telephone exchanges, extensions to, 369
Telephone expenses, 133
Teleprinter expenses, 134
Television
 advertising, 120, 122
 broadcasting companies, 50, 262, **272**
 communication systems, 133
 manufacturers, 85(a), 261(b)
 shops, 159(b), 223, 393
Telex, 133
Temporary premises after damage, damage at, 232, 233
Tennis clubs, 298
Term agreements, 21
Tests and experimental expenses, 169
Textile mills, 137, 144, 172, 173, 303, 320, 357, 361
Theatre ticket agents, 23(c), 369
Theatres, 39(a), 166, 252(a), 262, 297, 319
Theft, business interruption due to, 303
Thrift club interest, 113
Tiling contractors, 377
Timber merchants, 355
Time limit for claims
 in overseas policies, 79
 in U.K. policies, 245(a), 437
 in U.S. gross earnings policies, 463 (condition 9.h.)
"Time loss" insurance, 312
Tips to hotel, etc., employees, 192(b)
Tobacconists' bonus on sales, 223

583

INDEX

Totalisators at racetracks, 319
Tour operators and organisers, 123, 261(b), 369
Towel services, 169
Town offices of manufacturers, 23(c)
Toy manufacturers, 172(c)
Trade bonus on target sales, 223
Trade effluent charges, 137
Trade expenses, 183
Trade fairs and exhibitions
　extensions to, 361, 362
　policy for promoters of, 275(c)
"Trading profit" specification, 390, 391, Appendix G, 453
Trade levies, 139
Trade mark expenses, 169
Trade marks, purchase and depreciation of, 148
Trade show expenses, 120
Trade (journal, etc.) subscriptions, 138
Trade sundries, 183
Trade union's offices, policy for, 278(a)
Trade utensils, repairs and renewals, 172(a)
Trading account, 218
Trading estate boiler house, extensions to, 372
Trading loss, 95–96
Trailer renting, 128
Trainees, 199(d)
Training levy, 196
Training schemes for operatives, 169
Transit risks, 376
Transport undertakings, 39(a), 129, 275(e)
Travel agencies, 23(c), 123, 261(b), 275(a), 369
Travellers, reps, salespersons
　commission and bonus, 193
　expenses, 125
　salaries, 193
　samples, 303, 361
Travelling expenses, 125
Travelling saleshops, 127, 128
Trends of business, provision for, 52(c), 55–56, 82(b), (d), 96(b), **224**, 225(d)
"Trojan horses" 326
Tronc for hotel staffs, 192(b)
Trucks—*see* motor vehicles
Truckers—*see* haulage contractors
Trucking companies, 375
Turbines, breakdown of, 313, 314
Turnover, as index of loss, 2–4, 5, 36–38, 205(a)
　annual, **52(b)–(c)**, 55(a), (c)
　deferred, 246, 247
　elsewhere after damage, 58
　increased during indemnity period, 55(b), 247
　meaning of, 39(a)–(c)
　new businesses, 229
　payments in advance, stage or progress payments, 39(c)
　reduction in, 4(a)–(b), 7, 38
　specifications on turnover basis, 36–59, 449, 450

Turnover—*cont.*
　standard—*see* standard turnover
Tyre dealers, 223
Tyres, expenses of, as a standing charge, 127, 129

Uberrimae fides, 15, 18, 435
Uncompleted contracts, profit on, 94
Undamaged stock, deterioration of, 269, 323, 324
Under-insurance—*see* average proviso
Unearned standing charges, 95
Uniform Policy Conditions (UPC), 72
Uniforms, employees', 163
Uninsurable charges, 147, 159(a)
Uninsured standing charges, **46**, **49**, 51(b), 55(a), 96(a), **107**, **108**, **109**
　clause, **49**, 57, 109, 184
Uninsured ("specified") working expenses, **6**, 81, **83**, **84**, Chapter 9: 104–184

UNITED STATES OF AMERICA
Business interruption insurances.
　Note: paragraph numbers in heavier type denote they are applicable specifically to the United States and/or Canada. "B & M" means Boiler & Machinery b.i. insurance. Paragraph numbers in lighter type denote United Kingdom insurances of some particular relevance in the United States and Canada.

academies, policy for, 50, **63(b)**, 275(a)
accounts receivable insurance, **394(a)–(b)**, Chapter 19
actual loss sustained; contract to indemnify, 10, **61**, B & M **331**
additional coverages, **30**
adjustments for probable experience, **70**, **331**, **432**, and *see* U.K. "other circumstances clause"
agents' commission, policy for, 363, **364**
agreed value, **68**
aircraft, damage by, 287
all risks, 309
alterations and new buildings clause, **268(b)**
annual reports, **234(a)**, B & M **268(b)**
apartments, loss of rents coverage, 263(a)
appraisal clause, **443**
appraisers, policy for, **71(a)**, 275(b)
attorneys, policy for, **71(a)**, 276
base rate, **254(b)**
baseball stadiums, 319
blanket coverage, 382(a), **382(b)–(c)**
boiler and machinery b.i., **Chapter 16: 328–339**
bond specialists, policy for, **71(a)**, 275(b)
bowling alleys, 252(a)–(c), 319, **337**
brokers' commission, 363, **364**
building laws—contingent liability coverage, **65(b)**

584

INDEX

Business interruption insurances—*cont.*
Business Income Coverage, **24** *et seq.*, **61** *et seq.*, **97** *et seq.*, **234(b)**, Appendix S, **465**
candy manufacturers, 321
catalog sales merchants, **368**
causes of loss, 25(a)–(c)
certified public accountants—*see* U.K. accountants
claim representatives, 411(b)
claim statement, time limit, 437
claims. *See* Chapter 20: 411–446
   account books destroyed, 414
   action on damage occurring, 29, 411(a), **411(b)**, 411(c), 412–415
   appraisal clause, **443**
   death or injury of personnel, 421
   employees—employment during period of interruption, 422–429(a)
   finished stock exclusion, 418
   loss settlement, simple specimen, **Appendix Z, 472**
   period of interruption increased by extraneous causes, 420(a), **420(b)**, 421
   probable experience clause, **432**
   residual value, 419
   special exclusions, strikers, etc., 420(a), **420(b)**
   time limit for statement of claim, 437
   wages during period of interruption, 422–429(a)
clinics, policy for, 71(a), 275(b)
co-insurance clause, **31, 67**, 235, 236, B & M 333
colleges, insurance for, 50, **63(b)**, 275(g)
commencement of liability, B & M **332**
commissions of selling agents, factors and brokers, 363, **364**
conditions
   common policy, **32**
   commercial property, **32**
conditions for a valid claim, **27**
condominiums, loss of rent, 263(a)
consequential damage—spoilage, B & M, **338**
contingent b.i. coverages—*see* dependencies, outside
contract to indemnify, **61**
contribution clause, 32, **67(a)**, 440, B & M **333**
costs deducted from net sales, 98, 99
courtesy discounts and mark-downs, 192(a)
credit unions, policy for, 278(a), **278(b)**
Declarations, **33**
denial of access by civil authority, **65(a)**, 373
dependencies, outside, 28(b)
   contributing properties, **347**
   leader properties, **374**

Business interruption insurances—*cont.*
dependencies, outside—*cont.*
   recipient properties, 347, and all Chapter 17: 340–377
earnings (short form): monthly limitation, no co-insurance, **71(a)**
earthquake risks, **288(b)**
"economic limit" in expediting expenses, **64(b)**
educational establishments, 50, **63(b)**, 275(g)
electrical apparatus clause, 305
electricity supplies, failure of, 319, **337**, **348**
exclusions
   enforcement of law, **65(b)**
   finished stock (manufacturers), **97(b)**, **418**
   interference by strikers, **65(c)**
   lease cancellation, etc., **65(d)**
   nuclear radiation, **26**
expediting expenses, 45, **64(b)**, 66
expenses to reduce loss, 11, 45, **64(b)**, 66
Extended Business Income, **63(b)**
extended coverage endorsement, **281(b)**
Extended Period of Indemnity, **63(b)**
extra expense only policy, 278(a), **278(b)**
extra perils, **281(b)**, Chapter 14: 280–310
extraneous causes increasing loss, **65(b)–(d)**, 420
factors' commission, policy for, 363, **364**
finished stock exclusion—
   manufacturers, 27, **97(b), (c)**, 418
flood risks, 294
gas supplies, failure of, 319, **337**, 347
grace period, 20
gross earnings, 81
   manufacturing and mining risks, **97(b)**, **Appendix R, 464**
   mercantile and non-manufacturing risks, **97(a)**, **Appendix Q**, 463
group companies and corporations, 382
hail insurance, 204
honesty clause, 68, 237(a)
ice rinks, policy for, **71(a)**, 275(d)
industrial parks and trading estates, 372
Insurance Advisory Organisation (IAO), Canada, **73(a)**
Insurance Services Office (ISO), U.S., **24**
"interruption of business," 27
interruption of public utilities, 319, **337**, **348**
lawyers, policy for, 276(a)–(b), **278(b)**
leader properties, 374
leasehold interest policy, **266(b)**
licensed public accountants—*see* U.K. accountants
limitations
   electrical injury to appliances, etc., **305**
   media for electronic data processing, **63(c)**
loss adjusters, **411**

585

INDEX

Business interruption insurances—*cont.*
loss clause on gross earnings policy, **238**
loss determination, **417**, **433**
media for electronic data processing, **63(c)**
mini-storage premises, 275(d)
molten material clause, **293**
movers—*see* U.K. removal contractors
Net Income, **62**, **100**
nuclear exclusion clause, **26**
off-premises services, **369**
operating expenses, 69, 97(c), 101, 185
Optional Coverages, **63(b)**, **68**
ordinary payroll
   100 per cent. included in gross earnings, **97(a)–(b)**
   how it works, **217(a)**
   limited coverage only, **47(c)**
   total exclusion of, **217(b)**
   what "payroll" means, **189(b)**
other earnings, 102, 239
packing and processing plants, vegetable and fruit growers, **63(b)**, 252(a)–(c)
payroll tax, **195(b)**
"per diem", **71(b)**
perils insured, **25**
period of indemnity, **63(a)**, B & M **330**
period of indemnity extension endorsement, 63(b)
period of interruption extended by extraneous causes, **65(b)–(d)**
period of restoration, **278(b)**, **245(b)**
personal b.i.—managers, etc., **364**
policy, the standard, **24**
pollutants, **27**, **302**
premium adjustment (return of premium), **237(a)**, B & M **336**
premium rating table, **256(b)**
probable experience, **70**, B & M **331** and *see* U.K. "other circumstances clause"
profit (loss of) on finished goods, 97(b), 97(c), **418**
prolongation, 65
pro rata clause, **463**
protective safeguards condition, **463**
proximate cause, 44, 420(a), **420(b)**
public adjuster, 410 *et seq.*, **411(b)**
public utilities, failure of, 319, **337**, **347**
radio broadcasting companies—*see* U.K. entry
R & D establishments, 273
rain insurance—*see* U.K. "pluvius" policies, 298
realtors, policy for, **71(a)**, 275(b), 308
reduction of payment condition, B & M **335**
refrigeration, failure of, **337**, **347**
reinstatement of claim amounts, **238**
rental expense, 187
rental income, 263(a)
resumption of operations, **62**, **66**

Business interruption insurances—*cont.*
return of premium endorsement, **237(a)–(b)**
revenue covers, U.S. attitudes, 275(i)
riot risks, 289(a), **289(b)**
Sales Tax, **71(a)**
savings in charges and expenses after damage, **62**
schools and colleges, 50, **63(b)**, 275(g)
seasonal crops and foodstuffs, **63(b)**, 252(a)–(c)
selling agents, policy for, 363, **364**
severance pay schemes, 197(b)
shipping and handling charges, 132
small businesses, B & M **339**
Social Security Contributions, **195(b)**
special exclusions, 420
sports grounds and stadiums, 319
standard policy, 24
strikers, interference by, **65(c)**, 281(b)
subrogation, **32**, 441
subrogation waiver clause, 385
taxation, **188**
television broadcasting companies—*see* U.K. entry
time element, **63(a)**
title companies, policy for, **71(a)**, 275(b)
trading loss, 103
trading parks, 264
tuition fees, policy for, **63(b)**
use and occupancy, 71(b)
valued bases, 71
vehicles, damage by, extended coverage, **296(a)**
war, civil war, etc., risks excluded, **463**, **464**, **465**
water supplies, failure of, 319, **337**, **347**
windstorm, 294
worksheets, **234**

Universities, policy for, 278(a)
Unspecified premises, extensions to
   processors, 349, 350, 357–360
   storage, 354, 355
   suppliers, 349, 350, 359
Unspecified standing charges, 183
Uruguay, 74(f)

Value Added Tax (VAT), 118, 275(a), 408
Valued bases, 60
Variable charges, 3, 4(a), **6**, **81**, **84**, 104, 106, 108
Vegetable canners and preservers, 269, 306, 323, 354–356
Vegetable growers, 269
Venezuela, 74(g)
Ventilation engineers, 377
Vermin on the premises, 301
Veterinary surgeons, policy for, 275(b)
Viewdata and visual display systems, 133

INDEX

Vulcanisers, 172(a)

Wages insurance: Chapter 10: 189–217
  Acts of Parliament, liabilities under, 202(a)–(d), 203
  annual basis, 213
  apprentices and trainees, 199(d)
  claims for loss under, 214(b), 215, 422–427, 429(a)
  Contracts of Employment Act 1972, 202(a)
  debited under another item in accounts, 172(a)
  dual basis scheme, 200, 205–212—wages and payroll
    adjustment for trends, etc., 205(a)
    alternative period (option to consolidate), 205(c), 206(a)–(c)
    average proviso applicable, 210
    carry-over of savings, 205(c)–(d), 207(a)–(b)
    claim illustration—Appendix W, 469
    claims, how the cover works, 208(a)–(b), 422–428
    definitions of wages, 205(b)
    increase in cost of working, 47(b), 209
    increased ratio of wages after damage, 46, 424, 425
    initial period of 100 per cent. cover, 205(c)
    payroll cover, 212
      100 per cent. payroll cover, 204
    premium rates, 204, 206(c)
    remainder percentage, 205(a)–(c)
    remainder period, 205(a)–(c)
    specification—Appendix H, 454
    sum insured, 205(a), 212
    two or more premises, 215
  Employment Protection Act 1975, 202(a), 202(c), **202(d)**, 203
  Employment Protection (Consolidation) Act 1978, **197(a)**, 200, **202(a)**, **202(b)**, **203**
  gratuities and tips included with, 192(b)
  holiday pay insured with, 196
  increased ratio after damage, 46, **424**, **425**, 426, 427
  methods of describing, 214(a)
  National Insurance contributions with, 196
  notice wages, 213
  overtime pay
    included in insurance, 196
    payments after damage, 426, 427
  part-time, casual and seasonal workers, 203, 213
  payments pertaining to, 196, 242(a)
  payroll cover and 100 per cent. payroll cover—*see under* "dual basis," etc., above
  premium rating methods, 204, 206(c), 213

Wages insurance—*cont.*
  "pro rata" basis of insurance, 214(a), specification Appendix I, 455
  Redundancy Payments Act 1965, 202(a)–(b)
  return of premium clause, 216
  two or more premises, 215
  "weekly basis" of insurance—*see* pro rata basis entry above
Wallpaper trade, 144
War, effect on period for reinstatement, 420
War risks excluded
  in overseas policies, 62
  in U.K. policies, 13, 281
  in U.S. policies, 463, 464, 465
Warehouses—insured's property in
  private, 354, 356
  public, 60(a), 354–357
Washing machine manufacturers, 261(b)
Waste heat from electricity works, 372
Water damage, loss due to, 13, 294, 295, 297
Water charges and meter rents, 137
Water table level, change in, 294(a)
Water treatment charges, 137
Water tube boilers, 285
Waterworks, extensions to, 319, 371
Wayleaves, 169
Weavers' premises, property at, 357
Wharfingers, policy for, 275(d)
Whisky distilleries, 172(a), 172(b), **271**, 282(a)
Winding-up of business, **17**, 21, 436
Window-dressing and display expenses, 121
Wineries, 271
Wireworks, 319
Wool textile industry, 137, 144, 172, 173, 303, 357, 361
Work done elsewhere after damage, 58
Work in progress, 81, 85(a)
Workers' hostels, 23(c)
Workers' share of profits, 92, 93
Working men's clubs, 97
Works
  fire brigade expenses, 169
  locomotive and wagon expenses, 169
  overalls and protective clothing, 163
  social club, sports club, outings, 143
  vehicles, damage by, 296(a)
  welfare expenses, 143
Workwear clothing and servicing, 163
World-wide insurance, 80, 382, 446
Worsley v. *Wood* (1976), 439
Wrapping materials, 154
Writers to the signet, 276(a)
Writing down of stock values, 147, 225(c)

Yards, forming part of the premises, 23(c)

Zimbabwe, 76(c)